EPISTEMIC LOGIC FOR AI AND COMPUTER SCIENCE

Cambridge Tracts in Theoretical Computer Science

Titles in the series

1. G.Chaitin *Algorithmic Information Theory*
2. L.C.Paulson *Logic and Computation*
3. M.Spivey *Understanding Z*
4. G.Revesz *Lambda Calculus, Combinators and Functional Programming*
5. A.Ramsay *Formal Methods in Artificial Intelligence*
6. S.Vickers *Topology via Logic*
7. J-Y.Girard, Y.Lafont & P.Taylor *Proofs and Types*
8. J.Clifford *Formal Semantics & Pragmatics for Natural Language Processing*
9. M.Winslett *Updating Logical Databases*
10. K.McEvoy & J.V.Tucker (eds) *Theoretical Foundations of VLSI Design*
11. T.H.Tse *A Unifying Framework for Stuctured Analysis and Design Models*
12. G.Brewka *Nonmonotonic Reasoning*
14. S.G.Hoggar *Mathematics for Computer Graphics*
15. S.Dasgupta *Design Theory and Computer Science*
17. J.C.M.Baeten (ed) *Applications of Process Algebra*
18. J.C.M.Baeten & W. P.Weijland *Process Algebra*
21. D.A.Wolfram *The Clausal Theory of Types*
23. E.-R.Olderog *Nets, Terms and Formulas*
26. P.D.Mosses *Action Semantics*
27. W.H.Hesselink *Programs, Recursion and Unbounded Choice*
28. P.Padawitz *Deductive and Declarative Programming*
29. P.Gärdenfors (ed) *Belief Revision*
30. M.Anthony & N.Biggs *Computational Learning Theory*
31. T.F.Melham *Higher Order Logic and Hardware Verification*
32. R.L.Carpenter *The Logic of Typed Feature Structures*
33. E.G.Manes *Predicate Transformer Semantics*
34. F.Nielson & H.R.Nielson *Two Level Functional Languages*
35. L.Feijs & H.Jonkers *Formal Specification and Design*
36. S.Mauw & G.J.Veltink (eds) *Algebraic Specification of Communication Protocols*
37. V.Stavridou *Formal Methods in Circuit Design*
38. N.Shankar *Metamathematics, Machines and Gödel's Proof*
39. J.B.Paris *The Uncertain Reasoner's Companion*
40. J.Desel & J.Esparza *Free Choice Petri Nets*
41. J.-J. Ch. Meyer & W. van der Hoek *Epistemic Logic for AI and Computer Science*

EPISTEMIC LOGIC FOR AI AND COMPUTER SCIENCE

J.-J. Ch. Meyer

W. van der Hoek

University of Utrecht

PUBLISHED BY THE PRESS SYNDICATE OF THE UNIVERSITY OF CAMBRIDGE
The Pitt Building, Trumpington Street, Cambridge, United Kingdom

CAMBRIDGE UNIVERSITY PRESS
The Edinburgh Building, Cambridge CB2 2RU, UK
40 West 20th Street, New York NY 10011–4211, USA
477 Williamstown Road, Port Melbourne, VIC 3207, Australia
Ruiz de Alarcón 13, 28014 Madrid, Spain
Dock House, The Waterfront, Cape Town 8001, South Africa

http://www.cambridge.org

First published 1995
First paperback edition 2004

A catalogue record for this book is available from the British Library

ISBN 0 521 46014 X hardback
ISBN 0 521 60280 7 paperback

What one knows is not so much as what one does not know.

There is a great variety of things.

Ko Huang

TABLE OF CONTENTS

PREFACE

Epistemic logic concerns the notions knowledge and belief ('επιστημη — episteme — is Greek for 'knowledge'), and stems from philosophy where it has been developed to give a formal treatment of these notions. (Sometimes the logic of belief is separately referred to as *doxastic logic*, from the Greek word δοξα — doxa —, meaning 'surmise' or 'presumption'. In this book we shall use epistemic logic for the logic of knowledge *and belief*.) In [Hin62] the Finnish logician and philosopher Jaakko Hintikka presented a logic for knowledge and belief that was based on *modal logic*. Modal logic is a so-called philosophical logic dealing with the notions of necessity and contingency (possibility) ([Kri63], [Che80], [HC68, HC84]), and it appeared that epistemic logic could be viewed as an instance of this more general logic by interpreting necessity and possibility in an epistemic manner. For a thorough treatment of epistemic logic from the perspective of philosophy we refer to [Len80].

Especially in the last decade the use of logic and logical formalisms in artificial intelligence (AI) has increased enormously, including that of those logics that have been developed originally in and for philosophy. Epistemic logic is one of these so-called philosophical logics that has been 'discovered' by computer scientists and AI researchers. Particularly, the relevance of epistemic logic has been realised by researchers interested in the formal description of knowledge of agents in distributed and intelligent systems in order to specify or verify protocols, and represent knowledge and formalise reasoning methods, respectively. To mention a few propagators of the epistemic approach: J.Y. Halpern, Y.O. Moses, R. Fagin, M.Y. Vardi, D.J. Lehmann, H.J. Levesque and R.C. Moore. For instance, [HM85] is an excellent introduction in the area, and has provided a basis for this work.

This book grew out of lecture notes for a (part of a) course of applied logic for third-year undergraduate computer science students at the Free University in Amsterdam, and the Universities of Nijmegen and Utrecht. This book is an extended version of those notes, intended as a textbook on epistemic logic, treating both the basics and applications in computer science and, particularly, artificial intelligence. This text hopes to give an introduction to this topic accessible to undergraduates in computer science and AI. However, we also believe that the book will be of help to graduate students and researchers by rendering the specialist literature using epistemic logic accessible to them. Furthermore, it may be of interest to logicians and philosophers interested in the application of (philosophical) logic.

We now give an overview of the contents of the book. After an introduction to the topic of epistemic logic (Chapter 0), in Chapter 1 we start with the (modal) basics of multi-agent epistemic logic, including Kripke semantics and the well-known modal logics K, T, S4 and S5. In particular, we pause at single-agent S5-logic, where we treat the simple models as well as the issue of normal forms for this case. We then turn to the application of epistemic logic in the context of distributed systems, including the topic of protocol verification. This line is continued in Chapter 2, where we proceed with some notions that are particularly interesting in this context such as common and implicit (distributed) knowledge. We then consider more AI-oriented issues such as the difference between knowledge and belief; the problem of logical omniscience, involving various notions of explicit and implicit belief, combining knowledge and belief into one logic; the interplay between knowledge and time; and the interplay between knowledge and action. Finally some attention is paid to the use of graded (or numerical) modalities in epistemic logic. In Chapter 3 we occupy ourselves with the issue of knowledge vs ignorance: first we discuss Halpern & Moses' elegant theory of honesty, next we digress into the realm of nonmonotonic reasoning and preferential entailment, and we end Chapter 3 with a treatment of Moore's *auto*epistemic logic (AEL) in which an agent is able to reason about its own knowledge (or belief), and the related logic of 'all I know' of Hector Levesque. Then in Chapter 4, we show how one can base default and counterfactual reasoning on epistemic logic, including a treatment of well-known but complicated examples such as the Yale Shooting Problem. In particular, we consider a kind of default entailment based on the theory of Chapter 3. In appendixes we consider alternative approaches to knowledge and belief, namely Konolige's 'deduction model' and the 'knowledge structures' of Fagin, Halpern and Vardi. Finally we stress that the emphasis of the book is on *propositional* epistemic logic, since most interesting features of epistemic logic can already be appreciated in this simple setting. Nevertheless, we felt obliged to say something about first-order epistemic logic in an appendix.

An important part of the book is the answers to *all* exercises, from trivial to difficult, as well as some elaborations of the theory in the main text. Students may therefore use this section interactively: first try to obtain solutions themselves to get a feel for the problems, then discover further technical tools offered in the answers and next try the exercises again. This makes the book very suited for self-study. Students themselves may choose the level of mastering the material.

A word of warning is in order, however. There is a sense in which this book is not self-contained and does not provide the complete story (definitions, elementary propositions, etc.): namely with respect to the topic of classical logic. The main text does not give an introduction into classical logic, simply because there already exist so many good introductions in the literature (see e.g. [Gal90], [Gam91], [Men64], [Tha88]). However, in order to present answers to the exercises in a systematic and somewhat standardised way, and also for readers who want to measure their knowledge of the subject of classical logic against the level we like to assume familiar, we present a number of properties of classical logic that we used in the answers in Intermezzo E.1 in Appendix E.

Finally, a general remark about the text. Sections marked with * are rather technical, and may be skipped without loss of continuity. Exercises marked with * are more advanced (and may even need substantial further development of the theory, as is shown in the answers).

We gratefully acknowledge the help of Jan Willem Klop when we prepared the original lecture notes in Dutch for students at the Free University. He provided many valuable suggestions for improvement, as well as some of the drawings that appear in this book. Thanks are also due to Gerard Vreeswijk who did preliminary work for a part of Chapter 4 (in particular the sections dealing with AEL) and to Aart Middeldorp who did some groundwork for Appendix A2. We furthermore thank Johan van Benthem, Joeri Engelfriet, Jeroen Hoekstra, Marten van Hulst, Jeroen Krabbendam, Paul Spruit, Yao-Hua Tan, Hans Tonino and Gerard Vreeswijk for their comments on previous versions of (parts of) this work. We thank Jaco de Bakker for his encouragement to publish this text in this Cambridge University Press series. Moreover, we are grateful to David Tranah, publishing director of the Mathematical Sciences Department of Cambridge University Press, for his mediating role and, above all, his patience, and to Mairi Sutherland for the elaborate copy-editing she has performed to improve the readability of the book. Last but not least we are indebted to Coby Meyer-van Kol and Helen Appel for their efforts in the text processing of the original Dutch lecture notes, which we could use fruitfully as a basis for the present version.

0 INTRODUCTION

Knowledge and belief play an important role in everyday life. In fact, most of what we do has to do with the things we know or believe. Likewise, it is not so strange that when we have to specify the behaviour of artificial agents in order to program or implement them in some particular way, it is thought to be important to be interested in the 'knowledge' and 'belief' of such an agent. In many areas of computer science and artificial intelligence one is concerned with the description or representation of knowledge of users or even the systems themselves. For example, in database theory one tries to model knowledge about parts of reality in certain formal ways to render it implementable and accessible to users. In AI one tries to design knowledge-based decision-support systems that are intended to assist professional users in some specialistic field when making decisions by providing pieces of knowledge and preferably some deductions from the input data by means of some inference mechanism. The representation and manipulation of knowledge of some sort is ubiquitous in the information sciences.

This book is not about knowledge representation in general, but rather concentrates on the logic of knowledge and belief. What (logical) properties do knowledge and belief have? What is the difference between knowledge and belief? We do not intend to answer these questions in a deep philosophical discussion of these notions. (For this the reader is referred to the philosophical literature, e.g. [Pol86], [Hin86], or, more technically, [Voo92].) Rather, we will look at a basic logical approach of epistemic logic based on modal logic, and show how this can be applied to problems that concern computer science and AI, such as the characterisation of a state of knowledge of an artificially intelligent agent or a processor in a computer network.

In particular, we will study various modal operators that have to do with (various kinds of) knowledge and belief, and with (certain or uncertain) information available to an agent more in general. Sometimes, we shall also briefly encounter other modalities, like time. In fact, we shall often have occasion to use more than one modality at the same time. There are several justifications for using multiple modalities: apart from the need to express the knowledge of *several agents* (denoting persons or processors in a distributed system), it might be interesting to combine *different interpretations* of several boxes in one system, like that of *knowledge and belief*, or *knowledge and time.*

What kind of logical properties may we expect knowledge and belief to have? Let us consider an example. Let us assume the following situation: When John lies to me, his heart-beat doubles. And when his heart-beat doubles, I know that he is lying to me. Now I can conclude the following: whenever John lies to me, I know that he does so. Formally (letting $K\varphi$ stand for "I know that φ"):

$$\text{from } p,\ p \to q,\ q \to Kp \text{ conclude } Kp. \tag{1}$$

Even from the point of view of propositional logic this scheme is completely sound. If we think that this is an unpleasant situation in the case of our interpretation, we must have a closer look at the premises of (1). Indeed, the last premise ($q \to Kp$: "if John's heart-beat doubles, I know he is lying") does not seem to make sense: the doubling of John's heart-beat does not affect my knowledge as long I am not aware of this change in his physical condition. In other words, instead of the premise mentioned ($q \to Kp$), we probably prefer a premise with a shift of *scope* of the knowledge operator: I know that, if John's heart-beat doubles, he is lying to me. This would give the unsound scheme:

$$\text{from } p,\ p \to q,\ K(q \to p) \text{ conclude } Kp. \tag{2}$$

It is interesting to observe that the bare formal representation of the arguments, and the explicit use of modal operators, already enlightens matters tremendously. Moreover, formalisations like (1) and (2) offer a further analysis of the problem. For instance, under what circumstances *would* it be acceptable to conclude Kp? One way to think about this is to try another instantiation of (some of) the primitives. For example,

p: John lies to me (3)
q: John stammers while talking to me.

The difference between (1) and (3) is that, in (3), the evidence for John's lying will be clear to me, so it seems reasonable to add the premise that I know that John stammers to me (whenever he does), giving

$$\text{from } p,\ p \to q,\ q \to Kq,\ K(q \to p), \text{ conclude } Kp. \tag{4}$$

The reader may ask whether the argument in (4) is valid: the answer in the 'standard' modal epistemic logic that we shall treat in Chapter 1 would be positive, since it would use the following accepted subargument:

$$\text{from } K(q \to p) \text{ conclude } Kq \to Kp. \tag{5}$$

In fact, the argument (5) is considered a *characteristic scheme* for modal logic. It is valid in any approach in which the K-operator is considered as a modal (necessity-type) operator. However, we shall see in Chapter 2 that this validity is sometimes questionable.

How do we know whether inferences like (2) are unsound for the (modal) epistemic logic under consideration? The answer is that modal logic is provided with a very appealing *model theory,* in which exactly those conclusions that are derivable in the logic are valid. In this model theory, or *semantics*, the notion of *possible world* plays a vital role. This notion, for which the term *situation* is also used occasionally, goes back to Leibniz, and was further developed by philosophers like Carnap and Kanger. However, it was not until the formalisation by Kripke ([Kri63]) that this notion became fully recognised by modal logicians. To put it more strongly, Kripke's work was the start of a prosperous period in which all kinds of new modal logics were developed — not only dealing with knowledge and belief, but also with such notions as time, obligation and action — each of them equipped with its *possible world semantics* or *Kripke semantics.*

To get an idea of this Kripke-style semantics using possible worlds: consider a student in a classroom without a view to the outside of the building. As he is more interested in plans for the afternoon than in the lecture today, he is wondering whether it is raining outside (denoted by the proposition r). As he cannot see outside, he considers two situations (worlds) as possible, one in which r holds, and one in which ¬r holds. So he does not know (for sure) whether r holds. On the other hand, in both situations it holds that the lecture is boring (b) and (having completed primary school successfully) that $2 \times 2 = 4$. So, assuming that these two situations are the only ones that are considered possible by the student, he knows that b and that $2 \times 2 = 4$. In general, knowing an assertion φ is modelled by the property that all possible worlds (i.e. worlds that are considered possible on the basis of one's knowledge) satisfy φ.

In the example we formalized in (2), we had a situation, or world (say w), in which the premises express that the following hold: John lies to me (p), If John lies to me, his heart-beat doubles ($p \to q$) and I know that, if his heart-beat doubles, John lies to me: $K(q \to p)$. Assuming that p and q are the only propositions that are relevant, we are led to the following model of (epistemically) possible worlds:

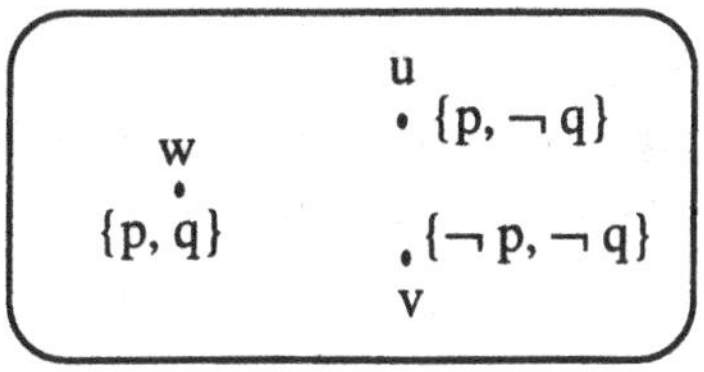

w: {p, q}
u: {p, ¬q}
v: {¬p, ¬q}

Figure 0.1

Note that, since the student knows (in world w) that q implies p, the only situations that are considered possible (epistemically) by him are worlds in which $(q \rightarrow p)$ is true (worlds u, v, and w itself). Now it is clear that the argument of (2) is not valid: in w, the formulas p, $p \rightarrow q$ and $K(q \rightarrow p)$ are true, but Kp is not; for, not in all worlds that were considered possible, p is true (it is not in v). We are deliberately slightly vague about what the the picture of Figure 0.1 denotes exactly (precise definitions will follow in Chapter 1): for the moment, let us assume it to be the set of worlds *that are epistemically compatible with the agent's knowledge at w*. In Chapter 1, we will make this idea of basing knowledge on possible worlds precise, and we shall see what consequences this approach has for the K-operator. In fact, here we shall lay a modal logic foundation of knowledge, treating both semantics and proof-theory. In Appendix A1 and A2 we shall also treat some alternative (non-modal) bases for epistemic logic that can be found in the literature. Furthermore in Chapter 1, we pay special attention to the logic of knowledge for one agent, where some simplifications can be made both semantically and syntactically (the latter pertaining to certain normal forms).

Specific applications of epistemic logic in the areas of computer science and artificial intelligence show up in a still growing variety. At the end of Chapter 1 and in Chapter 2, we shall discuss the use of epistemic logic for reasoning about distributed systems and intelligent systems. We shall see how epistemic logic is used for reasoning about protocols for communication (where processor A keeps sending a message until it knows that B knows the message — $K_A K_B m$; and B, on its turn, has to know whether A knows this — $K_B K_A K_B m$, in order to decide that a new message can be expected instead of the repetition of the old one). Furthermore, it is shown how modal epistemic logic can be fruitfully used to study other epistemic notions (like *explicit, implicit* (or *distributed*), and *common knowledge*) in the area of distributed systems. Finally, in this chapter attention is paid to other epistemic notions, such as various forms of *belief*, with some special focus on the problem of so-called logical omniscience: in standard epistemic (doxastic) logic, belief is closed under a number of idealized properties that are not always very realistic. We show several ways out of this problem at the expense of complicating the clear-cut modal semantics of the basic approach in some way or another. We also look briefly at the role of knowledge and belief in connection with other modalities such as *time* and *action*. Here we investigate expressions such as "believing that tomorrow I will believe that φ" and "I know that after the execution of the action α it will hold that ψ". These issues are especially important in the realm of AI research, for example in the area of *planning*. Chapter 2 ends with a treatment of a numerical version of standard epistemic logic, so-called *graded* modal logic, in which degrees of knowledge of a formula can be expressed by counting exceptions (in terms of worlds) to that formula.

Epistemic logic is especially useful as a 'meta'-tool to specify the contents and behaviour of, for instance, a knowledge base (KB). We may consider the facts that are stored in a KB as a set of formulas that are believed by that KB (we deliberately use the term 'belief' here, because a fact p in such a knowledge base need not be true, i.e. $Bp \wedge \neg p$ is consistent, which we do not allow for *known* formulas — cf. Chapter 2; $B\varphi$ stands for "I believe that φ"), and the modal language provides us (or the knowledge base itself) with a powerful tool to reason about its (non-) beliefs. We will discuss this in depth in Chapter 3, where we will give a number of theories to describe knowledge vs ignorance of an agent (or KB), such as *autoepistemic logic* (AEL), Levesque's logic of "all I know" and Halpern & Moses' theory of honest formulas.

However, as we shall see, the role of epistemic (and doxastic) logic in computer science and artificial intelligence goes even further. As we have said already, computer science is interlarded with *representation of* and *reasoning with* knowledge — where the reasoner may be *someone* or *something*, and the knowledge may pertain to some specified domain (the *Universe of Discourse* or *UoD*). A systematic description of "someone knows" is also relevant for the area of cognitive psychology and artificial intelligence, where we try to understand and represent *common-sense knowledge* and describe and simulate/implement *common-sense reasoning*, i.e. knowledge and reasoning about everyday things (in some UoD) in an everyday (human) way. This is less simple than it might appear at first glance. Contrary to what we are led to believe from lectures on logic, humans seldom employ just plain propositional or predicate logic while reasoning, but often (mostly?) use quite different reasoning methods as well. Most of these are even logically unsound. On the other hand, there are good reasons for a rational agent to use certain forms of these in practice. (It is not just reasoning in a wrong way.) A good example is *default reasoning*: unless it is known to the contrary, we assume (expect) something to hold. Reasoning by default is commonly used in daily life, e.g. when one is going to attend a(n announced) meeting: by default, i.e. unless something extraordinary is *known* to be the case (e.g. that the meeting is cancelled because of the illness of a speaker, etc.), we presume (expect) that the meeting will take place, and act accordingly (e.g. by taking the car to go to the place of meeting). As is clear from the way we put it, this involves the notion of *knowledge* again, and we shall treat the subject of default reasoning from an epistemic perspective in Chapter 4, along with a related topic, namely that of *counterfactual reasoning* ('reasoning against the facts'), that is to say, reasoning assuming some assertion φ while (you *know* that) φ is not actually the case. In this chapter we also encounter other default-related issues that are of great importance to AI, such as problems of representing the dynamics of systems like the infamous frame problem, and discuss these from an epistemic point of view. Furthermore, (in Chapter 3) we digress into the related topic of *non-monotonic* or *defeasible reasoning* in general, in which it is possible to lose previously inferred conclusions when more information becomes available. We shall discuss this issue, which has been a prominent AI research topic for the last 15 years, at some length as well.

Finally, a word on notation and some notions of classical logic that we shall use in this book. We assume the reader to be familiar with classical propositional logic (see for this any of the numerous introductions to logic, e.g. the 'classic' [Men64] or the more recent [Gal90] and [Gam91]). Throughout the book we shall use the following notions and notations regarding classical propositional logic: we use t and f for the semantic truth values 'true' and 'false', respectively. For a classical valuation w (i.e., a function that assigns truth (t) or falsehood (f) to the atomic propositions) we denote the fact that w satisfies a (propositional) formula φ by $w \models \varphi$. (This is defined inductively as usual.) Classical logical entailment is denoted $\models_{prop}$; $\varphi \models_{prop} \psi$ is defined formally as: for all valuations w: $w \models \varphi$ implies $w \models \psi$. A (classical) tautology φ, denoted $\models_{prop}\varphi$ (or simply $\models \varphi$, when no confusion can arise), is a formula that is satisfied by all classical valuations, that is to say, $w \models \varphi$ for all valuations w. A formula φ is (classically) satisfiable if there is a valuation w such that $w \models \varphi$. Satisfaction and logical entailment are lifted to sets of formulas: $w \models \Phi$ if $w \models \varphi$ for all $\varphi \in \Phi$; $\Phi \models_{prop} \Psi$ is defined as $w \models \Phi$ implies $w \models \Psi$, for all w. The (classically) propositional closure (or theory) of a set Φ of formulas is denoted $Th_{prop}(\Phi)$ or simply $<\Phi>$: $Th_{prop}(\Phi) = <\Phi> = \{\psi \mid \Phi \models_{prop} \psi\}$. We also use this notation for formulas: $Th_{prop}(\varphi) = <\varphi> = \{\psi \mid \varphi \models_{prop} \psi\} = Th_{prop}(\{\varphi\}) = <\{\varphi\}>$. On the syntactic level we use $\Phi \vdash_{PC} \psi$ to denote the derivability of ψ from the premises in the set Φ in (some sound and complete axiomatisation of) propositional calculus, and $\vdash_{PC} \psi$ (or $PC \vdash \psi$) that ψ is a theorem in propositional calculus. (We also extend this notation to $\Phi \vdash_{PC} \Psi$ for sets Φ and Ψ, in the obvious way.) We shall use the usual notion of propositional (in)consistency: φ is propositionally inconsistent if $\vdash_{PC} \neg\varphi$, and φ is consistent otherwise. Often we shall have occasion to use the well-known completeness result of classical propositional logic: $\vdash_{PC} \psi$ iff $\models_{prop} \psi$ or, more generally, $\Phi \vdash_{PC} \psi$ iff $\Phi \models_{prop} \psi$, so that $Th_{prop}(\Phi)$ can be alternatively given by $Th_{prop}(\Phi) = <\Phi> = \{\psi \mid \Phi \vdash_{PC} \psi\}$. Furthermore, by this completeness we also have that (classical) satisfiability and consistency are equivalent notions. Finally, we use occasionally $\Rightarrow$, $\Leftrightarrow$ and the 'outlined' symbols $\forall$ and $\exists$ as abbreviations for the meta-logical expressions 'implies', 'is equivalent to', 'for all' and 'there exist(s)', respectively. We also use the non-English but very convenient word 'iff' for 'if and only if'.

1 BASICS: THE MODAL APPROACH TO KNOWLEDGE

1.1. The Language: Epistemic Formulas

In this subsection we introduce the language of knowledge that we shall consider in the first instance. Let **P** be a set of propositional constants (atoms); $\mathbf{P} = \{p_n \mid n \in \mathbb{N}\}$ or $\mathbf{P} = \{p_0, ..., p_{n-1}\}$ for some $n \in \mathbb{N}$. We also refer to propositional constants as 'atomic' or 'primitive' propositions. Furthermore, let **A** be a set of m 'agents'. For notational convenience, we shall take $\mathbf{A} = \{1, ..., m\}$. The set $\mathcal{L}^m_\mathbf{K}(\mathbf{P})$ of epistemic formulas φ, ψ, ... over **A** is the smallest set closed under:

(i) If $p \in \mathbf{P}$ then $p \in \mathcal{L}^m_\mathbf{K}(\mathbf{P})$.

(ii) If $\varphi, \psi \in \mathcal{L}^m_\mathbf{K}(\mathbf{P})$ then $(\varphi \wedge \psi), \neg\varphi \in \mathcal{L}^m_\mathbf{K}(\mathbf{P})$.

(iii) If $\varphi \in \mathcal{L}^m_\mathbf{K}(\mathbf{P})$ then $K_i\varphi \in \mathcal{L}^m_\mathbf{K}(\mathbf{P})$, for all $i \in \mathbf{A}$.

Here $K_i\varphi$ is read as: "*agent* i *knows that* φ". From here on we omit the outermost parentheses, and write e.g. $p_1 \wedge \neg p_4$ instead of $(p_1 \wedge \neg p_4)$. Moreover we introduce $\varphi \vee \psi$, $\varphi \rightarrow \psi$ and $\varphi \leftrightarrow \psi$ as the usual abbreviations for $\neg(\neg\varphi \wedge \neg\psi)$, $\neg\varphi \vee \psi$ and $(\varphi \rightarrow \psi) \wedge (\psi \rightarrow \varphi)$, respectively, together with $\bot = p_0 \wedge \neg p_0$ (*falsum*). Occasionally we shall also use the abbreviation **true** for $\neg\bot$. When the set **P** of primitive propositions is understood, we omit it and write $\mathcal{L}^m_\mathbf{K}$ rather than $\mathcal{L}^m_\mathbf{K}(\mathbf{P})$. We may furthermore use the abbreviation $M_i\varphi$ for $\neg K_i\neg\varphi$, read as: "*agent* i *considers* φ *as possible* (on the basis of his / her knowledge)". When we only have one agent (i.e. **A** is a singleton set), we often omit subscripts, and just write Kφ and Mφ. Formulas without occurrences of the modal operators K and M are called *purely propositional* or *objective*. The set of objective formulas is denoted $\mathcal{L}_0(\mathbf{P})$ or simply $\mathcal{L}_0$.

1.1.1. EXAMPLE. The following are formulas in $\mathcal{L}^4_\mathbf{K}(\mathbf{P})$ (let $p, q \in \mathbf{P}$): p, K_1q, $\neg K_2p$, K_1K_2q, $K_2\neg K_1p$, $\neg K_1\neg M_1(p\vee q)$, $K_2(K_1q \vee K_1\neg q)$, $K_1(\neg K_3(K_4q \wedge M_1p) \vee K_2\neg q)$.

1.2. Kripke Structures

1.2.1. DEFINITION. A *Kripke structure* (or Kripke model) $\mathbb{M}$ is a tuple $\langle S, \pi, R_1, ..., R_m\rangle$ where:

(i) S is a non-empty set of *states*,

(ii) $\pi\colon S \to (\mathbf{P} \to \{t, f\})$ is a truth assignment to the propositional atoms per state,

(iii) $R_i \subseteq S \times S$ $(i = 1, ..., m)$ are the so-called *possibility/accessibility relations*.

A (Kripke) *world* w consists of a Kripke model $\mathbb{M}$ together with a distinguished state $s \in S$: $(\mathbb{M}, s)$. The interpretation of $(s, t) \in R_i$ is: in world $(\mathbb{M}, s)$ agent i considers world $(\mathbb{M}, t)$ as a *possible world*, that is to say a world that he considers as possible. In the context of epistemic logic these possible worlds are also called *epistemic alternatives*. This term emphasises that agent i considers such an alternative world as possible on the basis of his knowledge. For convenience, we may also write $R_i(s, t)$ instead of $(s, t) \in R_i$.

1.3. Kripke Semantics of Epistemic Formulas

We define the relation $w \models \varphi$ (φ *is true in* w, or w *satisfies* φ) by induction on the structure of the epistemic formula φ:

$$(\mathbb{M}, s) \models p \quad\Leftrightarrow\quad \pi(s)(p) = t \text{ for } p \in \mathbf{P}$$

$$(\mathbb{M}, s) \models \varphi \wedge \psi \quad\Leftrightarrow\quad (\mathbb{M}, s) \models \varphi \text{ and } (\mathbb{M}, s) \models \psi$$

$$(\mathbb{M}, s) \models \neg\varphi \quad\Leftrightarrow\quad (\mathbb{M}, s) \not\models \varphi$$

$$(\mathbb{M}, s) \models K_i\varphi \quad\Leftrightarrow\quad (\mathbb{M}, t) \models \varphi \text{ for all t with } (s, t) \in R_i.$$

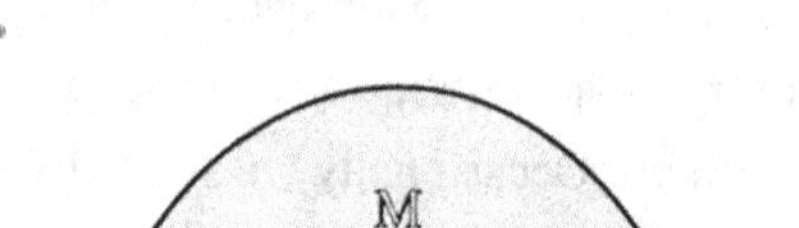
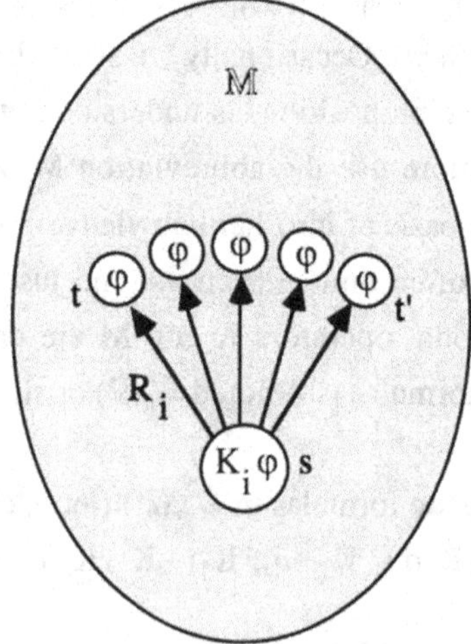

Figure 1.1

The last clause thus states "Agent i knows φ in world $(\mathbb{M}, s)$ iff φ is true in all worlds that i considers possible." (See Figure 1.1.) This can be explained as follows. In state s, the agent i has doubt about the true nature of the real world. So he considers several worlds as possible, namely the worlds t such that $R_i(s, t)$ holds. However, if in all possible worlds t with $R_i(s, t)$ it holds that φ, i has no doubts about the truth of φ: he *knows* φ (for certain).

1.3.0.1. EXERCISE. Show that regarding the abbreviations $\varphi \vee \psi$ and $\varphi \rightarrow \psi$ the following hold:

(i) $(\mathbb{M}, s) \models \varphi \vee \psi \Leftrightarrow (\mathbb{M}, s) \models \varphi$ or $(\mathbb{M}, s) \models \psi$,

(ii) $(\mathbb{M}, s) \models \varphi \rightarrow \psi \Leftrightarrow ((\mathbb{M}, s) \models \varphi \Rightarrow (\mathbb{M}, s) \models \psi)$.

1.3.0.2. EXERCISE. Show that: $(\mathbb{M}, s) \models M_i\varphi \Leftrightarrow$ there exists a t with $(s, t) \in R_i$ such that $(\mathbb{M}, t) \models \varphi$.

1.3.0.3. EXERCISE. Using the truth definition of formulas as given in this section, give the truth conditions for the formulas of Example 1.1.1.

1.3.1. EXAMPLE. Let $\mathbb{M}$ a Kripke model with $S = \{s_1, s_2, s_3\}$, $\mathbf{A} = \{\text{Alice, Bob}\}$, $\mathbf{P} = \{p\}$, and accessibility relations R_{Alice} (black arrows) and R_{Bob} (grey arrows) as in Figure 1.2.

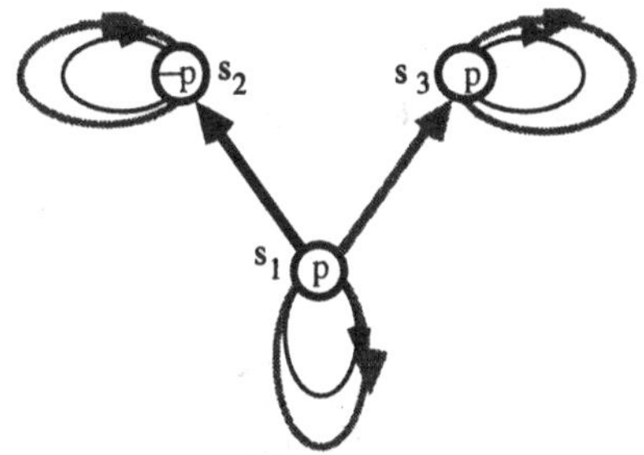

Figure 1.2

We now have (see Figure 1.2):

(i) $(\mathbb{M}, s_1) \models p$
(in s_1 p *holds)*

(ii) $(\mathbb{M}, s_1) \models \neg K_{Alice}p$
(Alice does not know in s_1 *that* p)

(iii) $(\mathbb{M}, s_1) \models \neg K_{Alice}p \wedge \neg K_{Alice}\neg p$
(Alice does not know in s_1 *whether* p *holds)*

(iv) $(\mathbb{M}, s_1) \models K_{Bob}p$
(Bob knows in s_1 *that* p, *since in* s_1 *and* s_3 p *holds)*

(v) $(\mathbb{M}, s_1) \models K_{Alice}(K_{Bob}p \vee K_{Bob}\neg p)$
(Alice knows in s_1 *that Bob knows whether* p *holds, since* $K_{Bob}p$ *holds in* s_1 *and* $K_{Bob}\neg p$ *in* s_2*.)*

(vi) $(\mathbb{M}, s_1) \models \neg K_{Bob}\neg K_{Alice}p$
(Bob does not know in s_1 *that Alice does not know that* p, *since in* s_1: $\neg K_{Alice}p$ *holds and in* s_3: $K_{Alice}p$ *holds.).*

1.3.1.1. EXERCISE. Check the above assertions.

1.3.2. EXERCISE. Let $\mathbf{P} = \{p, q\}$. Consider Kripke structure $\mathbb{M} = \langle S, \pi, R_A, R_B\rangle$ with $S = \{s_1, s_2, s_3, s_4\}$ and π, R_A, R_B as indicated in Figure 1.3 where black and grey arrows denote relations R_A and R_B, respectively.

Show that the following statements hold.

(i) $(\mathbb{M}, s_1) \models p$
(ii) $(\mathbb{M}, s_1) \models q$
(iii) $(\mathbb{M}, s_1) \models K_A p$
(iv) $(\mathbb{M}, s_1) \models \neg K_B p$
(v) $(\mathbb{M}, s_1) \models \neg K_A q$
(vi) $(\mathbb{M}, s_1) \models \neg K_B q$
(vii) $(\mathbb{M}, s_1) \models K_A K_A p$
(viii) $(\mathbb{M}, s_1) \models \neg K_B K_A p$
(ix) $(\mathbb{M}, s_1) \models \neg K_A \neg K_B p$
(x) $(\mathbb{M}, s_1) \models K_A \neg K_A q$
(xi) $(\mathbb{M}, s_1) \models \neg K_B \neg K_A q$
(xii) $(\mathbb{M}, s_1) \models \neg K_A \neg K_B q$
(xiii) $(\mathbb{M}, s_1) \models K_B \neg K_B q$

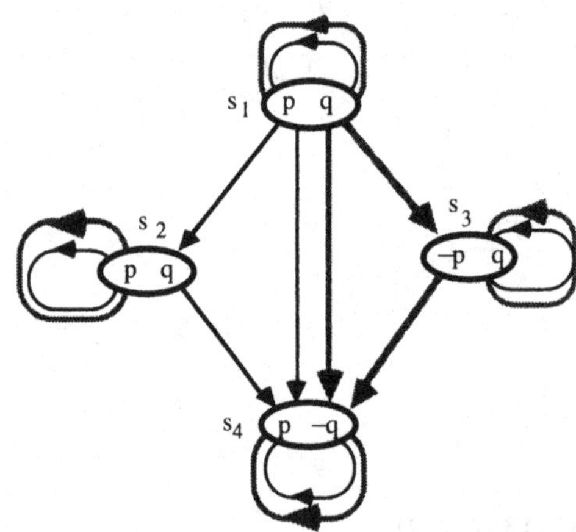

Figure 1.3

1.3.3. EXERCISE. Let $\mathbf{P} = \{p, q\}$. Construct Kripke structures $\mathbb{M} = \langle S, \pi, R_1, R_2\rangle$ such that for some $s \in S$:

(i) $(\mathbb{M}, s) \models K_1(K_1 p \wedge K_2 q) \wedge \neg K_1(p \wedge q)$

(ii) $(\mathbb{M}, s) \models K_1(K_1p \vee K_2q) \wedge \neg K_1p \wedge \neg K_1q$

(iii) $(\mathbb{M}, s) \models K_2(K_1p \wedge K_1K_2q) \wedge \neg K_2p \wedge \neg K_2K_1q$

1.3.4. DEFINITION. Let φ be an epistemic formula. Then:

(i) φ is *valid in a Kripke model* $\mathbb{M} = \langle S, \pi, R_1, ..., R_m\rangle$ if, for all $s \in S$, $(\mathbb{M}, s) \models \varphi$ (notation: $\mathbb{M} \models \varphi$);

(ii) φ is *valid*, notation $\models \varphi$, if $\mathbb{M} \models \varphi$ for all $\mathbb{M}$;

(iii) φ is *satisfiable* if there is a world $w = (\mathbb{M}, s)$ such that $w \models \varphi$.

1.3.4.1. EXERCISE. Prove that: φ is satisfiable $\Leftrightarrow\ \not\models \neg\varphi$.

1.3.5. PROPOSITION.

(i) *If* φ *is a(n instance of a) propositional tautology, then* $\models \varphi$.

(ii) $\models (K_i\varphi \wedge K_i(\varphi \rightarrow \psi)) \rightarrow K_i\psi$

(iii) *If* $\models \varphi$ *and* $\models \varphi \rightarrow \psi$ *then* $\models \psi$.

(iv) *If* $\models \varphi$ *then* $\models K_i\varphi$.

(v) $\not\models \varphi \rightarrow K_i\varphi$

(vi) $\not\models K_i\varphi \rightarrow \varphi$

(vii) $\not\models K_i\varphi \rightarrow K_iK_i\varphi$

PROOF. We only show (i), (ii) and (vi), leaving the rest to Exercise 1.3.5.1.

(i) (sketch) Considering formulas of the form $K_i\varphi$ as additional propositional atoms, take the set $\mathbf{P}^* = \mathbf{P} \cup \{K_i\varphi \mid \varphi \in \mathcal{L}_{\mathbf{K}}^m\}$, and consider truth assignment functions $\pi^* : S \rightarrow \mathbf{P}^* \rightarrow \{t, f\}$. Now define for models $\mathbb{M}^* = \langle S, \pi^*\rangle$ satisfaction of epistemic formulas as follows: $(\mathbb{M}^*, s) \models p \Leftrightarrow \pi^*(s)(p) = t$ for $p \in \mathbf{P}^*$ and for conjunction and negation we use the familiar clauses. (Note that we now do *not* have—or need—the modal clause interpreting $K_i\varphi$ by means of accessibility relations.) Clearly, these clauses regarding $\mathbb{M}^*$ are in complete accord with classical propositional logic, and thus we have that $\mathbb{M}^* \models \varphi$, for any (instance of a) propositional tautology and any model $\mathbb{M}^* = \langle S, \pi^*\rangle$. Finally we note that, for a formula φ, we have that if $\mathbb{M}^* \models \varphi$ for *all* models $\mathbb{M}^* = \langle S, \pi^*\rangle$, then also it holds that $\mathbb{M} \models \varphi$ for all models $\mathbb{M} = \langle S, \pi, R_1,...,R_m\rangle$. (Since apparently the truth value of a formula of the form $K_i\varphi$ does not matter for the formula φ to be true—this truth value varies according to the π^* concerned—it can be interpreted arbitrarily, in particular in the usual modal way by use of the accessibility relations!) So we have that $\mathbb{M} \models \varphi$, for any (instance of a) propositional tautology and any model $\mathbb{M} = \langle S, \pi, R_1, ..., R_m\rangle$, i.e. $\models \varphi$.

(ii) We have to show that, for arbitrary model $\mathbb{M} = \langle S, \pi, R_1, ..., R_m\rangle$ and state $s \in S$, it holds that $(\mathbb{M}, s) \models (K_i\varphi \wedge K_i(\varphi \rightarrow \psi)) \rightarrow K_i\psi$, i.e. if $(\mathbb{M}, s) \models K_i\varphi$ and $(\mathbb{M}, s) \models K_i(\varphi \rightarrow \psi)$, then $(\mathbb{M}, s) \models K_i\psi$. So suppose $(\mathbb{M}, s) \models K_i\varphi$ and $(\mathbb{M}, s) \models K_i(\varphi \rightarrow \psi)$. This means that, for all t

with $R_i(s, t)$, we both have that $(\mathbb{M}, t) \models \varphi$ and that $(\mathbb{M}, t) \models \varphi \to \psi$. So, by Exercise 1.3.0.1 (ii) we have that $(\mathbb{M}, t) \models \psi$ for all t with $R_i(s, t)$. Thus $(\mathbb{M}, s) \models K_i\psi$.
(vi) It is sufficient to give a model $\mathbb{M} = \langle S, \pi, R_1, ..., R_m \rangle$ and a state $s \in S$ such that $(\mathbb{M}, s) \not\models K_ip \to p$, for $p \in \mathbf{P}$, and some $1 \le i \le m$. We show that the model $\mathbb{M} = \langle \{s_1, s_2\}, \pi, R_1, ..., R_m \rangle$ with $\pi(s_1)(p) = f$, $\pi(s_2)(p) = t$, and $R_i = \{(s_1, s_2)\}$ satisfies the requirement: clearly $(\mathbb{M}, s_1) \models K_ip$, since $(\mathbb{M}, s_2) \models p$. On the other hand, $(\mathbb{M}, s_1) \not\models p$. So, $(\mathbb{M}, s_1) \not\models K_ip \to p$. ■

1.3.5.1. EXERCISE. Prove Proposition 1.3.5, parts (iii), (iv), (v) and (vii).

1.3.5.2. REMARKS. Proposition 1.3.5 (i) says that the modal logic that we have developed thus far is an extension of classical propositional logic: all classical propositional tautologies are still valid. (ii) gives us a first property of knowledge: it is closed under logical consequence. It is rather ironic that this property, in fact the only non-trivial property of knowledge so far, is one that is rather unrealistic for real agents. For instance, for human agents it is not to be expected that their knowledge is closed under logical consequence, since the mere fact that this would yield as a consequence that humans have the disposal of an infinite body of knowledge, makes this debatable already. On the other hand property (ii) is very intrinsically connected to the modal approach to knowledge: in Chapter 2 we shall discuss this issue further and we shall have to pull a number of tricks to get rid of it. (iii) is nothing more and nothing less than modus ponens. (iv) states that every valid formula is known to every agent. This, too, may be too idealistic a property, which we shall return to in Chapter 2. For the moment it suffices to distinguish (iv) from the formula in (v), which states something completely different, namely, if a formula is true, an agent would know it. This is (fortunately) not a valid formula! One would perhaps expect the converse, the formula mentioned in (vi): if some formula is known, it is true. Unfortunately, this is not a valid formula either, but we shall see that in the extensions of the present basic logic to be discussed later this formula will be indeed valid!

1.3.5.3. EXERCISE. Show that, for any epistemic formula φ and ψ, the following hold.

(i) $\models K_i(\varphi \wedge \psi) \leftrightarrow (K_i\varphi \wedge K_i\psi)$

(ii) $\models K_i\varphi \to K_i(\varphi \vee \psi)$

(iii) $\not\models K_i(\varphi \vee \psi) \leftrightarrow (K_i\varphi \vee K_i\psi)$

(iv) $\models M_i(\varphi \vee \psi) \leftrightarrow (M_i\varphi \vee M_i\psi)$

(v) $\not\models K_i\neg\varphi \to \neg K_i\varphi$

(vi) $\models \neg K_i\bot \leftrightarrow (K_i\varphi \to \neg K_i\neg\varphi)$

(vii) $\not\models \neg K_i\varphi \to K_i\neg\varphi$

In Proposition 1.3.5 and Exercise 1.3.5.3 we have encountered some first properties of knowledge. In the next section we shall give an axiom system for the logic so far. However, it is also evident that this logic will only be a first approximation of a logic of knowledge.

1.4. The Axiom System K

We now present a first and tentative (later we shall add more properties) axiomatic system for knowledge: $\mathbf{K_{(m)}}$, with respect to a set of agents $\mathbf{A} = \{1, ..., m\}$. The system consists of:

Axioms:

(A1) All (instances of) propositional tautologies

(A2) $(K_i\varphi \wedge K_i(\varphi \rightarrow \psi)) \rightarrow K_i\psi$ for $i = 1, ..., m$

Derivation rules:

(R1) $\dfrac{\varphi \quad \varphi \rightarrow \psi}{\psi}$ *Modus ponens*

(R2) $\dfrac{\varphi}{K_i\varphi}$ $(i = 1, ..., m)$ *Necessitation*

The name of the last rule, Necessitation, stems from the general modal framework, in which K (or denoted usually by $\Box$) has the meaning of necessity.

Concerning axiom (A1) we may remark that this also applies to instances of propositional tautologies that involve epistemic formulas such as e.g. $K_1p \rightarrow K_1p$. Axiom (A2), which is generally called the *K-axiom,* says that the knowledge of agent i is closed under classical logical consequence. Note that (A2) is equivalent to $K_i(\varphi \rightarrow \psi) \rightarrow (K_i\varphi \rightarrow K_i\psi)$, which is sometimes given as an alternative axiom.

1.4.1. DEFINITION. A *derivation* of a formula φ is a finite sequence of formulas $\varphi_1, \varphi_2, ..., \varphi_n = \varphi$, where each φ_i, for $1 \leq i \leq n$, is either an instance of the axioms (or rather axiom schemes) (A1) and (A2), or the conclusion of one of the rules (R1) and (R2) of which the premises have been derived already, i.e. appear as φ_j in the sequence with $j < i$. When we can derive an epistemic formula φ by using the axioms and rules of $\mathbf{K_{(m)}}$, we write $\mathbf{K_{(m)}} \vdash \varphi$ (φ *is* $\mathbf{K_{(m)}}$-*provable*). In this case, φ is called a $\mathbf{K_{(m)}}$-theorem. If $m = 1$, we often omit the subscript (1), and write **K**. We furthermore stress that the rules should thus only be applied in cases where the premises are already proven as theorems. In particular, one *cannot* use (R2) to derive a formula $\varphi \rightarrow K_i\varphi$, for arbitrary φ. This is not to be confused with a derivation of a formula $K_i\varphi$

for some particular φ that has been established already as a theorem (such as e.g. $p \vee \neg p$), which *is* allowed. We return to this very important issue later, after we have discussed the soundness of the system.

1.4.1.1. EXERCISE. (i) Prove that the following rule is derivable in system $\mathbf{K_{(m)}}$:

$$\frac{\varphi_1 \leftrightarrow \varphi_2}{K_i\varphi_1 \leftrightarrow K_i\varphi_2}$$

that is, prove: $\vdash \varphi_1 \leftrightarrow \varphi_2 \Rightarrow \vdash K_i\varphi_1 \leftrightarrow K_i\varphi_2$.

(ii) Prove the following powerful derived rule in system $\mathbf{K_{(m)}}$, which enables us to substitute equivalent formulas:

$$\frac{\varphi_1 \leftrightarrow \varphi_2}{\psi \leftrightarrow \psi[\varphi_1/\varphi_2]}$$

where $\psi[\varphi_1/\varphi_2]$ denotes the formula ψ in which φ_1 is replaced by φ_2. Semantically this rule means that formulas that are equivalent in all possible worlds may be substituted for each other in any epistemic formula while conserving truth: if $\vdash \varphi_1 \leftrightarrow \varphi_2$, then $\vdash \psi \leftrightarrow \psi\,[\varphi_1/\varphi_2]$.

1.4.1.2. EXERCISE. Prove that for any epistemic formulas φ and ψ the following hold.

(i) $\mathbf{K_{(m)}} \vdash K_i(\varphi \wedge \psi) \leftrightarrow (K_i\varphi \wedge K_i\psi)$

(ii) $\mathbf{K_{(m)}} \vdash (K_i\varphi \vee K_i\psi) \rightarrow K_i(\varphi \vee \psi)$

(iii) $\mathbf{K_{(m)}} \vdash \neg K_i\bot \leftrightarrow (K_i\varphi \rightarrow \neg K_i\neg\varphi)$

(iv) $\mathbf{K_{(m)}} \vdash M_i(\varphi \vee \psi) \leftrightarrow (M_i\varphi \vee M_i\psi)$

(v) $\mathbf{K_{(m)}} \vdash M_i(\varphi \wedge \psi) \rightarrow (M_i\varphi \wedge M_i\psi)$

1.4.2. DEFINITION.

(i) φ is *consistent* if $\mathbf{K_{(m)}} \nvdash \neg\varphi$.

(ii) A finite set $\{\varphi_1, ..., \varphi_k\}$ is *consistent* if the conjunction $\varphi_1 \wedge \cdots \wedge \varphi_k$ is consistent.

(iii) An infinite set Φ of epistemic formulas is *consistent* if any finite subset of Φ is consistent.

(iv) Formulas and sets of formulas are called *inconsistent* if they are not consistent.

(v) A set Φ of formulas is *maximally consistent* if:

  (1) Φ is consistent,

  (2) $\Phi \cup \{\psi\}$ is inconsistent for any epistemic formula $\psi \notin \Phi$.

Except for $\mathbf{K_{(m)}}$ these notions can be defined for every axiom system **S** for epistemic formulas. We then speak of **S**-theorems, **S**-(in)consistent and maximally **S**-consistent. We shall assume that any axiom system **S** for epistemic formulas is an extension of propositional logic, i.e. contains axiom (A1) and rule (R1). Strictly speaking, in Definition 1.4.2, we should say $\mathbf{K_{(m)}}$-consistent and maximally $\mathbf{K_{(m)}}$-consistent. However, for convenience, we shall omit the $\mathbf{K_{(m)}}$-prefix when no confusion can arise.

1.4.2.1. NOTATION. Let Δ be a finite set of formulas. For convenience, the *conjunction* of the formulas in Δ will also be denoted by Δ. Thus if $\Delta = \{\varphi_1, ..., \varphi_n\}$, $\neg\Delta$ stands for the formula $\neg(\varphi_1 \wedge ... \wedge \varphi_n)$. Note that this notation is in accord with Definition 1.4.2(i,ii).

1.4.2.2. EXERCISE. Let Δ be a finite set of formulas. Show that:

(i) Δ is **S**-inconsistent $\Leftrightarrow \mathbf{S} \vdash \Delta \to \bot$,

(ii) $\Delta \cup \{\varphi\}$ is **S**-inconsistent $\Leftrightarrow \mathbf{S} \vdash \Delta \to \neg\varphi$.

(Hint: Note that in propositional calculus $\neg\varphi \leftrightarrow (\varphi \to \bot)$ is a tautology for any φ.)

1.4.2.3. EXERCISE. Let Φ be an **S**-consistent set of epistemic formulas. Let Φ° denote the propositional closure of Φ, defined by $\Phi^\circ = \{\varphi \mid \{A1, R1\} \vdash \Phi \to \varphi\}$ $(= \langle\Phi\rangle)$. Show that Φ° is **S**-consistent as well.

1.4.3. LEMMA. *Let* **S** *be an axiom system for epistemic formulas. (So* **S** *contains* A1 *and* R1.*)*

(i) *Every* **S**-*consistent set of formulas* Φ *can be extended to a maximally* **S**-*consistent set.*

(ii) *Let* Φ *be a maximally* **S**-*consistent set of formulas. Then it holds for all* φ,ψ:

(1) *either* $\varphi \in \Phi$, *or* $\neg\varphi \in \Phi$;

(2) $\varphi \wedge \psi \in \Phi \Leftrightarrow \varphi \in \Phi$ *and* $\psi \in \Phi$;

(3) *if* $\varphi \in \Phi$ *and* $\varphi \to \psi \in \Phi$ *then* $\psi \in \Phi$;

(4) *if* $\mathbf{S} \vdash \varphi$ *then* $\varphi \in \Phi$.

PROOF. (i) We enumerate all epistemic formulas: $\varphi_0, \varphi_1, \varphi_2, ..., \varphi_n, ...$. We define a sequence of sets of formulas

$$\Phi_0 \subseteq \Phi_1 \subseteq \Phi_2 \subseteq ... \Phi_n \subseteq ...$$

as follows, with induction on n: $\Phi_0 = \Phi$, and, having defined Φ_n:

$$\Phi_{n+1} = \begin{cases} \Phi_n \text{, if } \Phi_n \cup \{\varphi_n\} \text{ is inconsistent;} \\ \Phi_n \cup \{\varphi_n\}, \text{ otherwise.} \end{cases}$$

Moreover we define

$$\Phi_\omega = \bigcup_{n\geq 0} \Phi_n.$$

CLAIM I. Φ_ω is **S**-consistent.

CLAIM II. Φ_ω is maximally **S**-consistent.

PROOF OF CLAIM I. Suppose Φ_ω is not **S**-consistent. Then by Definition 1.4.2 there exists a finite subset $\Psi \subseteq \Phi_\omega$ that is **S**-inconsistent. Now $\Psi \subseteq \Phi_n$ for some n. But Φ_n is **S**-consistent, by construction. This yields a contradiction. Hence Φ_ω is **S**-consistent. ■*Claim I*

PROOF OF CLAIM II. Suppose Φ_ω is not maximally **S**-consistent. Then there exists a fomula φ such that $\varphi \notin \Phi_\omega$ and $\Phi_\omega \cup \{\varphi\}$ is **S**-consistent. Let $\varphi = \varphi_m$ in the enumeration. Then apparently $\Phi_m \cup \{\varphi_m\}$ is **S**-inconsistent, since otherwise φ_m would have been included in Φ_ω. But then $\Phi_\omega \cup \{\varphi\}$ is **S**-inconsistent as well, contradicting what was stated above. Consequently, Φ_ω is maximally **S**-consistent. ■*Claim II*

(ii) PROOF OF (1). Suppose that the assertion does not hold. Then there exists φ with: $\varphi \notin \Phi$ and $\neg\varphi \notin \Phi$. Since Φ is maximally **S**-consistent, we have that both $\Phi \cup \{\varphi\}$ and $\Phi \cup \{\neg\varphi\}$ are **S**-inconsistent. So there exists a finite subset $\Gamma \subseteq \Phi$ such that $\Gamma \cup \{\varphi\}$ is **S**-inconsistent, and a finite subset $\Delta \subseteq \Phi$ such that $\Delta \cup \{\neg\varphi\}$ is **S**-inconsistent. Therefore also $\Gamma \cup \Delta \cup \{\varphi\}$ and $\Gamma \cup \Delta \cup \{\neg\varphi\}$ are **S**-inconsistent. Note that $\Gamma \cup \Delta$ is finite, say $\Gamma \cup \Delta = \{\psi_1, ..., \psi_m\}$. Then

$$\mathbf{S} \vdash \neg(\psi_1 \wedge ... \wedge \psi_m \wedge \varphi),$$
$$\mathbf{S} \vdash \neg(\psi_1 \wedge ... \wedge \psi_m \wedge \neg\varphi).$$

Since **S** allows inferences from propositional calculus (**S** contains A1 and R1), it follows that

$$\mathbf{S} \vdash \neg\psi_1 \vee ... \vee \neg\psi_m \vee \neg\varphi,$$
$$\mathbf{S} \vdash \neg\psi_1 \vee ... \vee \neg\psi_m \vee \varphi.$$

So $\mathbf{S} \vdash (\psi_1 \wedge ... \wedge \psi_m) \to \neg\varphi,$

$\mathbf{S} \vdash (\psi_1 \wedge ... \wedge \psi_m) \to \varphi.$

Thus $\mathbf{S} \vdash (\psi_1 \wedge ... \wedge \psi_m) \to (\neg\varphi \wedge \varphi)$

$\mathbf{S} \vdash (\psi_1 \wedge ... \wedge \psi_m) \to \bot$

$\mathbf{S} \vdash \neg(\psi_1 \wedge ... \wedge \psi_m).$

Hence Φ is **S**-inconsistent, which yields a contradiction. So the assertion holds.

PROOF OF (2). ($\Rightarrow$) Suppose $\varphi \wedge \psi \in \Phi$, and $\varphi \notin \Phi$. So $\Phi \cup \{\varphi\}$ is inconsistent, that is to say, for some finite subset Γ of Φ, $\Gamma \cup \{\varphi\}$ is inconsistent, i.e. $\mathbf{S} \vdash \neg(\Gamma \wedge \varphi)$. But then also $\Gamma \cup \{\varphi\wedge\psi\}$ is inconsistent (because $\Gamma \cup \{\varphi \wedge \psi\} \vdash_{PC} \Gamma \cup \{\varphi\}$), which contradicts the assumption that Φ is **S**-consistent.

($\Leftarrow$) Suppose $\varphi \in \Phi$, $\psi \in \Phi$ and $\varphi \wedge \psi \notin \Phi$. Then $\Phi \cup \{\varphi \wedge \psi\}$ is inconsistent, i.e. for some finite $\Gamma \subseteq \Phi$ it holds that $\mathbf{S} \vdash \neg(\Gamma \wedge \varphi \wedge \psi)$. This states that the set $\Gamma \cup \{\varphi, \psi\}$, which is a finite subset of Φ, is inconsistent. So Φ itself is **S**-inconsistent, yielding a contradiction. Hence, $\varphi \wedge \psi \in \Phi$.

PROOF OF (3). Assume $\varphi \in \Phi$ and $\varphi \rightarrow \psi \in \Phi$. Now suppose $\psi \notin \Phi$. So $\Phi \cup \{\psi\}$ is **S**-inconsistent, i.e. there is a finite $\Gamma \subseteq \Phi$ such that $\Gamma \cup \{\psi\}$ is **S**-inconsistent. But then also $\Gamma \cup \{\varphi, \varphi \rightarrow \psi\}$ is **S**-inconsistent (because $\Gamma \cup \{\varphi, \varphi \rightarrow \psi\} \vdash_{PC} \Gamma \cup \{\psi\}$); contradicting the **S**-consistency of Φ.

PROOF OF (4). See Exercise 1.4.3.2. ■

1.4.3.1. EXERCISE. Let Φ be maximally **S**-consistent. Show that, in addition to Lemma 1.4.3(ii), the following holds:

$$\varphi \vee \psi \in \Phi \quad \Leftrightarrow \quad \varphi \in \Phi \text{ or } \psi \in \Phi.$$

1.4.3.2. EXERCISE. Prove Lemma 1.4.3(ii) part 4.

1.4.3.3. EXERCISE. Give an alternative proof of Lemma 1.4.3(ii), part 2, using parts 3 and 4.

1.4.4. NOTATION.
(i) Let $\mathcal{M}$ be a class of Kripke models. Then $\mathcal{M} \models \varphi$ stands for: for all $\mathbb{M} \in \mathcal{M}$ it holds that $\mathbb{M} \models \varphi$.
(ii) $\mathcal{K}_{(\mathbf{m})}$ is the class of all Kripke models with m agents ($m \geq 1$). Instead of $\mathcal{K}_{(\mathbf{m})} \models \varphi$ we write $\models \varphi$, as we have seen already in Definition 1.3.4(ii). (Note that in the notation $\models \varphi$ the number m of agents is suppressed for convenience.)

1.4.5. DEFINITION. (i) Let **S** be an axiom system for epistemic formulas, and let $\mathcal{M}$ be a class of Kripke models. Then **S** is called *sound with respect to* $\mathcal{M}$, if $\mathbf{S} \vdash \varphi \Rightarrow \mathcal{M} \models \varphi$.
(ii) **S** is called *complete with respect to* $\mathcal{M}$, if $\mathcal{M} \models \varphi \Rightarrow \mathbf{S} \vdash \varphi$.

1.4.5.1. REMARK. Having discussed the soundness of the system **K**, it is worth while to return to the remarks we made in Definition 1.4.1 concerning the use of the necessitation rule (R2). Semantically speaking, the use of the necessitation rule amounts to the derivation of a valid formula from a valid formula: if $\models \varphi$, then $\models K_i\varphi$. This is true, witness Proposition 1.3.5 (iv). An appeal to (R2) within an assertion to derive something like $\varphi \rightarrow K_i\varphi$ is completely different, and not correct, witness Proposition 1.3.5 (v), which states $\not\models \varphi \rightarrow K_i\varphi$. This is especially treacherous, since in ordinary classical propositional logic we are used to confusing these two derivability notions. The reason for this is that in propositional logic we have a different notion of derivability $\vdash_{PC}$, for which it holds that: $\varphi \vdash_{PC} \psi \Leftrightarrow \models_{prop} \varphi \rightarrow \psi$. (This is a consequence of the so-called deduction theorem in propositional logic. In modal logic we do not have a deduction theorem in this way.) So we have to be careful when applying (R2).

1.4.6. THEOREM. $\mathbf{K_{(m)}}$ *is sound with respect to* $\mathcal{K}_{(m)}$.

PROOF. From Proposition 1.3.5 it follows that $\mathcal{K}_{(m)}$ satisfies the axioms (A1) and (A2) of system $\mathbf{K_{(m)}}$. Proposition 1.3.5 also shows that the rules (R1) and (R2) of system $\mathbf{K_{(m)}}$ hold in the sense that, if the premises of the rules are valid, then the consequents are valid as well. An inductive proof on the length of derivations then yields that every provable formula is true. ∎

1.4.7. THEOREM. $\mathbf{K_{(m)}}$ *is complete with respect to* $\mathcal{K}_{(m)}$.

PROOF. We have to show that, for all $\varphi \in \mathcal{L}^m_{\mathbf{K}}$,

$$\models \varphi \;\Rightarrow\; \mathbf{K_{(m)}} \vdash \varphi.$$

Or, equivalently,

$$\mathbf{K_{(m)}} \nvdash \varphi \;\Rightarrow\; \not\models \varphi,$$

i.e.:

$$\mathbf{K_{(m)}} \nvdash \varphi \;\Rightarrow \text{there is a model } \mathbb{M} \text{ with } \mathbb{M} \not\models \varphi.$$

In its turn this is equivalent to

$$\mathbf{K_{(m)}} \nvdash \varphi \;\Rightarrow \text{there is a world } (\mathbb{M}, s) \text{ such that } (\mathbb{M}, s) \not\models \varphi;$$

equivalently

$$\mathbf{K_{(m)}} \nvdash \varphi \;\Rightarrow \text{there is a world } (\mathbb{M}, s) \text{ such that } (\mathbb{M}, s) \models \neg\varphi;$$

equivalently (by replacing φ by $\neg\varphi$)

$$\mathbf{K_{(m)}} \nvdash \neg\varphi \;\Rightarrow \text{there is a world } (\mathbb{M}, s) \text{ such that } (\mathbb{M}, s) \models \varphi.$$

Thus proving completeness is equivalent to showing that every *consistent* formula is *satisfiable*. In order to prove this it is sufficient to show that every *consistent set* of formulas is satisfiable; and by Lemma 1.4.3(i) for this it is sufficient to show that every *maximally consistent set* Φ of formulas is satisfiable. This is established by means of the construction of a so-called *canonical* Kripke structure $\mathbb{M}^c$ for $\mathbf{K_{(m)}}$ containing a state s_Φ with $(\mathbb{M}^c, s_\Phi) \models \Phi$, for each maximally consistent set Φ.

The canonical Kripke model is defined as

$$\mathbb{M}^c = \langle S^c, \pi^c, R_1{}^c, \ldots, R_m{}^c \rangle$$

with $S^c = \{s_\Theta \mid \Theta \text{ is a maximally consistent set of formulas}\}$

$$\pi^c(s_\Theta)(p) = \begin{cases} \mathbf{t} \text{ if } p \in \Theta \\ \mathbf{f} \text{ if } p \notin \Theta \end{cases}$$

$$R_i{}^c = \{(s_\Theta, s_\Psi) \mid \Theta/K_i \subseteq \Psi\},$$

where $\Theta/K_i = \{\varphi \mid K_i\varphi \in \Theta\}$.

REMARKS.
1. In fact a state s_Θ is the maximally consistent set of formulas Θ itself. The notation s_Θ just serves the intuition.
2. Note that the definition of $R_i{}^c$ says that, for all states s_Θ, s_Ψ in the canonical model (and thus for every maximal consistent Θ and Ψ): $R_i{}^c(s_\Theta, s_\Psi) \Leftrightarrow \Theta/K_i \subseteq \Psi \Leftrightarrow (\forall\varphi: K_i\varphi \in \Theta \Rightarrow \varphi \in \Psi)$, which is in line with the definition of the interpretation of the modal operator K_i.

Below we shall prove the so-called 'coincidence lemma' or 'truth lemma' asserting:

$$\forall\varphi: \quad (\mathbb{M}^c, s_\Phi) \models \varphi \quad \Leftrightarrow \quad \varphi \in \Phi,$$

which implies $(\mathbb{M}^c, s_\Phi) \models \Phi$, for any maximally consistent set Φ, thus completing the completeness proof. ■

To prove the coincidence lemma, we prove by induction on the structure of φ that:

1.4.8. LEMMA. *For any maximally consistent* Θ *it holds that* $\forall\varphi : (\mathbb{M}^c, s_\Theta) \models \varphi \Leftrightarrow \varphi \in \Theta$.

PROOF. Here we use, for reasons that will become apparent below, that the complexity of $\neg\varphi$ is less than that of $K_i\varphi$. Actually, it suffices to take the length of formulas as the induction measure, counting the modal operator K_i for two symbols, as it is in the present representation using an index.

Case 1. $\varphi = p \in \mathbf{P}$, the set of primitive propositions: directly from the definition of π^c.

Case 2. $\varphi = \varphi_1 \wedge \varphi_2$:

$(\mathbb{M}^c, s_\Theta) \models \varphi_1 \wedge \varphi_2 \quad \Leftrightarrow$

$(\mathbb{M}^c, s_\Theta) \models \varphi_1$ and $(\mathbb{M}^c, s_\Theta) \models \varphi_2 \quad \Leftrightarrow$ (induction hypothesis)

$\varphi_1 \in \Theta$ and $\varphi_2 \in \Theta \quad \Leftrightarrow$ (maximal consistency of Θ)

$\varphi_1 \wedge \varphi_2 \in \Theta$.

Case 3. $\varphi = \neg\varphi_1$:

$(\mathbb{M}^c, s_\Theta) \models \neg\varphi_1 \quad \Leftrightarrow$

$(\mathbb{M}^c, s_\Theta) \not\models \varphi_1 \quad \Leftrightarrow$ (induction hypothesis)

$\varphi_1 \notin \Theta \quad \Leftrightarrow$ (maximal consistency of Θ)

$\neg\varphi_1 \in \Theta$.

Case 4. $\varphi = K_i\psi$.

($\Leftarrow$) Suppose $\varphi = K_i\psi \in \Theta$. Then $\psi \in \Theta/K_i$ and so by the definition of $R_i{}^c$

$(s_\Theta, s_\Psi) \in R_i{}^c \quad \Rightarrow$

$\psi \in \Theta/K_i \subseteq \Psi \quad \Rightarrow$ (induction hypothesis)

$(\mathbb{M}^c, s_\Psi) \models \psi$.

So $(\mathbb{M}^c, s_\Psi) \models \psi$ for all Ψ with $(s_\Theta, s_\Psi) \in R_i{}^c$, i.e.

$(\mathbb{M}^c, s_\Theta) \models K_i\psi$.

($\Rightarrow$) Assume that $(\mathbb{M}^c, s_\Theta) \models K_i\psi$. (*)

CLAIM. $(\Theta/K_i) \cup \{\neg\psi\}$ *is inconsistent.*

PROOF OF THE CLAIM. Suppose $(\Theta/K_i) \cup \{\neg\psi\}$ is consistent. Then by Lemma 1.4.3(ii) there exists a maximally consistent extension Ψ, and since $\Theta/K_i \subseteq (\Theta/K_i) \cup \{\neg\psi\} \subseteq \Psi$ we have $(s_\Theta, s_\Psi) \in R_i^c$. Furthermore, $\neg\psi \in \Psi$ and so by the induction hypothesis (having the remark concerning the induction measure in mind!) $(\mathbb{M}^c, s_\Psi) \models \neg\psi$, and so $(\mathbb{M}^c, s_\Theta) \models \neg K_i\psi$, since s_Ψ is R_i^c-accessible from s_Θ. This contradicts the assumption (*). ■*Claim*

From this it follows that some finite subset of $(\Theta/K_i) \cup \{\neg\psi\}$, say $\varphi_1, ..., \varphi_k, \neg\psi$, is inconsistent. (We may always include $\neg\psi$, since if a subset without $\neg\psi$ is already inconsistent, including $\neg\psi$ keeps the set inconsistent.) So $\vdash \neg(\varphi_1 \wedge ... \wedge \varphi_k \wedge \neg\psi)$. By propositional reasoning we now obtain:

$$\vdash \varphi_1 \rightarrow (\varphi_2 \rightarrow (...(\varphi_k \rightarrow \psi)...)).$$

Using (R2) this yields:

$$\vdash K_i(\varphi_1 \rightarrow (\varphi_2 \rightarrow (...(\varphi_k \rightarrow \psi)...))).$$

Since a maximally consistent set contains all theorems (Lemma 1.4.3(ii) part 4), we have

$$K_i(\varphi_1 \rightarrow (\varphi_2 \rightarrow (...(\varphi_k \rightarrow \psi)...))) \in \Theta. \tag{1}$$

We abbreviate $(\varphi_2 \rightarrow (...(\varphi_k \rightarrow \psi)...))$ by ξ. Since $\varphi_1,...,\varphi_k \in \Theta/K_i$, we have

$$K_i\varphi_1, ..., K_i\varphi_k \in \Theta. \tag{2}$$

With (A2):

$$\vdash K_i\varphi_1 \rightarrow (K_i(\varphi_1 \rightarrow \xi) \rightarrow K_i\xi).$$

Hence (since Θ contains all theorems)

$$K_i\varphi_1 \rightarrow (K_i(\varphi_1 \rightarrow \xi) \rightarrow K_i\xi) \in \Theta. \tag{3}$$

From (2),(3) and the maximal consistency of Θ it follows that

$$(K_i(\varphi_1 \rightarrow \xi) \rightarrow K_i\xi) \in \Theta. \tag{4}$$

From (1),(4) and the maximal consistency of Θ it follows that

$K_i\xi \in \Theta$.

Repetitive application of this argument yields $K_i\psi \in \Theta$. ■

1.4.8.1. EXERCISE. (i) Show that the consistency of Θ does *not* imply that Θ/K_i is consistent.

(ii) Show that, if Θ is maximally consistent and Θ/K_i is inconsistent, $K_i\varphi \in \Theta$, for *any* epistemic formula φ.

1.4.8.2. EXERCISE. Let **S** be an epistemic logic containing $\mathbf{K_{(m)}}$. Show that every **S**-theorem is valid in the canonical model $\mathbb{M}^c$, i.e. prove that $\mathbf{S} \vdash \varphi$ implies $\mathbb{M}^c \models \varphi$.

1.4.8.3. EXERCISE. Use the soundness theorem of $\mathbf{K_{(m)}}$ to prove that $\mathbf{K_{(m)}} \nvdash K_i(\varphi \vee \psi) \to K_i\varphi \vee K_i\psi$, $\mathbf{K_{(m)}} \nvdash K_i\neg\varphi \to \neg K_i\varphi$, and $\mathbf{K_{(m)}} \nvdash (M_i\varphi \wedge M_i\psi) \to M_i(\varphi \wedge \psi)$.

1.4.9. COROLLARY. *Let Φ be a set of epistemic formulas. Then*

$$\Phi \text{ is consistent} \Leftrightarrow \Phi \text{ is satisfiable.}$$

PROOF. Directly from Theorems 1.4.6 and 1.4.7. ■

1.4.9.1. EXERCISE. Let P = {p}. Are the following sets consistent (in system **K**)?

(i)	{p, ¬Kp}	(vi)	{p, Kp, ¬KKp}
(ii)	{p, K¬p}	(vii)	{p, Kp, K ¬Kp}
(iii)	{Kp, K¬p}	(viii)	{Kp, K¬K¬p}
(iv)	{Kp, ¬K¬p}	(ix)	{¬K¬Kp, ¬p}
(v)	{¬Kp, ¬K¬p}	(x)	{p, ¬Kp, K¬Kp, ¬K¬K¬Kp}

1.4.9.2. EXERCISE. Let P = {p, q}. Are the following sets consistent (in system **K**)?

(i)	{Kp, ¬Kq, p ∧ q}	(vi)	{K(p ∧ q), ¬Kp ∧ ¬Kq}
(ii)	{Kp, ¬Kq, ¬K¬Kq, p ∧ q}	(vii)	{K(Kp ∧ Kq), ¬Kp, p}
(iii)	{p, K(p ∨ q), Kp ∧ Kq}	(viii)	{Kp, K(p → q), ¬Kq}
(iv)	{K(p ∨ q), Kp, ¬Kq}	(ix)	{¬Kp, ¬K¬p, K(p → Kp)}
(v)	{K(p ∨ q), ¬Kp, K¬q}	(x)	{Kp, K ¬p, ¬Kq}

From the perspective of knowledge it is strange that e.g. {p, K¬p} and {Kp, ¬KKp} are consistent sets: in the former case it is intuitively inconsistent to state that p holds and nevertheless ¬p is known; in the latter case it seems to be inconsistent to state that an agent knows that p, but nevertheless (s)he does not know that (s)he knows p. We expect that $Kp \to p$ should hold, and $Kp \to KKp$. But, as we have seen earlier, this is not valid with respect to all

Kripke models (Proposition 1.3.5), and so by soundness of K also not derivable in **K**. This observation leads to an extension of the properties knowledge should enjoy.

1.5. Further Properties of Knowledge: The System S5

System $\mathbf{K}_{(\mathbf{m})}$ does not say much about knowledge yet. Knowledge is supposed to have additional properties, in particular it is the case that a known fact is true. Also other properties can be assumed depending on the applications concerned. Therefore, we introduce the following axioms (or rather axiom schemes):

(A3) $K_i\varphi \to \varphi$ (i = 1, ..., m)
Known facts are true.

(A4) $K_i\varphi \to K_iK_i\varphi$ (i = 1, ..., m; 'positive introspection')
An agent knows that he knows something.

(A5) $\neg K_i\varphi \to K_i\neg K_i\varphi$ (i = 1, ..., m; 'negative introspection')
An agent knows that he does not know something.

1.5.0.1. EXERCISE. Show that (A5) is equivalent to $M_i\varphi \to K_iM_i\varphi$.

We consider the following systems:

$$\mathbf{T}_{(\mathbf{m})} = \mathbf{K}_{(\mathbf{m})} + (A3)$$

$$\mathbf{S4}_{(\mathbf{m})} = \mathbf{T}_{(\mathbf{m})} + (A4)$$

$$\mathbf{S5}_{(\mathbf{m})} = \mathbf{S4}_{(\mathbf{m})} + (A5).$$

The subscript m indicates the number of agents again. One may wonder which system is the 'best' one to capture knowledge. The answer depends on the circumstances in applications. Axioms (A3) and (A4) are rather plausible; the corresponding system $\mathbf{S4}_{(\mathbf{m})}$ is generally accepted as a good representation of the properties of knowledge. If an agent knows an assertion, it is very plausible that (s)he knows that (s)he knows this. Axiom (A5), on the other hand, is very controversial, philosophically. If an agent is ignorant of the truth of an assertion, it is in general, and particularly for human agents, unlikely that (s)he knows this ignorance. However, system $\mathbf{S5}_{(\mathbf{m})}$ has nicer technical properties than the other systems (as we shall see later). Moreover, $\mathbf{S5}_{(\mathbf{m})}$ appears to be an adequate system for reasoning about distributed systems and intelligent systems with finite storage of information. For these reasons, $\mathbf{S5}_{(\mathbf{m})}$ is by far the most popular system for knowledge among computer scientists and AI researchers.

1.5.1. EXAMPLE. We give a formal proof of $\mathbf{T_{(m)}} \vdash \neg K_i(\varphi \wedge \neg K_i\varphi)$. Informally: an agent cannot know—under the **S5** assumptions concerning knowledge—both that φ holds and that he does not know that φ holds. For convenience we write K instead of K_i.

(i)	$K\neg K\varphi \vee \neg K\neg K\varphi$	(A1)
(ii)	$K\neg K\varphi \rightarrow \neg K\varphi$	(A3)
(iii)	$\neg K\varphi \vee \neg K\neg K\varphi$	(i), (ii)
(iv)	$\neg(K\varphi \wedge K\neg K\varphi)$	(iii), PC
(v)	$\varphi \wedge \neg K\varphi \rightarrow \varphi$	(A1)
(vi)	$K(\varphi \wedge \neg K\varphi \rightarrow \varphi)$	(v), (R2)
(vii)	$K(\varphi \wedge \neg K\varphi) \rightarrow K\varphi$	(vi), (A2)
(viii)	$\varphi \wedge \neg K\varphi \rightarrow \neg K\varphi$	(A1)
(ix)	$K(\varphi \wedge \neg K\varphi \rightarrow \neg K\varphi)$	(viii), (R2)
(x)	$K(\varphi \wedge \neg K\varphi) \rightarrow K\neg K\varphi$	(ix), (A2)
(xi)	$K(\varphi \wedge \neg K\varphi) \rightarrow K\varphi \wedge K\neg K\varphi$	(vii), (x)
(xii)	$\neg(K\varphi \wedge K \neg K\varphi) \rightarrow \neg K(\varphi \wedge \neg K\varphi)$	(xi), PC
(xiii)	$\neg K(\varphi \wedge \neg K\varphi)$	(iv), (xii), (R1)

1.5.1.1. EXERCISE.

(i) Prove $\mathbf{T_{(m)}} \vdash K_i\bot \leftrightarrow \bot$. Is this also true with respect to $\mathbf{K_{(m)}}$?

(ii) Prove $\mathbf{T_{(m)}} \vdash K_i\neg\varphi \rightarrow \neg K_i\varphi$.

1.5.1.2. EXERCISE. Show that the following formulas are derivable in $\mathbf{S5_{(1)}}$ (we write K instead of K_1).

(i) $\varphi \rightarrow \neg K\neg\varphi$

(ii) $K\varphi \rightarrow \neg K\neg\varphi$

(iii) $K\neg K\neg\, \varphi \leftrightarrow \neg K\neg\varphi$

(iv) $\neg K\varphi \leftrightarrow K\neg K\varphi$

(v) $\neg K\neg K\varphi \leftrightarrow K\varphi$

(vi) $K\varphi \leftrightarrow KK\varphi$ (without using A4! Note that this implies that in $\mathbf{S5_{(1)}}$ the axiom (A4) is redundant!)

(vii) $\neg K\neg\varphi \leftrightarrow \neg KK\neg\varphi$

(viii) $K\neg\bot$

(ix) $(\neg K\neg\varphi \wedge K(\varphi \rightarrow \psi)) \rightarrow \neg K\neg\psi$

(x) $K\neg K\neg K\varphi \leftrightarrow K\varphi$

(xi) $\neg K\neg K\neg K\neg\varphi \leftrightarrow \neg K\neg\varphi$

(xii) $K(\varphi \rightarrow K\varphi) \wedge \neg K\neg\varphi) \rightarrow K\varphi$

1.6. Kripke Models for Knowledge

It appears that the axioms (A3)—(A5) enforce interesting properties of the Kripke models that satisfy them. (In modal logic the study of the relations between axioms and properties of models is called *correspondence theory*, which is itself a large area.) We first introduce a number of properties for Kripke models and their accessibility relations in particular.

1.6.1. DEFINITION. Let S be the set of states of a Kripke model and $R \subseteq S \times S$ an accessibility relation.

(i) R is *reflexive* if $\forall s \in S\ (s, s) \in R$.

(ii) R is *transitive* if $\forall s, t, u \in S$: $(s, t) \in R \ \&\ (t, u) \in R \Rightarrow (s, u) \in R$.

(iii) R is *symmetrical* if $\forall s, t \in S$: $(s, t) \in R \Rightarrow (t, s) \in R$.

(iv) R is *euclidean* if $\forall s, t, u \in S$: $(s, t) \in R \ \&\ (s, u) \in R \Rightarrow (t, u) \in R$.

(v) R is *serial* if $\forall s \in S\ \exists t \in S\ (s, t) \in R$.

(vi) R is an *equivalence relation* if R is reflexive, transitive and symmetrical.

1.6.2. PROPOSITION.

(i) R *is symmetrical and transitive* $\Rightarrow$ R *is euclidean.*

(ii) R *is reflexive* $\Rightarrow$ R *is serial.*

(iii) R *is symmetrical, transitive and serial* $\Leftrightarrow$
R *is reflexive and euclidean* $\Leftrightarrow$
R *is an equivalence relation.*

PROOF. Exercise 1.6.2.1. ■

1.6.2.1. EXERCISE. Prove Proposition 1.6.2.

We call a Kripke model $\mathbb{M}$ reflexive (transitive, etc.) if all accessibility relations in $\mathbb{M}$ are reflexive (transitive, etc.).

1.6.3. DEFINITION.

(i) $\mathcal{T}_{(\mathbf{m})}$ is the class of all reflexive Kripke models with m agents.

(ii) $\mathcal{S4}_{(\mathbf{m})}$ is the class of all reflexive-transitive Kripke models with m agents.

(iii) $\mathcal{S5}_{(\mathbf{m})}$ is the class of all Kripke models with m agents with accessibility relations that are equivalence relations.

When m is irrelevant (particularly in case m = 1) we may omit the subscript (m), and write just $\mathcal{T}$, $\mathcal{S4}$ and $\mathcal{S5}$.

1.6.3.1. EXERCISE. Consider the Kripke model $\mathbb{M}$ of Exercise 1.3.2 (Figure 1.3). Is $\mathbb{M} \in \mathcal{T}_{(2)}, \mathcal{S4}_{(2)}, \mathcal{S5}_{(2)}$?

It is not difficult to see that $\mathcal{T}_{(\mathbf{m})}, \mathcal{S4}_{(\mathbf{m})}, \mathcal{S5}_{(\mathbf{m})}$ satisfy the axioms of the systems $\mathbf{T}_{(\mathbf{m})}$, $\mathbf{S4}_{(\mathbf{m})}$, $\mathbf{S5}_{(\mathbf{m})}$, respectively:

1.6.4. THEOREM (Soundness of **T**, **S4**, **S5**).

(i) $\mathbf{T}_{(\mathbf{m})} \vdash \varphi \Rightarrow \mathcal{T}_{(\mathbf{m})} \models \varphi$,

(ii) $\mathbf{S4}_{(\mathbf{m})} \vdash \varphi \Rightarrow \mathcal{S4}_{(\mathbf{m})} \models \varphi$,

(iii) $\mathbf{S5}_{(\mathbf{m})} \vdash \varphi \Rightarrow \mathcal{S5}_{(\mathbf{m})} \models \varphi$.

PROOF. We only show (iii), leaving (i) and (ii) to Exercise 1.6.4.1.
(iii). It is sufficient to show that every model in $\mathcal{S5}_{(\mathbf{m})}$ satisfies the axioms of $\mathbf{S5}_{(\mathbf{m})}$: let $\mathbb{M} = \langle S, \pi, R_1, ..., R_m \rangle \in \mathcal{S5}_{(\mathbf{m})}$, and $s \in S$. Since, for any $1 \leq i \leq m$, R_i is an equivalence relation, it is in particular reflexive and transitive. So, in particular, $\mathbb{M} \in \mathcal{T}_{(\mathbf{m})}$ and $\mathbb{M} \in \mathcal{S4}_{(\mathbf{m})}$. Hence, by (i) and (ii), we know that $\mathbb{M}$ satisfies (A3) and (A4). We now show that $\mathbb{M}$ satisfies (A5). Take $1 \leq i \leq m$. We have to show that $\mathbb{M} \models \neg K_i\varphi \rightarrow K_i\neg K_i\varphi$, i.e. $(\mathbb{M}, s) \models \neg K_i\varphi \rightarrow K_i\neg K_i\varphi$, for any $s \in S$. So suppose $(\mathbb{M}, s) \models \neg K_i\varphi$, for some arbitrary $s \in S$. This means that there is some t with $R_i(s, t)$ such that $(\mathbb{M}, t) \models \neg\varphi$. We have to show that $(\mathbb{M}, s) \models K_i\neg K_i\varphi$, i.e. for all u with $R_i(s, u)$ it holds that $(\mathbb{M}, u) \models \neg K_i\varphi$. Consider an arbitrary u such that $R_i(s, u)$. Since we already have that $R_i(s, t)$, and R_i is an equivalence relation, we obtain that also $R_i(u, t)$. Since we know that $(\mathbb{M}, t) \models \neg\varphi$, we may infer that indeed $(\mathbb{M}, u) \models \neg K_i\varphi$. ■

1.6.4.1. EXERCISE. Show that $\mathcal{T}$ and $\mathcal{S4}$ satisfy the axioms and rules of **T** and **S4**, respectively.

1.6.5. PROPOSITION. *Let* **S** *be an axiom system that contains* $\mathbf{K}_{(\mathbf{m})}$. *Let* $\mathbb{M}^c(\mathbf{S})$ *be the canonical Kripke structure as constructed in the proof of Theorem 1.4.6. Then*

(i) $A3 \in \mathbf{S} \Rightarrow \mathbb{M}^c(\mathbf{S})$ *is reflexive,*

(ii) $A4 \in \mathbf{S} \Rightarrow \mathbb{M}^c(\mathbf{S})$ *is transitive,*

(iii) $A5 \in \mathbf{S} \Rightarrow \mathbb{M}^c(\mathbf{S})$ *is euclidean.*

PROOF. (i) By the construction of $\mathbb{M}^c(\mathbf{S})$ we know that: $(s_\Theta, s_\Psi) \in R_i^c \Leftrightarrow \Theta/K_i \subseteq \Psi$ where $\Theta/K_i = \{\varphi \mid K_i\varphi \in \Theta\}$. Since A3: $K_i\varphi \rightarrow \varphi \in \Theta$ (since maximal consistent sets contain all theorems, and axioms in particular) we have that if $\varphi \in \Theta/K_i$, i.e. $K_i\varphi \in \Theta$, then $\varphi \in \Theta$, since Θ is maximally consistent and thus is closed under entailment: $K_i\varphi \in \Theta$ and $(K_i\varphi \rightarrow \varphi) \in \Theta$ imply $\varphi \in \Theta$. So $\Theta/K_i \subseteq \Theta$, i.e. $(s_\Theta, s_\Theta) \in R_i^c$. Since this holds for arbitrary $s_\Theta \in S^c$, R_i^c is reflexive.

(ii) Assume $(s_\Theta, s_\Psi) \in R_i^c$ and $(s_\Psi, s_\Xi) \in R_i^c$. Suppose $\varphi \in \Theta/K_i$, i.e. $K_i\varphi \in \Theta$. Since A4: $K_i\varphi \rightarrow K_iK_i\varphi \in \Theta$ we now have that $K_iK_i\varphi \in \Theta$ and so $K_i\varphi \in \Psi$ (since $\Theta/K_i \subseteq \Psi$) and $\varphi \in \Xi$ (since $\Psi/K_i \subseteq \Xi$). Hence $\Theta/K_i \subseteq \Xi$ and consequently $(s_\Theta, s_\Xi) \in R_i^c$.

(iii) Assume $(s_\Theta, s_\Psi) \in R_i^c$ and $(s_\Theta, s_\Xi) \in R_i^c$. Suppose $\varphi \in \Psi/K_i$, i.e $K_i\varphi \in \Psi$. We now have to prove $\varphi \in \Xi$. Suppose not: $\varphi \notin \Xi$. Then, since $\Theta/K_i \subseteq \Xi$, $\varphi \notin \Theta/K_i$. In other words, $K_i\varphi \notin \Theta$ (by definition of Θ/K_i). So, since Θ is maximally consistent, $\neg K_i\varphi \in \Theta$. Since A5: $\neg K_i\varphi \rightarrow K_i\neg K_i\varphi \in \Theta$, also $K_i\neg K_i\varphi \in \Theta$, and consequently, since $\Theta/K_i \subseteq \Psi$, we have that $\neg K_i\varphi \in \Psi$. This results in both $K_i\varphi \in \Psi$ and $\neg K_i\varphi \in \Psi$, contradicting the consistency of Ψ.
■

1.6.6. COROLLARY. *Let* $\mathbb{M}^c(\mathbf{S})$ *be an* $\mathbf{S5}_{(\mathbf{m})}$*-model. Then the accessibility relations of* $\mathbb{M}^c(\mathbf{S})$ *are equivalence relations.*

PROOF. Immediately from 1.6.2 and 1.6.5. ■

1.6.7. THEOREM (Completeness of **T**, **S4**, **S5**).
(i) $\mathbf{T}_{(\mathbf{m})}$ *is a complete axiomatisation of* $\mathcal{T}_{(\mathbf{m})}$.
(ii) $\mathbf{S4}_{(\mathbf{m})}$ *is a complete axiomatisation of* $\mathcal{S4}_{(\mathbf{m})}$.
(iii) $\mathbf{S5}_{(\mathbf{m})}$ *is a complete axiomatisation of* $\mathcal{S5}_{(\mathbf{m})}$.

PROOF. As in the proof of Theorem 1.4.6 we prove the equivalent assertion that a **T** (**S4**, **S5**)-consistent formula is satisfiable within the class $\mathcal{T}$ ($\mathcal{S4}$, $\mathcal{S5}$). To this end we again construct a canonical model $\mathbb{M}^c(\mathbf{S})$ for satisfying maximally consistent sets. By Proposition 1.6.5 these canonical models are of the right kind. ■

1.6.7.1. EXERCISE. Provide also a model-theoretical justification of the statements in Exercise 1.5.1.2 (in $\mathcal{S5}$).

1.6.7.2. EXERCISE. Give a model-theoretical proof of the redundancy of axiom (A4) in **S5**.

1.6.7.3. EXERCISE. Let $\mathbf{P} = \{p, q\}$. Check whether the sets which we considered in Exercises 1.4.9.1 and 1.4.9.2 are consistent in the systems **T**, **S4**, **S5**.

1.6.7.4. EXERCISE. Check whether the following formulas are valid with respect to $\mathcal{K}$, $\mathcal{T}$, $\mathcal{S4}$ and $\mathcal{S5}$.

(i) $\varphi \rightarrow K\varphi$

(ii) $\varphi \rightarrow K\neg K\neg\varphi$

(iii) $K\varphi \rightarrow \neg K\neg\varphi$

(iv) $\neg K\varphi \rightarrow K\neg\varphi$

(v) $K\neg\varphi \rightarrow \neg K\varphi$

(vi) $K\neg\varphi \vee K\varphi$

(vii) $(\varphi \wedge K(\varphi \rightarrow K\varphi)) \rightarrow K\varphi$

1.7. Remarks on $\mathbf{S5}_{(1)}$-Models

In this section we will examine $\mathbf{S5}_{(1)}$-models somewhat further. It will appear that the class of these models can be reduced to a class of very simple models without the loss of soundness and completeness of the system $\mathbf{S5}_{(1)}$. First we need a notion of equivalent worlds.

1.7.1. DEFINITION. Two worlds $(\mathbb{M}, s)$ and $(\mathbb{M}', s')$ are called *equivalent*, notation $(\mathbb{M}, s) \equiv (\mathbb{M}', s')$, if

$$\forall\varphi: \quad (\mathbb{M}, s) \models \varphi \Leftrightarrow (\mathbb{M}', s') \models \varphi.$$

1.7.2. PROPOSITION. *Suppose* $\mathbb{M} = \langle S, \pi, R\rangle$ *where* R *is an equivalence relation (i.e.* $\mathbb{M}$ *is an* $\mathbf{S5}_{(1)}$*-model) and* $s \in S$. *Then* $(\mathbb{M}, s) \equiv (\mathbb{M}', s)$ *where* $\mathbb{M}' = \langle S', \pi', R'\rangle$ *and*

$S' = \{t \mid (s, t) \in R\}$ *(i.e.* S' *is the equivalence class of* s*),*
$\pi' = \pi \mid S'$ *(the restriction of* π *to* S'*),*
$R' = \{(t, t') \mid t, t' \in S'\}$.

PROOF. Exercise 1.7.2.1. ∎

1.7.2.1. EXERCISE. Prove Proposition 1.7.2.

Proposition 1.7.2 states that for the determination of the truth of an $\mathbf{S5}_{(1)}$-formula in a given state s it is sufficient to consider the states that are reachable (regarded possible) from s. (See Figure 1.4.) So without loss of generality we may assume that $\mathbf{S5}_{(1)}$-models $\mathbb{M}$ have the form $\mathbb{M} = \langle S, \pi, R\rangle$, where for all $s, t \in S$ it holds that $(s, t) \in R$. We shall call these models *reduced* $\mathbf{S5}_{(1)}$-models. Since a maximal consistent set Φ of formulas is satisfiable in a(n ordinary) $\mathbf{S5}_{(1)}$-model, we know by Proposition 1.7.2 that Φ is satisfiable in a reduced $\mathbf{S5}_{(1)}$-model as well. Consequently, the system $\mathbf{S5}_{(1)}$ is also a (sound and) complete axiomatisation of the class of reduced $\mathbf{S5}_{(1)}$-models.

Note that $\mathbf{S5}_{(1)}$-models $\mathbb{M}$ may be represented even without mentioning the relation R: so $\mathbb{M} = \langle S, \pi\rangle$ suffices. If we do this, we must adapt the semantics of the K-operator, as follows:

$$(\mathbb{M}, s) \models K\varphi \Leftrightarrow (\mathbb{M}, t) \models \varphi \text{ for } all\ t \in S.$$

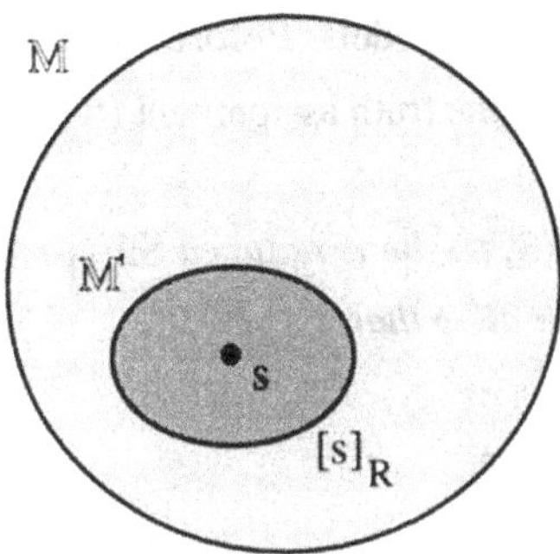

Figure 1.4

Obviously this definition is equivalent to the old one in the case where R(s, t) for all s, t ∈ S. In the literature this definition is often used when only (reduced) $\mathbf{S5_{(1)}}$-models are considered. (*Note:* the remarks in Section 1.7 do *not* hold for $\mathbf{S5_{(m)}}$ with m > 1.) As a direct consequence we obtain that in reduced $\mathbf{S5_{(1)}}$-models the dual M-operator has the following semantics:

$$(\mathbb{M}, s) \models M\varphi \;\Leftrightarrow\; (\mathbb{M}, t) \models \varphi \text{ for } \textit{some } t \in S.$$

Reduced models have the following pleasing property:

1.7.3. LEMMA. *Let* $\mathbb{M} = \langle S, \pi \rangle$ *be a reduced* $\mathbf{S5_{(1)}}$*-model, and* s ∈ S. *Then*

(i) $(\mathbb{M}, s) \models K\varphi \Leftrightarrow \forall u \in S\ (\mathbb{M}, u) \models K\varphi$.

(ii) $(\mathbb{M}, s) \models M\varphi \Leftrightarrow \forall u \in S\ (\mathbb{M}, u) \models M\varphi$.

PROOF. In both (i) and (ii), the direction from right to left is obvious. To prove '⇒' in the case of (i), suppose $(\mathbb{M}, s) \models K\varphi$. By the truth-definition of K in reduced models, as given above, this is equivalent to $\forall t \in S, (\mathbb{M}, t) \models \varphi$. Now let u ∈ S. Since all states in S are 'successors' of u, and they all verify φ, we have $(\mathbb{M}, u) \models K\varphi$. For (ii), assume $(\mathbb{M}, s) \models M\varphi$, implying that there is some t ∈ S for which $(\mathbb{M}, t) \models \varphi$. If we now choose an arbitrary u ∈ S, we see that u has a 'successor' satisfying φ, namely t, implying $(\mathbb{M}, u) \models M\varphi$. ∎

We may now proceed even further and note that with respect to $\mathbf{S5_{(1)}}$ it is even sufficient to consider models in which states are identified if they have the same truth assignment to the primitive propositions. To put it more precisely, all states with equal truth assignment are identified:

$$s = s' \;\Leftrightarrow\; \pi(s) = \pi(s').$$

These models can be denoted simply by a set S of states (= truth assignment functions). We shall call these models *simple* $\mathbf{S5}_{(1)}$-models. Before we justify this, we first remark that two states in a reduced model that have the truth assignment (function) satisfy the same formulas.

1.7.4. PROPOSITION. *Let* $\mathbb{M} = \langle S, \pi \rangle$ *be a reduced* $\mathbf{S5}_{(1)}$*-model. Let* s, s' *be two states such that* $\pi(s) = \pi(s')$. *Then it holds for all* φ *that*

$$(\mathbb{M}, s) \models \varphi \iff (\mathbb{M}, s') \models \varphi.$$

PROOF. We use induction on the structure of formula φ.
Basis. For $p \in \mathbf{P}$,

$$(\mathbb{M}, s) \models p \iff \pi(s)(p) = t \iff \pi(s')(p) = t \iff (\mathbb{M}, s') \models p.$$

Induction step. The only (potentially) interesting case is $\varphi = K\psi$:

$$(\mathbb{M}, s) \models K\psi \iff \forall t \in S \ (\mathbb{M}, t) \models \psi \iff (\mathbb{M}, s') \models K\psi. \ \blacksquare$$

The previous result already gives us some indication of the 'redundancy' of states with the same truth assignment in a reduced $\mathbf{S5}_{(1)}$-model. However, to prove this we need some additional notion that enable us to relate models to each other, namely that of a *bisimulation*.

1.7.4.1. DEFINITION (*Bisimulation* between two Kripke models). To avoid cumbersome notation, let us assume that we have Kripke models of the form $\mathbb{M} = \langle S, \pi, R \rangle$ and $\mathbb{M}' = \langle S', \pi', R' \rangle$. (Naturally, this notion can be also defined analogously on more general Kripke models.)

(i) For a relation $\mathfrak{R} \subseteq S \times S'$ we define the following properties:

(1) $\mathfrak{R}$ satisfies *forward-choice* if
$\forall s, t \in S \ \forall s' \in S' \ (\mathfrak{R}ss' \ \& \ (s, t) \in R) \Rightarrow \exists t' \in S'(\mathfrak{R}tt' \ \& \ (s', t') \in R')$;

(2) $\mathfrak{R}$ satisfies *back-choice* if
$\forall s \in S \ \forall s', t' \in S' \ (\mathfrak{R}ss' \ \& \ (s', t') \in R') \Rightarrow \exists t \in S(\mathfrak{R}tt' \ \& \ (s, t) \in R)$.

(ii) A relation $\mathfrak{R}$ between $\mathbb{M}$ and $\mathbb{M}'$ is a *bisimulation* if it satisfies forward-choice, back-choice, and moreover:

(3) $\forall s \in S\ \forall s' \in S'\ (\mathfrak{R}ss' \Rightarrow \pi(s) = \pi'(s'))$.

If there is a bisimulation between two models $\mathbb{M}$ and $\mathbb{M}'$, we call $\mathbb{M}$ and $\mathbb{M}'$ *bisimilar*.

(iii) A bisimulation $\mathfrak{R}$ between $\langle S, \pi, R\rangle$ and $\langle S', \pi', R'\rangle$ is a *zigzag-connection* if:
(4) domain($\mathfrak{R}$) = S; range($\mathfrak{R}$) = S'.

The notion of zigzag-connection was introduced in [Seg70] but then called a *p-relation* (or *pseudo-relation*) (see also [vB83] for *p-morphisms* or [vdH92a] for this notion with respect to a more general language).

Now we have the following theorem concerning bisimilar models:

1.7.4.2. THEOREM. *Suppose* $\mathbb{M} = \langle S, \pi, R\rangle$ *and* $\mathbb{M}' = \langle S', \pi', R'\rangle$ *are bisimilar (and bisimulated by* $\mathfrak{R}$*). Then, for all modal (i.e. epistemic) formulas* φ *and for all* $s \in S$ *and* $s' \in S'$ *with* $\mathfrak{R}ss'$: $(\mathbb{M}, s) \models \varphi \Leftrightarrow (\mathbb{M}', s') \models \varphi$.

PROOF. Use induction on the complexity of φ. If φ equals some $p \in \mathbf{P}$, the assertion is true by clause (3) of the definition of a bisimulation. The cases $\varphi = (\varphi_1 \wedge \varphi_2)$ and $\varphi = \neg\varphi_1$ are in the same spirit as in the proof of Exercise 1.7.2.1. Now suppose that $\varphi = K\varphi_1$, and $(\mathbb{M}, s) \models \varphi$. Then, for all t with $(s, t) \in R$, $(\mathbb{M}, t) \models \varphi_1$. Suppose that $(s', t') \in R'$. Since $\mathfrak{R}ss'$, by *back-choice,* there is a t with $(s, t) \in R$ and $\mathfrak{R}tt'$. We know that $(\mathbb{M}, t) \models \varphi_1$, and thus, by the induction hypothesis, $(\mathbb{M}', t') \models \varphi_1$, yielding $(\mathbb{M}', s') \models K\varphi_1$. The opposite direction is proven similarly, using *forward-choice.* ■

1.7.4.3. COROLLARY. *Two models* $\mathbb{M} = \langle S, \pi, R\rangle$ *and* $\mathbb{M}' = \langle S', \pi', R'\rangle$ *that are bisimulated by a zigzag-connection* $\mathfrak{R}$ *satisfy the same formulas, i.e., for every formula* φ*, for every* $s \in S$ *with* $(\mathbb{M}, s) \models \varphi$ *there is an* $s' \in S'$ *such that* $(\mathbb{M}', s') \models \varphi$*, and vice versa.*

PROOF. Suppose that $(\mathbb{M}, s) \models \varphi$ for some $s \in S$. We know that $\mathfrak{R}$ is a zigzag-connection, i.e. a bisimulation with domain($\mathfrak{R}$) = S and range($\mathfrak{R}$) = S'. So there is an $s' \in S'$ such that $\mathfrak{R}ss'$. By Theorem 1.7.4.2 we have that $(\mathbb{M}', s') \models \varphi$. The other direction is shown analogously. ■

1.7.4.4. PROPOSITION. *Every reduced* $\mathbf{S5}_{(1)}$*-model* $\mathbb{M} = \langle S, \pi, R\rangle$ *is bisimilar with a simple* $\mathbf{S5}_{(1)}$*-model* $\mathbb{M}'$*. Moreover, the bisimulation between* $\mathbb{M}$ *and* $\mathbb{M}'$ *can be chosen to be a zigzag-connection.*

PROOF. Denote by $[s]_\pi$ the set of states in $\mathbb{M}$ with the same truth assignment as s: $[s]_\pi = \{s' \mid \pi(s') = \pi(s)\}$. Then we can write $S = \bigcup_{s' \in S'} [s']_\pi$ for some set S' for which it holds that, for all $s_1', s_2' \in S'$, $[s_1']_\pi \neq [s_2']_\pi$, or equivalently, $\pi(s_1') \neq \pi(s_2')$. Now take $\mathbb{M}' = \langle S', \pi', R' \rangle$, where S' is as before, $\pi' = \pi \mid S'$ and $R' = \{(t, t') \mid t, t' \in S'\}$. We show that $\mathbb{M}'$ satisfies the requirement. First note that $\mathbb{M}'$ is a simple $\mathbf{S5}_{(1)}$-model. Next we have to find a bisimulation $\mathfrak{R}$ between the two models that satisfies domain($\mathfrak{R}$) = S and range($\mathfrak{R}$) = S'. Define $\mathfrak{R}$ by: for all $s' \in S'$ and all $s \in [s']_\pi$, $\mathfrak{R}ss'$ for all $s' \in S'$. Clearly, range($\mathfrak{R}$) = S'. Moreover, domain($\mathfrak{R}$) = S, since $S = \bigcup_{s' \in S'} [s']_\pi$. Furthermore, $\mathfrak{R}$ satisfies $\forall s \in S\ \forall s' \in S'\ (\mathfrak{R}ss' \Rightarrow \pi(s) = \pi'(s'))$, since $\mathfrak{R}ss'$ implies that $s \in [s']_\pi$, i.e. $\pi(s) = \pi(s') = \pi'(s')$. Finally we check the forward- and back-choice properties.

(Forward-choice) Suppose $\mathfrak{R}ss'$ for $s \in S$ and $s' \in S'$, and $(s, t) \in R$ for $t \in S$. We know that there is a $t' \in S'$ such that $t \in [t']_\pi$, i.e. $\mathfrak{R}tt'$. Since $s', t' \in S' \subseteq S$, and $\forall u, v \in S : R(u, v)$ holds ($\mathbb{M}$ is a reduced model), we have that R(s', t'). Furthermore, since both s' and t' are elements of S', and R' is just the restriction of R to S', we also have R'(s', t'). So we have found a $t' \in S'$ such that $\mathfrak{R}tt'$ and $(s', t') \in R'$.

(Back-choice) Suppose $\mathfrak{R}ss'$ for $s \in S$ and $s' \in S'$, and $(s', t') \in R'$ for $t' \in S'$. Since $S' \subseteq S$, we have that $t' \in S$. Since $\forall u, v \in S : R(u, v)$ holds ($\mathbb{M}$ is a reduced model), we have that $(s, t') \in R$. Moreover, clearly $\mathfrak{R}t't'$ (since $t' \in [t']_\pi$). So we have found a $t \in S$ (namely t') such that $\mathfrak{R}tt'$ and $(s, t) \in R$. ■

1.7.4.5. COROLLARY. *For every reduced* $\mathbf{S5}_{(1)}$*-model* $\mathbb{M} = \langle S, \pi, R \rangle$ *there exists a simple* $\mathbf{S5}_{(1)}$*-model* $\mathbb{M}' = \langle S', \pi', R' \rangle$ *that satisfies the same formulas, i.e., for every formula* φ*, for every* $s \in S$ *with* $(\mathbb{M}, s) \models \varphi$*, there is an* $s' \in S'$ *such that* $(\mathbb{M}', s') \models \varphi$*, and vice versa.*

PROOF. Suppose we have a reduced $\mathbf{S5}_{(1)}$-model $\mathbb{M} = \langle S, \pi, R \rangle$. By Proposition 1.7.4.4 we know that there is a simple $\mathbf{S5}_{(1)}$-model $\mathbb{M}' = \langle S', \pi', R' \rangle$ that is bisimilar by means of a zigzag-connection. Corollary 1.7.4.3 now says that $\mathbb{M}$ and $\mathbb{M}'$ satisfy the same formulas in the sense stated in the present corollary. ■

Again, we can now obtain a completeness result: by Corollary 1.7.4.5 a set of formulas that is satisfiable in a reduced $\mathbf{S5}_{(1)}$-model is satisfiable in a simple $\mathbf{S5}_{(1)}$-model; hence the system $\mathbf{S5}_{(1)}$ is (sound and) complete for the class of simple $\mathbf{S5}_{(1)}$-models as well:

1.7.4.6. COROLLARY. *The system* $\mathbf{S5}_{(1)}$ *is sound and complete for the class of simple* $\mathbf{S5}_{(1)}$*-models.* ■

From now on, when we speak about simple $\mathbf{S5}_{(1)}$-models, we may assume without loss of generality that such a model is a set S of truth assignments $\mathbf{P} \rightarrow \{t, f\}$. Particularly, in Chapter

3 we will employ this simple representation of an $\mathbf{S5_{(1)}}$-Kripke model, identifying s with $\pi(s)$, allowing a straightforward definition of the union of models and the subset relation between models:

1.7.4.7. DEFINITION (Union of and subset relation on simple $\mathbf{S5_{(1)}}$-models). Let $\mathbb{M}_1 = \langle S_1, \pi_1 \rangle$ and $\mathbb{M}_2 = \langle S_2, \pi_2 \rangle$ be $\mathbf{S5_{(1)}}$-models.
(i) We define $\mathbb{M}_1 \cup \mathbb{M}_2 = \langle S_1 \cup S_2, \pi_1 \cup \pi_2 \rangle$, where $(\pi_1 \cup \pi_2)(s) = \pi_1(s)$ if $s \in S_1$, and $= \pi_2(s)$, if $s \in S_2$. (Note that in case $s \in S_1 \cap S_2$, there is no disagreement between the two clauses, since we have identified states with their truth assignments, and hence both $\pi_1(s)$ and $\pi_2(s)$ have to give the same outcome.)

(ii) We define $\mathbb{M}_1 \subseteq \mathbb{M}_2$ iff $S_1 \subseteq S_2$.

We remark again that the 'reduction' of $\mathbf{S5_{(1)}}$-models to reduced and simple $\mathbf{S5_{(1)}}$-models does not apply to $\mathbf{S5_{(m)}}$ with $m > 1$.

Next we spend some time (and space) on issues of computational complexity.

We define the length $|\varphi|$ of a formula φ as follows: $|p| = 1$ $(p \in \mathbf{P})$, $|\varphi_1 \wedge \varphi_2| = |\varphi_1| + 1 + |\varphi_2|$, and $|\surd\psi| = 1 + |\psi|$, for $\surd \in \{\neg, K\}$.

1.7.5. PROPOSITION (Small model property, [Lad77]). *An $\mathbf{S5_{(1)}}$-formula φ is satisfiable if and only if φ is satisfiable in a world $(\mathbb{M}, s)$ where $\mathbb{M} \in \mathcal{S5}_{(1)}$ contains at most $|\varphi|$ states.*

PROOF. '$\Leftarrow$' is trivial. For '$\Rightarrow$' assume that φ is satisfiable in some reduced model $\mathbb{N} = \langle S', \pi' \rangle \in \mathcal{S5}_{(1)}$, say at state $s \in S'$. By our remarks about simple models, we may assume $\mathbb{N}$ to be simple. We now create a subset S of S': first we put s in S and add elements to S as witnesses for $\neg\psi$, for subformulas $K\psi$ of φ that are *not* true at s. Formally, we do the following. Let $Sub(\varphi)$ be the set of subformulas of φ. We define the function f_s: $Sub(\varphi) \rightarrow 2^{S'}$ as follows:

$f_s(p) = \{\ \}$, for all atoms $p \in Sub(\varphi)$;
$f_s(\varphi_1 \wedge \varphi_2) = f_s(\varphi_1) \cup f_s(\varphi_2)$, for any $\varphi_1 \wedge \varphi_2 \in Sub(\varphi)$;
$f_s(\neg\psi) = f_s(\psi)$, for $\neg\psi \in Sub(\varphi)$;
$f_s(K\psi) = \{t\}$, for some $t \in S'$ for which $(\mathbb{N}, t) \models \neg\psi$, in case $(\mathbb{N}, s) \not\models K\psi$;
$\quad = \{\ \}$, otherwise.

Now let $\mathbb{M} = \langle S, \pi, R \rangle$ with $S = \{s\} \cup \bigcup_{\psi \in Sub(\varphi)} f_s(\psi)$, $R = S \times S$ and $\pi = \pi' \mid S$. Note that $\mathbb{M}$ is a (simple) $\mathbf{S5_{(1)}}$-model again. Since f_s adds at most one world for subformulas $K\psi$, we obviously have $|S| \leq |\varphi|$. We claim that, for all $\psi \in Sub(\varphi)$ and all $u \in S$, $(\mathbb{M}, u) \models \psi$ iff $(\mathbb{N}, u) \models \psi$.

This is proven inductively. If $\psi = p \in Sub(\varphi)$, it is obvious. (Recall that $\mathbb{N}$ is simple, so we may identify the worlds u with (their) valuations.) The cases involving the logical connectives are straightforward, and are left as an exercise. Now consider $\psi = K\alpha$, and assume that the above statement is proven for α, i.e.

$$\text{for all } u \in S, (\mathbb{M}, u) \models \alpha \text{ iff } (\mathbb{N}, u) \models \alpha. \qquad (*)$$

Now let $u \in S$ and suppose $(\mathbb{M}, u) \models K\alpha$. Suppose we do *not* have $(\mathbb{N}, u) \models K\alpha$. This means that not all states in S' verify α, say $t \in S'$ does not satisfy α. Since also $s \in S'$ and $\mathbb{N}$ is a reduced model (it is even simple), we have that $(\mathbb{N}, s) \models \neg K\alpha$. Thus, by construction of f_s, we have added a state v to S, for which we have $(\mathbb{N}, v) \not\models \alpha$. By the induction hypothesis, (*), we then have $(\mathbb{M}, v) \not\models \alpha$, and, since $\mathbb{M}$ is also reduced, we have $(\mathbb{M}, u) \not\models K\alpha$: a contradiction, so that we must have $(\mathbb{N}, u) \models K\alpha$. Conversely, suppose we have $(\mathbb{N}, u) \models K\alpha$. It implies that, for all $x \in S'$ we have $(\mathbb{N}, x) \models \alpha$. Since $S \subseteq S'$, we then also have for all $x \in S$ that $(\mathbb{N}, x) \models \alpha$. We apply (*) to conclude that, for all $x \in S$, $(\mathbb{M}, x) \models \alpha$. Since $\mathbb{M}$ is a reduced model, we have $(\mathbb{M}, u) \models K\alpha$. ∎

1.7.5.1. EXERCISE. Complete the proof of Proposition 1.7.5.

As an immediate consequence of the small (finite) model property we obtain that the logic $\mathbf{S5_{(1)}}$ is *decidable*, i.e. there exists an effective procedure by which, for any given epistemic formula φ, it can be determined in a finite number of steps whether or not φ is an $\mathbf{S5_{(1)}}$-theorem. If φ is not a theorem, we know by the completeness of $\mathbf{S5_{(1)}}$ that φ is not $\mathbf{S5_{(1)}}$-valid. So its negation $\neg\varphi$ must be $\mathbf{S5_{(1)}}$-satisfiable. By Proposition 1.7.5 we only have to check models containing at most $|\varphi|$ states to decide whether $\neg\varphi$ is satisfiable.

For the other modal propositional systems, $\mathbf{K_{(m)}}$, $\mathbf{T_{(m)}}$, $\mathbf{S4_{(m)}}$ ($m \geq 1$) and $\mathbf{S5_{(m)}}$ ($m > 1$), one can also prove a finite model property by constructions that are somewhat more involved (see e.g. [HC84] and [Lad77] for m = 1, and [HM85] for m > 1), and therefore these logics are decidable as well. However, it can be shown (see e.g. [HM85]) that because the models are very small in the case of $\mathbf{S5_{(1)}}$, we can do even better and state the hardness of decidability in this case:

1.7.5.2. COROLLARY. *Decidability of* $\mathbf{S5_{(1)}}$*-satisfiability is NP-complete.* ∎

The decidability of $\mathbf{S5}_{(1)}$-satisfiability is thus as hard as the decidability of satisfiability in propositional calculus (see [Coo71]). To make a comparison: decidability of satisfiability in $\mathbf{K}_{(m)}$, $\mathbf{T}_{(m)}$, $\mathbf{S4}_{(m)}$ ($m \geq 1$) and $\mathbf{S5}_{(m)}$ ($m > 1$) is PSPACE-complete, which is much harder (see [Lad77], [HM85]). A good reference for an explanation of these notions of computational complexity is [HU79]. Halpern and Moses have given an excellent survey of complexity results for modal, and in particular epistemic logics, in [HM92].

1.7.6. Normal Forms

Finally in this subsection about $\mathbf{S5}_{(1)}$, we turn to another interesting special property of this logic. One can prove that every epistemic formula is equivalent (in $\mathbf{S5}_{(1)}$) to some formula without nestings of the modal operator K. Formally, we introduce a normal form of epistemic formulas, and show that in $\mathbf{S5}_{(1)}$ every formula is equivalent to a formula in normal form.

1.7.6.1. DEFINITION. We say a formula ψ is in *normal form* if it is a disjunction of conjunctions of the form $\delta = \alpha \wedge K\beta_1 \wedge K\beta_2 \wedge \ldots \wedge K\beta_n \wedge M\gamma_1 \wedge M\gamma_2 \wedge \ldots \wedge M\gamma_k$, where α, β_i and γ_j ($i \leq n$, $j \leq k$) are all purely propositional formulas. The formula δ is called a *canonical conjunction* and the subformulas $K\beta_i$ and $M\gamma_j$ are called *prenex* formulas.

The next lemma guarantees that prenex formulas can always be moved to the outermost level:

1.7.6.2. LEMMA. *If ψ is in normal form and contains a prenex formula σ, then ψ may be supposed to have the form $\pi \vee (\lambda \wedge \sigma)$, where π, λ and σ are all in normal form.*

PROOF. ψ is in normal form, so $\psi = \delta_1 \vee \delta_2 \vee \ldots \vee \delta_m$ where the δ_i's are canonical conjunctions. Suppose σ occurs in δ_m. Then σ must be either some conjunct $K\beta$ or $M\gamma$, so that δ_m can be written as $(\lambda \wedge \sigma)$. Taking π to be $(\delta_1 \vee \delta_2 \vee \ldots \delta_{m-1})$ gives the desired result $\psi = \pi \vee (\lambda \wedge \sigma)$. ■

1.7.6.3. LEMMA. *We have the following equivalences in $S5_{(1)}$:*

(i) $S5_{(1)} \models K(\pi \vee (\lambda \wedge K\beta)) \leftrightarrow [(K(\pi \vee \lambda) \wedge K\beta) \vee (K\pi \wedge \neg K\beta)]$;

(ii) $S5_{(1)} \models K(\pi \vee (\lambda \wedge M\beta)) \leftrightarrow [(K(\pi \vee \lambda) \wedge M\beta) \vee (K\pi \wedge \neg M\beta)]$.

PROOF. We only prove (i), by a semantical argument, leaving (ii) as an exercise. We have to show that, for any $\mathbf{S5}_{(1)}$-model $\mathbb{M}$ and s, $(\mathbb{M}, s) \models K(\pi \vee (\lambda \wedge K\beta)) \leftrightarrow [(K(\pi \vee \lambda) \wedge K\beta) \vee (K\pi \wedge \neg K\beta)]$. By the previous results of this section, it is sufficient to prove the assertion for reduced $\mathbf{S5}_{(1)}$-models. Thus, let $\mathbb{M} = \langle S, R, \pi \rangle$ be an arbitrary reduced $\mathbf{S5}_{(1)}$-model, and $s \in S$. We will show that

$$(\mathbb{M}, s) \models K(\pi \vee (\lambda \wedge K\beta)) \leftrightarrow [(K(\pi \vee \lambda) \wedge K\beta) \vee (K\pi \wedge \neg K\beta)] \tag{*}$$

To do so, we use the validity of

$$(\mathbb{M}, s) \models K\beta \vee \neg K\beta \tag{1}$$

to reason by cases, as follows.
Firstly, assume that

$$(\mathbb{M}, s) \models K\beta. \tag{2}$$

By Lemma 1.7.3 we then know that $K\beta$ is true in all states of S. Moreover, since $(\pi \vee (\lambda \wedge K\beta)) \rightarrow (\pi \vee \lambda)$ is a propositional tautology, the truth of $K(\pi \vee (\lambda \wedge K\beta))$ in s implies that of $K(\pi \vee \lambda)$ in s, so that we have:

$$(\mathbb{M}, s) \models K(\pi \vee (\lambda \wedge K\beta)) \rightarrow K(\pi \vee \lambda) \wedge K\beta. \tag{3}$$

For the converse, suppose that $(\mathbb{M}, s) \models K(\pi \vee \lambda) \wedge K\beta$. Again applying Lemma 1.7.3, we see that both $K(\pi \vee \lambda)$ and $K\beta$ are true in all t of S. But then also $(\pi \vee \lambda)$ and $K\beta$ are true in all t; so is $(\pi \vee \lambda) \wedge K\beta$ and the weaker $(\pi \vee (\lambda \wedge K\beta))$, implying $(\mathbb{M}, s) \models K(\pi \vee (\lambda \wedge K\beta))$;

$$(\mathbb{M}, s) \models K(\pi \vee \lambda) \wedge K\beta \rightarrow K(\pi \vee (\lambda \wedge K\beta)). \tag{4}$$

So that we conclude, from (2), (3) and (4),

$$(\mathbb{M}, s) \models K\beta \rightarrow (K(\pi \vee (\lambda \wedge K\beta)) \leftrightarrow (K(\pi \vee \lambda) \wedge K\beta)). \tag{5}$$

In the second case, we assume

$$(\mathbb{M}, s) \models \neg K\beta. \tag{6}$$

Since $\mathcal{S5}_{(1)} \models \neg K\beta \leftrightarrow M\neg\beta$, Lemma 1.7.3(ii) now gives us that $\neg K\beta$ is true in all worlds u $\in$ S, and thus $(\mathbb{M}, s) \models K\neg K\beta$. Suppose $(\mathbb{M}, s) \models K(\pi \vee (\lambda \wedge K\beta))$, and $(s, t) \in R$. Then we have both $(\mathbb{M}, t) \models \neg K\beta$ and $(\mathbb{M}, t) \models \pi \vee (\lambda \wedge K\beta)$, and hence $(\mathbb{M}, t) \models \pi$. Combining this with (6) we get for s:

$$(\mathbb{M}, s) \models K(\pi \vee (\lambda \wedge K\beta)) \rightarrow (K\pi \wedge \neg K\beta). \tag{7}$$

For the converse, since $\pi \rightarrow (\pi \vee \alpha)$ is a tautology, we also have

$$(\mathbb{M}, s) \models (K\pi \wedge \neg K\beta) \rightarrow K(\pi \vee (\lambda \wedge K\beta)). \tag{8}$$

so that we obtain, from (6), (7) and (8),

$$(\mathbb{M}, s) \models \neg K\beta \rightarrow (K(\pi \vee (\lambda \wedge K\beta)) \leftrightarrow (K\pi \wedge \neg K\beta)). \tag{9}$$

Finally we use the propositional tautology

$$[(p \rightarrow (q \leftrightarrow (p \wedge r)) \wedge (\neg p \rightarrow (q \leftrightarrow (\neg p \wedge s)))] \rightarrow [(q \leftrightarrow ((r \wedge p) \vee (s \wedge \neg p))]$$

together with (5) and (9) to conclude (*). ∎

1.7.6.3.1. EXERCISE. (a) Prove (ii) of Lemma 1.7.6.3.

(b) Give a proof-theoretical proof of Lemma 1.7.6.3.

Now we are ready for the main result of this subsection:

1.7.6.4. THEOREM. *In* $\mathbf{S5}_{(1)}$ *every epistemic formula* φ *is equivalent to a formula* ψ *in normal form.*

PROOF. By induction on φ. We only show the result for $\varphi = K\varphi_1$, where we suppose φ_1 to be in normal form (leaving the remaining cases as Exercise 1.7.6.4.1). We also assume that φ_1 contains some prenex formula σ (which is either $K\beta$ or $M\gamma$). (We are done otherwise.) Using Lemma 1.7.6.2 this subformula can be brought to the outermost level, giving $\varphi \leftrightarrow K(\pi \vee (\lambda \wedge \sigma))$. Lemma 1.7.6.3 then gives $K(\pi \vee (\lambda \wedge \sigma)) \leftrightarrow [(K(\pi \vee \lambda) \wedge \sigma) \vee (K\pi \wedge \neg\sigma)]$. In this way, we can bring all the nested prenex formulas of φ to the top level, thus obtaining a formula in normal form. ∎

1.7.6.4.1. EXERCISE. Complete the proof of Theorem 1.7.6.4 by doing the remaining inductive steps.

1.7.6.4.2. REMARK. The proof-theoretical proof of Lemma 1.7.6.3 (Exercise 1.7.6.3.1(b)) (and so that of Theorem 1.7.6.4) obviously depend only on (the presence of) the axioms (A1) —(A5) and the rules (R1) and (R2). A closer look at the proof shows that the only case in which (A3) is used is in theorems of the form $\vdash KK\beta \rightarrow K\beta$ and $\vdash K\neg K\alpha \rightarrow \neg K\alpha$.(*) Consequently, Lemma 1.7.6.3 also holds for logical systems which are like $\mathbf{S5}_{(1)}$, but for which the reflexivity axiom (A3) is replaced by (an axiom entailing) property (*). This will be of use when we consider systems for belief in Chapter 2.

1.8. Application to Distributed Systems (Halpern & Moses)

Consider a distributed system with processors 1, ..., m interconnected by a communication network. Every processor is a state machine. The local state of a processor is a function of the initial state, the messages received and possible internal actions. The precise way in which this function works is irrelevant for our present purposes. The global state **s** of the system is a vector of local states:

$$\mathbf{s} = (s_1, ..., s_m).$$

We can now associate a Kripke structure $\mathbb{M}$ with this distributed system:

$$\mathbb{M} = \langle S, \pi, R_1, ..., R_m \rangle,$$

where

$$S = \{(s_1, ..., s_m) \mid s_i \text{ is a local state of processor i}\},$$

$$\pi\colon S \to \mathbf{P} \to \{t, f\},$$

$$R_i = \{(\mathbf{s}, \mathbf{t}) \mid s_i = t_i\} \text{ for } i = 1, ..., m.$$

The set S thus contains all possible global states. One can imagine the set **P** of primitive propositions to include assertions such as: "*for the local variable* x_i *of processor* i *it holds that* $x_i = 0$". Again, the precise form of these primitive propositions is irrelevant for our present purposes. The justification of the definition of the relations R_i is the following: processor i is supposed to 'know' in which local state it is itself, but regarding the local states of the other parallel processors processor i is ignorant. Thus it considers all global states as possible provided these agree on the local state of i itself. Note that the R_i (i = 1, ..., m) are equivalence relations and hence the Kripke models associated with distributed systems are $\mathbf{S5}_{(\mathbf{m})}$-models.

We shall return to this 'concrete' model later when we discuss the notion of common knowledge. Here we end this section by some remarks concerning possible refinements of the above model. In this simple model two global states of a system are considered equivalent for agent i if they have the same i-local state. There are also more sophisticated options for the equivalence relation between states. In general, states may be replaced by so-called *points* (r, t) consisting of a *run* r of the system (i.e. a description of what the system is subsequently doing and will do in the future) together with a time stamp t according to a global clock of the system.

(In Chapter 2 we will make the notion of a run more precise, but for the moment we do not need a detailed description of this notion.) We suppose that t takes values from some time domain T. Now, given some set $\mathcal{R}$ of possible runs, we can consider a Kripke model $\langle\{(r, t) \mid r \in \mathcal{R}, t \in T\}, \pi, \cong_1, ..., \cong_m\rangle$, where π is a truth assignment function mapping points to maps from primitive proposition to truth values, and the $\cong_i$ are equivalence relations induced by some view of agent i deciding what has to be regarded equivalent. The view of agent i gives a criterion according to which the agent (processor) i considers points as 'the same' or, in other words, which points are regarded possible given the point i is at. One may interpret this as a kind of *observational equivalence*: agent i is not able to distinguish between processes that are equivalent in this sense. The view of agent i may just involve considering the local state of i, as above, but may be much more complex, involving the history of the process (and so also the run r) in a non-trivial way. For example, agent i's view may concern the global history of the process, or just its own local history (the actions that it has executed itself), but also its location in a program. The general approach of Halpern & Moses covers all these possibilities. The primitive and complex propositions are now interpreted in the usual way, e.g.:

$$(\mathcal{R}\times T, (r, t)) \models K_i\varphi \iff (\mathcal{R}\times T, (r', t')) \models \varphi \text{ for all } (r', t') \in \mathcal{R}\times T \text{ such that } (r, t) \cong_i (r', t').$$

This general model can be used to reason about (knowledge in/of) distributed processes. For more details about applications using this more advanced model we refer to e.g. [HM84a, 90], [ChM85, 86], [FV86], [FI86], [KT86], [HF89]. Although the framework above is generally used to model concurrency in an interleaving manner, it can also be adapted for modelling *'true' concurrency* (see e.g. [LMRT90]). For this we replace the points in Halpern & Moses' approach by pairs $(r, \mathfrak{L})$ of posets of actions, where r models the causality relation between the actions of the process concerned, and $\mathfrak{L}$ is a sub-poset of r, describing to what extent the process is advanced at the current moment (see [vHM92]).

Below we shall look briefly into the use of epistemic logic for the verification of protocols, and in the next chapter we shall also discuss in some depth the use of more refined epistemic notions to reason about distributed systems, in the setting of the simple model using global and local states we described above. We see that in this simple setting already very interesting results can be obtained.

1.9. Protocol Verification by Means of Epistemic Logic (Halpern & Zuck)

After our more general considerations on the use of epistemic logic in the context of distributed systems we consider in this section the possibilities of using epistemic logic in a more concrete area, namely that of *protocol verification*. We shall see how Halpern and Zuck [HZ87] have demonstrated that an epistemic analysis of protocols for sending messages in a computer network more or less naturally leads to 'alternating bit'-like algorithms.

For researchers like Halpern one of the reasons for occupying himself with epistemic logic was the application to *protocols*, programs that are able to guarantee the error-free transmission of messages over a distributed system (network). In the literature several more or less complicated protocols have been proposed. A very well-known one is the *'alternating bit protocol'*, in which messages are alternately ended with either a 0 or a 1. Of course it is of the greatest interest to know whether these protocols are adequate in the sense that they indeed guarantee a perfect transmission of messages.

However, *protocol verification*, proving the correctness of protocols, is non-trivial. Exercises done in this area often involve long and complicated formal calculation. Halpern *cum suis* got the idea to use the notion of knowledge to gain some insight in the functioning of protocols, which change the knowledge that is present at the nodes in a network by sending messages. In this manner Halpern & Zuck have investigated a number of protocols. It appears that by using epistemic operators it becomes possible to give compact and exact specifications of protocols, which can be transformed easily into a proper program. Here we discuss a simple case to get an impression of this approach.

Let two processes be given, a sender S and a receiver R. S has an input tape with an infinite sequence X of data elements:

$$X = \langle x_0, x_1, x_2, \ldots \rangle \text{ with } x_i \in \{0,1\}.$$

S reads these data elements and sends them to R, which writes the data received on an output tape. Reception, however, is NOT guaranteed by the network: *deletion errors* may occur. What we now need is a protocol that guarantees:

(a) *safety* — at any moment the sequence of data elements written by R is a prefix of X;

(b) *liveness* — every $x_i \in X$ will eventually be written by R (provided the communication medium satisfies certain *fairness* properties).

The problem above is called the *sequence transmission*-problem.

On the basis of the properties of knowledge possessed by S and R we obtain:

SOLUTION 1: PROTOCOL A

PROTOCOL for S:

```
i := 0;
while true do
   begin read x_i;
      send x_i until K_S K_R(x_i);
      send "K_S K_R(x_i)" until K_S K_R K_S K_R(x_i);
      i := i + 1
   end
```

PROTOCOL for R:

```
when K_R(x_0) set i := 0;
while true do
   begin write x_i;
      send "K_R(x_i)" until K_R K_S K_R(x_i);
      send "K_R K_S K_R(x_i)" until K_R(x_{i+1});
      i := i + 1
   end
```

Here "φ" stands for the message that a state has been reached in which φ holds. Intuitively, the protocols are clear: after reading a data element x, S sends it (i.e. x) repeatedly to R until it (i.e. S) knows that x has been received by R. Then S sends an acknowledgement that it (S) knows that R has received x, and keeps on sending this acknowledgement until it (S) knows that R has received this acknowledgement. On the other hand, when R receives a data element x, it writes it on its tape, and sends an acknowledgement repeatedly to S until it (R) knows that this acknowledgement has been received by S. Then it (R) sends a further acknowledgement stating that it (R) knows that S has received the first acknowledgement, and keeps on doing so until it (R) receives a new data element (indicating that the sender has also received the second acknowledgement).

Protocol A is put in terms of the knowledge operators K_S and K_R. These are not available in ordinary programming languages. We can implement Protocol A by means of acknowledgements ack, ack^2, ack^3, with respective meanings "$K_R(x_i)$", "$K_S K_R(x_i)$", and "$K_R K_S K_R(x_i)$", as follows:

PROTOCOL for S:

```
while true do
   begin read y;
```

```
        send y until ack is received;
        send ack² until ack³ is received
    end
```

PROTOCOL for R:

```
when receive y write y
while true do
    begin send ack until ack² is received;
        send ack³ until y is received;
        write y
    end
```

Note that e.g. for R an 'until' clause such as 'until K_R K_S $K_R(x_i)$' is implemented simply as 'until ack^2 is received', since this means exactly that the message (ack^2 =) "$K_SK_R(x_i)$" is received by R, i.e. R knows that $K_SK_R(x_i)$, i.e. $K_RK_SK_R(x_i)$, as desired. Likewise for the other 'until' clauses of R and S.

In [HZ87] it is shown that:

1.9.1. THEOREM. *Protocol* A *solves the sequence transmission problem. It guarantees safety, and — provided it is guaranteed that messages from* S *to* R *and from* R *to* S *arrive eventually — also liveness.* ■

One may construct extensions of protocol A such that the above theorem also holds in cases where, besides 'deletion errors', '*mutation errors*' (data elements may get mutilated, 0 may become 1 or vice versa) and '*insertion errors*' (undesired data elements are inserted) may also occur.

An interesting question is whether the protocol really needs *knowledge of depth 4*. This appears to be not the case when we extend our alphabet to {0, 0', 1, 1', ack, ack'}, in other words, when we have the disposal of two 'coloured' versions of {0, 1, ack}. So now we are able to code the acknowledgement of the receipt of the previous message directly into a new message, without having to send the acknowledgement separately ahead of it. The protocol becomes simpler in this case:

SOLUTION 2: PROTOCOL B

PROTOCOL for S:

```
i := 0;
while true do
   begin read x_i;
      send x_i ;"K_S K_R(x_{i-1})" until K_S K_R(x_i);
      i := i + 1
   end
```

PROTOCOL for R:

```
when K_R(x_0) set i := 0;
while true do
   begin write x_i;
      send "K_R(x_i)" until K_R(x_{i+1});
      i := i + 1
   end
```

Here x_i ;"K_S $K_R(x_{i-1})$" stands for the combined message of the data element x_i, with the message "K_S $K_R(x_{i-1})$" encoded in it (by using the 'colour' of the alphabet).

By means of the coloured alphabet we can now implement protocol B as follows, using

$$\text{var}(m, i) = \begin{cases} m, \text{ if } i \text{ is even} \\ m', \text{ if } i \text{ is odd} \end{cases}$$

PROTOCOL for S:

```
i := 0;
while true do
   begin read x_i;
      send var(x_i,i) until var(ack, i) is received;
      i := i + 1
   end
```

PROTOCOL for R:

```
when receive x_0 set i := 0;
while true do
   begin write x_i;
```

```
        send var(ack, i) until x_{i+1} is received;
        i := i + 1
    end
```

Halpern & Zuck [HZ87] prove that protocol B guarantees safety and liveness as well, and also this protocol can be extended in such a way that the transmitted data are protected against other errors than just 'deletion errors'.

Although process S in protocol B does not wait until knowledge of depth 4 is obtained before sending x_{i+1}, we can prove that S acquires knowledge of depth 4. More precisely it is shown in [HZ87] that:

1.9.2. THEOREM. $\models$ S *sends* $x_{i+1} \rightarrow K_S \Box$ (R *receives* $x_{i+1} \rightarrow K_R K_S K_R(x_i)$).
(Here $\Box$ denotes the temporal 'always'-operator.)

This, too, appears not to be essential for a satisfactory protocol. For example, alternatively S might send messages in packages of 5 according to protocol A or B.

Protocol B is closely related to the *alternating bit protocol.* To obtain this protocol one has to simulate the 'coloured' messages by the use of alternating closing bits:

$$\text{var}(m,i) = \begin{cases} m0, \text{ if i even} \\ m1, \text{ otherwise} \end{cases}$$

Finally we mention that Halpern & Zuck [HZ87] claim that their epistemic analysis is applicable to a whole class of related protocols that appear in the literature.

2 VARIOUS NOTIONS OF KNOWLEDGE AND BELIEF

In this chapter we consider extensions of the basic notion of knowledge, namely *common* knowledge and *implicit* knowledge in a group, and also consider notions of *belief* rather than knowledge. An important topic will be that of the *logical omniscience problem*. Besides this we shall also discuss the interplay between knowledge, belief and time, and that between knowledge and action. Finally we shall introduce so-called *graded modalities* for knowledge and belief. Throughout this chapter and subsequent ones, we will refer to formulas without any modal operators as *purely propositional* or *objective*.

To start with we extend the language $\mathcal{L}_{\mathbf{K}}^{m}$ by the operators E ("everyone knows") and C ('common knowledge'). We denote the extended language by $\mathcal{L}_{\mathbf{KEC}}^{m}$.

2.1. Common Knowledge

We introduce two new operators into our language: $E\varphi$ for "*everyone knows that* φ" and $C\varphi$ for "*it is common knowledge that* φ". Informally,

$$E\varphi = K_1\varphi \wedge \ldots \wedge K_m\varphi,$$

$$C\varphi = \varphi \wedge E\varphi \wedge EE\varphi \wedge EEE\varphi \wedge \ldots = \bigwedge_{i\geq 0} E^i\varphi.$$

Here $E^i\varphi$ is defined as $EEE\ldots\varphi$ (i operators E). The latter 'formula' can only be understood intuitively, for we do not consider infinite conjunctions. We shall now first give a proper semantics to these new operators, and next a sound and complete axiomatisation.

2.1.1. DEFINITION. Let the Kripke model $\mathbb{M} = \langle S, \pi, R_1, \ldots, R_m\rangle$ be given. Let $s, t \in S$.

(i) Then instead of $(s, t) \in R_i$ (t is reachable via R_i in one step) we write $s \rightarrow_{R_i} t$.

(ii) Instead of $(s, t) \in R_1 \cup \ldots \cup R_m$ we write $s \rightarrow t$. We write $s \rightarrow^k t$ if there is a sequence $s = s_0 \rightarrow s_1 \rightarrow \ldots \rightarrow s_k = t$, for some s_i $(0 \leq i \leq k)$.

(iii) The relation $\twoheadrightarrow$ is the *reflexive-transitive closure* of the one-step reachability relation $\rightarrow$. Thus $s \twoheadrightarrow t$ holds iff $s \rightarrow^k t$ for some $k \geq 0$.

2.1.2. DEFINITION. Let $\mathbb{M} = \langle S, \pi, R_1, ..., R_m \rangle$ and $s \in S$. Let φ be an epistemic formula in the language $\mathcal{L}^m_{\mathbf{KEC}}$. The semantics of such formulas is defined by the semantic definition in Section 1.3 extended with the following clauses:

$$(\mathbb{M}, s) \models E\varphi \Leftrightarrow (\mathbb{M}, t) \models \varphi \text{ for all } t \text{ with } s \rightarrow t,$$
$$(\mathbb{M}, s) \models C\varphi \Leftrightarrow (\mathbb{M}, t) \models \varphi \text{ for all } t \text{ with } s \twoheadrightarrow t.$$

In addition to the axiom schemes (A1), (A2) and rules (R1), (R2) in Section 1.4 and (A3)—(A5) in Section 1.5 we now give an axiomatisation for the E- and C-operators:

(A6) $E\varphi \leftrightarrow K_1\varphi \wedge ... \wedge K_m\varphi$

(A7) $C\varphi \rightarrow \varphi$

(A8) $C\varphi \rightarrow EC\varphi$

(A9) $(C\varphi \wedge C(\varphi \rightarrow \psi)) \rightarrow C\psi$

(A10) $C(\varphi \rightarrow E\varphi) \rightarrow (\varphi \rightarrow C\varphi)$

(R3) $\dfrac{\varphi}{C\varphi}$

Furthermore we define the following deduction systems (cf. $\mathbf{T}_{(m)}$, $\mathbf{S4}_{(m)}$, $\mathbf{S5}_{(m)}$ in Section 1.5):

$\mathbf{KEC}_{(m)} = \mathbf{K}_{(m)}$ + (A6)—(A10) + (R3)

$\mathbf{TEC}_{(m)} = \mathbf{T}_{(m)}$ + (A6)—(A10) + (R3)

$\mathbf{S4EC}_{(m)} = \mathbf{S4}_{(m)}$ + (A6)—(A10) + (R3)

$\mathbf{S5EC}_{(m)} = \mathbf{S5}_{(m)}$ + (A6)—(A10) + (R3)

2.1.2.1. EXERCISE. Prove the following theorems (where $i \leq m$).

(i) $\mathbf{KEC}_{(m)} \vdash C\varphi \rightarrow E\varphi$

(ii) $\mathbf{KEC}_{(m)} \vdash C\varphi \rightarrow K_i\varphi$

(iii) $\mathbf{KEC}_{(m)} \vdash C\varphi \leftrightarrow CC\varphi$

(iv) $\mathbf{TEC}_{(m)} \vdash C\varphi \leftrightarrow CE\varphi$

(v) $\mathbf{TEC}_{(m)} \vdash C\varphi \leftrightarrow K_iC\varphi$

(vi) $\mathbf{TEC_{(m)}} \vdash C\varphi \leftrightarrow EC\varphi$

(vii) $\mathbf{S5EC_{(m)}} \vdash \neg C\varphi \leftrightarrow K_i\neg C\varphi$ (Hint: Use (v).)

(viii) $\mathbf{S5EC_{(m)}} \vdash \neg C\varphi \leftrightarrow E\neg C\varphi$

(ix) $\mathbf{S5EC_{(m)}} \vdash \neg C\varphi \leftrightarrow C\neg C\varphi$

2.1.2.2. EXERCISE. Prove the following derived rules in the system $\mathbf{KEC_{(m)}}$.

(i) $\vdash \varphi \Rightarrow \vdash E\varphi$

(ii) $\vdash \varphi_1 \leftrightarrow \varphi_2 \Rightarrow \vdash \psi \leftrightarrow \psi[\varphi_1/\varphi_2]$ (cf. Exercise 1.4.1.1(ii))

2.1.2.3. EXERCISE. Prove that $\mathbf{KEC_{(m)}} \vdash C\varphi \rightarrow K_{i_1}K_{i_2}...K_{i_n}\varphi$ for any tuple $i_1, i_2, ..., i_n$ with $1 \leq i_1, i_2, ..., i_n \leq m$.

2.1.3. THEOREM (Soundness of $\mathbf{KEC_{(m)}}$, $\mathbf{TEC_{(m)}}$, $\mathbf{S4EC_{(m)}}$, $\mathbf{S5EC_{(m)}}$).

(i) $\mathbf{KEC_{(m)}} \vdash \varphi \quad \Rightarrow \quad \mathcal{K}_{(m)} \models \varphi$

(ii) $\mathbf{TEC_{(m)}} \vdash \varphi \quad \Rightarrow \quad \mathcal{T}_{(m)} \models \varphi$

(iii) $\mathbf{S4EC_{(m)}} \vdash \varphi \quad \Rightarrow \quad \mathcal{S4}_{(m)} \models \varphi$

(iv) $\mathbf{S5EC_{(m)}} \vdash \varphi \quad \Rightarrow \quad \mathcal{S5}_{(m)} \models \varphi$

PROOF. We only prove (i).
We only prove the soundness of axiom (A10), leaving the rest as Exercise 2.1.3.1. We have to show that $\mathcal{K}_{(m)} \models C(\varphi \rightarrow E\varphi) \rightarrow (\varphi \rightarrow C\varphi)$. To this end, we take a model $\mathbb{M} = \langle S, \pi, R_1, ..., R_m\rangle \in \mathcal{K}_{(m)}$, and an arbitrary $s \in S$. Now suppose that $(\mathbb{M}, s) \models C(\varphi \rightarrow E\varphi)$. This means that $(\mathbb{M}, t) \models \varphi \rightarrow E\varphi$ for all t with $s \twoheadrightarrow t$. Now suppose that $(\mathbb{M}, s) \models \varphi$. We have to show that $(\mathbb{M}, s) \models C\varphi$, i.e. that $(\mathbb{M}, t) \models \varphi$ for all t with $s \twoheadrightarrow t$. For this it is sufficient to show by induction on k that for all $k \geq 0$ it holds that $(\mathbb{M}, t) \models \varphi$ for all t with $s \rightarrow^k t$. The basic case that $k = 0$ is obvious, since the only t with $s \rightarrow^0 t$ is s itself, and we know that $(\mathbb{M}, s) \models \varphi$. Next, assume that the assertion holds for all $k < n$. We now prove the assertion for $k = n$: consider a state t such that $s \rightarrow^n t$. Then there is a state u such that $s \rightarrow^{n-1} u \rightarrow t$. By the induction assumption we have that $(\mathbb{M}, u) \models \varphi$. Since we also have that $s \twoheadrightarrow u$, we know that also $(\mathbb{M}, u) \models \varphi \rightarrow E\varphi$. Thus we have that $(\mathbb{M}, u) \models E\varphi$, i.e. $(\mathbb{M}, v) \models \varphi$ for all v with $u \rightarrow v$. In particular, we have that $(\mathbb{M}, t) \models \varphi$, which was to be proven. ■

2.1.3.1. EXERCISE. Complete the soundness proof of Theorem 2.1.3(i).

*2.1.4. Completeness of $\mathbf{KEC_{(m)}}$, $\mathbf{TEC_{(m)}}$, $\mathbf{S4EC_{(m)}}$, and $\mathbf{S5EC_{(m)}}$

In this subsection we will prove a completeness theorem that is a generalisation of Theorems 1.4.6, 1.6.4 and 1.6.7. This proof is non-trivial, since the C-operator involves a reflexive-transitive closure of the accessibility relation '$\rightarrow$' associated with the E-operator. This situation is similar to that in propositional dynamic logic (PDL), where there is a relation associated with an iterative program α^*; see [Gol87].

First we define the following classes of models: $\mathcal{KEC}_{(\mathbf{m})}$ is the class of models $\mathbb{M} = \langle S, \pi, R_1, ..., R_m, R_E, R_C\rangle$, where $R_E = R_1 \cup ... \cup R_m$, and $R_C = R_E{}^*$, the reflexive-transitive closure of the relation R_E. The classes $\mathcal{TEC}_{(\mathbf{m})}$, $\mathcal{S4EC}_{(\mathbf{m})}$ and $\mathcal{S5EC}_{(\mathbf{m})}$ are like $\mathcal{KEC}_{(\mathbf{m})}$, but here the relations R_i are reflexive, reflexive and transitive, and equivalence relations, respectively. It is easy to check that for every formula φ in the present extended language it holds that: $\mathcal{K}_{(\mathbf{m})} \models \varphi \Leftrightarrow \mathcal{KEC}_{(\mathbf{m})} \models \varphi$, and similarly for the remaining of the above classes.

2.1.4.1. EXERCISE. Show by induction on the structure of formula φ that for every φ it holds that $\mathcal{K}_{(\mathbf{m})} \models \varphi \Leftrightarrow \mathcal{KEC}_{(\mathbf{m})} \models \varphi$.

In order to achieve completeness with respect to the corresponding class of models, we again use the notion of a maximal consistent set and canonical model as in Section 1.4. Since we have that all modalities $K_1, ..., K_m$, E and C satisfy the basic properties of the basic system **K**, we have that all results of Section 1.4 are applicable in the present case. In particular, we can define a canonical model $\mathbb{M}^c = \langle S^c, \pi^c, R_1{}^c, ..., R_m{}^c, R_E{}^c, R_C{}^c\rangle$ with:

$$S^c = \{s_\Theta \mid \Theta \text{ is a maximally consistent set of formulas}\},$$

$$\pi^c(s_\Theta)(p) = \begin{cases} \mathfrak{t} \text{ if } p \in \Theta \\ \mathfrak{f} \text{ if } p \notin \Theta, \end{cases}$$

$$R_i{}^c = \{(s_\Theta, s_\Psi) \mid \Theta/K_i \subseteq \Psi\},$$
$$R_E{}^c = \{(s_\Theta, s_\Psi) \mid \Theta/E \subseteq \Psi\},$$
$$R_C{}^c = \{(s_\Theta, s_\Psi) \mid \Theta/C \subseteq \Psi\},$$

where $\Theta/K_i = \{\varphi \mid K_i\varphi \in \Theta\}$, $\Theta/E = \{\varphi \mid E\varphi \in \Theta\}$ and $\Theta/C = \{\varphi \mid C\varphi \in \Theta\}$. This canonical model satisfies the coincidence property, $\forall\varphi : (\mathbb{M}^c, s_\Phi) \models \varphi \Leftrightarrow \varphi \in \Phi$, and from this it follows as in Section 1.4 that we can satisfy any maximally consistent set of formulas in this canonical model. To have completeness it would now be sufficient to show that the canonical model is of the right type. Unfortunately, this is not (yet) the case, as we see in the following theorem (we focus on the most interesting case viewed in the light of epistemic logic, namely that of $\mathbf{S5EC}_{(\mathbf{m})}$):

2.1.4.2. THEOREM. *The canonical model* $\mathbb{M}^c = \langle S^c, \pi^c, R_1{}^c, ..., R_m{}^c, R_E{}^c, R_C{}^c\rangle$ *for the logic* $\mathbf{S5EC}_{(\mathbf{m})}$, *as defined above, satisfies the following properties.*

(i) R_i^c ($i \leq m$) is reflexive, transitive and euclidean, i.e. is an equivalence relation.

(ii) $R_E^c = R_1^c \cup \ldots \cup R_m^c$.

(iii) $(R_E^c)^* \subseteq R_C^c$.

PROOF. (i) is proved as in Section 1.6; (ii) is proved as follows.
($\subseteq$) Suppose $(s_\Theta, s_\Psi) \in R_E^c$, i.e. $\Theta/E \subseteq \Psi$. We have to show that $(s_\Theta, s_\Psi) \in R_1^c \cup \ldots \cup R_m^c$. For this it is sufficient to show that $(s_\Theta, s_\Psi) \in R_i^c$, i.e. $\Theta/K_i \subseteq \Psi$, for some $1 \leq i \leq m$. Suppose this is not the case. Then we have that, for all $1 \leq i \leq m$, $\Theta/K_i \not\subseteq \Psi$. This means that for all $1 \leq i \leq m$ there exists a $\varphi_i \in \Theta/K_i$ and $\varphi_i \notin \Psi$. So, for all i, $K_i\varphi_i \in \Theta$ and, by the maximal consistency of Ψ, $\neg\varphi_i \in \Psi$. Consequently, $\neg\varphi_1 \wedge \ldots \wedge \neg\varphi_m \in \Psi$. Let $\varphi = \varphi_1 \vee \varphi_2 \vee \ldots \vee \varphi_m$. Since $\vdash \varphi_i \rightarrow \varphi$, also $\vdash K_i(\varphi_i \rightarrow \varphi)$, and hence also $\vdash K_i\varphi_i \rightarrow K_i\varphi$. Since Θ is maximally consistent, $K_i\varphi_i \rightarrow K_i\varphi \in \Theta$, and therefore also $K_i\varphi \in \Theta$, for all i. Thus also $K_1\varphi \wedge \ldots \wedge K_m\varphi \in \Theta$. So, by the fact that (A6) holds, i.e. $E\varphi \leftrightarrow K_1\varphi \wedge \ldots \wedge K_m\varphi \in \Theta$ (since maximal consistent sets contain all theorems, and axioms in particular), we have that $E\varphi \in \Theta$, and hence $\varphi \in \Theta/E \subseteq \Psi$. On the other hand, $\neg\varphi_1 \wedge \ldots \wedge \neg\varphi_m \in \Psi$, and hence $\neg(\varphi_1 \vee \varphi_2 \vee \ldots \vee \varphi_m) \in \Psi$, i.e., $\neg\varphi \in \Psi$, which yields a contradiction. Thus $(s_\Theta, s_\Psi) \in R_i^c$, for some $1 \leq i \leq m$.
($\supseteq$) Suppose $(s_\Theta, s_\Psi) \in R_1^c \cup \ldots \cup R_m^c$. Then $(s_\Theta, s_\Psi) \in R_j^c$, i.e., $\Theta/K_j \subseteq \Psi$, for some $1 \leq j \leq m$. We have to show that $(s_\Theta, s_\Psi) \in R_E^c$, i.e., $\Theta/E \subseteq \Psi$. Take $\varphi \in \Theta/E$, i.e., $E\varphi \in \Theta$. Since (A6) $\in \Theta$, $K_1\varphi \wedge \ldots \wedge K_m\varphi \in \Theta$ as well, and hence $K_i\varphi \in \Theta$ for all $1 \leq i \leq m$. In particular, $K_j\varphi \in \Theta$, and so $\varphi \in \Theta/K_j \subseteq \Psi$. Since $\varphi \in \Theta/E$ was chosen arbitrarily, we indeed obtain $\Theta/E \subseteq \Psi$.
(iii). Suppose $(s_\Theta, s_\Psi) \in (R_E^c)^*$, which means that there is some sequence $s_\Theta = s_{\Gamma_0}, s_{\Gamma_1}, \ldots, s_{\Gamma_n} = s_\Psi$, such that $(s_{\Gamma_i}, s_{\Gamma_{i+1}}) \in R_E^c$, i.e. $\Gamma_i/E \subseteq \Gamma_{i+1}$ $(0 \leq i < n)$. We now have to show that $(s_\Theta, s_\Psi) \in R_C^c$, i.e. $\Theta/C \subseteq \Psi$. Take $\varphi \in \Theta/C$. Then $C\varphi \in \Theta$. By the fact that (A8) holds, $C\varphi \rightarrow EC\varphi \in \Theta = \Gamma_0$, we have that $EC\varphi \in \Gamma_0$, and thus $C\varphi \in \Gamma_0/E \subseteq \Gamma_1$. By repeating this argument n−1 times, we obtain that $C\varphi \in \Gamma_n = \Psi$. Since (A7) $C\varphi \rightarrow \varphi \in \Psi$, we obtain that $\varphi \in \Psi$. ■

We call a model that satisfies the properties mentioned in Theorem 2.1.4.2 a *quasi-$\mathcal{S5EC}_{(m)}$-model.* If we do this we immediately obtain the following corollary:

2.1.4.3. COROLLARY. *Every* **S5EC$_{(m)}$**-*consistent formula* φ *is satisfied in some quasi-$\mathcal{S5EC}_{(m)}$-model, and hence validity on the class of quasi-$\mathcal{S5EC}_{(m)}$-models implies derivability in* **S5EC$_{(m)}$**.

Although the properties (i) and (ii) in Theorem 2.1.4.2 are as desired, property (iii) is too weak: we would like to have that $R_C^c = (R_E^c)^*$. Unfortunately, this is not the case:

2.1.4.4. THEOREM. *For the canonical model* $\mathbb{M}^c = \langle S^c, \pi^c, R_1{}^c, ..., R_m{}^c, R_E{}^c, R_C{}^c\rangle$ *for the logic* $\mathbf{S5EC_{(m)}}$*, as defined above, we have that* $R_C{}^c \not\subseteq (R_E{}^c)^*$.

PROOF. Consider $\Phi = \{Ep, EEp, EEEp, ...\} \cup \{\neg Cp\}$.

CLAIM. Φ is $\mathbf{S5EC_{(m)}}$-consistent.

PROOF OF THE CLAIM. Let us write again $E^1\varphi$ for $E\varphi$, $E^2\varphi$ for $EE\varphi$, etc. Suppose that Φ is inconsistent. Then there is a finite set $\Gamma \subseteq \Phi$ that is already inconsistent, i.e. $\mathbf{S5EC_{(m)}} \vdash \Gamma \to \bot$. Say $\Gamma = \{E^{n_1}p, E^{n_2}p, ..., E^{n_k}p \mid n_i < n_{i+1} \text{ for } i < k\} \cup \{\neg Cp\}$. By the soundness of $\mathbf{S5EC_{(m)}}$ (Theorem 2.1.3), $\mathcal{S5EC}_{(m)} \models \Gamma \to \bot$, i.e. Γ is unsatisfiable in the class $\mathcal{S5EC}_{(m)}$. However, consider the following model $\mathbb{N} = \langle S, \pi, R_1, R_2, R_E, R_C\rangle$, where $W = \mathbb{N}$, $R_1 = \{(n, n) \mid n \in \mathbb{N}\} \cup \{(n, n+1), (n+1, n) \mid n \in \mathbb{N} \text{ and n is even}\}$, $R_2 = \{(n, n) \mid n \in \mathbb{N}\} \cup \{(n, n+1), (n+1, n) \mid n \in \mathbb{N} \text{ and n is odd}\}$, $R_E = R_1 \cup R_2 = \{(n, n) \mid n \in \mathbb{N}\} \cup \{(n, n+1), (n+1, n) \mid n \in \mathbb{N}\}$ and $R_C = (R_E)^*$. See Figure 2.1 below, in which R_1 is denoted at the upper half, R_2 below. Note that $\mathbb{N}$ is indeed a quasi-$\mathcal{S5EC}_{(m)}$-model.

Figure 2.1

Now we define $\pi(x)(p) = t \Leftrightarrow x \leq n_k + 1$. Then $(\mathbb{N}, 1) \models \Gamma$, so Γ is satisfiable, which completes the proof of the claim. ■ *Claim*

To complete the proof of Theorem 2.1.4.4, we use the fact that Φ is $\mathbf{S5EC_{(m)}}$-consistent and Lemma 1.4.3 (i) to find a maximal consistent set $\Phi' \supseteq \Phi$. Let $\Psi = \{\neg p\} \cup \{\psi \mid C\psi \in \Phi'\}$. Then Ψ is consistent, so again there is some maximal consistent set $\Psi' \supseteq \Psi$. Now observe that, in the canonical model $\mathbb{M}^c$, we have $(s_{\Phi'}, s_{\Psi'}) \in R_C$, but $(s_{\Phi'}, s_{\Psi'}) \notin R_E{}^*$. ■

Since the canonical model is not of the right kind, we do not immediately have completeness of $\mathbf{S5EC_{(m)}}$ with respect to the class $\mathcal{S5EC}_{(m)}$ of models. For this we need to apply some more sophisticated technique, namely that of filtrations, which we shall discuss in the next section.

Here we pause for a moment to wonder whether we do have completeness with respect to the class of quasi-$\mathcal{S5EC}_{(m)}$-models. However, this is not the case either, since axiom (A10) is not valid with respect to this class. In order to see this, consider the model $\mathcal{A} = \langle S, \pi, R_1, R_2, R_E, R_C\rangle$, with $S = \{a, b\}$, $R_1 = R_2 = R_E = \{(a, a), (b, b)\}$ and $R_C = \{(a, a), (b, b), (a, b)\}$. Note that $\mathcal{A}$ is a quasi-$S5EC_{(m)}$-model. Finally, let π be such that $\pi(x)(p) = (x = a)$ (see Figure 2.2). Then we have $(\mathcal{A}, a) \models C(p \to Ep) \wedge p \wedge \neg Cp$.

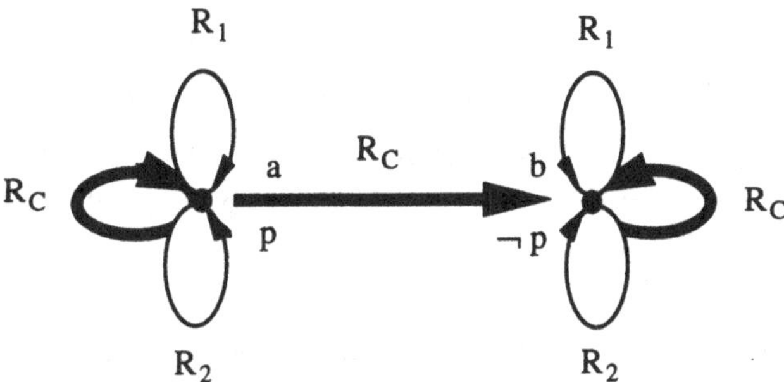

Figure 2.2

*2.1.5. Filtrations

We will now describe a way to turn the canonical model of the previous section into an $S5EC_{(m)}$-model. It will appear to be crucial (see Lemma 2.1.5.8) that the result is a *finite* model. Our technique to obtain this finite model is called *filtrating*. This method obtains, for any model $\mathbb{M} = \langle S, \pi, R\rangle$ and formula φ, a model $\mathbb{N} = \langle W, \pi_{\mathbb{N}}, T\rangle$ which is finite and for which there is some function $f: S \to W$ such that, for all $s \in S$ and subformulas ψ of φ, $(\mathbb{M}, s) \models \psi \Leftrightarrow (\mathbb{N}, f(s)) \models \psi$. The strategy to achieve this is the following. To transfer the truth of a modal formula φ at s in an infinite model to a finite one, we only need s itself and a number of s's successors v that are witnesses for subformulas of φ that are of the form $\neg\Box\neg\psi$, where $\Box$ is the modal operator denoting truth in successor states according to the relations R and T in the models $\mathbb{M}$ and $\mathbb{N}$, respectively. And, inductively, a finite number of successors of those v's as well. In fact, it turns out that we only need at most one witness for each subformula of φ. Moreover, we have some liberty in choosing the exact accessibility relation T. We will start out by setting the stage for the purely modal case.

2.1.5.1. DEFINITION. Let $\mathbb{M} = \langle S, \pi, R\rangle$ be some Kripke model. Furthermore, suppose that Φ is some finite set of formulas closed under subformulas. It is easily verified that the relation $\equiv_\Phi$ on S, defined as $s \equiv_\Phi t \Leftrightarrow$ for all $\psi \in \Phi$ $((\mathbb{M}, s) \models \psi \Leftrightarrow (\mathbb{M}, t) \models \psi)$ is an equivalence relation. The equivalence class of $s \in S$ will be denoted by $[s]_\Phi$. When no confusion can arise, we omit the subscript Φ. Now we define the model $\mathbb{N}_\Phi = \langle W, \pi_{\mathbb{N}_\Phi}, T\rangle$ as follows.

- $W = \{[s] \mid s \in S\}$.
- T satisfies the following conditions Min(T/R) and Max(T).

  Min(T/R): For all $[s], [t] \in W$, if there are $s', t' \in S$ with $(s', t') \in R$, $[s] = [s']$ and $[t] = [t']$, then $([s], [t]) \in T$.

Max(T): For any [s] and [t] $\in$ W, if ([s], [t]) $\in$ T, then for any $\Box\psi \in \Phi$: $((\mathbb{M}, s) \models \Box\psi \Rightarrow (\mathbb{M}, t) \models \psi)$.

- $\pi_{N_\Phi}([s])(p) = \pi(s)(p)$.

A relation T that satisfies both Min(T/R) and Max(T) is called a *filtration (through Φ)* of R. For a multi-modal model $\mathbb{M} = \langle S, \pi_{\mathbb{M}}, R_1, \ldots, R_m \rangle$, if we have $N_\Phi = \langle W, \pi_{N_\Phi}, T_1, \ldots, T_m \rangle$ such that for all $i \leq m$, T_i is a filtration of R_i, then the model N_Φ is also called a filtration (through Φ) of $\mathbb{M}$.

Note that, for our new set W of states, we just take the Φ-equivalence classes of S. Since the set Φ is finite, W is finite as well. Furthermore, note that Min(T/R) is indeed a minimal condition for T to simulate R: if $\Diamond\psi$ $(=\neg\Box\neg\psi)$ is true in s', then s' must have an R-successor t' in which ψ is true. We must mimic this situation for T in N_Φ, and this is exactly what Min(T/R) enables us to do. In addition, the condition Max(T) allows us, independently from the actual relation R upon which it is based, to add pairs to T, but only if the truth of modal formulas of Φ is respected. Note that we can always find a relation that fulfils both requirements: just take T to exactly satisfy Min(T/R). Finally, note that we can alternatively write condition Min(T/R) as:

Min(T/R): for all s, t $\in$ S, $(s, t) \in R \Rightarrow ([s], [t]) \in T$.

2.1.5.2. THEOREM. *Let* $N_\Phi = \langle W, \pi_{N_\Phi}, T_1, \ldots, T_m \rangle$ *be a filtration of* $\mathbb{M} = \langle S, \pi_{\mathbb{M}}, R_1, \ldots, R_m \rangle$ *through* Φ. *Then, for all* $\psi \in \Phi$ *and* $s \in S$, *we have* $((\mathbb{M}, s) \models \psi \Leftrightarrow (N_\Phi, [s]) \models \psi)$.

PROOF. We prove the theorem by induction on the structure of ψ. For atomic formulas this follows immediately from the definition of π_{N_Φ}. The logical connectives are straightforward and left as Exercise 2.1.5.3. Now suppose $\psi = \Box\alpha$ and assume the theorem proven for α. Suppose also $(\mathbb{M}, s) \models \Box\alpha$. Let [t] be such that $([s], [t]) \in T$. By Max(T), if $(\mathbb{M}, s) \models \Box\alpha$, then $(\mathbb{M}, t) \models \alpha$. By our induction hypothesis, $(N_\Phi, [t]) \models \alpha$, so $(N_\Phi, [s]) \models \Box\alpha$. Conversely, suppose $(N_\Phi, [s]) \models \Box\alpha$, so that for all [t] with $([s], [t]) \in T$, $(N_\Phi, [t]) \models \alpha$. If $(s, u) \in R$, then, by Min(T/R), $([s], [u]) \in T$, so $(N_\Phi, [u]) \models \alpha$, and, by the induction hypothesis, $(\mathbb{M}, u) \models \alpha$, so $(N_\Phi, [s]) \models \Box\alpha$. ■

2.1.5.3. EXERCISE. Show Theorem 2.1.5.2 for the cases that ψ is of the form $\neg\psi_1$ and $\psi_1 \wedge \psi_2$.

2.1.5.4. DEFINITION. Let φ be a formula, and

- $\Phi_1 = \{\psi, \neg\psi \mid \psi \text{ is a subformula of } \varphi, i \leq m\}$;

- $\Phi_2 = \{K_i\psi, \neg K_i\psi \mid E\psi \in \Phi_1, i \leq m\}$;
- $\Phi_3 = \{EC\psi, \neg EC\psi, K_iC\psi, \neg K_iC\psi \mid C\psi \in \Phi_1, i \leq m\}$.

Then $\Phi = \Phi_1 \cup \Phi_2 \cup \Phi_3$ is called a *suitable* set of subformulas of φ or, simply, Φ is suitable with respect to φ. Note that Φ is finite and that $\varphi \in \Phi$. Furthermore, note that a suitable set Φ is closed under subformulas, that for any formula $\psi \in \Phi$ there is some formula χ in Φ that is equivalent to $\neg\psi$, and that for each $C\psi \in \Phi$ we also have $EC\psi \in \Phi$ and for each $E\psi \in \Phi$ we have $K_i \in \Phi$. These three properties will be used in Lemma 2.1.5.8 and Theorem 2.1.5.9 below.

2.1.5.5. COROLLARY. *Let Φ be suitable with respect to φ, and let $\mathbb{M} = \langle S, \pi_{\mathbb{M}}, R_1, \ldots, R_m\rangle$ be such that $(\mathbb{M}, s) \models \varphi$. Then the filtration $\mathbb{N}_\Phi$ of $\mathbb{M}$ through Φ has the property that $(\mathbb{N}_\Phi, [s]) \models \varphi$.*

PROOF. Immediate from Theorem 2.1.5.2 and the fact that $\varphi \in \Phi$. ■

2.1.5.6. DEFINITION. Let $\mathbb{M}^c = \langle S^c, \pi^c, R_1{}^c, \ldots, R_m{}^c, R_E{}^c, R_C{}^c\rangle$ be the canonical model of the previous subsection, and let φ be a consistent formula. Furthermore, let Φ be suitable with respect to φ. Now define the model $\mathbb{N} = \langle W, \pi_{\mathbb{N}}, T_1, \ldots, T_m, T_E, T_C\rangle$ by:

- $W = \{[s]_\Phi \mid s \in S^c\}$. (Note that W is finite since Φ is finite.)
- For all T_i $(1 \leq i \leq m)$ it holds that:
  - (i) for any $[s]_\Phi$ and $[t]_\Phi \in W$, $([s]_\Phi, [t]_\Phi) \in T_i \Leftrightarrow$ for all $K_i\psi \in \Phi$: $((\mathbb{M}^c, s) \models K_i\psi \Leftrightarrow (\mathbb{M}^c, t) \models K_i\psi)$;
  - (ii) $T_E = (T_1 \cup \ldots \cup T_m)$;
  - (iii) $T_C = (T_E)^*$.
- $\pi_{\mathbb{N}}([s])(p) = \pi(s)(p)$.

2.1.5.7. LEMMA. *The model $\mathbb{N}$ as defined in Definition 2.1.5.6 is an $\mathcal{S5EC}_{(m)}$-model.*

PROOF. We only have to show that the T_i are equivalence relations, and this is immediate from the definition of T_i. ■

Not only is the model $\mathbb{N}$ of Definition 2.1.5.6 an $\mathcal{S5EC}_{(m)}$-model, but it is also *finite*. It is this fact that enables us to prove the following lemma, which states a crucial property when proving that $\mathbb{N}$ is indeed a filtration of $\mathbb{M}^c$.

2.1.5.8. LEMMA (Definability lemma). *Let* W *be as defined in Definition 2.1.5.6. Then, for each subset* $A \subseteq W$ *there is some formula* σ_A *such that, for all* $[s] \in W$, $(\mathbb{M}^c, s) \models \sigma_A \Leftrightarrow [s] \in A$.

PROOF. Let Form(s) be the conjunction of formulas $\psi \in \Phi$ that are true in $(\mathbb{M}^c, s)$. By the definition of [s], it is clear that $(\mathbb{M}^c, t) \models \text{Form}(s) \Leftrightarrow [s] = [t]$. Put σ_A to be the disjunction of all Form(s) for which $[s] \in A$, denoted $\bigvee_{[t]\in A} \text{Form}(t)$. (This is well-defined, since A is a subset of the finite set W, and therefore finite itself.) Now we have that:

$(\mathbb{M}^c, s) \models \sigma_A \Leftrightarrow$
$(\mathbb{M}^c, s) \models \bigvee_{[t]\in A} \text{Form}(t) \Leftrightarrow$
$(\mathbb{M}^c, s) \models \text{Form}(t)$ for some t with $[t] \in A \Leftrightarrow$
$[s] = [t]$ for some t with $[t] \in A \Leftrightarrow$
$[s] \in A$. ■

2.1.5.9. THEOREM. *The model* $\mathbb{N}$ *as defined in Definition 2.1.5.6 is a filtration of* $\mathbb{M}^c$ *through* Φ.

PROOF. We have to show that the accessibility relations $T_1, \ldots, T_m, T_E, T_C$ are filtrations through Φ of $R_1^c, \ldots, R_m^c, R_E^c$, and R_C^c, respectively.

1. We start out by showing this for the T_i, $i \leq m$, i.e., that T_i satisfies the minimality and maximality condition of 2.1.5.1. For the minimality condition, suppose that $[s], [t] \in W$, and $s', t' \in S^c$ with $(s', t') \in R_i^c$, $[s] = [s']$ and $[t] = [t']$. Let $K_i\psi \in \Phi$. Now,

$(\mathbb{M}^c, s) \models K_i\psi \Leftrightarrow$	$([s] = [s'])$
$(\mathbb{M}^c, s') \models K_i\psi \Leftrightarrow$	(R_i is an equivalence relation and $(s', t') \in R_i^c$)
$(\mathbb{M}^c, t') \models K_i\psi \Leftrightarrow$	$([t] = [t'])$
$(\mathbb{M}^c, t) \models K_i\psi$.	

So $([s], [t]) \in T_i$.

For the maximality condition, let $[s], [t] \in W$, and $([s], [t]) \in T_i$. Suppose $(\mathbb{M}^c, s) \models K_i\psi$. By the definition of T_i, we have $(\mathbb{M}^c, t) \models K_i\psi$, and, since R_i^c is reflexive, also $(\mathbb{M}^c, t) \models \psi$.

2. To prove that T_E satisfies $\text{Min}(T_E/R_E^c)$, suppose that $(s, t) \in R_E^c$. Since $\mathbb{M}^c$ is an $\mathcal{S5EC}_{(m)}$-model, we have that $R_1^c \cup \ldots \cup R_m^c = R_E^c$, and thus that $(s, t) \in R_i^c$ for some $i \leq m$. Since

we know that T_i is a filtration of R_i^c, we have $([s], [t]) \in T_i$, and thus, by definition of T_E, also $([s], [t]) \in T_E$.

To prove $Max(T_E)$, suppose $([s], [t]) \in T_E$, and $(\mathbb{M}^c, s) \models E\psi$, with $E\psi \in \Phi$. Since Φ is suitable, we have $K_i\psi \in \Phi$ for all $i \leq m$. Since $([s], [t]) \in T_E$ there must be an $i \leq m$ such that $([s], [t]) \in T_i$ and, since $(\mathbb{M}^c, s) \models K_i\psi$ and T_i is a filtration of R_i^c, we have $(\mathbb{M}^c, t) \models \psi$ and hence that T_E satisfies the maximality condition to be a filtration through R_E^c.

3. To prove that T_C satisfies $Min(T_C/R_C^c)$, suppose $(s, t) \in R_C^c$. Let $A \subseteq W$ be the set

$$A = \{[u] \in W \mid ([s], [u]) \in T_E^*\}.$$

We are done if we can prove that

$$(\mathbb{M}^c, s) \models C\sigma_A, \tag{0}$$

for this means that $(\mathbb{M}^c, t) \models \sigma_A$ and thus, by definition of σ_A, that $[t] \in A$, i.e., $[t]$ is a T_E^*-successor of $[s]$, and hence $([s], [t]) \in T_C$. To prove (0), we use the fact that $\mathbb{M}^c$ validates the induction axiom, in particular, that

$$(\mathbb{M}^c, s) \models C(\sigma_A \to E\sigma_A) \to (\sigma_A \to C\sigma_A). \tag{1}$$

It appears that also the antecedent of this formula is true at $(\mathbb{M}^c, s)$, i.e. that

$$(\mathbb{M}^c, s) \models C(\sigma_A \to E\sigma_A). \tag{2}$$

To see this, suppose $(s, x) \in R_C^c$, and $(\mathbb{M}^c, x) \models \sigma_A$; we have to show $(\mathbb{M}^c, x) \models E\sigma_A$. So suppose $(x, y) \in R_E^c$. Since $(\mathbb{M}^c, x) \models \sigma_A$, by definition of A, $[x] \in A$, so $([s], [x]) \in T_E^*$, i.e. $([s], [x]) \in T_E^n$ for some $n \in \mathbb{N}$. Since T_E is a filtration of R_E, we have also $([x], [y]) \in T_E$, and thus $([s], [y]) \in T_E^{n+1}$, and so $([s], [y]) \in T_E^*$. This implies that $[y] \in A$, and so $(\mathbb{M}^c, y) \models \sigma_A$, which completes the proof of (2).

Finally, we observe that $([s], [s]) \in T_E^*$, so that (by definition of A)

$$(\mathbb{M}^c, s) \models \sigma_A. \tag{3}$$

It is easily seen that (1), (2) and (3) together imply (0), so we are done.

Next we have to show that $Max(T_C)$ holds. Suppose $([s], [t]) \in T_C$ and $(\mathbb{M}^c, s) \models C\psi$, with $C\psi \in \Phi$. We have to show that $(\mathbb{M}^c, t) \models \psi$. By definition of T_C, we have that $([s]), [t]) \in T_E^n$

for some $n \in \mathbb{N}$. This means that there are $[s_1] = [s], [s_2], \ldots, [s_n] = [t]$ with $([s_i], [s_{i+1}]) \in T_E$, $i < n$. Since $\mathbb{M}^c$ is a model for (A8), we have that $(\mathbb{M}^c, s_i) \models C\psi \Rightarrow (\mathbb{M}^c, s_i) \models EC\psi$. Moreover, since $C\psi \in \Phi$ and Φ is suitable (with respect to φ), we also have $EC\psi \in \Phi$. Together with the fact that T_E is a filtration through Φ of $R_E{}^c$, the condition $Max(T_E)$ guarantees that $(\mathbb{M}^c, s_i) \models EC\psi \Rightarrow (\mathbb{M}^c, s_{i+1}) \models C\psi$. Altogether we get that $(\mathbb{M}^c, s_i) \models C\psi \Rightarrow (\mathbb{M}^c, s_{i+1}) \models C\psi$ for all $i < n$. Since $(\mathbb{M}^c, s_1) = (\mathbb{M}^c, s) \models C\psi$, we eventually derive by means of induction $(\mathbb{M}^c, t) = (\mathbb{M}^c, s_n) \models C\psi$. Since $R_C{}^c$ is reflexive, we have $(\mathbb{M}^c, t) \models \psi$. ∎

2.1.5.10. COROLLARY (Soundness and completeness of $\mathbf{S5EC_{(m)}}$). *For any formula* φ, *we have* $\mathbf{S5EC_{(m)}} \vdash \varphi \Leftrightarrow \mathcal{S5EC}_{(m)} \models \varphi$.

PROOF. The '$\Rightarrow$' part is Theorem 2.1.3. For the '$\Leftarrow$' part, suppose $\mathbf{S5EC_{(m)}} \nvdash \varphi$, i.e. $\neg\varphi$ is $\mathbf{S5EC_{(m)}}$-consistent. Then $\neg\varphi$ is contained in some maximal consistent set Θ and thus we have, for the canonical model $\mathbb{M}^c$ of Section 2.1.4, that $(\mathbb{M}^c, s_\Theta) \models \neg\varphi$. However, this model $\mathbb{M}^c$ is only a quasi-$\mathcal{S5EC}_{(m)}$-model, as shown in Corollary 2.1.4.3 and Theorem 2.1.4.4. But we can define a suitable set Φ of subformulas of $\neg\varphi$ and make (along the lines of Definition 2.1.5.6 and Lemma 2.1.5.7) an $\mathcal{S5EC}_{(m)}$-model $\mathbb{N}$, which, according to Theorem 2.1.5.9, turns out to be a filtration through Φ of $\mathbb{M}^c$, so that, by theorem 2.1.5.2, we have $(\mathbb{N}, [s_\Theta]) \models \neg\varphi$, which means that we have found an $\mathcal{S5EC}_{(m)}$-model $\mathbb{N}$ for which $\mathbb{N} \not\models \varphi$. ∎

2.1.5.11. COROLLARY. $\mathbf{S5EC_{(m)}}$ *has the finite model property, i.e. every* $\mathbf{S5EC_{(m)}}$-*consistent formula (i.e.* $\mathcal{S5EC}_{(m)}$*-satisfiable formula by completeness) is satisfiable in some finite model.*

PROOF. If φ is satisfiable, there is some $\mathcal{S5EC}_{(m)}$-model $\mathbb{M}$ and some state s in $\mathbb{M}$ such that $(\mathbb{M}, s) \models \varphi$. $\mathbb{M}$ is of course also a quasi-$\mathcal{S5EC}_{(m)}$-model, so that we can build a filtration $\mathbb{N}$ of $\mathbb{M}$ (through a suitable class of subformulas of φ) which is a finite $\mathcal{S5EC}_{(m)}$-model and for which $(\mathbb{N}, [s]) \models \varphi$. ∎

2.1.5.12. COROLLARY. $\mathbf{S5EC_{(m)}}$ *is decidable.*

PROOF. This is guaranteed by the fact that $\mathbf{S5EC_{(m)}}$ has a finite set of axioms and has the finite model property (see Theorem 8.15 of [HC84]). ∎

2.1.6. EXAMPLE ('Muddy children'). We are given the following problem. (See Figure 2.3.) A number, say n, of children are standing in a circle around their father. There are k $(1 \leq k \leq n)$ children with mud on their heads. The children can see each other but they cannot see themselves. In particular they do not know if they themselves have mud on their heads. There is no communication between the children. The children all attended a course on epistemic logic and they can reason with this in a perfect way. Furthermore, they are perfectly honest and do not cheat. Now Father says aloud:

> *"There is at least one child with mud on its head. Will all children who know they have mud on their heads please step forward?"*

In case $k > 1$, no child steps forward. Father repeats his question. If $k > 2$, again the children show no response. This procedure is repeated until, after the k-th time Father has asked the same question, all muddy children miraculously step forward. We will explain this event by using epistemic logic.

Figure 2.3

We view the n children as agents and model the situation formally as follows: we use a set $\mathbf{P} = \{p_0, p_1, ..., p_n\}$ of propositional atoms, where the atom p_i stands for child i is muddy. We define a Kripke model $\mathbb{M} = \langle S, \pi, R_1, ..., R_m \rangle$, where $S = \{s = <x_0, x_1, ..., x_n> \mid x_i \in \{0,1\}\}$ is a set of states describing the possible situations of the 'muddiness' of the n children: $x_i = 1$ means that child i is muddy; π is a truth assignment function such that $\pi(<x_0, x_1, ..., x_n>)(p_i) = t \Leftrightarrow x_i = 1$, which is obvious in the light of the definition of a state in this case; R_i is the accessibility relation associated with child i, given by the following definition: let $s = <x_0, x_1, ..., x_n>$ and $s' = <x_0', x_1', ..., x_n'>$. Then:

$$R_i(s, s') \Leftrightarrow x_i \neq x_i' \text{ and } x_j = x_j' \text{ for all } j \neq i.$$

The intuition behind this definition is that child i cannot observe whether s/he is muddy him/herself, but can observe exactly whether the other children are muddy.

We can now use our epistemic language to reason about the situation, including the E- and C-operators defined as usual. These operators then denote (E-)knowledge and common knowledge in the initial situation before Father makes his first public announcement. Let φ_j be the assertion that there are *at least* j muddy children. Furthermore, let ψ_j be the assertion that: there are *precisely* j muddy children. (Clearly, the assertions φ_j and ψ_j can be expressed in terms of the primitive propositions p_i; see Exercise 2.1.6.1.)

2.1.6.1. EXERCISE. Consider the case that $n = 5$ and $k = 3$.

(i) Write the assertions φ_1, φ_2, ψ_1 and ψ_2 in terms of the primitive propositions $p_1, ..., p_5$.

(ii) Consider state $<1, 0, 0, 1, 1>$. What are the states that are R_4-accessible (considered possible by agent 4) in this state?

(iii) Verify that, although $E\varphi_1$ holds in state $<1, 0, 0, 1, 1>$, it also holds there that e.g. $\neg K_1K_4K_5\varphi_1$!

We now prove by induction on j (with $1 \leq j \leq k$) that after the j-th round of questioning it holds that $C\varphi_j$. Then we are done, since then it holds in particular in the k-th round that $E\varphi_k$, thus every child knows that there are at least k muddy children. And since every *muddy* child sees only k−1 muddy children, it knows that it is muddy itself—and thus steps forward.

The proof is as follows. The basis of the induction is $j = 1$. After Father's announcement φ_1 it holds that $C\varphi_1$ (so, in particular, $E\varphi_1$). The induction hypothesis is: after the j-th round it holds that $C\varphi_j$ (and thus particularly that $E\varphi_j$). Since any muddy child sees only k−1 muddy children, no child is able to conclude that it is muddy itself (for $j < k$). Hence no muddy child steps forward, and we go to the (j+1)-th round. Since in the previous round no one has stepped forward (and every child knows this, as well as the reason for it), it holds that $C\neg\psi_j$, so $C\varphi_{j+1}$. ■

2.1.6.2. EXERCISE. Check how the model in Exercise 2.1.6.1 changes successively after Father's announcements.

The paradox in this muddy children puzzle occurs for $k \geq 2$. For in this case every child sees at least one muddy child. So it seems that the statement made publicly by Father is entirely redundant. This, however, is not true. If Father would, in the case that $k \geq 2$, only ask the muddy children to come forward, without making his initial statement that there is at least one muddy child, he can repeat his question indefinitely without ever getting a reaction from the children. Even stronger, if Father would initially whisper φ_1 in each child's ear, without another child hearing it, his (repeatedly) asking the muddy children to step forward would be in vain as well.

*2.1.6.3. EXERCISE. Explain this paradox. Note the difference between C and E, and the fact that $E\varphi_1$ would also be established, if Father whispered φ_1 in each child's ear.

2.2. Common Knowledge in Distributed Systems

As in Section 1.8 we consider a distributed system consisting of m processors 1, ..., m. We consider the Kripke model $\mathbb{M}$ associated with this distributed system, with the set S of global system states $\mathbf{s} = (s_1, ..., s_m)$ where the s_i ($i = 1, ..., m$) are local states of the processors 1, ..., m. The accessibility relations R_i are defined as in Section 1.8.

This associated Kripke model does not contain any information about the actual state transformations that the system executes or is subject to. The actual process is determined by the structure of the processors, the way they are programmed and the protocols by which they communicate. All these issues are beyond the scope of epistemic logic. Although epistemic logic cannot express anything about the way in which a process comes about, it can say something about the knowledge that is available at the processors in the system during a *run* of the system. In general, the notion of a run through a Kripke model is defined as follows:

2.2.1. DEFINITION. A *run* in a Kripke model $\mathbb{M}$, with set of states S, is a (finite or infinite) sequence of states $s^{(1)}, s^{(2)}, ...$ with $s^{(i)} \in S$ ($i = 1, 2, ...$). We denote such a run as:

$$s^{(1)} \Rightarrow s^{(2)} \Rightarrow \ldots$$

(***Warning:*** $\Rightarrow$ has nothing whatsoever to do with $\rightarrow$, the union of the accessibility relations R_i.)

One may now ask oneself whether one can say something about the course of common knowledge during a certain run. In particular we may pose this question in the context of Kripke models associated with distributed systems. Is it possible to devise a distributed system such that common knowledge *increases* during some run? That is to say, for some φ, $C\varphi$ does not hold in an initial part of $s^{(1)} \Rightarrow s^{(2)} \Rightarrow \ldots \Rightarrow s^{(k)}$ of the run (i.e. $(\mathbb{M}, s^{(i)}) \not\models C\varphi$ for $1 \le i \le k$), while $C\varphi$ holds after this initial part and continues to hold (i.e. $(\mathbb{M}, s^{(i)}) \models C\varphi$ for $i > k$). Somewhat surprisingly, this is *not* the case if we do not impose further restrictions on the reachability of the states of the system besides the ones we prescribed in Section 1.8, as we shall see presently. First we give a proposition and a definition.

2.2.2. PROPOSITION. (See Figure 2.4.) *Let* s *be a state in Kripke model* $\mathbb{M}$. *Let* K *be the 'upward cone' of* s, *i.e.* $K_s = \{s' \in S \mid s \twoheadrightarrow s'\}$. *Then:*

(i) $(\mathbb{M}, s) \models C\varphi$ *iff* $(\mathbb{M}, t) \models \varphi$ *for all* $t \in K_s$;

(ii) *if* $C\varphi$ *holds in* s (*i.e.* $(\mathbb{M}, s) \models C\varphi$) *then* $C\varphi$ *holds in the whole of* K_s.

PROOF. (i) $(\mathbb{M}, s) \models C\varphi \Leftrightarrow (\mathbb{M}, t) \models \varphi$ for all t with $s \twoheadrightarrow t \Leftrightarrow (\mathbb{M}, t) \models \varphi$ for all $t \in K_s$.
(ii) Suppose that $(\mathbb{M}, s) \models C\varphi$. By (i) we get that $(\mathbb{M}, t) \models \varphi$, for every $t \in K_s$ (*). Take some state $u \in K_s$, so $s \twoheadrightarrow u$. Let $K_u = \{u' \in S \mid u \twoheadrightarrow u'\}$. (Thus K_u is the upward cone of u.) Clearly, if $v \in K_u$, then $v \in K_s$, since then we have that $s \twoheadrightarrow u \twoheadrightarrow v$, and hence $s \twoheadrightarrow v$. Thus K_u is a 'subcone' of K_s: $K_u \subseteq K_s$. So, by (*), we obtain that $(\mathbb{M}, t) \models \varphi$, for every $t \in K_u$. Consequently, by (a) we have that $(\mathbb{M}, u) \models C\varphi$. This way of reasoning holds for any $u \in K_s$. ■

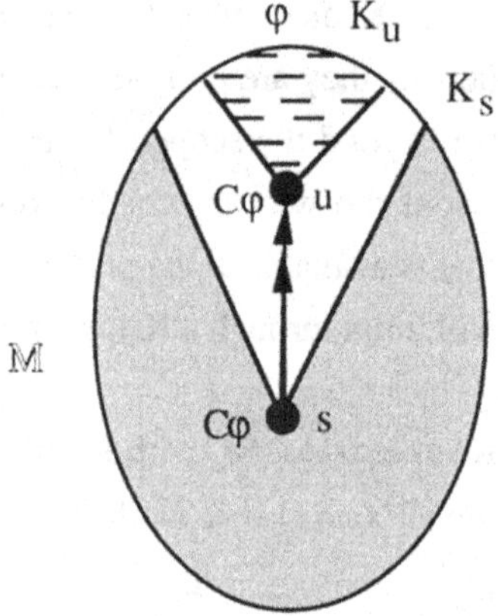

Figure 2.4

2.2.3. DEFINITION. Let $\mathbb{M} = \langle S, \pi, R_1, ..., R_m \rangle$, and $\twoheadrightarrow$ be defined as in Definition 2.1.2. Then $\mathbb{M}$ is called *strongly connected* if for all $s, t \in S$ it holds that $s \twoheadrightarrow t$.

2.2.3.1. PROPOSITION. *The Kripke model associated with a distributed system, as defined in Section 1.8, is strongly connected, provided that* $m > 1$.

PROOF. Let $\mathbb{M} = \langle S, \pi, R_1, ..., R_m \rangle$. We have to prove that for any $\mathbf{s}, \mathbf{t} \in S$ it holds that $\mathbf{s} \twoheadrightarrow \mathbf{t}$. Say that $\mathbf{s} = (s_1, s_2, ..., s_m)$ and $\mathbf{t} = (t_1, t_2, ..., t_m)$. Now we have that $\mathbf{s} = (s_1, s_2, ..., s_m) \rightarrow (s_1, t_2, ..., t_m) \rightarrow (t_1, t_2, ..., t_m) = \mathbf{t}$. The former '$\rightarrow$' holds on account of the relation R_1; the latter '$\rightarrow$' holds on account of any relation R_i for $i \neq 1$. Thus we have $\mathbf{s} \twoheadrightarrow \mathbf{t}$. ■

We now have the following general result:

2.2.4. THEOREM. *Let* 𝕄 *be a strongly connected Kripke model. Suppose that for some state* s *and formula* φ *it holds that* (𝕄, s) ⊨ Cφ. *Then* 𝕄 ⊨ Cφ.

PROOF. Directly from Proposition 2.2.2. ■

2.2.5. COROLLARY. *Let* 𝕄 *be the Kripke model associated with a distributed system with processors* 1, ..., m, (m > 1), *as defined in Section 1.8. Suppose that* (𝕄, s) ⊨ Cφ *for some state* s. *Then* 𝕄 ⊨ Cφ.

PROOF. Directly from Theorem 2.2.4 and Proposition 2.2.3.1. ■

2.2.6. COROLLARY. *Let* 𝕄 *be the Kripke model associated with a distributed system with processors* 1, ..., m, (m > 1), *as defined in 1.8. Then common knowledge is constant through every run of* 𝕄 *(see Figure 2.5).* ■

2.2.7. EXERCISE. Given a distributed system with three processors A,B,C. Each processor may be in two local states: 0 or 1. Let P = {p, q}. Describe the Kripke model 𝕄 associated with this distributed system, along with a truth assignment π such that:

(1) 𝕄 ⊨ Cp and

(2) there is a global state s such that (𝕄, s) ⊨ Eq, but not 𝕄 ⊨ Eq.

2.2.8. EXERCISE.

(i) Show that for any Kripke model 𝕄 it holds that: 𝕄 ⊨ φ ⇒ 𝕄 ⊨ Cφ.

(ii) Give a counter-example for 𝕄 ⊨ φ → Cφ.

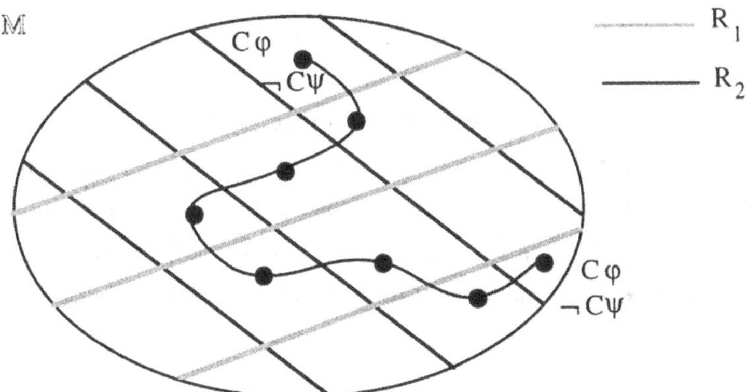

Figure 2.5

2.2.9. EXERCISE. Give a Kripke model 𝕄 and a run in 𝕄 along which common knowledge increases.

2.2.10. EXERCISE.

(i) Let $E^k\varphi$ $(k \geq 0)$ be defined by: $E^0\varphi = \varphi$, $E^{k+1}\varphi = E(E^k\varphi)$. Let $\mathbb{M}$ be an $S5_{(m)}$-Kripke model with n states. Prove that $\mathbb{M} \models E^n\varphi \leftrightarrow C\varphi$.

(ii) Devise an $S5_{(m)}$-Kripke model $\mathbb{M}$ and a formula φ such that for every $n \geq 0$ it holds that $\mathbb{M} \not\models E^n\varphi \leftrightarrow C\varphi$.

The results on common knowledge in distributed systems are somewhat surprising and may even seem counterintuitive. We would expect common knowledge in distributed systems to increase by communication. The solution of this paradox is the fact that in practice not every global state of the system is reachable. In this case it becomes possible that the associated Kripke model loses the property of being strongly connected, and thus escapes the results obtained so far.

So now we have to consider Kripke models $\mathbb{M} = \langle S, \pi, R_1, ..., R_m \rangle$, where $S \subseteq S_1 \times ... \times S_m$ (rather than $S = S_1 \times ... \times S_m$). Although in this case we cannot prove in general that C-knowledge is constant, we can still obtain a result of a somewhat more special nature. First we need a definition.

2.2.11. DEFINITION. A run $s^{(1)} \Rightarrow s^{(2)} \Rightarrow ...$ is called *non-simultaneous* if for every transition $s^{(k)} \Rightarrow s^{(k+1)}$ there exists a processor $1 \leq i \leq m$ with $s_i^{(k)} = s_i^{(k+1)}$.

2.2.12. THEOREM ([HM84a]). *In non-simultaneous runs common knowledge is constant.*

PROOF. Suppose $s \Rightarrow s'$ for $s = (s_1, s_2, ..., s_m)$ and $s' = (s_1', s_2', ..., s_m')$ with $s_i = s_i'$, and consequently $(s, s') \in R_i$, and suppose $(\mathbb{M}, s') \models C\varphi$. Now it holds that

$$(\mathbb{M}, s') \models C\varphi \Rightarrow (\mathbb{M}, s') \models EC\varphi \Rightarrow (\mathbb{M}, s') \models K_iC\varphi.$$

R_i is an equivalence relation, so in particular it holds that: $(s, s') \in R_i \Rightarrow (s', s) \in R_i$. From this it follows, by means of the definition of the semantics of the K_i-operator, that $(\mathbb{M}, s) \models C\varphi$. So any C-knowledge that is present in s' is also present in s. Analogously: any C-knowledge present in s is present in s' as well. Hence, C-knowledge is constant at the non-simultaneous transition $s \Rightarrow s'$. By induction it follows that C-knowledge is constant in a non-simultaneous run. ■

Concluding we may say that in a distributed system, in which not all global states are accessible, it is not the case that in general common knowledge is constant, although it must be constant along non-simultaneous runs. In other words, the only *possibility* for a change in common knowledge is via transitions that are 'simultaneous', in the sense of being not non-simultaneous.

2.2.13. EXERCISE.

(i) Give an example of a distributed system with $S \subset S_1 \times ... \times S_m$, together with a run along which C-knowledge changes. ('$\subset$' denotes *proper* inclusion.)

(ii) Give an example of a 'simultaneous' run in a distributed system with $S \subset S_1 \times ... \times S_m$, along which C-knowledge nevertheless is *constant*.

2.2.14. EXERCISE. Consider a distributed system with two processors A and B with three local states both, denoted 0, 1, 2. Now consider the following Kripke models, with respect to $\mathbf{P} = \{p\}$, associated with this system.

(a) Let $\mathbb{M} = \langle S, \pi, R_A, R_B \rangle$ with $S = (\{0, 1, 2\} \times \{0, 1, 2\})$, π as in Figure 2.6, $R_A(s, t) \Leftrightarrow (s_1 = t_1$ and $s, t \in S)$, and $R_B(s, t) \Leftrightarrow (s_2 = t_2$ and $s, t \in S)$.

(b) Let $\mathbb{M}'$ be as $\mathbb{M}$, but with S replaced by $S' = (\{0, 1, 2\} \times \{0, 1, 2\}) \setminus \{(2, 0), (0, 2)\}$.

(c) Let $\mathbb{M}''$ be as $\mathbb{M}$, but with S replaced by $S'' = \{(0, 0), (1, 1), (2, 2)\}$.

Is common knowledge the same in (0, 0) and (2, 2) in the models $\mathbb{M}$, $\mathbb{M}'$ and $\mathbb{M}''$?

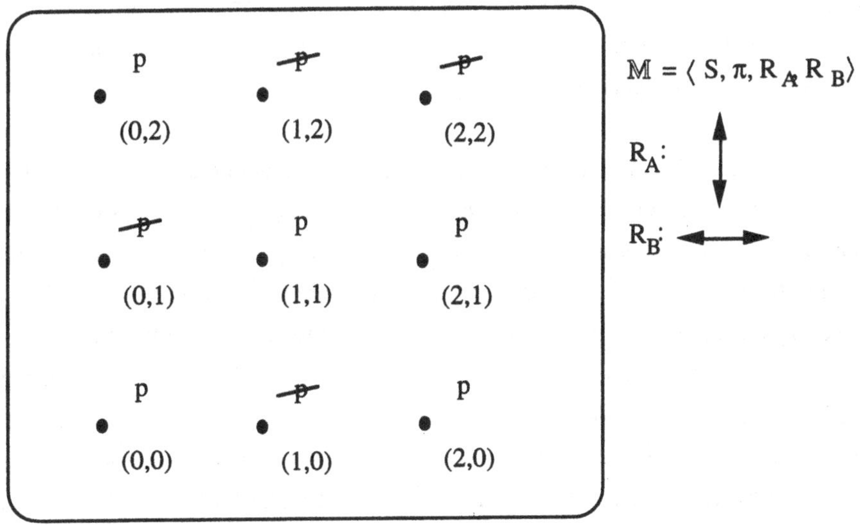

Figure 2.6

2.2.15. EXERCISE. Consider n children, of which some are muddy. Define a Kripke model $\mathbb{M}_n = (S, \pi, R_1, ..., R_n)$ as follows: $S = \{0, 1\}^n$ is the set of n-tuples over the set $\{0, 1\}$. An n-tuple $(i_1, ..., i_n)$ with $i_j \in \{0, 1\}$ $(1 \leq j \leq n)$ represents the state in which each child for which $i_j = 1$ is muddy, and all other children are not; π

gives, in each state $s \in S$, a truth value to the primitive propositions φ_j ($j \geq 0$), denoting that there are at least j muddy children. For example $\pi((1, 0, ..., 0))(\varphi_j) = t$ if j=0 or j=1, and f otherwise; the accessibility relations R_i ($1 \leq i \leq n$) are defined by $\forall s = (s_1, ..., s_n) \forall t = (t_1, ..., t_n) [(s, t) \in R_i \Leftrightarrow \forall j \neq i (s_j = t_j)]$. The Kripke model $\mathbb{M}_n$ represents the situation in which no knowledge has been made public; all states $(i_1, ..., i_n)$ are still possible. After an assertion φ_j has been made public, we may again construct a Kripke model $\mathbb{M}$ representing the new situation: $\mathbb{M}$ contains all states $(i_1, ..., i_n)$ that agree with φ_j, i.e., $\pi((i_1, ..., i_n))(\varphi_j) = t$. (The accessibility relations and the truth assignment function are defined as for $\mathbb{M}_n$.) Now consider the following questions / exercises.

(i) Draw a picture, representing the model $\mathbb{M}_2$.

(ii) For which j≥0 does it hold that $\mathbb{M}_2 \models C\varphi_j$?

(iii) Construct the model $\mathbb{M}' = \langle S', \pi', R_1', R_2' \rangle$ representing the situation after Father has made a public announcement that φ_1 holds, i.e. that there is at least one muddy child. Check again for which $j \geq 0$ it holds that $\mathbb{M}' \models C\varphi_j$. Answer the same questions concerning the situation that arises after it is announced publically that φ_2 holds.

There is more to be said about common knowledge in distributed systems. We already saw that special conditions have to be met to enable common knowledge to be changed. In practice it is even worse since in a network it is generally not guaranteed that messages come across. Communication channels may be faulty, so that messages can get lost. Halpern & Moses show in [HM84a, 90] that under these circumstances it is even impossible in principle to attain common knowledge in such a network. In order to get a feeling for this result we discuss the example of the Byzantine generals who want to launch a co-ordinated attack.

2.2.16. EXAMPLE ('Co-ordinated Attack Problem'). Consider a situation of two army regiments on two hills on both sides of a valley, in which a hostile army is situated. If the two regiments attack simultaneously, they will conquer the enemy. If only one of the two regiments attacks, it will be defeated by the enemy. There is no initial battle plan available which the two regiments agree upon. Neither general of the regiments would decide to attack without knowing for sure that the other one will also attack. The general of one of the two regiments, let us call him A, now wants to co-ordinate a simultaneous attack of the two regiments. To this end he may only use a messenger who has to go through enemy territory to convey the message 'm' ("attack!") to the other general, B. Unfortunately, not least for the messenger himself, his safe arrival is not guaranteed. In order to be certain that the message has been delivered (and that its recipient will attack) an *acknowledgement*, i.e. a message '$K_B m$', has to be sent by the recipient, general B, to the sender, general A. However, this has to be done again by a messenger, which is not safe either. So, in order for general B to be sure about the simultaneous attack he has to have an acknowledgement of the arrival of this acknowledgement. (Otherwise, it is *he* who might attack on his own, with dramatic consequences.) So there has to be sent a message about this, '$K_A K_B m$', from A to B. But A will need again a confirmation of this by means of a message '$K_B K_A K_B m$', *ad infinitum*. At any moment, however, there will be an assertion of the form '$K_B K_A K_B \dots m$' or '$K_A K_B K_A \dots m$' that is not (yet) true. This means that *common knowledge* of m, i.e. 'Cm', cannot be attained (in finite time).

Unfortunately for the two generals common knowledge of m ('Cm') is necessary to be (both) sure that they will attack simultaneously. (Otherwise, there will always be doubt in the mind of one of them whether the last acknowledgement that has been sent has been received by the other one.)

Halpern & Moses [HM90] have proven this rigorously by means of a theorem that says on the one hand that 'Cm' is necessary for solving the 'Co-ordinated Attack Problem', and on the other that 'C-knowledge' cannot be attained in a distributed system in which communication is not guaranteed. So the 'Co-ordinated Attack Problem' is fundamentally unsolvable.

There is a bright spot in this problem, however. Halpern & Moses and Fischer & Immerman have shown that in order to solve some practical problems of this nature certain weaker forms of common knowledge suffice which *are* attainable in practice. The interested reader is referred to [FI86] and [HM90]. The reader is also referred to [Mos92] for an overview of recent developments in this area.

2.3. Implicit Knowledge in a Group

After common knowledge we introduce yet another variant of knowledge: *implicit* or *distributed knowledge*. The intuition behind this notion is the following. We say that a group of agents has implicit knowledge of a fact if the knowledge of that fact is distributed over the members of that group. In a closed system a group of cooperating agents can only acquire knowledge that is already implicit in the group. This idea is formalised by the following definition of the implicit knowledge operator I, which we also add to the language $\mathcal{L}^m_{\mathbf{K}}$. The extended language is denoted by $\mathcal{L}^m_{\mathbf{KI}}$.

2.3.1. DEFINITION. Given a Kripke structure $\mathbb{M} = \langle S, \pi, R_1, \dots, R_m \rangle$, we define

$$(\mathbb{M}, s) \models I\varphi \iff (\mathbb{M}, t) \models \varphi \text{ for all t such that } (s, t) \in R_1 \cap \dots \cap R_m.$$

Thus if all agents could pool their knowledge, they would only consider those worlds as possible which are epistemic alternatives for each of them in isolation. One can summarise this intuition by using the reading of $I\varphi$ as: "*a wise man knows* φ", as opposed to that of $C\varphi$: "*any fool knows* φ". Indeed, if some agent in the group knows that t is not an epistemic alternative for him, then the 'wise man' knows this as well. The 'wise man' does not consider any state as a possible one that, according to at least one of the agents, is not considered possible either.

From the definition it is directly clear that implicit knowledge is only interesting for $m \geq 2$ agents. For $m = 1$, $I\varphi$ coincides with $K\varphi$. Axiomatisation of implicit knowledge for the case $m = 1$ is therefore trivial. For $m \geq 2$, however, the question of axiomatisation is quite another matter. We cannot use a clear-cut correspondence result as in the case of the E-operator, since – contrary to the union of accessibility relations – there is no axiom that corresponds directly to the intersection of accessibility relations (see [vdHM92b], Theorem 2.17). We can, however, profit from the fact that in these modal logics we cannot distinguish models in which we have relations that are intersections of the accessibility relations associated with the (knowledge of the) agents involved from models in which we have relations that are *contained within* these intersections.

And with respect to the latter weaker property we *do* have a corresponding axiom, namely

(A11) $K_i\varphi \rightarrow I\varphi$ $(i = 1, ..., m)$

It is easy to show that this axiom corresponds with the property that $R_I \subseteq R_i$, for $1 \leq i \leq m$, where R_I stands for the accessibility relation associated with the modal operator I.

2.3.1.1. EXERCISE. Show that (A11) is sound.

2.3.1.2. EXERCISE. Show that if (A11) is added to the system **K**, we have in the canonical model $\mathbb{M}^c = \langle S^c, \pi^c, R_1{}^c, ..., R_m{}^c, R_I{}^c\rangle$ that $R_I{}^c \subseteq R_i{}^c$, for all $1 \leq i \leq m$.

So, if we now introduce the following axiom systems:

$$\mathbf{KI}_{(m)} = \mathbf{K}_{(m)} + (A11) + \mathbf{K}_I$$
$$\mathbf{TI}_{(m)} = \mathbf{T}_{(m)} + (A11) + \mathbf{T}_I$$
$$\mathbf{S4I}_{(m)} = \mathbf{S4}_{(m)} + (A11) + \mathbf{S4}_I$$
$$\mathbf{S5I}_{(m)} = \mathbf{S5}_{(m)} + (A11) + \mathbf{S5}_I$$

where $\mathbf{S}_I$ stands for the logic $\mathbf{S}_{(1)}$, where, in each axiom, the operator K is replaced by the operator I, we can now prove soundness and completeness again, with respect to the models with the appropriate properties, and an accessibility relation R_I associated with the I-operator that is the intersection of the accessibility relations associated with (the knowledge of) the m agents (see [HM85], [vdHM92b]).

2.3.2. THEOREM (Soundness and completeness of $\mathbf{KI_{(m)}}$, $\mathbf{TI_{(m)}}$, $\mathbf{S4I_{(m)}}$, $\mathbf{S5I_{(m)}}$).

(i) $\mathbf{KI_{(m)}} \vdash \varphi \quad \Leftrightarrow \quad \mathcal{K}_{(\mathbf{m})} \models \varphi$

(ii) $\mathbf{TI_{(m)}} \vdash \varphi \quad \Leftrightarrow \quad \mathcal{T}_{(\mathbf{m})} \models \varphi$

(iii) $\mathbf{S4I_{(m)}} \vdash \varphi \quad \Leftrightarrow \quad \mathcal{S4}_{(\mathbf{m})} \models \varphi$

(iv) $\mathbf{S5I_{(m)}} \vdash \varphi \quad \Leftrightarrow \quad \mathcal{S5}_{(\mathbf{m})} \models \varphi$

PROOF. The proof of this theorem follows by the usual construction of a canonical model for a maximally consistent set of formulas, employing the correspondence result from Exercise 2.3.1.1, and a non-trivial result, proved in [vdHM92b], stating that, for all φ, we have that $\mathcal{K}^{\cap}_{(\mathbf{m+1})} \models \varphi \Leftrightarrow \mathcal{K}^{\cap\supseteq}_{(\mathbf{m+1})} \models \varphi$, where $\mathcal{K}^{\cap}_{(\mathbf{m+1})}$ stands for the class of Kripke models $\mathbb{M} = \langle S, \pi, R_1, ..., R_m, R_I \rangle$ with $R_1 \cap ... \cap R_m = R_I$, and $\mathcal{K}^{\cap\supseteq}_{(\mathbf{m+1})}$ stands for the class of Kripke models $\mathbb{M} = \langle S, \pi, R_1,..., R_m, R_I \rangle$ with $R_1 \cap ... \cap R_m \supseteq R_I$. Moreover, analogous results can be obtained with respect to the classes $\mathcal{T}_{(\mathbf{m})}$, $\mathcal{S4}_{(\mathbf{m})}$ and $\mathcal{S5}_{(\mathbf{m})}$. ■

2.3.2.1. REMARK. Strictly speaking, in the statement of Theorem 2.3.2, we should also use $\mathcal{K}^{\cap}_{(\mathbf{m+1})}$ rather than $\mathcal{K}_{(\mathbf{m})}$ (and likewise for the other classes mentioned), for this would make it explicit that the accessibility relation associated with the modality I is the intersection of the other accessibility relations. However, we have not done so to avoid notational overkill. For more information on this topic we refer the reader to [vdHM92b].

From the intuitive description of implicit knowledge we would expect that the following rule holds:

$$\text{(R4)} \quad \frac{(\psi_1 \wedge \ldots \wedge \psi_m) \to \varphi}{(K_1\psi_1 \wedge \ldots \wedge K_m\psi_m) \to I\varphi}$$

We elaborate on the intuition behind this rule by means of an example. Let m = 3 and assume φ to be 'P = NP'. We furthermore assume that three researchers 1, 2, 3 work on this long-standing and famous problem in order to discover a proof of this theorem. Suppose that the actual situation is such that φ follows from three lemmas: ψ_1, ψ_2 and ψ_3. Researcher 1 has proved ψ_1 — so he knows ψ_1. Analogously for researchers 2 and 3 with respect to ψ_2 and ψ_3, respectively. Thus in this situation we have that $K_1\psi_1$, $K_2\psi_2$, $K_3\psi_3$, i.e. $K_1\psi_1 \wedge K_2\psi_2 \wedge K_3\psi_3$. If the researchers would contact each other at a congress on theoretical computer science, they would be able to gather their partial knowledge and thereby know (a proof of) φ.

Rule (R4) indeed appears to be deducible from (A2), (A11) and propositional logic. Conversely, (A11) is also deducible from (R4) and the other axioms. So we can replace (A11) by (R4) and obtain an alternative complete axiomatisation of implicit knowledge.

2.3.3. EXERCISE. Prove the statements above on the mutual derivability of (A11) and (R4) in the presence of the other axioms and rules.

In [FV86] R. Fagin & M. Vardi consider a somewhat more concrete model of distributed systems and show in this setting how the notion of implicit knowledge can be applied in these systems with unreliable message exchange in order to characterise attainable states of knowledge and to obtain a 'message logic'. First they show a kind of *conservation principle for implicit knowledge* for distributed systems that satisfy certain conditions, stating that implicit knowledge about objective (i.e. non-modal) formulas remains constant during runs of the system in which no information from the outside environment is communicated, but all communications are internal (i.e. between agents of the system).

Next, in order to obtain a '*message logic*' $\mathbf{ML_{(m)}}$ for a certain class of distributed systems they add the following axiom to the system $\mathbf{S5I_{(m)}}$:

(ML) $I\neg\alpha \rightarrow (K_1\neg\alpha \vee \ldots \vee K_m\neg\alpha)$,

where α is a so-called primitive state formula uniquely and exactly describing a state of the system. The axiom (ML) says that, if it is implicit knowledge that a state is impossible, then the stronger formula is true that some agent knows that the state is impossible. That is, if by pooling their knowledge, the agents can rule out a state, then some agent can do this already on his / her own. The axiom (ML) is shown to be invalid for arbitrary formulas, even for primitive propositions. Finally, the logic $\mathbf{ML_{(m)}}$ is proven sound and complete for $m \geq 2$. Since a proper treatment of this topic would be too involved, we refer for details to [FV86]. Finally we mention [HHM93] and [vHM93], where the notion of implicit knowledge is employed for reasoning about the correctness of programs written in a CSP-like programming language with parallelism and communication.

2.4. Belief

In this section we treat briefly a variant of knowledge, namely *belief.* As Levesque remarks in [Lev84], knowledge in e.g. a knowledge base need not be necessarily true. We shall call such 'knowledge that need not be true' belief. We use the same language as for the logic of knowledge from the first chapter, but we replace K_i by B_i, denoting belief by agent i. The language that we obtain in this way is denoted $\mathcal{L}_B^m$. The semantics of the formulas in this language is the same as that for knowledge, but the accessibility relations are now associated with the agent's belief instead of knowledge:

$$(\mathbb{M}, s) \models B_i\varphi \quad \Leftrightarrow \quad (\mathbb{M}, t) \models \varphi \text{ for all t with } (s, t) \in R_i.$$

As a logic for belief we adopt a variant of the system $\mathbf{S5_{(m)}}$: we replace K_i by B_i everywhere, and we delete axiom (A3), since belief does not need to be true! We keep (A4) and (A5). So we still assume that our agents (including knowledge bases) can perform introspection (A4, A5). Furthermore we introduce by way of partial compensation of (A3):

(D) $\neg B_i(\bot)$
(A knowledge base is not inconsistent.)

Note that indeed (A3) implies that $\neg K_i(\bot)$, that is to say that — apart from the notational difference between K and B — (D) is a weakening of (A3). We shall now consider the following axiom system:

$$\mathbf{KD45_{(m)}} = (R1) + (R2) + (A1) + (A2) + (D) + (A4) + (A5).$$

This system is referred to as 'weak $\mathbf{S5_{(m)}}$'. The system consisting of (R1), (R2), (A1), (A2), (A4), (A5) (so without (D)) is referred to as $\mathbf{K45_{(m)}}$. Axiom (D) has the following effect on the accessibility relations R_i^c in the canonical model associated with this system:

2.4.1. PROPOSITION. *Let* **S** *be a proof system for epistemic formulas (containing* $\mathbf{K_{(m)}}$*). Suppose* **S** *contains the axiom* (D). *Then it holds for the canonical model* $\mathbb{M}^c(\mathbf{S})$ *that all accessibility relations* R_i^c *are serial.*

PROOF. (See the proof of Theorem 1.4.6 for the construction of the canonical model $\mathbb{M}^c(\mathbf{S})$; also cf. Proposition 1.6.5 for analogous facts.)
Suppose R_i^c is not serial. Take some s; then there is no t with $R_i^c(s, t)$. So for all t it holds that not $R_i^c(s, t)$. So, for all t, $R_i^c(s, t) \Rightarrow$ f, and thus $R_i^c(s, t) \Rightarrow (\mathbb{M}^c, t) \models \bot$. This means that $(\mathbb{M}^c, s) \models B_i(\bot)$.

However, since $\mathbf{S} \vdash \neg B_i(\bot)$, and $s = s_\Phi$ for some maximally **S**-consistent set of formulas Φ, $\neg B_i(\bot) \in \Phi$. Thus, by the coincidence lemma (cf. the proof of Theorem 1.4.6),

$$(\mathbb{M}^c, s) \models \neg B_i(\bot).$$

This contradicts $(\mathbb{M}^c, s) \models B_i(\bot)$. Hence R_i^c is serial. ■

2.4.2. COROLLARY. *The canonical model* $\mathbb{M}^c(\mathbf{KD45_{(m)}})$ *possesses accessibility relations* R_i^c *that are serial, transitive and euclidean.*

PROOF. 'Seriality' follows from Proposition 2.4.1. 'Transitivity' and 'euclidicity' follow from the presence of (A4) and (A5), and Proposition 1.6.5. ■

We denote the class of serial, transitive and euclidean Kripke models by $\mathcal{KD}45_{(m)}$. We can now state the following completeness result:

2.4.3. THEOREM. $\mathbf{KD45_{(m)}}$ *is sound and complete with respect to the class* $\mathcal{KD}45_{(m)}$.

PROOF. We may combine Corollary 2.4.2 with the observation that serial, transitive and euclidean Kripke models are models for (D), (A4) and (A5), respectively. Since for (A4) we know this already from Theorem 1.6.4(ii), and for (A5) from Exercise 1.6.7.1(v). So we only have to consider the soundness of the axiom (D):

Suppose $\mathcal{KD}45_{(m)} \nvDash \neg B_i\bot$. Then there would be an $\mathcal{KD}45_{(m)}$-model $\mathbb{M}$ with a state s such that $(\mathbb{M}, s) \models B_i\bot$. This would mean that all R_i-successors of s would verify $\bot$, which is only possible if s does not have any R_i-successor. However, by seriality, we know that s does have them, so our assumption, i.e. that $\mathcal{KD}45_{(m)} \nvDash \neg B_i\bot$, must be false. Hence we have $\mathcal{KD}45_{(m)} \models \neg B_i\bot$. ■

2.4.3.1. EXERCISE.

(a) Check whether the following formulas are satisfiable in $\mathcal{KD}45_{(1)}$.

(i) $B(p\wedge q) \wedge \neg Bp \wedge \neg Bq$

(ii) $B(p\wedge q) \wedge B\neg p \wedge B\neg q$

(iii) $B(p\wedge q) \wedge B\neg p \wedge \neg Bq$

(iv) $B(p\vee q) \wedge \neg Bp \wedge \neg Bq$

(v) $B(p\vee q) \wedge B\neg p \wedge B\neg q$

(vi) $B(p\vee q) \wedge B\neg p \wedge \neg Bq$

(b) What happens in the above examples when we consider $\mathcal{K}45_{(1)}$, the class of transitive and euclidean Kripke models, instead of $\mathcal{KD}45_{(1)}$?

2.4.3.2. EXERCISE.

(i) State an analogous soundness and completeness result for $\mathbf{K45_{(m)}}$.

*(ii) Let us define a *simple* $\mathbf{K45_{(1)}}$-model as a tuple (S, s_0, π, R), where S is a set of states, $s_0 \in S$ is a special state, to be interpreted as the 'real' or 'actual' state, π is a truth assignment function as usual, and R is an accessibility relation such that $R = (\{s_0\} \times \{S\backslash\{s_0\}\}) \cup (S\backslash\{s_0\}) \times (S\backslash\{s_0\}))$. (So a simple $\mathbf{K45_{(1)}}$-model is a

'simple $\mathbf{S5_{(1)}}$-model on a broom stick', see Figure 2.7.) Show that the system $\mathbf{K45_{(1)}}$ is *sound* and *complete* with respect to the class of simple $\mathbf{K45_{(1)}}$-models.

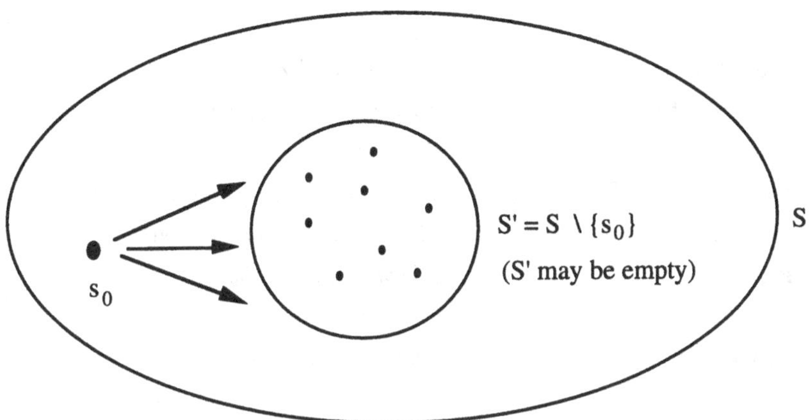

Figure 2.7

(iii) Prove (semantically and/or proof-theoretically) that:
$\mathbf{K45_{(1)}} \vdash B(B\varphi \leftrightarrow BB\varphi)$ and $\mathbf{K45_{(1)}} \vdash B(\neg B\varphi \leftrightarrow B\neg B\varphi)$.

(iv) Does $\mathbf{K45_{(1)}} \vdash B\varphi \rightarrow \varphi$ hold? Explain your answer.

We finally remark that in the systems **K45** and **KD45** (A4) is not redundant, as the reader may check for himself in Exercise 2.4.3.3 below.

2.4.3.3. EXERCISE. Check that (A4) is not redundant in $\mathbf{K(D)45_{(m)}}$ by using a completeness result for $\mathbf{K(D)5_{(m)}}$, which is $\mathbf{K(D)45_{(m)}}$ without the axiom (A4), and the construction of a model with (serial,) euclidean but non-transitive relations.

Finally we note that as the system $\mathbf{KD45_{(1)}}$ contains the axioms (A1), (A2), (A4) and (A5), Remark 1.7.6.4.2 is applicable, so that for this logic we have the same normal form theorem as for $\mathbf{S5_{(m)}}$ (of course, with K replaced by B).

2.5. The Problem of Logical Omniscience

In the theory of knowledge and belief thus far there appears the natural question of whether these notions are captured adequately and realistically. There is indeed a problem with the notions so far, known as the problem of '*logical omniscience*". This problem pertains to a notion of knowledge and belief that is too idealistic. Consider, for instance, the property that 'beliefs' are closed under logical consequences. Especially for a notion of belief, which should be more fallible if human everyday beliefs are to be captured, this property is obviously not true. On the other hand, this property holds for the *S5*-notion of knowledge and the **KD45**-

notion of belief. But there are also other (related) properties that are not very realistic, which nevertheless hold in **S5** and **KD45**. We list some of them (for **KD45**-belief) below, including the one mentioned already:

(LO1)	$B\varphi \wedge B(\varphi \rightarrow \psi) \rightarrow B\psi$	*(Closure under implication)*
(LO2)	$\models \varphi \Rightarrow \models B\varphi$	*(Belief of valid formulas)*
(LO3)	$\models \varphi \rightarrow \psi \Rightarrow \models B\varphi \rightarrow B\psi$	*(Closure under valid implication)*
(LO4)	$\models \varphi \leftrightarrow \psi \Rightarrow \models B\varphi \leftrightarrow B\psi$	*(Belief of equivalent formulas)*
(LO5)	$(B\varphi \wedge B\psi) \rightarrow B(\varphi \wedge \psi)$	*(Closure under conjunction)*
(LO6)	$B\varphi \rightarrow B(\varphi \vee \psi)$	*(Weakening of belief)*
(LO7)	$B\varphi \rightarrow \neg B \neg \varphi$	*(Consistency of beliefs)*
(LO8)	$B(B\varphi \rightarrow \varphi)$	*(Belief of having no false beliefs)*
(LO9)	B **true**	*(Believing truth)*

2.5.1. EXERCISE. Check that (LO1)—(LO9) are validities in **KD45**.

These properties are clearly undesirable when modelling a (human or artificial) agent's belief. For example:

(LO1/3) For an agent with limited resources it is very unrealistic that he has every logical consequence of his set of beliefs at his disposal.

(LO2) Every valid assertion has to be believed by the agent no matter how complicated it is.

(LO4) For two logically equivalent assertions, if the agent believes the one, he has also to believe the other, no matter how complicated these assertions may be.

Most of these problems are even really fundamental in the sense that they lie in the very nature of using Kripke-style modal semantics for modelling (knowledge and) belief: apart from (LO7) and (LO8), all problematic properties above hold in every 'belief-as-necessity' approach, i.e. every approach that employs a 'necessity'-type modal operator — i.e. an operator $\Box$ that is interpreted by means of an accessibility relation R in the usual way: $\Box\varphi$ is true in a state s if φ is true in all states with R(s, t) — in a modal system that is an extension of **K**. Therefore, in the next sections, we will look for alternatives to the standard modal approach without throwing away too much of the comfortable Kripke-style semantics. But before we pursue this line, we remark that (LO7) and (LO8) can, of course, be denied in the standard modal framework, by dropping seriality (axiom(D)) and euclidicity (A5), respectively. But, as if this price is not yet high enough, there still remains the following modified problem concerning inconsistent beliefs:

(LO10) $(B\varphi \wedge B\neg\varphi) \rightarrow B\bot$ *(No non-trivial inconsistent belief)*

(LO10) states that, if an assertion and its negation are both believed, every assertion has to be believed. So, dropping axiom (D), we may now represent inconsistent belief, but only in a very trivial manner. Since (LO10) is already a theorem in system **K** — it is, in fact, a consequence of (LO5) — this problem cannot be solved within the standard modal framework either.

2.6. Belief-as-Possibility: The System Dual-KD45 (van der Hoek & Meyer)

A first and perhaps slightly naive attempt to overcome the problems with the 'belief-as-necessity' approach is to turn to the dual approach: namely 'belief-as-possibility' ([vdHM89]). Here we model belief by the dual operator M of the operator B in **KD45**: $M = \neg B \neg$.

For a **KD45**-model $\mathbb{M} = (S, \pi, R)$ we have: $(\mathbb{M}, s) \models M\varphi \Leftrightarrow \exists\, t\, [R(s, t) \,\&\, (\mathbb{M}, t) \models \varphi]$.

Of course, in this way we circumvent a number of the typical problems of a necessity operator mentioned in the previous section, while still maintaining desirable ones, like the introspection properties:

2.6.1. PROPOSITION. *The following properties hold in* **Dual-KD45**:

(i) $\not\models M\varphi \wedge M(\varphi \rightarrow \psi) \rightarrow M\psi$
(ii) $\not\models (M\varphi \wedge M\psi) \rightarrow M(\varphi \wedge \psi)$
(iii) $\not\models M\varphi \rightarrow \neg M \neg\varphi$
(iv) $\models M(M\varphi \rightarrow \varphi)$
(v) $\not\models \varphi \rightarrow M\varphi$
(vi) $\models M\varphi \leftrightarrow MM\varphi$
(vii) $\models \neg M\varphi \leftrightarrow M\neg M\varphi$
(viii) $\models \varphi \leftrightarrow \psi \Rightarrow\ \models M\varphi \leftrightarrow M\psi$

PROOF. See Exercise 2.6.1.1. ■

2.6.1.1. EXERCISE. Prove Proposition 2.6.1.

However, the law of conservation of misery is also applicable in this case: we retain some of the problems, and even obtain a number of extra undesirable properties:

2.6.2. PROPOSITION. *The following properties hold in* **Dual-KD45**:

(i) $\models \varphi \Rightarrow\ \models M\varphi$ (LO2)
(ii) $\models \varphi \rightarrow \psi \Rightarrow\ \models M\varphi \rightarrow M\psi$ (LO3)

(iii) $\models M\varphi \rightarrow M(\varphi \vee \psi)$ (LO6)

(iv) $\models M$ **true** (LO9)

(v) $\models M(\varphi \vee \psi) \leftrightarrow M\varphi \vee M\psi$ (weak belief I)

PROOF. See Exercise 2.6.2.1. ■

2.6.2.1. EXERCISE. Prove Proposition 2.6.2.

Note that here (LO2) and (LO9) can be denied by dropping seriality (axiom (D)). Note that (v) is not very desirable viewed in the light of a standard notion of belief. This becomes even more pregnant in the context of **Dual-S5** rather than **Dual-KD45**, since here we even have a further property:

$\models \varphi \rightarrow M\varphi$ (weak belief II)

Properties weak belief I and II may be defended in the context of a very weak notion of belief that is associated with the idea of considering something as a possibility (i.e. not certain that not). As we point out in [vdHM89], this notion is related to a kind of *default* belief (if it is considered possible, assume it to be true) or *auto-epistemic* belief (if it is true, I'd know it) that is considered in [Moo85a] and [Sho88], [SM89]. We shall return to the topics of default reasoning and auto-epistemic reasoning more extensively in subsequent chapters.

To conclude this section we may state that the 'belief-as-possibility' approach may be useful for some (weak) forms of belief. It does not suffer from all the 'standard' properties of logical omniscience, but instead it possesses some other properties that are certainly not appropriate for all notions of belief. Thus, in order to try to solve the problems of logical omniscience in a more general way, we have to do something different, and deviate from the standard modal approach even further.

2.7. Implicit versus Explicit Belief (Levesque)

Levesque [Lev84] tries to solve the logical omniscience problem by distinguishing *implicit* and *explicit* belief. For implicit belief, i.e. belief one may be unaware of, one may assume logical omniscience. Implicit belief is an ideal form of belief. By definition, one has to be aware of explicit belief, however, and one need not be aware of the consequences of one's belief. So for explicit belief it is not adequate to assume logical omniscience. We denote explicit belief in φ as $B_e\varphi$. The language of doxastic logic in which B_e is present rather than the normal (implicit) operator B is denoted as $\mathcal{L}_{B,e}(\mathbf{P})$. (For convenience, we restrict ourselves to the single agent case.)

Levesque bases the (formal) semantics of formulas with operators B_e on so-called '*situations*', that is to say *partial* possible worlds. In a situation a formula may possess also both truth values at once, or no truth value at all. So in this way we deviate from standard modal logic.

A model for explicit belief now becomes a structure

$$\mathbb{M} = \langle S, \mathcal{B}, \pi_T, \pi_F \rangle,$$

where S is a non-empty set of situations, $\mathcal{B} \subseteq S$ is a set of situations that are explicitly considered as possible, and on which the semantics of a formula $B_e\varphi$ is based, and where $\models_T$, $\models_F \subseteq \mathbb{M} \times S \times \mathcal{L}_{\mathbf{B},e}(\mathbf{P})$ are truth and falsehood support relations that — given a structure and a situation — determine whether an assertion in the language $\mathcal{L}_{\mathbf{B},e}(\mathbf{P})$ with explicit belief is true, false, both or none. The precise definition of $\models_T$, $\models_F$ reads as follows. Let π_T, π_F: $S \to (\mathbf{P} \to \{t, f\})$ be truth and falsehood assignments to the primitive propositions for every situation. Now:

$$
\begin{array}{lcl}
(\mathbb{M}, s) \models_T p & \Leftrightarrow & \pi_T(s)(p) = t \\
(\mathbb{M}, s) \models_F p & \Leftrightarrow & \pi_F(s)(p) = t \\
(\mathbb{M}, s) \models_T (\varphi \vee \psi) & \Leftrightarrow & (\mathbb{M}, s) \models_T \varphi \text{ or } (\mathbb{M}, s) \models_T \psi \\
(\mathbb{M}, s) \models_F (\varphi \vee \psi) & \Leftrightarrow & (\mathbb{M}, s) \models_F \varphi \text{ and } (\mathbb{M}, s) \models_F \psi \\
(\mathbb{M}, s) \models_T (\varphi \wedge \psi) & \Leftrightarrow & (\mathbb{M}, s) \models_T \varphi \text{ and } (\mathbb{M}, s) \models_T \psi \\
(\mathbb{M}, s) \models_F (\varphi \wedge \psi) & \Leftrightarrow & (\mathbb{M}, s) \models_F \varphi \text{ or } (\mathbb{M}, s) \models_F \psi \\
(\mathbb{M}, s) \models_T \neg\varphi & \Leftrightarrow & (\mathbb{M}, s) \models_F \varphi \\
(\mathbb{M}, s) \models_F \neg\varphi & \Leftrightarrow & (\mathbb{M}, s) \models_T \varphi \\
(\mathbb{M}, s) \models_T B_e\varphi & \Leftrightarrow & (\mathbb{M}, s') \models_T \varphi \text{ for all } s' \in \mathcal{B} \\
(\mathbb{M}, s) \models_F B_e\varphi & \Leftrightarrow & (\mathbb{M}, s) \not\models_T B_e\varphi
\end{array}
$$

Furthermore we define $\models\varphi$ (φ is *valid*) if $(\mathbb{M}, s) \models_T \varphi$ for all structures $\mathbb{M}$ and *complete* situations $s \in S$, i.e., for every $p \in \mathbf{P}$, either $\pi_T(s)(p) = t$ or $\pi_F(s)(p) = t$, but not both. A formula is *satisfiable* if there is a structure $\mathbb{M}$ and a complete situation $s \in S$ with $(\mathbb{M}, s) \models_T \varphi$.

2.7.1. EXERCISE. Extend the language $\mathcal{L}_{\mathbf{B},e}(\mathbf{P})$ with the 'classical' (implicit) belief operator B, and extend the semantics of this section in order to include formulas $B\varphi$. Is it possible to choose this semantics in such a way that the relation $B_e\varphi \to B\varphi$ between the two notions of belief becomes a validity?

2.7.2. EXERCISE.

(a) We use again $\varphi \to \psi$ as an abbreviation for $\neg\varphi \vee \psi$.

(i) Give the truth-definition of $(\mathbb{M}, s) \models_T \varphi \rightarrow \psi$, in terms of the truth and falsity conditions of φ and ψ in s.

(ii) Is it the case that, for *all* situations s, we have:

$$(\mathbb{M}, s) \models_T \varphi \rightarrow \psi \Leftrightarrow ((\mathbb{M}, s) \models_T \varphi \Rightarrow (\mathbb{M}, s) \models_T \psi)?$$

(iii) The same question as in (ii) for the case that we restrict ourselves to *complete* situations s.

(b) Check whether the following formulas are valid in Levesque's logic:

(i) $(B_e\varphi \wedge B_e(\varphi \rightarrow \psi)) \rightarrow B_e\psi$

(ii) $\neg B_e\bot$. (Here the interpretation of $\bot$ is given by $(\mathbb{M}, s) \not\models_T \bot$ and $(\mathbb{M}, s) \models_F \bot$, for any $\mathbb{M}$ and s.)

(iii) $B_e\varphi \rightarrow B_eB_e\varphi$

(iv) $\neg B_e\varphi \rightarrow B_e\neg B_e\varphi$

2.7.3. EXERCISE. Check whether the following formulas are satisfiable in Levesque's logic.

(i) $B_e(p \wedge q)$

(ii) $\neg B_e((p \wedge q) \rightarrow p)$

(iii) $B_e(p \wedge q) \wedge \neg B_ep \wedge \neg B_eq$

(iv) $B_e(p \wedge q) \wedge B_e\neg p \wedge B_e\neg q$

(v) $\neg B_ep \wedge \neg B_e\neg p$

(vi) $B_e(p \vee \neg p) \wedge \neg B_ep \wedge \neg B_e\neg p$

This notion of explicit belief does not suffer much from the problem of logical omniscience, witness the following proposition.

2.7.4. PROPOSITION. *The following 'non-omniscient' assertions are all satisfiable in Levesque's approach.*

(i) $\{B_ep, B_e(p \rightarrow q), \neg B_eq\}$

(ii) $\{\neg B_e(p \vee \neg p)\}$

(iii) $\{B_ep, \neg B_e(p \wedge (q \vee \neg q))\}$

(iv) $\{B_ep, B_e\neg p, \neg B_eq\}$

(v) $\{B_ep \wedge B_e\neg p\}$

(vi) $\{B_e(p \wedge \neg p)\}$

PROOF. See Exercise 2.7.4.1. ■

2.7.4.1. EXERCISE. Prove Proposition 2.7.4.

2.7.4.2. EXERCISE. Check whether the problems regarding logical omniscience (LO1)—(LO10) are solved in Levesque's approach.

Finally we remark that Levesque's system for explicit belief has an interesting connection to a philosophical logic with an non-material implication, namely *(first-degree) relevance logic* (cf. [Dun86]). Relevance logic is a so-called paraconsistent logic, in which the assertion $\varphi \wedge \neg\varphi \rightarrow_{relevant} \psi$ is *not* valid, and it takes its name from the fact that in a valid implication the premise is relevant in some precise sense for the conclusion. More precisely, one can prove that

$$\models (B_e\varphi \rightarrow B_e\psi) \Leftrightarrow \varphi \rightarrow_{relevant} \psi.$$

In other words: explicit belief is logical omniscient with respect to relevance logic. This is a reason for researchers such as Fagin & Halpern not to consider Levesque's solution as entirely satisfactory, and propose their own solution.

2.8. Awareness and Explicit Belief (Fagin & Halpern)

Fagin and Halpern ([FH88]) propagate a more *syntactical* approach to solve the logical omniscience problem. They introduce the notion of *awareness* to indicate which formulas the agent has at his/her disposal. This is a strong medicine indeed, by which undesirable consequences can be banned to the realm of the unknown. The operator that is used to indicate that the agent is aware of a formula is denoted A. The language obtained in this way is $\mathcal{L}^m_{BA}$. For the interpretation of this language a structure

$$\mathbb{M} = \langle S, \pi, \mathcal{A}_1, ..., \mathcal{A}_n, R_1, ..., R_n \rangle$$

is introduced, where S is a non-empty set of states, $\pi(s)$ a truth assignment to primitive propositions for every $s \in S$, and R_i is a serial, transitive and euclidean relation on S for every agent i. Furthermore, $\mathcal{A}_i$: $S \rightarrow \wp(\mathcal{L}^m_{BA})$ is a function that yields, for any $s \in S$, the set of formulas of which the agent is aware.

The semantics of formulas is as usual, only now we have to add a clause for $A_i\varphi$:

$$(\mathbb{M}, s) \models A_i\varphi \Leftrightarrow \varphi \in \mathcal{A}_i(s).$$

Explicit belief $B_{E,i}\varphi$ is now defined with the aid of awareness:

$$(\mathbb{M}, s) \models B_{E,i}\varphi \Leftrightarrow \varphi \in \mathcal{A}_i(s) \text{ and } (\mathbb{M}, t) \models \varphi \text{ for all t such that } (s, t) \in R_i.$$

That is, we have that $B_{E,i}\varphi \leftrightarrow (A_i\varphi \wedge B_i\varphi)$; explicit belief is (implicit) belief of which one is aware.

Validity of φ, $\models \varphi$, is defined again as $(\mathbb{M}, s) \models \varphi$ for all structures $\mathbb{M}$ and all states s. Note that the quantification over structures also includes a quantification over awareness functions $\mathcal{A}_i$. Satisfiability of a formula is defined again as non-validity of its negation.

2.8.1. EXERCISE. (a) Check whether the following formulas are valid in awareness logic.

(i) $(B_{E,i}\varphi \wedge B_{E,i}(\varphi \rightarrow \psi)) \rightarrow B_{E,i}\psi$

(ii) $\neg B_{E,i}\bot$

(iii) $B_{E,i}\varphi \rightarrow B_{E,i}B_{E,i}\varphi$

(iv) $\neg B_{E,i}\varphi \rightarrow B_{E,i}\neg B_{E,i}\varphi$

(b) For the properties in (a) that are not valid, try to find natural conditions on the model to enforce them.

2.8.2. EXERCISE. Check whether the following formulas are satisfiable in awareness logic.

(i) $B_{E,i}(p \wedge q)$

(ii) $\neg B_{E,i}((p \wedge q) \rightarrow p)$

(iii) $B_{E,i}(p \wedge q) \wedge \neg B_{E,i}p \wedge \neg B_{E,i}q$

(iv) $B_{E,i}(p \wedge q) \wedge B_{E,i}\neg p \wedge B_{E,i}\neg q$

(v) $\neg B_{E,i}p \wedge \neg B_{E,i}\neg p$

(vi) $B_{E,i}(p \vee \neg p) \wedge \neg B_{E,i}p \wedge \neg B_{E,i}\neg p$

Also this approach of Fagin & Halpern's avoids some forms of logical omniscience that we saw earlier.

2.8.3. PROPOSITION. *Of the following 'non-omniscient' assertions:*

(i) $\{B_{E,i}p, B_{E,i}(p \rightarrow q), \neg B_{E,i}q\}$

(ii) $\{\neg B_{E,i}(p \vee \neg p)\}$

(iii) $\{B_{E,i}p, \neg B_{E,i}(p \wedge (q \vee \neg q))\}$

(iv) $\{B_{E,i}p, B_{E,i}\neg p, \neg B_{E,i}q\}$

(v) $\{B_{E,i}p \wedge B_{E,i}\neg p\}$

(vi) $\{B_{E,i}(p \wedge \neg p)\}$

(i)—(iii) *are satisfiable in the 'awareness' approach of Fagin & Halpern, and* (iv)—(vi) *are not.*

PROOF. See Exercise 2.8.3.1. ■

2.8.3.1. EXERCISE. Prove Proposition 2.8.3.

2.8.3.2. EXERCISE. Check whether the problems (or which of them) regarding logical omniscience (LO1)—(LO10) are solved in the awareness approach.

Note that the awareness function $\mathcal{A}_i$ can filter out any (undesired) belief, a property which we shall return to in Section 2.10. In its most general form, the operator A_i may diverge dramatically from the intuition behind 'awareness'. For instance, $A_i(p \wedge q) \wedge \neg A_i(q \wedge p)$ is satisfiable, as is $A_i A_i p \wedge \neg A_i p$. Moreover, the set-up of **KD45**-like belief is destroyed by the incorporation of the function $\mathcal{A}_i$, since all instances of the introspection properties $B_{E,i}\varphi \rightarrow B_{E,i}B_{E,i}\varphi$, and $\neg B_{E,i}\varphi \rightarrow B_{E,i}\neg B_{E,i}\varphi$ can be denied by suitable functions $\mathcal{A}_i$. In [vdHM89], but also in [FH88] itself and in [HK91], the addition of special conditions on $\mathcal{A}_i$ in order to obtain intuitive notions of explicit belief is studied. In [Hua90] Zhisheng Huang uses the awareness framework to model *belief dependence*, which in [HvEB91] is used to solve problems of distributed belief (which is much less straightforward than the analogous notion of distributed (or implicit) knowledge of Section 2.3, cf. [Sch86]). In the same vein, Moses [Mos88] tries to capture *resource bounded* awareness by interpreting / employing the awareness function as a bounded computability predicate. Furthermore, Gillet & Gochet ([GG90]) give a solution to logical omniscience based on a notion of awareness that is related to the syntactical complexity of the formulas involved.

The logic of Fagin & Halpern treated in this section is called the logic of *general* awareness. The term 'general' refers to the definition of the awareness function $\mathcal{A}$ allowing us to assign sets of *arbitrary* formulas to be aware of. In their paper [FH88] Fagin & Halpern also give a logic of *special* awareness, in which the awareness function only involves primitive propositions. This simplification allows for a recursive definition of explicit belief without the need to use the special awareness operator A_i. We refer the interested reader to [FH88].

2.9. Local Reasoning (Fagin & Halpern) and Opaque Knowledge (Gochet & Gillet)

Although the logic of the previous section is very flexible, we cannot express *inconsistent* beliefs in it, as we could do with Levesque's logic. Consequently Fagin and Halpern proposed in [FH88] yet another approach, in which this can be done as well without the use of incoherent states (i.e. Levesque's situations). The basic idea behind this treatment is that an agent may have several (inconsistent) opinions, depending on the frame of reference. One may think of a researcher in physics who may consider an electron alternately as a particle or as a wave, depending on whether s/he thinks classically or quantum-physically.

Formally 'local reasoning', as Fagin & Halpern call this approach, is given by the introduction of a so-called 'cluster model'

$$\mathbb{M} = \langle S, \pi, \mathcal{C}_1, \ldots, \mathcal{C}_n \rangle,$$

where S is again a non-empty set of states and π is a truth assignment function per state. The $\mathcal{C}_i$, however, are now functions $S \to \wp(\wp(S))$: for every s, $\mathcal{C}_i(s)$ is a non-empty collection of non-empty subsets (*clusters*) of S (See Figure 2.8). Thus $\mathcal{C}_i(s)$ indicates which clusters (frames of reference) are considered by the agent. We may now distinguish '*weak*' versus '*strong*' belief:

$B_i\varphi$: agent i believes φ in a *weak* sense, i.e. within *some* cluster;
$S_i\varphi$: agent i believes φ in a *strong* sense, i.e. in *all* clusters.

The language that is obtained by considering weak and strong belief in this sense is denoted $\mathcal{L}^m_{BS}$, and the formal semantics of the weak and strong belief operators read as follows:

$$(\mathbb{M}, s) \models B_i\varphi \iff \exists T \in \mathcal{C}_i(s)\ \forall t \in T\ (\mathbb{M}, t) \models \varphi,$$
$$(\mathbb{M}, s) \models S_i\varphi \iff \forall T \in \mathcal{C}_i(s)\ \forall t \in T\ (\mathbb{M}, t) \models \varphi.$$

Validity and satisfiability are defined as usual again.

2.9.1. EXERCISE. (a) Check whether the following formulas are valid in the local reasoning approach.

(i) $(B_i\varphi \wedge B_i(\varphi \to \psi)) \to B_i\psi$

(ii) $\neg B_i\bot$.

(iii) $B_i\varphi \to B_iB_i\varphi$

(iv) $\neg B_i\varphi \to B_i\neg B_i\varphi$

(b) The same questions as in (a) for S_i instead of B_i.

(c) ([Lok94]) Show that $(S_i\varphi \wedge B_i\psi) \to B_i(\varphi \wedge \psi)$ is valid.

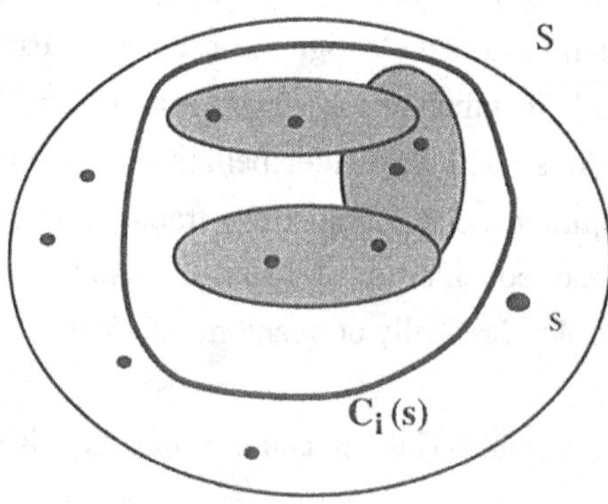

Figure 2.8

2.9.2. EXERCISE. Check whether the following formulas are satisfiable in the local reasoning approach.

(i) $B_i(p \wedge q)$

(ii) $\neg B_i((p \wedge q) \rightarrow p)$

(iii) $B_i(p \wedge q) \wedge \neg B_i p \wedge \neg B_i q$

(iv) $B_i(p \wedge q) \wedge B_i \neg p \wedge B_i \neg q$

(v) $\neg B_i p \wedge \neg B_i \neg p$

(vi) $B_i(p \vee \neg p) \wedge \neg B_i p \wedge \neg B_i \neg p$

This set-up is such that inconsistent (weak) beliefs can be believed. On other points it is less flexible again, as can be seen from the following:

2.9.3. PROPOSITION. *Of the following 'non-omniscient' assertions:*

(i) $\{B_i p, B_i(p \rightarrow q), \neg B_i q\}$

(ii) $\{\neg B_i(p \vee \neg p)\}$

(iii) $\{B_i p, \neg B_i(p \wedge (q \vee \neg q))\}$

(iv) $\{B_i p, B_i \neg p, \neg B_i q\}$

(v) $\{B_i p \wedge B_i \neg p\}$

(vi) $\{B_i(p \wedge \neg p)\}$

(i), (iv) *and* (v) *are satisfiable in the 'local reasoning' approach of Fagin & Halpern, and* (ii), (iii) *and* (vi) *are not.*

PROOF. See Exercise 2.9.3.1. ■

2.9.3.1. EXERCISE. Prove Proposition 2.9.3.

2.9.3.2. EXERCISE. Check whether the problems (or which of them) regarding logical omniscience (LO1)—(LO10) are solved in the local reasoning approach.

As in traditional modal logic, we may impose restrictions to the functions $\mathcal{C}_i$ to enforce certain desirable properties of the operators B_i (and S_i).

2.9.4. EXERCISE.

(i) Show that under the condition

$$s' \in T \in \mathcal{C}_i(s) \Rightarrow T \in \mathcal{C}_i(s')$$

we have that $\models B_i\varphi \rightarrow B_iB_i\,\varphi$.

(ii) Show that under the condition

$$\forall T \in \mathcal{C}_i(s)\ \forall t \in T\ \mathcal{C}_i(t) \subseteq \mathcal{C}_i(s)$$

we have that $\models \neg B_i\varphi \rightarrow B_i\neg B_i\varphi$.

Let us close this section with a brief discussion of work by Gochet & Gillet [GG91], who use another kind of local reasoning inspired by [Wei82] to solve problems of logical omniscience for *knowledge between* agents. For example, in standard epistemic logic we have the validity $K_1K_2\varphi \rightarrow K_1\varphi$. (Convince yourself of this.) That this is sometimes problematic can be seen from the following example from [Wei92]: Consider a child who says that he knows that his father knows that something is the case. "Although it should then follow [...] that the father knows that p [...] one does not assume [...] in general the consequence that the child also knows that p". If knowledge of φ is to mean 'has verified for himself that φ' or even, in a mathematical environment — the father is a mathematician, for instance — 'claims to have a (mathematical) proof of φ', *and it is not sufficient to trust an authority (Father)*, the inference of the child knowing p is indeed questionable if not just simply false. In mathematics, claiming to have a proof of an assertion should not be sufficiently convincing for other mathematicians to believe / know that assertion, witness the controversy about Fermat's Last 'Theorem', which has plagued mathematicians for so many years.

This form of lack of logical omniscience, which is called *opaque* (vs *transparent*) knowledge, is dealt with by considering agent-dependent (*local*) worlds as well as agent-dependent (local) accessibility relations in the model. Thus agent i is deprived of the ability to consult freely the alternatives that agent j considers as compatible with i's alternatives of the 'real' world. The model allows some epistemic alternatives to be shared while others remain private.

Formally, Gochet & Gillet achieve this by introducing models of the form $\mathbb{M} = \langle \mathbf{S}, \rho, \pi, \mathbf{R} \rangle$, where $\mathbf{S} = (S_1, ..., S_n)$ with S_i the set of states associated with agent i, $\rho \in \bigcap_i S_i$ is the 'real' state, π is a truth assignment function per state, and $\mathbf{R} = (R_1, ..., R_n)$ with R_i a reflexive, transitive and euclidean accessibility relation over S_i, associated with agent i. The K_i-operator is now interpreted by the clause: $(\mathbb{M}, s) \models K_i\varphi$ iff [if $s \in S_i$ then for every t with $R_i(s, t)$: $(\mathbb{M}, t) \models \varphi$]. Now Gochet & Gillet consider two types of validity:

(1) a formula φ is valid_1 iff for every model $\mathbb{M} = \langle \mathbf{S}, \rho, \pi, \mathbf{R} \rangle$ and for any $s \in \bigcup_i S_i$: $(\mathbb{M}, s) \models \varphi$.

(2) a formula φ is valid_2 iff for every model $\mathbb{M} = \langle \mathbf{S}, \rho, \pi, \mathbf{R} \rangle$, $(\mathbb{M}, \rho) \models \varphi$. Note the role of the real state ρ in this notion of validity!

Now e.g. $K_i(\varphi \to \psi) \to (K_i\varphi \to K_i\psi)$ is both valid_1 and valid_2, whereas, in general, $K_i\varphi \to \varphi$ is valid_2, but invalid_1. (Take, for $\varphi = p \in \mathbf{P}$, a model with a state s such that $\pi(s)(p) = f$, and such that $s \notin S_i$. Then $(\mathbb{M}, s) \models K_ip$, but $(\mathbb{M}, s) \not\models p$; note that we cannot give an analogous counter-example with respect to validity_2, since in this notion we have to evaluate the formula in the real world ρ, and by definition $\rho \in S_i$, for any i.) Finally, returning to our original motivating example: it is readily shown that $K_iK_jp \to K_ip$ is neither valid_1 nor valid_2, as desired, by taking a model with two states $s \in S_i$ and $t \notin S_j$, such that $R_i(s, t)$ and $\pi(t)(p) = f$.

2.10. Principles and Implicit Belief (van der Hoek & Meyer)

In [vdHM89] we experimented with a kind of dual approach to the awareness one by Fagin & Halpern. Whereas the awareness approach enables one to filter out some unwanted validities, simply by choosing the awareness function in such a way that these validities are not aware of, *principles* allow one to add some validities to model a kind of blind faith or prejudice in possibly incoherent beliefs. Just as with awareness this is done in a purely syntactical way. We extend the language with operators P_i, denoting that some assertion is a principle. This gives rise to a new notion of belief, which is 'even more implicit' than the original notion of belief. For that reason we refer to this *new* notion as *implicit belief* in this section, and denote it by operators $B_{I,i}$. The extended language is denoted as $\mathcal{L}^m_{\mathbf{BP}}$.

With respect to semantics, ordinary Kripke models are extended by functions $\mathcal{P}_i$: $S \to \wp(\mathcal{L}^m_{\mathbf{BP}})$, yielding per state a set of formulas that are considered as principles in that state. Thus models are of the form

$$\mathbb{M} = \langle S, \pi, \mathcal{P}_1, \ldots, \mathcal{P}_n, R_1, \ldots, R_n \rangle,$$

where S is a non-empty set of states, π is the usual truth assignment function, and the R_i are serial, transitive and euclidean accessibility relations. The semantics of the formulas is very similar to that of the awareness logic. The clause for the new operator P_i is as follows:

$$(\mathbb{M}, s) \models P_i\varphi \quad \Leftrightarrow \quad \varphi \in \mathcal{P}_i(s).$$

Implicit belief $B_{I,i}\varphi$ is now defined as $B_i\varphi \vee P_i\varphi$, expressing that something is implicitly believed if it is believed (in the traditional sense) or if it is a principle. Thus we have that $(\mathbb{M}, s) \models B_{I,i}\varphi \;\Leftrightarrow\; \varphi \in \mathcal{P}_i(s)$ or $(\mathbb{M}, t) \models \varphi$ for all t such that $(s, t) \in R_i$. Validity and satisfiability are defined as usual. Note that in this setting the incoherent belief $B_{I,i}(\varphi \wedge \neg\varphi)$ is satisfiable, by choosing $\varphi \wedge \neg\varphi \in P_i(s)$ for some state s. Although this is a rather simplistic approach, it shows that incoherent beliefs can be represented without resort to incoherent worlds (à la Levesque) or multiple frames (clusters à la Fagin & Halpern).

2.10.1. EXERCISE. (a) Check whether the following formulas are valid in the principle approach.

(i) $(B_{I,i}\varphi \wedge B_{I,i}(\varphi \to \psi)) \to B_{I,i}\psi$

(ii) $\neg B_{I,i}\bot$

(iii) $B_{I,i}\varphi \to B_{I,i}B_{I,i}\varphi$

(iv) $\neg B_{I,i}\varphi \to B_{I,i}\neg B_{I,i}\varphi$

(b) For the introspection properties that do not hold, try to find natural conditions on the model to enforce them.

2.10.2. EXERCISE. Check whether the following formulas are satisfiable in the principle approach.

(i) $B_{I,i}(p \wedge q)$

(ii) $\neg B_{I,i}((p \wedge q) \to p)$

(iii) $B_{I,i}(p \wedge q) \wedge \neg B_{I,i}p \wedge \neg B_{I,i}q$

(iv) $B_{I,i}(p \wedge q) \wedge B_{I,i}\neg p \wedge B_{I,i}\neg q$

(v) $\neg B_{I,i}p \wedge \neg B_{I,i}\neg p$

(vi) $B_{I,i}(p \vee \neg p) \wedge \neg B_{I,i}p \wedge \neg B_{I,i}\neg p$

Concerning the problem of logical omniscience we have the following:

2.10.3. PROPOSITION. *Of the following 'non-omniscient' assertions:*

(i) $\{B_{I,i}p, B_{I,i}(p \to q), \neg B_{I,i}q\}$

(ii) $\{\neg B_{I,i}(p \vee \neg p)\}$

(iii) $\{B_{I,i}p, \neg B_{I,i}(p \wedge (q \vee \neg q))\}$

(iv) $\{B_{I,i}p, B_{I,i}\neg p, \neg B_{I,i}q\}$

(v) $\{B_{I,i}p \wedge B_{I,i}\neg p\}$

(vi) $\{B_{I,i}(p \wedge \neg p)\}$

only (ii) ***is not** satisfiable in the 'principle' approach of Van der Hoek & Meyer; the rest are.*

PROOF. See Exercise 2.10.3.1. ■

2.10.3.1. EXERCISE. Prove Proposition 2.10.3.

2.10.3.2. EXERCISE. Check whether the problems (or which of them) regarding logical omniscience (LO1)—(LO10) are solved in the principle approach.

2.11. Fusion Models (Jaspars)

Inspired by work by Rescher & Brandom ([RB80]) on representing inconsistencies in a meaningful manner, Jaspars ([Jas91], [Jas93]) proposes a model of 'confused' belief, in which it is possible to represent some inconsistencies in an agent's beliefs 'without resulting in total mental collapse'. This approach is reminiscent of Fagin & Halpern's local reasoning one, but is set up somewhat differently from a model-theoretic point of view. Jaspars considers Kripke structures of the form

$$\mathbb{M} = \langle S, \pi, R_1, \ldots, R_n \rangle,$$

where S and π are the usual (non-empty) set of states and truth assignment function, respectively, but the R_i are accessibility relations of type $R_i \subseteq S \times (\wp(S) \setminus \{\emptyset\})$, thus associating with a state a set of accessible non-empty *sets of* states (See Figure 2.9). Note that, in principle, it is allowed that there are s for which there is *no* T such that $R_i(s, T)$. Belief B_i is now interpreted by:

$$(\mathbb{M}, s) \models B_i\varphi \;\Leftrightarrow\; \forall T \subseteq S\ [R_i(s, T) \Rightarrow \exists t \in T\ (\mathbb{M}, t) \models \varphi],$$

expressing that φ is believed by agent i in state s iff for all accessible sets of states there is at least one state in which φ holds. A way to view this is by regarding the accessible *sets of* states as a kind of *superstates* in which a local form of inconsistency may be present: it may be the case that in such an accessible superstate both some evidence (modelled by an ordinary state contained in the superstate) for a formula ψ and some evidence for the formula $\neg\psi$ is available. In some sense this approach is dual to the local reasoning one of Fagin & Halpern: there a possible inconsistency is modelled by referring to different accessible sets, which in themselves are consistent (or rather represent a consistent set of beliefs). In Jaspars' approach inconsistencies are already modelled *within* the accessible sets.

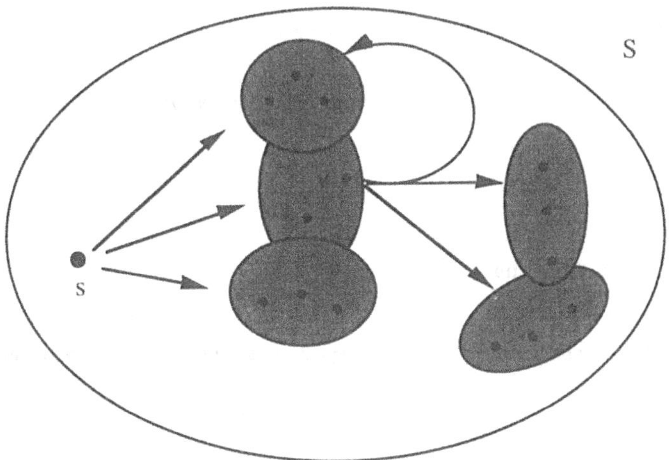

Figure 2.9

Validity and satisfiability are defined as usual again.

2.11.1. EXERCISE. Check whether the following formulas are valid in the fusion model approach.

(i) $(B_i\varphi \wedge B_i(\varphi \to \psi)) \to B_i\psi$

(ii) $\neg B_i\bot$ (Here $\bot$ stands for $p \wedge \neg p$, for some primitive proposition p.)

(iii) $B_i\varphi \to B_iB_i\varphi$

(iv) $\neg B_i\varphi \to B_i\neg B_i\varphi$

2.11.2. EXERCISE. Check whether the following formulas are satisfiable in the fusion approach.

(i) $B_i(p \wedge q)$

(ii) $\neg B_i((p \wedge q) \to p)$

(iii) $B_i(p \wedge q) \wedge \neg B_ip \wedge \neg B_iq$

(iv) $B_i(p \wedge q) \wedge B_i\neg p \wedge B_i\neg q$

(v) $\neg B_ip \wedge \neg B_i\neg p$

(vi) $B_i(p \vee \neg p) \wedge \neg B_ip \wedge \neg B_i\neg p$

This set-up is such that inconsistent (weak) beliefs can be believed. On other points it is less flexible again, as can be seen from the following:

2.11.3. PROPOSITION. *From the following 'non-omniscient' assertions:*

(i) $\{B_ip, B_i(p \to q), \neg B_iq\}$

(ii) $\{\neg B_i(p \vee \neg p)\}$

(iii) $\{B_ip, \neg B_i(p \wedge (q \vee \neg q))\}$

(iv) $\{B_ip, B_i\neg p, \neg B_iq\}$

(v) $\{B_ip \wedge B_i\neg p\}$

(vi) $\{B_i(p \wedge \neg p)\}$

(i), (iv), (v) *and* (vi) *are satisfiable in the 'fusion model' approach, and* (ii) *and* (iii) *are not.*

PROOF. See Exercise 2.11.3.1. ■

2.11.3.1. EXERCISE. Prove Proposition 2.11.3.

2.11.3.2. EXERCISE. Check whether the problems (or which of them) regarding logical omniscience (LO1)—(LO10) are solved in the fusion model approach.

As we have seen in Exercise 2.11.1 above, the logic thus far does not validate the introspective properties, so that in fact it is not yet suited as a logic for modelling belief. In fact, in [Jas93]

Jaspars puts additional constraints on his model to obtain a genuine logic of 'confused belief'. First we need some additional not(at)ions to facilitate the expression of these constraints:

2.11.4. DEFINITION. The relations $R_i^{\uparrow}$, $\overline{R}_i$ and $\underline{R}_i$ are given by:

(i) $xR_i^{\uparrow}Y \Leftrightarrow \exists Y' \subseteq Y: xR_iY'$;

(ii) $X\overline{R}_iY \Leftrightarrow \forall x \in X: xR_i^{\uparrow}Y$;

(iii) $X\underline{R}_iY \Leftrightarrow \exists x \in X: xR_i^{\uparrow}Y$.

Now in order to let B_i satisfy the axioms (D), (A4) and (A5), Jaspars imposes the following restrictions on R:

2.11.5. DEFINITION (F-seriality, F-transitivity and F-euclidicity).

(i) a (fusion model) relation R is *F-serial* iff: $\forall x\, \exists Y : xR_iY$;

(ii) a (fusion model) relation R is *F-transitive* iff: $\forall x, Y, Z : xR_i^{\uparrow}Y \;\&\; Y\overline{R}_iZ \Rightarrow xR_i^{\uparrow}Z$;

(iii) a fusion model) relation is *F-euclidean* iff: $\forall x, Y, Z : xR_i^{\uparrow}Y \;\&\; xR_i^{\uparrow}Z \Rightarrow Y\underline{R}_iZ$.

2.11.6. PROPOSITION. Fusion models that satisfy (F-seriality), (F-transitivity) and (F-euclidicity) validate the axioms (D), (A4) and (A5).

PROOF. See Exercise 2.11.6.1. ■

2.11.6.1. EXERCISE. Show that the above conditions on R_i indeed imply the validity of (D), (A4) and (A5).

2.12. Impossible World Semantics (Rantala) and Non-Modal Approaches

Rantala [Ran82] has proposed a theory to overcome logical omniscience in epistemic / doxastic logic, based on Kripke's theory of non-standard or impossible worlds [Kri65]. In this approach normal possible worlds are extended with a set S* of so-called *impossible* worlds, which may behave very 'illogically'. Formally, such a (Rantala) model looks like this:

$$\mathbb{M} = \langle S, S^*, \pi, \pi^*, R_1, ..., R_n \rangle,$$

where S and S* are sets of *possible* and *impossible* worlds, respectively, with $S \neq \emptyset$, π is a truth assignment function to primitive propositions on S, π^* is a valuation function of *arbitrary* formulas on S*, and the R_i are accessibility relations of type $R_i \subseteq (S \cup S^*) \times (S \cup S^*)$, thus associating with a (possible or impossible) world a set of accessible (possible or impossible) worlds. All clauses for the interpretation of the language in possible worlds of these models are standard (*including* those for the modal belief operator B_i); the truth condition for impossible worlds (in which one may have to evaluate formulas when considering modal formulas), however, is *completely free*. Validity (and satisfiability) of a formula in a model $\langle S, S^*, \pi, R_1, ..., R_n \rangle$ is now defined as the truth of that formula in all (some) *possible* world(s) $s \in S$. And, as usual, validity (satisfiability) of a formula is defined as validity (satisfiability) of that formula in all Rantala models of the above form.

Owing to the freedom in interpretation when encountering a non-normal world, impossible world semantics provides a very powerful means to get rid of logical omniscience. In fact, in this framework an agent may have no general logical principle at all. In particular, one can show that all forms of logical omniscience (LO1)—(LO10) can be avoided. For instance, a contradiction in belief may be represented by a model with an impossible world where this contradiction is stipulated to hold within this world.

2.12.1. EXERCISE. Show that in impossible world semantics all forms (LO1)—(LO10) of logical omniscience can be avoided.

Of course, this method is rather crude: by using the right choice of impossible worlds S^* (and the associated valuation function π^* on these) one may accomplish the avoidance of logical omniscience in a trivial manner. In fact, the semantics is not at all logical with regard to the impossible worlds. The semantics is not even recursively compositional in these worlds. This is a reason why researchers in the field are mostly not satisfied with this semantics. The fact remains, however, that it is the most powerful method to avoid logical omniscience: [Wan90] shows that the approaches of Levesque (Section 2.7), Fagin & Halpern (Sections 2.8, 2.9), Van der Hoek & Meyer (§2.10) can be interpreted in impossible world semantics. Moreover, Thijsse [Thy92] shows that all approaches to the avoidance of logical omniscience can be embedded in his framework of so-called *sieve semantics*, which can be viewed as a generalisation of the general awareness logic of Fagin & Halpern (Section 2.8) by dropping the structural conditions on the accessibility relations R_i, and which he shows to be equivalent with Rantala impossible world semantics. [Thy92] also gives (partial) solutions to the logical omniscience problem using *partial* semantics.

Finally let us mention even more radical methods to solve the problem of logical omniscience. As we mentioned already in Section 2.5, the problem of logical omniscience is connected intrinsically with the Kripke-structure-based modal approach. So one way to avoid the problem is to deviate from Kripke-style semantics for knowledge and belief. In appendixes A1 and A2 we deal with two such approaches, namely Konolige's deduction model of belief [Kon86] and Fagin, Halpern & Vardi's knowledge structures [FHV84, 91]. Although the original treatment of [FHV84, 91] does not solve the logical omniscience problem — it is originally proposed as an alternative for the standard approach — Lejoly & Minsoul [LM91] show how to use the more flexible framework of knowledge structures to eliminate some forms of logical omniscience.

In conclusion of all this we may safely state that the problem of logical omniscience has received a lot of attention in the literature, but, although there exist very general methods to overcome logical omniscience (such as Rantala's impossible world semantics and Thijsse's sieve semantics), it is not always clear what is the right model. The general methods seem to be too 'illogical', whereas the more special and 'logical' methods seem to suffer from some remnants of logical omniscience. Perhaps a perfectly logical solution to the logical omniscience problem is a *contradictio in terminis*, and we must satisfy ourselves in practical situations with a particular choice of the available models that more or less captures the extent of logical (non)omniscience that is acceptable in that particular situation.

2.13. A System for Knowledge and Belief (Kraus & Lehmann)

In [KL86] knowledge and belief are considered within one single system. In this system it becomes possible to speak about belief of knowledge, knowledge of belief, etc. Furthermore, apart from an operator for 'common knowledge' this system contains an operator for the notion of 'common belief' as well. The authors stress that these notions possess entirely different properties with respect to communication in distributed systems. We know that without simultaneous runs common knowledge could not increase (change); for common belief this property does not hold. We shall come back to this after we have presented the formal system.

2.13.1. NOTATION.

$K_i\varphi$: " i knows that φ "

$B_i\varphi$: " i believes that φ "

$C\varphi$: " φ is common knowledge "

$D\varphi$: " φ is common belief "

$E\varphi$: " every agent knows that φ " $\equiv \bigwedge_{i\in A} K_i\varphi$

$F\varphi$: " every agent believes that φ " $\equiv \bigwedge_{i\in A} B_i\varphi$

2.13.2. The Language $\mathcal{L}^m_{\mathbf{KB}}(\mathbf{P})$

Let **P** be a set of primitive propositions. The language $\mathcal{L}^m_{\mathbf{KB}}(\mathbf{P})$ is the combination of $\mathcal{L}^m_{\mathbf{K}}(\mathbf{P})$, including the E and C-operators, and $\mathcal{L}^m_{\mathbf{B}}$, extended with a clause for common belief (D):

$$\textit{if } \varphi \in \mathcal{L}^m_{\mathbf{KB}}(\mathbf{P}) \ \textit{ then } \ D\varphi \in \mathcal{L}^m_{\mathbf{KB}}(\mathbf{P})$$

2.13.3. Kripke Models for $\mathcal{L}^m_{KB}(P)$

A model for $\mathcal{L}^m_{KB}(P)$ is a structure $\mathbb{M} = \langle S, \pi, R_1, \ldots, R_m, T_1, \ldots, T_m \rangle$ where

S is a set of states
$\pi : S \to (P \to \{t, f\})$ is a truth assignment function
$R_i \subseteq S \times S$ are the accessibility relations with respect to knowledge
$T_i \subseteq S \times S$ are the accessibility relations with respect to belief

such that:

(a) R_i is an equivalence relation
(b) T_i is serial
(c) $T_i \subseteq R_i$
(d) for all s, t, u ∈ S: $R_i(s, t)$ and $T_i(t, u)$ implies $T_i(s, u)$.

2.13.3.1. REMARKS.

1. Condition (a) means that the relations R_i are *S5*-relations.
2. Condition (b) states that in every state an agent i may be, there is at least one state he considers possible.
3. Condition (c) expresses that if an agent knows something, he also believes it: if a state is considered possible on the basis of belief, it is considered possible on the basis of knowledge as well. However, it is easier to believe something than to know something, so there might be states s, t ∈ S such that $R_i(s, t)$, but $\neg T_i(s, t)$. For example (see Figure 2.10, for the case that m = 1):

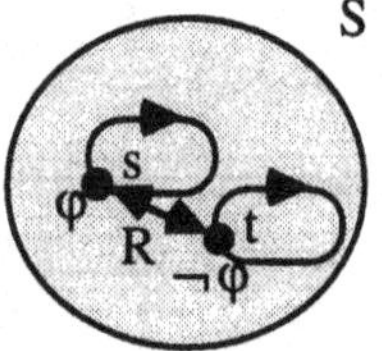

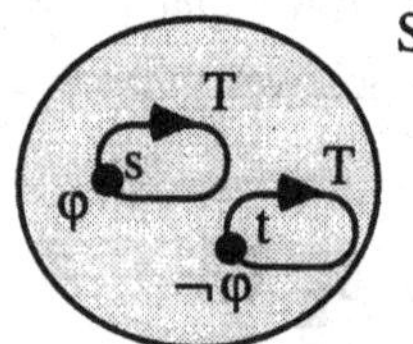

Figure 2.10

Here it holds that $s \models B\varphi$, but $s \not\models K\varphi$.

4. Condition (d) is the most interesting: this says that if s, t are both possible on the basis of the *knowledge* of agent i, and if i *believes* in state t that u is possible, then i also believes

that u is possible if he (i) is in state s, since he cannot distinguish s from t. See Figure 2.11.

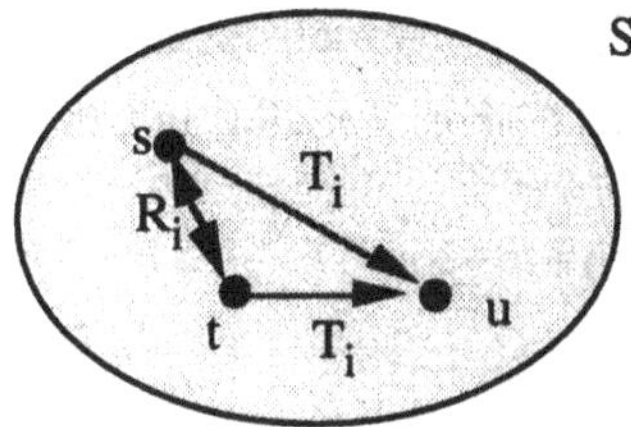

Figure 2.11

In other words, within an R_i-equivalence class every state possesses the same T_i-alternatives!

2.13.3.2. PROPOSITION.
(i) $T_i(s, t) \Rightarrow R_i(s, t)$;
(ii) T_i *is transitive and euclidean.*

PROOF. (i) direct from (c).
(ii) Transitivity: $T_i(s, t) \wedge T_i(t, u) \Rightarrow^{(i)} R_i(s, t) \wedge T_i(t, u) \Rightarrow^{(d)} T_i(s, u)$.
Euclidicity: $T_i(s, t) \wedge T_i(s, u) \Rightarrow R_i(s, t) \wedge T_i(s, u) \Rightarrow$ (R_i symmetrical) $R_i(t, s) \wedge T_i(s, u) \Rightarrow^{(d)} T_i(t, u)$.

Thus B is, just as in Section 2.4, a $\mathbf{KD45_{(m)}}$-modality (T_i was already serial according to (b)). Furthermore, we define the relations $R^+ = (\bigcup_{i \in \mathbf{A}} R_i)^{tr}$ and $T^+ = (\bigcup_{i \in \mathbf{A}} T_i)^{tr}$, where tr stands for the transitive closure.

2.13.3.3. PROPOSITION. R^+ *is reflexive and symmetrical, i.e.* R^+ *equals* R^* *(cf. Section 2.1.4).*

PROOF. Follows directly since every R_i is reflexive and symmetrical. ■

2.13.4. Semantics for $\mathcal{L}^m_{\mathbf{KB}}(\mathbf{P})$

We base the semantics of $\mathcal{L}^m_{\mathbf{KB}}(\mathbf{P})$-expressions on models $\mathbb{M} = \langle S, \pi, R_1, \ldots, R_m, T_1, \ldots, T_m \rangle$, as follows:

$(\mathbb{M}, s) \models p \quad \Leftrightarrow \pi(s)(p) = \mathbf{t}$ for $p \in \mathbf{P}$;

$$\begin{array}{lll}
(\mathbb{M}, s) \models \varphi \wedge \psi & \Leftrightarrow & (\mathbb{M}, s) \models \varphi \text{ and } (\mathbb{M}, s) \models \psi \\
(\mathbb{M}, s) \models \neg\varphi & \Leftrightarrow & (\mathbb{M}, s) \not\models \varphi \\
(\mathbb{M}, s) \models K_i\varphi & \Leftrightarrow & (\mathbb{M}, t) \models \varphi \text{ for all t such that } (s, t) \in R_i; \\
(\mathbb{M}, s) \models B_i\varphi & \Leftrightarrow & (\mathbb{M}, t) \models \varphi \text{ for all t such that } (s, t) \in T_i; \\
(\mathbb{M}, s) \models C\varphi & \Leftrightarrow & (\mathbb{M}, t) \models \varphi \text{ for all t such that } (s, t) \in R^*; \\
(\mathbb{M}, s) \models D\varphi & \Leftrightarrow & (\mathbb{M}, t) \models \varphi \text{ for all t such that } (s, t) \in T^*;
\end{array}$$

As usual we define:

$$\begin{array}{lll}
\mathbb{M} \models \varphi & \Leftrightarrow & (\mathbb{M}, s) \models \varphi \text{ for all } s \in S; \\
\models \varphi & \Leftrightarrow & \mathbb{M} \models \varphi \text{ for all models } \mathbb{M} \text{ of the form above.}
\end{array}$$

2.13.5. The System KL

The logical system **KL** consists of four levels of axioms and rules:

I. *PC - level:*

(KL0) axioms of propositional calculus (PC)

(KLR0) modus ponens: $\dfrac{\varphi, \varphi \to \psi}{\psi}$

II. *Knowledge and common knowledge:*

(KL1) $K_i(\varphi \to \psi) \to (K_i\varphi \to K_i\psi)$

(KL2) $K_i\varphi \to \varphi$

(KL3) $\neg K_i\varphi \to K_i\neg K_i\varphi$

(KL4) $C(\varphi \to \psi) \to (C\varphi \to C\psi)$

(KL5) $C\varphi \to K_i\varphi$

(KL6) $C\varphi \to K_iC\varphi$

(KL7) $C(\varphi \to E\varphi) \to (\varphi \to C\varphi)$

(KLR1) (common knowledge-generalisation:)

$$\frac{\varphi}{C\varphi}$$

Here $E\varphi$ abbreviates $K_1\varphi \wedge \ldots \wedge K_m\varphi$, as before. Note that this part is the logic $\mathbf{S5EC_{(m)}}$ of Section 2.1, since we know that the positive introspection property $K_i\varphi \to K_iK_i\varphi$ is derivable from the other axioms.

III. *Belief and common belief:*

(KL8) $B_i(\varphi \to \psi) \to (B_i\varphi \to B_i\psi)$ *(belief is closed under MP)*

(KL9) $\neg B_i\bot$ *(an agent does not believe contradictions)*

(KL10) $D(\varphi \to \psi) \to (D\varphi \to D\psi)$ *(common belief is closed under MP)*

(KL11) $D\varphi \to F\varphi$ *(if something is common belief, everyone believes it)*

(KL12) $D\varphi \to FD\varphi$ *(if something is common belief, everyone believes that it is)*

(KL13) $D(\varphi \to F\varphi) \to (F\varphi \to D\varphi)$ *(induction)*

(Here $F\varphi$ abbreviates $B_1\varphi \wedge \ldots \wedge B_m\varphi$)

IV. *Interrelation between knowledge and belief, common knowledge and common belief:*

(KL14) $K_i\varphi \to B_i\varphi$ *(an agent believes an assertion he knows)*

(KL15) $B_i\varphi \to K_iB_i\varphi$ *(an agent knows his beliefs: 'belief is conscious')*

(KL16) $C\varphi \to D\varphi$ *(common knowledge implies common belief)*

2.13.5.1. THEOREM. **KL** *is sound and complete with respect to the Kripke models in Section 2.13.3.*

PROOF. See Exercise 2.13.5.1.1. ■

*2.13.5.1.1. EXERCISE. Prove the soundness and completeness of system **KL** as stated in Theorem 2.13.5.1.

2.13.6. Some Theorems of System KL

(T1) $K_i\neg\varphi \to \neg B_i\varphi$

(T2) $B_i\varphi \leftrightarrow K_iB_i\varphi$

(T3) $\neg B_i\varphi \leftrightarrow K_i\neg B_i\varphi$

!(T4) $K_i\varphi \leftrightarrow B_iK_i\varphi$

(T5) $\neg K_i\varphi \leftrightarrow B_i\neg K_i\varphi$

(T6) $B_i\varphi \leftrightarrow B_iB_i\varphi$

(T7) $\neg B_i\varphi \leftrightarrow B_i\neg B_i\varphi$

(T8) $B_i(B_i\varphi \to \varphi)$

(T9) $D\varphi \leftrightarrow DF\varphi$

(T10) $D\varphi \leftrightarrow FD\varphi$

(T11) $FD\varphi \leftrightarrow DFD\varphi$

(T12) $D\varphi \leftrightarrow DD\varphi$

(T13) $C(\varphi \wedge \psi) \leftrightarrow C\varphi \wedge C\psi$

(T14) $D(\varphi \wedge \psi) \leftrightarrow D\varphi \wedge D\psi$

2.13.6.1. EXERCISE. Prove these theorems.

2.13.6.2. REMARK. Note that the addition of a rather intuitive axiom $B_i\varphi \rightarrow B_iK_i\varphi$ ("an agent believes to know what he believes") would have very nasty consequences for the system **KL**, since then $B_i\varphi \rightarrow K_i\varphi$ would become derivable via (T4), collapsing the notions of knowledge and belief in the system. In [vdH91a] the causes of this collapse are investigated thoroughly, and a system is proposed that is 'as close as possible to' **KL** but contains the axiom mentioned above without the undesirable collapse of knowledge and belief. Essentially, the axiom (KL3) of negative introspection for knowledge is replaced by the positive introspection axiom $K_i\varphi \rightarrow K_iK_i\varphi$, after which as many properties of **KL** are added as possible without collapsing $K_i\varphi$ and $B_i\varphi$. In particular, it is shown in [vdH91a] that in this situation the following properties can be added (simultaneously) without problems (i.e. inconsistency or collapse of K and B):

(KL17) $B_iB_i\varphi \rightarrow B_i\varphi$;

(KΛ18) $B_i\neg B_i\varphi \rightarrow \neg B_i\varphi$;

(KL19) $B_i\varphi \rightarrow B_iK_i\varphi$;

(KL20) $\neg B_i\varphi \rightarrow K_i\neg B_i\varphi$;

(KL21) $\neg K_i\varphi \rightarrow B_i\neg K_i\varphi$;

Another solution to the problem of a sensible synthesis of knowledge and belief appears in [Voo91a] and [Voo93], where it is argued that negative introspection for knowledge is incompatible with the principle that knowledge implies ('rational') belief (the former is claimed to concern so-called 'objective' knowledge of an information processing device such as a thermometer, as captured by **S5**-logic, whereas the latter is a property of a different notion of knowledge such as 'justified true belief'), and the latter is dropped rather than the former as in the solution of Van der Hoek. Furthermore, in [Voo93] the notion of justified true belief ('justified knowledge') and its purported logic are discussed extensively, and the latter is identified as a logic between **S4** and **S5**, namely **S4.2**, consisting of the axioms and rules of **S4** plus the axiom $MK\varphi \rightarrow KM\varphi$. We will not pursue this here, but refer to [Voo93] for further details.

2.14. Knowledge, Belief and Time

The previous system has been extended by Kraus & Lehmann (also in [KL86]) to include the notion of time. This has been done by adding well-known operators from temporal logic: O (next), □ (always), and Until.

Kraus & Lehmann distinguish two notions of belief that concern change in time:

(1) Belief in the sense of willingness to bet: e.g. "i believes that it will rain tomorrow". Such a belief may cause a certain way of acting (for example that i will take an umbrella with him tomorrow), but it does not matter if the belief will not be confirmed. (In the example of carrying an umbrella if it is not needed this is awkward at worst.) It may well be that I will have given up my belief tomorrow, because it is contradicted by the facts, but it seems to be the case nevertheless that if I believe that tomorrow φ will hold, I believe that I will believe this tomorrow. Thus an axiom for this kind of belief is

(KL22) $B_iO\varphi \to B_iOB_i\varphi$.

(2) 'Serious' belief, the undermining of which would cause a crisis. Therefore in this sense only those things will be believed that will never be contradicted under any circumstances. In some sense this is a kind of 'religious belief'. For this interpretation we may add the following axiom to **KL**:

(KL23) $B_iO\varphi \to K_iO\neg K_i\neg\varphi$.

(If agent i believes that something will be true tomorrow, he knows that he will not discover tomorrow that he was wrong.)

Under the serious interpretation of belief one might even replace (KL23) by

(KL24) $B_iO\varphi \to OB_i\varphi$.

(If i believes that φ will be true tomorrow, then tomorrow he will believe in φ, since — under the serious interpretation — he will not be convinced of the opposite.)

2.14.1. EXERCISE. Show that (KL24) $\vdash_{\mathbf{KL}}$ (KL23), under the assumption that both $O(\varphi \to \psi) \to (O\varphi \to O\psi)$ is valid and O-necessitation $\varphi / O\varphi$ is sound.

Analogously we have for common belief:

(KL25) $DO\varphi \to OD\varphi$.

Returning to the first kind of belief, one may postulate an analogue to (KL24) for this:

(KL24') $B_iO\varphi \to OB_i\varphi \vee OK_i\neg\varphi$,

that is to say: if i believes φ then he will still believe φ tomorrow, unless he will know the opposite. In any case the following weaker assertion is defensible:

(KL24") $B_i O\varphi \rightarrow OB_i\varphi \vee OB_i\neg\varphi$,

that is to say, if i believes φ, then he will still believe φ tomorrow, unless he *believes* that he was/is wrong. As far as is known to us, it is still an open problem to find a natural family of models with respect to which these systems are complete, although there have appeared some papers about (models for) combinations of (modal) logics ([KW91], [FS9?]), including combinations with temporal logics in particular ([Tho84], [FG92]).

Finally a remark on common belief versus common knowledge. We had seen earlier that a necessary condition for an increase of common knowledge is a certain kind of *simultaneity (synchronicity)* in the system (Theorem 2.2.13). This was a direct consequence of the theorem $C\varphi \leftrightarrow EC\varphi$.

The analogue for common belief, $D\varphi \leftrightarrow FD\varphi$, however, is *not* a valid theorem. So now we cannot prove the analogue of Theorem 2.2.13: in general, common belief is *not* constant in non-simultaneous runs. Indeed it may happen that $\neg B_2D\varphi \wedge \ldots \wedge \neg B_mD\varphi \wedge \Box B_1D\varphi$ (now the agents 2 to m do not believe $D\varphi$, but always from now on, agent 1 will believe $D\varphi$) and $O(\neg B_3D\varphi \wedge \ldots \wedge \neg B_mD\varphi \wedge \Box B_2D\varphi)$ (at the next time unit, the agents 3 to m still do not believe $D\varphi$, but from this time onwards, agents 2 will always believe $D\varphi$) and $OO(\neg B_4D\varphi \wedge \ldots \wedge \neg B_mD\varphi \wedge \Box B_3D\varphi)$ (at the second time unit from now, the agents 4 to m still do not believe $D\varphi$, but, from this time on, agent 3 will always believe $D\varphi$) and … and $O^m\Box B_mD\varphi$ (from the m-th time unit from now, also agent m will always believe $D\varphi$), and thus $O^m\Box FD\varphi$ is true, expressing that $D\varphi$ will be common belief from the m-th time unit from now, whereas this was not the case at times earlier than the m-th time unit. This may very well happen in an asynchronous system! A typical situation is the broadcast of a message where the belief that the content of that message is common belief among themselves will spread over the agents. Hence common belief may increase in such a system. On the other hand common belief may also get lost: if φ is common belief ('$D\varphi$') and at a certain moment agent i_0 no longer believes that φ holds ($B_{i_0}\neg\varphi$), then from this moment on it holds that $\neg D\varphi$, although (*ceteris paribus*) it still holds that $B_iD\varphi$ for $i \neq i_0$, i.e. everyone except for i_0 believes not only φ, but even $D\varphi$!

2.15. Knowledge and Action

Knowledge and action influence each other: on the basis of certain foreknowledge we may decide to perform certain actions, and on the other hand the performance of actions has an effect on our knowledge. Concerning the latter, executing actions according to a computer program, for example, influences (our knowledge of) the values of program variables. Regarding the former, this is of the highest importance in action planning and problem solving, and as such particularly in artificial intelligence applications.

Bob Moore from the Artificial Intelligence Center of SRI International has proposed an integrated theory of knowledge and action in [Moo85b], in which both aforementioned aspects of knowledge and action are treated. With respect to knowledge he employs the modal system **S4** rather than **S5**, which is more in line with the philosophical view of epistemic logic. As usual, the modal operators K_i are associated with (**S4**-)relations R_i. (He uses in fact a first-order version of **S4**, but here we shall restrict ourselves to a propositional version; first-order modal logic contains additional problems concerning the interpretation of predicate (function) and constant symbols in the diverse worlds and completeness, cf. the appendix A3 and [Gam91].)

For the treatment of actions he uses the notion '*event*' for which he introduces accessibility relations $r_e \subseteq S \times S$ that denote the state transitions induced by the event e. Furthermore he introduces an operator RES(e, φ) with intended meaning that event e has φ as a result. We shall, however, use the notation that is common in dynamic logic ([Har84]). Dynamic logic is a logic devised specially to reason about the *effects of actions* (i.e. *events*). Propositional dynamic logic (PDL) consists of the language of propositional logic extended by the clause: if e is an event and φ is an assertion then $[e]\varphi$ is an assertion in the language. So Moore's RES(e, φ) can be expressed in dynamic logic as $[e]\varphi$. Later we also deviate somewhat from the semantical treatment of RES or [e] to keep in line with standard practice in computer science (and program verification in particular). Regarding r_e we now postulate the following property:

(determ) $\quad r_e(s_1, s_2) \wedge r_e(s_1, s_3) \Rightarrow (s_2 = s_3)$,

that is to say, r_e is a (partial) function and e is a *deterministic* event. Furthermore, the interpretation of the expression $[e]\varphi$ is given a normal modal interpretation by means of the accessibility relation r_e:

([e]) $\quad s \models [e]\varphi \iff \forall s' \, [r_e(s, s') \Rightarrow s' \models \varphi]$.

(This expresses that $[e]\varphi$ is the weakest precondition (with respect to *partial* correctness) of event e with respect to postcondition φ. In fact, Moore uses in [Moo85b] a *total* correctness variant of this weakest precondition, but for the present purposes this difference is not relevant.)

Moore now considers a class of actions that is well-known, given by the following Backus-Nauer Form (BNF) [Nau63]:

$$\text{act} ::= \text{a} \mid \text{skip} \mid \text{fail} \mid \text{act}_1 \,;\, \text{act}_2 \mid \text{if } \varphi \text{ then act}_1 \text{ else act}_2 \text{ fi} \mid \text{while } \varphi \text{ do act}_1 \text{ od}$$

with meanings, subsequently: atomic action, sequential composition, conditional composition, and repetitive composition. These actions can be turned into events by their execution by an agent. For this we use an expression $do_i(act)$ to denote that agent i performs action act.

Semantically, the expression $do_i(act)$ is interpreted by the functional relation $r_{do_i(act)} \subseteq S \times S$, yielding the state transition associated with the event $do_i(act)$. Note that in a way we consider parametrised events, since the performance of act by agent i may (and generally will) depend on the initial state. However, we have chosen for this approach to facilitate technicalities (cf. [Moo85b], where this is done differently). Since, for an event e, r_e is taken to be a functional relation, we shall also, for convenience, use the notation of a function r_e: $S \rightarrow S$. So, e.g. $r_{do_i(act)}(s_0)$ denotes the resulting state after the event $do_i(act)$ has occurred, i.e. after agent i has performed action act in s_0. We may also employ a lambda expression: $r_e = \lambda s.\ r_e(s)$, indicating that r_e is a function with argument $s \in S$.

Now we may write down expressions such as $\varphi' := K_1([do_2(act)]\varphi)$ with meaning: "1 knows that the execution of act by agent 2 will establish the truth of assertion φ". The formal semantics of the expression φ' reads as follows: φ' is true in state s_0, if

$$\forall s_1\, [R_1(s_0, s_1) \Rightarrow \forall s_2\, [r_{do_2(act)}(s_1, s_2) \Rightarrow s_2 \models \varphi]].$$

This situation is depicted in Figure 2.12.

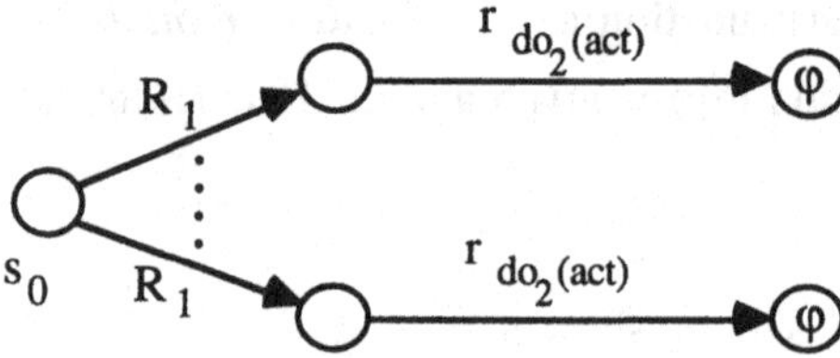

Figure 2.12

Concerning the events e we postulate the following expected properties of the accessibility relation associated with e:

(if) If $s \models \varphi$ then $r_{do_i(\text{if } \varphi \text{ then act}_1 \text{ else act}_2 \text{ fi})}(s) = r_{do_i(act_1)}(s)$ and

If $s \not\models \varphi$ then $r_{do_i(\text{if } \varphi \text{ then } act_1 \text{ else } act_2 \text{ fi})}(s) = r_{do_i(act_2)}(s)$

(while) $r_{do_i(\text{while } \varphi \text{ do act od})}(s) = r_{do_i(\text{if } \neg\varphi \text{ then skip else fail fi})}((r_{do_i(\text{if } \varphi \text{ then act else skip fi})})^*(s))$
where $r^*(s)$ stands for the union of the relations $r^n(s) = r(r(\ldots r(s)\ldots))$, ($n$ applications of r, $n \in \mathbb{N}$).

(;) $r_{do_i(act_1;\, act_2)}(s) = r_{do_i(act_2)}(r_{do_i(act_1)}(s))$

(skip) $r_{do_i(\text{skip})}(s) = s$

(fail) $\forall\, s, t : \mathit{not}\ r_{do_i(\text{fail})}(s, t)$

The (if) clause is straightforward. The clause (;) expresses that first action act_1 is applied in state s, and in the resulting state action act_2. (skip) states that the state remains unchanged after execution of skip. (fail) expresses that the action fail does not yield a successor state.

The clause (while) for the while-statement is slightly non-standard. Moore gives a fixed-point equation, but this is not well-defined unless some theory of the semantics of programming languages is introduced. So we have opted for a different solution here, inspired by the way in which the while-statement is usually treated in dynamic logic. Intuitively, (while) states that we have to repeat the 'body' act for a number of times (repeatedly checking that the 'guard' φ still holds). After this we check whether $\neg\varphi$ holds, in which case we stop. Otherwise, we fail, yielding no successor state. Note that in this way all repetitions that are stopped too early (i.e. φ still holds), do not contribute to the semantics of the while-statement. The only sequence of repetitions that *does* contribute, is the one that is stopped precisely at the moment that $\neg\varphi$ holds. Since this semantics for the while does not distinguish failure (of a guard) from non-termination, it is only correct with respect to *partial* correctness; for total correctness we must be somewhat more sophisticated and use partial orders and fixed points (see e.g. [Bak80]).

In this theory we can express various properties concerning the interplay between knowledge and (performing) actions. We consider briefly a few notions inspired by [Moo85b].

(1) We call an action act_1 *accordant* (or *according to plan*) for agent i if it holds for arbitrary assertion φ that if i knows that φ will hold after execution of the event $do_i(act_1)$, i will know after executing act that φ holds. Formally, this can be expressed by the formula

(K[]) $K_i[do_i(act_1)]\varphi \rightarrow [do_i(act_1)]K_i\varphi$.

In terms of the semantics this corresponds to the following constraint on the accessibility relations:

$$\forall s_1, s_2(r_{do_i(act_1)}(s_1, s_2) \Rightarrow$$

$$(\forall s_3(R_i(s_2, s_3) \Rightarrow \exists s_4(R_i(s_1, s_4) \wedge r_{do_i(act_1)}(s_4, s_3))))).$$

We can illustrate this by Figure 2.13 below.

2.15.1. EXERCISE. Show that in models that satisfy the above constraint the formula (K[]) is valid.

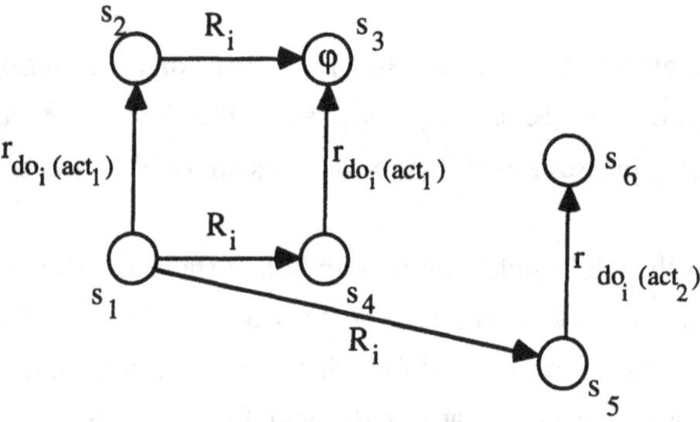

Figure 2.13

Figure 2.13 also shows that the execution of an accordant action may nevertheless have an unexpected influence upon his knowledge, e.g. with respect to other actions: in this example i considers it possible in s_1 that $do_i(act_2)$ is executable (i.e. delivers a next state), that is to say

$$s_1 \not\models K_i[do_i(act_2)]\bot$$

(or, equivalently, $s_1 \models \neg K_i[do_i(act_2)]\bot$); in s_2 (after executing act_1) i knows that $do_i(act_2)$ cannot be executed:

$$s_2 \models K_i[do_i(act_2)]\bot.$$

In case that the agent considers the performance of action act_2 as something favourable or even necessary, the discovery of not being able to perform act_2 any more may come as an unpleasant surprise. So, speaking informally, this says that, even if an action is according to plan, i.e. after performance of the action the agent knows indeed what he knew beforehand that would be the case after performance of the action, he still has to watch out for undesirable and unexpected side-effects of his action: he may also come to know other (possibly unpleasant) things that he did not foresee. (By the way, in the situation of Figure 2.13 this discovery is not that bad, since from the picture we can see that the agent was not able to perform act_2 in s_1 anyway. So, in some sense the performance of act_1 was informative. But by drawing an act_2-arrow from s_1 to some state, this is not true any more: in such a situation the agent was able to perform act_2 in s_1, but no longer in s_2 after performance of act_1.)

(2) An action act is called *informative for agent i with respect to* a formula φ_0, if φ_0 is learnt by agent i by means of executing act, i.e. *after execution of* act it holds that either he knows that φ_0 or he knows that $\neg\varphi_0$. We can express this by the formula

$$[do_i(act)](K_i\varphi_0 \vee K_i\neg\varphi_0).$$

Semantically this can be imposed by the following condition:
With respect to formula φ_0 it holds that

$$\forall\, s_1, s_2(r_{do_i(act)}(s_1, s_2) \Rightarrow (\forall\, s_3(R_i(s_2, s_3) \Rightarrow (s_2 \models \varphi_0 \Leftrightarrow s_3 \models \varphi_0)).$$

So this puts a requirement on the states that are considered possible (epistemically) in s_2. One has to have that s_2 and states considered possible in s_2 assign the same truth value to φ_0:

$$\forall\, s_3\ (R_i(s_2, s_3) \Rightarrow (s_2 \models \varphi_0 \Leftrightarrow s_3 \models \varphi_0)),$$

i.e. after executing act it holds (in s_2) that $\varphi_0 \to K_i\varphi_0$ and $\neg\varphi_0 \to K_i\neg\varphi_0$, i.e. $(\varphi_0 \wedge K_i\varphi_0) \vee (\neg\varphi_0 \wedge K_i\neg\varphi_0)$, i.e. $K_i\varphi_0 \vee K_i\neg\varphi_0$ by the requirement that knowledge implies truth.

An accordant action of which it is known that its execution leads to φ is informative with respect to φ:

2.15.2 PROPOSITION. *If* act *is accordant, and* $K_i[do_i(act)]\varphi$ *holds in a state* s, *then* act *is informative with respect to* φ *in that state.*

PROOF. Since in s both $K_i[do_i(act)]\varphi \to [do_i(act)]K_i\varphi$ and $K_i[do_i(act)]\varphi$ hold, $[do_i(act)]K_i\varphi$ also holds, and thus $[do_i(act)](K_i\varphi \vee K_i\neg\varphi)$. ■

On the other hand, of course, an (trivially accordant) action can also be informative without $K_i[do_i(act)]\varphi$ being true. We see this clearly in the following example (see Figure 2.14). So, for example in Figure 2.14, in s_1, before the execution of act, i does not know whether his performance of act leads to φ_0: $s_1 \models \neg K_i[do_i(act)]\varphi_0$ (since $s_5 \not\models [do_i(act)]\varphi_0$). After his performance of act, i *does* know that φ_0 holds: $s_2 \models K_i\varphi_0$, and thus $s_1 \models [do_i(act)]K_i\varphi_0$, and hence $s_1 \models [do_i(act)](K_i\varphi_0 \vee K_i\neg\varphi_0)$.

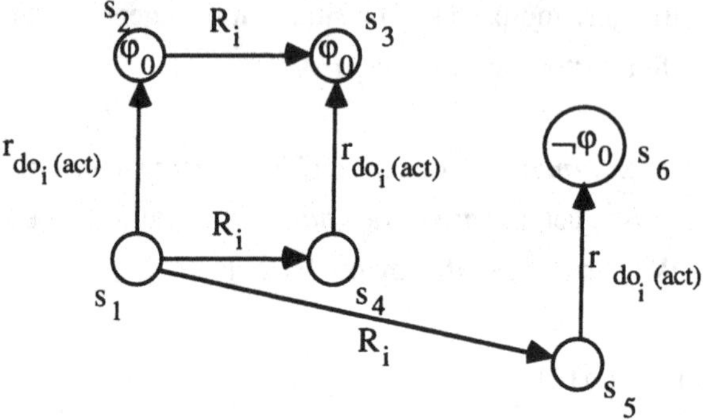

Figure 2.14

Note that informativeness of an action act (with respect to an assertion φ_0) in this sense does not include the requirement that the truth value of φ_0 was not known before the performance of act. For instance, every action is informative with respect to **true**, although **true** was known before execution of the action. One may want to consider the stronger notion of act being *strictly informative for agent i with respect to* φ_0, given by:

(i) act is informative for agent i with respect to φ_0, and

(ii) $\exists s_5(R_i(s_1, s_5) \wedge s_5 \models \varphi) \wedge \exists s_6(R_i(s_1, s_6) \wedge s_6 \not\models \varphi)$, i.e. in s_1 it holds that $\neg K_i\neg\varphi \wedge \neg K_i\varphi$ (that is to say, nothing is known about φ).

One might also consider variants of this notion, which state that *before* execution of act it is not only unknown whether φ holds, but it is also *a priori* unknown to the agent that φ will hold after execution of act, and the truth value of φ becomes known to the agent only *after* execution of act (as we saw in the example of Figure 2.14). In fact, much more can be said about a theory of knowledge and action, e.g. as a framework for reasoning about plans. For instance, there are some criticisms to Moore's approach in the literature, mainly having to do with the theory's lack of expressibility to treat practical problems in planning (e.g. [Mor86]). Here we will not pursue this issue further, having given only some basic idea of an integrated theory of knowledge and action. For further developments in this direction we refer to [HLM94a,b] and [LHM94a,b,c], where we also address the issue of *capabilities* of agents to perform actions (and tests) in this context.

2.16. Graded Modalities in Epistemic Logic (van der Hoek & Meyer)

'Infallible' computers are computers that have multiple processors (usually each from a different company and programmed in a different way using different programming languages) to check and double-check on the results. Decisions are taken on a kind of democratic basis: the results that come up the most as the results of a certain calculation count and are used to make the decision. The idea is just based on statistics: the chance that n independent processors are faulty in the same way is p^n for an already very small probability p. Typically, infallible computers are used in situations where the failure of a computer would have disastrous consequences, such as the stock exchange, certain security situations, and the so-called flying-by-wire (i.e. using a steering computer) of an airplane such as the Airbus A320. Decision Support Systems working on infallible computers, and devices with several input sensors in general, may have knowledge that is source dependent. In this section we will propose an epistemic logic that can deal with knowledge (or perhaps some may prefer the term belief here) that is not absolutely true in all worlds, but may have exceptions in the sense that there are exceptional worlds in which the assertion believed is nevertheless not true, such as in the case of a faulty processor or sensor in the situation described above.

Consider an agent getting its input from three different sources w_1, w_2 and w_3. Suppose furthermore, that two types of information are relevant for this agent, say p and q. All the sources agree on p: they mark p as true. Finally, in w_1 and w_2, q is true, whereas in w_3 it is false. When using 'standard' modal logic to model epistemic logic (as discussed in Chapter 1), one would consider the resources w_i ($i \leq 3$) to be worlds in an $\mathbf{S5}_{(1)}$-Kripke model, and observe that the agent knows p, i.e. Kp holds, but does not know q or $\neg q$, since he considers both alternatives to be possible, i.e. $Mq \wedge M\neg q$ holds.

This is about the limit of the expressibility of standard modal epistemic logic, where the only operators that are available are K and M, to express 'truth in all accessible words' and 'truth in some accessible word', respectively. Since the favourite system for knowledge ($\mathbf{S5}_{(1)}$) may be interpreted on Kripke models in which the accessibility relation is universal (i.e. what we called reduced $\mathbf{S5}_{(1)}$-models in Section 1.7), we may leave out the reference to this relation, so that one is left with a system in which one can associate 'K' with 'all (worlds)' and M with 'some (world)'.

However, in the above example, it might be desirable to be able to express that the agent might have more confidence in q than in $\neg q$. One way to achieve this is to add a qualitative modality '>', enabling the agent to judge ($q > \neg q$), as is done in [vdH91b]. Here, we will take an alternative approach, in which we add quantitative modalities to the language (M_n, $n \in \mathbb{N}$), so that, in the above example, we can describe the agent's point of view in a more precise manner, like for instance the fact that he considers exactly two q-alternatives possible, and exactly one ¬q-alternative.

Actually, adding such 'graded modalities' to the modal language is not new. In 1970, K. Fine was one of the first to study these operators [Fin72] whereas, in the 1980s, they were rediscovered by some Italian logicians ([FC85], [FC88], [dCar88]). While in those contributions the completeness of several graded modal systems was the central theme, a rough investigation in the expressibility and definability of this graded language is to be found in [vdH92b]. An application of those graded modalities, especially of the graded analogue of S5, is established in the area of *generalised quantifiers*, as studied in [HR93].

In [vdHM92c] we showed how the greater expressibility of graded modalities may be used in epistemic logic. Here we give a summary of that paper.

2.16.1. The System Gr(S5)

In this subsection, we introduce our basic language, together with a system for graded epistemic logic. To get some intuition, it may be useful to keep in mind standard modal logic (together with its semantics) for knowledge, in which $K\varphi$ (φ is known) is defined to be true in a Kripke model $(\mathbb{M}, s)$ iff, in all worlds t accessible from s, $(\mathbb{M}, t)$ is a model for φ. Also, $M\varphi$ is defined to be $\neg K \neg \varphi$, which will be true in s iff φ is true in some accessible world t. The intended interpretation of $M_n\varphi$ ($n \in \mathbb{N}$) will be that there are more than n accessible worlds verifying φ. Then, $K_n\varphi$ is true iff at most n accessible worlds refute φ.

In terms of epistemic operators, note that $K_0\varphi$ is equal to $K\varphi$, so that we may interpret K_0 as our (certain) knowledge operator. Generally, $K_n\varphi$ means that the agent reckons with at most n exceptions for φ. Dually, $M_n\varphi$ then means that the agent considers more than n alternatives possible, in which φ is true. Now, what would be the appropriate properties of these 'defeasible' necessity operators? For instance, what kind of introspective properties are desirable? Since there are many possibilities in which our infinitely many operators may be interwoven, as a starting point, we choose that graded modal system, which is known to be sound and complete with respect to **S5**-Kripke models, so that, at least semantically, we will remain on solid ground.

The language $\mathfrak{L}_{\mathbf{grad}}$ is built, in the usual way, from propositional atoms p, q, ... ∈ **P**, using the standard connectives ∧, ∨ , ¬, → and ↔. Moreover, if $\varphi \in \mathfrak{L}_{\mathbf{grad}}$, then so is $M_n\varphi$ ($n \in \mathbb{N}$). From now on, we will assume that $n, m, k \in \mathbb{N}$. We use K_n as an abbreviation for $\neg M_n \neg$. Finally we introduce the abbreviation $M!_n\varphi$, where $M!_0\varphi \equiv K_0\neg\varphi$, $M!_n\varphi \equiv (M_{n-1}\varphi \wedge \neg M_n\varphi)$, if $n > 0$. From the definitions above, it is clear that $M!_n$ means 'exactly n'.

2.16.2. DEFINITION. The system **Gr(S5)** is defined as follows [HR93]. It has rules *modus ponens* and *necessitation*:

(R1) $\vdash \varphi, \vdash \varphi \rightarrow \psi \Rightarrow \vdash \psi$

(R2) $\vdash \varphi \Rightarrow \vdash K_0\varphi$.

It also has the following axioms (for each n, m $\in \mathbb{N}$):

(Gr0) all propositional tautologies

(Gr1) $K_0(\varphi \rightarrow \psi) \rightarrow (K_n\varphi \rightarrow K_n\psi)$

(Gr2) $K_n\varphi \rightarrow K_{n+1}\varphi$

(Gr3) $K_0\neg(\varphi \wedge \psi) \rightarrow ((M!_n\varphi \wedge M!_m\psi) \rightarrow M!_{n+m}(\varphi \vee \psi))$

(Gr4) $\neg K_n\varphi \rightarrow K_0\neg K_n\varphi$

(Gr5) $K_0\varphi \rightarrow \varphi$

Before elaborating on the impact of the axioms on the (meaning of) our intended epistemic reading of the operators, which we will do in the following section, let us pause here for a moment to increase our understanding of the postulates as such. The system with rules (R1) and (R2), axioms (Gr0)—(Gr3) is the graded modal analogue of K, the basic modal system — so let us refer to it as **Gr(K)**. In **Gr(K)**, (Gr1) is a kind of 'generalised K-axiom' (cf. 2.16.1.3), (Gr2) is a way to 'decrease grades' in the possibility operator ((Gr2) is equivalent to $M_{n+1}\varphi \rightarrow M_n\varphi$) and using (Gr3), one can go to 'higher grades'. To ensure that these definitions work out right, we take from [vdH92b] (Proposition 1.9):[1]

2.16.3. PROPOSITION. The following are derivable in **Gr(K)** (and hence in **Gr(S5)**).

(i) $M_n(\varphi \wedge \psi) \rightarrow (M_n\varphi \wedge M_n\psi)$

(ii) $M!_n\varphi \wedge M!_m\varphi \rightarrow \bot \quad (n \neq m)$

(iii) $K_n\neg\varphi \leftrightarrow (M!_0\varphi \,\nabla\, M!_1\varphi \,\nabla \ldots \nabla\, M!_n\varphi)$ (∇ denotes 'exclusive or')

(iv) $\neg M_n(\varphi \vee \psi) \rightarrow \neg M_n\varphi$

(v) $M_{n+m}(\varphi \vee \psi) \rightarrow (M_n\varphi \vee M_m\psi)$

(vi) $M!_n\varphi \wedge M_m\varphi \rightarrow \bot \quad (m \geq n)$

(vii) $M_n(\varphi \wedge \psi) \wedge M_m(\varphi \wedge \neg\psi) \rightarrow M_{n+m+1}\varphi$

(viii) $(K_0\neg(\varphi \wedge \psi) \wedge (M_n\varphi \wedge M_m\psi)) \rightarrow M_{n+m+1}(\varphi \vee \psi)$

PROOF. See Exercise 2.16.3.1. ∎

[1] Since here the use of graded modalities in epistemic logic is the central theme, we present axioms and properties using the K_n-operator. It may be really verified that the axioms presented here are indeed equivalent to those in [vdH92b].

2.16.3.1. EXERCISE. Prove Proposition 2.16.3.

To see the system in action, we will give a derivation of a theorem which is a generalisation of the K-axiom from standard modal logic.

2.16.4. PROPOSITION. The following is derivable in **Gr(K)** (and in **Gr(S5)**).

$$K_n(\varphi \to \psi) \to (K_m\varphi \to K_{n+m}\psi)$$

PROOF. We implicitly use the (**Gr(K)**-derivable) rule of substitution: $\vdash \alpha \leftrightarrow \beta \Rightarrow \vdash \varphi \leftrightarrow \varphi[\alpha/\beta]$. Then, observe that $\vdash$ (Gr1) $\leftrightarrow$ $(K_0(\varphi \to \psi) \to (M_n\varphi \to M_n\psi))$ (*). To see this, note that $\vdash K_0(\varphi \to \psi) \leftrightarrow K_0(\neg\psi \to \neg\varphi)$, and $\vdash (M_n\varphi \to M_n\psi) \leftrightarrow (K_n\neg\psi \to K_n\neg\varphi)$.

1	$\vdash \neg\psi \to (\varphi \wedge \neg\psi) \vee (\neg\varphi \wedge \neg\psi)$	(Gr0)
2	$\vdash K_0(\neg\psi \to (\varphi \wedge \neg\psi) \vee (\neg\varphi \wedge \neg\psi))$	(R0), 1
3	$\vdash M_{n+m}\neg\psi \to M_{n+m}((\varphi \wedge \neg\psi) \vee (\neg\varphi \wedge \neg\psi))$	(*), 2
4	$\vdash M_{n+m}((\varphi \wedge \neg\psi) \vee (\neg\varphi \wedge \neg\psi)) \to (M_m(\varphi \wedge \neg\psi) \vee M_n(\neg\varphi \wedge \neg\psi))$	2.16.3(v)
5	$\vdash ((\varphi \wedge \neg\psi) \to \neg(\varphi \to \psi)) \wedge ((\neg\varphi \wedge \neg\psi) \to \neg\varphi)$	(Gr0)
6	$\vdash M_m(\varphi \wedge \neg\psi) \to M_m\neg(\varphi \to \psi)) \wedge M_n(\neg\varphi \wedge \neg\psi) \to M_n\neg\varphi)$	(R0),1, (Gr1)
7	$\vdash M_{n+m}\neg\psi \to (M_m\neg(\varphi \to \psi) \vee M_n\neg\varphi)$	(Gr1), 3, 4, 6
8	$\vdash \neg M_n\neg(\varphi \to \psi) \to (\neg M_m\neg\varphi \to \neg M_{n+m}\neg\psi)$	(Gr1),7
9	$\vdash K_n(\varphi \to \psi) \to (K_m\varphi \to K_{n+m}\psi)$	def. K_j,8

■

Note that, by taking n = m = 0 in 1.3, we have what is known as the K-axiom in **Gr(S5)**. Together with the presence of the necessitation rule, this means that we have a 'normal' modal logic. In fact, the axioms (Gr4) and (Gr5) are graded versions of euclidicity and reflexivity, respectively. Before making this explicit, we give the definition of the models on which we want to interpret formulas of $\mathcal{L}_{\mathbf{grad}}$.

We now also employ Kripke structures to interpret our graded modal language.

2.16.5. DEFINITION. For a Kripke structure $\mathbb{M} = (S, \pi, R)$ we define the *truth of* φ at s inductively as follows.

(i) $(\mathbb{M}, s) \models p$ iff $\pi(s)(p) = t$, for all $p \in \mathsf{P}$
(ii) $(\mathbb{M}, s) \models \neg\varphi$ iff not $(\mathbb{M}, s) \models \varphi$
(iii) $(\mathbb{M}, s) \models \varphi \vee \psi$ iff $(\mathbb{M}, s) \models \varphi$ or $(\mathbb{M}, s) \models \psi$
(iv) $(\mathbb{M}, s) \models M_n\varphi$ iff $|\{t \in S \mid R(s, t) \text{ and } (\mathbb{M}, t) \models \varphi\}| > n$, $n \in \mathbb{N}$

Here $|W|$ stands for the cardinality of the set $W \subseteq S$.

Note that $(\mathbb{M}, t) \models K_n\varphi$ iff $|\{t \in S \mid R(s, t) \text{ and } (\mathbb{M}, t) \models \neg\varphi\}| \leq n$.

As usual, we say that φ is true in $\mathbb{M}$ at s if $(\mathbb{M}, s) \models \varphi$. If such an $\mathbb{M}$ and exist for φ, we say that φ is satisfiable. φ is true in $\mathbb{M}$ ($\mathbb{M} \models \varphi$) if $(\mathbb{M}, s) \models \varphi$ for all $s \in S$, and φ is called valid ($\models \varphi$) if $\mathbb{M} \models \varphi$ for all $\mathbb{M}$. If $\mathcal{C}$ is a class of models (like $\mathcal{S5}$), $\mathcal{C} \models \varphi$ means that, for all $\mathbb{M} \in \mathcal{C}$, $\mathbb{M} \models \varphi$.

2.16.6. REMARK. The modal operators K and M ($=\neg K\neg$) are special cases of our indexed operators: $K\varphi \equiv K_0\varphi$ and $M\varphi \equiv M_0\varphi$.

We end this introduction into **Gr(S5)** by recalling the following results:

2.16.7. THEOREM (Completeness: [Fin72], [FC88]). *For all* $\varphi \in \mathcal{L}_{\mathbf{grad}}$, $\vdash \varphi$ *iff* $\mathcal{S5} \models \varphi$. ■

Thus $\mathcal{S5}$ also characterizes **Gr(S5)**.

2.16.7.1. EXERCISE. Prove the soundness part of Theorem 2.16.7.

Let us now explain how **Gr(S5)** can serve as an appropriate starting point to study epistemic entities. To start with, (R1) and (Gr0) express that we are dealing with a (extension of propositional, classical) logic: we may use Modus Ponens and reason 'classically' (Gr0). By taking **S5** as a 'standard' system for knowledge, using the observations in the preceding section, we know that we may read $K_0\varphi$ as "φ is known".

Then, (R1), (R2), (Gr0) and (Gr5) find their motivation in the same fashion as the corresponding properties in **S5**, i.e. we may use *modus ponens*, the agent knows all (**Gr(S5)**)-derivable facts, we are dealing with an extension of propositional logic (Gr0) and moreover the agent cannot know facts that are not true (Gr5).

In order to interpret the other axioms, we need to have some intuition about the meaning of $K_n\varphi$. The semantics suggest that this should mean something like "the agent reckons with at most n exceptional situations for φ", or "the agent 'knows-modulo-n-exceptions' φ". What should be clear at least is that, the greater n is in $K_n\varphi$, the less confidence in φ is uttered by that sentence. The latter observation immediately hints at (Gr2), $K_n\varphi \to K_{n+1}\varphi$: if the agent foresees at most n exceptions to φ, he also does so with at most n+1 exceptions. Of course, the generalisation of (Gr3), $K_n\varphi \to \varphi$, for $n > 0$, is *not* valid: if the agent does not know φ for sure, i.e. if he allows for exceptions on φ, he cannot conclude that φ is the case. Thus $K_n\varphi$ expresses a form of 'uncertain knowledge' or 'belief'.

In standard **S5**, we have the axiom $\neg K\varphi \rightarrow K\neg K\varphi$, expressing the agent's negative introspection: if he does not know a given fact, he knows that he does not (this is of course an 'over-idealised' property of knowledge, especially if we have in mind to capture human knowledge). We may write this introspection axiom equivalently as $M\varphi \rightarrow KM\varphi$ (**), saying that the agent has knowledge of what he considers to be possible. Now that we have at hand a more fine-tuned mechanism to distinguish between 'grades' of possibility, it seems straightforward to strengthen the bare (**) to $M_n\varphi \rightarrow K_0M_n\varphi$ (***), saying that the agent knows the fact that he considers more than n φ-situations possible. (***) is equivalent to our axiom (Gr4). Note that (***) is at the same time the 'most general' way to generalise (**): it implies (using (Gr2) m−1 times) for instance $M_n\varphi \rightarrow K_mM_n\varphi$. Moreover, note that (***) is the proper justification for (Gr4): they are equivalent.

In the same spirit, we can interpret (Gr1): if the agent knows that φ implies ψ, then, if he believes there are at most n exceptions to φ, he will not imagine more than n exceptions to ψ, since every exception to ψ will be an exception to φ as well, i.e. $K_0(\varphi \rightarrow \psi) \rightarrow (K_n\varphi \rightarrow K_n\psi)$, or equivalently (cf. 1.3), $K_0(\varphi \rightarrow \psi) \rightarrow (M_n\varphi \rightarrow M_n\psi)$ (Gr1').

Finally, to understand (Gr3), we must recall that $M!_n\varphi$ means that the agent is aware of exactly n possible situations in which φ is true. But then, (Gr3) simply states this property of additivity: if the agent knows that φ and ψ are mutual exclusive events, and he is thinking of exactly n situations in which φ is true and, at the same time, m situations in which ψ is true, altogether he has to reckon with (n + m) situations in which one of these two alternatives is the case.

Up to now, we have been deliberately slightly vague about what $M_n\varphi$ and $M!_n\varphi$ exactly should mean. For instance, is this index n in the scope of the agent's knowledge? That is, does the agent himself know of (exactly) n concrete situations in which φ holds, and if so is it possible that there are still other situations he does not know about where φ holds as well? Or, are these n situations only known to the reasoner using the system at a meta-level, interpreting K_n as some abstract n-degree of knowledge (or perhaps belief, if n > some threshold)? We believe that the logic can be used in all these cases, and will not fix the interpretation.

In a previous section it was argued that the axiom which distinguishes knowledge (K) from belief (B) is $(K\varphi \rightarrow \varphi)$, which is, for belief, substituted by (the weaker) $\neg B\bot$. Now that we have (infinitely) many operators around, we might see how they behave in this respect. In

Gr(S5), $\neg K_n\bot$ (meaning that more than n possibilities are reckoned with) is derivable only for n = 0. If we would have (add) $\neg K_n\bot$, it would mean that the agent does not know too much (for 'big' n); he allows for more than n possibilities. And indeed, as long as the agent considers at least one possible world, it means that he does not know everything ($\neg K\bot$). In case he has no epistemic alternative left his knowledge is all encompassing but inconsistent ($K\varphi$, for any φ). This is, of course, excluded in **S5** (and hence in **Gr(S5)**), but so far, there was no way to exclude this extreme case. Semantically speaking, there was no way to define the class of Kripke models in which each world had more than one successor. It is stressed, that, using graded modalities, a lot of classes of Kripke structures become definable (cf. [vdH92b], [vdHM89]). Another example is an agent considering exactly one alternative (characterised by $M!_1$**true**), having perfect knowledge ($\varphi \leftrightarrow K\varphi$).

2.16.8. Examples

When interpreting K_n as an 'n-degree of knowledge', we recall that, the higher the degree, the less certain the knowledge. In case the number of alternative worlds is *infinite*, we have the infinite chain:

$$K_0\varphi \rightarrow K_1\varphi \rightarrow \ldots \rightarrow K_n\varphi \rightarrow K_{n+1}\varphi \ldots \Rightarrow \ldots M_{n+1}\varphi \rightarrow M_n\varphi \rightarrow \ldots \rightarrow M_1\varphi \rightarrow M_0\varphi.$$

Here, the '$\rightarrow$' denotes logical implication. If, semantically speaking, the number of alternatives is infinite, the sequence is an infinite one, and '$\Rightarrow$' denotes implication in the sense that all M_i-formulas are logically weaker than all the K_j-formulas. We could, as argued above, interpret the strongest formula in this chain ('$K_0\varphi$') as "φ is known", and the weakest ('$M_0\varphi$') as "φ is not impossible" — but even as "φ is believed"; see [vdHM89].

If, however, the number of alternatives is *finite*, say N, we get the sequence

$$K_0\varphi\ (\equiv M_{N-1}\varphi) \rightarrow K_1\varphi\ (\equiv M_{N-2}\varphi) \rightarrow \ldots \rightarrow K_n\varphi\ (\equiv M_{N-n-1}\varphi) \rightarrow \ldots \rightarrow K_{N-1}\varphi\ (\equiv M_0\varphi)$$
$$\rightarrow K_N\varphi\ (\equiv \mathbf{true})$$

In fact, this is the case in the situation of the introduction, where the agent is capable of summing up a complete description of the model by listing a (finite) number of possible situations determined by some finite set of propositional atoms.

We can consider an **S5**-model to be a collection of 'points' (worlds) that can have certain properties (summarised by the atomic formulas that are true in each world), the language $\mathcal{L}_{\mathbf{grad}}$ being sufficiently expressive to sum up the quantitative distribution of those properties over the model. Alternatively, identifying worlds with truth assignments to primitive propositions, as is usual in standard **S5**-models, we can view a **Gr(S5)**-model as a multi-set of truth assignments rather than a set of these as in standard, ungraded modal logic. A special case, of course, is that situations (= truth assignments) occur only once in a description. We shall refer to these models as *simple* (referring to the original Latin meaning of this word). Note that in simple models it is still sensible to use graded modalities, since an assertion (even a primitive proposition) may nevertheless hold in more than one situation, as e.g. p in the situations {p is true, q is false} and {p is true, q is true}.

To be more specific, let us consider a simple example. Suppose we are given that the agent knows $(p \vee q)$ and also $(p \vee r)$. Since q and r are 'independent' propositional atoms, we try to formalise our intuition that the agent has more confidence in p than in q (or r). Given the three propositional atoms, the agent will consider five of the eight (*a priori*) possible worlds: the worlds in which $(\neg p \wedge (\neg q \vee \neg r))$ is true, left out. Thus, assuming that we have a simple model in the sense above, we get $(M!_5\mathbf{true} \wedge M!_4 p \wedge M!_3 q \wedge M!_3 r)$, indicating that indeed p is the 'most frequent' atom.

In epistemic logic, the K-axiom, $K(\varphi \rightarrow \psi) \rightarrow (K\varphi \rightarrow K\psi)$, has been considered a source of *logical omniscience* (see Section 2.5), which, in its turn, yields a too idealistic notion of knowledge (and certainly of belief). It would mean that the agent is capable of closing his knowledge (belief) under logical implication. However, now we allow for weaker notions of knowledge, it appears that the K-axiom is only valid for K_0, which we may consider as a kind of 'ideal' knowledge. Instead of a K-axiom for each K_n, we have the much more realistic (cf. 2.16.4)

(****) $K_n(\varphi \rightarrow \psi) \rightarrow (K_m\varphi \rightarrow K_{n+m}\psi)$, and in particular $K_n(\varphi \rightarrow \psi) \rightarrow (K_n\varphi \rightarrow K_{2n}\psi)$.

This seems very reasonable (suppose $n, m > 0$): if the agent has some confidence that φ implies ψ, and also has some confidence in φ, his conclusion that ψ holds should be stated with even less certitude than that of the two assertions separately. This is also reminiscent of *plausible* [Res76] or *defeasible reasoning* (see Chapter 4), where reasoning under uncertainties is also the topic of investigation. Note that (****) guarantees that, the longer the chain of reasoning with uncertain arguments, the less certain the conclusion that can be stated by the agent.

Note that in the example of the introduction the number of worlds (sources) is fixed. This gives rise to considering $\mathbf{Gr_n(S5)}$, with fixed $n \in \mathbb{N}$, which is obtained from **Gr(S5)** by adding $M!_n\mathbf{true}$. Let $\hat{n} = \min\{m \in \mathbb{N} \mid m \geq \frac{1}{2}n\} - 1$. We may now introduce a modality $\hat{B}$, and express the democratic principle of infallible computers in $\mathbf{Gr_n(S5)}$, with n denoting the number of computers, as $\hat{B}\varphi \leftrightarrow K_{\hat{n}}\varphi$, that is, φ is preferred (is a practical or working belief) iff it is true in more than the half of all sources. This means that there is no logical omniscience in this respect, resembling the local reasoning approach of Fagin & Halpern (Section 2.9).

The modality $\hat{B}$ is not a normal modality like the usual epistemic operators K and B, since, as follows from our discussion about the K-axiom, $\hat{B}(\varphi \to \psi) \to (\hat{B}\varphi \to \hat{B}\psi)$ is not valid. To illustrate this, consider the case with three sensors in which 'it is foggy' (φ) is true according to w_1 and w_2, and 'permission to take off' (ψ) is true according to sensor w_1. Then we have that both $\hat{B}(\varphi \to \psi)$ — since $\varphi \to \psi$ is true in w_1 and w_3 — and $\hat{B}\varphi$ — since φ is true in w_1 and w_2 — are working beliefs, without the conclusion 'permission to take off' being one.

One might contrast this with the situation where *rules* are added to the system (in the form of (certain) knowledge: cf. [MH91a]). For instance, in the above example, $K_0(\varphi \to \neg\psi)$ might be a rule (it is *known* by the decision support system, independently of information the sources supply, that fog is sufficient to deny permission to leave). If now additionally $P\varphi$ would be the case (the systems supposes φ based on the information of its sources), it would take as a working belief $\neg\psi$, i.e. there is no permission to fly! (This follows directly from axiom (A1): $K_0(\varphi \to \neg\psi) \to (K_{\hat{n}}\varphi \to K_{\hat{n}}\neg\psi)$, i.e. $K_0(\varphi \to \psi) \to (P\varphi \to P\neg\psi)$.)

Finally, we mention the use of graded operators to express 'numerical syllogisms' (cf. [AP88]) such as:

$M!_7 d$	exactly 7 days of the week are known
$M!_5(w \wedge d)$	I know 5 of them to be working days
$M_3(s \wedge d)$	at least 4 days are shopping days
-----------------	---
$\therefore M_1(w \wedge s)$	$\therefore$ I know at least 2 days to go working and shopping.

To prove such a conclusion formally, it appears to be worth while to split up the set of formulas in d, w and s, in a set of partitions as follows:

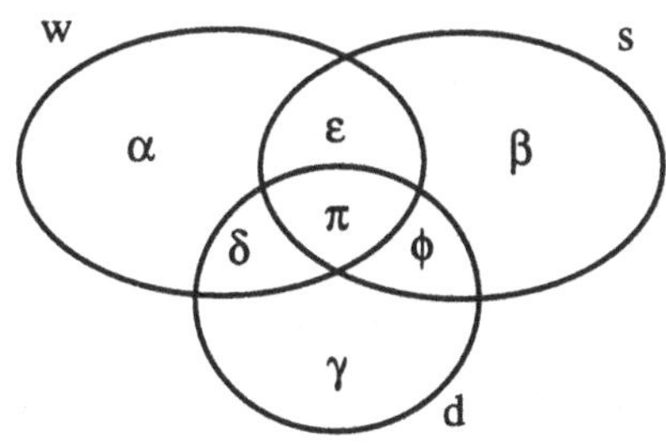

Figure 2.15

For example, it is understood that $w \leftrightarrow (\alpha \vee \delta \vee \varepsilon \vee \pi)$. If $\Gamma = \{\alpha, \beta, \gamma, \delta, \varepsilon, \phi, \pi\}$, then, for all different $x1, \ldots, xk \in \Gamma$ $(2 \leq k \leq 7)$:

(*) $\vdash \neg(x1 \wedge \ldots \wedge xk)$

The formal derivation now reads as follows (note $\Gamma = \{\alpha, \beta, \gamma, \delta, \varepsilon, \phi, \pi\}$):

(1) $M!_7(\gamma \vee \delta \vee \phi \vee \pi)$ translation of 1 (cf. Figure 2.15)

(2) $M!_5(\delta \vee \pi)$ translation of 2

(3) $M_3(\phi \vee \pi)$ translation of 3

(4) $K_0\neg((\phi \vee \pi) \wedge (\gamma \vee \delta))$ definition of Γ

(5) $\neg M_7(\gamma \vee \delta \vee \phi \vee \pi)$ (1), def. M !

(6) $\neg M_3(\gamma \vee \delta)$ 1.2(viii), (3), (4), (5)

(7) $(K_0(\delta \rightarrow (\gamma \vee \delta)) \rightarrow (M_3\delta \rightarrow M_3(\gamma \vee \delta))) \wedge K_0(\delta \rightarrow (\gamma \vee \delta))$ (Gr1') and (Gr0), (R2)

(8) $\neg M_3\delta$ (Gr0), (6), (7)

(9) $M!_0\delta \vee M!_1\delta \vee M!_2\delta$ (8), 1.2(iii)

(10) $\neg M_1\pi \rightarrow (M!_0\pi \vee M!_1\pi)$ 1.2(iii)

(11) $K_0\neg(\delta \wedge \pi) \rightarrow [((M!_0\delta \vee M!_1\delta \vee M!_2\delta) \wedge (M!_0\pi \vee M!_1\pi)) \rightarrow$
$(M!_0(\delta \vee \pi) \vee M!_1(\delta \vee \pi) \vee M!_2(\delta \vee \pi)]$ (Gr0), (Gr3)

(12) $\neg M_1\pi \rightarrow (M!_0(\delta \vee \pi) \vee M!_1(\delta \vee \pi) \vee M!_2(\delta \vee \pi)$ (9)(10)(11), $\vdash K_0\neg(\delta \wedge \pi)$

(13) $[(M!_0(\delta \vee \pi) \vee M!_1(\delta \vee \pi) \vee M!_2(\delta \vee \pi)] \rightarrow \neg M_2(\delta \vee \pi)$ (Gr0), def. M !

(14) $(M!_5(\delta \vee \pi) \rightarrow M_4(\delta \vee \pi)) \wedge (M_4(\delta \vee \pi) \rightarrow M_2(\delta \vee \pi))$ def. M !, (Gr2) twice

(15) $(\neg M_2(\delta \vee \pi) \wedge M!_5(\delta \vee \pi)) \rightarrow \bot$ (Gr0), (14)

(16) $(\neg M_1\pi \wedge M!_5(\delta \vee \pi)) \rightarrow \bot$ (Gr0), (12), (13), (15)

(17) $M_1\pi$ (2), (16)

(18) $M_1(\pi \vee \varepsilon)$ (17), (Gr1')

Since the last formula is equivalent to $M_1(w \wedge s)$, we are done.

Γνωθι σεαυτον

3 KNOWLEDGE AND IGNORANCE

In previous chapters we have looked at the basic theory of knowledge and belief, along with some extensions and applications in the realms of computer science and artificial intelligence. The emphasis in this theory (or rather these theories and applications) was put upon the question of what is known or believed by the agent, and the logical systems that we have seen enable one to derive the knowledge or belief of such an agent.

In this chapter we shall switch the emphasis to the other side of the picture, namely whether one can say something about the ignorance of an agent as well. This is not as easy as it might seem at first glance. Of course, we can employ epistemic logic to express ignorance of the agent as well as its knowledge, e.g. by formulas of the form $\neg K\varphi$, expressing that φ is not known, and that the agent is thus ignorant about the truth of φ. One may even express a kind of total ignorance of the agent about the assertion φ by considering a formula of the form $\neg K\varphi \wedge \neg K\neg\varphi$: the agent does not know φ nor does he know $\neg\varphi$. This is all perfectly fine, but how can one *infer* that the agent knows neither φ nor $\neg\varphi$ in an actual situation? Of course, epistemic logic enables one to derive the agent's ignorance in some cases. For instance, since $Kp \rightarrow \neg K\neg p$ is valid in **S5**, we can derive that, given Kp, the agent knows p, it holds that the agent must be ignorant about $\neg p$ (i.e. $\neg K\neg p$). However, now consider the following situation. Given some base set of (the agent's) knowledge, say $Th_{S5}(\{p\})$, one is tempted to say that the agent knows p but not a different atom q. However, this does not follow in the epistemic logic **S5** or in any other logic that we have seen so far! Epistemic logic in itself does not provide a mechanism to infer this kind of ignorance from what is known. This is not really surprising, since as far as this logic is concerned it might be that the agent also knows *more* than just $Th_{S5}(\{p\})$!

The reason that in the example above we are tempted to say that the agent does not know q, is that we assume implicitly that the base set given, i.e. $Th_{\mathbf{S5}}(\{p\})$, is a *complete* description or representation of the agent in question. This additional information, however, is not included nor represented in regular epistemic logic. Models that satisfy $Th_{\mathbf{S5}}(\{p\})$ may certainly satisfy q as well. So epistemic logic *per se* is not yet fit to treat the ignorance of an agent in the above sense.

Halpern & Moses [HM84b] have proposed a theory of *epistemic states* in which one can express that a base set of knowledge, such as the set $Th_{S5}(\{p\})$ above, is the *only* set of formulas that is known, and so they are able to infer from this what is *not* known to a rational introspective agent by means of a special entailment relation. We shall deal with this theory in Section 3.1.

Very much related, but yet different, is Moore's [Moo84, Moo85a] *autoepistemic logic* (AEL), a logic which is very similar to (regular) epistemic logic and in which one may represent the beliefs (knowledge) of a rational introspective agent by means of so-called extensions of a base set of knowledge. Also in this approach a kind of closure operation on the knowledge based on the base set is present that enables one to reason about the ignorance of an agent.

Finally, we look at Levesque's logic of "All I know" [Lev90], which again has the same flavour as the previous approaches, but contains a special modal operator $O\varphi$ expressing that φ is all that is known. So, where the approach of Halpern & Moses deals with the agent's ignorance by defining a (special) entailment relation, and that of Moore's focusses on the notion of extensions of base sets, the main gain of Levesque's contribution is that it studies minimisation of the agent's knowledge at the object level — rather than at the meta-level.

3.1. Halpern & Moses' Theory of Epistemic States

Suppose that a person or an intelligent system, with positive and negative introspective qualities as we have assumed earlier, claims that he or it *only* knows that $Kp \vee Kq$ (including the logical consequences of this). In this case he (it) must be *dishonest*, for if he (it) only knows that $Kp \vee Kq$, he (it) knows neither Kp nor Kq (since these assertions are not implied by what *is* known). But then it is impossible for him / it to know $Kp \vee Kq$ either, as we shall show more formally later: an honest introspective person cannot know $Kp \vee Kq$ without knowing either Kp or Kq themselves. Note that we do *not* claim that the agent would be dishonest to say that he only knows that $K(p \vee q)$. On the contrary, as we shall see, in this case he is perfectly honest about his ignorance, and can honestly state that he does not know either Kp or Kq.

This issue is relevant for a definition of the epistemic state of an agent. The statement "I only know that φ" is extremely unclear. We saw already that some statements of this kind are logically impossible for honest agents. But we also have other problems. For example, consider the following inference: "If I only know that φ, then I also *know* that I do *not* know that ψ (which has nothing to do with φ)." So I have to be very careful, when I claim to know only some proposition φ!

Halpern & Moses [HM84b] have proposed a very elegant mathematical treatment of this phenomenon, using the notions of a '*stable set*' of epistemic formulas and **S5** Kripke models. In this section we shall briefly discuss some ingredients of their approach. First of all we introduce the notion of a stable set of epistemic formulas.

3.1.1. DEFINITION. A set Σ of epistemic formulas is *stable* if it satisfies the following:

(St 1) all instances of propositional tautologies are elements of Σ

(St 2) if $\varphi \in \Sigma$ and $\varphi \to \psi \in \Sigma$ then $\psi \in \Sigma$

(St 3) $\varphi \in \Sigma \Leftrightarrow K\varphi \in \Sigma$

(St 4) $\varphi \notin \Sigma \Leftrightarrow \neg K\varphi \in \Sigma$

(St 5) Σ is propositionally consistent

Here (St 5) means that from Σ one cannot derive a contradiction ($\bot$) by means of propositional logic (A1, R1) only. By (St 1) and (St 2), this is equivalent to stating that $\bot \notin \Sigma$, which in turn is equivalent to the condition that $\Sigma \neq \mathcal{L}^1_{\mathbf{K}}(\mathbf{P})$.

3.1.1.1. EXERCISE. Let Σ be a stable set. Show that

(i) $\varphi, \psi \in \Sigma \Leftrightarrow \varphi \wedge \psi \in \Sigma$;

(ii) if $\varphi \leftrightarrow \psi$ is a propositional tautology, then $\varphi \in \Sigma \Leftrightarrow \psi \in \Sigma$.

3.1.1.2. EXERCISE. Let w be a 'word' over the alphabet $\{\neg, K\}$. For example, $w = K\neg KK\neg\neg$. If φ is an epistemic formula, we write, in the case of the example, $w\varphi$ to denote $K\neg KK\neg\neg\varphi$.

Prove that if Σ is a stable set of epistemic formulas, then:

(i) $\varphi \in \Sigma \Rightarrow \neg K\neg\varphi \in \Sigma$;

(ii) $\varphi \in \Sigma \Rightarrow w\varphi \in \Sigma$ for all w which contain an even number of $\neg$'s (and an arbitrary number of K's).

A first property of stable sets can be found in [Moo85a]. Recall that by a '*purely propositional* formula' we mean a formula in which there are no occurrences of the K-operator. We denote by Prop(Σ) the subset of Σ that exactly contains all purely propositional formulas, i.e., Prop(Σ) = $\Sigma \cap \mathcal{L}_0$.

3.1.2. PROPOSITION. *A stable set of epistemic formulas is uniquely determined by the purely propositional formulas it contains, i.e. for all stable sets Σ and Σ' we have that:* Prop(Σ) = Prop(Σ') $\Rightarrow \Sigma = \Sigma'$.

This proposition is proved by means of the following lemma:

3.1.3. LEMMA. *Let Σ be a stable set of epistemic formulas. Then it holds for all formulas φ, ψ $\in \mathcal{L}^1_{\mathbf{K}}(\mathbf{P})$ that*

(i) $(K\varphi) \vee \psi \in \Sigma \quad \Leftrightarrow \quad \varphi \in \Sigma$ or $\psi \in \Sigma$;

(ii) $(\neg K\varphi) \vee \psi \in \Sigma \quad \Leftrightarrow \quad \varphi \notin \Sigma$ or $\psi \in \Sigma$.

PROOF. (i) ($\Leftarrow$) If $\psi \in \Sigma$ then also $(K\varphi) \vee \psi \in \Sigma$, since $\psi \rightarrow ((K\varphi) \vee \psi) \in \Sigma$ (tautology, St 1) and Σ is closed under modus onens (St 2). If $\varphi \in \Sigma$, then $K\varphi \in \Sigma$ as well (St 3) and so $(K\varphi) \vee \psi \in \Sigma$ (analogously to the previous case).
($\Rightarrow$) Suppose $(K\varphi) \vee \psi \in \Sigma$. If $\varphi \in \Sigma$, we are done. So now suppose $\varphi \notin \Sigma$. Then $\neg K\varphi \in \Sigma$ (St 4). Since $(\neg K\varphi) \rightarrow \psi$ ($\equiv (K\varphi) \vee \psi)) \in \Sigma$, we obtain $\psi \in \Sigma$ (St 2).

(ii) ($\Leftarrow$) If $\psi \in \Sigma$ then also $(\neg K\varphi) \vee \psi \in \Sigma$ (cf. the proof of part (i) $\Leftarrow$). If $\varphi \notin \Sigma$, then $\neg K\varphi \in \Sigma$ (St 4) and so $(\neg K\varphi) \vee \varphi \in \Sigma$.
($\Rightarrow$) Suppose $(\neg K\varphi) \vee \psi \in \Sigma$. If $\varphi \notin \Sigma$, we are done. Otherwise: $\varphi \in \Sigma$, and so $K\varphi \in \Sigma$ (St 3). Hence, since $(K\varphi \rightarrow \psi) \in \Sigma$, also $\psi \in \Sigma$ (St 2). ■

3.1.3.1. EXERCISE. Let Σ be a stable set. Show that: $\neg K\varphi \vee K\psi \vee \chi \in \Sigma \quad \Leftrightarrow \quad \varphi \notin \Sigma$ or $\psi \in \Sigma$ or $\chi \in \Sigma$.

3.1.3.2. EXERCISE. Let Σ be a stable set and let φ be a formula of the form $K\psi \blacklozenge K\chi$, where $\blacklozenge$ stands for either $\vee$ or $\wedge$. Show that exactly one of φ or $\neg\varphi$ is an element of S.

The proof of Proposition 3.1.2 now proceeds as follows:

PROOF of Proposition 3.1.2. Suppose Σ and Σ' are two stable sets containing exactly the same purely propositional formulas, i.e. $Prop(\Sigma) = Prop(\Sigma')$. We now prove by induction on the depth $|\varphi|$ of the nesting of the K-operators in a formula φ that:

$$\varphi \in \Sigma \Leftrightarrow \varphi \in \Sigma', \qquad (*)$$

yielding $\Sigma = \Sigma'$, as desired. Here the depth $|\varphi|$ is defined by:

$$|p| = 0 \text{ for } p \in \mathbf{P}$$
$$|K\varphi| = |\varphi| + 1$$
$$|\varphi \otimes \psi| = \max(|\varphi|, |\psi|) \text{ for } \otimes = \vee, \wedge, \rightarrow$$
$$|\neg\varphi| = |\varphi|.$$

For purely propositional formulas, which have depth 0, (*) is given. Now assume (*) to hold for all formulas ψ with $|\psi| < n$, and suppose φ is a formula of depth n. By propositional reasoning φ can be proven equivalent to a formula φ' in *conjunctive normal form:* φ' possesses the form $\bigwedge_i \delta_i$, where every δ_i is a disjunction of the form

$$K\psi_1 \vee \ldots \vee K\psi_k \vee \neg K\psi_{k+1} \vee \ldots \vee \neg K\psi_m \vee \rho,$$

$(m \geq k \geq 0)$ with $|\psi_i| < n$ and $|\rho| = 0$. By (St 1) and (St 2) we have (cf. Exercise 3.1.1.1):

$$\varphi \in \Sigma \iff \varphi' \in \Sigma$$

$$(\bigwedge_i \delta_i) \in \Sigma \iff \delta_i \in \Sigma \text{ for every i.}$$

By repeated application of Lemma 3.1.3 we obtain:

$$\delta_i \in \Sigma \iff \rho \in \Sigma \text{ or } \psi_1 \in \Sigma \text{ or } \ldots \text{ or } \psi_k \in \Sigma \text{ or } \psi_{k+1} \notin \Sigma \text{ or } \ldots \text{ or } \psi_m \notin \Sigma.$$

Analogous properties hold regarding Σ'. Since by the induction hypothesis Σ and Σ' contain the same formulas of depth $< n$, we obtain $\delta_i \in \Sigma \iff \delta_i \in \Sigma'$ for all i. Consequently, $\varphi' \in \Sigma \iff \varphi' \in \Sigma'$ and thus $\varphi \in \Sigma \iff \varphi \in \Sigma'$. ■

Now suppose that φ is a formula that describes all the facts that have been learnt by the agent. (If the agent is an intelligent system it is realistic to assume that the set of facts that have been input is finite, so that we can indeed describe these facts by means of a finite conjunction.) What then is the epistemic state of the agent if he "only knows φ"? Clearly, this epistemic state has to contain φ, but what else is contained in it? The state must be *minimal* in some sense. However, unfortunately it is not the minimal stable set with respect to *set inclusion* that contains φ, since different stable sets are incomparable with respect to $\subseteq$, because of the following proposition.

3.1.4. PROPOSITION. *Let Σ, Σ' be stable sets of epistemic formulas such that $\Sigma \subseteq \Sigma'$. Then $\Sigma = \Sigma'$.*

PROOF. Suppose that Σ, Σ' are stable such that $\Sigma \subseteq \Sigma'$ and $\Sigma \neq \Sigma'$. Then there is a formula φ such that $\varphi \in \Sigma'$ and $\varphi \notin \Sigma$. By (St 3) and (St 4) it then holds that $K\varphi \in \Sigma'$ and $\neg K\varphi \in \Sigma$. Since $\Sigma \subseteq \Sigma'$, also $\neg K\varphi \in \Sigma'$, so that both $K\varphi$ and $\neg K\varphi$ are elements of Σ'. This contradicts (St 5). ■

3.1.4.1. EXAMPLE (see Figure 3.1). Let Σ_1 and Σ_2 be stable sets with $\text{Prop}(\Sigma_1) = <\{p\}> \cap \mathcal{L}_0$ and $\text{Prop}(\Sigma_2) = <\{p, q\}> \cap \mathcal{L}_0$. Although $\text{Prop}(\Sigma_1) \subseteq \text{Prop}(\Sigma_2)$, it holds neither that $\Sigma_1 \subseteq \Sigma_2$ nor $\Sigma_2 \subseteq \Sigma_1$, since $\neg Kq \in \Sigma_1$ and $\neg Kq \notin \Sigma_2$, and $Kq \notin \Sigma_1$ and $Kq \in \Sigma_2$.

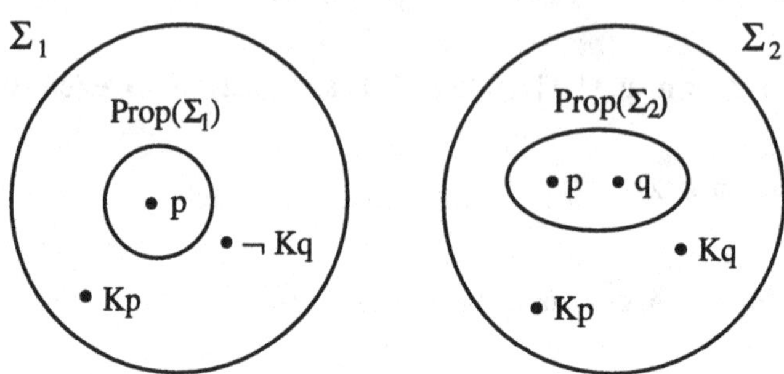

Figure 3.1

So minimisation with respect to set inclusion does not work in order to obtain a characterisation of the epistemic state of only knowing φ. However, by Proposition 3.1.2 a stable set Σ of epistemic formulas (which we identify with an epistemic state) is uniquely determined by the purely propositional formulas that it contains. Now we may try as the 'least' epistemic state containing φ the stable set that contains φ and for which the purely propositional part is the least (with respect to $\subseteq$). Such a least stable set is not defined for every formula φ.

3.1.4.2. EXAMPLE. Consider $\varphi = Kp_1 \vee Kp_2$. Every stable set Σ that contains φ, has to contain either p_1 or p_2, since by Lemma 3.1.3 and (St 3):

$$\varphi \in \Sigma \;\Leftrightarrow\; p_1 \in \Sigma \text{ or } Kp_2 \in \Sigma \;\Leftrightarrow\; p_1 \in \Sigma \text{ or } p_2 \in \Sigma.$$

However, there are stable sets Σ_1, Σ_2 such that

$$\varphi, p_1 \in \Sigma_1, p_2 \notin \Sigma_1,$$

$$\varphi, p_2 \in \Sigma_2, p_1 \notin \Sigma_2.$$

Thus $\text{Prop}(\Sigma_1) \cap \text{Prop}(\Sigma_2)$ contains neither p_1 nor p_2. So there is no stable set Σ that contains φ such that $\text{Prop}(\Sigma) \subseteq \text{Prop}(\Sigma_1)$ and $\text{Prop}(\Sigma) \subseteq \text{Prop}(\Sigma_2)$.

3.1.4.3. DEFINITION. A formula φ is *honest*$_S$ if there is a stable set Σ^φ containing φ such that for all stable sets Σ containing φ it holds that $\text{Prop}(\Sigma^\varphi) \subseteq \text{Prop}(\Sigma)$.

*3.1.4.3.1. EXERCISE. Check whether the following formulas are honest$_S$ ($p, q \in \mathbf{P}$).

(i)	$p \vee Kq$	(iv)	$Kp \vee K\neg p$	(vii)	$Kp \wedge Kq$
(ii)	$p \wedge K\neg q$	(v)	$p \vee q$	(viii)	$p \wedge \neg K\neg q$
(iii)	$\neg Kp \vee Kq \vee r$	(vi)	$Kp \vee \neg Kp$	(ix)	$p \vee \neg K\neg q$

The intention is that Σ^{φ} denotes the stable set representing the epistemic state of the agent who "knows only φ" (if φ is honest). We can also characterise the notion of 'honest$_S$' by means of an **S5**-Kripke model:

3.1.4.4. DEFINITION. Let $\mathbb{M} = \langle S, \pi\rangle$ be an **S5**-Kripke model. Then $K(\mathbb{M})$ is the set of facts that are known in $\mathbb{M}$: $K(\mathbb{M}) = \{\varphi \in \mathcal{L}(\mathbf{P}) \mid \mathbb{M} \models K\varphi\}$ $(= \{\varphi \in \mathcal{L}(\mathbf{P}) \mid \mathbb{M} \models \varphi\})$. $K(\mathbb{M})$ is called the *knowledge in* $\mathbb{M}$ or *theory of* $\mathbb{M}$.

3.1.5. PROPOSITION.
(i) $\varphi \in K(\mathbb{M}) \Leftrightarrow K\varphi \in K(\mathbb{M})$
(ii) $\varphi \notin K(\mathbb{M}) \Leftrightarrow \neg K\varphi \in K(\mathbb{M})$

PROOF. (i) If $\varphi \in K(\mathbb{M})$, then $\mathbb{M} \models \varphi$, i.e. $(\mathbb{M}, s) \models \varphi$ for all $s \in S$. But then by (R2), $(\mathbb{M}, s) \models K\varphi$ for all $s \in S$, i.e. $K\varphi \in K(\mathbb{M})$. Conversely, if $K\varphi \in K(\mathbb{M})$, then by definition $(\mathbb{M}, s) \models K\varphi$ for all $s \in S$. However, by (A3), $(\mathbb{M}, s) \models K\varphi \rightarrow \varphi$. Using (R1) we obtain $(\mathbb{M}, s) \models \varphi$ for all s, i.e. $\varphi \in K(\mathbb{M})$.

(ii) If $\neg K\varphi \in K(\mathbb{M})$, then $K\varphi \notin K(\mathbb{M})$ (since $K(\mathbb{M})$ is consistent) and so by (i) $\varphi \notin K(\mathbb{M})$. If $\varphi \notin K(\mathbb{M})$, then there exists $s_0 \in S$ with $(\mathbb{M}, s_0) \not\models \varphi$.
Suppose also $\neg K\varphi \notin K(\mathbb{M})$, then there is $s_1 \in S$ with $(\mathbb{M}, s_1) \not\models \neg K\varphi$, so there is s_1 with $(\mathbb{M}, s_1) \models K\varphi$. But then, for all $s \in S$, $(\mathbb{M}, s) \models \varphi$, which yields a contradiction. ■

3.1.6. LEMMA. $K(\mathbb{M})$ *is a stable set.*

PROOF. We check whether $K(\mathbb{M})$ satisfies (St 1)—(St 5).
(St 1): Yes, by the fact that every $\mathbb{M}$ satisfies (A1).
(St 2): Yes, by the fact that every $\mathbb{M}$ satisfies (A2). Suppose $\varphi \in K(\mathbb{M})$ and $(\varphi \rightarrow \psi) \in K(\mathbb{M})$. Then $(\mathbb{M}, s) \models K\varphi$ and $(\mathbb{M}, s) \models K(\varphi \rightarrow \psi)$ for all s. By (A2), $(\mathbb{M}, s) \models K(\varphi \rightarrow \psi) \rightarrow (K\varphi \rightarrow K\psi)$, for all s. By the semantics of the propositional connectives this states that, for all s, if $(\mathbb{M}, s) \models K(\varphi \rightarrow \psi)$ and $(\mathbb{M}, s) \models K\varphi$, then $(\mathbb{M}, s) \models K\psi$. Altogether, we may conclude that $\psi \in K(\mathbb{M})$.
(St 3): Yes, by Proposition 3.1.5: $\varphi \in K(\mathbb{M}) \Leftrightarrow K\varphi \in K(\mathbb{M})$.
(St 4): Yes, by Proposition 3.1.5: $\varphi \notin K(\mathbb{M}) \Leftrightarrow \neg K\varphi \in K(\mathbb{M})$.

(St 5): Suppose K(M) is not propositionally consistent. That is to say, from some finite subset $\Gamma \subseteq K(M)$ a contradiction is derivable by using only propositional calculus: $\mathbf{PC} \vdash \Gamma \to \bot$. So also $\mathbf{S5} \vdash \Gamma \to \bot$, since **S5** includes **PC**. By the soundness theorem (1.6.4) for **S5** we now know that $\Gamma \to \bot$ is valid in all **S5**-models. In particular, $M \models \Gamma \to \bot$. However, by $M \models \Gamma$ (because of $M \models K(M)$) we have $M \models \bot$, a contradiction. So K(M) is propositionally consistent. ∎

3.1.6.1. EXERCISE. Show, by devising a suitable Kripke model, that in Exercise 3.1.1.2(i) the converse implication does not hold.

3.1.6.2. EXERCISE. Let M, M' be simple *S5*-models such that $M' \models K(M)$. Show that $K(M') = K(M)$.

3.1.7. DEFINITION. (i) A *valuation* is a function from **P** to {t, f}. The set of all valuations is denoted $\mathbb{W}$.

(ii) We recall the definition of a *simple* **S5**-Kripke model M: an **S5**-Kripke model M is a *simple* **S5**-*model* if $M = \langle S, \pi \rangle$ for some (non-empty) subset $S \subseteq \mathbb{W}$ and π such that $\pi(s)(p) = s(p)$ for all $s \in S$ and $p \in \mathbf{P}$.

(iii) Furthermore, we repeat the definitions of union and intersection of simple **S5**-Kripke models. If $M_1 = \langle S_1, \pi_1 \rangle$ and $M_2 = \langle S_2, \pi_2 \rangle$ are two simple models, their union is defined as: $M_1 \cup M_2 = \langle S_1 \cup S_2, \pi_1 \cup \pi_2 \rangle$, where $(\pi_1 \cup \pi_2)(s) = \pi_1(s)$ if $s \in S_1$, and $= \pi_2(s)$, if $s \in S_2$ (cf. Section 1.7.) Likewise, their intersection is defined as: $M_1 \cap M_2 = \langle S_1 \cap S_2, \pi_1 \cap \pi_2 \rangle$, where $(\pi_1 \cap \pi_2)(s) = \pi_1(s)$ $(= \pi_2(s))$, if $s \in S_1 \cap S_2$. Moreover, we define the subset relation by: $M_1 \subseteq M_2$ iff $S_1 \subseteq S_2$.

3.1.7.1. EXERCISE. Let M_1, M_2 be simple models such that $M_1 \subseteq M_2$.

(i) Prove $\mathrm{Prop}(K(M_1)) \supseteq \mathrm{Prop}(K(M_2))$.

(ii) Show by giving a counter-example that $K(M_1) \supseteq K(M_2)$ does not need to hold.

3.1.7.2. EXERCISE. Let M_1, M_2 be simple models. Prove that:

(i) $\mathrm{Prop}(K(M_1 \cup M_2)) = \mathrm{Prop}(K(M_1)) \cap \mathrm{Prop}(K(M_2))$

(ii) $\mathrm{Prop}(K(M_1 \cap M_2)) \supseteq \mathrm{Prop}(K(M_1)) \cup \mathrm{Prop}(K(M_2))$ (Furthermore, show that the converse inclusion does not hold.)

In what follows we will assume that **S5**-models are simple. This is justified by Propositions 1.7.2 and 1.7.5, and the discussion following them, in which we have seen that it is sufficient to consider **S5**-models with the property that all states with the same truth assignment are identified. So note again that a simple **S5**-model $\langle S, \pi \rangle$ is completely determined by the set S alone!

3.1.8. PROPOSITION. *Every stable set* Σ *of epistemic formulas determines an* **S5**-*Kripke model* $\mathbb{M}_\Sigma$ *for which it holds that* $\Sigma = K(\mathbb{M}_\Sigma)$. *Moreover, if* **P** *is a finite set, then* $\mathbb{M}_\Sigma$ *is the unique* **S5**-*Kripke model with this property.*

PROOF. Let $S = \{s \in \mathbb{W} \mid s \models Prop(\Sigma)\}$. Since Σ is propositionally consistent, S is non-empty. Now consider the (simple) model $\mathbb{M}_\Sigma = \langle S, \pi\rangle$. By Lemma 3.1.6 $K(\mathbb{M}_\Sigma)$ is a stable set. From the definitions and the stability of Σ it follows immediately that $Prop(K(\mathbb{M}_\Sigma)) = Prop(\Sigma)$ (Exercise 3.1.8.1). So by Proposition 3.1.2 this implies that $\Sigma = K(\mathbb{M}_\Sigma)$.

Now assume **P** is finite, say $\mathbf{P} = \{p_1, ..., p_n\}$. To show uniqueness of $\mathbb{M}_\Sigma$ it is sufficient to show that if $\mathbb{M}$ and $\mathbb{M}'$ are two **S5**-Kripke models with $\mathbb{M} \neq \mathbb{M}'$, then $K(\mathbb{M}) \neq K(\mathbb{M}')$. So suppose $\mathbb{M} = \langle S, \pi\rangle$ and $\mathbb{M}' = \langle S', \pi'\rangle$ such that $\mathbb{M} \neq \mathbb{M}'$. Since in simple **S5**-models states are identified with (their) truth assignments, we may assume that $S \neq S'$. Without loss of generality we may assume that there is a state s_0 with $s_0 \in S$ and $s_0 \notin S'$. Now let q_0 be the propositional formula that describes state s_0 completely: $q_0 = q_1 \wedge ... \wedge q_n$, where $q_i = p_i$ if $\pi(s_0)(p_i) = \mathbf{t}$ and $q_i = \neg p_i$ if $\pi(s_0)(p_i) = \mathbf{f}$.

Now it holds that $\neg q_0 \in K(\mathbb{M}')$ because $s_0 \notin S'$ (since, for all $s \in S'$, $(\mathbb{M}', s) \not\models q_0$ and so $(\mathbb{M}', s) \models \neg q_0$). However, since $(\mathbb{M}, s_0) \models q_0$, it does *not* hold that $(\mathbb{M}, s) \not\models q_0$ for all $s \in S$, i.e. *not* $(\mathbb{M}, s) \models \neg q_0$ for all $s \in S$, i.e. $\neg q_0 \notin K(\mathbb{M})$. Thus $K(\mathbb{M}) \neq K(\mathbb{M}')$. ■

3.1.8.1. EXERCISE. (Cf. Proposition 3.1.8.) Prove $Prop(K(\mathbb{M}_\Sigma)) = Prop(\Sigma)$.

*3.1.8.2. EXERCISE (based on an idea of Jan Willem Klop). In this exercise we will show that the finiteness condition in Proposition 3.1.8 is necessary. Let **P**, the set of primitive propositions, be countably infinite: $\mathbf{P} = \{p_n \mid n \geq 1\}$. Now consider the following two simple models. $\mathbb{M}_1 = \langle \mathbb{N}, \pi_1\rangle$, $\mathbb{M}_2 = \langle \mathbb{N} \cup \{\infty\}, \pi_2\rangle$. For all $p_i \in \mathbf{P}$, $i, j \in \mathbb{N}$, we define $\pi_1(j)(p_i) = \pi_2(j)(p_i) = \mathbf{t}$ if and only if $i \geq j$ (so the atom p_i is true 'from world i on'); and moreover $\pi_2(\infty)(p_i) = \mathbf{t}$ for all i. We define $\infty \geq n$ for all $n \in \mathbb{N}$.

(i) Let MI (for *maximal index)* be defined on formulas as $MI(p_i) = i$, $MI(\varphi \otimes \psi) = \max\{MI(\varphi), MI(\psi)\}$ for any of the connectives $\otimes \in \{\wedge, \vee, \rightarrow, \leftrightarrow\}$ and $MI(\surd\varphi) = MI(\varphi)$ for $\surd \in \{K, \neg\}$.
Show that, for all $i \in \mathbb{N}$, all φ with $MI(\varphi) \leq i$, and all $x, y \geq i$: $((\mathbb{M}_2, x) \models \varphi \Leftrightarrow (\mathbb{M}_2, y) \models \varphi)$.

(ii) Prove that, for all φ: $(\mathbb{M}_2, \infty) \models \varphi \Rightarrow \exists n \in \mathbb{N}: (\mathbb{M}_2, n) \models \varphi$.

(iii) Prove that, for all φ, all $n \in \mathbb{N}$: $((\mathbb{M}_1, n) \models \varphi \Leftrightarrow (\mathbb{M}_2, n) \models \varphi)$.

(iv) Prove that $K(\mathbb{M}_1) = K(\mathbb{M}_2)$.

(v) Conclude that the finiteness condition in Proposition 3.1.8 is really necessary.

3.1.8.3. EXERCISE. Suppose that **P** is finite, and let $\mathbb{M}, \mathbb{M}'$ be simple *S5*-models. Prove that: $\mathbb{M} = \mathbb{M}' \Leftrightarrow K(\mathbb{M}) = K(\mathbb{M}')$.

3.1.8.4. EXERCISE (cf. Exercise 3.1.6.2). Assume that **P** is finite and let $\mathbb{M}$, $\mathbb{M}'$ be simple *S5*-models such that $\mathbb{M}' \models K(\mathbb{M})$. Show that $\mathbb{M}' = \mathbb{M}$.

3.1.9. COROLLARY. *Stable sets are closed under* **S5***-consequences.*

PROOF. Let Σ be a stable set and let $\mathbf{S5} \vdash \Gamma \to \varphi_0$ for some finite $\Gamma \subseteq \Sigma$. We have to prove that $\varphi_0 \in \Sigma$. Associated with Σ there is an **S5**-Kripke model $\mathbb{M}_\Sigma = \langle \Sigma, \pi \rangle$ such that $\Sigma = K(\mathbb{M}_\Sigma) = \{\varphi \mid \mathbb{M}_\Sigma \models \varphi\}$. Since **S5** is sound with respect to (simple) **S5**-Kripke models, the implication $\Gamma \to \varphi_0$ is valid in any **S5**-model $\mathbb{M}$. In particular:

$$\mathbb{M}_\Sigma \models \Gamma \to \varphi_0.$$

Since also $\mathbb{M}_\Sigma \models \Gamma$ we have that $\mathbb{M}_\Sigma \models \varphi_0$, i.e. $\varphi_0 \in K(\mathbb{M}_\Sigma) = \Sigma$. ■

This implies that in the definition of a stable set (St 1) can be replaced by

(St 1') Σ contains all instances of **S5**-valid formulas.

Which Kripke model is associated with the epistemic state of an agent that "only knows φ"? From Exercise 3.1.7.1 we know the bigger the model the less is known. Therefore we take the union of all (simple) **S5**-models $\mathbb{M} = \langle S, \pi \rangle$ in which it holds that $K\varphi$:

$$\mathbb{M}_\varphi = \bigcup \{\mathbb{M} \mid \mathbb{M} \models K\varphi\} \; (= \bigcup \{\mathbb{M} \mid \mathbb{M} \models \varphi\})$$

It appears that this 'greatest model' is not always a model of $K\varphi$, i.e. not always $\mathbb{M}_\varphi \models K\varphi$! So we define:

3.1.10. DEFINITION. φ is *honest*$_{\mathbb{M}}$ $\Leftrightarrow \varphi \in K(\mathbb{M}_\varphi)$.

3.1.10.1. EXAMPLE. $\varphi = Kp \vee Kq$ is not honest$_{\mathbb{M}}$.
PROOF. Consider the models

$$\mathbb{M}_1 = \{s \mid \pi(s)(p) = \mathbf{t}\},$$
$$\mathbb{M}_2 = \{s \mid \pi(s)(q) = \mathbf{t}\}.$$

Clearly, $(\mathbb{M}_1, s) \models K\varphi$ for all s and $(\mathbb{M}_2, s) \models K\varphi$ for all s. Now take

$$\mathbb{M}_3 = \mathbb{M}_1 \cup \mathbb{M}_2.$$

M_3 is a submodel of M_φ and so $Prop(K(M_3)) \supseteq Prop(K(M_\varphi))$. Since p, q $\notin Prop(K(M_3))$, also p, q $\notin Prop(K(M_\varphi))$, i.e. $M_\varphi \nvDash p$ and $M_\varphi \nvDash q$. Hence, by Proposition 3.1.5, $M_\varphi \vDash \neg Kp$ and $M_\varphi \vDash \neg Kq$. Consequently, $M_\varphi \vDash \neg Kp \wedge \neg Kq$, i.e. $M_\varphi \vDash \neg\varphi$. So $M_\varphi \nvDash \varphi$. ■

3.1.10.2. EXERCISE. Show that every consistent purely propositional formula is $honest_M$.

3.1.10.3. EXERCISE. Check whether the formulas from Exercise 3.1.4.3.1 are $honest_M$.

3.1.11. THEOREM. *For any epistemic formula φ it holds that:*

(i) *φ is* $honest_S \Leftrightarrow$ *φ is* $honest_M$,

(ii) *φ is* $honest_S \Rightarrow K(M_\varphi) = \Sigma^\varphi$.

(iii) *Let* **P** *be finite. Then: φ is* $honest_S \Rightarrow M_{\Sigma^\varphi} = M_\varphi$.

PROOF. (i) ($\Leftarrow$) φ is $honest_M \Rightarrow \varphi \in K(M_\varphi) \Rightarrow M_\varphi \vDash K\varphi$. Now

$$M_\varphi = \bigcup \{M \mid M \vDash K\varphi\}$$

and thus M_φ is itself the largest M that satisfies $M \vDash K\varphi$; that is to say $\varphi \in K(M_\varphi)$ and $M_\varphi \supseteq M$ for all M with $\varphi \in K(M)$. We know that K(M) and $K(M_\varphi)$ are stable. Now define

$$\Sigma^\varphi = K(M_\varphi).$$

Then $\varphi \in \Sigma^\varphi$ (= $K(M_\varphi)$) and $Prop(K(M_\varphi)) \subseteq Prop(K(M))$ for all M with $\varphi \in K(M)$ (since $M \subseteq M_\varphi$). Now we also have that $Prop(\Sigma^\varphi) \subseteq Prop(\Sigma)$ for all stable Σ with $\varphi \in \Sigma$, since by Proposition 3.1.8 we know that every stable set Σ is equal to K(M) for some S5-model M. Thus Σ^φ is a set Σ with the property that $\varphi \in \Sigma$ and $Prop(\Sigma^\varphi)$ is the least set under the condition $\varphi \in \Sigma$.

($\Rightarrow$) φ is $honest_S$, i.e. there is a set Σ^φ which is a stable set Σ with the property that $\varphi \in \Sigma$ and such that $Prop(\Sigma^\varphi)$ is the least set under the condition $\varphi \in \Sigma$. Consider $M_\varphi = \bigcup\{M \mid M \vDash K\varphi\} = \bigcup\{M \mid \varphi \in K(M)\}$. We have to prove that φ is $honest_M$, i.e. $\varphi \in K(M_\varphi)$, i.e. $M_\varphi \vDash K\varphi$. By Exercise 3.1.7.2. it holds that:

$$Prop\ K(\bigcup_i M_i) = \bigcap_i Prop\ K(M_i)$$

for any sequence of models $(M_i)_i$. So in particular

$$Prop\ K(M_\varphi) = \bigcap \{Prop\ K(M) \mid M \vDash K\varphi\} = \bigcap \{Prop\ K(M) \mid \varphi \in K(M)\}.$$

We know that there is a stable set Σ^φ such that

$$\forall\Sigma : \Sigma \text{ stable } \& \ \varphi \in \Sigma \ \Rightarrow \ \mathrm{Prop}(\Sigma^\varphi) \subseteq \mathrm{Prop}(\Sigma).$$

Since K(M) is stable for every M, $\mathrm{Prop}(\Sigma^\varphi) \subseteq \mathrm{Prop}(K(M))$ holds for all M such that $\varphi \in K(M)$. Hence

$$\mathrm{Prop}(\Sigma^\varphi) \subseteq \bigcap\{\mathrm{Prop}\ K(M) \mid \varphi \in K(M)\}.$$

On the other hand by Proposition 3.1.8 it holds that $\Sigma^\varphi = K(M_{\Sigma^\varphi})$ for some model M_{Σ^φ}. Note that $\varphi \in \Sigma^\varphi = K(M_{\Sigma^\varphi})$; so M_{Σ^φ} has itself the property that $\varphi \in K(M_{\Sigma^\varphi})$ (i.e., $M_{\Sigma^\varphi} \models K\varphi$). So now

$$\begin{aligned}
&\bigcap\{\mathrm{Prop}\ K(M) \mid \varphi \in K(M)\} \subseteq \\
&\mathrm{Prop}(\ K(M_{\Sigma^\varphi})) = \\
&\mathrm{Prop}(\Sigma^\varphi) \subseteq \\
&\bigcap\{\mathrm{Prop}\ K(M) \mid \varphi \in K(M)\}.
\end{aligned}$$

Hence:

$$\begin{aligned}
&\bigcap\{\mathrm{Prop}\ K(M) \mid \varphi \in K(M)\} = \\
&\mathrm{Prop}(\ K(M_{\Sigma^\varphi})) = \\
&\mathrm{Prop}(\Sigma^\varphi).
\end{aligned}$$

Since stable sets Σ are uniquely determined by $\mathrm{Prop}(\Sigma)$, we know $\Sigma^\varphi = K(M_\varphi)$. Consequently, $\varphi \in (\Sigma^\varphi =)\ K(M_\varphi)$.

(ii) Suppose that φ is honest$_S$. In the proof of '(i)$\Rightarrow$' we have seen that in this case $\Sigma^\varphi = K(M_\varphi)$.

(iii) Suppose again that φ is honest$_S$. By (ii), $K(M_\varphi) = \Sigma^\varphi$, and by and Proposition 3.1.8, $K(M_{\Sigma^\varphi}) = \Sigma^\varphi$. By the second part of Proposition 3.1.8, we obtain $M_{\Sigma^\varphi} = M_\varphi$. ■

The theorem says that both notions of honesty, namely honest$_S$ and honest$_M$, are *a posteriori* the same. Therefore, from now on we may refer to the notion of 'honest' without mentioning a subscript S or M. From this theorem we obtain a few corollaries, which have to do with objective (i.e. non-modal) formulas.

3.1.12. COROLLARY. *Let φ be an objective formula, then φ is honest.*

PROOF. By Theorem 3.1.11 it is sufficient to prove that an objective formula is honest$_M$. But this obvious, since clearly for an objective formula φ it holds that the 'greatest model' $\mathbb{M}_\varphi = \bigcup\{\mathbb{M} \mid \mathbb{M} \models \varphi\}$ satisfies φ again. ■

Furthermore, we have a nice property concerning the non-modal kernel of the stable set associated with only knowing the objective formula φ. (Recall that $\models_{prop}$ stands for classical propositional entailment and Th_{prop} stands for the classical propositional theory: $Th_{prop}(\varphi) = \{\psi \mid \varphi \models_{prop} \psi\}$.)

3.1.13. COROLLARY. *Let φ be an objective formula, then:*

$$Prop(\Sigma^\varphi) = Th_{prop}(\varphi) \cap \mathcal{L}_0.$$

PROOF. Since φ is objective and $\varphi \in \Sigma^\varphi$, we have that $\varphi \in Prop(\Sigma^\varphi)$. Since Σ^φ is closed under classical propositional entailment, we have that $Th_{prop}(\varphi) \subseteq Prop(\Sigma^\varphi)$.

Conversely, suppose that $\psi \in Prop(\Sigma^\varphi)$. We have to show that $\psi \in Th_{prop}(\varphi)$, i.e. $\varphi \models_{prop} \psi$, i.e. for all classical valuations w, $w \models \varphi \Rightarrow w \models \psi$. Since $\psi \in Prop(\Sigma^\varphi) =$ (Theorem 3.1.11) $Prop(K(\mathbb{M}_\varphi))$, we have that $\mathbb{M}_\varphi \models \psi$. Since $\mathbb{M}_\varphi = \bigcup\{\mathbb{M} \mid \mathbb{M} \models \varphi\} =$ (since φ is objective) $\{w \mid w \models \varphi\}$, we obtain what we had to prove, namely $\{w \mid w \models \varphi\} \models \psi$. ■

3.1.13.1. EXERCISE. Let φ and ψ be objective. Show that: $\psi \in \Sigma^\varphi \Leftrightarrow\ \models \varphi \to \psi$.

As we have seen in Example 3.1.10.1, honesty is clearly not preserved by disjunction. (Both Kp and Kq are honest, but Kp $\vee$ Kq is not.) Moreover, honesty is not preserved by conjunction either, witness the following example: both p and $\neg$Kp are honest, while the conjunction p $\wedge$ $\neg$Kp is not honest.

3.1.14. EXERCISE. Check that both p and $\neg$Kp are honest, while p $\wedge$ $\neg$Kp is not.

*3.1.15. REMARK. In the case of more than one agent (St 1) is not strong enough, as becomes apparent from the following example.

3.1.15.1. EXAMPLE. Suppose i knows that j does not know p. Then i's knowledge state Σ_i contains $\neg K_j p$. Since i is supposed to know that j can perform introspection, i knows that j knows that j does not know p. So we expect the following to hold:

$$\neg K_j\varphi \in \Sigma_i \Leftrightarrow K_j\neg K_j\varphi \in \Sigma_i.$$

However, this is implied by neither (St 1) nor (St 4) (i's *own* introspection). Thus (St 1) needs to be strengthened to (St 1'): Σ_i *contains all* **S5**-*theorems*. This (together with (St 2)) yields the desired result. Note that in the case of a single agent (St 1') is equivalent to (St 1), in the context of the rest of the requirements (St 2)—(St 5) for a stable set.

A set satisfying (St 1'), (St 2), ... , (St 5) is called *stable with respect to* i or i-*stable*. There are in the multi-agent case additional complications, however. To start with, an i-stable set is no longer uniquely determined by its purely propositional kernel, and not even by the K_i-free formulas (cf. [HM84b]).

By the complication above it becomes totally unclear how to characterise an epistemic state in which "i only knows φ". Furthermore, a notion like honest$_S$ becomes unclear, in which we try to approach things in a more refined manner.

In spite of the above problems it appears to be possible to define a notion of honest$_M$ by the use of Kripke models ($\mathcal{S5}_{(m)}$, $m > 1$). (To be able to unite $\mathbf{S5}_{(m)}$-Kripke models one needs to be extra careful, since this is not as trivial as in the single-agent case.) For this we refer again to [HM84b].

We now return to the much simpler case of a single agent.

3.1.16. Epistemic States and Entailment

On the basis of epistemic states Halpern & Moses [HM84b] define an entailment relation $\mathrel{|\!\!\sim}$ associated with the agent, as follows. Let φ be honest. Then we define

$$\varphi \mathrel{|\!\!\sim} \psi \Leftrightarrow \psi \in \Sigma^\varphi.$$

Please note that this definition is only meaningful if φ is honest, since Σ^φ is not defined otherwise.

The relation $\varphi \mathrel{|\!\!\sim} \psi$ indicates which consequences can be derived by the agent from an honest formula φ (i.e. a formula that characterises an epistemic state). This is possible, since φ describes exactly what is known to the agent and what is not. In particular, we have:

3.1.17. PROPOSITION. *For any honest formula* φ, $\varphi \mathrel{|\!\!\sim} \varphi$.

PROOF. Immediate, since by definition $\varphi \in \Sigma^{\varphi}$. ■

From Theorem 3.1.11 (ii) we now obtain immediately :

3.1.18. COROLLARY. $\varphi \vdash \psi \iff M_\varphi \models K\psi$ ($\iff M_\varphi \models \psi$). ■

This corollary gives us a semantical characterisation of the entailment relation $\vdash$.

3.1.19. EXAMPLE. Let p and q be two distinct primitive propositions. Then the following hold.

(i) $p \vdash p$
(ii) $p \vdash p \vee q$
(iii) $p \vdash Kp$
(iv) $p \vdash \neg Kq$
(v) $p \vdash K(p \vee q)$
(vi) $p \wedge (p \rightarrow q) \vdash Kq$
(vii) $p \vee q \vdash K(p \vee q)$
(viii) $p \vee q \vdash \neg Kp \wedge \neg Kq$
(ix) $p \wedge q \vdash Kp \wedge Kq$
(x) $p \rightarrow q \vdash \neg Kp \wedge \neg Kq \wedge K(p \rightarrow q)$
(xi) $K(p \rightarrow q) \vdash Kp \rightarrow Kq$

3.1.19.1. EXERCISE. (i) Prove the examples above.
(ii) Does $p \vee \neg p \vdash Kp \wedge \neg KKp$ hold? Explain your answer.

3.1.19.2. EXERCISE. (i) Let α be an honest formula. Check whether $\alpha \vdash \beta$ implies the honesty of β.
(ii) Prove that for each honest formula α it holds that $\alpha \vdash (K\varphi) \vee \psi \iff \alpha \vdash \varphi$ or $\alpha \vdash \psi$.

In general, honesty is not preserved by $\vdash$ (cf. Exercise 3.1.19.2(i)). However, we *do* have preservation in the sense that the conclusion in conjunction with the (honest) premise is again honest:

3.1.20. PROPOSITION. *Let φ be honest. Then $\varphi \vdash \psi$ implies that $\varphi \wedge \psi$ is honest.*

PROOF. Since $\varphi \vdash \psi$, by Corollary 3.1.18 we have that $M_\varphi \models \psi$. i.e. $\bigcup \{M \mid M \models \varphi\} \models \psi$. So we have that $\forall M\ [M \models \varphi \Rightarrow M \models \psi]$. But then also $\forall M\ [M \models \varphi \Rightarrow M \models \varphi \wedge \psi]$. Obviously, also $\forall M\ [M \models \varphi \wedge \psi \Rightarrow M \models \varphi]$. So $\forall M\ [M \models \varphi \iff M \models \varphi \wedge \psi]$. Consequently, $M_{\varphi\wedge\psi} = \bigcup \{M \mid M \models \varphi \wedge \psi\} = \bigcup \{M \mid M \models \varphi\} = M_\varphi \models \psi$. Moreover, since

$\varphi \vdash \varphi$, also by Corollary 3.1.18, $M_\varphi \models \varphi$. Altogether we obtain $M_{\varphi\wedge\psi} = M_\varphi \models \varphi \wedge \psi$, i.e. $\varphi \wedge \psi$ is honest. ∎

Note that the proof of the Proposition 3.1.20 yields a corollary:

3.1.20.1. COROLLARY. *Let φ be honest. Then $\varphi \vdash \psi$ implies that* $M_{\varphi\wedge\psi} = M_\varphi$. ∎

3.1.21. DEFINITION. Let Γ be a finite set of epistemic formulas, and φ an epistemic formula. Then we define $\Gamma \vdash \varphi$ iff $\Gamma^* \vdash \varphi$ (i.e. $\varphi \in \Sigma^{\Gamma^*}$), where Γ^* stands for the conjunction of the formulas in Γ. We call the set Γ honest if Γ^* is an honest formula.

Next we prove a useful property of $\vdash$:

3.1.22. LEMMA. *If $\Gamma \vdash \varphi$ then* $\Sigma^{\Gamma^*\wedge\varphi} = \Sigma^{\Gamma^*}$. (Note that — under the implicit assumption that Γ is honest — by Proposition 3.1.20 also $\Gamma^* \wedge \varphi$ is honest, so $\Sigma^{\Gamma^*\wedge\varphi}$ is well-defined.)

PROOF. Suppose $\Gamma \vdash \varphi$. So $\varphi \in \Sigma^{\Gamma^*}$ (#). By definition,

(1) $\Gamma^* \wedge \varphi \in \Sigma^{\Gamma^*\wedge\varphi}$;

(2) for all stable sets Σ with $\Gamma^* \wedge \varphi \in \Sigma$ it holds that $\text{Prop}(\Sigma^{\Gamma^*\wedge\varphi}) \subseteq \text{Prop}(\Sigma)$.

Also by definition,

(1') $\Gamma^* \in \Sigma^{\Gamma^*}$;

(2') for all stable sets Σ' with $\Gamma^* \in \Sigma'$ it holds that $\text{Prop}(\Sigma^{\Gamma^*}) \subseteq \text{Prop}(\Sigma')$.

By (#) and (1'), $\Gamma^* \wedge \varphi \in \Sigma^{\Gamma^*}$, since stable sets are closed under logical consequence.
Thus, by (2), $\text{Prop}(\Sigma^{\Gamma^*\wedge\varphi}) \subseteq \text{Prop}(\Sigma^{\Gamma^*})$.
By (1) and the fact that $\models \Gamma^* \wedge \varphi \to \Gamma^*$, $\Gamma^* \in \Sigma^{\Gamma^*\wedge\varphi}$, since stable sets are closed under logical consequence. So by (2'), $\text{Prop}(\Sigma^{\Gamma^*}) \subseteq \text{Prop}(\Sigma^{\Gamma^*\wedge\varphi})$.
Hence, $\text{Prop}(\Sigma^{\Gamma^*\wedge\varphi}) = \text{Prop}(\Sigma^{\Gamma^*})$. Consequently, by Proposition 3.1.2, $\Sigma^{\Gamma^*\wedge\varphi} = \Sigma^{\Gamma^*}$. ∎

3.1.22.1. EXERCISE. Give a proof of Lemma 3.1.22 using Corollary 3.1.20.1.

The entailment relation $\vdash$ possesses a peculiar property: *when we strengthen the premises, it may be that a formula that was derivable becomes not derivable.*

3.1.23. EXAMPLE.

(i) $p \vdash \neg Kq$

(ii) $p \wedge q \vdash Kq$

(iii) *not* $p \wedge q \vdash \neg Kq$

3.1.23.1. EXERCISE. Convince yourself of the correctness of Example 3.1.23.

3.1.23.2. EXERCISE. Show that the entailment relation $\vdash$ also lacks the property of transitivity.

Thus for $\vdash$ it does ***not*** hold that

$$\varphi \vdash \chi \;\Rightarrow\; \varphi \wedge \psi \vdash \chi.$$

This property renders $\vdash$ a so-called *non-monotonic* entailment relation. Non-monotonic logics constitute a vast research area by themselves. (See [Rei87] for an overview.) For now, it suffices to give the intuition of the non-monotonicity in this particular case: if χ follows from the fact that the agent knows *only* φ, then χ need not follow from the fact that s/he only knows φ *and* ψ! In the following section we will digress on this point, and show that Halpern & Moses' non-monotonic entailment relation can be viewed semantically in terms of a preference relation on the models: some models of the premise are more preferred than others.

3.2. Digression: Non-monotonic Reasoning and Preferential Entailment

In this section we will touch briefly upon an area of knowledge representation which is still under full investigation, namely *non-monotonic* or *defeasible reasoning*. Although rather a young domain of research a full treatment of this topic would easily warrant a complete book in itself. Actually, such enterprises have already been undertaken (e.g. [Bes89] and [Luk90]). Here we shall focus on that part of non-monotonic reasoning that is related to epistemic logic, in particular in connection with Halpern & Moses' theory of epistemic states.

Non-monotonic reasoning is a general term that indicates a way of reasoning in which some assertions change truth value from 'true' to 'false' or vice versa in the course of reasoning. In contrast with traditional forms of reasoning, in which assertions stated remain true, non-monotonic reasoning is characterised by situations in which assertions stated earlier (or rather with less information available) have to be retracted. Viewed in a procedural manner, this amounts to *belief revision*.

An example of *monotonic* reasoning is reasoning by means of a (classical) formal proof system. For this kind of systems we always have the following property, called *monotonicity*:

$$\text{If } \varphi_1, ..., \varphi_n \vdash \psi \text{ then } \varphi_1, ..., \varphi_n, \varphi \vdash \psi.$$

Mathematical reasoning, of course, should ideally be monotonic: it would be very unpleasant if obtaining a new mathematical theorem would invalidate theorems that were derived at an earlier stage.

Nevertheless, in daily life there is an abundance of examples of non-monotonic reasoning: for example, in *probabilistic*, *plausible*, *hypothetical* and *counterfactual* reasoning, and *a fortiori* in reasoning by *default*, we encounter phenomena of non-monotonicity in which statements that were established at an earlier stage have to be revoked. Often this has to do with *uncertain* or *partial* information. Some examples:

1. "Most A are B" does *not* imply that "most A-and-C are B". For instance "Most birds can fly", but *not*: "most broken-winged birds can fly". So "if A then probably B" does *not* imply"if A-and-C then probably B". A similar example can be given with 'plausible' instead of 'probable'.
2. Assertions that are assumed by default might be retracted. For instance, we know that Tweety is a bird. In the absence of further information we assume that Tweety is able to fly. When we discover later on that Tweety is a penguin, we have to drop the assertion that Tweety can fly.
3. More generally, in case we are unsure about something, we may assume some assertion hypothetically, until we discover that this leads to contradiction and we are forced to drop our hypothesis.
4. Furthermore, also in the case we may assume something which we know to be untrue, i.e. is *contra* the facts, as in counterfactual reasoning we may encounter non-monotonic phenomena. For instance, consider the following situation:

Julius Caesar was a general and no lion	$G(c) \wedge \neg L(c)$
Generals do not have tails	$G(x) \rightarrow \neg T(x)$
Lions do have tails	$L(x) \rightarrow T(x)$

Consider now the following counterfactual:

Suppose Caesar had been a lion	$L(c)$

What can we deduce from this?

(i) To start with we have to retract $\neg L(c)$.
(ii) By $L(c) \rightarrow T(c)$ we might deduce:

Caesar was a general with a tail	$G(c) \wedge T(c)$

If we do this we also have to withdraw $G(x) \rightarrow \neg T(x)$.

(iii) We could also retract $L(x) \rightarrow T(x)$ and infer by $G(c) \rightarrow \neg T(c)$:

Caesar was a lion without a tail $L(c) \wedge \neg T(c)$

Which choice has to be made in this case is not clear. In general we might assign a higher priority to certain principles $A(x) \rightarrow B(x)$ in order to enforce a decision in this kind of situation. Counterfactuals occur frequently in natural language: "If Julius Caesar had been a lion, then ... ". They therefore play an important role in 'natural language processing'. For more on counterfactuals and their relation with defaults and the phenomenon of non-monotonicity we refer to Chapter 4.

Non-monotonicity is strongly related to problems of *change* and *revision*. By *change* we mean that assertions change their truth value over time. This is to be interpreted in a purely ontological way: in the real world things are subject to changes, e.g. because of actions that are performed or events that occur, and we may employ some logic to describe these changes. Here it is not the case that there is uncertainty but rather that we are interested in the effects of the execution of (trans)actions changing the world (situation) over time. An example of this kind of problem is the behaviour of computer systems due to programs written in imperative languages in which assignments change the state of the system. So, for example, when we are in a state where a program variable (or some other memory device) x has the value 0, and we perform the action (program) x:=x+1, we get into a state in which x has the value 1. This kind of change is well-understood in the context of imperative programming languages and can be treated by program logics such as Hoare's logic [Hoa69] and dynamic logic [Har84]. In the example above, we may express this as $\{x=0\}$ x:=x+1 $\{x=1\}$ in Hoare's logic, and as $x=0 \rightarrow [x:=x+1]$ $x=1$ in dynamic logic. Moreover, dynamic logic (and especially the propositional version of it) lends itself to a description of the effects of actions (by humans or otherwise) more in general.

In the context of databases we encounter a similar situation when considering database updates manipulating data by insertions, deletions and modifications. Here the problem is already much harder because in databases there is generally some form of uncertainty involved in the form of *disjunctive information*. This complicates the description of the effects of the actions (updates) on the database considerably, especially when considering deletions. For example, consider a database consisting of the formula $p \vee q$. What does it mean if we delete p from this database. Does this have no effect, since the formula did not occur in the database, or do we lose the information $p \vee q$, since it may have been the case that p was true, and we now do not know p any more (cf. [DR92]). As the word 'know' already indicates, not only pure ontological issues are at stake here, but also epistemological ones: i.e. having to do with what one *knows*. In fact, when one has disjunctive information one is uncertain about what holds in the real world, and considers multiple states, which have to be updated. This is a non-trivial problem (cf. e.g. [Win90], [SWM95]).

Moreover, matters are even more complicated by the use in databases of a self-imposed form of uncertainty for reasons of efficient storage of data, namely the closed world assumption (CWA), which is a way of deliberately disposing of complete information by omitting negative information and maintaining that negative knowledge should follow from the absence of positive knowledge: if p is not found in the database, it is concluded that $\neg$p. This enables one to dispense with the storage of explicit negative information. The CWA itself introduces a form of non-monotonicity, that is closely related to the use of negation-as-failure in logic programming, and there is already a vast amount of literature on this topic (e.g. [Min88], [Tha88], [Tha89]).

Very closely related to this is the issue of *belief revision*. Here we directly address the problem of changing our beliefs because of newly discovered information. Where in database theory we still have the database itself as a 'hard' source of information, albeit sometimes incomplete, here the problem is that the knowledge that one has, or rather the beliefs that one holds, is (are) even more implicit. Where in database updates the contents of the database one starts with are not questioned (but may be giving just insufficient information), here the beliefs that are held are much more uncertain: these sets may contain assertions that are simply not true. So, no wonder that in belief revision the newly discovered information plays an even more important role: the old beliefs have to be changed to fit the new information. This comes, of course, very close to non-monotonic or defeasible reasoning, the difference being that in belief revision the modification and possible retraction of 'theorems' (beliefs) that have been obtained earlier is operationalised. In non-monotonic logic, we just have that after adding premises we have to do our derivations all over again, in the process possibly invalidating theorems that were obtained in the old situation; in belief revision it is indicated how these sets of beliefs change over time, when adding new information. Of course, this operationalisation is again even more concrete in so-called truth (or reason) maintenance systems, in which a bookkeeping is employed to keep track of all dependencies in derivations, so that in case some assertion has to be retracted, it also takes the consequences of this by adjusting dependent assertions (beliefs). For more about belief revision we refer to the book of Gärdenfors [Gär88]. More about truth maintenance systems can be found in [Doy79], [SK88].

Here we concentrate on non-monotonic logic (/ reasoning) in the more strict sense, namely as a logical system with an inference relation $\mid\!\sim$ that lacks monotonicity.

Unfortunately, non-monotonic logic is problematic from a theoretical point of view. In [McDD80] for the first time there has been an attempt to propose a theory of non-monotonic logic. As one of the authors, Drew McDermott, explained later in [McD82], this theory was not quite adequate. Although Moore [Moo84, Moo85a] improved things considerably with his autoepistemic logic (AEL), this theory is still not adequate as an all-embracing theory of non-monotonic reasoning, not in the least since AEL was proposed to capture how ideal, rational introspective agents reason, which is a rather different objective.

Y. Shoham has proposed in [Sho87, Sho88] a general model-theoretical approach of non-monotonic reasoning. According to Shoham non-monotonic logics are obtained by putting a preference criterion on models of standard logics. These standard logics may be propositional logic, first-order predicate logic, but also modal (epistemic) logic. In the rest of this section we use $\mathcal{M}$ to denote a 'model': in the case of propositional logic this is just a propositional valuation, in that of first-order logic it is an interpretative structure with the right signature, and for modal / epistemic logic it is a world $(\mathbb{M}, s)$, consisting of a Kripke structure and a state in this structure, as in previous sections. Thus for all three set-ups the semantics is Tarskian or compositional, at least regarding the propositional connectives $\neg, \wedge, \vee, \rightarrow$:

$$\begin{array}{lll} \mathcal{M} \models \neg\varphi & \Leftrightarrow & \mathcal{M} \not\models \varphi \\ \mathcal{M} \models \varphi \wedge \psi & \Leftrightarrow & \mathcal{M} \models \varphi \;\&\; \mathcal{M} \models \psi \\ \mathcal{M} \models \varphi \vee \psi & \Leftrightarrow & \mathcal{M} \models \varphi \text{ of } \mathcal{M} \models \psi \\ \mathcal{M} \models \varphi \rightarrow \psi & \Leftrightarrow & (\mathcal{M} \models \varphi \Rightarrow \mathcal{M} \models \psi) \end{array}$$

(Note that for $\mathbb{M} \models \varphi$ in epistemic logic this compositionality does not hold, but this is the reason why we consider $(\mathbb{M}, s) \models \varphi$ in this case, which *is* compositional.)

Let **L** be a standard logic and φ an assertion in this logic. We denote (standard) validity by $\models$: $\models \varphi$ iff $\mathcal{M} \models \varphi$ for all models $\mathcal{M}$ of **L**. On the models of **L** we postulate a strict partial ordering $\lhd$: $\mathcal{M}_1 \lhd \mathcal{M}_2$ means that model $\mathcal{M}_2$ is preferred to model $\mathcal{M}_1$. The logic **L** and ordering $\lhd$ constitute a new logic (a *preferential logic*) $\mathbf{L}_\lhd$, the syntax of which is the same as that of **L**, but with a different semantics:

3.2.1. DEFINITION. $\mathcal{M} \models_\lhd \varphi$ if $\mathcal{M} \models \varphi$ and there is no $\mathcal{M}'$ such that $\mathcal{M} \lhd \mathcal{M}'$ and $\mathcal{M}' \models \varphi$. (So $\mathcal{M}$ is a *maximal* model of φ with respect to the partial ordering $\lhd$.) In this case $\mathcal{M}$ is called a *preferred model* of φ.

3.2.2. DEFINITION. φ is *preferentially satisfiable* if there exists an $\mathcal{M}$ such that $\mathcal{M} \models_\lhd \varphi$.

Note that all preferentially satisfiable formulas are also satisfiable, but not necessarily the other way around.

3.2.3. DEFINITION. φ is *preferentially valid*, denoted $\models_{\lhd} \varphi$, if $\neg\varphi$ is not preferentially satisfiable.

3.2.4. PROPOSITION. $\models_{\lhd} \varphi$ *if for every* $\mathcal{M}$ *either*

(i) $\mathcal{M} \not\models \neg\varphi$, *or*

(ii) $\exists\, \mathcal{M}' (\, \mathcal{M} \lhd \mathcal{M}'$ *and* $\mathcal{M}' \models \neg\varphi)$.

PROOF. Immediate from the definitions. ■

This notion of preferential validity possesses some curious properties.

3.2.5. EXERCISE. Let $\lhd$ be *serial*, i.e. $\forall \mathcal{M} \exists \mathcal{M}'\ \mathcal{M} \lhd \mathcal{M}'$. Show that if $\models \varphi$ then both $\models_{\lhd} \varphi$ and $\models_{\lhd} \neg\varphi$.

Moreover, if we require $\lhd$ to be *bounded*, i.e. there is no infinite sequence $\mathcal{M}_1 \lhd \mathcal{M}_2 \lhd \ldots$, then $\models_{\lhd}$ coincides with $\models$:

3.2.6. PROPOSITION. *Let* $\lhd$ *be a bounded partial ordering on the models of* **L** *and let* φ *be a formula in* **L**. *Then* φ *is satisfiable* $\Leftrightarrow$ φ *is preferentially satisfiable.*

PROOF. $\Leftarrow$ is trivial. ($\Rightarrow$) Suppose $\mathcal{M}_0 \models \varphi$. Now define sequences $\langle \mathcal{M}_0, \mathcal{M}_1, \mathcal{M}_2, \ldots \rangle$ with properties:

(a) $\mathcal{M}_i \models \varphi$ for any i,

(b) if there is an $\mathcal{M}_{i+1}$ in the sequence, then $\mathcal{M}_i \lhd \mathcal{M}_{i+1}$.

Clearly at least one such sequence exists, namely the singleton sequence $\langle \mathcal{M}_0 \rangle$. Since $\lhd$ is bounded, there is *no* infinite sequence of this kind: all sequences are finite. So there is a *maximal* finite sequence $\langle \mathcal{M}_0, \mathcal{M}_1, \ldots, \mathcal{M}_n \rangle$, i.e. this sequence cannot be extended any further. Hence by definition $\mathcal{M}_n \models_{\lhd} \varphi$. ■

3.2.7. COROLLARY. *Under the same assumptions as in Proposition 3.2.6:*

$$\models \varphi \;\Leftrightarrow\; \models_{\lhd} \varphi.$$

PROOF. Exercise 3.2.7.1. ■

3.2.7.1. EXERCISE. Show that Corollary 3.2.7 follows directly from Proposition 3.2.6 and the definitions of $\models$ and $\models_{\triangleleft}$.

Although 'preferentially satisfiable' and 'preferentially valid' are somewhat peculiar notions, this is not really important, since actually we only need the notion of *preferential model* ($\mathcal{M} \models_{\triangleleft} \varphi$) in the definition of *preferential entailment*:

3.2.8. DEFINITION. φ *implies* ψ *preferentially* (denoted $\varphi \models_{\triangleleft} \psi$) if for every $\mathcal{M}$

$$\mathcal{M} \models_{\triangleleft} \varphi \;\Rightarrow\; \mathcal{M} \models \psi.$$

So $\varphi \models_{\triangleleft} \psi$ holds precisely if the collection of ψ-models (preferred or not) includes that of the preferred φ-models, in other words, if, in every maximal model of φ, ψ also holds.

3.2.9. DEFINITION. We say that a logic $\mathbf{L}_{\triangleleft}$ is *monotonic* if

$$\forall \varphi, \psi, \chi \in \mathbf{L}\ (\varphi \models_{\triangleleft} \chi \;\Rightarrow\; \varphi \wedge \psi \models_{\triangleleft} \chi).$$

3.2.9.1. REMARKS. (i) Thus a logic is monotonic if all *preferred* models of $\varphi \wedge \psi$ are *preferred* models of φ.

(ii) It appears that in general a preferential logic is not monotonic. (This is, of course, not surprising seen in the light of the reason the concept was developed, namely as a logical basis for non-monotonic reasoning!) For an example we refer to Exercise 3.2.9.1.1(ii) below, and Section 3.3.

(iii) If $\mathbf{L}_{\triangleleft}$ is a preferential logic, it may happen that both $\varphi \models_{\triangleleft} \psi$ and $\varphi \models_{\triangleleft} \neg\psi$ without φ being inconsistent.

3.2.9.1.1. EXERCISE. (i) Prove 3.2.9.1(i).

(ii) As an example of a non-monotonic preferential logic (cf. 3.2.9.1(ii)) we take propositional logic together with its classical models, namely propositional valuations, as the underlying logic. Now we define the preference ordering $\triangleleft$ on valuations as follows: $w_1 \triangleleft w_2$ iff, for all propositional atoms p, $w_1(p) = t$ implies $w_2(p) = t$. Show that this preferential logic is non-monotonic.

(iii) Give an example that satisfies the conditions as stated in 3.2.9.1(iii).

3.2.10. THEOREM. *Let* $\mathbf{L}_{\triangleleft}$ *be a preferential logic and let* $\varphi \in \mathbf{L}$. *Then:*

$$\varphi \textit{ is preferentially satisfiable } \Leftrightarrow\; \neg\exists\psi \in \mathbf{L}_{\triangleleft}\ (\varphi \models_{\triangleleft} \psi \textit{ and } \varphi \models_{\triangleleft} \neg\psi).$$

PROOF. ($\Rightarrow$) Suppose φ is preferentially satisfiable. Then there exists an $\mathcal{M}$ with $\mathcal{M} \models_{\triangleleft} \varphi$. Suppose there was a ψ such that $\varphi \models_{\triangleleft} \psi$ *and* $\varphi \models_{\triangleleft} \neg\psi$. Then $\mathcal{M} \models \psi$ and $\mathcal{M} \models \neg\varphi$, which is a contradiction.
($\Leftarrow$) We prove that: φ is not preferentially satisfiable $\Rightarrow \exists \psi \in \mathbf{L}_{\triangleleft}$ ($\varphi \models_{\triangleleft} \psi$ *and* $\varphi \models_{\triangleleft} \neg\psi$). Suppose φ is not preferentially satisfiable. Then there is no $\mathcal{M}$ with $\mathcal{M} \models_{\triangleleft} \varphi$. But this means that the implication $\varphi \models_{\triangleleft} \psi$ is trivially true for any ψ (for $\varphi \models_{\triangleleft} \psi$ is defined as: for all $\mathcal{M}$ it holds that $\mathcal{M} \models_{\triangleleft} \varphi \Rightarrow \mathcal{M} \models \psi$). In the same way the implication $\varphi \models_{\triangleleft} \neg\psi$ is trivially true. ■

3.2.11. LEMMA. *If $\mathcal{M} \models \psi$ and $\mathcal{M} \models_{\triangleleft} \varphi$, then $\mathcal{M} \models_{\triangleleft} \varphi \wedge \psi$.*

PROOF. Suppose $\mathcal{M} \models \psi$ *and* $\mathcal{M} \models_{\triangleleft} \varphi$. In particular, $\mathcal{M} \models \varphi$. So $\mathcal{M} \models \varphi \wedge \psi$. This $\mathcal{M}$ is a maximal model of $\varphi \wedge \psi$, since $\mathcal{M}$ is not a maximal model of φ otherwise. This means that $\mathcal{M} \models_{\triangleleft} \varphi \wedge \psi$. ■

3.2.12. THEOREM (Weak deduction theorem).

$$\varphi \wedge \psi \models_{\triangleleft} \chi \quad \Rightarrow \quad \varphi \models_{\triangleleft} \psi \rightarrow \chi.$$

PROOF. Suppose $\varphi \wedge \psi \models_{\triangleleft} \chi$ and not $\varphi \models_{\triangleleft} \psi \rightarrow \chi$. Then there is $\mathcal{M}_0$ such that $\mathcal{M}_0 \models_{\triangleleft} \varphi$ but $\mathcal{M}_0 \not\models \psi \rightarrow \chi$. From the latter it follows that $\mathcal{M}_0 \models \psi$ and $\mathcal{M}_0 \not\models \chi$ (here we use the compositionality of the semantics). Furthermore, $\mathcal{M}_0 \not\models_{\triangleleft} \varphi \wedge \psi$, since $\mathcal{M}_0 \not\models \chi$ and $\varphi \wedge \psi \models_{\triangleleft} \chi$. But also $\mathcal{M}_0 \models_{\triangleleft} \varphi \wedge \psi$, since $\mathcal{M}_0 \models_{\triangleleft} \varphi$ and $\mathcal{M}_0 \models \psi$ (by Lemma 3.2.11). Contradiction. Hence $\varphi \models_{\triangleleft} \psi \rightarrow \chi$. ■

*3.2.12.1. EXERCISE. Show that in Theorem 3.2.12 the converse implication does not hold in general.

When the converse of the weak deduction theorem does hold, the logic $\mathbf{L}_{\triangleleft}$ must be monotonic:

3.2.13. THEOREM.

$$\mathbf{L}_{\triangleleft} \textit{ is monotonic} \iff \forall \varphi, \psi, \chi \in \mathbf{L}_{\triangleleft} (\varphi \models_{\triangleleft} \psi \rightarrow \chi \Rightarrow \varphi \wedge \psi \models_{\triangleleft} \chi) \qquad (*)$$

PROOF. ($\Rightarrow$) $\mathbf{L}_{\triangleleft}$ is monotonic, so

$$\forall \varphi, \psi, \chi \in \mathbf{L}_{\triangleleft} (\varphi \models_{\triangleleft} \chi \Rightarrow \varphi \wedge \psi \models_{\triangleleft} \chi).$$

Now suppose $\varphi \models_{\triangleleft} \psi \rightarrow \chi$. Then $\varphi \wedge \psi \models_{\triangleleft} \psi \rightarrow \chi$, that is to say:

$$\forall \mathcal{M}(\mathcal{M} \models_{\triangleleft} \varphi \wedge \psi \;\Rightarrow\; \mathcal{M} \models \psi \rightarrow \chi).$$

Now take an arbitrary $\mathcal{M}$ with $\mathcal{M} \models_{\triangleleft} \varphi \wedge \psi$. Then $\mathcal{M} \models \psi \rightarrow \chi$ and $\mathcal{M} \models \varphi \wedge \psi$. So also $\mathcal{M} \models \chi$. Since this holds for arbitrary $\mathcal{M}$ with $\mathcal{M} \models_{\triangleleft} \varphi \wedge \psi$, we have thus proved $\varphi \wedge \psi \models_{\triangleleft} \chi$ under the assumption that $\varphi \models_{\triangleleft} \psi \rightarrow \chi$. With this we have proved the right-hand side (*) of the statement in the theorem.

($\Leftarrow$) Suppose that (*) and $\varphi \models_{\triangleleft} \chi$. We have to show that $\varphi \wedge \psi \models_{\triangleleft} \chi$. Since $\varphi \models_{\triangleleft} \chi$, i.e.

$$\forall \mathcal{M}(\mathcal{M} \models_{\triangleleft} \varphi \;\Rightarrow\; \mathcal{M} \models \chi),$$

we also have that

$$\forall \mathcal{M}(\mathcal{M} \models_{\triangleleft} \varphi \;\Rightarrow\; \mathcal{M} \models \psi \rightarrow \chi)$$

for arbitrary ψ. Hence $\varphi \models_{\triangleleft} \psi \rightarrow \chi$ and by (*) we get $\varphi \wedge \psi \models_{\triangleleft} \chi$. ■

Shoham's preferential entailment enjoys some other interesting properties as well:

3.2.14. THEOREM (Cut).

$$\varphi \wedge \psi \models_{\triangleleft} \chi \textit{ and } \varphi \models_{\triangleleft} \psi \;\Rightarrow\; \varphi \models_{\triangleleft} \chi.$$

PROOF. Suppose $\varphi \wedge \psi \models_{\triangleleft} \chi$ and $\varphi \models_{\triangleleft} \psi$. We have to show that $\varphi \models_{\triangleleft} \chi$. Let $\mathcal{M} \models_{\triangleleft} \varphi$. We now prove that $\mathcal{M} \models \chi$. By $\varphi \models_{\triangleleft} \psi$ we obtain that $\mathcal{M} \models \psi$. By Lemma 3.2.11 we then get that $\mathcal{M} \models_{\triangleleft} \varphi \wedge \psi$. So now $\mathcal{M} \models \chi$, since $\varphi \wedge \psi \models_{\triangleleft} \chi$. ■

3.2.15. THEOREM (Cautious monotonicity). *Let $\triangleleft$ be a bounded partial ordering on the models of* **L**. *Then we have that:*

$$\varphi \models_{\triangleleft} \psi \textit{ and } \varphi \models_{\triangleleft} \chi \;\Rightarrow\; \varphi \wedge \psi \models_{\triangleleft} \chi.$$

PROOF. Suppose $\varphi \models_{\triangleleft} \psi$ and $\varphi \models_{\triangleleft} \chi$. We have to show that $\varphi \wedge \psi \models_{\triangleleft} \chi$. Let $\mathcal{M} \models_{\triangleleft} \varphi \wedge \psi$. We now prove that $\mathcal{M} \models \chi$. Since $\mathcal{M} \models \varphi \wedge \psi$, we have that $\mathcal{M} \models \varphi$. We prove that $\mathcal{M} \models_{\triangleleft} \varphi$. Let us assume for contradiction that $\mathcal{M} \not\models_{\triangleleft} \varphi$. Then there is a model $\mathcal{M}'$ such that $\mathcal{M} \triangleleft \mathcal{M}'$ and $\mathcal{M}' \models \varphi$. Since $\triangleleft$ is bounded, there must also be a $\triangleleft$-*maximal* model $\mathcal{M}''$ such that $\mathcal{M} \triangleleft \mathcal{M}''$ and $\mathcal{M}'' \models \varphi$. This means that there is a model $\mathcal{M}''$ such that $\mathcal{M} \triangleleft \mathcal{M}''$ and $\mathcal{M}'' \models_{\triangleleft} \varphi$. By $\varphi \models_{\triangleleft} \psi$ we then have that $\mathcal{M}'' \models \psi$, and hence by Lemma 3.2.11 $\mathcal{M}'' \models_{\triangleleft} \varphi \wedge \psi$. Since $\mathcal{M} \triangleleft \mathcal{M}''$, this contradicts the fact that $\mathcal{M} \models_{\triangleleft} \varphi \wedge \psi$. Thus we may conclude that $\mathcal{M} \models_{\triangleleft} \varphi$, and consequently, by the fact that $\varphi \models_{\triangleleft} \chi$, that $\mathcal{M} \models \chi$. ■

We further have some additional intuitive simple properties:

3.2.16. THEOREM.
(i) $\varphi \models_{\triangleleft} \varphi$ *(Reflexivity)*
(ii) *If* $\models \varphi \leftrightarrow \psi$ *and* $\varphi \models_{\triangleleft} \chi$ *then* $\psi \models_{\triangleleft} \chi$. *(Left logical equivalence)*
(iii) *If* $\models \varphi \rightarrow \psi$ *and* $\chi \models_{\triangleleft} \varphi$ *then* $\chi \models_{\triangleleft} \psi$. *(Right weakening)*

PROOF. (i) Clear, since $\mathcal{M} \models_{\triangleleft} \varphi$ implies that $\mathcal{M} \models \varphi$.
(ii) Assume $\varphi \models_{\triangleleft} \chi$ and suppose that $\models \varphi \leftrightarrow \psi$. Then $\mathcal{M} \models \varphi \leftrightarrow \psi$, for all models $\mathcal{M}$. This implies that for all models $\mathcal{M}$ it holds that $\mathcal{M} \models \varphi \Leftrightarrow \mathcal{M} \models \psi$, i.e. φ and ψ have the same models. But then they also have the same preferred models (Exercise 3.2.16.1). So if $\mathcal{M} \models_{\triangleleft} \psi$, we also have $\mathcal{M} \models_{\triangleleft} \varphi$, which by the assumption $\varphi \models_{\triangleleft} \chi$ yields that $\mathcal{M} \models \chi$, which had to be shown.
(iii) Assume $\chi \models_{\triangleleft} \varphi$ and suppose that $\models \varphi \rightarrow \psi$. Since $\models \varphi \rightarrow \psi$, we have that $\mathcal{M} \models \varphi \rightarrow \psi$, for all models $\mathcal{M}$, and hence that for all models $\mathcal{M}$ it holds that $\mathcal{M} \models \varphi$ implies $\mathcal{M} \models \psi$. Now, if $\mathcal{M} \models_{\triangleleft} \chi$, we have by the assumption $\chi \models_{\triangleleft} \varphi$ that $\mathcal{M} \models \varphi$, and hence $\mathcal{M} \models \psi$. ■

3.2.16.1. EXERCISE. Show that if φ and ψ have the same models, they also have the same preferred models.

3.2.16.2. EXERCISE. Show that in general we do not have left strengthening: if $\models \varphi \rightarrow \psi$ and $\psi \models_{\triangleleft} \chi$, then $\varphi \models_{\triangleleft} \chi$ does not need to hold. (Of course, this is akin to the very notion of non-monotonicity!)

In the literature on non-monotonic logic ([Gab85], [Mak89], [KLM90]) entailment relations that enjoy the properties of reflexivity, left logical equivalence, right weakening, cut and cautious monotonicity are called *cumulative*. This is generally considered to be a desirable property of nonmonotonic entailments. A cumulative nonmonotonic logic is — although non-monotonic — well-behaved in some sense and is not completely 'wild'. So Shoham's general semantical theory captures cumulative approaches to non-monotonic reasoning (cf. [Sho87, Sho88]), in particular that of Halpern & Moses' $\mid\!\sim$ of Section 3.1, as we shall see below. Many other approaches to non-monotonic logic in the literature appear also to be cumulative, and can be treated as a special case of Shoham's approach. There are some notable exceptions, however, such as Reiter's default logic ([Rei80]). On the other hand, Voorbraak ([Voo91b]) has given a preferential semantics to default logic by modifying the notion of a preferred model. *A fortiori*, in [Voo93] it is shown that by relaxing the requirement of (strict) partial orders on the standard models to *arbitrary relations*, also non-cumulative approaches such as default logic can be given a preferential model semantics using the *original* definition of preferred model. We shall return to the notion of cumulativity in Section 4.5.

3.3. Halpern & Moses' Theory of Epistemic States Revisited

Halpern & Moses' theory of "I only know that φ" as discussed in Section 3.1 shows non-monotonic behaviour: if the agent only knows that φ then s/he also knows that s/he does *not* know that ψ (where ψ has nothing to do with φ). If, however, s/he later discovers that ψ, then s/he *does* know that ψ and s/he does *not* know any longer that s/he does *not* know ψ!

We have seen before that a stable set Σ^φ such that $\varphi \in \Sigma^\varphi$ and with smallest Prop(Σ^φ) represents the knowledge associated with "all I know is φ". As we saw earlier, this set Σ^φ can also be characterised as the set of formulas that are true in the 'greatest' model $\mathbb{M}_\varphi$ satisfying φ, provided this exists: $\Sigma^\varphi = K(\mathbb{M}_\varphi)$. By using Shoham's theory of preferred models we can reformulate Halpern & Moses' theory as follows.

3.3.1. DEFINITION. Let $\mathcal{M}_1 = (\mathbb{M}_1, s_1)$ and $\mathcal{M}_2 = (\mathbb{M}_2, s_2)$ be simple $\mathbf{S5}_{(1)}$-Kripke worlds. Then $(\mathbb{M}_1, s_1) \lhd (\mathbb{M}_2, s_2)$ if

(i) for each pure proposition α: $(\mathbb{M}_2, s_2) \models K\alpha \Rightarrow (\mathbb{M}_1, s_1) \models K\alpha$, and

(ii) there is some pure proposition α: $(\mathbb{M}_1, s_1) \models K\alpha$ and $(\mathbb{M}_2, s_2) \not\models K\alpha$.

3.3.1.1. REMARK. (i) In fact, the state s in ($\mathbb{M}$, s) in the above definition is not essential, since for the class of models concerned we know that:

$$(\mathbb{M}, s) \models K\alpha \Leftrightarrow \mathbb{M} \models K\alpha \Leftrightarrow \mathbb{M} \models \alpha.$$

(ii) An equivalent formulation of the definition above reads:

$$(\mathbb{M}_1, s_1) \lhd (\mathbb{M}_2, s_2) \Leftrightarrow \text{Prop}(K(\mathbb{M}_2)) \subset \text{Prop}(K(\mathbb{M}_1))$$

where $\subset$ denotes strict inclusion.

Thus the *most preferred* models, in this case simple **S5**-Kripke worlds ($\mathbb{M}$, s), are those worlds in which the *propositional knowledge is the smallest*. The content of the statement "I only know φ" is now represented by the model-theoretical assertion "$K\varphi$ is preferentially satisfiable", that is, there is a world ($\mathbb{M}$, s) with $(\mathbb{M}, s) \models_{\lhd} K\varphi$, i.e. ($\mathbb{M}$, s) is $\lhd$-maximal such that $(\mathbb{M}, s) \models K\varphi$.

In general there may be more than one distinct $\lhd$-maximal world $(\mathbb{M}, s)$ with $(\mathbb{M}, s) \models K\varphi$. Of course, defining the meaning of "I only know φ" by "$K\varphi$ is preferentially satisfiable" is therefore only sensible if all these maximal worlds $(\mathbb{M}, s)$, $(\mathbb{M}', s')$, ... contain the same propositional knowledge, i.e. $Prop(K(\mathbb{M})) = Prop(K(\mathbb{M}')) = \ldots$. Indeed this holds under the assumption that φ is *honest* (cf. Section 3.1).

3.3.2. THEOREM. *if* φ *is honest, then*

(i) $\exists(\mathbb{M}, s)\ (\mathbb{M}, s) \models_{\lhd} K\varphi$,

(ii) $\forall(\mathbb{M}_1, s_1), (\mathbb{M}_2, s_2) : (\mathbb{M}_1, s_1), (\mathbb{M}_2, s_2) \models_{\lhd} K\varphi \ \Rightarrow\ K(\mathbb{M}_1) = K(\mathbb{M}_2)$.

PROOF. (i) We know that, if φ is honest, $\varphi \in K(\mathbb{M}_\varphi)$, that is to say, $\mathbb{M}_\varphi \models K\varphi$. Moreover, it holds for all $(\mathbb{M}, s)$ with $(\mathbb{M}, s) \models K\varphi$ and for all t that $(\mathbb{M}, s) \unlhd (\mathbb{M}_\varphi, t)$, where $\unlhd$ stands for the reflexive closure of $\lhd$, since

$$Prop(K(\mathbb{M}_\varphi)) = \bigcap \{Prop(K(\mathbb{M})) \mid \mathbb{M} \models K\varphi\} \subseteq Prop(K(\mathbb{M}))$$

for all $\mathbb{M}$ with $\mathbb{M} \models K\varphi$ (or, equivalently, for all $(\mathbb{M}, s)$ with $(\mathbb{M}, s) \models K\varphi$).

(ii) Suppose that $(\mathbb{M}_1, s_1), (\mathbb{M}_2, s_2) \models_{\lhd} K\varphi$. In particular, $\mathbb{M}_1, \mathbb{M}_2 \models K\varphi$. By the above,

$$Prop(K(\mathbb{M}_\varphi)) \subseteq Prop(K(\mathbb{M}_i)) \qquad (i = 1, 2).$$

In fact this holds with '=' rather than '$\subseteq$'; for suppose, for i = 0 or i = 1,

$$Prop(K(\mathbb{M}_\varphi)) \subset Prop(K(\mathbb{M}_i))$$

(where $\subset$ denotes strict inclusion), then we have (by definition of $\lhd$), for all s, t,

$$(\mathbb{M}_i, s) \lhd (\mathbb{M}_\varphi, t).$$

But then $(\mathbb{M}_i, s) \not\models_{\lhd} K\varphi$, since $(\mathbb{M}_\varphi, t) \models K\varphi$. So $Prop(K(\mathbb{M}_\varphi)) = Prop(K(\mathbb{M}_i))$ $(i = 1, 2)$. Hence $Prop(K(\mathbb{M}_1)) = Prop(K(\mathbb{M}_2))$, and consequently $K(\mathbb{M}_1) = K(\mathbb{M}_2)$, by Proposition 3.2. ∎

Finally we see the connection with the non-monotonic entailment relation $\mid\!\sim$ from Section 3.1:

3.3.3. THEOREM. *If* φ *is honest, then*

$$K\varphi \models_{\triangleleft} K\psi \;\Leftrightarrow\; \varphi \mid\!\sim \psi.$$

PROOF. Let φ be honest. Then:

$$\begin{array}{l} K\varphi \models_{\triangleleft} K\psi \;\Leftrightarrow \\ \forall \mathbb{M}\,(\mathbb{M} \models_{\triangleleft} K\varphi \Rightarrow \mathbb{M} \models K\psi) \;\Leftrightarrow^* \\ \psi \in K(\mathbb{M}_{\varphi}) \;\Leftrightarrow \\ \psi \in \Sigma^{\varphi} \;\Leftrightarrow \\ \varphi \mid\!\sim \psi. \end{array}$$

We still owe a justification of $\Leftrightarrow^*$:
($\Rightarrow$) Since φ is honest, we know that $\mathbb{M}_{\varphi} \models_{\triangleleft} K\varphi$. So also $\mathbb{M}_{\varphi} \models K\psi$, i.e. $\psi \in K(\mathbb{M}_{\varphi})$.
($\Leftarrow$) By Theorem 3.3.2 we have that for all $\mathbb{M}_1$, $\mathbb{M}_2$ with $\mathbb{M}_1, \mathbb{M}_2 \models_{\triangleleft} K\varphi$ it holds that $K(\mathbb{M}_1) = K(\mathbb{M}_2)$. So now in particular (since $\mathbb{M}_{\varphi} \models_{\triangleleft} K\varphi$) it holds that $K(\mathbb{M}) = K(\mathbb{M}_{\varphi})$ for all $\mathbb{M}$ with $\mathbb{M} \models_{\triangleleft} K\varphi$. Hence for all $\mathbb{M}$ with $\mathbb{M} \models_{\triangleleft} K\varphi$ we have $\psi \in K(\mathbb{M}_{\varphi}) = K(\mathbb{M})$, i.e. $\mathbb{M} \models K\psi$. ■

In fact, since for (*all*) simple $\mathbf{S5}_{(1)}$-Kripke models $\mathbb{M}$ we have that $\mathbb{M} \models K\varphi \Leftrightarrow \mathbb{M} \models \varphi$ (and thus *a posteriori* this holds for *preferred* models as well), we obtain a correspondence result that is even more straightforward:

3.3.4. COROLLARY. *For honest φ we have that* $\varphi \models_{\triangleleft} \psi \;\Leftrightarrow\; \varphi \mid\!\sim \psi$. ■

Since from Section 3.2 we know that the relation is cumulative, we can now apply this general insight to this particular case, and obtain immediately:

3.3.5. COROLLARY. *The entailment relation* $\mid\!\sim$ *is cumulative.* ■

3.4. Autoepistemic Logic (Moore)

In the previous section we have seen how we can characterise epistemic states with the aid of (**S5**-) epistemic logic: these states represent the (exact) knowledge (or perhaps rather beliefs) of agents that have introspection capabilities. On the basis of these epistemic states we were able to determine what is known and what is unknown to the agent. We saw that by the use of (minimal) epistemic states it was possible to define an entailment relation to infer the precise knowledge and ignorance of the agent.

Motivated by much the same considerations as Halpern & Moses, Moore [Moo84, Moo85a] introduced a logic to express the way rational introspective agents reason. His aim was to provide a sound basis to McDermott & Doyle's non-monotonic logic ([McDD80], [McD82]).

The logic he employed is closely related to the epistemic logic(s) we saw earlier, but since the emphasis is here on the agents' reasoning about their *own* knowledge and ignorance, this logic is called ***auto**epistemic logic* (AEL) (αυτος(Gr.) = self).

More precisely, like Halpern & Moses' approach, AEL concerns forms of logical introspective reasoning that are idealised as follows: precisely the logical consequences of an initial set of epistemic formulas are known, together with the consequences of positive and negative introspection. Like Halpern & Moses, Moore is concerned with the exact knowledge (or *belief set*) of a rational, introspective agent, given some base set of knowledge. But we shall see that, although naturally there are strong similarities between the two approaches, there are also marked differences between them. For example, while Halpern & Moses stress the importance of honest formulas to represent an epistemic state, and the minimal objective knowledge associated with the base set, Moore is more concerned with a requirement that the beliefs of the agent should be completely justified (*grounded*) by the base set. So although also Moore considers stable sets to represent belief sets, he is not so much interested in the minimality of the objective formulas in the belief sets, but rather in another kind of minimality concerning these sets, namely the condition whether the formulas in these sets follow exactly from the base set, taking into account deductive closure and introspection. Another difference is that where Halpern & Moses start out from traditional epistemic logic, as we have introduced in Chapter 1, Moore's AEL starts with a language which looks modal, but is not directly given a modal semantics *à la* Kripke. It is only when additional apparatus (the so-called AE-extensions which are meant to represent the AE-beliefs of an agent) is introduced that *a posteriori* one can establish relations with modal logic, and S5(-like) logic(s) in particular.

The language of AEL strongly resembles that of ordinary epistemic logic. We again start with a set **P** of propositional symbols (atoms). For technical reasons, we assume **P** to be finite in what follows: $\mathbf{P} = \{p_0, p_1, \ldots, p_m\}$. The class $\mathcal{L}_{\mathbf{AE}}(\mathbf{P})$ of *autoepistemic* (or *AE-)formulas* φ, ψ is the least set closed under:

(i) if $p \in \mathbf{P}$ then $p \in \mathcal{L}_{\mathbf{AE}}(\mathbf{P})$;

(ii) if $\varphi, \psi \in \mathcal{L}_{\mathbf{AE}}(\mathbf{P})$ then $\neg\varphi, \varphi \wedge \psi\ (, \varphi \vee \psi, \varphi \rightarrow \psi, \ldots) \in \mathcal{L}_{\mathbf{AE}}(\mathbf{P})$;

(iii) if $\varphi \in \mathcal{L}_{\mathbf{AE}}(\mathbf{P})$ then $L\varphi \in \mathcal{L}_{\mathbf{AE}}(\mathbf{P})$ and $M\varphi \in \mathcal{L}_{\mathbf{AE}}(\mathbf{P})$.

Here $L\varphi$ stands for "the agent knows/believes φ" and $M\varphi$ for "the agent considers φ as possible on the basis of his knowledge", or $\neg L\neg\varphi$: "it is not the case that the agent knows/believes $\neg\varphi$".

The semantics of AE-formulas resembles that of ordinary epistemic logic, but does not employ Kripke structures (in the first instance) to treat the modal operators. AE-formulas without modal operators are called *objective*, and refer to the '*objective external world*'; AE-formulas of the form $L\varphi$ are called *subjective*, and refer to the '(*subjective*) *internal* world' of the beliefs of the agent.

Formally we proceed as follows: An *AE-valuation* of the language $\mathcal{L}_{\mathbf{AE}}(\mathbf{P})$ is a pair [w, X] where w is a propositional valuation $w: \mathbf{P} \to \{\mathfrak{t}, \mathfrak{f}\}$ and $X \subseteq \mathcal{L}_{\mathbf{AE}}(\mathbf{P})$ is a set of AE-formulas that functions as the knowledge of the agent. Any AE-valuation may serve as an *AE-interpretation* of sentences of the language $\mathcal{L}_{\mathbf{AE}}(\mathbf{P})$. Any interpretation of the form $[\cdot, X]$ is called an X-*interpretation*. An AE-interpretation [w, X] of AE-sentences is defined inductively by :

$$
\begin{aligned}
&[w, X] \models p && \Leftrightarrow w(p) = \mathfrak{t} \text{ for } p \in \mathbf{P}\\
&[w, X] \models \neg\varphi && \Leftrightarrow [w, X] \not\models \varphi\\
&[w, X] \models \varphi \wedge \psi && \Leftrightarrow [w, X] \models \varphi \text{ and } [w, X] \models \psi\\
&[w, X] \models L\varphi && \Leftrightarrow \varphi \in X
\end{aligned}
$$

Moreover, $M\varphi$ is considered as an abbreviation of $\neg L \neg\varphi$.

An AE-interpretation [w, X] such that $[w, X] \models \varphi$ is called an *AE-model* of φ. An AE-formula that has an AE-model is called *AE-satisfiable*. An AE-formula φ *implies* an AE-formula ψ *autoepistemically*, notation $\varphi \models_{AE} \psi$, if every AE-model of φ is also an AE-model of ψ; φ *implies* ψ *with respect to index* X, notation $\varphi \models_X \psi$, if all X-interpretations that are AE-models of φ are also AE-models of ψ. Analogous definitions can be given for sets of AE-formulas. If $\varnothing \models_{AE} \Phi$, notation $\models_{AE} \Phi$, Φ is called *AE-valid.* Analogously, if $\varnothing \models_X \Phi$, notation $\models_X \Phi$, Φ is called *AE-valid with respect to index X.* Intuitively speaking, $\varphi \models_X \psi$ means that an agent with knowledge base set X is able to derive ψ from φ. AE-semantics 'without index' (i.e. $\models_{AE}$) is not very interesting, seen in the light of the following proposition.

3.4.1 PROPOSITION. $\Phi \models_{AE} \varphi \Leftrightarrow \Phi \models_{prop} \varphi$. ■
(Recall that $\models_{prop}$ stands for the ordinary semantical entailment in propositional logic.)

We denote $LX = \{L\varphi \mid \varphi \in X\}$ and $\neg L\overline{X} = \{\neg L\varphi \mid \varphi \notin X\}$.

3.4.2. LEMMA. $\forall w, X, Y$: $[w, X] \models LY \cup \neg L\overline{Y} \Leftrightarrow X = Y$.

PROOF.

$$
\begin{aligned}
&[w, X] \models LY \cup \neg L\overline{Y} \Leftrightarrow\\
&\forall \varphi \in LY \cup \neg L\overline{Y} \ : \ [w, X] \models \varphi \Leftrightarrow
\end{aligned}
$$

$$\forall\varphi \in LY : [w, X] \models \varphi \text{ and } \forall\varphi \in \neg L\overline{Y} : [w, X] \models \varphi \Leftrightarrow$$
$$\forall\psi \in Y : [w, X] \models L\psi \text{ and } \forall\psi \notin Y : [w, X] \models \neg L\psi \Leftrightarrow$$
$$\forall\psi \in Y : \psi \in X \text{ and } \forall\psi \notin Y : \psi \notin X \Leftrightarrow$$
$$Y \subseteq X \text{ and } X \subseteq Y \Leftrightarrow X = Y. \quad \blacksquare$$

By means of this lemma we can establish a relation between indexed entailment $\models_X$ and $\models_{AE}$.

3.4.3. PROPOSITION. $\Phi \models_X \Psi \Leftrightarrow \Phi \cup LX \cup \neg L\overline{X} \models_{AE} \Psi$.

PROOF.

$$\Phi \cup LX \cup \neg L\overline{X} \models_{AE} \Psi \Leftrightarrow$$
$$(\forall w, Y : [w, Y] \models \Phi \cup LX \cup \neg L\overline{X} \Rightarrow [w, Y] \models \Psi) \Leftrightarrow$$
$$(\forall w, Y : ([w, Y] \models \Phi \text{ and } [w, Y] \models LX \cup \neg L\overline{X}) \Rightarrow [w, Y] \models \Psi) \Leftrightarrow \text{(Lemma 3.4.2)}$$
$$(\forall w, Y : ([w, Y] \models \Phi \text{ and } X = Y) \Rightarrow [w, Y] \models \Psi) \Leftrightarrow$$
$$(\forall w : [w, X] \models \Phi \Rightarrow [w, X] \models \Psi) \Leftrightarrow$$
$$\Phi \models_X \Psi. \quad \blacksquare$$

3.4.3.1. EXERCISE. Show:

(i) $Mp \to q \models_{\{p\}} q$

(ii) $Mp \to q \models_{\varnothing} q$

(iii) $Mp \to q \not\models_{\{\neg p\}} q$

To define the belief set associated with some base set of knowledge, we define the notion of an AE-extension below, and to this end we need the following definitions.

3.4.4. DEFINITION.

(i) Φ is *semantically closed* if Φ contains all its AE-consequences, i.e.

$$\forall\varphi: \Phi \models_{AE} \varphi \Rightarrow \varphi \in \Phi.$$

(ii) X is *semantically sound with respect to* Φ if every formula in X is a consequence of Φ with respect to index X:

$$\forall\varphi \in X: \Phi \models_X \varphi.$$

(iii) X is *semantically sound* if X is semantically sound with respect to $\varnothing$.

(iv) X is *semantically complete with respect to* Φ if every formula that is a consequence of Φ with respect to X is an element of X:

$$\forall\varphi:\ \Phi \models_X \varphi \Rightarrow \varphi \in X.$$

(v) X is *semantically complete* if X is semantically complete with respect to $\emptyset$.

Speaking intuitively, semantical soundness of X means that all facts known already in X can be derived by the agent. On the other hand semantical completeness means that all knowledge derivable from X is already known to the agent.

3.4.5. DEFINITION. X is called an *AE-extension* of Φ if X is propositionally consistent,[1] and semantically sound and complete with respect to Φ, i.e.

$$X = \{\varphi \mid \Phi \models_X \varphi\}.$$

One may view an AE-extension of a base set Φ as a coherent set of beliefs induced by Φ, or even as a set of consequences of Φ. Note, however, that one may have more than one of these sets (which are typically incompatible) or even none at all. The notion of an AE-extension is the central notion of AEL rendering the logic *non-monotonic*, since, in general, extending the base set yields a completely different set of extensions. (We will see this subsequently.)

As is to be expected, there is a relation between AE-extensions and the epistemic states of the previous section. We define stable sets of *auto*epistemic formulas in the same way as in the case of epistemic formulas:

3.4.6. DEFINITION. A set Φ of autoepistemic formulas is *stable* if it satisfies:

(St 1) Φ contains all instances of propositional tautologies

(St 2) $\varphi, \varphi \rightarrow \psi \in \Phi \Rightarrow \psi \in \Phi$

(St 3) $\varphi \in \Phi \ \Leftrightarrow\ L\varphi \in \Phi$

(St 4) $\varphi \notin \Phi \ \Leftrightarrow\ \neg L\varphi \in \Phi$

(St 5) Φ is propositionally consistent.[2]

3.4.7. LEMMA. *Let Φ be a set of AE-formulas such that:*

(St 1) *Φ contains all instances of propositional tautologies*

(St 2) *Φ is propositionally closed*

---

[1]Actually, [Moo84] does not require propositional consistency for either stability or AE-extensions (or expansions as it is called there), but we impose this requirement here to keep in line with the previous section. This line is also followed in e.g. [MT93].

[2]See above.

(St 3') $\varphi \in \Phi \Rightarrow L\varphi \in \Phi$

(St 4') $\varphi \notin \Phi \Rightarrow \neg L\varphi \in \Phi$

(St 5) *Φ is propositionally consistent.*

Then Φ is stable.

PROOF. It is sufficient to prove that

(i) $L\varphi \in \Phi \Rightarrow \varphi \in \Phi$ and

(ii) $\neg L\varphi \in \Phi \Rightarrow \varphi \notin \Phi$.

(i) Suppose $L\varphi \in \Phi$ and $\varphi \notin \Phi$. Then both $L\varphi \in \Phi$ and $\neg L\varphi \in \Phi$. Contradiction with (St 5).

(ii) Suppose $\neg L\varphi \in \Phi$ and $\varphi \in \Phi$. Then both $\neg L\varphi \in \Phi$ and $L\varphi \in \Phi$. Contradiction with (St 5). ■

3.4.7.1. EXERCISE. Show:

(i) $LLp \models_X Lp$ for any stable set X;

(ii) $Mp \to q \models_X q$ for any stable set X with $Lp \in X$.

Now we may state the following:

3.4.8. THEOREM. *Let Φ and Ψ be sets of AE-formulas. Then:*
Φ is propositionally consistent, semantically closed and complete with respect to $\Psi \Leftrightarrow \Phi$ is stable and contains Ψ.

PROOF. ($\Rightarrow$) Suppose that Φ is semantically closed and complete with respect to Ψ. We first prove that $\Phi \supseteq \Psi$. Suppose $\varphi \in \Psi$. Then $\Psi \models_\Phi \varphi$. Hence, since Φ is semantically complete with respect to Ψ, it holds that $\varphi \in \Phi$. Next we prove that Φ is stable:

(i) $\varphi \in \Phi \Rightarrow \Psi \models_\Phi L\varphi$ (by the truth definition of $[w, \Phi] \models L\varphi$)
$\Rightarrow L\varphi \in \Phi$ (semantical completeness with respect to Ψ)

(ii) $\varphi \notin \Phi \Rightarrow \Psi \models_\Phi \neg L\varphi$ (by the truth definition of $[w, \Phi] \models L\varphi$)
$\Rightarrow \neg L\varphi \in \Phi$ (semantical completeness with respect to Ψ)

Furthermore, by assumption Φ is propositionally consistent and propositionally closed ($\Leftarrow$ semantically closed and $\models_{AE}$ and $\models_{prop}$ coincide). Moreover, since for any propositional tautology τ it holds that $\models_{prop} \varphi \to \tau$, for any formula $\varphi \in \Phi$, we also get $\tau \in \Phi$, by propositional closedness. So (Lemma 3.4.7) Φ is stable.

($\Leftarrow$) Suppose Φ is stable and $\Phi \supseteq \Psi$. Then $\Phi \supseteq \Psi \cup L\Phi \cup \neg L\overline{\Phi}$ (stability).

We now prove that Φ is semantically complete with respect to Ψ (semantical closedness follows directly from the fact that Φ is propositionally closed). Let $\Psi \models_\Phi \varphi$. Then it holds that

$$\Psi \cup L\Phi \cup \neg L\overline{\Phi} \models_{AE} \varphi.$$

Since $\Psi \cup L\Phi \cup \neg L\overline{\Phi} \subseteq \Phi$, also $\Phi \models_{AE} \varphi$. So $\Phi \models_{prop} \varphi$ and thus $\varphi \in \Phi$, since Φ is propositionally closed. ■

3.4.9. COROLLARY. *Semantically closed AE-extensions are stable sets.*

PROOF. Since AE-extensions are propositionally consistent and semantically complete with respect to some set by definition, the statement in the corollary follows directly from the previous theorem. ■

According to this corollary semantically closed AE-extensions are epistemic states in the sense of the previous section. However, they possess yet another property:

3.4.10. DEFINITION. A set Φ of AE-formulas is *grounded in a set* Ψ of AE-formulas if it holds that

$$\Phi \subseteq \langle \Psi \cup L\Phi \cup \neg L\overline{\Phi} \rangle,$$

where $\langle X \rangle$ stands for the propositional closure of X, i.e. $\langle X \rangle = \{\varphi \mid X \vdash_{PC} \varphi\}$.

Note that this notion is the 'converse' of that of a Ψ-containing stable set:

3.4.11. PROPOSITION. *Let* $\Phi \supseteq \Psi$. *Then it holds that*

$$\Phi \textit{ is stable } \Leftrightarrow \Phi \textit{ is propositionally closed and consistent and } \langle \Psi \cup L\Phi \cup \neg L\overline{\Phi} \rangle \subseteq \Phi.$$

PROOF. First suppose that Φ is stable. By stability we immediately have that Φ is propositionally closed and consistent. Next we show that $\langle \Psi \cup L\Phi \cup \neg L\overline{\Phi} \rangle \subseteq \Phi$. We know that $\Psi \subseteq \Phi$. Furthermore, since Φ is stable, it holds that

$$L\Phi \subseteq \Phi \text{ and } \neg L\overline{\Phi} \subseteq \Phi.$$

Since Φ is stable and thus propositionally closed, it holds that

$$\langle \Psi \cup L\Phi \cup \neg L\overline{\Phi} \rangle \subseteq \Phi.$$

Conversely, suppose that Φ is propositionally closed and consistent and that $< \Psi \cup L\Phi \cup \neg L\overline{\Phi} > \subseteq \Phi$. Since we already know that Φ is propositionally closed (and thus also contains all instances of propositional tautologies) and consistent, we only have to show the introspective properties to get the stability of Φ:
Let $\varphi \in \Phi$. Then, since $L\Phi \subseteq \Phi$, we have that $L\varphi \in \Phi$.
Let $\varphi \notin \Phi$. Then, since $\neg L\overline{\Phi} \subseteq \Phi$, we have that $\neg L\varphi \in \Phi$.
By Lemma 3.4.7 we now directly obtain stability of Φ. ■

Regarding groundedness we have the following:

3.4.12. THEOREM. *Let Φ and Ψ be sets of AE-formulas.Then:*
Φ is semantically sound with respect to Ψ $\Leftrightarrow$ Φ is grounded in Ψ.

PROOF.

Φ is semantically sound with respect to Ψ $\Leftrightarrow$

$\Psi \models_{\Phi} \Phi$ $\Leftrightarrow$

$\Phi \subseteq \{\varphi \mid \Psi \models_{\Phi} \varphi\}$ $\Leftrightarrow$

$\Phi \subseteq \{\varphi \mid \Psi \cup L\Phi \cup \neg L\overline{\Phi} \models_{AE} \varphi\}$ $\Leftrightarrow$

$\Phi \subseteq \{\varphi \mid \Psi \cup L\Phi \cup \neg L\overline{\Phi} \models_{prop} \varphi\}$ $\Leftrightarrow$

$\Phi \subseteq < \Psi \cup L\Phi \cup \neg L\overline{\Phi} >$ $\Leftrightarrow$

Φ grounded in Ψ. ■

This theorem has the following consequence for AE-extensions:

3.4.13. COROLLARY. *AE-extensions of Ψ are grounded in Ψ.*

PROOF. Direct, since by definition AE-extensions of Ψ are semantically sound with respect to Ψ. ■

From Corollaries 3.4.9 and 3.4.13 we may conclude that semantically (or propositionally) closed AE-extensions of Ψ are stable sets grounded in Ψ. By a more careful analysis we can prove that AE-extensions are automatically semantically closed; we may strengthen the previous result and state that every AE-extension of Ψ is a stable set grounded in Ψ:

3.4.14. THEOREM.
(i) *Φ is an AE-extension of Ψ $\Leftrightarrow$*
Φ is propositionally consistent and $\Phi = < \Psi \cup L\Phi \cup \neg L\overline{\Phi} >$.
(ii) *AE-extensions of Ψ are stable sets grounded in Ψ.*

PROOF. (i) Let Φ be an AE-extension of Ψ. Then Φ is propositionally consistent, and

$$\Phi = \{\varphi \mid \Psi \models_{\overline{\Phi}} \varphi\}. \qquad (*)$$

Hence, for every φ, it holds that

$$\begin{aligned}
&\varphi \in \Phi \Leftrightarrow \text{(by (*))}\\
&\Psi \models_{\Phi} \varphi \Leftrightarrow \text{(by Proposition 3.4.3)}\\
&\Psi \cup L\Phi \cup \neg L\overline{\Phi} \models_{AE} \varphi \Leftrightarrow \text{(by Proposition 3.4.1)}\\
&\Psi \cup L\Phi \cup \neg L\overline{\Phi} \models_{prop} \varphi \Leftrightarrow\\
&\varphi \in < \Psi \cup L\Phi \cup \neg L\overline{\Phi} >.
\end{aligned}$$

So, $\Phi = < \Psi \cup L\Phi \cup \neg L\overline{\Phi} >$.

Conversely, suppose $\Phi = < \Psi \cup L\Phi \cup \neg L\overline{\Phi} >$ (and hence Φ is propositionally closed!) and Φ is propositionally consistent. By the propositional closedness and consistency of Φ, the fact that $< \Psi \cup L\Phi \cup \neg L\overline{\Phi} > \subseteq \Phi$ and Proposition 3.4.11, we have that Φ is stable, and hence Φ is semantically closed and complete with respect to Ψ, by Theorem 3.4.8. By the fact that $\Phi \subseteq < \Psi \cup L\Phi \cup \neg L\overline{\Phi} >$ and Theorem 3.4.12, we also have that Φ is semantically sound with respect to Ψ. Consequently, Φ is an AE-extension of Ψ.
(ii) Let Φ be an AE-extension of Ψ. From (i)$\Rightarrow$, we obtain that Φ is propositionally consistent and $\Phi = < \Psi \cup L\Phi \cup \neg L\overline{\Phi} >$. From '$\supseteq$', the fact that clearly Φ is propositionally closed and consistent, and Proposition 3.4.11, we get that Φ is stable. From '$\subseteq$' we immediately get that Φ is grounded in Ψ. ■

From all this we may conclude that AE-extensions of Ψ are those epistemic states (= stable sets) that are grounded in Ψ. This is not so strange, because one should expect that an AE-extension of a set Ψ still has something to do with Ψ.

3.4.14.1. EXERCISE ([MT91]).

(i) Show that two sets Ψ_1 and Ψ_2 of AE-formulas such that $<\Psi_1> = <\Psi_2>$, have the same AE-extensions.

(ii) Prove that if Φ is an AE-extension of Ψ and $\Psi \subseteq \Psi' \subseteq \Phi$, then Φ is an AE-extension of Ψ' as well, and that, in particular, Φ is its own AE-extension.

Not every set Ψ has an AE-extension:

3.4.15. EXAMPLE. The set {Lp} has no AE-extension.

PROOF. Suppose {Lp} does have an AE-extension, say Φ. Then Φ is a stable set that contains Lp. So also $p \in \Phi$ (stability). Moreover, Φ is semantically sound with respect to {Lp}, i.e. Lp $\models_{\Phi} \Phi$. That is to say that every Φ-interpretation $[w, \Phi]$ validating Lp has to validate Φ. However, for $[w_0, \Phi]$ with $w_0 = \lambda p \cdot \mathbb{f}$ it holds that $[w_0, \Phi] \models Lp$ (because $p \in \Phi$), but $[w_0, \Phi] \not\models p$. Contradiction. ■

Of course there are also sets that have AE-extensions. (The notion would not be very interesting, otherwise.)

3.4.16. EXAMPLE. Every (finite) set of objective formulas has a (unique) AE-extension.

PROOF. We know by Corollary 3.1.13 that a (finite) set Ψ of objective formulas determines a unique stable set Φ with $\text{Prop}(\Phi) = \langle \Psi \rangle \cap \mathcal{L}_0$. (Actually, $\Phi = \Sigma^{\Psi}$, where the notation Ψ is also (ab)used for the conjunction of the elements of the set Ψ.) Since Φ is a stable set containing Ψ, it follows from Theorem 3.4.8 that Φ is semantically complete with respect to Ψ (and semantically closed). It remains to be proved that Φ is grounded in Ψ, i.e.

$$\Phi \subseteq \langle \Psi \cup L\Phi \cup \neg L\overline{\Phi} \rangle.$$

We prove by induction on the structure of φ that

$$\varphi \in \Phi \Rightarrow \varphi \in \langle \Psi \cup L\Phi \cup \neg L\overline{\Phi} \rangle.$$

Assume that φ is in conjunctive normal form (composed of purely propositional formulas and formulas of the form $L\psi$, $\neg L\psi$).

(i) The assertion is true for purely propositional formulas, and for formulas of the form $L\psi$, $\neg L\psi$. Hence, if e.g. $L\psi \in \Phi$ then $\psi \in \Phi$ (Φ stable) and so $L\psi \in L\Phi$. If $\neg L\psi \in \Phi$ then $\psi \notin \Phi$ (Φ stable) and so $\neg L\psi \in \neg L\overline{\Phi}$.

(ii) If $\varphi = \varphi_1 \wedge \varphi_2 \in \Phi$, then $\varphi_1 \in \Phi$ and $\varphi_2 \in \Phi$ (Φ stable), and we may apply the induction hypothesis: $\varphi_1, \varphi_2 \in \langle \Psi \cup L\Phi \cup \neg L\overline{\Phi} \rangle$, and hence

$$\varphi_1 \wedge \varphi_2 \in \langle \Psi \cup L\Phi \cup \neg L\overline{\Phi} \rangle \qquad \text{(property } \langle \cdot \rangle\text{)}.$$

(iii) If $\varphi = \varphi_1 \vee \varphi_2$, φ no longer contains $\wedge$-symbols (by assumption of conjunctive normal form). If φ is not a purely propositional formula (otherwise we are in case (i)), either φ_1 or φ_2 is not a purely propositional formula either. Without loss of generality we assume that φ_1 is not purely propositional, i.e. of the form $L\varphi_3$ or $\neg L\varphi_3$. Then $\varphi = L\varphi_3 \vee \varphi_2$ or $\varphi = \neg L\varphi_3 \vee \varphi_2$. Now we use the 'AEL-analogue' of Lemma 3.1.3 and conclude, since $\varphi \in \Phi$ (Φ stable), $\varphi_3 \in \Phi$ or $\varphi_2 \in \Phi$, in the first case, and $\varphi_3 \notin \Phi$ or $\varphi_2 \in \Phi$, in the second. Hence (by stability of Φ)

$$L\varphi_3 \in \Phi \text{ or } \varphi_2 \in \Phi, \text{ and } \neg L\varphi_3 \in \Phi \text{ or } \varphi_2 \in \Phi, \text{ respectively.}$$

So in any case $\varphi_1 \in \Phi$ or $\varphi_2 \in \Phi$. Now we may apply the induction hypothesis and conclude that $\varphi_1 \in <\Psi \cup L\Phi \cup \neg L\overline{\Phi}>$ or $\varphi_2 \in <\Psi \cup L\Phi \cup \neg L\overline{\Phi}>$, and so in any case:

$$\varphi = \varphi_1 \vee \varphi_2 \in <\Psi \cup L\Phi \cup \neg L\overline{\Phi}>. \blacksquare$$

3.4.16.1. EXERCISE.

(i) Let Φ be stable. Prove that Φ is the unique AE-extension of its objective kernel Prop(Φ), i.e. $\Phi = <\text{Prop}(\Phi) \cup L\Phi \cup \neg L\overline{\Phi}>$.

(ii) Let Φ be a stable set. Prove that: $[w, \Phi] \models \text{Prop}(\Phi) \Rightarrow [w, \Phi] \models \Phi$.

3.4.17. EXERCISE. Check whether the following sets of AE-formulas have extensions, and if so which ones.

(i) $\{p\}$

(ii) $\{p, q\}$

(iii) $\{p \rightarrow Lp\}$

(iv) $\{Mp \rightarrow p\}$

(v) $\{p \rightarrow L\neg p\}$

(vi) $\{Mp \rightarrow \neg q, Mq \rightarrow \neg p\}$

The semantics of AEL as we have seen it does not seem to have much in common with (ordinary) epistemic logic, since in it there is no direct reference to Kripke models. On the other hand, we have seen that AE-extensions are stable sets, just like theories of **S5**-models, as we saw in the previous section. Next we establish a closer relationship between AEL and the logic **S5**. (The following is based primarily on [Vre91].)

First we give some additional definitions. Recall the definition of a *simple* **S5**-model as given in Section 1.7.

3.4.18. DEFINITION. Let $\mathbb{M} = (S, \pi)$ be a simple **S5**-model. The *universal* S5-model **M** *derived from* $\mathbb{M}$ is a Kripke model with $\mathbf{M} = (\mathbb{U}, \mathcal{R})$, where $\mathbb{U}$ is the universe of all classical propositional valuations, i.e. $\mathbb{U} = \{\pi \mid \pi : P \rightarrow \{\mathfrak{t}, \mathfrak{f}\}\}$, and $\mathcal{R}$ is given by S in the following way: $(s, t) \in \mathcal{R}$ iff $t \in S$. (Or, in other words, $\mathcal{R} = \mathbb{U} \times S$.)

We now interpret the modality L on a universal **S5**-model $\mathbf{M} = (\mathbb{U}, \mathcal{R})$ as expected: for $s \in \mathbb{U}$, $(\mathbf{M}, s) \models L\varphi$ iff $(\mathbf{M}, t) \models \varphi$ for all $t \in \mathbb{U}$ such that $\mathcal{R}(s, t)$. Thus for a universal **S5**-model $\mathbf{M} = (\mathbb{U}, \mathcal{R})$ derived from a simple **S5**-model $\mathbb{M} = (S, \pi)$, we have that, for $s \in \mathbb{U}$, $(\mathbf{M}, s) \models L\varphi$ iff $(\mathbf{M}, s) \models \varphi$ for all $s \in S$. This leads to the following simple observation.

3.4.19. PROPOSITION. *Let* $\mathbf{M}$ *be the universal* **S5**-*model derived from the simple* **S5**-*model* $\mathbb{M} = (S, \pi)$. *Then* $K(\mathbb{M}) = \{\varphi \mid \mathbf{M} \models L\varphi\}$.

PROOF. $\mathbf{M} \models L\varphi \iff \forall s \in \mathbb{U} : (\mathbf{M}, s) \models L\varphi \iff \forall s \in S : (\mathbf{M}, s) \models \varphi \iff \forall s \in S : (\mathbb{M}, s) \models \varphi \iff \mathbb{M} \models \varphi$. ■

3.4.20. LEMMA [Moo84, Moo85a]. *For every simple* **S5**-*model* $\mathbb{M} = (S, \pi)$, *it holds that* $(\mathbf{M}, s) \models K(\mathbb{M}) \Leftrightarrow s \in S$, where $\mathbf{M}$ is the universal **S5**-model derived from $\mathbb{M}$.

PROOF. First, suppose that $s \in S$. Because, for every formula φ, $\varphi \in K(\mathbb{M})$ iff $\forall s \in S : (\mathbb{M}, s) \models \varphi$ iff $\forall s \in S : (\mathbf{M}, s) \models \varphi$, we have that $(\mathbf{M}, s) \models K(\mathbb{M})$. Conversely, suppose that $s \notin S$. Recall that, in a universal **S5**-model, states s in S are identified with the valuation $\pi(s)$ assigned to s. Because of $s \notin S$, every element (valuation) t in S disagrees with s on at least one propositional constant p_t. Take, for each $t \in S$, the constant p_t or its negation $\neg p_t$, whichever is true in t (and thus false in s), and form their disjunction. (This will be finite disjunction, since we have assumed **P** to be finite and thus S must be finite!) This disjunction is true at every element t of S, so it is in $K(\mathbb{M})$, but it is false at $(\mathbf{M}, s)$. Hence, $(\mathbf{M}, s) \not\models K(\mathbb{M})$, and we are done. ■

3.4.21. LEMMA. *Suppose* Σ *is a stable set, and* $\mathbb{M}$ *is a simple* **S5**-*model such that* $\Sigma = K(\mathbb{M})$. *Then for the universal* **S5**-*model* $\mathbf{M}$ *derived from* $\mathbb{M}$ *we have that:* $(\mathbf{M}, s) \models \varphi \Leftrightarrow [s, \Sigma] \models \varphi$.

PROOF. Since epistemic and AE-satisfiability already coincide on atomic formulas and with respect to the propositional connectives, it suffices to show that, for any φ and s, $(\mathbf{M}, s) \models L\varphi$ iff $[s, \Sigma] \models L\varphi$. This follows immediately from the fact that $\Sigma = K(\mathbb{M})$, since now we have that, for any s, $(\mathbf{M}, s) \models L\varphi \iff \mathbf{M} \models L\varphi \iff$ (Proposition 3.4.19) $\varphi \in K(\mathbb{M}) \iff \varphi \in \Sigma \iff [s, \Sigma] \models L\varphi$. ■

3.4.22. THEOREM [Vre91]. *Suppose* Σ *is a stable set, and* $\mathbb{M} = (S, \pi)$ *is a simple* **S5**-*model such that* $\Sigma = K(\mathbb{M})$. *Then:* Σ *is an AE-extension of* $\Phi \Leftrightarrow S = \{s \mid (\mathbf{M}, s) \models \Phi\}$, *where* $\mathbf{M}$ *is the universal* **S5**-*model derived from* $\mathbb{M}$.

PROOF. First, suppose that $S = \{s \mid (\mathbf{M}, s) \models \Phi\}$. We have to prove that $\Sigma = K(\mathbb{M})$ is an AE-extension of Φ. By Definition 3.4.5 this means that we have to show that Σ is semantically sound and complete with respect to Φ. We first show that Σ is semantically complete with respect to Φ. Using Theorem 3.4.8, this amounts to showing that Σ is a stable set that contains Φ. The stability of Σ is given, and $\Phi \subseteq \Sigma$ follows from the fact that $\mathbb{M} \models \Phi$. Next, we show that Σ is semantically sound with respect to Φ, i.e. that $\Phi \models_\Sigma \varphi$ for all $\varphi \in \Sigma$. Recall that $S = \{s \mid (\mathbf{M}, s) \models \Phi\}$ and suppose that $[s, \Sigma]$ is an AE-interpretation of Φ. We have to show that $[s, \Sigma] \models \Sigma$. By Lemma 3.4.21 we obtain that $(\mathbf{M}, s) \models \Phi$, which implies that $s \in S$. So, according to Lemma 3.4.20, $(\mathbf{M}, s) \models K(\mathbb{M})$. Hence, by the fact that $\Sigma = K(\mathbb{M})$, we have that $(\mathbf{M}, s) \models \Sigma$. Using Lemma 3.4.21 again yields $[s, \Sigma] \models \Sigma$.

Conversely, suppose that Σ is an AE-extension of Φ. First we prove $\{s \mid (\mathbf{M}, s) \models \Phi\} \subseteq S$: suppose $(\mathbf{M}, s) \models \Phi$. By Lemma 3.4.21, this is equivalent with $[s, \Sigma] \models \Phi$. Since AE-extensions of Φ are semantically sound with respect to Φ, this gives us $[s, \Sigma] \models \Sigma$. Again, by Lemma 3.4.21 it is allowed to replace the AE-interpretation by a Kripke interpretation, yielding $(\mathbf{M}, s) \models \Sigma$. Hence, with Lemma 3.4.20, $s \in S$. Next we prove $S \subseteq \{s \mid (\mathbf{M}, s) \models \Phi\}$: suppose $s \in S$, so that $(\mathbf{M}, s) \models \Sigma$ (by Lemma 3.4.20). Since $\Phi \subseteq \Sigma$, we immediately obtain our desired result, namely $(\mathbf{M}, s) \models \Phi$. ■

We may even push the connection between AEL and modal logic further, when we introduce the notion of a *complementary* structure:

3.4.23. DEFINITION. Let $\mathbf{M}$ be a universal **S5**-model derived from a simple **S5**-model $\mathbb{M} = \langle S, \pi \rangle$. The simple S5-model $\mathbb{M}^* = \langle S^*, \pi^* \rangle$, where $S^* = \mathbb{U} \setminus S$ ($\setminus$ stands for the set-theoretic difference), and π^* is defined appropriately to match the valuations in $\mathbb{U} \setminus S$, is called the *complementary* structure of $\mathbb{M}$. See Figure 3.2.

On a universal model $\mathbf{M}$ we may now refer to its complementary structure by means of an additional modality L^*, of which the semantics is given by: $(\mathbf{M}, s) \models L^*\varphi \Leftrightarrow \mathbb{M}^* \models \varphi$. (The L^*-operator is the same in essence as the N-operator, 'believing at most to be false', of [Lev90].) When we need it we shall denote the accessibility relation associated with the modality L^* by $\mathcal{R}^*$. (So $\mathcal{R}^* = \mathbb{U} \times S^*$.) Now we can state the following theorem which is useful when determining whether a set has an AE-extension. Also we shall use $M\varphi$ for $\neg L \neg \varphi$, and $M^*\varphi$ for $\neg L^* \neg \varphi$.

3.4.24. THEOREM [Vre91]. *Let Φ be a set of L^*-free formulas. Then Φ has an AE-extension if and only if $L\Phi \wedge L^*\neg\Phi$ is satisfiable in a universal* **S5***-model.*

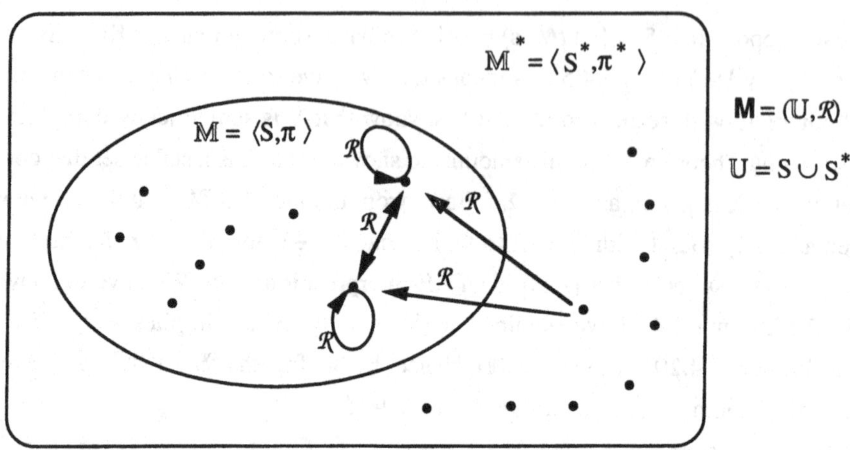

Figure 3.2

PROOF. By Theorem 3.4.22 it is sufficient to prove that $L\Phi \wedge L^*\neg\Phi$ is S5-satisfiable in a universal **S5**-model iff $S = \{s \mid (\mathbf{M}, s) \models \Phi\}$ for some universal model **M** derived from a simple model $\mathbb{M} = \langle S, \pi\rangle$. First, suppose that $L\Phi \wedge L^*\neg\Phi$ is S5-satisfiable in a universal **S5**-model $\mathbf{M} = (\mathbb{U}, \mathcal{R})$ in state $t \in \mathbb{U}$. So $(\mathbf{M}, t) \models L\Phi \wedge L^*\neg\Phi$. Let $S = \{s \mid \mathcal{R}(t, s)\}$, and $S^* = \{s \mid \mathcal{R}^*(t, s)\} = \{s \mid \neg\mathcal{R}(t, s)\}$. Then $\forall s : \mathcal{R}(t, s) \Rightarrow (\mathbf{M}, s) \models \Phi$, and $\forall s : \mathcal{R}^*(t, s) \Rightarrow (\mathbf{M}, s) \models \neg\Phi$. Thus we have that $\forall s \in S : (\mathbf{M}, s) \models \Phi$, and $\forall s \notin S : (\mathbf{M}, s) \not\models \Phi$, i.e. $S \subseteq \{s \mid (\mathbf{M}, s) \models \Phi\}$ and $S \supseteq \{s \mid (\mathbf{M}, s) \models \Phi\}$. Consequently, $S = \{s \mid (\mathbf{M}, s) \models \Phi\}$.
Conversely, suppose that $S = \{s \mid (\mathbf{M}, s) \models \Phi\}$ for some universal model **M** derived from a simple model $\mathbb{M} = (S, \pi)$. Now $\forall s \in S : (\mathbf{M}, s) \models \Phi$, and $\forall s \notin S : (\mathbf{M}, s) \not\models \Phi$. Thus, for any $t \in \mathbb{U}$, $\forall s : \mathcal{R}(t, s) \Rightarrow (\mathbf{M}, s) \models \Phi$, and $\forall s : \mathcal{R}^*(t, s) \Rightarrow (\mathbf{M}, s) \models \neg\Phi$. So, for any $t \in \mathbb{U}$, $(\mathbf{M}, t) \models L\Phi \wedge L^*\neg\Phi$, i.e. $L\Phi \wedge L^*\neg\Phi$ is satisfied in the universal **S5**-model **M**. ∎

Following Levesque [Lev90] we can now proceed to introduce a special operator O to denote 'knowing only' or 'knowing exactly'. In fact, we can define $O\varphi$, 'knowing only (exactly) φ', as an abbreviation of $L\varphi \wedge L^*\neg\varphi$, 'knowing at least φ and at most φ'. Alternatively, one can define the semantics of the O-operator on a universal model as follows:

Let **M** be a universal **S5**-model derived from a simple **S5**-model $\mathbb{M} = \langle S, \pi\rangle$. Then:

$$(\mathbf{M}, s) \models O\varphi \text{ iff, for every } t,\ t \in S \Leftrightarrow (\mathbf{M}, t) \models \varphi.$$

Note the similarity between the semantics of the O-operator and the L- and L*-operators, since it also holds that:

$(\mathbf{M}, s) \models L\varphi$ iff, for every t, $t \in S \Rightarrow (\mathbf{M}, t) \models \varphi$;
$(\mathbf{M}, s) \models L^*\varphi$ iff, for every t, $t \notin S \Rightarrow (\mathbf{M}, t) \models \varphi$, or equivalently,
$(\mathbf{M}, s) \models L^*\varphi$ iff, for every t, $(\mathbf{M}, t) \not\models \varphi \Rightarrow t \in S$, or equivalently,
$(\mathbf{M}, s) \models L^*\neg\varphi$ iff, for every t, $(\mathbf{M}, t) \models \varphi \Rightarrow t \in S$.

Finally for convenience we associate with a universal S5-model $\mathbf{M} = (\mathbb{U}, \mathcal{R})$ 'universal' modalities $\Box$ and $\Diamond$, expressing the ontological necessity with respect to such a model:

$(\mathbf{M}, s) \models \Box\varphi$ iff, for every t, $t \in \mathbb{U} \Rightarrow (\mathbf{M}, t) \models \varphi$;
$(\mathbf{M}, s) \models \Diamond\varphi$ iff, for some $t \in \mathbb{U}$, $(\mathbf{M}, t) \models \varphi$.

Thus the universal modalities do not take the dichotomy between S and S* into account, nor the state in which they are evaluated, but are just the S5-modalities associated with the model **M**, viewed as a simple S5-model $(\mathbb{U}, \pi)$ in itself. When it is convenient we write the accessibility relation associated with the modality $\Box$ as $\mathcal{R}^{\Box}$. Thus $\mathcal{R}^{\Box} = \mathbb{U} \times \mathbb{U}$. The modal language that includes all these modalities $\Box$, $\Diamond$, L, L*, M, M*, and O is denoted by $\mathcal{L}_O$.

As we have extended the number of modalities, we also need to reconsider the notion of a subjective formula. We define a *subjective formula* as a formula of the form $\otimes\varphi$, where $\otimes$ stands for one of the modalities $\Box$, $\Diamond$, L, L*, M, M*, and O. For technical convenience, we also define the notion of a *basic subjective formula* as a formula of the form $\otimes\varphi$, where $\otimes$ stands for one of the modalities $\Box$, $\Diamond$, L, L*, M, and M* (thus excluding O).

We can now give a sound and complete axiom system for the logic **S5O** of 'only knowing' as follows (this system is similar to those given in [Lev90] and [Vre91], but because of the use of an ontological necessity operator we can use familiar correspondences):

(O0) All propositional tautologies
(O1) $\Box(\varphi \to \psi) \to (\Box\varphi \to \Box\psi)$
(O2) $\Box\varphi \to \varphi$
(O3) $\neg\Box\varphi \to \Box\neg\Box\varphi$
(O4) $\Diamond\varphi \leftrightarrow \neg\Box\neg\varphi$
(O5) $\Diamond\varphi$, for every satisfiable objective formula φ
(O6) $\Box\varphi \leftrightarrow (L\varphi \wedge L^*\varphi)$
(O7) $\varphi \to \Box\varphi$, for every basic subjective formula φ
(O8) $L(\varphi \to \psi) \to (L\varphi \to L\psi)$
(O9) $L^*(\varphi \to \psi) \to (L^*\varphi \to L^*\psi)$
(O10) $\varphi \to L\varphi$, for every basic subjective formula φ

(O11) $\varphi \rightarrow L^*\varphi$, for every basic subjective formula φ

(O12) $\neg L\bot \rightarrow (L\varphi \rightarrow \varphi)$, for every basic subjective formula φ

(O13) $\neg L^*\bot \rightarrow (L^*\varphi \rightarrow \varphi)$, for every basic subjective formula φ

(O14) $\neg(M\varphi \wedge M^*\varphi)$, for every uniquely satisfiable objective formula φ

(O15) $O\varphi \leftrightarrow L\varphi \wedge L^*\neg\varphi$

The system is completed by *modus ponens* and the necessitation rule for $\Box$. (Note that the necessitation rules for L and L* follow from this and (O6).)

Note that this implies having S5 for $\Box$, and K45 for both L and L*. Moreover, (O5) states that every satisfiable objective formula is satisfied in a state of the universal model, i.e. the universal model **M** is really universal in the sense that every valuation is present. As we see below this also means that $S \cup S^* = \mathbb{U}$, since (O6) corresponds to $\mathcal{R}^{\Box} = \mathcal{R} \cup \mathcal{R}^*$. (O7), (O10) and (O11) express that, if a formula is already basically subjective, and thus referring to either the whole set $\mathbb{U}$, or the sets S or S*, it also does so in the same way when considering it from another point in $\mathbb{U}$, S or S*: the 'pointers' $\Box$, L, and L*, refer to the same sets (namely $\mathbb{U}$, S and S*, respectively) again. In some sense, (O2), (O12) and (O13) say the converse: if there is a basically subjective reference via an extra reference using the modalities $\Box$, L, and L*, we may leave out this intermediate reference (provided that in the cases of L and L* the sets that are referred to in the intermediate manner, namely S and S*, respectively, are non-trivial (i.e. non-empty)). (O14) states that S and S* are disjoint in the strong sense that they also do not contain the same valuations.

Some useful theorems of the logic are listed below:

3.4.25. PROPOSITION. *The following are theorems in the logic* **S5O**:

(O16) $M\varphi \vee M^*\varphi$, for satisfiable objective formulas φ

(O17) $L^*\psi \rightarrow \neg L\psi$, for falsifiable objective formulas ψ

(O18) $L^*\bot \rightarrow \neg L\bot$, and symmetrically $L\bot \rightarrow \neg L^*\bot$

(O19) $\neg L\bot \vee \neg L^*\bot$ ('distributed D-axiom')

(O20) $(L\varphi \vee L^*\psi) \rightarrow (\varphi \wedge \psi)$

(O21) $M\varphi \rightarrow L^*\neg\varphi$, for uniquely satisfiable objective formulas φ.

PROOF.

(O16) By (O5), $\Diamond\varphi$ for every satisfiable objective formula φ. Hence by (O4), $\neg\Box\neg\varphi$. So by (O6), $\neg(L\neg\varphi \wedge L^*\neg\varphi)$, i.e. $\neg L\neg\varphi \vee \neg L^*\neg\varphi$, i.e. $M\varphi \vee M^*\varphi$.

(O17) From the previous considerations, it also follows directly that $L^*\neg\varphi \rightarrow \neg L\neg\varphi$ for any satisfiable objective formula φ. But this implies in its turn that $L^*\psi \rightarrow \neg L\psi$ for any falsifiable objective formula φ.

(O18) Follows directly from (O17), since $\bot$ is a falsifiable objective formula.

(O19) Follows directly from (O18).

(O20) $(L\varphi \wedge L^*\psi) \Rightarrow (L(\varphi \vee \psi) \wedge L^*(\varphi \vee \psi)) \Rightarrow \Box(\varphi \vee \psi) \Rightarrow \varphi \vee \psi$.

(O21) By (O14), $\neg(M\varphi \wedge M^*\varphi)$ for any uniquely satisfiable objective formula φ. So also $\neg M\varphi \vee \neg M^*\varphi$, i.e., $M\varphi \rightarrow L^*\neg\varphi$, for uniquely satisfiable objective formulas φ. ∎

3.4.26. REMARKS. (O16) states semantically that a classical propositional valuation is in either S or S*; (O17) appears as an axiom in Levesque's logic [Lev90]. Note that we have the 'distributed D-axiom' (O19), which means that at least one of the two sets S and S* is non-empty. This is a difference with [Vre91], where it is assumed that both S and S* are non-empty, and therefore both $\mathbb{M}$ and $\mathbb{M}^*$ satisfy the D-axiom. (O20) appears as an axiom in Vreeswijk's approach [Vre91]; (O21) is similar to an axiom in [Vre91].

Note that now we have an axiom system for assessing validity in universal S5-models we can reformulate Theorem 3.4.24 as follows:

3.4.27. THEOREM. *Let Φ be a set of* L*-*free formulas. Then Φ has* ***no*** *AE-extension if and only if* **S5O** $\vdash \neg(L\Phi \wedge L^*\neg\Phi)$ *(or, equivalently,* **S5O** $\vdash M\neg\Phi \vee M^*\Phi$*)).* ∎

In closing this section on autoepistemic logic, we can state that, given some set of formulas that represents the knowledge and ignorance of an agent, we now have two ways to associate epistemic states with this set. If the set of formulas can be written as a single *honest* formula, we may choose to use Halpern & Moses' method, and employ the 'least' stable set that contains this honest formula to represent the epistemic state of the agent. In some cases we may also determine Moore's AE-extensions and use these as representations. Unfortunately, these methods are *not* equivalent. They involve different notions of 'minimality': Halpern & Moses employ the stable set that contains the *least propositional knowledge*; Moore uses the stable sets that are *grounded* in the knowledge given. One may try to combine these two methods, as is proposed by Konolige in [Kon88].

Konolige considers *minimal* AE-extensions of a set Φ which are AE-extension for which there is no stable set containing Φ that has a strictly smaller propositional kernel. One may characterise such minimal AE-extensions as sets Ψ satisfying $\Phi = \mathrm{Cons}_{\mathbf{K45}}(\Psi \cup L\Psi \cup \neg L\overline{\Phi})$, where $\mathrm{Cons}_{\mathbf{K45}}(\Theta)$ stands for the set $\{\varphi \mid \mathbf{K45} \vdash \varphi_1 \wedge \ldots \wedge \varphi_n \rightarrow \varphi$ for some $\varphi_1, \ldots,$

$\varphi_n \in \Theta\}$, whereas ordinary AE-extensions can be shown to satisfy $\Phi = Cons_{\mathbf{K45}}(\Psi \cup L\Phi \cup \neg L\overline{\Phi})$. In fact, Konolige considers a few further restricted extensions to relate AEL with Reiter's default logic, which is another well-known nonmonotonic formalism. We shall not pursue this further. The interested reader is referred to [Kon88] or [Luk90].

Finally we nóte that although AEL is a logic to reason about the self-knowledge of a rational introspective agent, in the literature it is often regarded as a logic for default reasoning (or reasoning by default). In the next chapter we shall see that this is problematic, and moreover, that although default reasoning involves epistemic reasoning, other ingredients must also be included to obtain a truthful theory of default reasoning.

4 DEFAULT REASONING BY EPISTEMIC LOGIC

In this chapter we shall occupy ourselves with default reasoning, or reasoning by default. In fact we indicate how default logic can be based on epistemic logic, and particularly how we may employ Halpern & Moses' minimal epistemic states for this purpose. In this way we obtain a simple and natural S5-based logic for default reasoning that is well-behaved in a certain way. (We show the logic to be cumulative in the sense of Kraus, Lehmann and Magidor [KLM90].)

Default logic, autoepistemic logic (AEL) and other approaches to non-monotonic reasoning suffer from a technical complexity that is not in line with naive common-sense reasoning. They employ fixed-point constructions or higher-order logic in order to define the belief sets that one would like to associate with some base set of knowledge.

Here we present a modal logic, called **EDL**, which is an extension of the epistemic logic of Chapter 1. The logic **EDL** was introduced in [MH91a, MH92], and in [MH93a, 95] we connected it to the theory of Halpern & Moses, as treated in Section 3.1, to obtain a logic for default reasoning. The combined approach is relatively simple compared with AEL, but, more importantly, it is better suited as a default logic than AEL, as we shall show subsequently.

Our approach — unlike AEL — does not involve any fixed points or higher-order formulas. The basis for this logic is the simple **S5**-modal logic of Chapter 1. **EDL** contains a knowledge (certainty) operator and (dual) possibility operator. Furthermore, the logic contains special modalities to indicate that some assertions hold by default. This results in a number of desirable properties with respect to e.g. transitivity and contraposition, which troubled AEL, when interpreted as a logic for default reasoning. Also reasoning by cases is supported by this logic in contrast with e.g. Reiter's default logic.

To motivate the origin of the certainty, and even more importantly, the possibility of an assertion in a particular situation, we employ Halpern & Moses' minimal epistemic states. As a result we obtain a simple and natural non-monotonic logic for default reasoning. We furthermore show that the logic is cumulative in the sense of Kraus, Lehmann & Magidor [KLM90].

4.1. Default Reasoning and Reiter's Default Logic

Default reasoning is a form of reasoning that is very important in AI applications and knowledge representation in particular. It is relevant when one considers inheritance hierarchies with exceptions, such as in reasoning with frames (see e.g. [RD88], [LvdG91]), in diagnostic reasoning, in natural language processing, etc. This is not so strange when one realises that reasoning by default is a very common-sense type of reasoning. In daily life we use it all the time. For instance, when we make appointments or other agreements with people we assume by default that they will adhere to (and remember) these, so that we can act accordingly. In fact, in many situations we lack certain knowledge about the situation at hand, but nevertheless we have to take decisions. In such cases we often use defaults: normally, p, so I decide to do a.

Imagine a zoo keeper, who wants to extend his zoo with some birds. So he sends one of his employees off to other zoos to buy some. If he is told that some birds will arrive in a week, but he does not get any further information, he will reserve a cage with a roof for these birds, otherwise they may fly away, since — he reasons — birds can normally fly. Of course, it is still possible that on the day of arrival of the animals he will discover that the delivery concerns a collection of penguins, emus and ostriches, so that the cage did not have to have a roof after all (and that the cage he reserved is probably too small, by an instance of Murphy's law!).

So in practice we often have to work with uncertain or defeasible information that is obtained by jumping to (default) conclusions. Also when doctors make diagnoses they often reason by default: if the patient has symptoms so and so, he will normally have illness so and so.

Although very similar to plausible and probable reasoning, default reasoning *per se* does not have to involve statistics. It can also concern typicality which is not connected directly (or even at all) with high frequencies of occurrence. For instance, we can say that normally birds lay eggs, turtles live to be a hundred years or more, rats carry the plague and mosquitos carry malaria, while this is known to be *contra* statistic data. (For instance, 50% of the birds, the male ones, do not lay eggs at all!) (Cf. [Vel91], [Morr92].)

When reasoning with inheritance hierarchies of classes or concepts where we have exceptions, we also make use of defaults in order to avoid having to also store all information about superclasses at (the slots of) instances of subclasses. Here default reasoning comes into play as an economic measure. We see the same in database theory, where the *closed world assumption*

(CWA) is employed to limit stored data to positive facts, and it is assumed by default that any fact that is not stored is not true. Also in reasoning about the dynamics of systems we often do not want to record complete information about the (non-)effects of the actions that may take place. Since there are generally (possibly infinitely) many non-effects of these actions, we only specify their positive effects, and leave it implicit that any effect that is not specified does not occur. This is called the *frame assumption* in AI literature [Bro87], and often implemented in a default manner. This is important in a large area of AI, involving *planning* or reasoning about plans [AKPT91].

Reiter [Rei80] was the first to propose a logic for default reasoning. A *default theory* in Reiter's sense is a pair (Φ, D), where Φ is a set of propositions[2] and D is a set of *default rules*. Default rules have the form

$$\varphi : \psi_1, ..., \psi_n / \chi.$$

Here φ, $\psi_1, ..., \psi_n$, and χ are propositional formulas.[3] φ is called the *prerequisite*, $\psi_1, ..., \psi_n$ the *justifications*, and χ the *consequent* of the default. The reading of such a default rule is: "If φ is believed, and every ψ_i is consistent with what is believed, then χ is to be believed. But you have to check whether the ψ_i remain consistent with what is known then." If φ = **true**, i.e. the prerequisite is trivially fulfilled, we write $: \psi_1, ..., \psi_n / \chi$. In what follows we shall restrict ourselves to defaults with n = 1. For example, the default rule

$$: \neg \text{can\_fly(object)} / \neg \text{can\_fly(object)}$$

has as its meaning that, if it is consistent to assume that the object cannot fly, then you may assume this to be true. A default rule is called *normal*, if it has the following form: $\varphi : \psi / \psi$, i.e. n = 1 and $\chi = \psi$.

Reiter [Rei80] treats defaults by means of so-called *extensions*. Let Ψ be a set of closed formulas, and let $\Delta = (\Phi, D)$ be a default theory in Reiter's sense. Now define:

$$\Psi_0 = \Phi$$

---

[2]Actually, Reiter considers first-order sentences in Φ and first-order formulas in default rules. As we only consider propositional logic in this book, we shall not do this. The interested reader is referred to [Rei80] and [Luk90]. In examples we shall sometimes abuse the language, and use a pseudo-first-order language.

[3]As above.

$$\Psi_{i+1} = <\Psi_i> \cup \{\chi \mid (\varphi : \psi_1, ..., \psi_n / \chi) \in D, \varphi \in \Psi_i \text{ and } \neg\psi_i \notin \Psi\}$$

where $<\Xi>$ stands for the set of all propositional (monotonic) consequences of Ξ. (Please note the occurrence of Ψ in the definition of Ψ_{i+1}. It does *not* read Ψ_i!) Now Ψ is called an *extension* of Δ if $\Psi = \bigcup_i \Psi_i$.

4.1.1. EXAMPLE.

Φ = {bird(Polly), bird(Polly) $\rightarrow$ can_fly(Polly), rabbit(Bugs)}

D = { : ¬can_fly(Polly) / ¬can_fly(Polly),
: ¬can_fly(Bugs) / ¬can_fly(Bugs)}

Now (Φ, D) has one single extension, namely

Ψ = < Φ ∪ {¬can_fly(Bugs)} >,

since $\Psi_1 = <\Psi_0> \cup$ {¬can_fly(Bugs)}, where $\Psi_0 = \Phi$. (Note that ¬¬can_fly(Bugs) $\notin \Psi$.) Furthermore, $\Psi_i = <\Psi_1>$, for $i \geq 2$. So $\Psi = <\Psi_1>$.

In general a default theory may have multiple extensions or none at all. However, normal defaults can be shown to have at least one extension. More about Reiter's default theory can be found in e.g. [Rei80] and [Luk90].

We now proceed to treat default reasoning in a (modal) epistemic logic framework.

4.2. Epistemic Default Logic (EDL)

The statement that normally birds fly is represented in Reiter's default logic (cf. [Rei80], [Luk90]) by a formula 'b : f / f', expressing that if we consider a bird, and *it is consistent to assume* that it can fly, then we conclude that it can. First of all we note that in this inference a rather dangerous jump is made from 'consistent to assume f' to 'f' itself. We may avoid this jump by using a special modality to indicate that belief in assertion f is preferred, but by no means certain. This will be done by the use of special modalities. (This is in contrast with other attempts to treat defaults by means of modal logic, such as McDermott & Doyle's NML [McDD80] and Moore's AEL,)

Here, however, we would like to draw attention to the statement "it is consistent to assume". In Reiter's default logic this is interpreted as being consistent with the resulting belief set ('extension' in the jargon of default logic). Since in Reiter's default logic we cannot distinguish between real facts and assumptions on the basis of a default, this results in the need for some fixed-point construction.

On the other hand, if one *does* make a distinction between (certain) facts and (default) assumptions, this need for such a construction disappears, and we may use a simple modal semantics. The certainty and possibility operators refer immediately to the possible epistemic alternatives in the model, and there is no dependency on the assertions that are assumed (by default) as in Reiter's default logic and AEL. The question now remains, how these epistemic alternatives collected in the (S5-) model — which represents so to speak the amount of knowledge that is available to the agent — come about. One may think of a process in which one starts with some certain base knowledge (possibly empty) and during which certain information is added. For the change in certain knowledge from one state of knowledge to another we use dynamic logic in [MH91a, MH92]. Since in [MH91a, MH92] we always included in our reasoning the assumption that an assertion is possible, and never made jumps, the approach there was entirely monotonic. One may view it as a logic of expectations given certain possibilities.

Here we follow the approach presented in [MH93a, 95], and we make precise how the certainties and possibilities mentioned above are obtained. By doing this we turn the approach into a truly non-monotonic one. But we emphasise that we still keep an important difference with AEL and default logic. In our approach we still have special P-modalities to indicate that an assertion is made by default. Thus we still make no jumps in this sense, as in the other approaches. Instead, we infer from a base set of certain knowledge the assertions that are not known, and hence which possibilities remain. So we employ a kind of closure on the facts in the sense that what is not explicitly known, is not known. (This is not the same as enforcing a closed world assumption (CWA) as it is meant generally in the literature, stating that an assertion that is not known is assumed to be false! Here we just say that it is not known.)

As we have seen in Section 3.1, Halpern & Moses [HM91a] have proposed a theory for doing just this, to derive ignorance from knowledge given. In summary, what the approach amounted to is a minimisation of the amount of objective (i.e. non-modal) knowledge given a set of (certain) base facts. As we have seen, in a way it is the logic of 'knowing only', and we saw that the entailment relation based on this is non-monotonic: knowing only p implies not knowing q (where q is an atom different from p), whereas knowing only p *and q*, does obviously not imply not knowing q. But the non-monotonicity emerges at a different place than in other approaches such as Reiter's default logic. In our framework the non-monotonicity lies in the determination of what one knows and what not, rather than jumping to conclusions with respect to some default. Halpern & Moses' theory as such does not treat defaults at all. It was devised to reason about the knowledge and ignorance of processes in a distributed computer system. But it fits very nicely into our view of default reasoning to determine the knowledge and ignorance of an agent, since we claim that defaults are applied on the basis of what is known to the agent and what is not! Moreover, as we have seen, it is a typical example of non-monotonic reasoning by means of a preference criterion, and thus yields a non-monotonic logic in a very natural manner.

We now start with the introduction of the modal logic **EDL**, which is an extension of the epistemic logic **S5** by means of special modal operators P_i denoting *preference* or *practical belief* (with respect to frame or situation i). In what follows we shall explain why we need several of these operators rather than just one.

The language $\mathcal{L}_{\mathbf{EDL}}$ is an extension of the language $\mathcal{L}_{\mathbf{EL}}$ of epistemic formulas we used above, defined as the minimal set of formulas closed under the following rules:

(i) $\mathbf{P} \subseteq \mathcal{L}_{\mathbf{EDL}}$;
(ii) if $\varphi, \psi \in \mathcal{L}_{\mathbf{EDL}}$, then $\neg\varphi, \varphi \wedge \psi(, \varphi \vee \psi, \varphi \rightarrow \psi, \varphi \leftrightarrow \psi, \bot) \in \mathcal{L}_{\mathbf{EDL}}$;
(iii) if $\varphi \in \mathcal{L}_{\mathbf{EDL}}$, then $K\varphi$, $M\varphi$, $P_i\varphi \in \mathcal{L}_{\mathbf{EDL}}$ $(i = 1, ..., n)$.

Informally, $P_i\varphi$ is read as "φ is *preferred* or a *practical belief* (within frame of reference i)" or even "*presumably* (within frame i), φ". As we shall see below, a frame of reference (or mind) refers to a preferred subset of the set of *a priori* possible worlds that together constitute a body of knowledge or, rather, preferred or practical belief. We will also see the need for multiple P-modalities, since, speaking intuitively, we may have to distinguish multiple frames of reference, in (more or less) the same way as in Reiter's default logic we may need / get multiple 'extensions'. This operator is very close to the PA (possible assumption) of [TT] and the D (default) operator of [Do]. We refer to formulas in $\mathcal{L}_{\mathbf{EDL}}$ as *EDL-formulas.*

Formally, EDL-formulas are interpreted on Kripke-structures of the form $\langle S, \pi, S_1, ..., S_n, \wp, \wp_1, ..., \wp_n\rangle$, where S is a collection of states, π: $\mathbf{P} \rightarrow S \rightarrow \{t, f\}$ is a truth assignment to the primitive propositions per state, $S_i \subseteq S$ are sets ('frames') of preferred states, $\wp = S \times S$ (and $\wp$ is hence reflexive, transitive and euclidean), and $\wp_i = S \times S_i \subseteq \wp$ is transitive and euclidean. Thus we have that $\forall s, t: \wp_i(s, t) \Leftrightarrow t \in S_i$. Like before, without loss of generality, we may identify states s and (their) truth assignments $\pi(s)$. We let $\mathcal{S5P}$ denote the collection of Kripke-structures of the above form (the $\mathcal{P}$ in $\mathcal{S5P}$ referring to preferences). The formal interpretation of the language now reads: for $\mathbb{M} = \langle S, \pi, S_1, ..., S_n, \wp, \wp_1, ..., \wp_n\rangle$,

$(\mathbb{M}, s) \models p$ iff $\pi(p)(s)=t$

$(\mathbb{M}, s) \models \neg\varphi$ iff not $(\mathbb{M}, s) \models \varphi$
$(\mathbb{M}, s) \models \varphi \wedge \psi$ iff $(\mathbb{M}, s) \models \varphi$ and $(\mathbb{M}, s) \models \psi$
$(\mathbb{M}, s) \models K\varphi$ iff $(\mathbb{M}, t) \models \varphi$ for all t with $\wp(s, t)$ (i.e. all $t \in S$)
$(\mathbb{M}, s) \models M\varphi$ iff $(\mathbb{M}, t) \models \varphi$ for some with $\wp(s, t)$ (i.e. some $t \in S$)
$(\mathbb{M}, s) \models P_i\varphi$ iff $(\mathbb{M}, t) \models \varphi$ for all t with $\wp_i(s, t)$ (i.e. all $t \in S_i$).

Thus the last clause states that $P_i\varphi$ is true (φ is a practical belief with respect to frame S_i) if φ is true in all states of S_i.

Moreover, $\mathbb{M} \models \varphi$ iff $(\mathbb{M}, s) \models \varphi$ for all $s \in S$, and $\models \varphi$ iff $\mathbb{M} \models \varphi$ for all $\mathbb{M} \in \mathcal{S5P}$. We may occasionally write $\mathbb{M} \models_{\mathbf{EDL}} \varphi$ and $\models_{\mathbf{EDL}} \varphi$, respectively, when confusion may arise as to the kind of validity (i.e. with respect to the class of models concerned).

We say that a model $\mathbb{M} = \langle S, \pi, S_1,..., S_n, \wp, \wp_1,..., \wp_n\rangle \in \mathcal{S5P}$ *extends* a model $\mathbb{M} = \langle S', \pi', \wp'\rangle \in \mathcal{S5}$, if $S = S'$, $\pi = \pi'$ and $\wp = \wp'$. Moreover, in this case we say that $\mathbb{M}'$ is the $\mathcal{S5}$-reduction of $\mathbb{M}$.

It is possible to axiomatise (the theory of) $\mathcal{S5P}$ as follows (cf. [MH91a, MH92]): take the **S5** system for the modality K (and dual M, i.e. $M\varphi \leftrightarrow \neg K\neg\varphi$) and use **K45** (cf. Section 2.4) for the P-modalities, together with the relating axioms:

(AP6)	$K\varphi \rightarrow P_i\varphi$	('certain' implies 'preferred' in any frame)
(AP7)	$KP_i\varphi \leftrightarrow P_i\varphi$	
(AP8)	$\neg P_i\bot \rightarrow (P_iP_j\varphi \leftrightarrow P_j\varphi)$	
(AP9)	$\neg P_i\bot \rightarrow (P_iK\varphi \leftrightarrow K\varphi)$	

Semantically, these extra axioms express the following properties: the $\wp_i$ are subrelations of the relation $\wp$ (AP6); they reach the same set S_i no matter where one starts from in S (AP7), or from another non-empty frame (AP8); and $\wp$ always refers to the whole set S no matter where one starts in some non-empty frame (AP9). (AP7) through (AP9) essentially convey that we have no nested modalities: a nested modality always refers to the frame corresponding to the innermost one. (Apart from technical convenience, we also have no clear intuition what these nested modalities should mean.) The condition $\neg P_i\bot$ in (AP8) and (AP9), expressing that the frame S_i is non-empty, is needed, since otherwise the left-hand sides of the equivalences concerned are trivially true.

Interestingly, this logic can be viewed as a variant of the system **KL** for knowledge and belief as discussed in Section 2.13 (as far as the K- and B-operators are concerned), where the B-operator in **KL** corresponds to a P-operator in the present setting. The differences being that here we consider only *one* agent, a P-operator is a **K45**-modality rather than a **KD45** one, and here we consider *multiple* belief operators P_i.

4.2.0.1. EXERCISE. (i) Check the soundness of the above system with respect to the class $\mathcal{S5P}$.

*(ii) Check the completeness of the above system.

We call the resulting system **EDL** and write $\Gamma \vdash_{\mathbf{EDL}} \varphi$ or $\varphi \in Th_{\mathbf{EDL}}(\Gamma)$ to indicate that φ is an **EDL**-consequence of Γ. We mean this in the more liberal sense: it is possible to derive φ from the assertions in Γ by means of the axioms and rules of the system **EDL**, *including the use of the necessitation rule on premises in* Γ. So, in effect we consider the assertions in Γ as additional axioms: $\Gamma \vdash_{\mathbf{EDL}} \varphi$ iff $\vdash_{\mathbf{EDL} \cup \Gamma} \varphi$ (i.e. φ is derivable in the system **EDL** extended with Γ) iff $\models_{\mathbf{EDL} \cup \Gamma} \varphi$ (i.e. φ is valid with respect to all $\mathcal{S5P}$-models that satisfy Γ).

In the language $\mathcal{L}_{\mathbf{EDL}}$ we have two natural ways to express defaults of the form $\varphi : \psi / \chi$ (using Reiter's notation), making use of our modalities K (and its derivative M) and P: a *strong* or *flexible* representation, and a *weak* or *rigid* one.

1. (Strong representation)

$\varphi \wedge M\psi \rightarrow P\chi$ *(If φ is* true *and ψ is (considered) possible, then χ is preferred)*

2. (Weak representation).

$K\varphi \wedge M\psi \rightarrow P\chi$ *(If φ is* known *and ψ is (considered) possible, then χ is preferred)*

Here φ, ψ and χ are supposed to be objective (non-modal) formulas. When $\psi = \chi$ (where '=' stands for syntactical equality), the default is called *normal*. Multiple defaults $\{\varphi_i : \psi_i / \chi_i\}_i$ are represented by formulas $(K)\varphi_i \wedge M\psi_i \rightarrow P_{f(i)}\chi_i$, where φ_i, ψ_i and χ_i are again objective formulas, and f is a function of type $\{1, ..., n\} \rightarrow J$, where $J \subseteq \{1, ..., n\}$. So, in effect, f assigns a frame $\Sigma_{f(i)}$ (and corresponding operator $P_{f(i)}$) to the i-th default. In particular, some of the $P_{f(i)}$-operators may be the same. The use of this ability will be clear when we consider some examples later.

The difference between the strong and weak representations of a default is quite essential. Clearly, the strong representation implies the weak one, but not conversely. The strong representation is applicable in any world where the 'prerequisite' φ holds (assuming the 'justification' $M\psi$ holds as well), whereas the weak representation is only possible if φ holds in *all* epistemic alternatives (under the same condition regarding $M\psi$). In fact, since we will assume that defaults are known and hence hold in every epistemic alternative (in proof-theoretical terms this means that we may apply necessitation to defaults; see Section 4.4, and Definition 4.4.1 in particular), the strong / flexible representation is applicable already if there is *any* epistemic alternative where φ holds. Actually, one can show that under these conditions the weak representation can be expressed equivalently by $M\varphi \wedge M\psi \rightarrow P\chi$, which might even be considered too strong for an adequate representation of a default. (Note, by the way that this is different from — and *not* equivalent to — $M(\varphi \wedge \psi) \rightarrow P\chi$, which would perhaps be even more undesirable.) The reason why we still admit the strong representation is that it enjoys a number of often desirable properties such as transitivity and reasoning by cases, as we shall show presently. In what follows we will therefore mostly use the strong representation. In most examples it does not really matter so much, as the reader may check for him/herself.

Before giving a number of examples of how to employ our approach we now examine briefly some of the advantages of our approach as opposed to other ones on the basis of a few general properties which are also discussed in [Gin87]. In particular, we show that in our approach, because of the use of P-modalities, we do not encounter the problem with contraposition and (by taking the strong representation) may avoid that with transitivity that are present in other modal approaches such as AEL. (This was reported first in [MH91a, MH92].)

1. *Strengthening the antecedent.* In every modal approach, and hence also in ours, we may strengthen the antecedent. So, if $p \wedge Mq \rightarrow Pq$, then also $p \wedge r \wedge Mq \rightarrow Pq$. For example, if birds normally fly, then also red birds normally fly. This is perfectly reasonable. Even in the context that we know that red birds do not fly for certain (expressed as $r \rightarrow L\neg q$), this does not lead to a contradiction, because in that case — given r — we have evidence that $\neg Mq$ holds, and we can not apply the default rule to infer that the flying of red birds is preferred.

On the other hand, we may also infer $p \wedge \neg q \wedge Mq \rightarrow Pq$. According to Ginsberg this is counterintuitive, but in our approach it is perfectly understandable, since, in fact, we can derive the stronger assertion $p \wedge \neg q \wedge Mq \rightarrow \neg q \wedge Pq$, which expresses that although q does not hold right now, we prefer a (counterfactual, but possible) situation in which q *does* hold.

2. *Transitivity.* Intuitively, one expects that defaults obey transitivity. If robins are birds and birds normally fly, then one expects to derive that robins normally fly.[4] However, in McDermott & Doyle's non-monotonic logic [McDD80] and Moore's autoepistemic logic

[4]Again this is also a sound form of reasoning when one encounters penguins instead of robins, because in this case we have the additional information that penguins are not normal birds, so that we simply cannot use the derived default rule "penguins normally fly".

[Moo84, Moo85a] we have a rather strange form of transitivity of default assertions: from $p \wedge Mq \rightarrow q$ and $q \wedge Mr \rightarrow r$ we can derive $p \wedge Mq \wedge Mr \rightarrow (q \wedge r)$, which is not really a default rule. In our approach (using the strong representation of defaults) this works out somewhat differently: from $p \wedge Mq \rightarrow P_1q$ and $q \wedge Mr \rightarrow P_2r$ we may derive $p \wedge Mq \wedge Mr \rightarrow P_1q$ but not $p \wedge Mq \wedge Mr \rightarrow P_1q \wedge P_2r$! What we *can* derive is $P_1q \wedge P_1Mr \rightarrow P_1P_2r$, which implies in case we know that $\neg P_1\bot$, i.e. if $\Sigma_1 \neq \emptyset$,[5] $P_1q \wedge Mr \rightarrow P_2r$. Hence we may derive: $p \wedge Mq \wedge Mr \rightarrow (P_1q \wedge Mr \rightarrow) P_2r \wedge P_1q$.[6]

Perhaps one wants to establish a relationship between the two preferred clusters associated with the operators P_1 and P_2. This can be done by forcing these two to be the same and using P for both P_1 and P_2. Then we obtain $p \wedge Mq \wedge Mr \rightarrow Pq \wedge Pr$ ($\leftrightarrow P(q \wedge r)$). This is very intuitive: we have set a preferred cluster which is the intersection of the clusters which are determined by the default assertions separately.

Note that when we would use the *weak* representation of defaults the property of transitivity in the above form is lost. From $Kp \wedge Mq \rightarrow P_1q$, we may derive $Kp \wedge Mq \wedge Mr \rightarrow P_1q$, but since, in general, $P_1q \wedge P_1Mr \rightarrow P_1P_2r$ is *not* derivable from $Kq \wedge Mr \rightarrow P_2r$, the above conclusion $p \wedge Mq \wedge Mr \rightarrow P_2r \wedge P_1q$ cannot be obtained.

3. *Contraposition.* When we put in a modal approach such as autoepistemic logic a default like $b \wedge Mf \rightarrow f$ in contraposition we obtain the assertion $\neg f \wedge Mf \rightarrow \neg b$, which is of no use whatsoever, according to Ginsberg [Gin87]. What is worse, the contraposed version does not seem to have the same informal reading as the original default. When we put our **EDL** version(s) $(K)b \wedge Mf \rightarrow Pf$ into contraposition we get $\neg Pf \rightarrow (\neg(K)b \vee \neg Mf)$, or $\neg Pf \rightarrow (Mf \rightarrow \neg(K)b)$, or $(\neg Pf \wedge Mf) \rightarrow \neg(K)b$. This is intuitively clearer: if it is the case that, although f is considered possible, f is nevertheless not preferred, it cannot be the case that b is true or known, depending on the strong or weak representation, respectively (or otherwise we should have preferred f!).

---

[5]Note that in case $P_1\bot$, i.e. the cluster Σ_1 is empty, we cannot draw any further conclusion from the second default, since now $P_1q \wedge P_1Mr \rightarrow P_1P_2r$ is vacuously true.

[6]Alternatively, if one likes to prevent transitivity altogether, one might opt for the representation of a default $\alpha : \beta / \gamma$ as $L\alpha \wedge M\beta \rightarrow P\gamma$. If one now has defaults $Lp \wedge Mq \rightarrow Pq$ and $Lq \wedge Mr \rightarrow Pr$, the second default cannot be applied to the conclusion Pq of the first one, since Pq does not imply Lq. This is also similar to the approach of [Doh91].

In conclusion we may say that **EDL** behaves rather well when we use it to represent defaults, as far as these well-known problems of modal logics are concerned. Next in order to get more acquainted with **EDL** we shall treat a number of examples that are taken from the literature. These are generally called bench-mark problems to test theories of common-sense reasoning, and are more or less ubiquitous in the literature. Although it is generally difficult to trace their origins, we have indicated their inventors to the best of our knowledge (cf. e.g. [Lif89], but we also included some material from handouts on bench-mark problems compiled by Ron Loui at the Workshop on Defeasible Reasoning with Specificity and Multiple Inheritance, held at St Louis in 1989).

4.2.1. EXAMPLE (Non-normal defaults). Consider the non-normal default : $p / \neg p$. In Reiter's approach [Rei80] this default theory has no extension. As is discussed in [Luk84], this is not according to common-sense intuition. In our approach we get the following representation of the above default: $Mp \rightarrow P\neg p$. In case Mp holds, i.e. p is an *a priori* possibility, this indeed has as a consequence that $\neg p$ is preferred. In fact, this means that although we must check whether p is (*a priori*) possible, we prefer the cluster of those worlds in which $\neg p$ holds: in terms of Reiter we do have an extension in this case in our approach.

4.2.2. EXAMPLE (Multiple 'extensions'). Consider the following defaults:

$$\frac{p : q}{q}, \quad \frac{p : \neg q}{\neg q}$$

These default rules, which have two extensions, can be formulated in our language as

$$p \wedge Mq \rightarrow P_1 q\,;$$
$$p \wedge M\neg q \rightarrow P_2 \neg q.$$

So in our framework we now obtain two preferred frameworks corresponding to the two extensions in Reiter's approach.

4.2.3. EXAMPLE (Disjunctive information). We assume that we have incomplete information about the failure of a high-tech device: either its power supply is faulty or its transformer is. On the other hand, by default, everything works fine. In **EDL** we may represent the above situation as:

(1a)	$\neg p \vee \neg t$	*(Either the power supply or the transformer is faulty.)*
(2a)	$Mp \rightarrow P_1 p$	*(By default, the power supply is OK.)*
(3a)	$Mt \rightarrow P_2 t$	*(By default, the transformer is OK.)*

We may now, for example, make the following inference: $\neg p \vee \neg t \vdash K(\neg p \vee \neg t) \vdash P_1(\neg p \vee \neg t)$. Now, if we have that Mp (we shall show in the next section how we might obtain this), we also have $\vdash P_1 p$, and consequently $P_1(p \wedge \neg t)$. Likewise, we can infer $P_2(t \wedge \neg p)$. This means that we have two preferred clusters, associated with the modal operators P_1 and P_2, respectively: one in which $p \wedge \neg t$ holds and another in which $t \wedge \neg p$ holds. (This corresponds, admittedly in a rather loose way, to the two extensions one obtains when using Reiter's default logic for this situation.) This example is closely related to the notion of closed world assumption (CWA) in database theory. We shall return to this in a later example, after we have seen how to infer ignorance from a set of premises.

4.2.4. EXAMPLE (Contradicting justifications). In [Luk84] an example is given where Reiter's default logic does not work properly. Let s stand for the proposition "it is Sunday", h for "I am on holidays", f for "I go fishing", and l for "I woke up late". Consider the following default theory:

$$\frac{s : (f \wedge \neg l)}{f}, \quad \frac{h : l}{l}, \quad s \wedge h.$$

This default theory is intended to express the situation that (i) normally on Sundays I go fishing when I do not wake up late, (ii) normally I wake up late on holidays, and (iii) it is now the case that it is both a sunday and I am on a holiday. Applying the second default rule first yields l, which blocks further application of the first default, so in this case we obtain an extension given by $<\{s, h, l\}>$, where $< >$ stands again for the propositional closure. In Reiter's default logic, if one applies the first default first (yielding f), one is forced to apply the second default as well, yielding l, which contradicts the justification of the application of the first default. In Reiter's theory this amounts to no further extension. Lukaszewicz argues rightly that this is not in accord with common-sense intuition, and remedies this situation by adopting a more refined definition of extension, involving a more restricted view on the applicability of default rules. In our approach we can avoid problems right away by representing the above situation by the assertions:

(1) $s \wedge h$ *(It is Sunday and a holiday.)*

(2) $s \wedge M(f \wedge \neg l) \rightarrow P_1 f$ *(Normally on Sundays I go fishing unless I wake up late.)*

(3) $h \wedge Ml \rightarrow P_2 l$ *(Normally on holidays I wake up late.)*

Given $M(f \wedge \neg l) \wedge Ml$ (which is not contradictory!), we now obtain the conclusion

(*) $P_1(s \wedge h \wedge f) \wedge P_2(s \wedge h \wedge l)$

expressing that the theory gives rise to two clusters of preferred worlds: one in which it is a Sunday and a holiday, and I go fishing, and one in which it is a Sunday and a holiday, and I wake up late.

4.2.4.1. EXERCISE. Check formally in **S5P** how in Example 4.2.4 the conclusion (*) follows from the premises.

4.2.4.2. REMARK. Note that in the above example we may require that these two clusters coincide by taking P for both P_1 and P_2. In this case we can infer that $P(f \wedge l)$, which is counterintuitive, and reminiscent of the problems Reiter's default logic encounters in this example. In fact, this strange outcome forces one to be more precise about the formalisation and represent the situation given as

(1a) $s \wedge h$

(2a) $s \wedge M(f \wedge \neg l) \rightarrow P(f \wedge \neg l)$

(3a) $h \wedge Ml \rightarrow Pl$

This set of assertions has as a consequence that $M(f \wedge \neg l) \wedge Ml \rightarrow P(f \wedge \neg l \wedge l)$, the conclusion of which is equivalent to $P\bot$, meaning that the associated preferred cluster is empty!

4.2.5. EXAMPLE. The so-called Lottery Paradox (due to Kyburg & Pollock) can also be treated in our approach. A version of this paradox reads as follows: consider a lottery where there are 1000 tickets. Now we can state:

Probably, ticket 1 will not win.
Probably, ticket 2 will not win.
...
Probably, ticket 1000 will not win.
On the other hand, ticket 1 or ticket 2 or ... or ticket 1000 will win.

In some probabilistic approaches one can infer the contradictory statement: "Probably none of the tickets will win". In our approach we can represent this situation as follows (taking the liberty to represent "probably" with "preferably", and using w sub i for the assertion "ticket i will win"):

$M\neg w_1 \rightarrow P_1\neg w_1$
$M\neg w_2 \rightarrow P_2\neg w_2$

$M\neg w_{1000} \rightarrow P_{1000}\neg w_{1000}$
$w_1 \vee w_2 \vee \ldots \vee w_{1000}$

From these statements we can infer: $K(w_1 \vee w_2 \vee \ldots \vee w_{1000})$, and so

$$\neg M(\neg w_1 \wedge \neg w_2 \wedge \ldots \wedge \neg w_{1000}). \qquad (*)$$

On the other hand we can derive: $(M\neg w_1 \wedge M\neg w_2 \wedge \ldots \wedge M\neg w_{1000}) \rightarrow (P_1\neg w_1 \wedge P_2\neg w_2 \wedge \ldots \wedge P_{1000}\neg w_{1000})$. So we have 1000 clusters and each cluster corresponds to the belief set of a person who has ticket i and does not believe that he will win. This is not contradictory to the statement (*) which states that it is certain that one of the 1000 tickets will win. Note that again it is in this case crucial to use different P_i operators in the formalisation of the problem. If one only uses, say, P_1, it is still the case that the formalisation itself is not inconsistent, it is true, but we get inconsistent *beliefs*, since we obtain both $P_1(\neg w_1 \wedge \neg w_2 \wedge \ldots \wedge \neg w_{1000}))$, or equivalently $P_1\neg(w_1 \vee w_2 \vee \ldots \vee w_{1000}))$, and $P_1(w_1 \vee w_2 \vee \ldots \vee w_{1000})$ from $K(w_1 \vee w_2 \vee \ldots \vee w_{1000})$ (so that we have $P_1\bot$, corresponding to an empty cluster S_1!).

Next we consider again an example from [Luk84], with which we can show that in **EDL** we can reason by cases in contrast to what can be done in Reiter's default logic.

4.2.6. EXAMPLE (Reasoning by cases). We consider the following variation on Example 4.2.4. If it is a Sunday, I normally go fishing; if it is a holiday, I normally go fishing. Now it is given that it is either a Sunday or a holiday (but it is not specified which of the two cases). On the basis of common-sense intuition we expect to conclude that in any case — provided that everything is normal — I go fishing. In default logic, the situation above is represented by the default theory:

$$\frac{s:f}{f}, \quad \frac{h:f}{f}, \quad s \vee h.$$

However, in default logic (both in Reiter's original and in Lukaszewicz' modified interpretation) we cannot derive that I go fishing, simply because I cannot deduce either s or h. In our approach, there is again no problem. We formulate the situation above by:

(1) $s \vee h$ *(It is Sunday or a holiday.)*
(2) $s \wedge Mf \rightarrow P_1f$ *(On Sundays I normally go fishing.)*
(3) $h \wedge Mf \rightarrow P_2f$ *(On holidays I normally go fishing.)*

Now we can infer $(s \wedge Mf) \rightarrow (P_1f \vee P_2f)$ and $(h \wedge Mf) \rightarrow (P_1f \vee P_2f)$, and so $((s \wedge Mf) \vee (h \wedge Mf)) \rightarrow (P_1f \vee P_2f)$, and therefore $((s \vee h) \wedge Mf)) \rightarrow (P_1f \vee P_2f)$, and consequently we can indeed conclude that $P_1f \vee P_2f$, i.e. in any case f is preferred (provided that Mf holds).

4.2.6.1. REMARKS. (i) Note that the above example also works well in case we use P instead of both P_1 and P_2. In this case we can infer directly that Pf, which is even more clear, intuitively.
(ii) Note that we see here an essential difference between (1)—(3) (using the strong representation) and

(1') $K(s \vee h)$
(2') $Ks \wedge Mf \rightarrow P_1f$
(3') $Kh \wedge Mf \rightarrow P_2f$

where the weak representation is employed. The formulation (1')—(3') suffers from the same drawback as its representation in default logic: we cannot infer either Ks or Kh from $K(s \vee h)$, and hence we cannot apply the default assertions to derive the conclusion that f is preferred! Thus, in **EDL** it is possible to both allow for reasoning by cases (by adopting the strong representation (1)—(3)) and disallow it (by adopting the weak representation (1')—(3')).

4.2.7. EXAMPLE (Nixon Diamond, [RC81]). Let r stand for being a republican, p for being a pacifist, and q for being a quaker. Now we consider the following situation:

(1) $r \wedge M\neg p \rightarrow P_1\neg p$ *(Republicans are non-pacifists by default.)*
(2) $q \wedge Mp \rightarrow P_2p$ *(Quakers are pacifists by default.)*
(3) $r \wedge q$ *(Nixon is both a republican and a quaker.)*

Given the consistency of both p and $\neg p$, i.e. given $Mp \wedge M\neg p$, we can now derive that $P_1\neg p \wedge P_2p$. That is to say, we have two subframes S_1 and S_2 of S: in the one $\neg p$ holds, in the other p. This is intuitively correct since there is in this particular case no preference of the one over the other whatsoever. Note also the need for different modalities P_1 and P_2 (or frames S_1 and S_2) in this case: the use of only one such modality results in an empty frame.

4.2.7.1. EXERCISE (Cascaded ambiguity, Touretzky). Formalise the following scenario:

Republicans tend to be non-pacifists and football fans.

Quakers tend to be pacifists.

Pacifists tend to be anti-military.

Football fans tend to be non-anti-military.

Nixon is a republican quaker.

Is Nixon (presumably) anti-military (given the appropriate assumptions about consistency)?

In more complicated cases, where there appears to be a preference of one subframe over the other, it may be adequate to put an ordering on the various subframes. A prominent example of this situation is that involving *specificity*:

4.2.8. EXAMPLE (Multiple defaults with specificity). We consider the case in which we have multiple defaults where some defaults apply to a more general case and some other ones apply to a more specific case. For example, consider the defaults "ravens are generally black" and "albino ravens are generally not black", represented by:

(1) $r \wedge Mb \rightarrow P_1 b$ *(Normally ravens are black.)*

(2) $r \wedge a \wedge M\neg b \rightarrow P_2 \neg b$ *(Normally albino ravens are not black.)*

Note that if we know that we have an albino raven ($r \wedge a$), and that both b and $\neg b$ are possible ($Mb \wedge M\neg b$), we can infer both $P_1 b$ and $P_2 \neg b$. This is not counterintuitive — we may subsequently impose an additional ordering on the subframes (that is to say, by putting a preference order on the subframes Σ_i in the semantics), and consequently impose also a corresponding priority relation on the P-operators, such that in this case P_2, which is associated with the more specific default, gets a higher priority. (We leave the details of this approach to the reader.) However, it is perhaps not the best answer one can get either. One might prefer an approach in which this priority ordering follows directly from the specification of the rules themselves. In comparison, consider the case in which we take (1) together with

(2*) $r \wedge a \rightarrow \neg b$

which simply states that an albino raven is always non-black. (In network terminology [Tou86], this is represented by a strict, i.e. nondefeasible link). Note that if we know that $r \wedge a$ in this case, we can infer $K(r \wedge a)$ and hence $K\neg b$, which blocks the application of the default (1). So in this case there is no need to additionally prioritise frames. One may wonder whether this can also be done in a similar way in case we consider our original problem. The answer is affirmative, if we are willing to represent defaults in a slightly different way. So now we consider (2) together with

(1*) $r \wedge \neg P_2 \neg b \rightarrow P_1 b$.

Now we may infer from $r \wedge a$, given $M\neg b$, that $P_2\neg b$, which *blocks* the application of (1*)! As in the case of (1) together with (2*), we now do not need to define an additional preference ordering on the subframes. The preference of Σ_2 over Σ_1 already follows from the formulation of the rule (1*): b is preferred with respect to cluster Σ_1 if $\neg b$ is not already preferred with respect to cluster Σ_2. (Note, by the way, that the premise $\neg P_2\neg b$ in (1*) is stronger than Mb in (1), since it holds that $\neg P\neg\varphi \Rightarrow \neg K\neg\varphi \Leftrightarrow M\varphi$.) So this is a way to specify or 'program' priorities in multiple defaults explicitly. We do not state a preference for the one method over the other, but rather believe that it depends on the concrete applications we may have in mind what is the best thing to do. The only thing we can say at this moment is that, in general, when not only specificity is at stake in the representation of some piece of knowledge, the knowledge engineer may more conveniently use an additional ordering on frames than programming them explicitly into the (possibly large) set of rules involved, which may result in a rather disordered and opaque representation. In a sense the difference between the two methods is that of a procedural ('explicitly programmed') specification versus a declarative one. In contemporary computer science the latter is mostly preferred. For now we close this issue by remarking that our setting is sufficiently flexible to choose either one of both methods or even combine them in a sensible way. More on this issue, in particular how to construct a 'layered' representation by stratification and how to reason with it, can be found in our paper [MH93c].

4.2.8.1. EXERCISE (Royal elephants, Sandewall). Formalise in **EDL** the following situation.

Royal elephants are elephants.

Elephants tend to be grey.

Royal elephants tend to be non-grey.

Clyde is a royal elephant.

Check whether it is derivable from your formalisation that Clyde is presumably grey or presumably non-grey.

4.2.8.2. EXERCISE (Pennsylvania Dutch, Horty & Thomason). Formalise in **EDL** the following scenario.

Native speakers of German tend not to be born in America.

All native speakers of Pennsylvania Dutch are native speakers of German.

Native speakers of Pennsylvania Dutch tend to be born in Pennsylvania.

Hermann is a native speaker of Pennsylvania Dutch.

Check whether it is derivable from your formalisation that Hermann is presumably born in America.

4.2.8.3. EXERCISE (Hidden presumptions, Geffner). Formalise:

People usually wake up before noon.

Tom usually wakes up after noon.

Does Tom presumably wake in the afternoon?

4.2.8.4. EXERCISE (University students and adults, Delgrande / Geffner & Pearl). Formalise in **EDL** the following situations:

(i) *Adults tend to be employed.*

University students tend to be unemployed.

University students tend to be adults.

Fred is a university student and an adult.

Is it derivable from your formalisation that Fred is presumably unemployed? And that he is presumably employed? Would specificity be of any use as a criterion here? Would this alter if we replaced the last premise, saying that Fred is a university student and an adult, by the premise that Fred is a university student?

(ii) *Adults tend to be employed.*

University students tend to be unemployed.

University students tend to be adults.

Adults under 22 tend to be university students.

Tom is an adult under 22.

Is Tom (presumably) unemployed?

4.2.8.5. EXERCISE (Dancers and Ballerinas, Loui). Formalise in **EDL** the following situation.

Dancers tend not to be ballerinas.

Dancers tend to be graceful.

Graceful dancers tend to be ballerinas.

Noemi is a dancer.

Is Noemi (presumably) a ballerina?

From the examples above we may conclude that reasoning in $\mathbf{EDL}_{(\mathbf{n})}$ is less complicated than in default logic or autoepistemic logic, and, more importantly, is more in line with commonsense intuition.

4.3. Dynamic Epistemic Default Logic and the Frame Problem

By combining EDL with dynamic logic, as discussed in Section 2.11 we also give a treatment of dynamic problems that involve a kind of default reasoning, such as the *frame problem* (cf. [Bro87], [McD87]). The essence of this problem is the fact that in practice actions have far more non-effects than effects upon the world, and we do not want or even are not able to specify all non-effects of actions that we are interested in. So a solution to this is only to specify the effects of an action, and then assume a frame axiom, stating that nothing else changes. Or, to put it concisely, nothing changes by an action unless specified explicitly (or known as a consequence of an explicit specification). We thus enforce a kind of *law of inertia*. Or, to put it differently still, in a default-like manner: by default, an action does not change the truth value of a proposition.

This idea can now be expressed rather straightforwardly in our framework, once we have included dynamic logic expressions in our logic. We shall do this in this section, after which we illustrate the theory by means of a well-known example, namely the Yale Shooting Problem and some variants.

4.3.1. Dynamic Epistemic Default Logic (DEDL)

In Section 2.11 we already saw how Bob Moore [Moo85b] has combined both epistemic and a version of dynamic logic into what we may call *dynamic epistemic logic*. As we have seen, in this logic it is possible to describe both the effect of actions on the knowledge an agent possesses and the effect that knowledge has on the actions of an agent. In this section we use a similar logic, but, of course, extended with our P-modalities.

We extend our epistemic default logic **EDL** to include dynamic logic expressions as follows.

Assume again a fixed collection **P** of primitive propositions and a fixed collection **ACT** of elementary actions. The language $\mathcal{L}_{\mathbf{DEDL}}$ we shall use is the minimal set of formulas closed under the following rules:

(i) $\mathbf{P} \subseteq \mathcal{L}_{\mathbf{DEDL}}$.

(ii) If $\varphi, \psi \in \mathcal{L}_{\mathbf{DEDL}}$, then $\neg\varphi, \varphi \wedge \psi, \varphi \vee \psi\ (, \varphi \rightarrow \psi, \varphi \leftrightarrow \psi) \in \mathcal{L}_{\mathbf{DEDL}}$.

(iii) If $\varphi \in \mathcal{L}_{\mathbf{DEDL}}$, then $K\varphi,\ M\varphi,\ P_i\varphi \in \mathcal{L}_{\mathbf{DEDL}}$ (i=1, ..., n).

(iv) If $\varphi \in \mathcal{L}_{\mathbf{DEDL}}$ and $\alpha \in \mathbf{ACT}$, then $[\alpha]\varphi \in \mathcal{L}_{\mathbf{DEDL}}$.

Recall, that, informally, $[\alpha]\varphi$ is read as "performance of α results in a state in which φ holds". Formally, expressions of **L** are interpreted by $\mathcal{S5P}^+$-structures of the form $\langle S, \pi, \wp, \{([s]_1,..., [s]_n, \wp_1{}^s,..., \wp_n{}^s) \mid s \in S\}, \{R_\alpha \mid \alpha \in \mathbf{ACT}\}\rangle$, where S is a collection of possible worlds, π: $\mathbf{P} \rightarrow S \rightarrow \{t, f\}$ is a truth assignment to the primitive propositions per world, $\wp$ is an equivalence relation on S (with equivalence classes $\{[s] \mid s \in S\}$), $[s]_i \subseteq [s]$ are sets (frames) of preferred worlds within the $\wp$-equivalence class [s] of $s \in S$, $\wp_i{}^s = [s] \times [s]_i \subseteq [s]$ for every $s \in S$, and $R_\alpha \subseteq S \times S$ ($\alpha \in \mathbf{ACT}$), such that $\forall s \in S\ \exists_1 t \in S\ [R_\alpha(s, t)]$ (total, deterministic actions).

Intuitively, these rather complicated structures must be viewed as a set of states, divided into equivalence classes with respect to knowledge, and actions may cause a transition to another state. But, of course, a change of state may involve a transition to another equivalence class, i.e. another epistemic context. If one views the equivalence classes as $\mathcal{S5P}$-models in their own right, then this comes down to an action changing state *and* (local) $\mathcal{S5P}$-model pertaining to the change of knowledge and preferences involved.

Although it is also possible to pose a fine structure on the actions (as is done in e.g. dynamic logic [Har84]), we shall not do this here, since we do not need this fine structure for the treatment of problems like the Yale Shooting Problem.

The formal interpretation of the language now reads: for $M = \langle S, \pi, \wp, \{([s]_1,..., [s]_n, \wp_1{}^s,..., \wp_n{}^s) \mid s \in S\}, \{R_\alpha \mid \alpha \in \mathbf{ACT}\}\rangle \in \mathcal{S5P}^+$,

$(M, s) \models p$ iff $\pi(p)(s) = t$

$(M, s) \models \neg\varphi$ iff $(M, s) \not\models \varphi$

$(M, s) \models \varphi \wedge \psi$ iff $(M, s) \models \varphi$ and $(M, s) \models \psi$

$(M, s) \models K\varphi$ iff $(M,t) \models \varphi$ for all $t \in [s]$

$(M, s) \models M\varphi$ iff $(M,t) \models \varphi$ for some $t \in [s]$

$(M, s) \models P_i\varphi$ iff $(M,t) \models \varphi$ for all $t \in [s]_i$

$(M, s) \models [\alpha]\varphi$ iff $\forall t \in S : R_\alpha(s, t) \Rightarrow (M, t) \models \varphi$

and, as usual, $M \models \varphi$ iff $(M, s) \models \varphi$ for all $s \in S$, and $\models \varphi$ iff $(M, s) \models \varphi$ for all $M \in \mathcal{S5P}^+$.

It is again possible to give an axiomatisation of the modal logic above. Extend the system **EDL** by a K-axiomatisation for the $[\alpha]$-modality for every action α:

(K) $([\alpha]\varphi \wedge [\alpha](\varphi \rightarrow \psi)) \rightarrow [\alpha]\psi$ for every $\alpha \in \mathbf{ACT}$,

and the rule

(NEC(α)) $\varphi / [\alpha]\varphi$

Furthermore, we need an axiom corresponding with the totality and determinacy of actions:

(TD) $[\alpha]\varphi \leftrightarrow \neg[\alpha]\neg\varphi$.

(Alternatively but equivalently, we can opt for the pair of axioms $\neg[\alpha]\bot$ (totality or seriality) and $\neg[\alpha]\neg\varphi \rightarrow [\alpha]\varphi$ (determinacy).)

The resulting system is called **DEDL**. In fact, it a straightforward combination of our logic **EDL** with a version of propositional dynamic logic (**PDL**, cf. [Har84]).

4.3.1.1. THEOREM. *The system* **DEDL** *is sound and complete for the class of* $S5\mathcal{P}^+$*-structures.*

4.3.1.1.1. EXERCISE. Check soundness and completeness of the logic **DEDL**.

As before, we express defaults of the form $\varphi : \psi / \chi$ (using Reiter's notation) as $\varphi \wedge M\psi \rightarrow P\chi$, and multiple defaults $\{\varphi_i : \psi_i / \chi_i\}_i$ are represented by formulas $\varphi_i \wedge M\psi_i \rightarrow P_i\chi_i$.

4.3.2. EXAMPLE (Yale Shooting Scenario). In the AI literature [HMcD87] the so-called Yale Shooting Problem has caused problems of formalisation in such a way that intuitively incorrect inferences can be made. A version of this problem reads as follows:

John loads his gun.
John waits one second.
John fires his gun aiming at Fred.
Fred is dead.

In order to give a formal representation of this situation we need to explicate facts that are presupposed in it: we need to say that loading a gun results in a state in which the gun is (known to be) loaded. Moreover, when a gun is fired (or rather when the trigger is pulled) in a loaded state, Fred will be hit and die (and the gun will be unloaded again). Of course, it is also presupposed that Fred is alive at the beginning of the story, although it does not say so explicitly. But finally, and most importantly, it is understood that *by default* an action does not change the truth value of an assertion unless it is given otherwise specifically. Semantically speaking, this is to say that an action does not change an aspect of a state unless it is specified otherwise. This way of representing knowledge concerning the effect of actions is efficient (it saves a lot of work in specifying explicitly all possible effects of all possible actions), but introduces a form of non-monotonic reasoning originating from dealing with uncertainties: by default, an action is not supposed to change an aspect of a state. So it is assumed that this is not the case until we run across information (knowledge) that implies the opposite.

This default nature of the situation causes the problems in the formalisation. Hanks & McDermott have shown in [HMcD87] that by using the circumscription formalism of McCarthy [McC80] one obtains two models of the above situation: either one gets the intended model in which the gun is still loaded after the second's wait and then the firing of the gun (i.e.

pulling the trigger) results in Fred's death, or one gets another unintended model in which the gun mysteriously gets unloaded after waiting for a second, and then firing the gun (i.e. pulling the trigger) does *not* result in the death of Fred. On the other hand, the default nature of the problem is imperative, since in these situations we cannot or won't specify all *non*-effects of all actions in all possible states under consideration. This issue is known in AI as the Frame Problem (see e.g. [Bro87]).

Here (following [Mey90]) we shall analyse the Yale Shooting Problem by the use of **DEDL**, and see that in this way we may also represent its common-sense reading. Moreover, we shall see that in this approach we are able to represent the problem in such a way that no confusion arises concerning the intended model. That *epistemic* logic is useful in the treatment of this problem may be argued as follows: the Yale Shooting Problem is — as is the Frame Problem in general — a problem concerning the availability (or rather lack of) information (knowledge) concerning the situations at hand. Owing to the need for an efficient representation of the situation to be described not all information is represented in order to render its interpretation unambiguous. This is in fact the problem's default nature again, and the lack of information results in unintended (non-standard) models of the representation as is the case in the representation by means of circumscription. So we need to keep track of the *knowledge* (or *belief*) available in order to decide on the problem's solution.

The Yale Shooting Scenario as stated above is now represented in **DEDL** by:

(Y1) $[\text{load}]\, K\, \text{loaded}$

(Y2) $\varphi \wedge M\, [\alpha]\varphi \rightarrow P\, [\alpha]\varphi$

(Y3) $\text{loaded} \rightarrow [\text{fire}]\, (\neg\text{alive} \wedge \neg\text{loaded})$

Y2 is called a *frame assumption*: it represents that, by default, i.e. unless there is evidence to the contrary, an action leaves an assertion true if it was so before the action was performed.

From this representation, letting φ_0 stand for alive $\wedge$ M[load] alive, we can derive the following assertions:

(Y4) $P\, [\text{load}]\, K\, \text{loaded}$ (from (Y1), using the necessitation rule)[7]

(Y5) $\varphi_0 \rightarrow P\, [\text{load}]\, \text{alive}$ (from (Y2))

(Y6) $\varphi_0 \rightarrow P\, [\text{load}]\, (\text{alive} \wedge K\, \text{loaded})$

[7]Recall that we have adopted the approach in which the necessitation rule is applicable to theorems derivable in S5 together with the additional axioms (Y1)—(Y3), cf. Section 4.2.

(from Y4 and Y5, using properties of necessity-like modalities)

(Y7) K loaded $\wedge$ M [wait] K loaded $\rightarrow$ P [wait] K loaded (from (Y2))

(Y8) P [load] (K loaded $\wedge$ M [wait] K loaded $\rightarrow$ P [wait] K loaded) (from (Y7))

(Y9) P [load] K loaded $\wedge$ P [load] M [wait] K loaded $\rightarrow$ P [load] P [wait] K loaded

(from (Y8))

(Y10) P [load] M [wait] K loaded $\rightarrow$ P [load] P [wait] K loaded (from (Y4), (Y9))

Analogously,

(Y11) P [load] alive $\wedge$ P [load] M [wait] alive $\rightarrow$ P [load] P [wait] alive (from (Y2))

(Y12) φ_0 $\wedge$ P [load] M [wait] alive $\rightarrow$ P [load] P [wait] alive (from (Y5) and (Y11))

(Y13) K (loaded $\rightarrow$ [fire] $\neg$alive) (from (Y3))

(Y14) K loaded $\rightarrow$ K [fire] $\neg$alive (from (Y13))

(Y15) K loaded $\rightarrow$ K $\neg$ [fire] alive (since $[\alpha]\neg\varphi \rightarrow \neg[\alpha]\varphi$ for serial actions α)

(Y16) K loaded $\rightarrow$ $\neg$ M [fire] alive (from (Y15))

(Y17) P [load] P [wait] K loaded $\rightarrow$ P [load] P [wait] $\neg$ M [fire] alive (from (Y16))

Note that — unless P [load] P $\perp$ holds, in which (uninteresting) case the cluster associated with the modality P [load] P is empty and every assertion of the form P [load] Pφ is trivially true — (Y17) blocks the application of the derived (generalised) default (Y20) below:

(Y18) alive $\wedge$ M [fire] alive $\rightarrow$ P [fire] alive (from (Y2))

(Y19) P [load] P [wait] alive $\wedge$ P [load] P [wait] M [fire] alive

$\rightarrow$ P [load] P [wait] P [fire] alive (from (Y18))

(Y20) φ_0 $\wedge$ P [load] M [wait] alive $\wedge$ P [load] P [wait] M [fire] alive

$\rightarrow$ P [load] P [wait] P [fire] alive (from (Y12), (Y19))

On the other hand, we can derive:

(Y21) P [load] P [wait] K loaded $\rightarrow$ P [load] P [wait] K [fire] ($\neg$alive) (from (Y3))

(Y22) P [load] M [wait] K loaded $\rightarrow$ P [load] P [wait] K [fire] ($\neg$alive) (from (Y10), (Y21))

(Y23) P [load] M [wait] K loaded $\rightarrow$ P [load] P [wait] P [fire] ($\neg$alive) (from (Y22)) reading that it is believed that loading the gun leads to a situation where it believed that waiting leads to a situation where in its turn it is believed that after firing the gun Fred is dead, provided that it is believed that loading the gun leads to a state where *possibly* waiting leads to a state where it is *known* that the gun is loaded.

4.3.2.1. REMARKS. 1. There are some subtleties to be noted in this treatment of the Yale Shooting Problem. First of all, note that in our derivation we use 'K loaded' rather than just 'loaded': this is first encountered in (Y1). Although it is also true that

(Y1') [load] loaded

this is essentially weaker, since in (Y1) also the *epistemic* aspect is stated that it is not only the case that the gun is loaded after loading, but also that this is *known*.[8] Moreover, this epistemic assertion K loaded is carried through the argument, and is essential in the blocking of the default Y20. If we give the derivation with 'loaded' instead of 'K loaded', we cannot derive that the default is blocked by showing that one of its premises is not true. In this case we obtain that if both P[load]M[wait]alive $\wedge$ P[load]P[wait]M[fire]alive and P[load]M[wait] loaded hold then there is a preferred cluster for Fred's being alive (P[load]P[wait]P[fire]alive), although it also holds that P[load]P[wait][fire]$\neg$alive. This is not unreasonable, since because of *ignorance* it is not known what is really the case: note the difference between P[α]φ and P[α]Pφ; the former expresses that it is believed (preferred) that the performance of α leads to a state in which φ, whereas the latter states that it is believed (preferred) that if α is performed one is in a state in which φ is (still) believed (preferred).[9] (Under certain conditions — by imposing certain restrictions — it is perhaps possible and desirable that nested occurrences of P-operators as in P[load]P[wait]P[fire]φ collapse, so that simple expressions of the form P[α][β] [γ] ... can be used, but we have not chosen for this option here in order to maintain generality.) In the above situation it holds that although it is believed (preferred) after loading that waiting leads to a state where firing results in Fred's being dead, it is nevertheless the case that in the (preferred) state after loading *and subsequent waiting* it is believed (preferred) that firing does *not* result in Fred's death. Although this is not inconsistent, it is not the intended

---

[8]Note, that, on the contrary, the use of L-assertions in normal 'static' defaults $\alpha \wedge M\beta \supset P\beta$ is nil: for instance, for β=Lp, $\alpha \wedge M\beta \supset P\beta$ becomes $\alpha \wedge MLp \supset PLp$, which is equivalent to the tautology $\alpha \wedge Lp \supset Lp$.

[9]This is similar to the difference in [KL86], as discussed briefly in Section 2.12, between the epistemic temporal expressions BOφ and BOBφ: the former states that it is believed that tomorrow φ holds, whereas the latter expresses that it is believed that tomorrow it is (still) believed that φ.

meaning of the situation. Here we see the need for an *epistemic* approach: using "K loaded" does not yield this strange situation.

2. Also note that although, in principle, it is possible and allowed to use different P-modalities (say P_α) for every instance of α in formula (Y2), it is not needed in our analysis of the Yale Shooting, and it would, in fact, only lead to cumbersome notation in this case.

4.3.3. EXAMPLE (The Hiding Turkey Scenario). E. Sandewall [San91, San95] has proposed a number of variants of the Yale Shooting Scenario in order to stress several aspects of the frame problem in combination with e.g. disjunctive information. He was thus able to show shortcomings in the approaches of the frame problem in the literature.

The Hiding Turkey Scenario is a problem that emphasises the role of disjunctive information. Many approaches in the literature involve some kind of minimisation, and Sandewall showed that, although these minimisation techniques are able to treat the standard Yale Shooting Scenario adequately, they often choose the wrong solution in the case of the Hiding Turkey Scenario variant. It is a particularly interesting problem from an epistemic logic point of view, since it involves an aspect of incomplete information (on top of that involving the frame assumption).

Given is the following problem concerning a hunter and a living, non-hiding turkey, which may be deaf (or not; this is not specified):

After loading the gun, the gun will be loaded.

If the turkey is not deaf, it will hide after the hunter's loading of his gun.

If the gun is loaded and the turkey is hiding, [the hunter will miss it when firing, so] it will still be alive after the hunter has fired his gun at it.

If the gun is loaded and the turkey is not hiding, the hunter will kill it by firing his gun.

Furthermore, after firing a loaded gun the gun will get unloaded.

What will be the situation after the hunter has loaded and then fired his gun?

The Hiding Turkey Scenario can be represented in **DEDL** as follows:

(H1) [load] K loaded (, so also K [load] K loaded)

(H2) $\neg$deaf $\rightarrow$ [load] hiding

(H3) alive $\wedge$ loaded $\wedge$ hiding $\rightarrow$ [fire] (alive $\wedge$ $\neg$loaded)

(H4) loaded $\wedge$ $\neg$hiding $\rightarrow$ [fire] ($\neg$alive $\wedge$ $\neg$loaded)

(H5) $\varphi \wedge M\,[\alpha]\varphi \rightarrow P\,[\alpha]\varphi$

First we show that this representation as it is is inadequate to give the expected results! Suppose we are given the initial condition alive $\wedge$ $\neg$hiding $\wedge$ $\neg$loaded, together with the assumption M [load] alive $\wedge$ (deaf $\rightarrow$ M [load] (deaf $\wedge$ $\neg$hiding)) $\wedge$ ($\neg$deaf $\rightarrow$ M [load] $\neg$deaf). Moreover, at this point there is also no reason to disallow the assumption M [load] $\neg$hiding. This enables us to derive the following:

alive $\wedge$ $\neg$hiding $\wedge$ $\neg$loaded $\Rightarrow$ P[load]$\neg$hiding (by using (H5)),

which is a undesirable belief viewed in the light of (H2). If you think about it, this is not so strange. This blocking of the inference above can only occur if one *knows for certain* that $\neg$[load]$\neg$hiding is true. From (H2) we cannot know this for sure, since $\neg$deaf is not known for sure. (In fact, what happens here, is the fact that we only know deaf $\vee$ $\neg$deaf (i.e. K(deaf $\vee$ $\neg$deaf)), and *not* K deaf $\vee$ K$\neg$deaf)!)

However, in our logic containing epistemic operators we may indeed state that it is known which of the two cases is true without committing ourselves to either one, namely just by stating the extra information that:

(H6) K deaf $\vee$ K$\neg$deaf

One of the cases is true, but we just do not specify which one. So on the level of the specification we have incomplete information, while the agent (knower) knows exactly which of deaf and $\neg$deaf is the case!

By applying necessitation to H2 we obtain K($\neg$deaf $\rightarrow$ [load] hiding), which in its turn implies that K$\neg$deaf $\rightarrow$ K[load] hiding. This gives us K$\neg$deaf $\rightarrow$ $\neg$M$\neg$ [load] hiding, and *(under the assumption that load does not fail)* K$\neg$deaf $\rightarrow$ $\neg$M [load] $\neg$hiding (*)

Given the initial condition alive $\wedge$ $\neg$hiding $\wedge$ $\neg$loaded, together with the assumption M [load] alive $\wedge$ (deaf $\rightarrow$ M [load] (deaf $\wedge$ $\neg$hiding)) $\wedge$ ($\neg$deaf $\rightarrow$ M [load] $\neg$deaf), we can now derive the following:

alive $\wedge$ ¬hiding $\wedge$ ¬loaded $\Rightarrow$ (using H6)

(alive $\wedge$ ¬hiding $\wedge$ ¬loaded $\wedge$ K deaf) $\vee$ (alive $\wedge$ ¬hiding $\wedge$ ¬loaded $\wedge$ K¬deaf) $\Rightarrow$

(Note that (*) now blocks the inference P[load]¬hiding *in the case of the second disjunct, as desired!)*

(P [load] (alive $\wedge$ deaf $\wedge$ ¬hiding) $\wedge$ K [load] K loaded) $\vee$ (P [load] (alive $\wedge$ ¬deaf) $\wedge$ K [load] (loaded $\wedge$ hiding)) $\Rightarrow$

(P [load] (alive $\wedge$ deaf $\wedge$ ¬hiding) $\wedge$ P [load] loaded) $\vee$ (P [load] (alive $\wedge$ ¬deaf) $\wedge$ P [load] (loaded $\wedge$ hiding)) $\Rightarrow$

(P [load] (alive $\wedge$ deaf $\wedge$ ¬hiding $\wedge$ loaded) $\vee$ (P [load] (alive $\wedge$ ¬deaf $\wedge$ hiding $\wedge$ loaded) $\Rightarrow$

(under the assumptions deaf $\rightarrow$ M [fire] deaf *and* ¬deaf $\rightarrow$ M [fire] ¬deaf*))*

(P [load] [fire] (¬alive $\wedge$ ¬loaded) $\wedge$ P [fire] deaf) $\vee$ (P [load] [fire] (alive $\wedge$ ¬loaded) $\wedge$ P [fire] ¬deaf)

This states that either we believe that after loading it holds that firing the gun results in a state where the turkey is dead and the gun unloaded and we believe that after firing the turkey is still deaf (we did not explicitly exclude being both deaf and dead!), or we believe that after loading: it holds that the turkey is still alive, the gun is unloaded, and we believe that after firing the gun the turkey is still not deaf. (Note that this belief is defeasible (namely by default): firing the gun may have caused such a noise that it damaged the turkey's hearing ability.)

4.3.3.1. REMARKS. Note that in order to derive the desired result we need to make the following assumptions and choices:

1. load does not fail, i.e. ¬[load] $\perp$. This is reasonable. If the gun can fail to be loaded, we are in an entirely different situation.
2. In fact, by inspecting the proof in this case it is sufficient to stipulate

(H1') [load] loaded

without a reference to the stronger notion of *knowing* that loaded holds after loading the gun. We used this to keep in line with the Yale Shooting Scenario we discussed in Example 4.3.2.

Moreover, we need it if we extend the Hiding Turkey Scenario to a combination with the Yale Shooting Scenario by including a wait in the sequence of actions (see Exercise 4.3.3.2).

3. We may even obtain a more elegant outcome if 3 and 4 are strengthened to

(H3') loaded $\wedge$ hiding $\rightarrow$ **K** [fire] (alive $\wedge$ $\neg$loaded)

(H4') loaded $\wedge$ $\neg$hiding $\rightarrow$ **K** [fire] ($\neg$alive $\wedge$ $\neg$loaded),

which means that firing a loaded gun not only results in killing (depending on hiding or not) and unloading, but this is also *known* to be the case. In this case we get:

P [load] P [fire] (alive $\wedge$ deaf) $\vee$ P [load] P [fire] ($\neg$alive $\wedge$ $\neg$deaf).

4. In the representation of the Hiding Turkey Scenario by means of (H1)—(H6), and (H3) in particular, we stated explicitly that in case the turkey is alive but hiding, it will survive a firing action, as opposed to the case it is not hiding (H4). Another, more sophisticated solution would be that (H3) and (H4) are changed into

(H3") loaded $\rightarrow$ [fire] $\neg$loaded
(H4") $\neg$hiding $\rightarrow$ [fire] $\neg$alive

stating that firing makes the gun unloaded (H3") and the turkey's not hiding results in certain death after firing the gun (H4"). The fact that firing the gun when the turkey is alive and hiding would then be captured by the law of inertia (H5): unless stated (known) explicitly otherwise (e.g. in case the turkey is *not* hiding, where [fire] $\neg$alive is assumed to imply $\neg$[fire] alive) the turkey stays alive when firing the gun. In this case we essentially use (H4") as a more specific rule than the general rule (an instance of the law of inertia (H5)) that says that firing does not change the status of being alive. We have not chosen to do this above in order not to complicate matters further. Moreover, the above interpretation of using (H4") as a more specific rule than the general law of inertia does not quite seem to match the intuition in this case, where we have two distinct cases to be distinguished, namely whether the turkey is hiding or not. Both cases have their own rules, as captured exactly by (H3) and (H4), respectively. Furthermore, this solution enables us to derive the conclusion P [load] [fire] alive (in case the turkey is not deaf), whereas the former solution would introduce (by an application of the law of inertia) further uncertainty, namely P [load] *P* [fire] alive (in the case again that the turkey is not deaf).

4.3.3.2. EXERCISE. What will be the situation that results in the Hiding Turkey Scenario after the hunter has loaded, **waited** and then fired his gun? Will the turkey be alive? Note that this problem is a combination of the Yale Shooting and Hiding Turkey Scenarios, with both a waiting period and disjunctive information.

4.3.3.3. EXERCISE (Potato in Tail-pipe Scenarios, McCarthy, cf. [San91]). Formalise the following scenarios concerning a car which is expected to run unless a potato is put in the tail-pipe.

(i) *Initially the car engine is not running.*
Normally, the engine runs after starting the car. Nothing is known about a potato in the tail-pipe.
If the tail-pipe is blocked by a potato, the engine will not run after starting the car.
The car is started.
Is the engine running?

(ii) The same scenario and question as in (i), but now additionally it is known that there is a tail-pipe destroyer around, which may block the tail-pipe by a potato.

4.4. Default Theories and Default Entailment

In this section we introduce a notion of default theory comparable with that of Reiter's. The most important difference is that we use our modal (epistemic) language $\mathcal{L}_{EDL}$ to express default rules and interpret formulas on Kripke models, as we did in Section 4.2. As in Reiter's approach we define a default theory as a pair, consisting of a set of formulas describing the world and a set of default rules.

4.4.1. DEFINITION. A default theory Θ is a pair (W, Δ), where W is a finite consistent set of objective (i.e. non-modal) formulas describing (necessary) facts about the world, and Δ is a finite set of defaults $\{\varphi_i \wedge M\psi_i \rightarrow P_{f(i)}\chi_i \mid i = 1, ..., n\} \in \mathcal{L}_{EDL}$,[10] where φ_i, ψ_i and χ_i are again objective formulas, and f is a function of type $\{1, ..., n\} \rightarrow J$, where $J \subseteq \{1, ..., n\}$. So, in effect, f assigns a frame $\Sigma_{f(i)}$ (and corresponding operator $P_{f(i)}$) to the i-th default. (In particular, some of the $P_{f(i)}$-operators may be the same.) The sets W and Δ are to be considered as sets of axioms, and we may apply necessitation to the formulas in them.

4.4.2. DEFINITION. Given a default theory $\Theta = (W, \Delta)$, we define the non-monotonic inference relation $\vdash_\Theta$ as follows. Let W* be the conjunction of the formulas in W. Note that W is a finite set, and that, moreover, W only consists of objective formulas. Furthermore, let φ be an epistemic formula such that the formula $\varphi \wedge W^*$ is honest, and thus $\Sigma^{\varphi \wedge W^*}$ is well-defined. Then (for $\psi \in \mathcal{L}_{EDL}$):

[10]Instead of $\mathcal{L}_{EDL}$ we can also take $\mathcal{L}_{DEDL}$ to include dynamic reasoning as in the examples of Section 4.3. We shall not pursue this option in this section.

$$\varphi \vdash_\Theta \psi \Leftrightarrow_{def} \psi \in Th_{\mathbf{EDL}}(\Sigma\varphi{\wedge}W^* \cup \Delta).$$

We shall call the relation $\vdash_\Theta$ the *default entailment relation* with respect to default theory Θ. The set of *consequences* $Cons_\varphi(\Theta)$ of a default theory Θ is the set of default entailments $\{\psi \mid \varphi \vdash_\Theta \psi\}$. When φ = **true**, we just write $Cons(\Theta)$.

4.4.3. EXAMPLE (Tweety). Consider the following default theory $\Theta = (W, \Delta)$ with $W = \{p \to \neg f\}$ and $\Delta = \{b \wedge Mf \to Pf\}$, representing that penguins do not fly, and that by default birds fly. Now consider the following inferences (to stress the application of Δ we denote such a step by $\vdash_{\mathbf{EDL},\Delta}$; moreover, recall that $\vdash$ stands for the Halpern & Moses entailment of Chapter 3):

(i) $b \wedge W^* \vdash b \wedge \neg K \neg f \vdash_{\mathbf{EDL}} b \wedge Mf \vdash_{\mathbf{EDL},\Delta} Pf$, i.e. $b \vdash_\Theta Pf$,

meaning that, from the mere fact that Tweety is a bird, we conclude that Tweety is assumed to fly; which must be contrasted with the inference:

(ii) $b \wedge p \wedge W^* \vdash Kp \vdash_{\mathbf{EDL}} K\neg f \vdash_{\mathbf{EDL}} \neg Mf \nvdash_{\mathbf{EDL},\Delta} Pf$, i.e. **not** $b \wedge p \vdash_\Theta Pf$,

meaning that, in case Tweety is a penguin, we cannot infer that Tweety is assumed to fly, but instead we can derive to know for certain that Tweety does not fly.

Note that we can determine whether $\nvdash_{\mathbf{EDL}} \varphi$, as above in (ii), by means of the completeness theorem for the logic **EDL** with respect to the models in $\mathcal{S5P}$, since this amounts to showing $\nvDash_{\mathbf{EDL}} \varphi$, i.e. giving a countermodel of φ in $\mathcal{S5P}$.

4.4.4. EXAMPLE (Closed world assumption, CWA). The difference between a closed and an open world assumption [Rei1] can be very succinctly expressed by the following two **EDL**-expressions:

(a) $M\neg p \to P\neg p$ (for $p \in \mathbf{P}$)

which expresses that, if $\neg p$ is possible, it is preferred, or believed in practice (closed world assumption), as opposed to

(b) $M\neg p \to \neg Pp$ (for $p \in \mathbf{P}$)

which expresses the weaker statement that, if $\neg p$ is possible, p is not preferred (believed in practice), which is in accord with the *open world assumption*. The CWA should be handled with care to avoid inconsistencies, particularly in connection with disjunctions. For example, under the CWA the set $\{q \vee r\}$ is inconsistent, since $q \vee r \vdash_{CWA} (q \vee r) \wedge \neg q \wedge \neg r \vdash_{CWA} \perp$. In our framework we would get an empty frame in this case: let $\Delta_{CWA} = \{M\neg p \rightarrow P\neg p \mid p \in \mathbf{P}\}$: $q \vee r \mathrel{|\!\sim} K(q \vee r) \wedge \neg Kq \wedge \neg Kr \vdash_{\mathbf{EDL}} K(q \vee r) \wedge M\neg q \wedge M\neg r \vdash_{\mathbf{EDL},\Delta_{CWA}} K(q \vee r) \wedge P\neg q \wedge P\neg r \vdash_{\mathbf{EDL}} P(q \vee r) \wedge P\neg q \wedge P\neg r \vdash_{\mathbf{EDL}} P((q \vee r) \wedge \neg q \wedge \neg r) \vdash_{\mathbf{EDL}} P\perp$, i.e. $q \vee r \mathrel{|\!\sim}_{\Theta} P\perp$, for $\Theta = (\{\mathbf{true}\}, \Delta_{CWA})$.

However, in our approach we can do better, by employing distinct frames: take $\Delta'_{CWA} = \{M\neg q \rightarrow P_1\neg q, M\neg r \rightarrow P_2\neg r\}$. Now we obtain $q \vee \mathrel{|\!\sim} K(q \vee r) \wedge \neg Kq \wedge \neg Kr \vdash_{\mathbf{EDL}} K(q \vee r) \wedge M\neg q \wedge M\neg r \vdash_{\mathbf{EDL},\Delta'_{CWA}} K(q \vee r) \wedge P_1\neg q \wedge P_2\neg r \vdash_{\mathbf{EDL}} P_1(q \vee r) \wedge P_1\neg q \wedge P_2(q \vee r) \wedge P_2\neg r \vdash_{\mathbf{EDL}} P_1(q \vee r) \wedge \neg q) \wedge P_2(q \vee r) \wedge \neg r) \vdash_{\mathbf{EDL}} P_1(r \wedge \neg q) \wedge P_2(q \wedge \neg r)$, i.e. $q \vee r \mathrel{|\!\sim}_{\Theta} P_1(r \wedge \neg q) \wedge P_2(q \wedge \neg r)$, for $\Theta = (\{\mathbf{true}\}, \Delta'_{CWA})$. This means that we obtain two frames S_1 and S_2, where $S_1 \models r \wedge \neg q$ and $S_2 \models q \wedge \neg r$. Note that this implies that in e.g. S_1 it holds that (r and) $P_1 r$, but, of course, it still holds that $\neg Kr$, meaning that here we *believe* (or *prefer*) r, but still do not *know* r for certain. This illustrates the flexibility of the epistemic logic **EDL**.

4.4.4.1. EXERCISE. Consider the default theory $\Theta = (W, \Delta)$, with

$W = \{q \rightarrow (\neg p \wedge \neg r)\}$, and

$\Delta = \{Mp \rightarrow P_1 p, Mq \rightarrow P_1 q, Mr \rightarrow P_2 r\}$.

Determine Cons(Θ).

4.4.4.2. EXERCISE. Reconsider the examples from Section 4.2 (including the exercises), now treating these as default theories and determine their consequences. (Note that now it is not necessary to *assume* the consistency of certain assertions: it can now be *proved* non-monotonically.)

4.4.4.3. EXERCISE (Lifschitz). Formalise as a default theory and determine its set of consequences:

(i) *Blocks A and B are heavy.*

Heavy blocks are normally located on the table.

A is not on the table.

Check whether "B is on the table" is a consequence of this default theory.

(ii) *Blocks A and B are heavy.*

Heavy blocks are normally located on the table.

Heavy blocks are normally red.

A is not on the table.

B is not red.

Check whether "B is on the table and A is red" is a consequence of this default theory.

In the same spirit as it was done for the entailment relation $\vdash$, we can give a semantical characterisation for $\vdash_\Theta$, which we state here without proof.

4.4.5. THEOREM. *Consider a default theory* $\Theta = (W, \Delta)$, *where* Δ *is finite, and let* $\varphi \in \mathcal{L}(\mathbf{P})$ *(thus not containing P-modalities) be an epistemic formula such that* $\varphi \wedge W^*$ *is honest. Then we have that (denoting the conjunction of elements of* Δ *by* Δ^**):*

$$\varphi \vdash_\Theta \psi \Leftrightarrow \mathbb{M} \models_{\mathbf{EDL}} K\Delta^* \rightarrow \psi \textit{ for all } \mathbb{M} \in \mathcal{S5P} \text{ such that } K(\mathbb{M}_{\varphi \wedge W^*}) \subseteq \{\psi \in \mathcal{L}(\mathbf{P}) \mid \mathbb{M} \models \psi\}$$

Moreover, if **P** is finite, we have:

$$\varphi \vdash_\Theta \psi \quad \Leftrightarrow \quad \mathbb{M} \models_{\mathbf{EDL}} K\Delta^* \rightarrow \psi \textit{ for all } \mathbb{M} \in \mathcal{S5P} \textit{ extending } \mathbb{M}_{\varphi \wedge W^*} \in \mathcal{S5}.$$

PROOF. See [MH95]. ∎

The significance of Theorem 4.9 is most easily seen in the case that the number of primitive propositions is finite. Then it states that, in order to check (model-theoretically) whether $\varphi \vdash_\Theta \psi$ holds, we first have to consider the model $\mathbb{M}_{\varphi \wedge W^*}$ that is determined (uniquely) by the honest formula $\varphi \wedge W^*$ describing the premise that we have (φ) together with the background information about the world (W^*). Then we consider all $\mathcal{S5P}$-models $\mathbb{M}$ that have $\mathbb{M}_{\varphi \wedge W^*}$ as a kernel (i.e. reduction), and check whether imposing the defaults on them — i.e. letting them satisfy the *global* (that is pertaining to *all* worlds in the model) condition $K\Delta^*$ — implies the consequence ψ.

Finally, we define the entailment relation $\vdash_\Theta$ for a finite premise set of epistemic formulas:

4.4.6. DEFINITION. Let $\Theta = (W, \Delta)$ be a default theory. Let Γ be a finite set of epistemic formulas, such that for the conjunction Γ^* of the formulas in Γ it holds that $\Gamma^* \wedge W^*$ is honest, and let ψ be an **EDL**-formula. Then we define: $\Gamma \vdash_\Theta \psi$ iff $\Gamma^* \vdash_\Theta \psi$. ∎

4.5. Cumulativity

Gabbay [Gab85], Makinson [Mak89] and Kraus, Lehmann & Magidor [KLM90] have provided some yardsticks for examining non-monotonic logics in the form of meta-properties that may be desirable for these logics. One of the criteria that in their opinion these logics should satisfy is that of *cumulativity*. As is observed by Makinson in [Mak89], Reiter's very influential default logic fails to satisfy cumulativity. In this section we show that our epistemic default logic (EDL) does satisfy cumulativity, thus establishing a desirable property for a logic dealing with default reasoning. Also Brewka ([Bre91]) has proposed a cumulative default logic, but as he starts out with Reiter's logic, mending cumulativity results in a substantially more complicated logic than ours. Finally we mention that Doherty in [Doh91] has proposed a cumulative logic for non-monotonic reasoning that is similar to ours in syntactical respects. His logic, however, is based on partial rather than modal interpretations.

In what follows we shall concentrate on the notion of (finistic) cumulativity as defined in [KLM90] as follows:

4.5.1. DEFINITION. An entailment relation $\vdash\!\sim$ is called *cumulative* iff the following conditions hold (Here Γ, Γ_1, Γ_2 stand for an arbitrary finite set of epistemic formulas, and Γ^* denotes again the conjunction of the formulas in Γ.):

(i) $\Gamma \vdash\!\sim \varphi$, for every $\varphi \in \Gamma$ (Reflexivity)
(ii) If $\models \Gamma_1^* \leftrightarrow \Gamma_2^*$ and $\Gamma_1 \vdash\!\sim \varphi$ then $\Gamma_2 \vdash\!\sim \varphi$ (Left logical equivalence)
(iii) If $\models \varphi \rightarrow \psi$ and $\Gamma \vdash\!\sim \varphi$ then $\Gamma \vdash\!\sim \psi$ (Right weakening)
(iv) If $\Gamma \cup \{\varphi\} \vdash\!\sim \psi$ and $\Gamma \vdash\!\sim \varphi$, then $\Gamma \vdash\!\sim \psi$ (Cut)
(v) If $\Gamma \vdash\!\sim \varphi$ and $\Gamma \vdash\!\sim \psi$ then $\Gamma \cup \{\varphi\} \vdash\!\sim \psi$ (Cautious monotonicity)

The term '*cumulativity*' pertains to condition (v), *cautious monotonicity*, which states that conclusions may be cumulated into the set of premises without altering (neither gaining nor losing) the power of this set of premises. This means that theorems may be added to the premises without changing the set of derivable formulas. This seems to be a reasonable (weak) form of monotonicity that one would like to have, even for non-monotonic logics (cf. [Gab85], [Mak89] and [KLM90]).

We now show that $\vdash\!\sim_\Theta$ is cumulative, where it has to be understood that it is only meaningful to consider $\Gamma \vdash\!\sim_\Theta \varphi$ when $\Gamma^* \wedge W^*$ is an honest epistemic formula, and thus Γ does not contain P-modalities. Thus we check cumulativity for meaningful expressions only!

4.5.2. THEOREM. *For any default theory* $\Theta = (W, \Delta)$, *the entailment relation* $\vdash\!\sim_\Theta$ *is cumulative.*

PROOF. We prove the requirements for cumulativity:

(i) We prove for $\varphi \in \Gamma$ that $\Gamma^* \vdash\!\sim_\Theta \varphi$: Let $\varphi \in \Gamma$. Obviously, $\Gamma^* \wedge W^* \in \Sigma^{\Gamma^* \wedge W^*}$. Therefore, by the logical closure of stable sets, we also have $\varphi \in Th_{\mathbf{EDL}}(\Sigma^{\Gamma^* \wedge W^*} \cup \Delta)$, since $\models \Gamma^* \wedge W^* \rightarrow \varphi$, i.e., $\Gamma^* \vdash\!\sim_\Theta \varphi$.

(ii) Suppose $\models \Gamma_1^* \leftrightarrow \Gamma_2^*$ and $\Gamma_1 \mathrel{|\!\sim_\Theta} \varphi$, i.e. $\Gamma_1^* \mathrel{|\!\sim_\Theta} \varphi$. First we verify that if Γ_1^* is honest also Γ_2^* is: if Γ_1^* is honest, then $M_{\Gamma_1^*}$ exists and $M_{\Gamma_1^*} \models \Gamma_1^*$. So also $M_{\Gamma_1^*} \models \Gamma_2^*$. Moreover, $M_{\Gamma_1^*} = \bigcup\{M \mid M \models \Gamma_1^*\} = \bigcup\{M \mid M \models \Gamma_2^*\} = M_{\Gamma_2^*}$. Hence $M_{\Gamma_2^*}$ exists and $M_{\Gamma_2^*} \models \Gamma_2^*$. So also Γ_2^* is honest.
Next we show that $\Gamma_1^* \mathrel{|\!\sim_\Theta} \psi$. First we note that $M_{\Gamma_1^* \wedge W^*} = \bigcup\{M \mid M \models \Gamma_1^* \wedge W^*\} = \bigcup\{M \mid M \models \Gamma_2^* \wedge W^*\} = M_{\Gamma_2^* \wedge W^*}$, since for every M, $M \models \Gamma_1^* \wedge W^* \Leftrightarrow M \models \Gamma_2^* \wedge W^*$. So by $\Gamma_1^* \mathrel{|\!\sim_\Theta} \varphi$ we know that $\varphi \in Th_{\mathbf{EDL}}(\Sigma^{\Gamma_1^* \wedge W^*} \cup \Delta) = Th_{\mathbf{EDL}}(K(M_{\Gamma_1^* \wedge W^*}) \cup \Delta) = Th_{\mathbf{EDL}}(K(M_{\Gamma_2^* \wedge W^*}) \cup \Delta) = Th_{\mathbf{EDL}}(\Sigma^{\Gamma_2^* \wedge W^*} \cup \Delta)$. So $\Gamma_2^* \mathrel{|\!\sim_\Theta} \varphi$, as desired.
(iii) Suppose $\models \varphi \to \psi$ and $\Gamma \mathrel{|\!\sim_\Theta} \varphi$. Then $\varphi \in Th_{\mathbf{EDL}}(\Sigma^{\Gamma^* \wedge W^*} \cup \Delta)$. Thus, $\Sigma^{\Gamma^* \wedge W^*} \cup \Delta \vdash_{\mathbf{EDL}} \varphi \vdash \psi$. So $\psi \in Th_{\mathbf{EDL}}(\Sigma^{\Gamma^* \wedge W^*} \cup \Delta)$, i.e. $\Gamma \mathrel{|\!\sim_\Theta} \psi$.
(iv) Suppose $\Gamma \cup \{\varphi\} \mathrel{|\!\sim_\Theta} \psi$ and $\Gamma \mathrel{|\!\sim_\Theta} \varphi$. Note that from the latter it follows that $\varphi \in Th_{\mathbf{EDL}}(\Sigma^{\Gamma^* \wedge W^*} \cup \Delta)$, i.e. $\Sigma^{\Gamma^* \wedge W^*} \cup \Delta \vdash_{\mathbf{EDL}} \varphi$. So either $\varphi \in \Sigma^{\Gamma^* \wedge W^*}$, or $\varphi \notin \Sigma^{\Gamma^* \wedge W^*}$ and then there is some finite $\Sigma \subseteq \Sigma^{\Gamma^* \wedge W^*}$ such that $\Sigma \cup \Delta \vdash_{\mathbf{EDL}} \varphi$.
Let us first consider the former case: $\varphi \in \Sigma^{\Gamma^* \wedge W^*}$, i.e. $\Gamma^* \wedge W^* \vdash \varphi$.
From Lemma 3.1.22 it follows that $\Sigma^{\Gamma^* \wedge \varphi \wedge W^*} = \Sigma^{\Gamma^* \wedge W^*}$. So now by $\Gamma \cup \{\varphi\} \mathrel{|\!\sim_\Theta} \psi$, i.e. $\Gamma \wedge \varphi \mathrel{|\!\sim_\Theta} \psi$ and hence $\psi \in Th_{\mathbf{EDL}}(\Sigma^{\Gamma^* \wedge \varphi \wedge W^*} \cup \Delta) = Th_{\mathbf{EDL}}(\Sigma^{\Gamma^* \wedge W^*} \cup \Delta)$. Thus, $\Gamma \mathrel{|\!\sim_\Theta} \psi$.
Next, consider the latter case: $\varphi \notin \Sigma^{\Gamma^* \wedge W^*}$ and there is some finite $\Sigma \subseteq \Sigma^{\Gamma^* \wedge W^*}$ such that $\Sigma \cup \Delta \vdash_{\mathbf{EDL}} \varphi$. Since a stable set is closed under S5-consequences, and still $\varphi \notin \Sigma^{\Gamma^* \wedge W^*}$, this last **EDL**-inference must involve (the 'P-part' and thus) some rule from Δ. But then φ must contain some P-modality, which case we had ruled out. (φ appears as a premise of $\mathrel{|\!\sim_\Theta}$ and here we only use epistemic formulas as defined in Chapter 1, containing no P-modalities.) So this case does not arise.
(v) Suppose $\Gamma \mathrel{|\!\sim_\Theta} \varphi$ and $\Gamma \mathrel{|\!\sim_\Theta} \psi$. We want to prove that $\Gamma \cup \{\varphi\} \mathrel{|\!\sim_\Theta} \psi$, in case ψ is an honest epistemic formula. By the latter again either $\varphi \in \Sigma^{\Gamma^* \wedge W^*}$, or $\varphi \notin \Sigma^{\Gamma^* \wedge W^*}$ and then there is some finite $\Sigma \subseteq \Sigma^{\Gamma^* \wedge W^*}$ such that $\Sigma \cup \Delta \vdash_{\mathbf{EDL}} \varphi$. As in case (iv) we can argue that the latter case does not arise under the condition that ψ must be an epistemic formula (and thus P-less). So we need only consider the former case: we use again that $\Sigma^{\Gamma^* \wedge \varphi \wedge W^*} = \Sigma^{\Gamma^* \wedge W^*}$, and obtain that $\psi \in Th_{\mathbf{EDL}}(\Sigma^{\Gamma^* \wedge W^*} \cup \Delta) = Th_{\mathbf{EDL}}(\Sigma^{\Gamma^* \wedge \varphi \wedge W^*} \cup \Delta)$. Thus, $\Gamma \wedge \varphi \mathrel{|\!\sim_\Theta} \psi$, i.e. $\Gamma \cup \{\varphi\} \mathrel{|\!\sim_\Theta} \psi$. ■

Of course, this result should not really surprise us, since we have seen in Section 3.3, that Halpern & Moses' entailment relation is already cumulative, and we use this notion as an underlying relation for our default entailment, only extended by the monotonic logic **EDL**.

4.5.3. The entailment relation $\mathrel{|\!\sim_\Theta}$ does not satisfy another property that is discussed in [KLM90], namely
(vi) If $\Gamma \mathrel{|\!\sim_\Theta} \varphi$ and **not** $\Gamma \mathrel{|\!\sim_\Theta} \neg\psi$ then $\Gamma \cup \{\psi\} \mathrel{|\!\sim_\Theta} \varphi$ (rational monotonicity),

as we can easily show that this does not hold already for Halpern & Moses' $\mid\!\sim$. (Note that $\mid\!\sim\ = \mid\!\sim_\Theta$ for $\Theta = (\emptyset, \emptyset)$.)

4.5.4. EXAMPLE. $p \mid\!\sim \neg Kq$, and **not** $p \mid\!\sim \neg q$, and still **not** $p \wedge q \mid\!\sim \neg Kq$. ∎

Finally, we discuss two examples taken from [Tan92] and [Mak89], the latter showing the non-cumulativity of Reiter's default logic, and see how this works in our approach.

4.5.5. EXAMPLE. Consider $\Theta = (W, \Delta)$ with $W = \{q \rightarrow \neg p\}$ and $\Delta = \{Mp \rightarrow Pq\}$. This default theory is the translation of what in Reiter's logic would be given by the default theory $W = \{q \rightarrow \neg p\}$ and $\Delta = \{ : p / q\}$. One can show that in Reiter's approach this theory has an extension in which both q and ¬p are true. However, one can also show that adding ¬p to the set W of premises leads to a situation in which q is no longer present in any extension, thus showing failure of cumulativity in Reiter's default logic.

In our approach when trying to mimic this failure of cumulativity we get the following. Let Θ be as before and let $\Theta' = (W', \Delta)$ with $W' = \{q \rightarrow \neg p, \neg p\}$ and $\Delta = \{Mp \rightarrow Pq\}$. Then (using again the *ad hoc* notations $\vdash_{\mathbf{EDL},\Delta}$ and $\vdash_W$ to indicate the kind of step taken; both are actually regular **EDL**-inferences) **true** $\mid\!\sim_\Theta Mp \vdash_{\mathbf{EDL},\Delta} Pq \vdash_W P\neg p$, so both q and ¬p are preferred. However, although **true** $\mid\!\sim_{\Theta'} K\neg p \vdash_{\mathbf{EDL}} \neg Mp \nvdash_{\mathbf{EDL},\Delta} Pq$, cumulativity is saved by the fact that, using Θ, **P**¬p rather than ¬p, which is contained in W', is derivable. In our set-up it is even illegal to put a P-formula in the set of premises. However, even if we were more liberal for the moment and allowed this, we would obviously still obtain the desirable result **true** $\mid\!\sim_{\Theta''} Mp \vdash_{\mathbf{EDL},\Delta} Pq$ ($\vdash_{W''} P\neg p$) for $\Theta'' = (W'', \Delta)$ and $W'' = \{q \rightarrow \neg p, P\neg p\}$ and Δ as before, since, in contrast to K¬p, P¬p does not entail ¬Mp and therefore cannot block the application of the default!

4.5.6. EXAMPLE. Consider $\Theta = (W, \Delta)$ with $W = \{\mathbf{true}\}$ and $\Delta = \{Mp \rightarrow P_1p, (p \vee q) \wedge M\neg p \rightarrow P_2\neg p\}$. This default theory is the translation of what in Reiter's logic would be given by the default theory $W = \{\ \}$ and $\Delta = \{:p / p, p \vee q :\neg p / \neg p\}$. One can show that in Reiter's approach this theory has one extension, namely $Th_{prop}(\{p\})$, where Th_{prop} stands for the propositional theory. However, one can also show that adding $p \vee q$ to the set W of premises leads to a situation in which also $Th_{prop}(\{\neg p, q\})$ is an extension, thus showing failure of cumulativity in Reiter's default logic. In our approach when trying to mimic this failure of cumulativity we get the following: let Θ be as before and let $\Theta' = (W', \Delta)$ with $W' = \{p \vee q\}$ and $\Delta = \{Mp \rightarrow P_1p, (p \vee q) \wedge M\neg p \rightarrow P_2\neg p\}$. Then (using again the *ad hoc* notations $\vdash_{\mathbf{EDL},\Delta}$ and $\vdash_{\mathbf{EDL},W}$ to indicate the kind of step taken; both are actually regular **EDL**-inferences) **true** $\mid\!\sim_\Theta Mp \vdash_{\mathbf{EDL},\Delta} P_1p \vdash_{\mathbf{EDL},W} P_1(p \vee q)$, so indeed p and $p \vee q$ are preferred, like in default logic. But we also have in our approach **true** $\mid\!\sim_\Theta M\neg p$, and thus **true** $\mid\!\sim_\Theta P_1($p

$\vee q) \wedge M\neg p \vdash_{\mathbf{EDL},\Delta} P_1P_2\neg p \vdash_{\mathbf{EDL}} P_2\neg p$ (under the assumption that $\neg P_1 \perp$, i.e. S_1 is non-empty). On the other hand, also **true** $\vdash_{\Theta'} Mp \vdash_{\mathbf{EDL},\Delta} P_1p \vdash_{\mathbf{EDL},W} P_1(p \vee q)$, and directly **true** $\vdash_{\Theta'} (p \vee q) \wedge M\neg p \vdash_{\mathbf{EDL},\Delta} P_2\neg p$. So we see that in default theory Θ' we can still derive the assertions $P_1(p \vee q)$ and $P_2\neg p$. Of course, in Θ' we may proceed further and derive stronger assertions: since we have **true** $\vdash_{\Theta'} K(p \vee q) \vdash_{\mathbf{EDL},\Delta} P_2(p \vee q)$, we obtain altogether: **true** $\vdash_{\Theta'} P_2\neg p \wedge P_2(p \vee q) \vdash_{\mathbf{EDL}} P_2(\neg p \wedge q)$, yielding a striking similarity with the second extension in Reiter's default logic for this case. We see, however, that cumulativity is maintained here, mainly due to a coincidence of two features in our approach: (1) the possibility of separating extensions in an explicit manner by means of distinct P_i-modalities, blocking less applications of defaults, and (2) a (somewhat restricted) form of transitivity of defaults, so that the outcome of the first default can be used at the second one (without getting contradictions in this case due to the distinct P_i-modalities again).

In this chapter so far we have proposed a default logic based on Halpern & Moses' epistemic states and the entailment associated with these. Although the resulting entailment relation for default reasoning is non-monotonic, this is not due to the infamous 'jumping to conclusions' as in other default logics like Reiter's. On the contrary, we distinguish facts from assertions that are assumed by default. In this respect we are very close to the approaches of [Doh91] and [TT91, Tan92]. They, however, employ partial semantics for their operators rather than modal (Kripke-style) semantics. Here we must also mention related work of Lin & Shoham [LS90, LS92]: they also felt the need to introduce additional modal operators, but in some sense they use them the other way around. Instead of translating a default à la Reiter $\varphi : \psi / \chi$ as $\varphi \wedge \neg K\neg\psi \supset P\chi$, as we do, in which the *default conclusion* is marked by a special modal operator, they treat the *assumption* by means of a special operator A, and translate the above default as $K\varphi \wedge \neg A\neg\psi \supset K\chi$. The emphasis of their paper, however, is somewhat different. They show how, by putting a suitable preference order on the models of their logic, both default logic and autoepistemic logic can be given an epistemic semantics. We, however, wanted to employ epistemic semantics to obtain a new logic that is simple and natural, and has the desirable property of cumulativity as we have seen.

The non-monotonicity in our approach arises from the way we reason about epistemic states, or about knowledge *versus* ignorance, as Halpern & Moses put it. Here we have an inference mechanism that may conclude from a set of premises that something is (as yet) unknown, which is clearly non-monotonic. In retrospect we may conclude that by disentangling the nature of non-monotonicity in other default logics, one obtains a logic that is well-behaved in the sense that it is cumulative in the sense of Kraus, Lehmann & Magidor. We also believe that — in comparison with approaches that employ preferential entailment after Shoham [Sho87, Sho88], like e.g. NM3 [Doh91] — in our approach it is exhibited in a clear-cut manner where preferences play a role in default reasoning. In our opinion the most important place is that where it is determined what is known and what is not. Then, on the basis of the outcome of this, default rules may be applied in a monotonic manner, after which it may be necessary again to put a preference order on the outcomes of this, which we believe is very domain- and even user-dependent. In other approaches it is often attempted to replace this whole process by the use of a single preference order, which is perhaps too ambitious and which, in any case, obscures matters considerably.

We next look at an extension of our framework, in which we can use our approach to defaults to perform *counterfactual* reasoning.

4.6. Counterfactual Reasoning

In this section we show how defaults can be used for counterfactual reasoning, which we already mentioned briefly in Section 3.2. To this end we slightly extend our logic **EDL** by means of an operator with which we can also express facts that hold in the actual or 'real' world. We also discuss some properties of our approach in relation to other approaches in the literature. An earlier version of this work was first reported in [MH93b].

Counterfactual reasoning, reasoning 'against the facts', has been studied extensively in philosophical literature (see [Sta68], [Lew73], [Sos75], [Nut84]). This is not surprising since traditionally philosophers have always been interested in (more or less ideal) worlds different from our actual (much less ideal) world, where other propositions hold. But also in (the philosophy of) the exact sciences counterfactuals play an important role in describing and applying laws of nature. In fact, every such law can be used in an argument that employs counterfactuals. For example, let us consider the law of gravity. This law can be applied in an academic or engineering argument as follows: "If this building was not sufficiently secured, it would collapse."

Recently, however, it has been realised [Gin86], that counterfactuals are also important in the area of artificial intelligence. It has uses in questions of database maintenance, in planning, in diagnosis and in natural language understanding, to mention a few applications. (See [Gin86].) For instance, if a robot has to plan lines of actions, it needs to examine possibilities, which are generally not true at the moment of examination. It should, so to speak, have the ability to perform 'experiments of thought'. Similar experiments of thought are needed in the other applications mentioned above.

Traditionally, counterfactuals are (a kind of) implications $p>q$, with intended meaning "if p were true, q would be (have been) true as well", with the underlying presumption that p is not actually true at the moment of utterance. This makes this kind of reasoning go beyond classical propositional and predicate logic, in which the paradox of material implication holds: $\perp \Rightarrow q$ for any q. Thus classical logic is obviously not sufficiently sophisticated to treat counterfactuals. In philosophy counterfactuals are treated by means of so-called conditional logic, which is based upon a more refined (conditional) implication involving worlds that satisfy the counterfactual premise but are 'as similar to' the actual world as is possible. This is presented in a very abstract setting. (See [Sta68], [Lew73], [Nut84].)

On the other hand, as we have seen, much effort in AI research has been given to the study of a class of reasoning methods (or logics) which is motivated from an entirely different point of view, namely logics in which defaults may occur, and non-monotonic logics more in general. *A posteriori* it has, perhaps somewhat surprisingly, been realised that these logics are related to conditional logic. For instance, the work of Shoham [Sho87, Sho88], which we have discussed in Section 3.2, and *a fortiori* that of Delgrande [Del88] can be viewed as attempts to 'implement' non-monotonic logics by means of conditional logic.

In this section (following [MH93b]) we view the relationship the other way around, so to speak, and investigate counterfactuals from the perspective of default reasoning (or, more generally, non-monotonic logic) implementing the 'as similar to' clause in the semantic definition of counterfactuals by means of defaults: by default, the hypothetical worlds under investigation are 'the same as' the actual one. To be able to express this we need a logical language in which we can express defaults as well as actualities.

To illustrate the similarity between counterfactuals and defaults on a more concrete level, let us consider (informally) the phenomenon of *ambiguity*. Counterfactual reasoning, like default reasoning, is not always unambiguous in the sense that there is a unique conclusion if one assumes a premise that is not actually true. Consider a 'classical' example from [Res75]:

(1a) *If Julius Caesar had been a lion, there would have been a lion without a tail.*

This statement sounds correct. However, we can also state:

(1b) *If Julius Caesar had been a lion, there would have been a Roman general with a tail.*

Although a little more peculiar, (1b) seems to be correct as well.

Whether one asserts (1a) or (1b) depends on the 'frame of mind' one sticks to. In the case of (1a), one considers Caesar — without tail — as a 'declared lion'; in the case of (1b) one imagines Caesar to be an actual lion including the property of having a tail. In the first case, the image of Caesar (and the fact that generals have no tails) dominates, in the second the image of a lion (including the fact that lions have tails) does. Moreover, the conclusions of the counterfactual implications (1a) and (1b) are inconsistent.

This example of an ambiguous counterfactual implication is similar to examples of default reasoning, where ambiguous conclusions may also occur, such as that of the Nixon Diamond (Example 4.2.7). There we saw that we could also draw two mutually inconsistent answers, namely with respect to the question of whether Nixon is a pacifist or not, depending on which 'frame of mind', a typical quaker or a typical republican, dominates.

In this section we investigate this similarity of counterfactuals and defaults in some more depth, using a logic in which both counterfactual and default reasoning can be represented. This logic will be a slight extension of the **S5**-like logic that we used for defaults. In particular, we show how counterfactual reasoning resembles (or, rather, involves a kind of) default reasoning. In this way we will provide further evidence of the similarities between defaults (non-monotonic logic) and counterfactuals (conditional logic) by implementing the latter by the former, and, moreover, obtain a 'less abstract' semantics for counterfactuals compared with the traditional approach initiated by Stalnaker ([Sta68], cf. also [Lew73]). In some sense the traditional counterfactual implication is too coarse. In our setting it is possible to differentiate between 'frames of mind' when reasoning about counterfactuals.

4.6.1. The Logic ECL (Epistemic Counterfactual Logic)

In previous sections we have extended the basic epistemic logic **S5** by special P-modalities, denoting preference or practical belief, to treat defaults. The resulting logic was called **EDL**, epistemic default logic. In order to treat counterfactuals we need to extend the logic once more, now by an A-operator denoting 'actuality'. This operator is needed to speak about (the assertions that hold in) the actual or 'real' world as opposed to other possible worlds. Moreover, we also put more structure on the clusters of preferred worlds, which, in the present context, will also be called 'focuses'. We shall call the resulting logic **ECL**, epistemic counterfactual logic.

The language $\mathcal{L}_{\mathbf{ECL}}$ of the logic **ECL** is defined as follows:

Assume again a fixed collection **P** of primitive propositions. Furthermore, let $I \subseteq \mathbb{N}$ be a set of indexes (which we shall use to name clusters), and let I^* denote the set of sequences over I. We denote elements $\sigma \in I^*$ by $<i_1, i_2, ..., i_n>$, dropping the brackets when convenient.

Concatenation of sequences is denoted by a comma ','. The language **L** we shall use is the minimal set of formulas closed under the following rules:

(i) $\mathbf{P} \subseteq \mathcal{L}_{\mathbf{ECL}}$.

(ii) If $\varphi, \psi \in \mathcal{L}_{\mathbf{ECL}}$, then $\neg\varphi, \varphi \wedge \psi(, \varphi \vee \psi, \varphi \rightarrow \psi, \varphi \leftrightarrow \psi) \in \mathcal{L}_{\mathbf{ECL}}$.

(iii) If $\varphi \in \mathcal{L}_{\mathbf{ECL}}$, then $K\varphi, M\varphi, A\varphi, P_\sigma\varphi \in \mathcal{L}_{\mathbf{ECL}}$ ($\sigma \in I^*, \sigma \neq \langle\rangle$).

Informally, the new operator $A\varphi$ is read as "φ is actually true (true in the real world)", and the other operators are read as we did before. The focus operator P_σ refers to a cluster which is named by the sequence σ reflecting a hierarchy of clusters. To locate a cluster referred to by $P_{i_1,i_2,\ldots,i_n}$ one considers the i_1-th cluster within the whole set of states, and next within this cluster the i_2-th, etc. For example, $P_{1,2,1}$ denotes the first cluster within the second cluster within the first cluster in the set of states. For convenience, we let $P_{\langle\rangle}$ stand for K. We refer to formulas in $\mathcal{L}_{\mathbf{ECL}}$ as *ECL-formulas*.

Formally, ECL-formulas are interpreted by Kripke-structures of the form $\langle\{S_\sigma \mid \sigma \in I^*\}, \pi, \rho, \{\wp_\sigma \mid \sigma \in I^*\}\rangle$, where $S_{\langle\rangle}$, also denoted S, is a collection of possible worlds, and the S_σ are subsets of S such that $S_{\sigma,i} \subseteq S_\sigma$, the so-called 'clusters' or 'focuses', $\pi: \mathbf{P} \rightarrow \Sigma \rightarrow \{t, f\}$ is a truth assignment to the primitive propositions per world, $\rho \in S$ is the *real or actual* world, $\wp_{\langle\rangle}$ (also denoted $\wp$) $= S \times S$, and $\wp_\sigma = S \times S_\sigma \subseteq \wp$. We let $\mathcal{S5AP}$ denote the collection of Kripke-structures of the above form (the **A** in $\mathcal{S5AP}$ referring to actualities).

Let $\mathcal{S5AP}^+$ denote the collection of pairs (M, s) with $M = \langle\{S_\sigma \mid \sigma \in I^*\}, \pi, \rho, \{\wp_\sigma \mid \sigma \in I^*\}\rangle \in \mathcal{S5AP}$ and $s \in S$. Elements of $\mathcal{S5AP}^+$ are referred to as *worlds*. The formal interpretation of the language now reads: for $M = \langle\{S_\sigma \mid \sigma \in I^*\}, \pi, \rho, \{\wp_\sigma \mid \sigma \in I^*\}\rangle$,

$(M, s) \models p$ iff $\pi(p)(s) = t$

$(M, s) \models \neg\varphi$ iff $(M, s) \not\models \varphi$

$(M, s) \models \varphi \wedge \psi$ iff $(M, s) \models \varphi$ and $(M, s) \models \psi$

$(M, s) \models K\varphi$ iff $(M, t) \models \varphi$ for all $t \in S$

$(M, s) \models M\varphi$ iff $(M, t) \models \varphi$ for some $t \in S$

$(M, s) \models A\varphi$ iff $(M, \rho) \models \varphi$

$(M, s) \models P_\sigma\varphi$ iff $(M, t) \models \varphi$ for all $t \in S_\sigma$.

Moreover, $M \models \varphi$ iff $(M, s) \models \varphi$ for all $s \in S$, and $\models \varphi$ iff $(M, s) \models \varphi$ for all $M \in \mathcal{S5AP}$.

Some words about the A- and P_σ-operators are in order at this point. As to the A-operator, one may wonder why a special actuality operator is needed at all, for usually the world of evaluation is taken to be the actual world, so that propositions without modal operators refer to this actual world automatically. In our approach, however, we like to be able to refer to the actual world independent of the status of the world of evaluation, that is to say, whether this world is regarded as actual or not. So we use the A-modality to refer to the actual world, even if we are evaluating in a hypothetical world (that is not thought of being actual). A further advantage of this approach is that one can continue our view of a (generalised) epistemic state associated with an S5-like Kripke model as a whole. In particular, whether $A\varphi$ holds is a property of a *model* rather than of a particular *state* in the model, since we have that $\mathbb{M} \models A\varphi$ iff there exists an $s \in S$ such that $(\mathbb{M}, s) \models A\varphi$. This is also related to the pleasing fact that we can continue to apply the K-necessitation rule to assumptions, even if these contain A-formulas. Clearly, representing formulas that actually hold by means of objective formulas (i.e. without the use of modal operators, and, particularly, A-modalities) this would not be possible: contingent facts that hold in the actual world, do not necessarily hold in all possible worlds. This is the very *raison d'être* of modal logic, and is in line with the fact that that we do *not* have for objective formulas φ that $\mathbb{M} \models \varphi$ iff there exists an $s \in S$ such that $(\mathbb{M}, s) \models \varphi$.

As to the P_σ-operators: in what follows we need to refer to clusters of worlds as we did in **EDL**. However, as we shall see we also need to set up frames (focuses) within frames (etc.), and we need to be specific about where exactly these frames are located. To this end we use the structure of the index sequences as introduced above.

The theory of $\mathcal{S5AP}$ is axiomatised by the system **ECL**, which is obtained as follows (cf. [MH92]): take the system **EDL** for the modalities K (and dual M) and the P_σ, together with the following extra axioms regarding the A-modality:

(AP10) $A(\varphi \wedge \psi) \leftrightarrow A\varphi \wedge A\psi$

(AP11) $A\neg\varphi \leftrightarrow \neg A\varphi$

(AP12) $K\varphi \rightarrow A\varphi$

(AP13) $A\varphi \rightarrow KA\varphi$

(AP14) $AP_\sigma\varphi \leftrightarrow P_\sigma\varphi$

(AP15) $\neg P_\sigma \bot \rightarrow (P_\sigma A\varphi \leftrightarrow A\varphi)$

and

(AP16) $P_\sigma\varphi \rightarrow P_{\sigma,i}\varphi$,

reflecting the internal structure of the clusters S_σ, that is $S_{\sigma,i} \subseteq S_\sigma$.

In the following we will write $\Gamma \vdash_{\mathbf{ECL}} \varphi$ or $\varphi \in \mathrm{Th}_{\mathbf{ECL}}(\Gamma)$ to indicate that φ is an **ECL**-consequence of Γ. We mean this again in the sense as explained in Section 4.2 when we considered **EDL**. Intuitively, these extra axioms express that the actual world ρ is unique in S, and that by means of the operator A one always points at ρ no matter where one starts in S or in some non-empty subframe (cf. [MH92] for a more technical justification of the correspondences between these axioms and the properties of the various accessibility relations).

4.6.1.1 EXERCISE. Check the soundness and completeness of **ECL**.

4.6.2. Towards Counterfactual Reasoning in ECL

In this section we shall discuss how to represent counterfactual implications in the setting of **ECL**. Here we use the idea that counterfactuals possess a default nature. To be more precise, when we reason counterfactually, we hypothesise about some assertion we know that (possibly) does not hold in actuality, but, of course, we do like to inherit as many as assertions that are true in the actual world. We want to reason *contra* reality in as few respects as possible, since in practice we would like the results of our reasoning to still have as much bearing on reality as possible! (A thought experiment of a completely deranged person with an imagination that has no bearing on reality is easy: just create some wild frame of mind S_0 and reason with the associated modality P_0. Here no relation with the actual world is necessary or even desirable. This is perhaps an explanation of the success of the program PARRY simulating a psychiatric patient with paranoia [Hei80].) Clearly this reminds us of defaults (and is a kind of *law of inertia* that one also encounters in the frame problem in AI, as discussed in Section 4.3). To put it in terms of defaults: by default, we take over the true assertions of the actual world. Suppose we hypothesise a frame S_0, in which some 'counterfacts' hold. For the moment, we need not be specific about which counterfacts. We now want to express that, if it is possible (consistent) to assume that some truth in the actual world also holds in the frame S_0, we prefer this actual truth to hold in S_0 as well. Or rather, we declare this assertion to be a preferred (or default) belief within the frame S_0. To put it in more operational terms, we set up a subframe (focus) $S_{0,i}$ of S_0, in which the assertion holds. Formally, this is captured by the following schema:

$$A\psi \wedge \neg P_0 \neg\psi \rightarrow P_{0,i}\psi \qquad \text{(for some } i \in I) \qquad (\Delta)$$

which states that if ψ holds in the actual world and ψ is not inconsistent within the frame S_0 (i.e. if there is a world in S_0 where ψ holds), then we assume that ψ holds within *some* (*not* required *every*) subframe $S_{0,i}$ of S_0. The latter condition allows for several possibilities (like the extensions in default logic). This is best illustrated by again considering the Caesar-lion example we mentioned in Section 3.2, which we shall discuss in detail presently.

Furthermore, we have to put an important restriction on the general schema (Δ). Although what we have said so far appears to be valid for any assertion ψ that is true in the actual world, we encounter some nasty and undesirable ramifications when we take ψ to be a material implication involving the formula we want to 'reason against': say that $\psi = p \rightarrow q$, where p is not true in the actual world. Suppose that we want to hypothesise that p holds (in some frame S_0). If we put no restrictions on the schema (Δ), we can apply it to ψ, and obtain that $\psi = p \rightarrow q$ holds in S_0. Since also p holds in S_0, we obtain that q holds in S_0 as well. This may be very undesirable, since the only reason why ψ (= $p \rightarrow q$) may hold in the actual world is the very fact that p does not hold there. For instance, take for p the assertion that "Caesar is a lion", and q the unrelated assertion that "Caesar is an American president", or even something more absurd like "Caesar is green". Now, if we may apply (Δ) unrestrictedly, because of the fact that p is not actually true, we may assume (under the further assumption that there were no other assertions true in S_0 that would contradict this) that $p \rightarrow q$, and thus q, is true in the frame S_0. This is clearly unwanted. So we restrict schema (Δ) to the case where ψ is a literal, i.e. a formula that is either a primitive proposition or a negation of this.

Before actually giving a representation of counterfactual implication in our logic, we now first illustrate the use of schema (Δ) by an example. We consider the Caesar-lion example again:

4.6.2.1. EXAMPLE. We take the following propositional constants: g stands for 'being a Roman general', ℓ stands for 'being a lion', and t for 'having a tail'. (Actually, this example is best represented in predicate logic, but we consider here a propositional approximation.)

1. Ag *(Actually, Caesar is a Roman general.)*
2. $A\neg\ell$ *(Actually, Caesar is not a lion.)*
3. $P_0\ell$ (We now hypothesise that Caesar is a lion, creating a frame S_0 in which this holds.)
4. $g \wedge \neg P_0 t \supset P_{0,1}\neg t$ *(Normally Roman generals do not have tails.)*
5. $\ell \wedge \neg P_0\neg t \supset P_{0,2} t$ *(Normally lions* do *have tails.)*
6. $Ag \wedge \neg P_0\neg g \supset P_{0,3} g$ (application of (Δ))
7. $A\neg\ell \wedge \neg P_0\ell \supset P_{0,4}\neg\ell$ (application of (Δ))

It is interesting to see what we can now derive under the assumption that

(a) $\neg P_0\neg g \wedge \neg P_0\neg t \wedge \neg P_0 t$

which states that the consistency checks in 4, 5 and 6 are satisfied. In particular, it says that in frame S_0 t is contingent, i.e. there are possible worlds both with t and ¬t. In some sense this merely says that it is possible to organise within S_0 a subframe with t and one with ¬t.

First we note that, by 3, the application of 7 is blocked. This means that we cannot derive that $P_0P_4\neg\ell$, which is clearly desirable in this situation. Next, we obtain:

8.	$K(\ell \wedge \neg P_0\neg t \supset P_{0,2}t)$	(from 5, applying necessitation)
9.	$P_0(\ell \wedge \neg P_0\neg t \supset P_{0,2}t)$	(from 8, and $K\varphi \supset P_0\varphi$)
10.	$P_0\ell \wedge \neg P_0\neg t \supset P_{0,2}t$	(from 9, by modal reasoning)
11.	$P_{0,2}t$	(from 10, 3 and (a))

Moreover, also we have that:

12.	$P_{0,3}g$	(from 1, 6 and (a))

and furthermore that:

13.	$P_{0,3}g \wedge \neg P_0 t \supset P_{0,1}\neg t$	(from 4 and modal reasoning, cf. 8—10)
14.	$P_{0,1}\neg t$	(from 12, 13 and (a))

Finally, we obtain:

15.	$P_{0,1}\ell$	(from 3 and the fact that is a subframe S_1 of S_0)
16.	$P_{0,1}(\ell \wedge \neg t)$	(from 14 and 15, by modal reasoning)

The formulas 14 and 11 state that there are two subframes $S_{0,1}$, $S_{0,2}$ within the frame S_0 such that: in the former, Caesar has no tail and (by 16) is a lion without a tail, and, in the latter, Caesar has a tail. This is exactly what is to be expected in this situation. Note, however, that from the above representation it *cannot* be inferred that in the frame $S_{0,2}$ Caesar is a Roman general with a tail, since although both $S_{0,2}$ and $S_{0,3}$ are subframes of S_0, they need not coincide, or even have some overlap. If one would like to represent the property that $S_{0,2}$ and $S_{0,3}$ coincide, one should replace $P_{0,3}$ by $P_{0,2}$ in 6.

4.6.3. Counterfactual Implication in ECL

We are now ready to try and capture the counterfactual implication '>' in **ECL**. Note that (Δ) is not yet intended to represent the counterfactual implication itself. (Δ) only provides a necessary background for such an implication. So now we search for an adequate representation of $\varphi > \psi$. If we look at the Caesar example, we should be able to say that in this case both $\ell > t$ and $\ell > \neg t$.

What we have here is of an inferential nature, using a background theory. This background theory will at least contain the scheme (Δ). We use $\varphi \mid\!\sim_T \psi$ for the meta-statement "from φ, ψ can be inferred with respect to background theory T" (in **ECL** using the appropriate consistency requirements of the form $\neg P_0 \neg \psi$ — like in schema (Δ) — which must hold as well). $\mid\!\sim_T$ is a nonmonotonic inference relation, extending $\vdash_{\mathbf{ECL}}$, with background theory T in a similar vein to the default entailment relation $\mid\!\sim_\Theta$ of Section 4.4, extending $\vdash_{\mathbf{EDL}}$. So $\varphi \mid\!\sim_T \psi$ implies that the inference actually can take place (or may 'fire' as we shall call it) as far as the consistency (within T) is concerned, which excludes, for instance, that $\varphi \mid\!\sim_T \bot$. (In this case firing is blocked since $\neg P_0 \neg \bot \leftrightarrow \bot$.) So this is very similar to what we have seen in default reasoning, where we also had to consider consistency. For instance, in the Tweety example, in order to show that b $\mid\!\sim$ Pf, we needed to prove b $\mid\!\sim$ Mf ($\Leftrightarrow \neg K \neg f$) to be able to use the default $b \wedge Mf \rightarrow Pf$ (see Example 4.4.3). A difference is that in the context of counterfactual reasoning we are concerned with deriving the possibility of an assertion ψ within frame $S_0 \subseteq S$ (denoted by $\neg P_0 \neg \psi$) rather than with deriving the possibility of an assertion ψ within the entire set S (denoted by $\neg K \neg \psi$ or $M\psi$), as in the default theories of Section 4.4.

We now define:

$$T \mid\!\sim \varphi >_{0,i} \psi \text{ as } P_0\varphi \mid\!\sim_T P_{0,i}\psi.$$

To put it more precisely, we have that $T \mid\!\sim \varphi >_{0,i} \psi \Leftrightarrow [T \cup \{P_0\varphi\} \mid\!\sim \neg P_0 \neg \psi \;\&\; T \cup \{P_0\varphi\} \mid\!\sim P_{0,i}\psi]$, where $\mid\!\sim$ is some non-monotonic inference relation extending $\vdash_{\mathbf{ECL}}$ with which we may infer the consistency of ψ (within the frame S_0) with the theory $T \cup \{P_0\varphi\}$ as well as the consistency checks needed to apply instances of the scheme (Δ). Without going into too many details we assume here that we have some means to derive $T \cup \{P_0\varphi\} \mid\!\sim \neg P_0 \neg \psi$, meaning that if φ is supposed to hold in the hypothetical frame S_0, then — given theory T — the assertion ψ is considered possible within that frame S_0. This derivation may be done in a non-monotonic way similar to the derivation of $\neg K \neg \varphi$ (or $M\varphi$) in the approach of Halpern & Moses (cf. Section 3.1.16). We, furthermore, assume that the non-monotonic entailment relation $\mid\!\sim$ maintains consistency. For consistent theory T, we have that $T \not\mid\!\sim \bot$, and, moreover, we assume that it is *not* the case that both $T \mid\!\sim \varphi$ and $T \mid\!\sim \neg\varphi$ or, to put it in other words: for all consistent T, $T \mid\!\sim \varphi \Rightarrow T \not\mid\!\sim \neg\varphi$. (This has as a consequence that, for instance, establishing $T \cup \{P_0\varphi\} \mid\!\sim P_0 \neg \psi$ implies that also $T \cup \{P_0\varphi\} \not\mid\!\sim \neg P_0 \neg \psi$ holds, in effect blocking the firing of the non-monotonic inference $P_0\varphi \mid\!\sim_T P_{0,i}\psi$, and thus the counterfactual implication $\varphi >_{0,i} \psi$ above.) Now we may say, in analogy with the default theories of Section 4.4, that $T \mid\!\sim \varphi >_{0,i} \psi \Leftrightarrow P_{0,i}\psi \in Th_{\mathbf{ECL}}(Poss_{0,\varphi} \cup T)$, where $Poss_{0,\varphi}$ consists of the formulas of the form $\neg P_0 \neg \chi$ denoting possibilities within frame S_0, given the constraints entailed by the theory $T \cup \{P_0\varphi\}$.

Next we define:

$$T \vdash \varphi >_0 \psi \text{ iff } T \vdash \varphi >_{0,i} \psi \text{ for some i,}$$

and finally we arrive at our definition of couterfactual implication:

$$T \vdash \varphi > \psi \text{ iff } T \vdash \varphi >_0 \psi \text{ for some frame } S_0.$$

(When the theory T is understood or irrelevant, and no confusion can arise, we omit the prefix '$T \vdash$' and the subscript 'T' from $\vdash_T$.) Now, the theory T_{Caesar} consisting of 1 to 7, together with the assumption (a), yields indeed $T_{Caesar} \vdash \ell >_{0,1} \neg t$ and $T_{Caesar} \vdash \ell >_{0,2} t$, and so $T_{Caesar} \vdash \ell >_0 \neg t$ and $T_{Caesar} \vdash \ell >_0 t$.

Given a collection $\{S_{0,i} \mid i \in I_0\}$ ($I_0 \subseteq I^*$) of subframes of S_0, one can also imagine a stronger notion of counterfactual $T \vdash \varphi \gg_{0,I_0} \psi$ defined as $T \vdash \varphi >_{0,i} \psi$ for *all* $i \in I_0$. This expresses that the consequent ψ must hold in all subframes $S_{0,i} \subseteq S_0$ with $i \in I_0$. This is similar to Lewis' notion of counterfactual [Lew73], and also to cautious approaches with respect to extensions in default logic [Rei80]. With respect to the Caesar example above, where $I_0 = \{1, 2\}$, we can now neither conclude $T_{Caesar} \vdash \ell \gg_{0,I_0} t$ nor $T_{Caesar} \vdash \ell \gg_{0,I_0} \neg t$, since neither in $S_{0,1}$ nor in $S_{0,2}$ the worlds both satisfy t and $\neg t$. We can also imagine that sometimes we need an ordering on frames $S_{0,i}$, $i \in I_0$, as in default reasoning, to indicate that some frames are more relevant (or preferred) than other ones.

4.6.3.1. EXAMPLE. We next consider a problem discussed by Ginsberg in [Gin86], namely the issue of non-monotonicity of counterfactual implication. As our approach is derived from our approach to non-monotonic reasoning in earlier sections, one may expect that this issue is also captured correctly in our setting. The example of Ginsberg reads as follows: consider the following counterfactual assertions:

(i) $p > d$ *(If the power had not failed, diner would have been on time.)*

(ii) $p \wedge e > \neg d$ *(If the power had not failed, but I had been elected president, diner would have been late.)*

(iii) $p \wedge e \wedge n > d$ *(If the power had not failed, and I had been elected president, but nobody had bothered to tell me, diner would have been on time.)*

As Ginsberg argues correctly, this example — which is intuitively completely sound and consistent — demonstrates the non-monotonicity of > in an evident manner. We now show how this example works out in our framework. We translate (i)—(iii) as

(i*) $P_0 p \vdash P_{0,1} d$ (under the consistency assumption $\neg P_0 \neg d$)
(ii*) $P_0(p \wedge e) \vdash P_{0,2} \neg d$ (under the consistency assumption $\neg P_0 d$)
(iii*) $P_0(p \wedge e \wedge n) \vdash P_{0,3} d$ (under the consistency assumption $\neg P_0 \neg d$)

We can rewrite this as:

(i*) $P_0 p \vdash P_{0,1} d$ (under the consistency assumption $\neg P_0 \neg d$)
(ii*) $P_0 p \wedge P_0 e \vdash P_{0,2} \neg d$ (under the consistency assumption $\neg P_0 d$)
(iii*) $P_0 p \wedge P_0 e \wedge P_0 n \vdash P_{0,3} d$ (under the consistency assumption $\neg P_0 \neg d$)

Under the assumption that $K(e \rightarrow \neg d)$, or sufficiently $P_0(e \rightarrow \neg d)$, (i*) and (ii*) are consistent, since this implies $P_0 e \rightarrow P_0 \neg d$, which together with $P_0 e$ yields $P_0 \neg d$, blocking application of (i*). So it is safe to apply (ii*). Likewise (ii*) and (iii*) are consistent under the assumptions $K(n \rightarrow d)$ or directly $K(e \rightarrow \neg n)$. (In the latter case we have $P_0(e \rightarrow \neg n)$, and so $P_0 \neg n$ by the antecedent of (iii*) (i.e. $P_0 e$). However, now assuming the antecedent of (iii*) we obtain $P_0 n \wedge P_0 \neg n$, i.e. $P_0(n \wedge \neg n)$, i.e. $P_0 \bot$, implying $P_0 d$, blocking firing of (ii*).)

4.6.3.2. EXERCISE. Check whether the following assertions hold:

(i). $(\varphi_1 >_0 \psi_1)$ & $(\varphi_2 >_0 \psi_2) \Rightarrow (\varphi_1 \wedge \varphi_2 >_0 \psi_1 \wedge \psi_2)$

(ii). $A\varphi$ & $(\varphi >_0 \psi) \Rightarrow A\psi$

(iii). $A\varphi$ & $(\varphi >_0 \psi) \Rightarrow P_{0,i}\psi$, for some i

4.6.4. Properties of the ECL Approach to Counterfactuals

Finally in this section we shall examine the properties of our set-up compared with Gärdenfors' postulates for conditional logic [Gär78], which are known to be equivalent to the Lewis approach, and which one can use — as Ginsberg does in [Gin86] — as a standard against which one can measure other systems for conditionals. Paraphrased into our language they read as follows (Here we use the notation $K\varphi$ for the meta-statement **ECL** $\vdash \varphi$ or, equivalently, **ECL** $\vdash K\varphi$, in order to stay in line with the notation of Gärdenfors as much as possible.):

(G1) $(\varphi >_0 \psi)$ & $(\varphi >_0 \chi) \Rightarrow (\varphi >_0 \psi \wedge \chi)$

(G2) $\varphi >_0$ **true**

(G3) $K(\psi \rightarrow \chi)$ & $(\varphi >_0 \psi) \Rightarrow (\varphi >_0 \chi)$

(G4) $\varphi >_0 \varphi$

(G5) $K(\varphi \leftrightarrow \psi)$ & $(\varphi >_0 \chi) \Rightarrow (\psi >_0 \chi)$

(G6) $K(\varphi \wedge \psi) \Rightarrow (\varphi >_0 \psi)$

(G7) $(\varphi >_0 \psi) \Rightarrow (K\varphi \Rightarrow K\psi)$

(G8) $(\varphi >_0 \chi)$ & $(\psi >_0 \chi)$ $\Rightarrow$ $(\varphi \vee \psi >_0 \chi)$

(G9) $(\varphi >_0 \psi)$ & *not* $(\varphi >_0 \neg\chi)$ $\Rightarrow$ $(\varphi \wedge \chi >_0 \psi)$

We check which of these hold in our approach:
(G1) does not hold. We do not regard this as a flaw in our approach. In fact, the Caesar example was already a counter-example demonstrating that (G1) is not always desirable a property. The crux of the matter is that the consequences ψ and χ may hold in different and disjoint subframes;
(G2) holds under the condition that $\neg P_0 \bot$, i.e. $S_0 \neq \varnothing$;
(G3) holds. We prove this case by way of an example:

PROOF of (G3). Suppose that $\vdash K(\psi \rightarrow \chi)$, and that $\varphi >_0 \psi$, i.e., for some i, $[T \cup \{P_0\varphi\} \vdash \neg P_0\neg\psi$ & $T \cup \{P_0\varphi\} \vdash P_{0,i}\psi]$. Since $\vdash K(\psi \rightarrow \chi)$, we also have that $\vdash P_0(\psi \rightarrow \chi)$, and hence $\vdash P_0(\neg\chi \rightarrow \neg\psi)$. Hence we obtain $\vdash P_0\neg\chi \rightarrow P_0\neg\psi$, and so $\vdash \neg P_0\neg\psi \rightarrow \neg P_0\neg\chi$. Moreover, we have $\vdash P_{0,i}(\psi \rightarrow \chi)$, and so $\vdash P_{0,i}\psi \rightarrow P_{0,i}\chi$. Thus we have that $[T \cup \{P_0\varphi\} \vdash \neg P_0\neg\chi$ & $T \cup \{P_0\varphi\} \vdash P_{0,i}\chi]$. Consequently, we obtain $\varphi >_0 \chi$. ■

A direct corollary of (G3) is:

(G3*) $K(\psi \leftrightarrow \chi)$ & $(\varphi >_0 \psi)$ $\Rightarrow$ $(\varphi >_0 \chi)$.

(G4) holds under the consistency condition that $\neg P_0\neg\varphi$. So, e.g. $\bot >_0 \bot$ does *not* hold;
(G5) holds; but it is important to note that we do *not* have the stronger assertion

(G5*) $K(\varphi \rightarrow \psi)$ & $(\psi >_0 \chi)$ $\Rightarrow$ $(\varphi >_0 \chi)$,

which would be a form of monotonicity. As we have seen in Ginsberg's power/diner example, we do *not* have this, because of the non-monotonicity in the consistency checks.

Note in passing that (G3*) and (G5) together imply a natural property concerning substitutivity of equivalent assertions:

(G35) $K(\varphi_1 \leftrightarrow \varphi_2)$ & $K(\psi_1 \leftrightarrow \psi_2)$ $\Rightarrow$ $((\varphi_1 >_0 \psi_1) \Leftrightarrow (\varphi_2 >_0 \psi_2))$.

(G6) holds under the condition that $\neg P_0\bot$, i.e. $S_0 \neq \varnothing$. (Admittedly, we have re-shaped the original form of (G6), which looks like $(\varphi \wedge \psi) \rightarrow (\varphi >_0 \psi)$ and which could not be fit in our framework immediately because it is not a well-formed formula; the same holds for (G7).) A related, simpler assertion

(G6*) $K\varphi \Rightarrow (\psi >_0 \varphi)$

also holds under the same condition of $\neg P_0\bot$.

(G7) (even in adjusted form) does not hold. However, we do have, under the consistency condition that $\neg P_0\neg\psi$:

(G7*) $(\varphi >_{0,i} \psi) \Rightarrow (K\varphi \Rightarrow P_{0,i}\psi)$,

which is not so strange: we cannot expect a counterfactual experiment to have an influence on the whole collection of *a priori* worlds as in (G7), but it *has* an influence on the subframe S_i. (This is even more intuitive and useful than what is stated in (G7), witness the Caesar example!)

(G8) does not hold, because $P_0(\varphi \vee \psi) \rightarrow P_0\varphi \vee P_0\psi$ does not hold.
(G9) is related to Example 4.6.3.1. It holds almost trivially (without using the second premise) under the assumption that $P_0\chi$ does not block the validity of the conclusion (which is admittedly very close to the intention of the second premise in (G9), stating something about the consistency of φ and χ). However, also the consistency of ψ and χ should be considered in our approach. Thus a version of (G9) that holds in our setting is:

(G9*) $(\varphi >_0 \psi)$ & $T \cup \{P_0\varphi, P_0\chi\} \vdash \neg P_0\neg\psi \Rightarrow (\varphi \wedge \chi >_0 \psi)$.

The second premise expresses the consistency (within frame S_0) of ψ with *both* φ and χ. Moreover, in order to derive $\varphi \wedge \chi >_0 \psi$, φ and χ must also be consistent (within S_0), since otherwise we have that $P_0\varphi \wedge P_0\chi \vdash P_0\bot$, so that we cannot derive the consistency check $\neg P_0\neg\psi$.

Also, as discussed in [Gin86], we should not have contraposition of counterfactual implication, i.e. $\varphi >_0 \psi \Rightarrow \neg\psi >_0 \neg\varphi$, which we obviously do not have in our framework (cf. Section 4.2).

4.6.4.1. EXERCISE. Check the above results concerning the Gärdenfors postulates (G1)—(G9) formally.

We finally discuss (non-)transitivity of counterfactual implication. Let us consider a (perhaps somewhat outdated) example from [Gin86] again:

4.6.4.2. EXAMPLE. Consider the following three counterfactual statements:

(a) If J. Edgar Hoover had been born a Russian, he would have been a Communist.

(b) If he had been a Communist, he would have been a traitor.

(c) If Hoover had been born a Russian, he would have been a traitor.

In our set-up we formalise (a)—(c) as:

(a*) $r > c$

(b*) $c > t$

(c*) $r > t$

Ginsberg rightly observes that (a) and (b) do not imply (c) by common-sense reasoning. So one would also expect that we do not have transitivity in (a*)—(c*): $r > c \;\&\; c > t \;\not\Rightarrow\; r > t$. In fact, the reason for the failure of transitivity in the example above can be explained by means of frames. Suppose (a*) concerns a frame S_0, for which obviously $P_0 r$ holds. So actually (a*) stands for $r >_0 c$. However, (b*) concerns a frame S_1, for which $P_1 a$, where 'a' stands for "Hoover is an American". It is this interpretation that makes (b*) a reasonable implication. Since we may for simplicity assume that $K(r \to \neg a)$, and thus that there is no state where $r \wedge a$ is true, we have that $S_0 \cap S_1 = \emptyset$. (Note that an attempt to derive that $P_{0,i}a$ for some subframe $S_{0,i}$ of S_0 by an application of $Aa \wedge \neg P_0 \neg a \to P_{0,i}a$ fails due to the fact that $P_0 r$ and thus $P_0 \neg a$ holds, blocking the inference to $P_{0,i}a$.) But under this assumption it is obvious that we do not have transitivity: $r >_0 c \;\&\; c >_1 t \;\not\Rightarrow\; r >_j t$ for some j.

It is nevertheless interesting that in our framework we are able to allow for a restricted form of transitivity by exploiting the fact that we can put a structure on our focuses, and by generalising our notion $\varphi >_{0,i} \psi$ slightly to a notion $\varphi >_{\sigma,\tau} \psi$ denoting $P_\sigma \varphi \vdash P_{\sigma,\tau}\psi$. Suppose that $S_{0,1,2} \subseteq S_{0,1} \subseteq S_0$. Then it holds that $\varphi >_{0,1} \psi \;\&\; \psi >_{<0,1>,2} \chi \;\Rightarrow\; \varphi >_{0,<1,2>} \chi$! (Since in this case $P_0\varphi \vdash P_{0,1}\psi$ and $P_{0,1}\psi \vdash P_{0,1,2}\chi$ imply that $P_0\varphi \vdash P_{0,1,2}\chi$; note that the consistency checks work out right as well!). An example of such a transitive counterfactual is: if John had broken a leg yesterday, he would have stayed at home today, and if he stayed at home today, he would not have been involved in this car accident, indeed imply: if John had broken a leg yesterday, he would not have been involved in this car accident.

In the setting of the logic **ECL** we have shown how to treat counterfactuals by means of defaults. It is interesting to view our result in connection to the recently discovered relation between preference-based semantics of non-monotonic reasoning [Sho87, Sho88] and conditional logic [Del88]. In some sense we have established the relation both in the other direction and on a lower (more concrete) level. We have investigated some properties of our approach compared with Gärdenfors' axioms for conditionals, and discussed the issues of contraposition and transitivity of counterfactual implication. Finally we remark that in [MH91b] we have shown how (a variant of) the logic **ECL** can also be of use in the context of analysing the meaning of linguistic conjunctions that express contrast such as ‘but’.

A APPENDIXES

A1. Konolige's Deduction Model of Belief

In [Kon86] Kurt Konolige gave an alternative approach to knowledge or belief of agents in intelligent systems. As an AI researcher he tried to find a model for the notions of knowledge and belief that would be closer to 'reality' than the modal approach based on Kripke models. Furthermore, like others such as [FHV84, 91] and [Lev84], he was interested in a model able to deal with *imperfect* reasoning.

The resulting model, called the *deduction model*, is a mixture of syntax (in the sense of proof-theoretical notions) and semantics (in the sense of model-theoretical notions), but appeals certainly to the imagination considering e.g. collaborating robots that each have certain beliefs and associated ways to reason with these. Therefore, a short treatment of this model is in order.

Konolige uses a first-order language without function symbols. We shall restrict ourselves again to a propositional fragment. Let $\mathfrak{L}_0$ be the basic language of propositional expressions with the usual semantics. On the basis of $\mathfrak{L}_0$ we can now define two other languages: the so-called 'internal' language $\mathcal{L}_I$ and 'external' language $\mathcal{L}_E$. The internal language is the one that is used by the agents (i.e. robots) themselves; the external language is used by the external observers of the system. In this language the beliefs of the agents should be expressible.

We immediately see that we have an enormous freedom to choose $\mathcal{L}_I$ and $\mathcal{L}_E$, but the most straightforward choices are the following:

1. $\mathcal{L}_I = \mathfrak{L}_0$, and $\mathcal{L}_E = \mathcal{L}_B$, given by the clauses:

    (i) $\mathfrak{L}_0 \subseteq \mathcal{L}_B$;
    (ii) $\varphi, \psi \in \mathcal{L}_B \Rightarrow \neg\varphi, \varphi \wedge \psi \in \mathcal{L}_B$
    (we can use $\varphi \vee \psi$ and $\varphi \rightarrow \psi$ again as the usual abbreviations);
    (iii) $\varphi \in \mathfrak{L}_0 \Rightarrow K_i\varphi \in \mathcal{L}_B$ (all $i \in \mathbf{A}$).

2. $\mathcal{L}_I = \mathcal{L}_E = \mathcal{L}_B$, as defined in 1.

The difference between 1 and 2 is that in case 1 the agents can express themselves only by means of the basic propositional language, and in particular cannot speak *about* their beliefs or the beliefs of other agents. The external observer of the system, on the other hand, *is* able to do this. In case 2 the agents and the external observers have the same expressive abilities: they can both speak about the knowledge (beliefs) of the agents in the system. We shall use the epistemic operator K_i to express the knowledge (or beliefs; this depends on the properties of the K-operators, to be discussed later).

In general an external language $\mathcal{L}_E$ could look like this:

(i) $\mathfrak{L}_0 \subseteq \mathcal{L}_E$ ($\mathcal{L}_E$ should contain at least the basic language),
(ii) $\varphi, \psi, \in \mathcal{L}_E \Rightarrow \neg\varphi, \varphi \wedge \psi \in \mathcal{L}_E$ (and abbreviations $\varphi \vee \psi, \varphi \rightarrow \psi$),
(iii) $\varphi \in \mathcal{L}_I \Rightarrow K_i\varphi \in \mathcal{L}_E$
($\mathcal{L}_E$ contains at least the expressions "agent i believes that φ", where φ is an expression in the internal language of i).

A1.1. REMARK. In these definitions we have assumed that there is one uniform internal language $\mathcal{L}_I$ that is used by *all* agents. In case we consider identical agents (robots) this is a reasonable assumption. In general (when considering human agents, for instance), it is perhaps more appropriate to consider distinct internal languages $\mathcal{L}_I^{(i)}$ per individual agent i. This option is not treated by Konolige, and, for the sake of simplicity, we will not do so either.

We next define a model for the external language $\mathcal{L}_E$, based on the basic propositional language $\mathfrak{L}_0$ and the internal language $\mathcal{L}_I \supseteq \mathfrak{L}_0$.

A1.2. DEFINITION. A *deduction system* d_i is a pair (B_i, ρ_i) with $B_i \subseteq \mathcal{L}_I$ (the so-called 'base set') and ρ_i is a set of inference rules.

A1.3. DEFINITION. Let ρ be a function from **A** to deduction systems. An $(\mathcal{L}_I, \rho)$-*deduction model* for the external language $\mathcal{L}_E$ with basic language $\mathfrak{L}_0$ and internal language $\mathcal{L}_I$ is a pair $M = (\pi, D)$, where π is a truth assignment to the primitive propositions of $\mathfrak{L}_0$ and $D = \{d_0, d_1, ...\}$ is a set of deduction systems, such that $d_i = (B_i, \rho(i))$ for a base set B_i.

A1.4. REMARK. The idea behind a deduction model as defined above is the following: first of all the model determines which primitive propositions of $\mathfrak{L}_0$ are true (in the actual or 'real' world). Furthermore it determines the belief sets of every individual agent (by means of the set of axioms B_i), and what rules of inferences he employs (namely $\rho(i)$). We may picture this as follows:

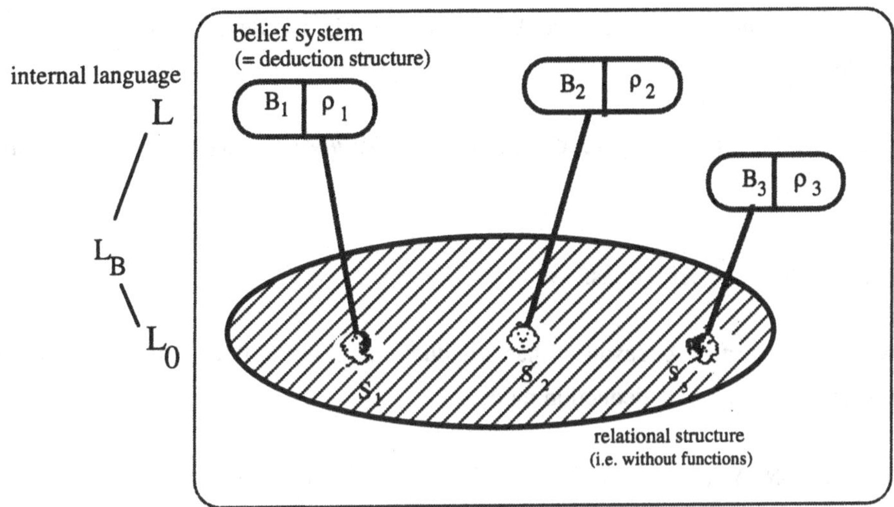

B(L,ρ)-model

Figure A.1

The truth of a formula in an $(\mathcal{L}_1, \rho)$-model is now given by:

A1.5. DEFINITION. $M \vDash \varphi$ where $M = (\pi, D)$ is an $(\mathcal{L}_1, \rho)$-model is defined inductively by:

(1) $M \vDash p \quad \Leftrightarrow \quad \pi \vDash p$ (p primitive proposition)

(2) $M \vDash \varphi \wedge \psi \quad \Leftrightarrow \quad M \vDash \varphi$ and $M \vDash \psi$

(3) $M \vDash \neg\varphi \quad \Leftrightarrow \quad M \nvDash \varphi$

(4) $M \vDash K_i\varphi \quad \Leftrightarrow \quad \varphi \in bel(d_i)$,

where $bel(d_i) = \{\varphi \in \mathcal{L}_1 \mid B_i \vdash_{\rho(i)} \varphi\}$, the *belief set* of agent i.

A1.6. DEFINITION. A formula φ is $(\mathcal{L}_1, \rho)$-valid, denoted $\vDash_\rho \varphi$, if $M \vDash \varphi$ for every model M of the form (π, D) with $D = \{d_1, d_2, ...\}$ and $d_i = (B_i, \rho(i))$. A formula φ is $(\mathcal{L}_1, \rho)$-satisfiable, if there is a model $M = (\pi, D)$ and $D = \{d_1, d_2, ...\}$, $d_i = (B_i, \rho(i))$ such that $M \vDash \varphi$.

A1.7. REMARK. Note that at this moment there is little use in defining validity of φ ($\vDash \varphi$) by: $M \vDash \varphi$ for all deduction models $M = (\pi, D)$, since nothing can be said about the sets D. (These may contain the most weird and 'non-logical' rules of inference!) However, it seems reasonable to consider validity with respect to special classes of deduction models.

Let $\mathbb{B}$ be the class of all deduction models and let $\mathcal{X} \subseteq \mathbb{B}$. We define: $\mathcal{X} \vDash \varphi$ iff $M \vDash \varphi$ for every deduction model $M \in \mathcal{X}$. We now say that agent i is a '*perfect $\mathcal{X}$-reasoner*' if for all $\varphi \in \mathcal{L}_1$ it holds that: $\mathcal{X} \vDash \varphi \Leftrightarrow \varphi \in bel(d_i)$. That is to say, i is a perfect $\mathcal{X}$-reasoner if i is able to deduce all facts true in the models in X by means of his private deduction system d_i, and *nothing more*.

A1.8. PROPOSITION. *For a perfect X-reasoner* i *it holds that:* $X \models \varphi \Leftrightarrow B_i \vdash_{\rho(i)} \varphi$ *for all* $\varphi \in \mathcal{L}_I$.

PROOF. Direct from the definitions. ∎

In other words, a perfect X-reasoner i has a deduction system d_i that is sound and complete with respect to the class of X-deduction models.

A1.9. DEFINITION. An $(\mathcal{L}_I, \rho)$-deduction model $M = (\pi, D)$ is called X-saturated if *every* agent $i \in \mathbf{A}$ is a perfect X-reasoner.

We can now also define a restricted form of validity:

A1.10. DEFINITION. φ is X-valid (denoted $\models_X \varphi$) if $M \models \varphi$ for any X-saturated deduction model M.

Note that we always have the following (PC stands for propositional calculus):

A1.11. LEMMA. *For every $X \subseteq \mathbb{B}$, for all objective φ (i.e. containing no K's!) it holds that:* $\models_X \varphi \Leftrightarrow \vdash_{PC} \varphi$.

PROOF. Let $X \subseteq \mathbb{B}$ and $p \in \mathbf{P}$. Then: $\models_X \varphi \Leftrightarrow M \models \varphi$ for all X-saturated $M = (\pi, D) \Leftrightarrow \pi(\varphi) = t$ for all truth assignments π (with a slight abuse of language) $\Leftrightarrow PC \vdash \varphi$ (by completeness of PC). ∎

A1.12. LEMMA. *For every $X \subseteq \mathbb{B}$ it holds that, for **any** $\varphi \in \mathcal{L}_E$, $\vdash_{PC} \varphi \Rightarrow \models_X \varphi$.*

PROOF. Let $\vdash_{PC} \varphi$. By Lemma A1.11 the assertion holds already for K-free φ. If φ contains K's, we use 'supervaluations' π' such that:

$$\pi'(\varphi) = \begin{cases} \pi(\varphi) & \text{if } \varphi \in \mathbf{P} \\ t & \text{if } \psi \in bel(d_i) \\ f & \text{if } \psi \notin bel(d_i) \end{cases} \quad \left.\begin{matrix} \\ \\ \end{matrix}\right\} \text{if } \varphi = K_i\psi$$

Since the assertion '$\psi \in bel(d_i)$' has classically propositional properties, e.g. $\psi \in bel(d_i)$ or $\psi \notin bel(d_i)$, it now also holds that $\vdash_{\mathcal{X}} \varphi$ for arbitrary $\mathcal{X}$. ■

We now consider a natural subclass $\mathcal{X}_1$, of which deduction models may be saturated:

$$\mathcal{X}_1 = Mod(\mathrm{PC}) = \{M \mid M \models \mathrm{PC}\}.$$

Now it holds for every agent i that

$$\mathrm{B}_i \vdash_{\rho(i)} \varphi \Leftrightarrow \mathcal{X}_1 \models \varphi \Leftrightarrow \mathrm{PC} \vdash \varphi.$$

Thus $d_i = (B_i, \rho(i))$ precisely yields the theorems of PC, i.e. d_i is itself a deductive system for P.C.

Let $\Phi = \{\varphi_1, \varphi_2, \ldots\} \subseteq \mathcal{L}_1$ be a countable set. Then we use notations $K_i\Phi$ for $\{K_i\varphi_1, K_2\varphi_2, \ldots\}$ and $\neg K_i\Phi$ for $\{\neg K_i\varphi_1, \neg K_i\varphi_2, \ldots\}$.

Now the following holds:

A1.13. LEMMA. *Let $\Phi_1, \Phi_2 \subseteq \mathcal{L}_1$. The set $K_i\Phi_1 \cup \neg K_i\Phi_2$ is not $(\mathcal{L}_1, \rho)$-satisfiable $\Leftrightarrow$ there is a $\varphi \in \Phi_2$ such that $\Phi_1 \vdash_{\rho(i)} \varphi$.*

PROOF. ($\Rightarrow$) Suppose that for all $\varphi \in \Phi_2$ it holds that $\Phi_1 \nvdash_{\rho(i)} \varphi$. Then it holds for the deduction system $d_i =_{\text{def}} (\Phi_1, \rho(i))$: $\varphi \notin bel(d_i)$ for all $\varphi \in \Phi_2$. Of course, it does hold that $\varphi_1 \in bel(d_i)$ for all $\varphi_1 \in \Phi_1$. So there is a deduction model $M = (\pi, D)$ with $d_i \in D$, with the property that $M \vdash K_i\varphi_1$ for all $\varphi_1 \in \Phi_1$ and $M \nvDash K_i\varphi$ for all $\varphi \in \Phi_2$, i.e. $M \models \neg K_i\varphi$ for all $\varphi \in \Phi_2$. So the set $K_i\Phi_1 \cup \neg K_i\Phi_2$ is $(\mathcal{L}_1, \rho)$-satisfiable.
($\Leftarrow$) Suppose that $K_i\Phi_1 \cup \neg K_i\Phi_2$ is $(\mathcal{L}_1, \rho)$-satisfiable. Then there is a deduction model $M = (\pi, D)$ with $D = \{d_1, d_2, \ldots\}$ and $d_i = (B_i, \rho(i))$ such that

$M \models K_i\varphi_1$	for all $\varphi_1 \in \Phi_1$ and
$M \nvDash K_i\varphi_2$	for all $\varphi_2 \in \Phi_2$, i.e.
$\varphi_1 \in bel(d_i)$	for all $\varphi_1 \in \Phi_1$ and
$\varphi_2 \notin bel(d_i)$	for all $\varphi_2 \in \Phi_2$, i.e.
$d_i = (B_i, \rho(i))$	such that
$B_i \vdash_{\rho(i)} \varphi_1$	(all $\varphi_1 \in \Phi_1$), so $B_i \vdash_{\rho(i)} \Phi_1$ and
$B_i \nvdash_{\rho(i)} \varphi_2$	(all $\varphi_2 \in \Phi_2$).

It is given that $\Phi_1 \vdash_{\rho(i)} \varphi$ for a $\varphi \in \Phi_2$. But then also $B_i \vdash_{\rho(i)} \varphi \in \Phi_2$. Contradiction. ■

A1.14. THEOREM. *Suppose* $\Phi \vdash_{PC} \varphi$. *Then* $\models_{Mod(PC)} K_i\Phi \rightarrow K_i\varphi$.

PROOF. We have that $\Phi \vdash_{PC} \varphi$. So for a *Mod*(PC)-perfect reasoner i with $d_i = (B, \rho(i))$ it holds that $\Phi \vdash_{\rho(i)} \varphi$ (using the deduction theorem for propositional logic). So by Lemma A1.13 we know that $K_i\Phi \cup \neg K_i\varphi$ is not $(\mathcal{L}_1, \rho)$-satisfiable. That is to say, for all $(\mathcal{L}_1, \rho)$-deduction models $M = (\pi, D)$ with $D = \{d_1, d_2, ...\}$ and $d_i = (B_i, \rho(i))$ (where i is a *Mod*(PC)-perfect reasoner) it holds that:

$$M \models \neg(K_i\Phi \wedge \neg K_i\varphi), \text{ i.e.}$$
$$M \models \neg K_i\Phi \vee K_i\varphi, \text{ i.e.}$$
$$M \models K_i\Phi \rightarrow K_i\varphi.$$

In other words, for all $(\mathcal{L}_1, \rho)$-deduction models $M = (\pi, D)$ with $d_i = (B_i, \rho(i)) \in D$ such that $\forall \varphi\, [PC \vdash \varphi \Leftrightarrow B_i \vdash_{\rho(i)} \varphi]$ it holds that $M \models K_i\,\Phi \rightarrow K_i\varphi$. Hence, $\models_{Mod(PC)} K_i\Phi \rightarrow K_i\varphi$. ■

A1.15. COROLLARY.

(i) *If* $\vdash_{PC} \varphi$ *then* $\models_{Mod(PC)} K_i\varphi$

(ii) $\models_{Mod(PC)} (K_i\varphi \wedge K_i(\varphi \rightarrow \psi)) \rightarrow K_i\psi$.

PROOF. (i) Suppose $\vdash_{PC} \varphi$. Then $\varnothing \vdash_{PC} \varphi$. So, by Theorem A1.14, $\models_{Mod(PC)} K_i\,\varnothing \rightarrow K_i\varphi$, i.e. $\models_{Mod(PC)} K_i\varphi$.

(ii) It holds that $\{\varphi\, ,\, \varphi \rightarrow \psi\} \vdash_{PC} \psi$. So, by Theorem A1.14, $\models_{Mod(PC)} K_i\{\varphi\, ,\, \varphi \rightarrow \psi\} \rightarrow K_i\psi$, i.e. $\models_{Mod(PC)} (K_i\varphi \wedge K_i(\varphi \rightarrow \psi)) \rightarrow K_i\psi$. ■

Thus a *Mod*(PC)-perfect reasoner indeed possesses the expected property that he knows propositional tautologies. Furthermore, his knowledge is closed under propositional consequence. We recognise, of course, the latter property as axiom (A2) of system K from Chapter 1. This suggests a relation between *Mod*(PC)-perfect reasoners in the deduction model and system K, and it can indeed be shown (cf. [Kon86]), that the *Mod*(PC)-saturated deduction models constitute an alternative for Kripke models: they also exactly characterise the system K:

A1.16. THEOREM. *For all* $\varphi \in \mathcal{L}_E$: $\models_{Mod(PC)} \varphi \Leftrightarrow \vdash_K \varphi$.

PROOF. See [Kon86]. ■

A further natural subclass of models is:

$$\mathcal{X}_2 = \{M \in \mathcal{X}_1 \mid M = (\pi, D) \text{ with } \forall i\, [\varphi \in bel(d_i) \Rightarrow M \models \varphi]\}.$$

A1.17. PROPOSITION. $\models_{\mathcal{X}_2} K_i\varphi \to \varphi$.

PROOF. Let $M \in \mathcal{X}_2$. Then: $\varphi \in bel(d_i) \Rightarrow M \models \varphi$, i.e. $M \models K_i\varphi \Rightarrow M \models \varphi$, i.e. $M \models K_i\varphi \to \varphi$. ■

A1.18. COROLLARY. $\vdash_T \varphi \;\Rightarrow\; \models_{\mathcal{X}_2} \varphi$.

In fact we have again:

A1.19. THEOREM. $\models_{\mathcal{X}_2} \varphi \;\Rightarrow\; \vdash_T \varphi$.

PROOF. See [Kon86]. ■

Further interesting subclasses are:

$$\mathcal{X}_3 = \{M \in \mathcal{X}_2 \mid M = (\pi, D) \text{ with } \forall i \in D\, [\varphi \in bel(d_i) \Rightarrow K_i\varphi \in bel(d_i)]\},$$
$$\mathcal{X}_4 = \{M \in \mathcal{X}_2 \mid M = (\pi, D) \text{ with } \forall i \in D\, [\varphi \notin bel(d_i) \Rightarrow \neg K_i\varphi \in bel(d_i)]\}.$$

It can be shown that:

A1.20. THEOREM.

(i) $\models_{\mathcal{X}_3} \varphi \;\Leftrightarrow\; \vdash_{S4} \varphi$

(ii) $\models_{\mathcal{X}_4} \varphi \;\Leftrightarrow\; \vdash_{S5} \varphi$

Thus Konolige's deduction model approach can be viewed as a generalisation of the standard one on the basis of Kripke models. Of course, this is not really surprising seen in the light of the theory of Chapter 3. The 'belief sets' $bel(d_i)$ of an $\mathcal{X}_4$-perfect reasoner are stable sets: they are propositionally closed, (propositionally) consistent and closed under positive and negative introspection. And thus they may be considered as theories of S5-Kripke models. However, Konolige's approach goes beyond the standard modal approach, since in deduction models also 'imperfect' reasoners may be treated by varying ρ (see [Kon86]).

A2. Knowledge Structures (Fagin, Halpern & Vardi)

In this section of the appendix we shall treat an alternative approach to knowledge, as proposed in [FHV84, 91]. This approach is not based on the rather 'Platonic' Kripke structures, but instead on the somewhat more computational looking *knowledge structures*. The knowledge structures model will turn out to be more 'constructive' than the modal one, but a price must be paid for this with respect to mathematical clarity and elegance. The theory of knowledge structures is somewhat troublesome and demands the utmost concentration on the part of the reader. Of course, seen in the context of computer science the more constructive nature of the theory must be considered an advantage. We shall discuss a part of the theory.

We again start from our familiar language $\mathcal{L}^m_{\mathbf{K}}(\mathbf{P})$ of epistemic expressions. $\mathcal{L}^m_{\mathbf{K}}(\mathbf{P})$ contains primitive propositions in $\mathbf{P}$, $\mathcal{L}^m_{\mathbf{K}}(\mathbf{P})$ is closed under $\wedge$ and $\neg$, and contains expressions $K_i\varphi$ ($i \in \mathbf{A} = \{1, ..., m\}$, the set of agents). For the semantics of the language $\mathcal{L}^m_{\mathbf{K}}(\mathbf{P})$ we now consider models based on *knowledge structures*.

A2.1. DEFINITION. Knowledge structures are defined inductively as follows:

(0) An *0-order knowledge assignment*, f_0, is a function $\mathbf{P} \to \{t, f\}$, also denoted as the set in $\mathcal{P}(\mathbf{P} \cup \neg \mathbf{P})$ that consists of true propositions; the structure $\langle f_0 \rangle$ is called an *1-ary world.*

(k) Suppose that k-ary worlds $\langle f_0, ..., f_{k-1} \rangle$ are defined already. Let W_k be the set of all k-ary worlds. A *k-order knowledge assignment* is a function f_k: $\mathbf{A} \to \mathcal{P}(W_k)$. $\langle f_0, ..., f_k \rangle$ is called a *k+1-ary world.*

(∞) An infinite sequence $\langle f_0, f_1, f_2, ... \rangle$ is called a *knowledge structure*, if every prefix $\langle f_0, ..., f_{k-1} \rangle$ is a k-ary world. The intention of these concepts is that an agent i considers sets $f_k(i)$ of k-ary worlds as possible. These worlds must satisfy certain restrictions:

A2.2. RESTRICTIONS. For every $i \in \mathbf{A}$ and every k, the set $f_k(i)$ of k-ary worlds satisfies the following restrictions: Given a k+1-ary world $\langle f_0, ..., f_k \rangle$,

(K1) If $k > 1$ then $\langle f_0, ..., f_{k-1} \rangle \in f_k(i)$ (i.e. for any agent i the 'real' k-ary world is one of the possibilities).

(K2) If $k > 1$ and $\langle g_0, ..., g_{k-1} \rangle \in f_k(i)$, then $g_{k-1}(i) = f_{k-1}(i)$ (i.e. agent i knows exactly what he knows).

(K3) If $k > 1$ then: $\langle g_0, ..., g_{k-2} \rangle \in f_{k-1}(i) \Leftrightarrow$ there is a (k−1)-order knowledge structure g_{k-1}, such that $\langle g_0, ..., g_{k-2}, g_{k-1} \rangle \in f_k(i)$ (i.e. agent i's higher-order knowledge is an extension of his/her lower-order knowledge).

A2.3. COROLLARY. *From* (K2) *and* (K3) *it follows that if* $k > 1$ *and* $\langle g_0, ..., g_{k-1} \rangle \in f_k(i)$ *then* $g_j(i) = f_j(i)$ *for* $0 < j < k$. *[NB **not** j = 0].*

PROOF. By (K2), $g_{k-1}(i) = f_{k-1}(i)$. So $<g_0, ..., g_{k-2}, f_{k-1}(i)> \in f_k(i)$. By (K3), $<g_0, ..., g_{k-2}> \in f_{k-1}(i)$. So again by (K2), $g_{k-2}(i) = f_{k-2}(i)$. By (K3) again, $<g_0, ..., g_{k-3}> \in f_{k-2}(i)$, etc. ■

A2.4. COROLLARY. Let $0 < j < k$. *Then:* $<g_0, ... , g_{j-1}> \in f_j(i) \Leftrightarrow \exists\, g_j, ..., g_{k-1}: <g_0, ..., g_{j-1}, g_j, ... , g_{k-1}> \in f_k(i)$.

PROOF. Immediate by induction. ■

Corollaries A1.3 and A1.4 imply that agent i's lower-order knowledge is determined by door his/her higher-order knowledge.

A2.5. EXAMPLE. Let $\mathbf{P} = \{p\}$ and $\mathbf{A} = \{\text{Alice, Bob}\}$. Let the 2-ary world $w_1 = <f_0, f_1>$ be given by:

(i) $f_0(p) = t$ ("p is true"; also denoted by $f_0 = \{p\}$.)

(ii) $f_1(\text{Alice}) = \{\{p\},\{\neg p\}\}$ ("Alice considers both p and ¬p as possible", i.e., "Alice does not know whether p".)

(iii) $f_1(\text{Bob}) = \{\{p\}\}$ ("Bob only considers p as possible", i.e., "Bob knows p".)

We may denote w_1 as:

$$w_1 = <\{p\}, (\text{Alice} \rightarrow \{\{p\},\{\neg p\}\}, \text{Bob} \rightarrow \{\{p\}\}) >.$$

Let w_2 and w_3 be two other 2-ary worlds:

$$w_2 = <\{\neg p\}, (\text{Alice} \rightarrow \{\{p\}, \{\neg p\}\}, \text{Bob} \rightarrow \{\{\neg p\}\}) >,$$
$$w_3 = <\{p\}, (\text{Alice} \rightarrow \{\{p\}\}, \text{Bob} \rightarrow \{\{p\}\}) >.$$

If Alice knows that Bob knows whether p is true, and Bob does not know whether Alice knows p, then this is modelled by the 2nd-order knowledge assignment f_2 with $f_2(\text{Alice}) = \{w_1, w_2\}$ and $f_2(\text{Bob}) = \{w_1, w_3\}$.

We check whether the restrictions hold:

(K1) Indeed it holds that $p \in f_1(\text{Alice})$ and $p \in f_1(\text{Bob})$. Furthermore it holds that $<f_0, f_1> = w_1 \in f_2(\text{Alice})$ and $<f_0, f_1> = w_1 \in f_2(\text{Bob})$. So Alice and Bob consider the 'real' world w_1 as possible.

(K2) For instance, $w_2 = \langle g_0, g_1\rangle = \langle\{\neg p\}, (\text{Alice} \to \{\{p\}, \{\neg p\}\}, \text{Bob} \to \{\{\neg p\}\})\rangle \in f_2(\text{Alice})$ and also $g_1(\text{Alice}) = \{\{p\}, \{\neg p\}\} = f_1(\text{Alice})$: this is all right.
Also, e.g. $w_3 = \langle g'_0, g'_1\rangle = \langle \{p\}, (\text{Alice} \to \{\{p\}\}, \text{Bob} \to \{\{p\}\})\rangle \in f_2(\text{Bob})$ and $g'_1(\text{Bob}) = \{\{p\}\} = f_1(\text{Bob})$: all right.

Note that the restriction (K2) only concerns $k \geq 1$; for $k = 1$ the requirement does not hold in the example.

A2.5.1. EXERCISE. Show that for k=1 the requirement mentioned in (K2) does not hold in Example A2.5.

(K3) For example, $f_1(\text{Alice}) = \{\{p\}, \{\neg p\}\}$: Alice considers both p and $\neg p$ as possible. So $g_0 =_{def} \{p\} \in f_1(\text{Alice})$. Indeed there is a g_1 such that $\langle g_0, g_1\rangle \in f_2(\text{Alice})$: namely $\langle g_0, g_1\rangle = w_1$. On the other hand, also $g'_0 =_{def} \{\{\neg p\}\} \in f_1(\text{Alice})$, and there is also a g'_1 such that $\langle g'_0, g'_1\rangle \in f_2(\text{Alice})$, namely $w_2 \in f_2(\text{Alice})$. Conversely, both $\langle g_0, g_1\rangle =_{def} w_1$ and $\langle g'_0, g'_1\rangle =_{def} w_2$ are elements of $f_2(\text{Alice})$. And for both $g_0 = \{p\}$ and $g'_0 = \{\neg p\}$ it holds that $g_0, g'_0 \in \{\{p\}, \{\neg p\}\} = f_1(\text{Alice})$.

A2.6. POSSIBLE WORLDS. Let **f** be the knowledge structure $\langle f_0, f_1, \ldots\rangle$. Define i's *view* on *f*, denoted $\pi_i(\mathbf{f})$, as the sequence $\langle f_1(i), f_2(i), \ldots\rangle$. Knowledge structures **f** and **f'** are called *i-equivalent*, denoted $\mathbf{f} \sim_i \mathbf{f'}$, if $\pi_i(\mathbf{f}) = \pi_i(\mathbf{f'})$. We are now able to define the notion of *possible world* in two ways.

1. Agent i considers k-ary world w as *possible*$_1$ in knowledge structure $\mathbf{f} = \langle f_0, f_1, \ldots\rangle$, if $w \in f_k(i)$.
2. Agent i considers world w as *possible*$_2$ in knowledge structure **f**, if w is a prefix of a knowledge structure **f'** with $\mathbf{f} \sim_i \mathbf{f'}$.

A2.7. THEOREM. *w is possible*$_1$ *in* **f** $\Leftrightarrow$ *w is possible*$_2$ in **f**.

PROOF. ($\Leftarrow$) Suppose w is *possible*$_2$ in **f**. Then $w = \langle f'_0, \ldots, f'_{k-1}\rangle$ is a prefix of a knowledge structure $\mathbf{f'} = \langle f'_0, \ldots, f'_{k-1}, \ldots\rangle$ with $\mathbf{f} \sim_i \mathbf{f'}$, i.e. $f_k(i) = f'_k(i)$ for all $k \geq 1$. Thus, by (K1), $w = \langle f'_0, \ldots, f'_{k-1}\rangle \in f'_k(i) = f_k(i)$. Hence w is *possible*$_1$ in **f**.
($\Rightarrow$) Suppose w is *possible*$_1$ in $\mathbf{f} = \langle f_0, f_1, \ldots\rangle$. So $w \in f_k(i)$ for some k. Consequently, $w = \langle f'_0, \ldots, f'_{k-1}\rangle \in f_k(i)$ for some $f'_0, \ldots, f'_{k-1}$. So now, by Corollary A2.3, $f'_j(i) = f_j(i)$ for all $0 < j < k$. Thus $w = \langle f'_0, \ldots, f'_{k-1}\rangle$ is a prefix of a structure $\mathbf{f'} = \langle f'_0, \ldots, f'_{k-1}, f'_k, \ldots\rangle$ such that $f_j(i) = f'_j(i)$ for all $j \geq 1$. (Take $f'_j(i) = f_j(i)$ for $j \geq k$). Thus $\mathbf{f} \sim_i \mathbf{f'}$. Hence w is *possible*$_2$ in **f**.

We define the depth of a formula φ, *depth*(φ), inductively by:

(i) $depth(p) = 0$, $p \in \mathbf{P}$

(ii) $depth(\neg\varphi) = depth(\varphi)$

(iii) $depth(\varphi_1 \wedge \varphi_2) \max \{depth(\varphi_1), depth(\varphi_2)\}$

(iv) $depth(K_i\varphi) = 1 + depth(\varphi)$

Thus $depth(\varphi)$ yields the number of nestings of K_i-operators in the epistemic formula φ.

A2.9. SEMANTICS. A formula φ is satisfiable in an $(r + 1)$-ary world $<f_0, ..., f_r>$, denoted $<f_0, ..., f_r> \models \varphi$, if $depth(\varphi) \leq r$ and the following holds:

(i) $f_0(p) = t$, if $\varphi = p \in \mathbf{P}$

(ii) $<f_0, ..., f_r> \not\models \psi$, if $\varphi = \neg\psi$

(iii) $<f_0, ..., f_r> \models \varphi_1$ and $<f_0, ..., f_r> \models \varphi_2$, if $\varphi = \varphi_1 \wedge \varphi_2$

(iv) $<g_0, ..., g_{r-1}> \models \psi$ for all $<g_0, ..., g_{r-1}> \in f_r(i)$, if $\varphi = K_i\psi$.

A2.10. EXAMPLE. In Example A2.5 we have that

(i) $w_1 = <f_0, f_1> \models K_{Bob}p$, since $g_0 \in f_1(Bob) = \{\{p\}\}$ implies $g_0 = \{p\}$ and for this it holds $<g_0> = <\{p\}> \models p$.

(ii) $w_2 = <f'_0, f'_1> \models K_{Bob}\neg p$, since $g'_0 \in f'_1(Bob) = \{\{\neg p\}\}$, and for this we have $<g'_0> = <\{\neg p\}> \models \neg p$.

(iii) $w_1 = <f_0, f_1> \models K_{Bob}p \vee K_{Bob}\neg p$, since $w_1 \models K_{Bob}\, p$.

(iv) $w_2 = <f'_0, f'_1> \models K_{Bob}p \vee K_{Bob}\neg p$, since $w_2 \models K_{Bob}\neg p$.

(v) $<f_0, f_1, f_2> \models K_{Alice}(K_{Bob}p \vee K_{Bob}\neg p)$, since $g_1 \in f_2(Alice) = \{w_1, w_2\}$ implies $g_1 = w_1$ or $g_1 = w_2$, and for $i = 1, 2$, $w_i \models K_{Bob}p \vee K_{Bob}\neg p$. Thus $<f_0, f_1, f_2> \models K_{Alice}(K_{Bob}p \vee K_{Bob}\neg p)$.

A2.11. LEMMA. *Suppose* $depth(\varphi) = k$ *and* $r \geq k$. *Then:* $<f_0, ..., f_r> \models \varphi \Leftrightarrow <f_0, ..., f_k> \models \varphi$.

PROOF. (by induction on the complexity of φ, using 'induction loading': proving the assertion for general $<g_0, ..., g_r>$ and $<g_0, ..., g_k>$, respectively, and all $r \geq k$). Consider the case $\varphi = K_i\psi$. Then: $<f_0, ..., f_r> \models K_i\psi \Leftrightarrow <g_0, ..., g_{r-1}> \models \psi$ for all $<g_0, ..., g_{r-1}> \in f_r(i) \overset{(*)}{\Leftrightarrow} <g_0, ..., g_{k-1}> \models \psi$ for all $<g_0, ..., g_{k-1}> \in f_k(i) \Leftrightarrow <f_0, ..., f_k> \models K_i\psi$.

We still owe the proof of (*): ($\Rightarrow$) Suppose $<g_0, ..., g_{k-1}> \in f_k(i)$. We have to show that $<g_0, ..., g_{k-1}> \models \psi$. We know that $<g_0, ..., g_{r-1}> \models \psi$ for all $<g_0, ..., g_{r-1}> \in f_r(i)$. From

$<g_0, ..., g_{k-1}> \in f_k(i)$ it follows that $<g_0, ..., g_{r-1}> \in f_r(i)$, and so $<g_0, ..., g_{r-1}> \vDash \psi$. So now (by the induction hypothesis for ψ) also $<g_0, ..., g_{k-1}> \vDash \psi$ (since $k - 1 \geq r - 1$).
($\Leftarrow$) Supposing $<g_0, ..., g_{r-1}> \in f_r(i)$, we now have to show: $<g_0, ..., g_{r-1}> \vDash \psi$. We have that $<g_0, ..., g_{k-1}> \vDash \psi$ for all $<g_0, ..., g_{k-1}> \in f_k(i)$. From $< g_0, ..., g_{r-1} > \in f_r(i)$ it follows that there exists an extended sequence $<g_0, ..., g_{r-1}, ..., g_{k-1}> \in f_k(i)$. For $<g_0, ..., g_{k-1}> \in f_k(i)$ it thus holds that $<g_0, ..., g_{k-1}> \vDash \psi$. And hence (by the induction hypothesis for ψ) $<g_0, ..., g_{r-1}> \vDash \psi$. ∎

A formula φ is *satisfiable* in a knowledge structure $\mathbf{f} = < f_0, f_1, ... >$, denoted $\mathbf{f} \vDash \varphi$, if $< f_0, ... ,f_k > \vDash \varphi$ for $k = depth(\varphi)$. A formula φ is *satisfiable* if there is a knowledge structure $\mathbf{f}$ with $\mathbf{f} \vDash \varphi$. A formula φ is *valid*, denoted $\vDash \varphi$, if for every knowledge structure $\mathbf{f}$ it holds that $\mathbf{f} \vDash \varphi$.

A2.12. THEOREM. The following properties hold:
(i) *If φ is a propositional tautology, then $\vDash \varphi$.*
(ii) $\vDash K_i(\varphi_1 \rightarrow \varphi_2) \rightarrow (K_i\varphi_1 \rightarrow K_i\varphi_2)$
(iii) $\vDash K_i\varphi \rightarrow \varphi$
(iv) $\vDash K_i\varphi \rightarrow K_iK_i\varphi$
(v) $\vDash \neg K_i\varphi \rightarrow K_i\neg K_i\varphi$
(vi) *If $\vDash \varphi_1$ and $\vDash \varphi_1 \rightarrow \varphi_2$, then $\vDash \varphi_2$.*
(vii) *If $\vDash \varphi$, then $\vDash K_i\varphi$.*

PROOF. (ii) Suppose $depth(\varphi_1) = k_1$ and $depth(\varphi_2) = k_2$, and so $depth(K_i(\varphi_1 \rightarrow \varphi_2)) = 1 + depth(\neg(\varphi_1 \wedge \neg\varphi_2)) = 1 + depth(\varphi_1 \wedge \neg\varphi_2) = 1 + \max\{depth(\varphi_1), depth(\neg\varphi_2)\} = 1 + \max\{k_1, k_2\}$. Let $\mathbf{f} = < f_0, f_1, ... >$ be a knowledge structure, such that $\mathbf{f} \vDash K_i(\varphi_1 \rightarrow \varphi_2) \wedge K_i(\varphi_1)$. We have to show that $\mathbf{f} \vDash K_i(\varphi_2)$, i.e. for all $<g_0, ..., g_{k_2}> \in f_{k_2+1}(i)$ it holds that $<g_0, ..., g_{k_2}> \vDash \varphi_2$. Take $<g_0, ..., g_{k_2}> \in f_{k_2+1}(i)$. We know that $\mathbf{f} \vDash K_i(\varphi_1 \rightarrow \varphi_2)$, so $<g'_0, ..., g'_{\ell-1}> \vDash (\varphi_1 \rightarrow \varphi_2)$ for all $<g'_0, ..., g'_{\ell-1}> \in f_\ell(i)$, where $\ell = depth(K_i(\varphi_1 \rightarrow \varphi_2))$. We furthermore have that $\mathbf{f} \vDash K_i(\varphi_1)$, so $<g''_0, ..., g''_{k_1}> \vDash \varphi_1$ for all $< g''_0, ..., g''_{k_1} > \in f_{k_1+1}(i)$. By (K3) there is an extension $<g_0, ..., g_{k_2}, g_{k_2+1}, ..., g_{\ell-1}> \in f_\ell(i)$, for which holds that $<g_0, ..., g_{k_2}, ..., g_{\ell-1}> \vDash (\varphi_1 \rightarrow \varphi_2)$. Since $< g_0, ..., g_{k_1} > \in f_{k_1+1}(i)$ ((K3) again; $k_1 + 1 \leq \ell$), we have $<g_0, ..., g_{k_1}> \vDash \varphi_1$ and hence (previous lemma; $k_1+1 \leq \ell$) also $<g_0, ..., g_{\ell-1}> \vDash \varphi_1$. So now *both* $<g_0, ..., g_{\ell-1}> \vDash \varphi_1$ *and:* $<g_0, ..., g_{\ell-1}> \vDash (\varphi_1 \rightarrow \varphi_2)$, i.e., $<g_0, ..., g_{\ell-1}> \vDash (\neg\varphi_1 \vee \varphi_2)$, i.e., $<g_0, ..., g_{\ell-1}> \vDash \neg\varphi_1$ or $<g_0, ..., g_{\ell-1}> \vDash \varphi_2$, i.e., $<g_0, ..., g_{\ell-1}> \nvDash \varphi_1$ or $<g_0, ..., g_{\ell-1}> \vDash \varphi_2$. Since $depth(\varphi_2) = k_2$, also (previous lemma) $<g_0, ..., g_{k_2}> \vDash \varphi_2$.

(iii) Suppose $depth(K_i\varphi) = k$. Let $\mathbf{f} = \langle f_0, f_1, \dots \rangle$ be knowledge structure such that $\mathbf{f} \models K_i\varphi$. Then, for all $\langle g_0, \dots, g_{k-1}\rangle \in f_k(i)$, $\langle g_0, \dots, g_{k-1}\rangle \models \varphi$. By (K1) it holds that $\langle f_0, \dots, f_{k-1}\rangle \in f_k(i)$, so $\langle f_0, \dots, f_{k-1}\rangle \models \varphi$, and $\mathbf{f} \models \varphi$ (since $depth(\varphi) = k - 1$).

(iv) Suppose $depth(K_i\varphi) = k$. Let $\mathbf{f} = \langle f_0, f_1, \dots\rangle$ such that $\mathbf{f} \models K_i\, \varphi$, i.e. for all $\langle g_0, \dots, g_{k-1}\rangle \in f_k(i)$ we have $\langle g_0, \dots, g_{k-1}\rangle \models \varphi$. To prove that $\mathbf{f} \models K_iK_i\varphi$, i.e. for all $\langle g'_0, \dots, g'_k\rangle \in f_{k+1}(i)$ it holds that $\langle g'_0, \dots, g'_k\rangle \models K_i\, \varphi$, i.e. for all $\langle g''_0, \dots, g''_{k-1}\rangle \in g'_k(i)$ we have $\langle g''_0, \dots, g''_{k-1}\rangle \models \varphi$. Suppose $\langle g'_0, \dots, g'_k\rangle \in f_{k+1}(i)$. By (K2), $g'_k(i) = f_k(i)$. So now it is immediate that for all $\langle g''_0, \dots, g''_{k-1}\rangle \in g'_k(i)$ $(= f_k(i))$ it holds that $\langle g''_0, \dots, g''_{k-1}\rangle \models \varphi$.

(v) Suppose $depth(K_i\varphi) = k$ and $\mathbf{f} = \langle f_0, f_1, \dots \rangle$ such that $\mathbf{f} \models \neg K_i\varphi$, i.e. there is some $\langle g_0, \dots, g_{k-1}\rangle \in f_k(i)$ with $\langle g_0, \dots, g_{k-1}\rangle \models \neg\varphi$. To show that $\mathbf{f} \models K_i\neg K_i\varphi$, i.e. for all $\langle g'_0, \dots, g'_k\rangle \in f_{k+1}(i)$ it holds that $\langle g'_0, \dots, g'_k\rangle \models \neg K_i\varphi$, i.e., there is some $\langle g''_0, \dots, g''_{k-1}\rangle \in g'_k(i)$ with $\langle g''_0, \dots, g''_{k-1}\rangle \models \neg\varphi$. Suppose $\langle g'_0, \dots, g'_k\rangle \in f_{k+1}(i)$. By (K2), $g'_k(i) = f_k(i)$. Thus there is a $\langle g_0, \dots, g_{k-1}\rangle \in f_k(i) = g'_k(i)$ with $\langle g_0, \dots, g_{k-1}\rangle \models \neg\varphi$.

(vi) It is given that, for every $\mathbf{f} = \langle f_0, f_1, \dots \rangle$, $\mathbf{f} \models \varphi_1$ and $\mathbf{f} \models \varphi_1 \to \varphi_2$. That is to say, for $k_1 = depth(\varphi_1)$ and $k = depth(\varphi_1 \to \varphi_2) \geq k_1$, $\langle f_0, \dots, f_{k_1}\rangle \models \varphi_1$ and $\langle f_0, \dots, f_k\rangle \models \varphi_1 \to \varphi_2$. So also (previous lemma; $k \geq k_1$) $\langle f_0, \dots, f_k\rangle \models \varphi_1$ and $\langle f_0, \dots, f_k\rangle \models \varphi_1 \to \varphi_2$, so $\langle f_0, \dots, f_k\rangle \models \varphi_1$ and $[\langle f_0, \dots, f_k\rangle \not\models \varphi_1$ or $\langle f_0, \dots, f_k\rangle \models \varphi_2]$. Hence, $\langle f_0, \dots, f_k\rangle \models \varphi_2$. And for $k_2 = depth(\varphi_2) \leq k$, $\langle f_0, \dots, f_{k_2}\rangle \models \varphi_2$, i.e. $\mathbf{f} \models \varphi_2$.

(vii) It is given that $\models \varphi$, i.e. $\mathbf{f} \models \varphi$ for every $\mathbf{f} = \langle f_1, f_2, \dots \rangle$. We have to show that $\models K_i\varphi$, i.e. $\mathbf{f} \models K_i\varphi$ for every $\mathbf{f}$, i.e. $\langle g_0, \dots, g_{r-1}\rangle \models \varphi$ for every $\langle g_0, \dots, g_{r-1}\rangle \in f_r(i)$, where $r = depth(K_i\, \varphi) = 1 + depth(\varphi)$. Since $depth(\varphi) = r - 1$, and $\mathbf{f} \models \varphi$, we have that $\langle f_1, \dots, f_{r-1}\rangle \models \varphi$ for *any* $\langle f_1, \dots, f_{r-1}\rangle$. Consequently, for every $\langle g_0, \dots, g_{r-1}\rangle \in f_r(i)$ it holds that $\langle g_0, \dots, g_{r-1}\rangle \models \varphi$.

(i) The proof of this is somewhat different from the proof of the other clauses. A proof by induction on the complexity of φ does not work, since parts of a tautology are generally no tautologies themselves. So this is done as follows (sketch). It is easy to check that the axioms of (PC) are valid (i.e. true in every knowledge structure). Moreover, (MP) is valid by (g). So every propositional tautology is valid. ■

A2.13. THEOREM. $\mathbf{f} \models K_i\varphi \;\Leftrightarrow\; \forall \mathbf{f}' (\mathbf{f} \sim_i \mathbf{f}' \;\Rightarrow\; \mathbf{f}' \models \varphi)$.

PROOF. Suppose $depth(K_i\varphi) = k$. Let $\mathbf{f} = \langle f_0, f_1, \dots \rangle$.

($\Rightarrow$) Let w be the k-ary world that is a prefix of $\mathbf{f}'$. So $w \in f_k(i)$, since $\mathbf{f} \sim_i \mathbf{f}'$. Since $\mathbf{f} \models K_i\varphi$, we now have $w \models \varphi$ and thus $\mathbf{f}' \models \varphi$.

($\Leftarrow$) We have to prove that $w \models \varphi$ for all $w \in f_k(i)$. So take $w \in f_k(i)$. So w is a prefix of some $\mathbf{f}'$ with $\mathbf{f} \sim_i \mathbf{f}'$. By the assumption we obtain $\mathbf{f} \models \varphi$ and so $w \models \varphi$. ■

In fact Theorem A2.13 says that an agent knows φ if and only if φ is true in every knowledge structure that s/he considers possible. This is reminiscent of the modal approach in which an agent exactly knows φ if φ is true in every (Kripke) world that s/he considers possible! In fact we can establish a close relation between knowledge structures and Kripke structures, as we see next. We show the following theorem:

A2.14. THEOREM. *To every Kripke world* $(\mathbb{M}, s)$ *there corresponds a knowledge structure* $\mathbf{f}_{\mathbb{M},s}$ *such that* $(\mathbb{M}, s) \models \varphi \Leftrightarrow \mathbf{f}_{\mathbb{M},s} \models \varphi$, *for any formula* φ. *Conversely, there is a Kripke structure* $\mathbb{M}_{knowstr} = (S_{knowstr}, \pi, R_1, ..., R_m)$ *such that for any knowledge structure* $\mathbf{f}$ *there is a state* $s_{\mathbf{f}} \in S_{knowstr}$ *such that* $\mathbf{f} \models \varphi \Leftrightarrow (\mathbb{M}_{kenstr}, s_{\mathbf{f}}) \models \varphi$, *for any formula* φ.

PROOF. Suppose $\mathbb{M} = \langle S, \pi, R_1, ..., R_m\rangle$ is a Kripke structure and $s_0 \in S$. We construct for *every* $s \in S$, $\mathbf{f}_{\mathbb{M},s} = \langle f_0^{(s)}, f_1^{(s)}, \ldots \rangle$ inductively, as follows:
$f_0^{(s)} = \pi(s)$; suppose $\langle f_0^{(s)}, f_1^{(s)}, \ldots, f_k^{(s)} \rangle$ have been constructed for *every* $s \in S$. Then we define $f_{k+1}^{(s)}(i) = \{\langle f_0^{(t)}, \ldots, f_k^{(t)} \rangle \mid (s, t) \in R_i\}$. Now it is simple to prove by induction on the complexity of φ that (for *all* s): $(\mathbb{M}, s) \models \varphi \Leftrightarrow \mathbf{f}_{\mathbb{M},s} \models \varphi$. We only consider the case $\varphi = K_i\psi$. Now $(\mathbb{M}, s) \models K_i\psi \Leftrightarrow (\mathbb{M}, t) \models \psi$ for all t such that $(s, t) \in R_i \Leftrightarrow$ (induction hypothesis) $\mathbf{f}_{\mathbb{M},t} \models \psi$ for all t with $(s, t) \in R_i \Leftrightarrow$ (suppose *depth*(t) = r) $\langle \mathbf{f}_0^{(t)}, \ldots, \mathbf{f}_r^{(t)} \rangle \models \psi$ for all t with $(s, t) \in R_i \Leftrightarrow \langle f_0^{(t)}, \ldots, f_r^{(t)} \rangle \models \psi$ for all $\langle f_0^{(t)}, \ldots, f_r^{(t)} \rangle$ with $(s, t) \in R_i \Leftrightarrow \langle g_0, ..., g_r \rangle \models \psi$ for all $\langle g_0, ..., g_r \rangle \in f_{r+1}^{(s)}(i) \Leftrightarrow \mathbf{f}_{\mathbb{M},s} \models K_i\psi$.

Conversely, define $\mathbb{M}_{knowstr} = (S_{knowstr}, \pi, R_1, ..., R_m)$ where $S_{knowstr}$ is the set of *all* knowledge structures, $\pi(\mathbf{f}) = f_0$, and $R_i = \{(\mathbf{f}, \mathbf{g}) \mid \mathbf{f} \sim_i \mathbf{g}\}$. Now it holds that $(\mathbb{M}_{kenstr}, \mathbf{f}) \models \varphi \Leftrightarrow \mathbf{f} \models \varphi$. We again only consider the case $\varphi = K_i\psi$. Then: $(\mathbb{M}_{knowstr}, \mathbf{f}) \models K_i\psi \Leftrightarrow (\mathbb{M}_{knowstr}, \mathbf{g}) \models \psi$ for all $\mathbf{g}$ with $R_i(\mathbf{f}, \mathbf{g}) \Leftrightarrow (\mathbb{M}_{knowstr}, \mathbf{g}) \models \psi$ for all $\mathbf{g}$ with $f \sim_i g \Leftrightarrow$ (induction hypothesis) $g \models \psi$ for all $\mathbf{g}$ with $f \sim_i g \Leftrightarrow$ (Theorem A2.13) $\mathbf{f} \models K_i\psi$. ∎

A2.15. COROLLARY. *Knowledge based on knowledge structures is axiomatized completely by the system* $\mathbf{S5}_{(\mathbf{m})}$.

The reader who has persevered up to now is rewarded at last for his effort. The direct relation with Kripke models certainly illuminates the theory of knowledge structures. Apparently, knowledge structures correspond to states in a 'universal' Kripke structure, where for agent i states are reachable from each other if they represent knowledge structures for which the knowledge of i (i.e. the π_i-projections) is the same.

Fagin, Halpern & Vardi have elaborated aspects of the theory of knowledge structures further [FHV84, 91]. However, it is significant that these authors mostly use Kripke models in more recent papers. Perhaps this theory will not survive in the long run; it contained sufficiently many interesting ingredients, however, to be discussed here. As the authors themselves say: "*Although [knowledge structures] do not replace the widely-used Kripke structures, they do complement them: There are times when we can gain more insight by modeling knowledge structures rather than with Kripke structures.*"

A3. First-Order Epistemic Logic

In this appendix we shall give a concise treatment of first-order epistemic logic, and say some words about the problems encountered when considering the first-order case.

A3.1. The Language: First-Order Epistemic Formulas

Let **P** and **F** be countable sets of predicate constants and function constants, respectively; with each $P \in \mathbf{P}$ and $f \in \mathbf{F}$ a unique non-negative integer is associated, the *arity* of P and f, denoted *ar*(P) and *ar*(f), respectively. 0-ary predicate constant are called propositional constants; 0-ary function constants are called individual or object constants. We denote the set of predicate and function constants of arity n by $\mathbf{P}_n$ and $\mathbf{F}_n$, respectively. Furthermore, let **V** be a denumerable set of individual variables: $\mathbf{V} = \{x_1, x_2, ...\}$. **A** be a set of m 'agents'. The set $\mathcal{T}(\mathbf{F}, \mathbf{V})$ of terms over **F** and **V** is the smallest set closed under:

(i) $\mathbf{V} \subseteq \mathcal{T}(\mathbf{F}, \mathbf{V})$;

(ii) if $\alpha_1, ..., \alpha_n \in \mathcal{T}(\mathbf{F}, \mathbf{V})$ $(n \geq 0)$ then $f(\alpha_1, ..., \alpha_n) \in \mathcal{T}(\mathbf{F}, \mathbf{V})$, for $f \in \mathbf{F}$ with $ar(f) = n$.

The set $\mathcal{L}^m_{\mathbf{K}}(\mathbf{P}, \mathbf{F}, \mathbf{V})$ of first-order epistemic formulas $\varphi, \psi,...$ over **A**, **P**, **F** and **V** is the smallest set closed under:

(i) if $\varphi_1, ..., \varphi_n \in \mathcal{L}^m_{\mathbf{K}}(\mathbf{P}, \mathbf{F}, \mathbf{V})$ $(n \geq 0)$ then $P(\varphi_1, ..., \varphi_n) \in \mathcal{L}^m_{\mathbf{K}}(\mathbf{P}, \mathbf{F}, \mathbf{V})$, for $P \in \mathbf{P}$

with $ar(P) = n$;

(ii) if $\alpha_1, \alpha_2 \in \mathcal{T}(\mathbf{F}, \mathbf{V})$ then $(\alpha_1 = \alpha_2) \in \mathcal{L}^m_{\mathbf{K}}(\mathbf{P}, \mathbf{F}, \mathbf{V})$;

(iii) if $\varphi, \psi \in \mathcal{L}^m_{\mathbf{K}}(\mathbf{P}, \mathbf{F}, \mathbf{V})$ then $(\varphi \wedge \psi), \neg\varphi \in \mathcal{L}^m_{\mathbf{K}}(\mathbf{P}, \mathbf{F}, \mathbf{V})$;

(iv) if $\varphi \in \mathcal{L}^m_{\mathbf{K}}(\mathbf{P}, \mathbf{F}, \mathbf{V})$ and $x \in \mathbf{V}$ then $\forall x(\varphi) \in \mathcal{L}^m_{\mathbf{K}}(\mathbf{P}, \mathbf{F}, \mathbf{V})$;

(v) if $\varphi \in \mathcal{L}^m_{\mathbf{K}}(\mathbf{P}, \mathbf{F}, \mathbf{V})$ then $K_i\varphi \in \mathcal{L}^m_{\mathbf{K}}(\mathbf{P}, \mathbf{F}, \mathbf{V})$, for all $i \in \mathbf{A}$.

We omit the outermost parentheses again. Moreover we again introduce $\varphi \vee \psi$, $\varphi \rightarrow \psi$ as the usual abbreviations for $\neg(\neg\varphi \wedge \neg\psi)$ and $\neg\varphi \vee \psi$, respectively, together with $\bot = P_0 \wedge \neg P_0$, for some 0-ary predicate constant. We shall also use the abbreviation **true** for $\neg\bot$. When the sets **P**, **F** and **V** are understood, we omit them and write $\mathcal{L}^m_{\mathbf{K}}$ rather than $\mathcal{L}^m_{\mathbf{K}}(\mathbf{P}, \mathbf{F}, \mathbf{V})$. We may furthermore again use the abbreviations $\exists x(\varphi)$ for $\neg\forall x(\neg\varphi)$, and $M_i\varphi$ for $\neg K_i\neg\varphi$. When we only have one agent (i.e. **A** is a singleton set), we often omit subscripts, and just write $K\varphi$ and $M\varphi$.

A3.2. Kripke Structures for First-Order Epistemic Logic

A3.2.1. DEFINITION. A *first-order Kripke structure (model)* $\mathbb{M}$ is a tuple $\langle D, S, \pi, R_1, ..., R_m\rangle$ where:

(i) D is a non-empty set, the *domain* of $\mathbb{M}$;

(ii) S is a non-empty set of *states*;

(iii) π: $(S \rightarrow ((\mathbf{P}_0 \rightarrow \{t, f\}) \cup \bigcup_{n\geq 1}(\mathbf{P}_n \rightarrow D^n)))$ is an interpretation function of the (n-ary) predicate constants (yielding (n-ary) relations) per state,

(iv) m: $\bigcup_{n\geq 0}(\mathbf{F}_n \rightarrow (D^n \rightarrow D))$ is an interpretation function of the (n-ary) function symbols yielding (n-ary) functions (Note that this interpretation function is state-independent!);

(iv) $R_i \subseteq S \times S$ $(i = 1, ..., m)$ are the *possibility/accessibility relations*.

A (Kripke) *world* w consists of a Kripke model $\mathbb{M}$ together with a distinguished state $s \in S$: $(\mathbb{M}, s)$. Besides a world we also need assignments a: $\mathbf{V} \rightarrow D$ to interpret individual variables. By $a_{[x/d]}$ we denote the assignment that is identical to a, possibly except for the value on x, which is equal to $d \in D$.

A3.3. Kripke Semantics of First-Order Epistemic Formulas

We first define the value $val_{w,a}(\alpha)$ of a term α in $\mathcal{T}(\mathbf{F}, \mathbf{V})$ in world $w = (\mathbb{M}, s)$ given assignment a as usual: $val_{w,a}(x) = a(x)$ for $x \in \mathbf{V}$; $val_{w,a}(f(\alpha_1, ..., \alpha_n)) = m(f)(val_{w,a}(\alpha_1), ..., val_{w,a}(\alpha_n))$.

We define the relation $w, a \models \varphi$ by induction on the structure of the epistemic formula φ:

$(\mathbb{M}, s), a \models P \Leftrightarrow \pi(s)(P) = t$ for $p \in \mathbf{P}_0$;

$(\mathbb{M}, s), a \models P(\varphi_1, ..., \varphi_n) \Leftrightarrow \pi(s)(P)(val_{w,a}(\varphi_1), ..., val_{w,a}(\varphi_n))$ for $p \in \mathbf{P}_n$, for $n \geq 1$;

$(\mathbb{M}, s), a \models (\alpha_1 = \alpha_2) \Leftrightarrow val_{w,a}(\alpha_1) = val_{w,a}(\alpha_n)$;

$(\mathbb{M}, s), a \models \varphi \wedge \psi \Leftrightarrow (\mathbb{M}, s), a \models \varphi$ and $(\mathbb{M}, s), a \models \psi$;

$(\mathbb{M}, s), a \models \neg\varphi \Leftrightarrow (\mathbb{M}, s) \not\models \varphi$;

$(\mathbb{M}, s), a \models \forall x(\varphi) \Leftrightarrow (\mathbb{M}, s), a_{[x/d]} \models \varphi$ for all $d \in D$;

$(\mathbb{M}, s), a \models K_i\varphi \Leftrightarrow (\mathbb{M}, t), a \models \varphi$ for all t with $(s, t) \in R_i$.

A3.3.1. DEFINITION. Let φ be an epistemic formula. Then:
(i) φ is *valid in a first-order Kripke model* $\mathbb{M} = \langle D, S, \pi, R_1, ..., R_m\rangle$ if for all $s \in S$ and all assignments $a \in \mathbf{V} \to D$: $(\mathbb{M}, s), a \models \varphi$ (notation: $\mathbb{M} \models \varphi$);
(ii) φ is *valid*, notation $\models \varphi$, if $\mathbb{M} \models \varphi$ for all first-order Kripke models $\mathbb{M}$;
(iii) φ is *satisfiable* if there is a world $w = (\mathbb{M}, s)$, where $\mathbb{M}$ is a first-order Kripke model, such that $w \models \varphi$.

As in the propositional case we may impose conditions on the accessibility relations of a first-order Kripke model. If there are no restrictions on the relations, we call the model a first-order K-model. If the relations are reflexive we call the model a first-order T-model; if the relations are reflexive and transitive we call it a first-order S4-model; if the relations are equivalence relations we call it a first-order S5-model. Validity may again be defined with respect to classes of models, e.g. K-validity, T-validity, S4-validity and S5-validity. For example, the formula $\forall x(K_i\varphi) \to K_i(\forall x\varphi)$ is K-valid. (Check this for yourself.)

We may axiomatise first-order epistemic logic as follows:

For first-order **K** we take the axioms:

(A1') All (instances of) validities in first-order predicate logic, including equality axioms
(A2) $(K_i\varphi \wedge K_i(\varphi \to \psi)) \to K_i\psi$ for $i = 1, ..., m$
(A12) $\forall x(K_i\varphi) \to K_i(\forall x\varphi)$ for $i = 1, ..., m$

and the rules:

(R1) $\dfrac{\varphi \quad \varphi \to \psi}{\psi}$ *Modus ponens*

(R2) $\dfrac{\varphi}{K_i\varphi}$ (i = 1, ..., m) *Necessitation*

(R4) $\dfrac{\varphi}{\forall x(\varphi)}$ *Generalisation*

For first-order **T** we add:

(A3) $K_i\varphi \rightarrow \varphi$ (i = 1, ..., m).

For first-order **S4** we add furthermore:

(A4) $K_i\varphi \rightarrow K_iK_i\varphi$ (i = 1, ..., m).

For first-order **S5** we add furthermore:

(A5) $\neg K_i\varphi \rightarrow K_i\neg K_i\varphi$ (i = 1,..., m).

It can be shown that these first-order systems are sound and complete with respect to the appropriate classes of models, so first-order **K** (**T**, **S4**, **S5**) is sound and complete with respect to the class of all first-order K (T, S4, S5)-models (cf. [HC84]).

Much more can be said about first-order epistemic logic. For example, concerning the K-validity of $\exists x(K_i\varphi) \rightarrow K_i(\exists x\varphi)$ (check). This states that if there is an object of which i knows that φ holds, then i knows that there is an object of which i holds. This seems to be very reasonable. The converse clearly does not hold intuitively, and one may show that indeed it does not in our logic (check).

Although this seems to be all very satisfactory, there are also serious problems to be reported: for instance concerning the K-validity of $\forall x(K_i\varphi) \rightarrow K_i(\forall x\varphi)$, the infamous *Barcan formula*. Since it is also easy to show that the converse $K_i(\forall x\varphi) \rightarrow \forall x(K_i\varphi)$ is K-valid (check), we in fact have that $\forall x(K_i\varphi) \leftrightarrow K_i(\forall x\varphi)$ is K-valid. This is an immediate consequence of the requirement in our definition of a first-order Kripke model that the function m is global and not state-dependent, since in particular this means that the domain of all objects (individuals) is the same in each world. This is not always obvious. Moreover, and even more seriously, the Barcan formula $\forall x(K_i\varphi) \rightarrow K_i(\forall x\varphi)$ is equivalent to the formula $M_i(\exists x\varphi) \rightarrow \exists x(K_i\varphi)$, which is rather questionable, also in epistemic contexts: from "i considers it possible that there is someone who is better at sports" it is rather dubious that it would follow that "there is (actually) someone of which i considers it possible that he is better at sports". As stated before, these matters have to do with the domains of individuals per state, and might be treated by introducing special existence predicates (cf. [Gam91]).

A4. Table of the Basic Logical Systems

A4.1. The Axiom System $K_{(m)}$

(A1) All (instances of) propositional tautologies

(A2) $(K_i\varphi \wedge K_i(\varphi \rightarrow \psi)) \rightarrow K_i\psi \quad (i = 1, ..., m)$

(R1) $$\frac{\varphi \quad \varphi \rightarrow \psi}{\psi}$$

(R2) $$\frac{\varphi}{K_i\varphi} \quad (i = 1, ..., m)$$

A4.2. The Axiom System $S5_{(m)}$

The axioms (A1) and (A2), the rules (R1) and (R2), together with:

(A3) $K_i\varphi \rightarrow \varphi \quad (i = 1, ..., m)$

(A4) $K_i\varphi \rightarrow K_iK_i\varphi \quad (i = 1, ..., m)$

(A5) $\neg K_i\varphi \rightarrow K_i\neg K_i\varphi \quad (i = 1, ..., m)$

A4.3. The Axiom System $S5EC_{(m)}$

The axioms (A1) to (A5), the rules (R1) and (R2), together with:

(A6) $E\varphi \leftrightarrow K_1\varphi \wedge ... \wedge K_m\varphi$

(A7) $C\varphi \rightarrow \varphi$

(A8) $C\varphi \rightarrow EC\varphi$

(A9) $(C\varphi \wedge C(\varphi \rightarrow \psi)) \rightarrow C\psi$

(A10) $C(\varphi \rightarrow E\varphi) \rightarrow (\varphi \rightarrow C\varphi)$

(R3) $$\frac{\varphi}{C\varphi}$$

A4.4. The Axiom System $S5I_{(m)}$

The axioms (A1) to (A5), the rules (R1) and (R2), together with:

(A2') $(I\varphi \wedge I(\varphi \rightarrow \psi)) \rightarrow I\psi$

(A3') $I\varphi \rightarrow \varphi$

(A4') $I\varphi \rightarrow II\varphi$

(A5') $\neg I\varphi \rightarrow I\neg I\varphi$

(A11) $K_i\varphi \rightarrow I\varphi \quad (i = 1, ..., m)$

A4.5. The Axiom System $KD45_{(m)}$

The axioms (A1), (A2), (A4), (A5), the rules (R1) and (R2), together with:

(D) $\neg B_i(\bot)$

A4.6. The System Gr(S5)

(Gr0)	all propositional tautologies
(Gr1)	$K_0(\varphi \to \psi) \to (K_n\varphi \to K_n\psi)$ $(n \in \mathbb{N})$
(Gr2)	$K_n\varphi \to K_{n+1}\varphi$ $(n \in \mathbb{N})$
(Gr3)	$K_0\neg(\varphi \wedge \psi) \to ((M!_n\varphi \wedge M!_m\psi) \to M!_{n+m}(\varphi \vee \psi))$ $(n, m \in \mathbb{N})$
(Gr4)	$\neg K_n\varphi \to K_0\neg K_n\varphi$ $(n \in \mathbb{N})$
(Gr5)	$K_0\varphi \to \varphi$
(R1)	$\vdash \varphi, \vdash \varphi \to \psi \Rightarrow \vdash \psi$
(R2)	$\vdash \varphi \Rightarrow \vdash K_0\varphi$

A4.7. The System S5O

(O0)	All propositional tautologies
(O1)	$\Box(\varphi \to \psi) \to (\Box\varphi \to \Box\psi)$
(O2)	$\Box\varphi \to \varphi$
(O3)	$\neg\Box\varphi \to \Box\neg\Box\varphi$
(O4)	$\Diamond\varphi \leftrightarrow \neg\Box\neg\varphi$
(O5)	$\Diamond\varphi$, for every satisfiable objective formula φ
(O6)	$\Box\varphi \leftrightarrow (L\varphi \wedge L^*\varphi)$
(O7)	$\varphi \to \Box\varphi$, for every basic subjective formula φ
(O8)	$L(\varphi \to \psi) \to (L\varphi \to L\psi)$
(O9)	$L^*(\varphi \to \psi) \to (L^*\varphi \to L^*\psi)$
(O10)	$\varphi \to L\varphi$, for every basic subjective formula φ
(O11)	$\varphi \to L^*\varphi$, for every basic subjective formula φ
(O12)	$\neg L\bot \to (L\varphi \to \varphi)$, for every basic subjective formula φ
(O13)	$\neg L^*\bot \to (L^*\varphi \to \varphi)$, for every basic subjective formula φ
(O14)	$\neg(M\varphi \wedge M^*\varphi)$, for every uniquely satisfiable objective formula φ
(O15)	$O\varphi \leftrightarrow L\varphi \wedge L^*\neg\varphi$

A4.8. The System EDL

The axioms (A1) to (A5) and rule (R2) for K, rule (R1), together with the axioms:

(AP2)	$(P_i\varphi \wedge P_i(\varphi \to \psi)) \to P_i\psi$ $(i = 1, ..., n)$
(AP4)	$P_i\varphi \to P_iP_i\varphi$ $(i = 1, ..., n)$
(AP5)	$\neg P_i\varphi \to P_i\neg P_i\varphi$ $(i = 1, ..., n)$
(AP6)	$K\varphi \to P_i\varphi$ $(i = 1, ..., n)$

(AP7) $KP_i\varphi \leftrightarrow P_i\varphi$ $(i = 1, ..., n)$

(AP8) $\neg P_i\bot \rightarrow (P_iP_j\varphi \leftrightarrow P_j\varphi)$ $(i, j = 1, ..., n)$

(AP9) $\neg P_i\bot \rightarrow (P_iK\varphi \leftrightarrow K\varphi)$ $(i = 1, ..., n)$

A4.9. The System ECL

The axioms (A1) to (A5) and rule (R2) for K, axioms (AP2), (AP3) to (AP9), rule (R1), together with the axioms:

(AP10) $A(\varphi \wedge \psi) \leftrightarrow A\varphi \wedge A\psi$

(AP11) $A\neg\varphi \leftrightarrow \neg A\varphi$

(AP12) $K\varphi \rightarrow A\varphi$

(AP13) $A\varphi \rightarrow KA\varphi$

(AP14) $AP_\sigma\varphi \leftrightarrow P_\sigma\varphi$ $(\sigma \in I^*)$

(AP15) $\neg P_\sigma \bot \rightarrow (P_\sigma A\varphi \leftrightarrow A\varphi)$ $(\sigma \in I^*)$

(AP16) $P_\sigma\varphi \rightarrow P_{\sigma,i}\varphi$ $(\sigma \in I^*, i \in I)$

A4.10. The System first-order K

The rules (R1) and (R2), together with:

(A1') All (instances of) validities in first-order predicate logic, including equality axioms

(A2) $(K_i\varphi \wedge K_i(\varphi \rightarrow \psi)) \rightarrow K_i\psi$ $(i = 1, ..., m)$

(A12) $\forall x(K_i\varphi) \rightarrow K_i(\forall x\varphi)$ $(i = 1, ..., m)$

(R4) $$\frac{\varphi}{\forall x(\varphi)}$$

To obtain first-order **S5** , add axioms (A3) to (A5).

E ANSWERS TO THE EXERCISES

Introduction

In this appendix, we provide the reader with a rather extensive presentation of the solutions to all exercises. We have chosen a thorough way of elaborating the exercises, for a number of reasons. Firstly, we consider the exercises, and, particularly, their solutions, as a way of deepening the material in the main text, 'off-line' so to speak, so that the main line of the book is not complicated too much. Secondly, we found the exercises a nice inducement to formulate and demonstrate in a precise way a host of results in epistemic modal logic that are part of folklore (to many logicians), but which we have not found published in this way elsewhere. Thirdly, the exercises show a great diversity in their degree of difficulty: from very simple and trivial to rather difficult. By providing complete solutions, each reader may go his/her own way through the exercises, allowing him/herself to skip the details of the more complicated technicalities whenever s/he wants, but on the other hand always having the security of having the disposal of a stock of technical solutions at hand (as, for instance, in the case of the elaborate completeness proofs), whenever s/he would like to inspect them. In our opinion this renders the book very suited for self-study on different levels of mastering the material.

As indicated already, solutions to the exercises sometimes also provide some theoretical elaboration: in many cases this appendix with answers is not just a way of providing readers with a way to verify their own solutions, but also a way to explore further directions of the material in the main text.

1.3.0.1 (i)

$(\mathbb{M}, s) \models (\varphi \vee \psi) \Leftrightarrow$	definition of '$\vee$'
$(\mathbb{M}, s) \models \neg(\neg\varphi \wedge \neg\psi) \Leftrightarrow$	truth definition '$\neg$'
not $(\mathbb{M}, s) \models \neg\varphi \wedge \neg\psi \Leftrightarrow$	truth definition '$\wedge$'
not $[(\mathbb{M}, s) \models \neg\varphi$ and $(\mathbb{M},s) \models \neg\psi] \Leftrightarrow$	truth definition '$\neg$'
not [not $(\mathbb{M}, s) \models \varphi$ and not $(\mathbb{M}, s) \models \neg\psi] \Leftrightarrow$	not (A and B) $\equiv$ not (A) or not (B)
not [not $(\mathbb{M}, s) \models \varphi$] or not [not $(\mathbb{M}, s) \models \psi] \Leftrightarrow$	not(not(A)) $\equiv$ A
$(\mathbb{M}, s) \models \varphi$ or $(\mathbb{M}, s) \models \varphi$.	

(ii)

$(\mathbb{M},s) \models \varphi \to \psi \Leftrightarrow$	def '$\to$'
$(\mathbb{M},s) \models (\neg\varphi \vee \psi) \Leftrightarrow$	Exercise 1.3.0.1(i)
$(\mathbb{M},s) \models \neg\varphi$ or $(\mathbb{M},s) \models \psi) \Leftrightarrow$	truth-definition '$\neg$'
not $(\mathbb{M},s) \models \varphi$ or $(\mathbb{M},s) \models \psi \Leftrightarrow$	not (A) or (B) $\equiv$ (A $\Rightarrow$ B)

$(\mathbb{M},s) \models \varphi \Rightarrow (\mathbb{M},s) \models \psi$

1.3.0.2 $(\mathbb{M},s) \models \neg K_i\psi \Leftrightarrow$ truth definition '$\neg$'
not $(\mathbb{M},s) \models K_i\psi \Leftrightarrow$ truth definition 'K_i'
not [for all t(R_ist $\Rightarrow (\mathbb{M},t) \models \psi$] $\Leftrightarrow$ not(for all x (A)) $\equiv$ there exists x(not(A))
there exists t (not (R_ist $\Rightarrow (\mathbb{M},t) \models \psi$) $\Leftrightarrow$ not (A $\Rightarrow$ B) $\equiv$ A and not(B)
there exists t (R_ist and not $(\mathbb{M},t) \models \psi$) $\Leftrightarrow$ truth definition '$\neg$'
there exists t (R_ist and $(\mathbb{M},t) \models \neg\psi$).

This has now been proven for arbitrary formulas ψ. Now choose $\psi \equiv \neg\varphi$, (then $\neg\psi \equiv \varphi$). Then
$(\mathbb{M}, s) \models \neg K_i\neg\varphi \Leftrightarrow$ definition φ
$(\mathbb{M}, s) \models \neg K_i\psi \Leftrightarrow$ cf. above
there exists t (R_ist and $(\mathbb{M},t) \models \neg\psi$) definition φ
there exists t (R_ist and $(\mathbb{M},t) \models \varphi$).

1.3.0.3 * From here on, 'td' means 'truth definition', and 'df' stands for 'definition'.
* A justification 'classical logic' means that we use properties like 'not all x satisfy A' $\equiv$ 'some x satisfies not A'.
* The justification 'type of π' refers to the equivalences '$\pi(x)(p) = t$' $\equiv$ 'not $\pi(x)(p) = f$'. This equivalence, in its turn, is justified by the fact that π is a function with range {t, f}
* All variables s, t u and v range over the set of states S of the model.

- p
$(\mathbb{M}, s) \models p \Leftrightarrow$ td of atoms
$\pi(s)(p) = t$

- K_1q
$(\mathbb{M}, s) \models K_1q \Leftrightarrow$ td of K_1
$(\mathbb{M}, t) \models q$ for all t with $(s, t) \in R_1$ td of atoms
$\pi(t)(q) = t$ for all t with $(s, t) \in R_1$

- $\neg K_2p$
$(\mathbb{M}, s) \models \neg K_2p \Leftrightarrow$ td of '$\neg$'
not $(\mathbb{M}, s) \models K_2p \Leftrightarrow$ td of K_2
not $(\mathbb{M}, t) \models p$ for all t with $(s, t) \in R_1 \Leftrightarrow$ classical logic
for some t, we have $(s, t) \in R_1$ and not $(\mathbb{M}, t) \models p \Leftrightarrow$ td of atoms
for some t, we have $(s, t) \in R_1$ and not $\pi(t)(p) = t \Leftrightarrow$ type of π
for some t, we have $(s, t) \in R_1$ and $\pi(t)(p) = f$

- K_1K_2q
$(\mathbb{M}, s) \models K_1K_2q \Leftrightarrow$ td of K_1
for all t with $(s, t) \in R_1$ $(\mathbb{M}, t) \models K_2q$ td of K_2
for all t with $(s, t) \in R_1$: (for all u with $(t, u) \in R_2$ $(\mathbb{M}, u) \models q$) td of atoms
for all t with $(s, t) \in R_1$: (for all u with $(t, u) \in R_2$ $\pi(u)(q) = t$

- $K_2\neg K_1p$

$(\mathbb{M}, s) \models K_2 \neg K_1 p \Leftrightarrow$ — td of K_2
for all t with $(s, t) \in R_2$ $(\mathbb{M}, t) \models \neg K_1 q \Leftrightarrow$ — td of '$\neg$'
for all t with $(s, t) \in R_2$: not $(\mathbb{M}, t) \models K_1 q \Leftrightarrow$ — td of K_1
for all t with $(s, t) \in R_2$: not for all u with $(t, u) \in R_1$: $(\mathbb{M}, u) \models q \Leftrightarrow$ — classical logic
for all t with $(s, t) \in R_2$: there is some u with $(t, u) \in R_1$ and not $(\mathbb{M}, u) \models q \Leftrightarrow$ — td of atoms
for all t with $(s, t) \in R_2$: there is some u with $(t, u) \in R_1$ and not $\pi(u)(q) = \mathbf{t} \Leftrightarrow$ — type of π
for all t with $(s, t) \in R_2$: there is some u with $(t, u) \in R_1$ and $\pi(u)(q) = \mathbf{f}$

- $\neg K_1 \neg M_1(p \vee q)$:
  $(\mathbb{M}, s) \models \neg K_1 \neg M_1(p \vee q) \Leftrightarrow$ — df of M_1
  $(\mathbb{M}, s) \models M_1 M_1(p \vee q) \Leftrightarrow$ — Exercise 1.3.0.2
  there is a t with $(s, t) \in R_1$ and $(\mathbb{M}, t) \models M_1(p \vee q)$ — Exercise 1.3.0.2
  there is a t with $(s, t) \in R_1$ with a u with $(t, u) \in R_1$ and $(\mathbb{M}, u) \models (p \vee q)$ — Exercise 1.3.0.1(i)
  there is a t with $(s, t) \in R_1$ with a u with $(t, u) \in R_1$ and $(\mathbb{M}, u) \models p$ or $(\mathbb{M}, u) \models q$ — df of atoms
  there is a t with $(s, t) \in R_1$ with a u with $(t, u) \in R_1$ and $\pi(u)(p) = \mathbf{t}$ or $\pi(u)(q) = \mathbf{t}$

- $K_2(K_1 q \vee K_1 \neg q)$
  $(\mathbb{M}, s) \models K_2(K_1 q \vee K_1 \neg q) \Leftrightarrow$ — td of K_2
  for all t with $(s, t) \in R_2$: $(\mathbb{M}, t) \models (K_1 q \vee K_1 \neg q) \Leftrightarrow$ — Exercise 1.3.0.1(i)
  for all t with $(s, t) \in R_2$: $[(\mathbb{M}, t) \models K_1 q$ or $(\mathbb{M}, t) \models K_1 \neg q] \Leftrightarrow$ — td of K_1 (twice)
  for all t with $(s, t) \in R_2$:
  [for all u with $(t, u) \in R_1$ $(\mathbb{M}, u) \models q$ or for all v with $(t, v) \in R_1$ $(\mathbb{M}, v) \models \neg q] \Leftrightarrow$ — td of '$\neg$'
  for all t with $(s, t) \in R_2$:
  [for all u with $(t,u) \in R_1$ $(\mathbb{M},u) \models q$ or for all v with $(t,v) \in R_1$ not $(\mathbb{M},v) \models q] \Leftrightarrow$ — td of atoms
  for all t with $(s, t) \in R_2$:
  [for all u with $(t, u) \in R_1$ $\pi(u)(q) = \mathbf{t}$ or for all v with $(t,v) \in R_1$ not $\pi(v)(q) = \mathbf{t}] \Leftrightarrow$ — type of π
  for all t with $(s, t) \in R_2$:
  [for all u with $(t, u) \in R_1$ $\pi(u)(q) = \mathbf{t}$ or for all v with $(t, v) \in R_1$ $\pi(v)(q) = \mathbf{f}$]

- $K_1(\neg K_3(K_4 q \wedge M_1 p) \vee K_2 \neg q)$
  $(\mathbb{M}, s) \models K_1(\neg K_3(K_4 q \wedge M_1 p) \vee K_2 \neg q)$ — td of K_1
  for all t with $(s, t) \in R_1$: $(\mathbb{M}, t) \models \neg K_3(K_4 q \wedge M_1 p) \vee K_2 \neg q$ — Exercise 1.3.0.1(i)
  for all t with $(s, t) \in R_1$: $[(\mathbb{M}, t) \models \neg K_3(K_4 q \wedge M_1 p)$ or $(\mathbb{M}, t) \models K_2 \neg q]$ — td of '$\neg$'
  for all t with $(s, t) \in R_1$:
  [not $(\mathbb{M},t) \models K_3(K_4 q \wedge M_1 p)$ or $(\mathbb{M},t) \models K_2 \neg q$] — td of K_2, K_3
  for all t with $(s, t) \in R_1$:
  [(not for all u with $(t, u) \in R_3$: $(\mathbb{M}, u) \models K_4 q \wedge M_1 p$)
  or for all v with $(t, v) \in R_2$: $(\mathbb{M}, v) \models \neg q$] — td of '$\wedge$', '$\neg$'
  for all t with $(s, t) \in R_1$:
  [(not for all u with $(t, u) \in R_3$: $((\mathbb{M}, u) \models K_4 q$ and $(\mathbb{M}, u) \models M_1 p))$
  or for all v with $(t, v) \in R_2$: not $(\mathbb{M}, v) \models q$] — td of K_4, 1.3.0.2
  for all t with $(s, t) \in R_1$:
  [(not for all u with $(t, u) \in R_3$:
  for all w with $(u, w) \in R_4$: $((\mathbb{M}, w) \models q$
  and for some x with $(u, x) \in R_1$, $(\mathbb{M}, x) \models p)$
  or for all v with $(t, v) \in R_2$: not $(\mathbb{M}, v) \models q$] — classical logic

for all t with $(s, t) \in R_1$:	
[(there is some u with $(t, u) \in R_3$ and	
for some w : $(u, w) \in R_4$ and not $((M, w) \models q$	
or for all x with $(u, x) \in R_1$, not $(M, x) \models p)$	
or for all v with $(t, v) \in R_2$: not $(M, v) \models q$]	td atoms, type of π
for all t with $(s, t) \in R_1$:	
[(there is some u with $(t, u) \in R_3$ and	
for some w : $(u, w) \in R_4$ and $\pi(w)(q) = f$	
or for all x with $(u, x) \in R_1$, $\pi(x)(p) = f)$	
or for all v with $(t, v) \in R_2$: $\pi(v)(q) = f$]	td atoms, type of π

1.3.1.1 We write 'K_A' for 'K_{Alice}' and 'K_B' for 'K_{Bob}'.

(i)

$(M, s_1) \models p \Leftrightarrow$	td for formulas of **P**
$(M, s_1) \models \pi(s_1)(p) \Leftrightarrow$	definition of π
true	

(ii)

$(M, s_1) \models \neg K_A p \Leftrightarrow$	td of '$\neg$'
not $(M, s_1) \models K_A p \Leftrightarrow$	td 'K_A'
not (for all t $(R_A s_1 t \Rightarrow (M, t) \models p)) \Leftrightarrow$	interplay 'for all' and 'exists'
there exists t with $R_A s_1 t$ and not $(M, t) \models p) \Leftarrow$	definition of 'exists'
$R_A s_1 s_2$ and not $(M, s_2) \models p \Leftrightarrow$	definition of R_A and π
true	

(iii)

$(M, s_1) \models \neg K_A p \wedge \neg K_A \neg p \Leftrightarrow$	td '$\wedge$'
$(M, s_1) \models \neg K_A p$ and $(M, s_1) \models \neg K_A \neg p \Leftrightarrow$	part (ii)
true and $(M, s_1) \models \neg K_A \neg p \Leftrightarrow$	(true and A) $\equiv$ A
$(M, s_1) \models \neg K_A \neg p \Leftrightarrow$	Exercise 1.3.0.2, definition of M
there is a t with $(R_A s_1 t$ and $(M, t) \models \neg p) \Leftarrow$	definition of 'exists'
$R_A s_1 s_2$ and $(M, s_2) \models \neg p \Leftrightarrow$	definition of the model
true	

(iv)

$(M, s_1) \models K_B p \Leftrightarrow$	td 'K_B'
for all t $(R_A s_1 t \Rightarrow (M, t) \models p) \Leftrightarrow$	definition of R_A
for all t $(t \in \{s_1, s_3\} \Rightarrow (M, t) \models p) \Leftrightarrow$	definition of the model
true	

(v)

$(M, s_1) \models K_A(K_B p \vee K_B \neg p) \Leftrightarrow$	td of 'K_A'
for all u $(R_A s_1 u \Rightarrow (M, u) \models K_B p \vee K_B \neg p) \Leftrightarrow$	td of '$\vee$'
for all u $(R_A s_1 u \Rightarrow ((M, u) \models K_B p$ or $(M, u) \models K_B \neg p)) \Leftrightarrow$	definition of R_A
for all u $(u \in \{s_1, s_2\} \Rightarrow ((M, u) \models K_B p$ or $(M, u) \models K_B \neg p)) \Leftarrow$	'for all', 'or'
$(M, s_1) \models K_B p$ and $(M, s_2) \models K_B \neg p \Leftrightarrow$	td of 'K_B'
for all t $(R_B s_1 t \Rightarrow (M, t) \models p)$ and for all u $(R_B s_2 u \Rightarrow (M, u) \models \neg p) \Leftrightarrow$	definition R_B
$(M, s_1) \models p$ and $(M, s_2) \models \neg p \Leftrightarrow$	definition of π
true	

(vi)	$(\mathbb{M}, s_1) \models \neg K_B \neg K_A p \Leftrightarrow$	Exercise 1.3.0.2, definition of M
	there exists a t with ($R_B s_1 t$ and $(\mathbb{M}, t) \models K_A p$) $\Leftrightarrow$	td 'K_A'
	there exists a t with ($R_B s_1 t$ and for all u ($R_A tu \Rightarrow (\mathbb{M}, u) \models p$)) $\Leftarrow$	definition of 'exists'
	$R_B s_1 s_3$ and for all u:($R_A s_3 u \Rightarrow (\mathbb{M}, u) \models p$) $\Leftrightarrow$	definition of R_B
	$R_B s_1 s_3$ and for all $u \in \{s_3\}$: $(\mathbb{M}, u) \models p \Leftrightarrow$	definition of the model
	true	

1.3.2 From now on, we occasionally write '∀' for 'for all' and '∃' for 'there exists', respectively. Moreover, for atomic formulas p, we directly decide about the truth of a condition like '$\forall t$ ($R_A s_1 t \Rightarrow (\mathbb{M}, t) \models p$)' by referring to the model immediately (instead of writing an intermediate step '$\forall t$ ($t \in \{s_1, s_2, s_3\} \Rightarrow (\mathbb{M}, t) \models p$)'). From item (vii) on, we will also stop presenting all the proofs by rewriting equivalences. In case of doubt, the reader should always be able to rewrite parts of a proof in a strict style.

(i)	$(\mathbb{M}, s_1) \models p \Leftrightarrow$	td of atoms from **P**
	$(\mathbb{M}, s_1) \models \pi(s_1)(p) \Leftrightarrow$	definition of π
	true	

(ii)	$(\mathbb{M}, s_1) \models q \Leftrightarrow$	td of atoms from **P**
	$(\mathbb{M}, s_1) \models \pi(s_1)(q) \Leftrightarrow$	definition of π
	true	

(iii)	$(\mathbb{M}, s_1) \models K_A p \Leftrightarrow$	td of 'K_A'
	$\forall t$ ($R_A s_1 t \Rightarrow (\mathbb{M}, t) \models p$) $\Leftrightarrow$	definition of the model
	true	

(iv)	$(\mathbb{M}, s_1) \models \neg K_B p \Leftrightarrow$	td of '¬'
	not $(\mathbb{M}, s_1) \models K_B p \Leftrightarrow$	definition of K_B
	not $\forall t$ ($R_B s_1 t \Rightarrow (\mathbb{M}, t) \models p$) $\Leftrightarrow$	not ∀ = ∃ not
	$\exists$ t ($R_B s_1 t$ and not $(\mathbb{M}, t) \models p$) $\Leftarrow$	∃-intro
	$R_B s_1 s_3$ and not $(\mathbb{M}, t) \models p \Leftrightarrow$	definition of the model
	true	

(v) as (iv) (now the witness of the existential quantifier is s_4)

(vi) as (iv) (now the witness is s_4)

(vii) To prove $(\mathbb{M}, s_1) \models K_A K_A p$, it is sufficient to prove that $(\mathbb{M}, u) \models K_A p$ holds for all u for which $R_A s_1 u$; that means that $(\mathbb{M}, u) \models K_A p$ holds for all $u \in \{s_1, s_2, s_4\}$. By looking at the model we see that indeed $(\mathbb{M}, s_1) \models K_A p$ (since p is true in all R_A-successors of s_1, namely s_1, s_2, and s_4); $(\mathbb{M}, s_2) \models K_A p$ (since p is true in s_2 and s_4) and $(\mathbb{M}, s_4) \models K_A p$ (p being true in s_4) simultaneously hold.

(viii)	$(\mathbb{M}, s_1) \models \neg K_B K_A p \Leftrightarrow$	$\neg\neg A \equiv A$
	$(\mathbb{M}, s_1) \models \neg K_B \neg\neg K_A p \Leftrightarrow$	definition of M
	$(\mathbb{M}, s_1) \models M_B \neg K_A \Leftrightarrow$	Exercise 1.3.0.2

there exists t (R_Bs_1t and $(\mathbb{M}, t) \models \neg K_Ap$) $\Leftrightarrow$ Exercise 1.3.0.2
there exists t (R_Bs_1t and (there exists u with R_Atu and $(\mathbb{M}, u) \models \neg p$))

By inspecting the model, and taking $t = u = s_3$, we see that the latter statement about $\mathbb{M}$ is true.

(ix) $(\mathbb{M}, s_1) \models \neg K_A\neg K_Bp \Leftrightarrow$ Exercise 1.3.0.2.
there exists t (R_As_1t and $(\mathbb{M}, t) \models K_Bp \Leftrightarrow$ td 'K_B'
there exists t (R_As_1t and for all u: ($R_Btu \Rightarrow (\mathbb{M}, u) \models p$))
We see that the latter statement is true in the model, by taking $t = s_2$: in all worlds R_B-accessible from s_2 (that is only s_2 itself) the atom p is true.

(x) $(\mathbb{M}, s_1) \models K_A\neg K_Aq \Leftrightarrow$ td 'K_A'
for all t ($R_As_1t \Rightarrow (\mathbb{M}, t) \models \neg K_Aq$) $\Leftrightarrow$ Exercise 1.3.0.2
for all t ($R_As_1t \Rightarrow$ there exists u (R_Atu and $(\mathbb{M}, u) \models \neg q$))
We see that the latter statement is true in the model, as follows: the only world in $\mathbb{M}$ in which $\neg q$ is true is the world s_4; so we have to show that for each t for which R_As_1t, it holds that R_Ats_4. And indeed, s_4 is R_A-accessible from s_1, s_2 and s_4, so R_A-accessible from all R_A-successor of s_1.

(xi) $(\mathbb{M}, s_1) \models \neg K_B\neg K_Aq \Leftrightarrow$ Exercise 1.3.0.2.
there exists t (R_Bs_1t and $(\mathbb{M}, t) \models K_Aq$) $\Leftrightarrow$ td 'K_A'
there exists t(R_Bs_1t and for all u ($R_Atu \Rightarrow (\mathbb{M}, u) \models q$))
The latter statement is true: take $t = s_3$; in all R_A-successors of s_3 (that is only s_3 itself) the atom q is true.

(xii) $(\mathbb{M}, s_1) \models \neg K_A\neg K_Bq \Leftrightarrow$ as in item (xi)
there exists t (R_As_1t and alle u($R_Btu \Rightarrow (\mathbb{M}, u) \models q$))
This is true: take $t = s_2$; in all R_B-successors of s_2 (that is only s_2 itself) the atom q is true.

(xiii) $(\mathbb{M}, s_1) \models K_B\neg K_Bq \Leftrightarrow$ td 'K_B'
for all t ($R_Bs_1t \Rightarrow (\mathbb{M}, t) \models \neg K_Bq$) $\Leftrightarrow$ Exercise 1.3.0.2.
for all t ($R_Bs_1t \Rightarrow$ (there exists u(R_Btu and $(\mathbb{M}, u) \models \neg q$))
To see that the latter is true, we have to show that all R_B-successors of s_1 (that are s_1, s_3 and s_4) have an R_B-successor verifying $\neg q$. But this is easy, since all states s_1, s_3 and s_4 are R_B-accessible to s_4, in which $\neg q$ is true.

1.3.3 The formulas are true in the following models. We denote R_1 with black arrows, R_2 with dashed arrows. We only give the truth of those atoms that are relevant:

(i) $K_1(K_1p \wedge K_2q) \wedge \neg K_1(p \wedge q)$ is satisfied in the model on the right. The first conjucnt is true, because for all R_1-successors of s (i.e. in t and u), we have that all their R_1-successors ({v, w} and {w}, respectively) satisfy p and all their R_2-successors ({w} and {x}, respectively) satisfy q. For the second conjunct, note that not all R_1-successors of s (i.e. t) satisfy p.

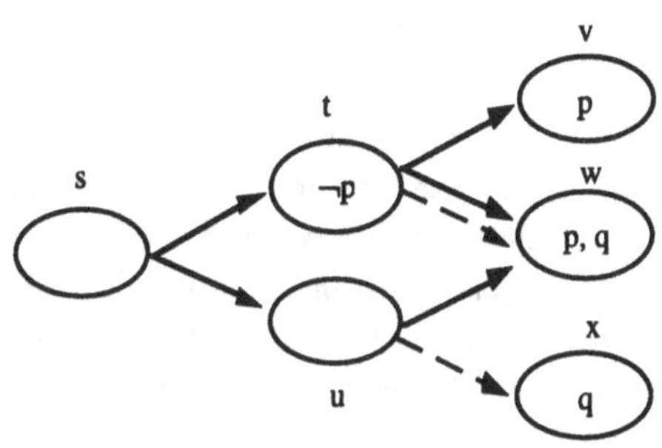

(ii) $K_1(K_1p \vee K_2q) \wedge \neg K_1p \wedge \neg K_1q)$ is satisfied in the model on the right. The first conjunct is true, because for all R_1-successors of s we have that $(K_1p \vee K_2q)$ is true (p is true in all R_1-successors of t, q is true in all R_2-successors of u) For the second conjunct, note that not all R_1-successors of s satisfy p (p is not true in t); for the third conjunct, note that not all R_1-successors of s satisfy q (q is not true in u).

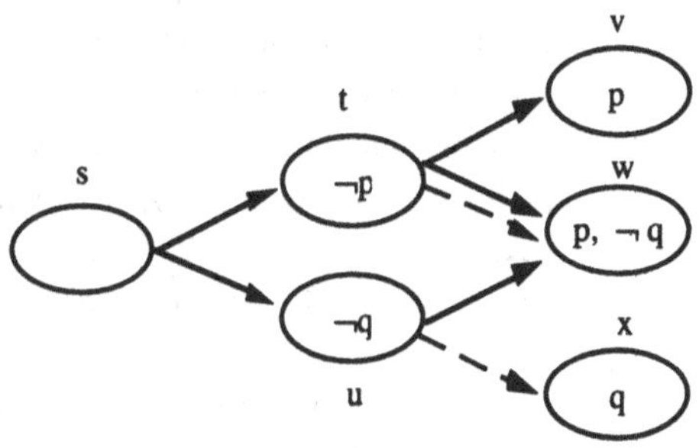

(iii) $K_2(K_1p \wedge K_1K_2q) \wedge \neg K_2p \wedge \neg K_2K_1q$ is satisfied in the model on the right. The first conjunct is true: for all R_2-successors of s we have that in all *their* R_1-successors ({u, v} and {v}) both the atom p is true and their R_2-successors (x, y and z) verify q. For the second conjunct, note that not all R_2-successors of s satisfy p (¬p is true in t); for the third conjunct, note that not for all R_2-successors of s (take t) the R_1-successors (take u) satisfy q.

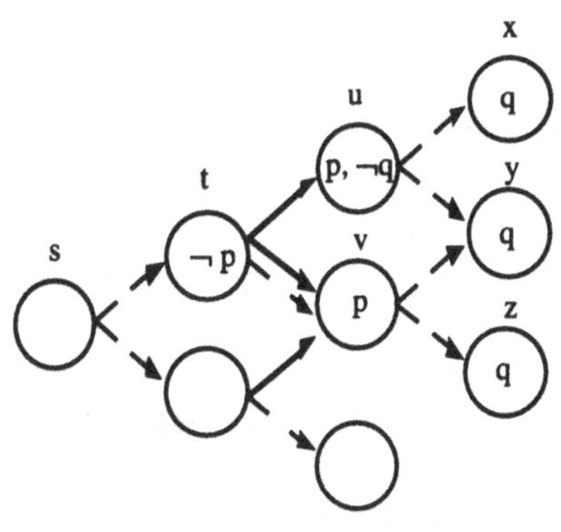

1.3.4.1

⊭ ¬φ	df⊭
not (⊨ ¬φ) ⇔	Def. 1.3.4(i)
not (for all M: M ⊨ ¬φ) ⇔	Def. 1.3.4(i)
not (for all M: (for all s: ((M, s) ⊨ ¬φ))) ⇔	not for all x P ≡ for some x not P

for some $\mathbb{M}$: (not for all s: (($\mathbb{M}$, s) $\models \neg\varphi$)) $\Leftrightarrow$ — not for all x P $\equiv$ for some x not P
there exists $\mathbb{M}$: (there exists s: (not (($\mathbb{M}$,s) $\models \neg\varphi$))) $\Leftrightarrow$ — td '$\neg$'
for some $\mathbb{M}$: (for some s: (not (not ($\mathbb{M}$, s) $\models \varphi$))) $\Leftrightarrow$ — not not P $\equiv$ P
for some $\mathbb{M}$: (for some s: (($\mathbb{M}$, s) $\models \varphi$)) $\Leftrightarrow$ — Def. 1.3.4(iii)
φ is satisfiable

1.3.5.1(iii) Suppose $\models \varphi$ and $\models (\varphi \to \psi)$. Then, for all $\mathbb{M}$ and all s, ($\mathbb{M}$, s) $\models \varphi$ and ($\mathbb{M}$, s) $\models (\varphi \to \psi)$. If we now take an arbitrary $\mathbb{M}$ and s, using Exercise 1.3.0.1.(ii), we conclude that ($\mathbb{M}$, s) $\models \psi$. Since this holds for arbitrary $\mathbb{M}$ and s, this proves $\models \psi$.

(iv) Suppose $\models \varphi$, that is, in all models $\mathbb{M}$ and states s, ($\mathbb{M}$, s) $\models \varphi$. Now take an arbitrary model $\mathbb{N}$, and states t and u in $\mathbb{N}$ with $R_i tu$. Since $\models \varphi$, we have that ($\mathbb{N}$, u) $\models \varphi$. This proves ($\mathbb{N}$, s) $\models K_i\varphi$, and, since $\mathbb{N}$ and s were arbitrarily chosen, we obtain $\models K_i\varphi$.

(v) To prove that $\not\models \varphi \to K_i\varphi$, it is sufficient to give some formula φ and one model $\mathbb{M}$ with a world s such that ($\mathbb{M}$, s) $\models \varphi \wedge \neg K_i\varphi$. Such a model $\mathbb{M} = \langle S, \pi, R_1, \ldots, R_m\rangle$ is obtained as follows: S = {a, b}, R_i = {(a, b)} and π(a)(p) = t while π(b)(p) = f. Then we have ($\mathbb{M}$, a) $\models p \wedge \neg K_i p$ (since p is not true in b and it holds that $R_i ab$).

(vii) We give a model $\mathbb{M} = \langle S, \pi, R_1, \ldots, R_m\rangle$ and a world s such that ($\mathbb{M}$, s) $\models K_i p \wedge \neg K_i K_i p$. Let S = {a, b, c}, R_i = {(a, b), (b, c)}and π(x)(p) = t iff x = b. It is easily verified that ($\mathbb{M}$, a) $\models K_i p \wedge \neg K_i K_i p$: p is true in all of a's R_i-successors (which is only world b) but not in all the R_i-successors of a's R_i-successors (which is only world c).

1.3.5.3 Let φ and ψ be arbitrary epistemic formulas, $\mathbb{M} = \langle S, \pi, R_1, \ldots, R_m\rangle$ an arbitrary Kripke model and s a state $\in$ S.

(i) ($\mathbb{M}$, s) $\models K_i(\varphi \wedge \psi)$
$\Leftrightarrow \forall t(R_i st \Rightarrow (\mathbb{M}, t) \models \varphi \wedge \psi)$
$\Leftrightarrow \forall t(R_i st \Rightarrow ((\mathbb{M}, t) \models \varphi$ and $(\mathbb{M}, t) \models \psi))$
$\Leftrightarrow \forall t(R_i st \Rightarrow ((\mathbb{M}, t) \models \varphi)$ and $\forall t(R_i st \Rightarrow (\mathbb{M}, t) \models \psi)$
$\Leftrightarrow (\mathbb{M}, s) \models K_i\varphi$ and $(\mathbb{M}, s) \models K_i\psi$
$\Leftrightarrow (\mathbb{M}, s) \models K_i\varphi \wedge K_i\psi$

(ii) ($\mathbb{M}$, s) $\models K_i\varphi$
$\Leftrightarrow \forall t(R_i st \Rightarrow (\mathbb{M}, t) \models \varphi)$
$\Rightarrow \forall t(R_i st \Rightarrow ((\mathbb{M}, t) \models \varphi$ or $(\mathbb{M}, t) \models \psi))$
$\Leftrightarrow \forall t(R_i st \Rightarrow ((\mathbb{M}, t) \models \varphi \vee \psi))$
$\Leftrightarrow (\mathbb{M}, s) \models K_i(\varphi \vee \psi)$.

(iii) The '$\to$' direction is not valid: take any model with R_i = {(s,t), (s,u)} and π(t)(p) = t, π(u)(p) = f. Then obviously ($\mathbb{M}$, s) $\models K_i(p \vee \neg p)$, but ($\mathbb{M}$, s) $\not\models (K_i p \vee K_i\neg p)$.

(iv) Immediate from (i) of this exercise: note that $M_i(\varphi \vee \psi) \equiv \neg K_i(\neg\varphi \vee \neg\psi)$.

(v) Let s have no R_i-successor. Then ($\mathbb{M}$, s) $\models K_i\neg p \wedge K_i p$, hence $\not\models K_i\neg p \to \neg K_i p$.

(vi) Suppose ($\mathbb{M}$, s) $\models \neg K_i\bot$, saying that not all of the R_i-successors of s verify $\bot$. This means that there must be at least one R_i-successor t satisfying $\neg\bot$, and in particular it implies that s has an R_i-successor t. Now suppose furthermore that ($\mathbb{M}$, s) $\models K_i\varphi$, saying that all R_i-successors of s satisfy φ. Then we know that in the state t the formula φ is true, and hence we see that s has an R_i-successor verifying φ: ($\mathbb{M}$, s) $\models \neg K_i\neg\varphi$. This proves ($\mathbb{M}$, s) $\models \neg K_i\bot \to (K_i\varphi \to \neg K_i\neg\varphi)$.

For the converse, suppose that $(\mathbb{M}, s) \models K_i\varphi \rightarrow \neg K_i\neg\varphi$. We distinguish two cases.

1 $(\mathbb{M}, s) \not\models K_i\varphi$. Then there is a t with R_ist and $(\mathbb{M}, t) \not\models \varphi$. Of course, $\bot$ is not true in t, hence $(\mathbb{M}, s) \models \neg K_i\bot$.

2 $(\mathbb{M}, s) \models K_i\varphi$. Then, by assumption, $(\mathbb{M}, s) \models \neg K_i\neg\varphi$, saying that not all R_i-successors of s verify $\neg\varphi$. So, there must be a t with R_ist and $(\mathbb{M}, t) \models \varphi$. Again, t does not satisfy $\bot$, so there is a state t such that R_ist and $(\mathbb{M}, t) \not\models \bot$. Hence, $(\mathbb{M}, s) \models \neg K_i\bot$.

(vii) In the situation of (iii) we have $(\mathbb{M}, s) \models \neg K_ip \wedge \neg K_i\neg p$, hence $\not\models \neg K_ip \rightarrow K_i\neg p$.

E.1. Intermezzo (including the answer to Exercise 1.4.1.1)

In order to write down derivations in what follows, we will use the following derived rules, which are derivable in **K(m)**. Most of these involve classical (non-modal) propositional logic, and are stated here both for easy reference and as help to the reader not well-versed in propositional logic.

i
$$\frac{\varphi \rightarrow \psi}{K_i\varphi \rightarrow K_i\psi}$$
K-distribution (KD)

ii
$$\frac{\begin{array}{c}\varphi \rightarrow \psi \\ \psi \rightarrow \varphi\end{array}}{\varphi \leftrightarrow \psi}$$
Equivalence-introduction (EI)

iii
$$\frac{\varphi \leftrightarrow \psi}{\varphi \rightarrow \psi}$$
Equivalence-elimination (EE)

$$\frac{\varphi \leftrightarrow \psi}{\psi \rightarrow \varphi}$$
Equivalence-elimination (EE)

iv
$$\frac{\varphi \leftrightarrow \psi}{K_i\varphi \leftrightarrow K_i\psi}$$
K-distribution $(\leftrightarrow)$ (KD$\leftrightarrow$)

v
$$\frac{\begin{array}{c}\varphi \rightarrow \varphi_1 \\ \varphi_1 \rightarrow \varphi_2 \\ \ldots \quad \ldots \\ \varphi_n \rightarrow \psi\end{array}}{\varphi \rightarrow \psi}$$
Hypothetical syllogism (HS)

vi
$$\frac{\begin{array}{c}\varphi \leftrightarrow \varphi_1 \\ \varphi_1 \leftrightarrow \varphi_2 \\ \ldots \quad \ldots \\ \varphi_n \leftrightarrow \psi\end{array}}{\varphi \leftrightarrow \psi}$$
Hypothetical syllogism $(\leftrightarrow)$ (HS$\leftrightarrow$)

vii $$\frac{\varphi \rightarrow \psi}{(\varphi \wedge \chi) \rightarrow (\psi \wedge \chi)}$$ *Left-right strengthening* (LR)

viii $$\frac{\varphi \rightarrow \psi}{\neg\psi \rightarrow \neg\varphi}$$ *Contra-position* (CP)

ix $$\frac{(\varphi \wedge \neg\psi) \rightarrow \bot}{\varphi \rightarrow \psi}$$ *No contradiction* (NC)

x $$\frac{\begin{array}{c}\varphi_1 \rightarrow \psi_1 \\ \varphi_2 \rightarrow \psi_2 \\ \ldots \quad \ldots \\ \varphi_n \rightarrow \psi_n\end{array}}{(\varphi_1 \wedge \ldots \wedge \varphi_n) \rightarrow (\psi_1 \wedge \ldots \wedge \psi_n)}$$ *Combining* (CO)

xi $$\frac{\begin{array}{c}\varphi_1 \leftrightarrow \psi_1 \\ \varphi_2 \leftrightarrow \psi_2 \\ \ldots \quad \ldots \\ \varphi_n \leftrightarrow \psi_n\end{array}}{(\varphi_1 \wedge \ldots \wedge \varphi_n) \leftrightarrow (\psi_1 \wedge \ldots \wedge \psi_n)}$$ *Combining($\leftrightarrow$)* ($CO^{\leftrightarrow}$)

xii $\vdash K_i(\varphi \rightarrow \psi) \rightarrow (K_i\varphi \rightarrow K_i\psi)$ (A2')

xiii $$\frac{\varphi_1 \leftrightarrow \varphi_2}{\psi \leftrightarrow \psi[\varphi_1/\varphi_2]}$$ *Substitution* (SUB)

Note that, except for the rule KD, all the derived rules are derivable in propositional logic already. In future derivations, the reader may either verify them by recognising them as propositionally valid, or check their specific format and derivability here. Moreover, when using these rules, we will implicitly use the commutivity of '$\wedge$'; so that, for instance, we asssume the rule NC also to stand for the rule

$$\frac{(\varphi \wedge \psi) \rightarrow \bot}{\psi \rightarrow \neg\varphi}$$ *No contradiction* (NC)

PROOFS.

i K-Distribution (KD):

1 $\vdash \varphi \rightarrow \psi$ (assumption)
2 $\vdash K_i(\varphi \rightarrow \psi)$ (R2; 1)
3 $\vdash K_i(\varphi \rightarrow \psi) \rightarrow (K_i\varphi \rightarrow K_i\psi)$ (A2)
4 $\vdash K_i\varphi \rightarrow K_i\psi$ (R1; 2,3)

REMARK. Note that, in the proof of KD, we do not assume (modal) formulas, but their derivability, which is, of course, a statement *about* such formulas (in the system **K(m)**, in this case).

ii Equivalence-introduction (EI):

1 $\vdash (\varphi \to \psi) \to ((\psi \to \varphi) \to (\varphi \leftrightarrow \psi))$ (A1)
2 $\vdash \varphi \to \psi$ (assumption)
3 $\vdash (\psi \to \varphi) \to (\varphi \leftrightarrow \psi)$ (R1; 1,2)
4 $\vdash \psi \to \varphi$ (assumption)
5 $\vdash \varphi \leftrightarrow \psi$ (R1; 3,4)

iii We omit the proof, which starts with the A1-instantiation $(\varphi \leftrightarrow \psi) \to (\varphi \to \psi)$

iv K-distribution($\leftrightarrow$) (KD$\leftrightarrow$):
Easy: use (EE), (KD), (R1) and then (EI).

v Hypothetical syllogism (HS)

1 $\vdash \varphi \to \varphi_1$ (assumption)
2 $\vdash \varphi_1 \to \varphi_2$ (assumption)
... ...
n+1 $\vdash \varphi_n \to \psi$ (assumption)
n+2 $\vdash (\varphi \to \varphi_1) \to ((\varphi_1 \to \varphi_2) \to (\varphi \to \varphi_2))$ (A1)
n+3 $\vdash (\varphi_1 \to \varphi_2) \to (\varphi \to \varphi_2)$ (R1; 1, n+2)
n+4 $\vdash \varphi \to \varphi_2$ (R1; 2, n+3)
n+5 $\vdash (\varphi \to \varphi_2) \to ((\varphi_2 \to \varphi_3) \to (\varphi \to \varphi_3))$ (A1)
... ...
3n+1 $\vdash \varphi \to \psi$ (R1; n+1,3n)

vi Hypothetical syllogism ($\leftrightarrow$) (HS$\leftrightarrow$):
The proof consists of applications of EE, HS and then EI.

vii Left-right strengthening (LR):

1 $\vdash \varphi \to \psi$ (assumption)
2 $\vdash (\varphi \to \psi) \to ((\varphi \wedge \chi) \to (\psi \wedge \chi))$ (A1)
3 $\vdash (\varphi \wedge \chi) \to (\psi \wedge \chi)$ (R1; 1,2)

viii-xii These proofs are left to the reader: they should all start with an appropriate instantiation of (A1).

xiii (A2')

1 $\vdash (K_i\varphi \wedge K_i(\varphi \to \psi)) \to K_i\psi$ (A2)
2 $\vdash ((K_i\varphi \wedge K_i(\varphi \to \psi)) \to K_i\psi) \to (K_i(\varphi \to \psi) \to (K_i\varphi \to K_i\psi))$ (A1)
3 $\vdash K_i(\varphi \to \psi) \to (K_i\varphi \to K_i\psi)$ (R1; 1,2)

xiv Substitution (SUB):
We have to prove the following rule, that we will call SUB. From the format of the

rule,

$$\frac{\varphi_1 \leftrightarrow \varphi_2}{\psi \leftrightarrow \psi[\varphi_1/\varphi_2]} \qquad \textit{Substitution} \qquad \text{(SUB)}$$

we see that we may assume that

$\vdash \varphi_1 \leftrightarrow \varphi_2$ (*)

We distinguish two cases: (A) $\psi = \varphi_1$ and (B) $\psi \neq \varphi_1$.

(A) In this case, $\psi[\varphi_1/\varphi_2] = \varphi_2$, and the conclusion $\vdash \varphi_1 \leftrightarrow \varphi_2$ follows directly from (*).

(B) In this case we have the following properties of substitutions:
$\psi[\varphi_1/\varphi_2] = (\psi_1[\varphi_1/\varphi_2] \otimes \psi_2[\varphi_1/\varphi_2])$ if $\psi = (\psi_1 \otimes \psi_2)$, $\otimes \in \{\wedge, \vee, \rightarrow, \leftrightarrow\}$; (**)
$\psi[\varphi_1/\varphi_2] = \lambda(\psi_1[\varphi_1/\varphi_2]$ if $\psi = \lambda\psi_1$, $\lambda \in \{\neg, K_i\}$. (***)
These properties express that substitution of φ_2 for φ_1 in ψ is compositional, provided that $\psi \neq \varphi_1$. This is intuitively clear, and we leave a proof to the reader (the notion of a 'well-formed formula' is needed here. For example, if we want to replace φ_1 by φ_2 in $(\psi_1 \wedge \psi_2)$, then φ_1 cannot be a string like '$(\psi_1 \wedge\ )$'. Thus, either $\varphi_1 = (\psi_1 \wedge \psi_2)$, or we may perform substitutions of φ_2 for φ_1 in ψ_1 and ψ_2 separately.

Now we continue our proof of the rule SUB, using induction on the complexity of formula ψ. By the interdefinability of the connectives, it is sufficient to do this for atomic formulas (I), for $\otimes = \wedge$ (II), and $\lambda \in \{\neg, K_i\}$ (III). Since the possibility of (A) has been taken care of already, we may assume that (B) holds, together with (*).

(I) Suppose now that ψ is atomic, say p. Since we know that $\psi \neq \varphi_1$, we immediately see that $\psi[\varphi_1/\varphi_2] = \psi$, so that the conclusion ($\vdash \psi \leftrightarrow \psi$ in this case) follows.

(II) Suppose that SUB has been proven for ψ_1 and ψ_2, and suppose $\psi = (\psi_1 \wedge \psi_2)$. We prove $\vdash \psi \leftrightarrow \psi[\varphi_1/\varphi_2]$ as follows:

1	$\vdash (\varphi_1 \leftrightarrow \varphi_2)$	(assumption (*))
2	$\vdash \psi_1 \leftrightarrow \psi_1[\varphi_1/\varphi_2]$	(induction hypothesis)
3	$\vdash \psi_2 \leftrightarrow \psi_2[\varphi_1/\varphi_2]$	(induction hypothesis)
4	$\vdash (\psi_1 \wedge \psi_2) \leftrightarrow (\psi_1[\varphi_1/\varphi_2] \wedge \psi_2[\varphi_1/\varphi_2])$	($CO^{\leftrightarrow}$; 2,3)
5	$\vdash (\psi_1 \wedge \psi_2)[\varphi_1/\varphi_2] \leftrightarrow (\psi_1[\varphi_1/\varphi_2] \wedge \psi_2[\varphi_1/\varphi_2])$	(**)
6	$\vdash (\psi_1 \wedge \psi_2) \leftrightarrow (\psi_1 \wedge \psi_2)[\varphi_1/\varphi_2]$	($HS^{\leftrightarrow}$; 4,5)
7	$\vdash \psi \leftrightarrow \psi[\varphi_1/\varphi_2]$	(definition of ψ)

(III) Now suppose that SUB has been proven for ψ_1, and suppose $\psi = \neg\psi_1$. Then:

1	$\vdash (\varphi_1 \leftrightarrow \varphi_2)$	(*)
2	$\vdash \psi_1 \leftrightarrow \psi_1[\varphi_1/\varphi_2]$	(induction hypothesis)
3	$\vdash (\psi_1 \leftrightarrow \psi_1[\varphi_1/\varphi_2]) \rightarrow (\neg\psi_1 \leftrightarrow \neg(\psi_1[\varphi_1/\varphi_2]))$	(A1)
4	$\vdash \neg\psi_1 \leftrightarrow \neg(\psi_1[\varphi_1/\varphi_2])$	(R1; 2,3)
5	$\vdash (\neg\psi_1)[\varphi_1/\varphi_2] \leftrightarrow \neg(\psi_1[\varphi_1/\varphi_2])$	(***)
6	$\vdash \neg\psi_1 \leftrightarrow (\neg\psi_1)[\varphi_1/\varphi_2]$	($HS^{\leftrightarrow}$; 4,5)
7	$\vdash \psi \leftrightarrow \psi[\varphi_1/\varphi_2]$	(definition of ψ)

Now suppose that SUB has been proven for ψ_1, and suppose $\psi = K_i\psi_1$. Then:

1	$\vdash (\varphi_1 \leftrightarrow \varphi_2)$	(*)
2	$\vdash \psi_1 \leftrightarrow \psi_1[\varphi_1/\varphi_2]$	(induction hypothesis)
3	$\vdash K_i\psi_1 \leftrightarrow K_i(\psi_1[\varphi_1/\varphi_2])$	(KD$\leftrightarrow$,2)
4	$\vdash (K_i\psi_1)[\varphi_1/\varphi_2] \leftrightarrow K_i(\psi_1[\varphi_1/\varphi_2])$	(***)
5	$\vdash K_i\psi_1 \leftrightarrow (K_i\psi_1)[\varphi_1/\varphi_2]$	(HS$^{\leftrightarrow}$; 3,4)
6	$\vdash \psi \leftrightarrow \psi[\varphi_1/\varphi_2]$	(definition of ψ)

1.4.1.2

(i)	1	$\vdash (\varphi \wedge \psi) \rightarrow \varphi$	(A1)
	2	$\vdash K_i(\varphi \wedge \psi) \rightarrow K_i\varphi$	(KD; 1)
	3	$\vdash (\varphi \wedge \psi) \rightarrow \psi$	(A1)
	4	$\vdash K_i(\varphi \wedge \psi) \rightarrow K_i\psi$	(KD; 3)
	5	$\vdash (K_i(\varphi \wedge \psi) \rightarrow K_i\varphi) \rightarrow ((K_i(\varphi \wedge \psi) \rightarrow K_i\psi) \rightarrow (K_i(\varphi \wedge \psi) \rightarrow (K_i\varphi \wedge K_i\psi)))$	(A1)
	6	$\vdash (K_i(\varphi \wedge \psi) \rightarrow K_i\psi) \rightarrow (K_i(\varphi \wedge \psi) \rightarrow (K_i\varphi \wedge K_i\psi))$	(R1; 2,5)
	7	$\vdash K_i(\varphi \wedge \psi) \rightarrow (K_i\varphi \wedge K_i\psi)$	(R1; 4,6)
	8	$\vdash \varphi \rightarrow (\psi \rightarrow (\varphi \wedge \psi))$	(A1)
	9	$\vdash K_i\varphi \rightarrow K_i(\psi \rightarrow (\varphi \wedge \psi))$	(KD; 8)
	10	$\vdash K_i(\psi \rightarrow (\varphi \wedge \psi)) \rightarrow (K_i\psi \rightarrow K_i(\varphi \wedge \psi))$	(A2)
	11	$\vdash K_i\varphi \rightarrow (K_i\psi \rightarrow K_i(\varphi \wedge \psi))$	(HS; 9,10)
	12	$\vdash (K_i\varphi \rightarrow (K_i\psi \rightarrow K_i(\varphi \wedge \psi))) \rightarrow ((K_i\varphi \wedge K_i\psi) \rightarrow K_i(\varphi \wedge \psi))$	(A1)
	13	$\vdash (K_i\varphi \wedge K_i\psi) \rightarrow K_i(\varphi \wedge \psi)$	(R1; 11,12)
	14	$\vdash K_i(\varphi \wedge \psi) \leftrightarrow (K_i\varphi \wedge K_i\psi)$	(EI; 7,8)

(ii)	1	$\vdash \varphi \rightarrow (\varphi \vee \psi)$	(A1)
	2	$\vdash K_i\varphi \rightarrow K_i(\varphi \vee \psi)$	(KD; 1)
	3	$\vdash \psi \rightarrow (\varphi \vee \psi)$	(A1)
	4	$\vdash K_i\psi \rightarrow K_i(\varphi \vee \psi)$	(KD, 3)
	5	$\vdash (K_i\varphi \rightarrow K_i(\varphi \vee \psi)) \rightarrow ((K_i\psi \rightarrow K_i(\varphi \vee \psi)) \rightarrow ((K_i\varphi \vee K_i\psi) \rightarrow K_i(\varphi \vee \psi)))$	(A1)
	6	$\vdash (K_i\psi \rightarrow K_i(\varphi \vee \psi)) \rightarrow ((K_i\varphi \vee K_i\psi) \rightarrow K_i(\varphi \vee \psi))$	(R1; 2,5)
	7	$\vdash (K_i\varphi \vee K_i\psi) \rightarrow K_i(\varphi \vee \psi)$	(R1; 4,6)

(iii)	1	$\vdash (K_i\bot \leftrightarrow (K_i\varphi \wedge K_i\neg\varphi)) \rightarrow (\neg K_i\bot \leftrightarrow (K_i\varphi \rightarrow \neg K_i\neg\varphi))$	(A1)
	2	$\vdash \bot \leftrightarrow (\varphi \wedge \neg\varphi)$	(A1)
	3	$\vdash K_i\bot \leftrightarrow K_i(\varphi \wedge \neg\varphi)$	(KD$\leftrightarrow$, 2)
	4	$\vdash K_i(\varphi \wedge \neg\varphi) \leftrightarrow (K_i\varphi \wedge K_i\neg\varphi)$	(this exercise, (i))
	5	$\vdash K_i\bot \leftrightarrow (K_i\varphi \wedge K_i\neg\varphi)$	(HS$\leftrightarrow$, 3,4)
	6	$\vdash \neg K_i\bot \leftrightarrow (K_i\varphi \rightarrow \neg K_i\neg\varphi$	(R1, 1)

(iv), (v) These proofs are left to the reader. One should use the definition of M_i: $M_i\varphi \equiv \neg K_i\neg\varphi$, together with A1-instantiations like $\neg(\varphi \wedge \psi) \leftrightarrow (\neg\varphi \vee \neg\psi)$

1.4.2.2

(i)	Δ is S-inconsistent $\Leftrightarrow$	Definition 1.4.2(iv)
	not (Δ is S-consistent) $\Leftrightarrow$	Definition 1.4.2(i)
	not ($S \nvdash \neg\Delta$) $\Leftrightarrow$	$\neg\neg A = A$

$\mathbf{S} \vdash \neg\Delta \Leftrightarrow$ introductory remark of this exercise

$\mathbf{S} \vdash \Delta \to \bot$

(ii) The set Δ is finite, say $\Delta = \{\delta_1, \ldots, \delta_n\}$. Now:

$\Delta \cup \{\varphi\}$ is **S**-inconsistent $\Leftrightarrow$ item (i)

$\mathbf{S} \vdash (\Delta \cup \{\varphi\}) \to \bot \Leftrightarrow$ definition Δ

$\mathbf{S} \vdash (\delta_1 \wedge \delta_2 \wedge \ldots \wedge \delta_n \wedge \varphi) \to \bot \Leftrightarrow$ $(A \wedge B) \to C \equiv A \to (B \to C)$

$\mathbf{S} \vdash (\delta_1 \wedge \delta_2 \wedge \ldots \wedge \delta_n) \to (\varphi \to \bot) \Leftrightarrow$ introductory remark of this exercise

$\mathbf{S} \vdash (\delta_1 \wedge \delta_2 \wedge \ldots \wedge \delta_n) \to \neg\varphi \Leftrightarrow$

$\mathbf{S} \vdash \Delta \to \neg\varphi$.

1.4.2.3 Assume that Φ is **S**-consistent, and suppose that Φ° is not **S**-consistent. Then, by Definition 1.4.2, there is some finite set $\Delta \subseteq \Phi^\circ$ that is **S**-inconsistent, so that $\mathbf{S} \vdash \neg\Delta$. By definition of Φ°, we have $\{A1, R1\} \vdash \Phi \to \Delta$. Since the logic **S** contains A1 and R1, we also have $\mathbf{S} \vdash \Phi \to \Delta$. We thus conclude $\mathbf{S} \vdash \Phi \to (\neg\Delta \wedge \Delta)$, i.e. $\mathbf{S} \vdash \Phi \to \bot$, so that Φ is **S**-inconsistent, which contradicts the assumption.

1.4.3.1 $(\varphi \vee \psi) \in \Phi \Leftrightarrow$ definition '$\vee$'

$\neg(\neg\varphi \wedge \neg\psi) \in \Phi \Leftrightarrow$ 1.4.3(ii)(1)

$(\neg\varphi \wedge \neg\psi) \notin \Phi \Leftrightarrow$ 1.4.3(ii)(2)

$\neg\varphi \notin \Phi$ or $\neg\psi \notin \Phi \Leftrightarrow$ 1.4.3(ii)(1)

$\varphi \in \Phi$ or $\psi \in \Phi$.

1.4.3.2 Suppose Φ is maximally **S**-consistent, and $\mathbf{S} \vdash \varphi$. If $\varphi \notin \Phi$, then, by item 1 of Lemma 1.4.3.(ii), $\neg\varphi \in \Phi$. But then $\Phi \vdash_{\mathbf{S}} \neg\varphi \wedge \varphi$, contradicting our assumption that Φ is **S**-consistent.

1.4.3.3 Let us assume the parts 3 and 4 of Lemma 1.4.3(ii). First we prove the '$\Rightarrow$' part. Let Φ be any **S**-maximal consistent set. Since **S** contains A1 and R1, we know that $\mathbf{S} \vdash (\varphi \wedge \psi) \to \varphi$ and, by part 4, $((\varphi \wedge \psi) \to \varphi) \in \Phi$. Now, if also $(\varphi \wedge \psi) \in \Phi$, we use part 3 to conclude that $\varphi \in \Phi$. In the same way, we see that $\psi \in \Phi$, if $(\varphi \wedge \psi) \in \Phi$. To prove the '$\Leftarrow$'part, suppose that $\varphi, \psi \in \Phi$. Now we observe that $\mathbf{S} \vdash \varphi \to (\psi \to (\varphi \wedge \psi))$, so, by part 4, $(\varphi \to (\psi \to (\varphi \wedge \psi))) \in \Phi$. Using $\varphi \in \Phi$ and part 3, we see that $(\psi \to (\varphi \wedge \psi)) \in \Phi$ and now, combining $\psi \in \Phi$ with part 3, we have that $(\varphi \wedge \psi) \in \Phi$.

1.4.8.1

(i) Let $\Theta = \{K_ip, K_i\neg p\}$. From Theorem 1.4.6, we know that $\mathbf{K_{(m)}}$ is sound with respect to all Kripke models $\mathcal{K}_{(m)}$: $\mathbf{K_{(m)}} \vdash \varphi \Rightarrow \mathcal{K}_{(m)} \models \varphi$. The set Θ is satisfiable, since it is true in a state s having no R_i-successors. Thus $\mathcal{K}_{(m)} \not\models \Theta \to \bot$, and hence $\mathbf{K_{(m)}} \nvdash \Theta \to \bot$, implying that Θ is $\mathbf{K_{(m)}}$-consistent. But, of course, $\Theta/K_i = \{p, \neg p\}$ is not consistent: $\mathbf{K_{(m)}} \vdash (p \wedge \neg p) \to \bot$.

(ii) Let Θ be maximally consistent such that Θ/K_i is inconsistent. This implies that some finite subset of Θ, say $\varphi_1, \ldots, \varphi_k$, is inconsistent, i.e. $\mathbf{K_{(m)}} \vdash \varphi_1 \wedge \ldots \wedge \varphi_k \to \bot$. But then also $\mathbf{K_{(m)}} \vdash \varphi_1 \wedge \ldots \wedge \varphi_k \wedge \neg\varphi \to \bot$, i.e., the set $\{\varphi_1, \ldots, \varphi_k, \neg\varphi\}$ is inconsistent as well, for any formula φ. Now we can mimic the proof of case 4 of Lemma 1.4.8, with the arbitrary formula φ instead of ψ, to obtain $K_i\varphi \in \Theta$.

1.4.8.2 Suppose that $\mathbf{S} \vdash \varphi$. By Lemma 1.4.3(ii)(4), we see that $\varphi \in \Phi$, for each maximal **S**-consistent set Φ. Now let s_Θ be any world of the canonical model M^c. In particular, we know that $\varphi \in \Theta$. By the claim in the proof of Theorem 1.4.7, we have $(\mathbb{M}^c, s_\Theta) \models \varphi$. Since s_Θ was arbitrary, we have $\mathbb{M}^c \models \varphi$.

1.4.8.3 By applying contraposition to Theorem 1.4.6 (soundness of $\mathbf{K_{(m)}}$ for $\mathcal{K}_{(m)}$) we know that $\mathcal{K}_{(m)} \not\models \varphi \Rightarrow \mathbf{K_{(m)}} \nvdash \varphi$. Thus, to show that $\mathbf{K_{(m)}} \nvdash \varphi$ for a given φ, it is sufficient to show that $\mathcal{K}_{(m)} \not\models \varphi$, which is equivalent to showing that $\neg\varphi$ is satisfied in some model $\mathbb{M}$ of $\mathcal{K}_{(m)}$. Moreover, to show that e.g. $\mathbf{K_{(m)}} \nvdash K_i(\varphi \vee \psi) \to (K_i\varphi \vee K_i\psi)$, it is sufficient to find a model that satisfies the negation $K_i(\varphi \vee \psi) \wedge \neg(K_i\varphi \vee K_i\psi)$ for *some instantiation* for φ and ψ.
For the cases of $K_i(\varphi \vee \psi) \to (K_i\varphi \vee K_i\psi)$ and $(K_i\neg\varphi \to \neg K_i\varphi)$ we refer to Exercise 1.3.5.3, item (iii) and (vii), respectively.
To show that $\mathbf{K_{(m)}} \nvdash (M_i\varphi \wedge M_i\psi) \to M_i(\varphi \wedge \psi)$, we choose p for φ, and $\neg p$ for ψ. Let s be such that R_ist and R_isu hold, and $\pi(t)(p) = t$, $\pi(u)(p) = f$. The reader may verify that $(\mathbb{M}, s) \models (M_ip \wedge M_i\neg p) \wedge \neg M_i(p \wedge \neg p)$

1.4.9.1 We claim that all sets of formulas of this exercise are satisfiable; moreover, in the model below, the set of item (i) is true in state i, the set of item (ii) in state ii, and so on. Note that, since P = {p}, at the atomic level, we only have to distinguish p- and $\neg$p-worlds.

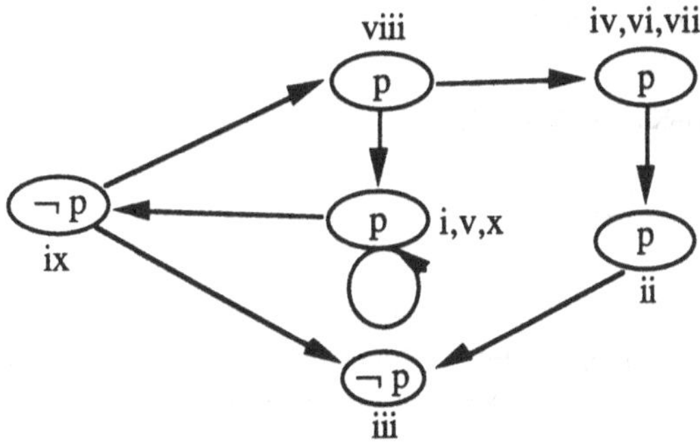

1.4.9.2 We claim that only the set given at (v), (vi), (viii) and (x) are inconsistent. The other sets are satisfied in the model below: the set of (i) is true in world i, and so on.

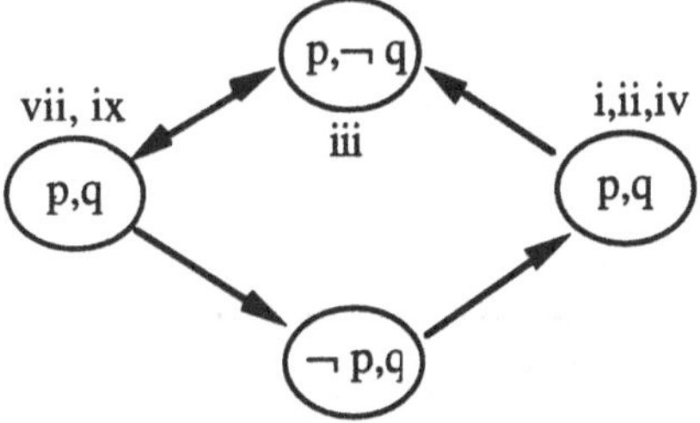

We proceed by showing that, for all sets Σ of items (v), (vi), (viii) and (x), there is some $\Delta \subseteq \Sigma$ such that $\mathbf{K_{(m)}} \vdash \Delta \to \bot$.

(v)	1	$(p \vee q) \to (\neg q \to p)$	(A1)
	2	$K(p \vee q) \to K(\neg q \to p)$	(KD; 1)
	3	$(K(p \vee q) \wedge \neg Kp \wedge K\neg q) \to (K(\neg q \to p) \wedge \neg Kp \wedge K\neg q)$	(LR; 2)
	4	$(K(\neg q \to p) \wedge K\neg q) \to Kp$	(A2')

	5	$(K(\neg q \to p) \wedge \neg Kp \wedge K\neg q) \to (Kp \wedge \neg Kp)$	(LR; 4)
	6	$(Kp \wedge \neg Kp) \to \bot$	(A1)
	7	$(K(\neg q \to p) \wedge \neg Kp \wedge K\neg q) \to \bot$	(HS; 5,6)

(vi)	1	$(p \wedge q) \to p$	(A1)
	2	$K(p \wedge q) \to Kp$	(KD; 1)
	3	$(K(p \wedge q) \wedge \neg Kp) \to (Kp \wedge \neg Kp)$	(LR; 2)
	4	$(Kp \wedge \neg Kp) \to \bot$	(A1)
	5	$(K(p \wedge q) \wedge \neg Kp) \to \bot$	(HS; 3,4)

(viii)	1	$(K(p \to q) \wedge Kp) \to Kq$	(A2')
	2	$(K(p \to q) \wedge Kp \wedge \neg Kq) \to (Kq \wedge \neg Kq)$	(LR; 2)
	3	$(Kq \wedge \neg Kq) \to \bot$	(A1)
	4	$(K(p \to q) \wedge Kp \wedge \neg Kq) \to \bot$	(HS; 2,3)

(x)	1	$p \to (\neg p \to q)$	(A1)
	2	$Kp \to K(\neg p \to q)$	(D; 1)
	3	$(Kp \wedge K\neg p) \to (K(\neg p \to q) \wedge K\neg p)$	(LR; 2)
	4	$(K(\neg p \to q) \wedge K\neg p) \to Kq$	(A2')
	5	$(Kp \wedge K\neg p) \to Kq$	(HS; 3,4)
	6	$(Kp \wedge K\neg p \wedge \neg Kq) \to (Kq \wedge \neg Kq)$	(LR; 5)
	7	$(Kq \wedge \neg Kq) \to \bot$	(A1)
	8	$(Kp \wedge K\neg p \wedge \neg Kq) \to \bot$	(HS; 6,7)

1.5.0.1 Note that axiom (A5) is an axiom *scheme*, that is: $\neg K_i\varphi \to K_i\neg K_i\varphi$ for *all* formulas φ. In particular, it is a property for the formula $\neg\varphi$, giving $\neg K_i\neg\varphi \to K_i\neg K_i\neg\varphi$. Now using the property that $\neg K_i\neg\varphi \equiv M_i\varphi$, we immediately obtain $M_i\varphi \to K_iM_i\varphi$.

1.5.1.1 REMARK. Since all the logics in this section are extensions of **K(m)**, we may use all previously derived formulas and rules. Moreover, in the following, we omit the symbol '$\vdash$' before derived theorems or axiom.

(i)	1	$\bot \to K\bot$	(A1)
	2	$K\bot \to \bot$	(A3)
	3	$K\bot \leftrightarrow \bot$	(EI; 1,2)

This is not derivable in $\mathbf{K}_{(m)}$, since $(K\bot \wedge \neg\bot)$ (which is equivalent to $K\bot$) is satisfied in any world $(\mathbb{M}, s)$ for which there is no t for which Rst.

(ii)	1	$K_i\neg\varphi \to \neg\varphi$	(A3)
	2	$K_i\varphi \to \varphi$	(A3)
	3	$\neg\varphi \to \neg K_i\varphi$	(CP; 2)
	4	$K_i\neg\varphi \to \neg K_i\varphi$	(HS;1, 3)

1.5.1.2

(i)	1	$K\neg\varphi \to \neg\varphi$	(A3)

	3	$\neg\neg\varphi \to \neg K\neg\varphi$	(CP; 1)
	4	$\varphi \leftrightarrow \neg\neg\varphi$	(A1)
	5	$\varphi \to \neg K\neg\varphi$	(SUB; 2, 3)
(ii)	1	$K\varphi \to \varphi$	(A3)
	2	$K\varphi \to \neg K\neg\varphi$	(HS; 1, item (i))
(iii)	1	$K\neg K\neg\varphi \to \neg K\neg\varphi$	(A3)
	2	$\neg K\neg\varphi \to K\neg K\neg\varphi$	(A5)
	3	$K\neg K\neg\varphi \leftrightarrow \neg K\neg\varphi$	(EI; 1,2)
(iv)	1	$\neg K\varphi \to K\neg K\varphi$	(A5)
	2	$K\neg K\varphi \to \neg K\varphi$	(A3)
	3	$\neg K\varphi \leftrightarrow K\neg K\varphi$	(EI; 1,2)
(v)	1	$\neg K\varphi \to K\neg K\varphi$	(A5)
	2	$\neg K\neg K\varphi \to \neg\neg K\varphi$	(CP; 1)
	3	$\neg\neg K\varphi \leftrightarrow K\varphi$	(A1)
	4	$\neg K\neg K\varphi \to K\varphi$	(SUB; 2,3)
	5	$K\neg K\varphi \to \neg K\varphi$	(A3)
	6	$\neg\neg K\varphi \to \neg K\neg K\varphi$	(CP; 5)
	7	$K\varphi \to \neg K\neg K\varphi$	(SUB; 6,3)
	8	$K\varphi \leftrightarrow \neg K\neg K\varphi$	(EI; 4,7)
(vi)	1	$K\varphi \leftrightarrow \neg K\neg K\varphi$	(item (v), for which we did not use A4)
	2	$KK\varphi \leftrightarrow K\neg K\neg K\varphi$	($KD^{\leftrightarrow}$; 1)
	3	$\neg K\neg K\varphi \to K\neg K\neg K\varphi$	(A5)
	4	$K\neg K\neg K\varphi \to \neg K\neg K\varphi$	(A3)
	5	$K\neg K\neg K\varphi \leftrightarrow \neg K\neg K\varphi$	(EI; 3,4)
	6	$KK\varphi \leftrightarrow \neg K\neg K\varphi$	($HS^{\leftrightarrow}$; 2,5)
	7	$K\varphi \leftrightarrow KK\varphi$	($HS^{\leftrightarrow}$; 1,6)
(vii)	1	$KK\neg\varphi \to K\neg\varphi$	(A3)
	2	$(\neg K\neg\varphi \wedge KK\neg\varphi) \to (\neg K\neg\varphi \wedge K\neg\varphi)$	(LR; 1)
	3	$(\neg K\neg\varphi \wedge K\neg\varphi) \to \bot$	(A1)
	4	$(\neg K\neg\varphi \wedge KK\neg\varphi) \to \bot$	(HS; 2,3)
	5	$\neg K\neg\varphi \to \neg KK\neg\varphi$	(NC; 4)
(viii)	1	$\neg\bot$	(A1)
	2	$K\neg\bot$	(R2; 1)
(ix)	1	$(\varphi \to \psi) \to (\neg\psi \to \neg\varphi)$	(A1)
	2	$K(\varphi \to \psi) \to K(\neg\psi \to \neg\varphi)$	(KD; 1)
	3	$(K\neg\psi \wedge K(\varphi \to \psi)) \to (K\neg\psi \wedge K(\neg\psi \to \neg\varphi))$	(LR; 2)
	4	$(K\neg\psi \wedge K(\neg\psi \to \neg\varphi)) \to K\neg\varphi$	(A2')
	5	$(K\neg\psi \wedge K(\varphi \to \psi)) \to K\neg\varphi$	(HS; 3,4)

	6	$(\neg K\neg\varphi \wedge K(\varphi \to \psi) \wedge K\neg\psi) \to (\neg K\neg\varphi \wedge K\neg\varphi)$	(LR; 5)
	7	$(\neg K\neg\varphi \wedge K\neg\varphi) \to \bot$	(A1)
	8	$(\neg K\neg\varphi \wedge K(\varphi \to \psi) \wedge K\neg\psi) \to \bot$	(HS; 6,7)
	9	$(\neg K\neg\varphi \wedge K(\varphi \to \psi)) \to \neg K\neg\psi$	(NC; 8)
(x)	1	$\neg K\neg K\varphi \leftrightarrow K\varphi$	(item (v))
	2	$K\neg K\neg K\varphi \leftrightarrow KK\varphi$	(K-SUB; 1)
	3	$K\varphi \leftrightarrow KK\varphi$	(item (vi))
	4	$K\neg K\neg K\varphi \leftrightarrow K\varphi$	($HS^{\leftrightarrow}$; 2,3)
(xi)	1	$\neg K\neg K\neg K\psi \leftrightarrow \neg K\psi$	(SUB; item (x))
	2	$\neg K\neg K\neg K\neg\varphi \leftrightarrow \neg K\neg\varphi$	(SUB; 1)
(xii)	1	$(K(\varphi \to K\varphi) \wedge \neg K\neg\varphi) \to \neg K\neg K\varphi$	(item (ix))
	2	$\neg K\neg K\varphi \to K\varphi$	(item (v).10)
	3	$(K(\varphi \to K\varphi) \wedge \neg K\neg\varphi) \to K\varphi$	(HS; 1,2)

1.6.2.1

(i) Suppose $(s, t) \in R$ and $(s, u) \in R$. By symmetry, we have $(t, s) \in R$. Using transitivity of R, together with $(t, s), (s, u) \in R$, we conclude that $(t, u) \in R$.

(ii) If R is reflexive, we have that $(s, s) \in R$ for any s. So, immediately we have that for every s there exists a t such that $(s, t) \in R$ (namely s itself).

(iii) We show the three equivalences in a cyclic way: first ⇒ second ⇒ third ⇒ first.
'first ⇒ second': Suppose R is symmetrical, transitive and serial, and let $s \in S$. By seriality, there is some $t \in S$ with $(s, t) \in R$. By symmetry, then also $(t, s) \in R$. Transitivity then yields $(s, s) \in R$, so that R is reflexive. The euclidicity of R follows from item (i) of this exercise.
'second ⇒ third': Suppose reflexivity and euclidicity of R. We only have to show that R is symmetrical and transitive. To show symmetry, suppose $(s, t) \in R$. Since R is reflexive, we also have $(s, s) \in R$. Euclidicity now immediately yields $(t, s) \in R$. To show transitivity, suppose both (s, t) and $(t, u) \in R$. By symmetry, we also have (t, s) and $(t, u) \in R$. Euclidicity now yields $(s, u) \in R$.
'third ⇒ first': Suppose R is an equivalence relation, i.e. reflexive, transitive and symmetrical. Since, by item (ii) of this exercise, reflexivity implies seriality, we are done.

1.6.3.1 Since both R_A and R_B are reflexive, $\mathbb{M} \in \mathcal{T}_{(2)}$. The relations are moreover both transitive, so that $\mathbb{M} \in \mathcal{S4}_{(2)}$. However, R_A is not euclidean: although both $(s_1, s_4) \in R$ and $(s_1, s_2) \in R$, we do not have $(s_4, s_2) \in R$. Hence $\mathbb{M} \notin \mathcal{S5}_{(2)}$.

1.6.4.1 Suppose $\mathbb{M} = \langle S, \pi, R_1, \ldots, R_m \rangle$ is a $\mathcal{T}$-model. In particular, the R_i's are reflexive. Let $s \in S$, and φ such that $(\mathbb{M}, s) \models K_i\varphi$. Then, for all t such that $(s, t) \in R_i$, we have $(\mathbb{M}, t) \models \varphi$. But then, reflexivity of R_i guarantees $(\mathbb{M}, s) \models \varphi$, which proves $(\mathbb{M}, s) \models K_i\varphi \to \varphi$. Since $\mathbb{M}$ and s were arbitrary (in $\mathcal{T}$), we have $\mathcal{T}_{(m)} \models$ (A3).
Now suppose that $\mathbb{M} = \langle S, \pi, R_1, \ldots, R_m \rangle$ is an $\mathcal{S4}_{(m)}$-model. We have again that $\mathbb{M} \models$ (A3). To show that moreover $\mathbb{M} \models$ (A4), let $s \in S$ and φ be any epistemic formula for which $(\mathbb{M}, s) \models K_i\varphi$, saying that for all $x \in S$ for which $(s, x) \in R_i$, we have $(\mathbb{M}, x) \models \varphi$ (*). In order to show that $(\mathbb{M}, s) \models K_iK_i\varphi$, let t be such that $(s, t) \in R_i$. Subsequently, in order to show that $(\mathbb{M}, t) \models K_i\varphi$,

suppose $(t, u) \in R_i$. By transitivity of R_i, we have $(s, u) \in R_i$. By (*), we observe that $(\mathbb{M}, u) \models \varphi$, which completes the proof.

1.6.7.1 In the following, $\mathbb{M}$ is an arbitrary $\mathcal{S5}_{(1)}$-model, and s a state in $\mathbb{M}$.

(i) Here, reflexivity of R is important. Suppose $(\mathbb{M}, s) \models \varphi$. Since Rss holds, it cannot be the case that all R-successors of s verify $\neg\varphi$, hence $(\mathbb{M}, s) \models \neg K\neg\varphi$.

(ii) We use reflexivity of R again: suppose $(\mathbb{M}, s) \models K\varphi$. Since R is reflexive, we find $(\mathbb{M}, s) \models \varphi$ and, by the argument given in (i), $(\mathbb{M}, s) \models \neg K\neg\varphi$.

(iii) Relating K to the $\forall$-quantifier, and $\neg K\neg = M$ to the $\exists$-quantifier, we see that the modal formula $K\neg K\neg\varphi \leftrightarrow \neg K\neg\varphi$ is true in a state s, if at s, it holds that

$$\forall t(Rst \Rightarrow \exists u(Rtu \text{ and } (\mathbb{M}, u) \models \varphi)) \Leftrightarrow \exists u(Rsu \text{ and } (\mathbb{M}, u) \models \varphi).$$

In this equivalence, the '$\Rightarrow$'-direction is guaranteed by reflexivity, and the '$\Leftarrow$'-direction by euclidicity.

(iv) One can use the same argument as in item (iii); replacing φ by $\neg\varphi$ does not affect it.

(v) We see that the modal formula is true at s if

$$\exists t(Rst \text{ and } \forall u(Rtu \Rightarrow (\mathbb{M}, u) \models \varphi)) \Leftrightarrow \forall v(Rsv \Rightarrow (\mathbb{M}, v) \models \varphi)$$

The '$\Leftarrow$'-direction is guaranteed by reflexivity, and the '$\Rightarrow$'-direction by euclidicity, which is seen as follows. Suppose $\exists t(Rst \text{ and } \forall u(Rtu \Rightarrow (\mathbb{M}, u) \models \varphi))$. Take any v with Rsv. By euclidicity we have Rtv, and by our assumption we get $(\mathbb{M}, v) \models \varphi$.

(vi) Since R is reflexive (at s), we obviously have $KK\varphi \rightarrow K\varphi$ (in s). Suppose $(\mathbb{M}, s) \models K\varphi$, saying that φ is true in all t for which Rst. Now suppose Rsu and Ruv. By transivity we have Rsv, so $(\mathbb{M}, v) \models \varphi$. This proves that $(\mathbb{M}, s) \models K\varphi \rightarrow KK\varphi$.

(vii) Note that the modal formula is equivalent with $K\varphi \leftrightarrow KK\varphi$ (replace $\neg\varphi$ by φ) in (vi) and use contraposition. Hence we can argue as in (vi).

(viii) This is not related to a property of R: in all R-successors t of s (whether they exist or not) we have $(\mathbb{M}, t) \not\models \bot$, so $(\mathbb{M}, t) \models \neg\bot$.

(ix) The formula is true, since, if s has an R-successor in which φ is true, and in all successors of s it is the case that $(\varphi \rightarrow \psi)$ is true, then there must be an R-successor of s in which ψ is true.

(x) We have to show that $(\mathbb{M}, s) \models KMK\varphi \leftrightarrow K\varphi$. Suppose $(\mathbb{M}, s) \models KMK\varphi$. Then, $\forall t(Rst \Rightarrow \exists u(Rtu \text{ and } \forall v(Ruv \Rightarrow (\mathbb{M}, v) \models \varphi)))$. Let x be any state with Rsx. We know that there is some u with Rxu and $\forall v(Ruv \Rightarrow (\mathbb{M}, v) \models \varphi)$. Since R is symmetric, we have in particular Rux, so $(\mathbb{M}, x) \models \varphi$.

Conversely, suppose $(\mathbb{M}, s) \models K\varphi$, i.e. all t with Rst satisfy φ. Let u be such that Rsu. By symmetry, Rus, so u is R-accessible to a state (namely s) in which $K\varphi$ is true. Since u was arbitrary, we have proved $(\mathbb{M}, s) \models KMK\varphi$.

(xi) Use (x) and contraposition.

(xii) Suppose $(\mathbb{M}, s) \models K(\varphi \rightarrow K\varphi) \wedge \neg K\neg\varphi$. It expresses that s has an R-successor t in which φ is true, and that in all successors of s the formula $(\varphi \rightarrow K\varphi)$ holds. Thus, in particular, we have $(\mathbb{M}, t) \models K\varphi$. Now, let u be (arbitrary) such that Rsu. By euclidicity, since Rst and Rsu, we also have Rtu, so that $(\mathbb{M}, u) \models \varphi$. This proves $(\mathbb{M}, s) \models K\varphi$.

1.6.7.2 Let us denote the logic which arises from **S5** by removing the axiom (A4), by **S5'**. Leaving out (A4) from the axioms of **S5** does of course not affect its soundness with respect to $\mathcal{S5}$-models. But let us now have a look at the canonical model $\mathbb{M}^c$ for the logic **S5'**. From Proposition 1.6.5, we see that $\mathbb{M}^c$ must be both reflexive and euclidean. By Proposition 1.6.2(iii) it then also must be transitive. Thus the **S5'** is complete with respect to $\mathcal{S5}$-models. Thus, we have: $\vdash_{\mathbf{S5}} \varphi \Leftrightarrow \mathcal{S5} \models \varphi$

$\Leftrightarrow \vdash_{S5'} \varphi$, so that $\vdash_{S5'}$ (A4).

1.6.7.3 REMARK. Let **X** be any of the mentioned logics. We recall that a formula φ is consistent in **X** iff it is satisfiable in the class of *models for X*! In particular, note that
Σ is **S5**-consistent $\Rightarrow$ Σ is **S4**-consistent $\Rightarrow$ Σ is **T**-consistent $\Rightarrow$ Σ is **K**-consistent, and
Σ is **K**-inconsistent $\Rightarrow$ Σ is **T**-inconsistent $\Rightarrow$ Σ is **S4**-inconsistent $\Rightarrow$ Σ is **S5**-inconsistent
In the answers, we only give the strongest of these statements that hold; moreover, we will not always specify the models in detail: when we give a model, we implicitly claim that the given set of formulas is true in (𝕄, s), and omit an explicit definition of S. Moreover, we will use an abbreviated (but self-explanatory) format to derive $\bot$ from Σ in any logic **X** when Σ is **X**-inconsistent (**X** $\in$ {**T**, **S4**, **S5**}).

The sets of Exercise 1.4.9.1:

(i) **S5**-consistent; let R = {s, t} × {s, t}; p only true in s (and not in t).
(ii) **T**-inconsistent: $(p \wedge K\neg p) \Rightarrow_{A3} (p \wedge \neg p) \Rightarrow_{A1} \bot$.
(iii) **T**-inconsistent: $(Kp \wedge K\neg p) \Rightarrow_{A3} (p \wedge \neg p) \Rightarrow_{A1} \bot$.
(iv) **S5**-consistent: let R = {(s, s)}, p true in s.
(v) **S5**-consistent: let R = {s, t} × {s,t}; p only true in s (and not in t).
(vi) **S4**-inconsistent: $(Kp \wedge \neg KKp) \Rightarrow_{A4} (KKp \wedge \neg KKp) \Rightarrow_{A1} \bot$;
T-consistent: R = {(s, s), (s, t), (t, t), (t, u), (u, u)}, p only true in s and t.
(vii) **T**-inconsistent: $(Kp \wedge K\neg Kp) \Rightarrow_{A3} (Kp \wedge \neg Kp) \Rightarrow_{A1} \bot$.
(viii) **S5**-consistent: let R = {(s, s)}, p true in s.
(ix) **S5**-inconsistent: $(\neg K\neg Kp \wedge \neg p) \Rightarrow_{\text{Exercise 1.5.1.2(v)}} (Kp \wedge \neg p) \Rightarrow_{A3} (p \wedge \neg p) \Rightarrow_{A1} \bot$
S4-consistent: let R = {(s, s), (s, t), (t, t)}; p true only in t.
(x) **S5**-consistent: let R = {s, t} × {s, t}; p only true in s.

The sets of Exercise 1.4.9.2:

(i) **S5**-consistent: let R = {s, t} × {s,t}; p, q true in s; p, ¬q true in t.
(ii) **S5**-inconsistent: $(\neg Kq \wedge \neg K\neg Kq) \Rightarrow_{A5} (\neg Kq \wedge K\neg Kq) \Rightarrow_{A1} \bot$
S4-consistent: let R = {(s, s), (s, t), (t, t), (t, u), (u, u), (s, u)}, p true in s, t and u; q true only in s and t.
(iii) **S5**-consistent: let R = {(s, s)}, p and q true in s.
(iv) **S5**-consistent: let R = {(s, s)}, p and ¬q true in s.
(v) **K**-inconsistent (cf. Exercise 1.4.9.2) and hence inconsistent for all extensions.
(vi) **K**-inconsistent (cf. Exercise 1.4.9.2).
(vii) **T**-inconsistent: $(K(Kp \wedge Kq) \wedge \neg Kp) \Rightarrow_{A3} (Kp \wedge Kq \wedge \neg Kp) \Rightarrow_{A1} \bot$.
(viii) **K**-inconsistent (cf. Exercise 1.4.9.2).
(ix) **S5**-inconsistent: $(\neg Kp \wedge \neg K\neg p \wedge K(p \rightarrow Kp)) \Rightarrow_{\text{Exercise 1.5.1.2(ix)}} (\neg Kp \wedge \neg K\neg Kp) \Rightarrow_{A5}$ $(K\neg Kp \wedge \neg K\neg Kp) \Rightarrow_{A1} \bot$.
(x) **K**-inconsistent (cf. Exercise 1.4.9.2).

1.6.7.4 For notational conventions regarding the truth of a formula in (𝕄, s): see Remark at Exercise 1.6.7.3. Moreover, recall from Exercise 1.3.0.2 that $(\mathbb{M}, s) \models \neg K\neg\varphi \Leftrightarrow$ there is some u with (s, u) $\in$ R and $(\mathbb{M}, u) \models \varphi$.

(i) Not even valid in *S5*: let R = {s, t} × {s, t}, p true only in s, then $(\mathbb{M}, s) \models \neg(p \rightarrow Kp)$
(ii) Not valid in *S4;* let R = {(s, s), (s, t), (t, t), (t, u), (u, u)}, p true only in s, then $(\mathbb{M}, s) \models \neg(p \rightarrow$

$K\neg K\neg p$).

However, the formula *is* valid in *S5*: let $\mathbb{M}$ be any *S5*-model, with state s, and suppose $(\mathbb{M}, s) \models \varphi$. Let u be arbitrary, with $(s, u) \in R$. Since R is symmetric, also $(u, s) \in R$, so $(\mathbb{M}, u) \models \neg K\neg\varphi$, and hence $(\mathbb{M}, s) \models \varphi \rightarrow K\neg K\neg\varphi$.

(iii) Valid in *T* already; suppose $\mathbb{M} \in T$ and $(\mathbb{M}, s) \models K\varphi$, that is, for all u with $(s, u) \in R$, $(\mathbb{M}, u) \models \varphi$. Since R is reflexive, $(s, s) \in R$, so s has an R-successor that verifies φ: $(\mathbb{M}, s) \models \neg K\neg\varphi$.

(iv) Not even valid in *S5*; let $R = \{s, t\} \times \{s, t\}$, p true only in s. Then $(\mathbb{M}, s) \models \neg(\neg Kp \rightarrow K\neg p)$.

(v) Valid in *T* already; suppose $\mathbb{M} \in T$ and $(\mathbb{M}, s) \models K\neg\varphi$, saying that all R-successors of s (including s itself) verify $\neg\varphi$; now, if at the same time we would have $(\mathbb{M}, s) \models K\varphi$, all R-successors (including s) would also verify φ, so that, in particular, we would have $(\mathbb{M}, s) \models \varphi \wedge \neg\varphi$, which is impossible. Thus $(\mathbb{M}, s) \models K\neg\varphi \rightarrow \neg K\varphi$.

(vi) Not even valid in *S5*: let $R = \{s, t\} \times \{s, t\}$, p true only in s. Then $(\mathbb{M}, s) \models \neg(K\neg p \vee Kp)$.

(vii) Valid in *T* already; suppose $\mathbb{M} \in T$ and $(\mathbb{M}, s) \models (\varphi \wedge K(\varphi \rightarrow K\varphi))$, i.e. in s both φ and $K(\varphi \rightarrow K\varphi)$ are true. Since $(s, s) \in R$ we have that s verifies both φ and $(\varphi \rightarrow K\varphi)$; but then we immediately conclude that $(\mathbb{M}, s) \models K\varphi$.

1.7.2.1 Let $\mathbb{M}$ and $\mathbb{M}'$ be as in Proposition 1.7.2. We will prove a stronger statement than just $(\mathbb{M}, s) \equiv (\mathbb{M}', s)$, i.e. we show that

$$\text{for all } t \in S'\text{: } (\mathbb{M}, t) \models \varphi \Leftrightarrow (\mathbb{M}', t) \models \varphi. \tag{1}$$

Proof. Using induction on the complexity of φ. If φ is atomic, say p, then, by the fact that π' is just the restriction of π to the states in S', we have that $(\mathbb{M}, t) \models p \Leftrightarrow (\mathbb{M}', t) \models p$ for all $t \in S'$. Now suppose that (1) holds for both φ_1 and φ_2, and let $\varphi = (\varphi_1 \wedge \varphi_2)$ and $t \in S'$. Then

$(\mathbb{M}, t) \models \varphi \Leftrightarrow (\mathbb{M}, t) \models \varphi_1$ and $(\mathbb{M}, t) \models \varphi_2 \Leftrightarrow (\mathbb{M}', t) \models \varphi_1$ and $(\mathbb{M}', t) \models \varphi_2 \Leftrightarrow (\mathbb{M}', t) \models \varphi$.

Also, if $\varphi = \neg\varphi_1$, then

$(\mathbb{M}, t) \models \neg\varphi \Leftrightarrow$ not $(\mathbb{M}, t) \models \varphi \Leftrightarrow$ not $(\mathbb{M}', t) \models \varphi \Leftrightarrow (\mathbb{M}', t) \models \neg\varphi$.

Finally, suppose $\varphi = K\varphi_1$ and $t \in S'$, i.e. $(s, t) \in R$. Note that, since R is an equivalence relation, we have, for all $u \in S$: $((t, u) \in R \Leftrightarrow (s, u) \in R)$ (*). Then

$(\mathbb{M}, t) \models K\varphi_1 \Leftrightarrow$	td of K
for all $u \in S$ such that $(t, u) \in R$, $(\mathbb{M}, u) \models \varphi_1 \Leftrightarrow$	(*)
for all $u \in S$ such that $(s, u) \in R$, $(\mathbb{M}, u) \models \varphi_1 \Leftrightarrow$	definition of S'
for all $u \in S'$, $(\mathbb{M}, u) \models \varphi_1 \Leftrightarrow$	induction hypothesis
for all $u \in S'$, $(\mathbb{M}', u) \models \varphi_1 \Leftrightarrow$	definition of R'
for all $u \in S'$ such that $(t, u) \in R'$, $(\mathbb{M}', u) \models \varphi_1 \Leftrightarrow$	td of K
$(\mathbb{M}', t) \models K\varphi_1$.	

1.7.6.3.1

a(ii) Let $\mathbb{M} = \langle S, \pi, R\rangle$ an arbitrary reduced *S5*-model, and $s \in S$. We will show that

$$(\mathbb{M}, s) \models K(\pi \vee (\lambda \wedge M\beta)) \leftrightarrow [(K(\pi \vee \lambda) \wedge M\beta) \vee (K\pi \wedge M\beta)] \tag{*}$$

To do so, we use the validity of

$$(\mathbb{M}, s) \models M\beta \vee \neg M\beta \tag{1}$$

to reason by cases, as follows.

Firstly, assume that

$$(\mathbb{M}, s) \models M\beta. \tag{2}$$

By Lemma 1.7.3(ii) we then know that $M\beta$ is true in all states of S. Since $((\pi \vee (\lambda \wedge M\beta)) \rightarrow (\pi$

$\vee \lambda)$ is a propositional tautology, the truth of $K(\pi \vee (\lambda \wedge M\beta))$ in s implies that of $K(\pi \vee \lambda)$ in s, so that we have:

$(\mathbb{M}, s) \models K(\pi \vee (\lambda \wedge M\beta)) \rightarrow K(\pi \vee \lambda) \wedge M\beta.$ (3)

For the converse, suppose that $(\mathbb{M}, s) \models K(\pi \vee \lambda) \wedge M\beta$. Again applying Lemma 1.7.3, we see that both $K(\pi \vee \lambda)$ and $M\beta$ are true in all t of S. But then also are $(\pi \vee \lambda)$ and $M\beta$ true in all t; so is $(\pi \vee \lambda) \wedge M\beta$ and the weaker $(\pi \vee (\lambda \wedge M\beta))$, implying $(\mathbb{M}, s) \models K(\pi \vee (\lambda \wedge M\beta))$;

$(\mathbb{M}, s) \models K(\pi \vee \lambda) \wedge M\beta \rightarrow K(\pi \vee (\lambda \wedge M\beta)).$ (4)

So that we conclude, from (2), (3) and (4):

$(\mathbb{M}, s) \models M\beta \rightarrow (K(\pi \vee (\lambda \wedge M\beta)) \leftrightarrow (K(\pi \vee \lambda) \wedge M\beta)).$ (5)

In the second case, we assume

$(\mathbb{M}, s) \models \neg M\beta$ (6)

and remember that $\neg M\beta = K\neg\beta$. Lemma 1.7.3(i) now gives us that $K\neg\beta$ is true in all worlds $u \in S$, and in particular $(\mathbb{M}, s) \models KK\neg\beta$, or $(\mathbb{M}, s) \models K\neg M\beta$. Now suppose $(\mathbb{M}, s) \models K(\pi \vee (\lambda \wedge M\beta))$. If $(s, t) \in R$, then both $(\mathbb{M}, t) \models \neg M\beta$ and $(\mathbb{M}, s) \models (\pi \vee (\lambda \wedge M\beta))$, so $(\mathbb{M}, t) \models \pi$, so that, with (6), we have for s:

$(\mathbb{M}, s) \models K(\pi \vee (\lambda \wedge M\beta)) \rightarrow (K\pi \wedge \neg M\beta).$ (7)

For the converse, since $\pi \rightarrow (\pi \vee \alpha)$ is a tautology, we also have

$(\mathbb{M}, s) \models (K\pi \wedge \neg M\beta) \rightarrow K(\pi \vee (\lambda \wedge M\beta))$ (8)

so that we obtain, from (6), (7) and (8):

$(\mathbb{M}, s) \models \neg M\beta \rightarrow (K(\pi \vee (\lambda \wedge M\beta)) \leftrightarrow (K\pi \wedge \neg M\beta)).$ (9)

Finally we use the propositional tautology

$[(p \rightarrow (q \leftrightarrow (p \wedge r)) \wedge (\neg p \rightarrow (q \leftrightarrow (\neg p \wedge s)))] \rightarrow [(q \leftrightarrow ((r \wedge p) \vee (s \wedge \neg p))]$

together with (5) and (9) to conclude (*).

b (i) We will prove, in $\mathbf{S5_{(1)}}$ that $\vdash K(\pi \vee (\lambda \wedge K\beta)) \leftrightarrow [(K(\pi \vee \lambda) \wedge K\beta) \vee (K\pi \wedge \neg K\beta)]$

1	$K\beta \rightarrow [(\pi \vee (\lambda \wedge K\beta)) \leftrightarrow ((\pi \vee \lambda) \wedge K\beta)]$	(A1)
2	$KK\beta \rightarrow K[(\pi \vee (\lambda \wedge K\beta)) \leftrightarrow ((\pi \vee \lambda) \wedge K\beta)]$	(KD, 1)
3	$K[(\pi \vee (\lambda \wedge K\beta)) \leftrightarrow ((\pi \vee \lambda) \wedge K\beta)] \rightarrow [K(\pi \vee (\lambda \wedge K\beta)) \leftrightarrow K((\pi \vee \lambda) \wedge K\beta)]$	(A2', twice)
4	$K\beta \rightarrow KK\beta$	(A4)
5	$K\beta \rightarrow [K(\pi \vee (\lambda \wedge K\beta)) \leftrightarrow K((\pi \vee \lambda) \wedge K\beta)]$	(HS, 4, 2, 3)
6	$K((\pi \vee \lambda) \wedge K\beta) \leftrightarrow (K(\pi \vee \lambda) \wedge KK\beta)$	(Exercise 1.4.1.1(i))
7	$K\beta \leftrightarrow KK\beta$	(A3, A4, A1)
8	$K((\pi \vee \lambda) \wedge K\beta) \leftrightarrow (K(\pi \vee \lambda) \wedge K\beta)$	(SUB, 6, 7)
9	$K\beta \rightarrow [K(\pi \vee (\lambda \wedge K\beta)) \leftrightarrow (K(\pi \vee \lambda) \wedge K\beta)]$	(SUB, 5, 8)
10	$\neg K\beta \rightarrow [(\pi \vee (\lambda \wedge K\beta)) \leftrightarrow (\pi \wedge \neg K\beta)]$	(A1)
11	$K\neg K\beta \rightarrow K[(\pi \vee (\lambda \wedge K\beta)) \leftrightarrow (\pi \wedge \neg K\beta)]$	(1, KD)
12	$K[(\pi \vee (\lambda \wedge K\beta)) \leftrightarrow (\pi \wedge \neg K\beta)] \rightarrow [K(\pi \vee (\lambda \wedge K\beta)) \leftrightarrow K(\pi \wedge \neg K\beta)]$	(A2', twice)
13	$\neg K\beta \rightarrow K\neg K\beta$	(A5)
14	$\neg K\beta \rightarrow [K(\pi \vee (\lambda \wedge K\beta)) \leftrightarrow K(\pi \wedge \neg K\beta)]$	(HS, 13, 11, 12)
15	$K(\pi \wedge \neg K\beta) \leftrightarrow (K\pi \wedge K\neg K\beta)$	(Exercise 1.4.1.1(i))
16	$\neg K\beta \leftrightarrow K\neg K\beta$	(A3, A5)
17	$K(\pi \wedge \neg K\beta) \leftrightarrow (K\pi \wedge \neg K\beta)$	(SUB, 15, 16)
18	$\neg K\beta \rightarrow [K(\pi \vee (\lambda \wedge K\beta)) \leftrightarrow (K\pi \wedge \neg K\beta)]$	(SUB, 14, 17)
19	$\{K\beta \rightarrow [K(\pi \vee (\lambda \wedge K\beta)) \leftrightarrow (K(\pi \vee \lambda) \wedge K\beta)]\} \wedge \{\neg K\beta \rightarrow [K(\pi \vee (\lambda \wedge K\beta)) \leftrightarrow (K\pi \wedge \neg K\beta)]\}$	(A1, 9, 18)

20 $\{p \to [q \leftrightarrow (r \wedge p)]\} \wedge \{\neg p \to [q \leftrightarrow (s \wedge \neg p)]\} \to$
$[(q \leftrightarrow ((r \wedge p) \vee (s \wedge \neg p))]$ (A1)

21 $\{K\beta \to [K(\pi \vee (\lambda \wedge K\beta)) \leftrightarrow (K(\pi \vee \lambda) \wedge K\beta)]\} \wedge \{\neg K\beta \to [K(\pi \vee (\lambda \wedge K\beta)) \leftrightarrow (K\pi \wedge \neg K\beta)]\} \to$
$[(K(\pi \vee (\lambda \wedge K\beta)) \leftrightarrow ((K(\pi \vee \lambda) \wedge K\beta) \vee (K\pi \wedge \neg K\beta))]$ (instantiation of 20)

22 $(K(\pi \vee (\lambda \wedge K\beta)) \leftrightarrow ((K(\pi \vee \lambda) \wedge K\beta) \vee (K\pi \wedge \neg K\beta))$ (R1, 19, 21)

(ii) We will prove, in $\mathbf{S5_{(1)}}$ that $\vdash K(\pi \vee (\lambda \wedge M\beta)) \leftrightarrow [(K(\pi \vee \lambda) \wedge M\beta) \vee (K\pi \wedge \neg M\beta)]$. Using the definition of M, and writing α for $\neg\beta$, this is the same as $\vdash K(\pi \vee (\lambda \wedge \neg K\alpha)) \leftrightarrow [(K(\pi \vee \lambda) \wedge \neg K\alpha) \vee (K\pi \wedge K\alpha)]$

1 $\neg K\alpha \to [(\pi \vee (\lambda \wedge \neg K\alpha)) \leftrightarrow ((\pi \vee \lambda) \wedge \neg K\alpha)]$ (A1)

2 $K\neg K\alpha \to K[(\pi \vee (\lambda \wedge \neg K\alpha)) \leftrightarrow ((\pi \vee \lambda) \wedge \neg K\alpha)]$ (KD, 1)

3 $K[(\pi \vee (\lambda \wedge \neg K\alpha)) \leftrightarrow ((\pi \vee \lambda) \wedge \neg K\alpha)] \to [K(\pi \vee (\lambda \wedge \neg K\alpha)) \leftrightarrow K((\pi \vee \lambda) \wedge \neg K\alpha)]$ (A2', twice)

4 $\neg K\alpha \to K\neg K\alpha$ (A5)

5 $\neg K\alpha \to [K(\pi \vee (\lambda \wedge \neg K\alpha)) \leftrightarrow K((\pi \vee \lambda) \wedge \neg K\alpha)]$ (HS, 4, 2, 3)

6 $K((\pi \vee \lambda) \wedge \neg K\alpha) \leftrightarrow (K(\pi \vee \lambda) \wedge K\neg K\alpha)$ (Exercise 1.4.1.1(i))

7 $\neg K\alpha \leftrightarrow K\neg K\alpha$ (A3, A5, A1)

8 $K((\pi \vee \lambda) \wedge \neg K\alpha) \leftrightarrow (K(\pi \vee \lambda) \wedge \neg K\alpha)$ (SUB, 6, 7)

9 $\neg K\alpha \to [K(\pi \vee (\lambda \wedge \neg K\alpha)) \leftrightarrow (K(\pi \vee \lambda) \wedge \neg K\alpha)]$ (SUB, 5, 8)

10 $K\alpha \to [(\pi \vee (\lambda \wedge \neg K\alpha)) \leftrightarrow (\pi \wedge K\alpha)]$ (A1)

11 $KK\alpha \to K[(\pi \vee (\lambda \wedge \neg K\alpha)) \leftrightarrow (\pi \wedge K\alpha)]$ (1, KD)

12 $K[(\pi \vee (\lambda \wedge \neg K\alpha)) \leftrightarrow (\pi \wedge K\alpha)] \to [K(\pi \vee (\lambda \wedge \neg K\alpha)) \leftrightarrow K(\pi \wedge K\alpha)]$ (A2', twice)

13 $K\alpha \to KK\alpha$ (A4)

14 $K\alpha \to [K(\pi \vee (\lambda \wedge \neg K\alpha)) \leftrightarrow K(\pi \wedge K\alpha)]$ (HS, 13, 11, 12)

15 $K(\pi \wedge K\alpha) \leftrightarrow (K\pi \wedge KK\alpha)$ (Exercise 1.4.1.1(i))

16 $K\alpha \leftrightarrow KK\alpha$ (A3, A4)

17 $K(\pi \wedge K\alpha) \leftrightarrow (K\pi \wedge K\alpha)$ (SUB, 15, 16)

18 $K\alpha \to [K(\pi \vee (\lambda \wedge \neg K\alpha)) \leftrightarrow (K\pi \wedge K\alpha)]$ (SUB, 14, 17)

19 $\{\neg K\alpha \to [K(\pi \vee (\lambda \wedge \neg K\alpha)) \leftrightarrow (K(\pi \vee \lambda) \wedge \neg K\alpha)]\} \wedge \{K\alpha \to [K(\pi \vee (\lambda \wedge \neg K\alpha)) \leftrightarrow (K\pi \wedge K\alpha)]\}$
(A1, 9, 18)

20 $\{\neg p \to [q \leftrightarrow (r \wedge \neg p)]\} \wedge \{p \to [q \leftrightarrow (s \wedge p)]\} \to$
$[(q \leftrightarrow ((r \wedge \neg p) \vee (s \wedge p))]$ (A1)

21 $\{\neg K\alpha \to [K(\pi \vee (\lambda \wedge \neg K\alpha)) \leftrightarrow (K(\pi \vee \lambda) \wedge \neg K\alpha)]\} \wedge \{K\alpha \to [K(\pi \vee (\lambda \wedge \neg K\alpha)) \leftrightarrow (K\pi \wedge K\alpha)]\} \to [(K(\pi \vee (\lambda \wedge \neg K\alpha)) \leftrightarrow ((K(\pi \vee \lambda) \wedge \neg K\alpha) \vee (K\pi \wedge K\alpha))]$ (instantiation of 20)

22 $(K(\pi \vee (\lambda \wedge \neg K\alpha)) \leftrightarrow ((K(\pi \vee \lambda) \wedge \neg K\alpha) \vee (K\pi \wedge K\alpha))$ (R1, 19, 21)

1.7.6.4.1 Recall that a normal form is a disjunction of canonical conjunctions of the form
$\delta = \alpha \wedge K\beta_1 \wedge K\beta_2 \wedge \ldots \wedge K\beta_n \wedge M\gamma_1 \wedge M\gamma_2 \wedge \ldots \wedge M\gamma_k$ (*)
where the α, β_i ($i \le n$) and γ_j ($j \le k$) are propositional. Let us call the formulas α, $K\beta_i$ ($i \le n$) and $M\gamma_j$ ($j \le k$) *damo* (depth_at_most_one)-formulas.

It is immediate that an atom p is in normal form. So suppose that φ is in normal form, say $\varphi = \delta_1 \vee \ldots \vee \delta_t$, with δ_i of the form (*), $i \le t$. Then:

$\neg\varphi \Leftrightarrow \neg(\delta_1 \vee \ldots \vee \delta_t) \Leftrightarrow \neg\delta_1 \wedge \ldots \wedge \neg\delta_t$; now $\neg\delta_i$ ($i \le t$) may be written as:

$$\neg\delta_i \Leftrightarrow \neg\alpha_i \vee \neg K\beta_{1_i} \vee \neg K\beta_{2_i} \vee \ldots \vee \neg K\beta_{n_i} \vee \neg M\gamma_{1_i} \vee \neg M\gamma_{2_i} \vee \ldots \vee \neg M\gamma_{k_i}$$

or

$$\neg\delta_i \Leftrightarrow \neg\alpha_i \vee M\neg\beta_{1_i} \vee M\neg\beta_{2_i} \vee \ldots \vee M\neg\beta_{n_i} \vee K\neg\gamma_{1_i} \vee K\neg\gamma_{2_i} \vee \ldots \vee K\neg\gamma_{k_i}.$$

Let us write $\neg\delta_i = (a_{i_1} \vee a_{i_2} \vee \ldots \vee a_{i_{n(i)}})$, with each a_{i_j} a damo-formula.
Then, using De Morgan,

$\neg\varphi \Leftrightarrow$ De Morgan

$\neg\delta_1 \wedge \neg\delta_2 \wedge \ldots \wedge \neg\delta_t \Leftrightarrow$ definition of δ_i

$((a_{1_1} \vee a_{1_2} \vee \ldots \vee a_{1_{n(1)}}) \wedge (a_{2_1} \vee a_{2_2} \vee \ldots \vee a_{2_{n(2)}}) \wedge \ldots \wedge (a_{t_1} \vee a_{t_2} \vee \ldots \vee a_{t_{n(t)}}) \Leftrightarrow$

Generalised distribution of '$\wedge$' over '$\vee$'

$\bigvee_{i_j \leq n(j)} (a_{1_{t_{i1}}} \wedge a_{2_{i_2}} \wedge \ldots \wedge a_{t_{i_t}})$

We now observe that the latter formula is a disjunction of conjunctions of formulas $a_{s_{i_s}}$, which are damo-formulas, so that (**) is again in normal form.

Now suppose that both φ_1 and φ_2 have a normal form, say
$\varphi_1 \Leftrightarrow \delta_{1_1} \vee \delta_{1_2} \vee \ldots \vee \delta_{1_k}$, and $\varphi_2 \Leftrightarrow \delta_{2_1} \vee \delta_{2_2} \vee \ldots \vee \delta_{2_m}$,
such that all the δ_{1_h} and δ_{2_i} ($h \leq k$, $i \leq m$) are as in (*). Then, obviously, $(\varphi_1 \vee \varphi_2)$ *is* in normal form too. Finally, let us consider $(\varphi_1 \wedge \varphi_2)$. Applying the generalised distribution of '$\wedge$' over '$\vee$' to this formula, we see that: $(\varphi_1 \wedge \varphi_2) \Leftrightarrow$

$(\delta_{1_1} \wedge \delta_{2_1}) \vee (\delta_{1_1} \wedge \delta_{2_2}) \vee \ldots \vee (\delta_{1_1} \wedge \delta_{2_m}) \vee \ldots \vee (\delta_{1_2} \wedge \delta_{2_1}) \vee \ldots \vee (\delta_{1_k} \wedge \delta_{2_m})$

We now observe that each conjunction $(\delta_{1_i} \wedge \delta_{2_j})$ ($i \leq k$, $j \leq m$) is a conjunction of damos; if we take the two propositional conjuncts α_{1_i} and α_{2_j} together as $(\alpha_{1_i} \wedge \alpha_{2_j})$, we see that $(\delta_{1_i} \wedge \delta_{2_j})$ is equivalent to a canonical conjunction of the form (*) so that $\varphi_1 \wedge \varphi_2$ is indeed equivalent to a disjunction of canonical conjunctions, i.e. a formula in normal form.

2.1.2.1. REMARK. Note that we can use (A8) and (R3) to derive the following rule for C, in exactly the same way as we derived (KD) for K:

$$\frac{\varphi \rightarrow \psi}{C\varphi \rightarrow C\psi} \qquad \textit{C-distribution} \qquad \text{(CD)}$$

Moreover, for E, we have a similar rule (immediate from (KD) and (A6)):

$$\frac{\varphi \rightarrow \psi}{E\varphi \rightarrow E\psi} \qquad \textit{E-distribution} \qquad \text{(ED)}$$

In the proofs, we omit reference to the specific logics; the reader is invited to check that we indeed only use the axioms of the denoted systems.

(i) 1 $C\varphi \rightarrow EC\varphi$ (A8)
2 $EC\varphi \rightarrow E\varphi$ (ED; A7)
3 $C\varphi \rightarrow E\varphi$ (HS; 1,2)

(ii) 1 $C\varphi \rightarrow E\varphi$ (item (i))
2 $E\varphi \rightarrow (K_1\varphi \wedge \ldots \wedge K_m\varphi)$)EE; A6)
3 $(K_1\varphi \wedge \ldots \wedge K_m\varphi) \rightarrow K_i\varphi$ (A1 ($i \leq m$))
4 $C\varphi \rightarrow K_i\varphi$ (HS; 1,2,3)

(iii)	1	$C(C\varphi \rightarrow EC\varphi)$	(R3; A8)
	2	$C(C\varphi \rightarrow EC\varphi) \rightarrow (C\varphi \rightarrow CC\varphi)$	(A10)
	3	$C\varphi \rightarrow CC\varphi$	(HS; 1,2)
	4	$CC\varphi \rightarrow C\varphi$	(A7)
	5	$C\varphi \leftrightarrow CC\varphi$	(EI; 3,4)

(iv)	1	$C\varphi \rightarrow CC\varphi$	(item (iii).3)
	2	$C\varphi \rightarrow E\varphi$	(item (i))
	3	$CC\varphi \rightarrow CE\varphi$	(CD; 2)
	4	$C\varphi \rightarrow CE\varphi$	(HS; 1,3)
	5	$E\varphi \rightarrow K_i\varphi$	(HS; item (ii)2,3)
	6	$E\varphi \rightarrow \varphi$	(HS; 5,A2)
	7	$CE\varphi \rightarrow C\varphi$	(CD; 6)
	8	$C\varphi \leftrightarrow CE\varphi$	(EI; 4,7)

(v)	1	$CC\varphi \rightarrow K_iC\varphi$	(item (ii))
	2	$C\varphi \rightarrow K_iC\varphi$	(HS; 2,item (iii)3)
	3	$C\varphi \leftrightarrow K_iC\varphi$	(EI; 2,A2)

(vi)	1	$C\varphi \leftrightarrow EC\varphi$	(EI; A8,item (iv)6)

(vii)	1	$K_i\neg C\varphi \rightarrow \neg C\varphi$	(A2)
	2	$\neg K_iC\varphi \leftrightarrow \neg C\varphi$	(item (v), A1)
	3	$K_i\neg K_iC\varphi \rightarrow K_i\neg C\varphi$	(KD; 2)
	4	$\neg K_i\neg C\varphi \rightarrow \neg K_i\neg K_iC\varphi$	(CP; 3)
	5	$\neg K_i\neg K_iC\varphi \rightarrow K_iC\varphi$	(1.5.1.3.(v))
	6	$K_iC\varphi \rightarrow C\varphi$	(A2)
	7	$\neg K_i\neg C\varphi \rightarrow C\varphi$	(HS; 4,5,6)
	8	$\neg C\varphi \rightarrow K_i\neg C\varphi$	(CP; 7)
	9	$\neg C\varphi \leftrightarrow K_i\neg C\varphi$	(EI; 1,8)

(viii)	1	$E\neg C\varphi \rightarrow K_i\neg C\varphi$	(A6, A1)
	2	$K_i\neg C\varphi \rightarrow \neg C\varphi$	(A2)
	3	$E\neg C\varphi \rightarrow \neg C\varphi$	(HS; 1,2)
	4	$\neg C\varphi \rightarrow (K_1\neg C\varphi \wedge K_2\neg C\varphi \wedge \ldots \wedge K_m\neg C\varphi)$	(item (vi), in which i was arbitrary)
	5	$(K_1\neg C\varphi \wedge K_2\neg C\varphi \wedge \ldots \wedge K_m\neg C\varphi) \rightarrow E\neg C\varphi$	(EE; A6)
	6	$\neg C\varphi \leftrightarrow E\neg C\varphi$	(EI; 3,5)

(ix)	1	$C\neg C\varphi \rightarrow \neg C\varphi$	(A7)
	2	$\neg C\varphi \rightarrow E\neg C\varphi$	(EE; item viii)
	3	$C(\neg C\varphi \rightarrow E\neg C\varphi)$	(R3; 2)
	4	$C(\neg C\varphi \rightarrow E\neg C\varphi) \rightarrow (\neg C\varphi \rightarrow C\neg C\varphi)$	(A10)
	5	$\neg C\varphi \rightarrow C\neg C\varphi$	(R1; 3,4)

2.1.2.2

(i)	1	$\vdash \varphi$	(assumption)

2	$\vdash C\varphi$	(R3; 1)
3	$\vdash C\varphi \rightarrow E\varphi$	(2.1.2.1(i))
4	$\vdash E\varphi$	(R1; 2,3)

(ii) Again, we will refer to this rule as the Substitution rule. It turns out to be valid in all the logics of Definition 2.1.2.

$$\frac{\varphi_1 \leftrightarrow \varphi_2}{\psi \leftrightarrow \psi[\varphi_1/\varphi_2]} \qquad \textit{Substitution} \qquad \text{(SUB)}$$

To prove the validity of this rule in the logics introduced in in this chapter, we only have to extend the inductive proof we gave in Exercise 1.5.1.2 for the cases $\psi = E\psi_1$ and $\psi = C\psi_1$. These steps, in their turn, are exact copies of the case $\psi = K\psi_1$ of Exercise 1.5.1.2. That step heavily relied upon the K-SUB for K, saying that $\mathbf{K(m)} \vdash \varphi_1 \leftrightarrow \varphi_2$ implies $\mathbf{K(m)} \vdash K\varphi_1 \leftrightarrow K\varphi_2$. It is easily seen that we now also have that $\mathbf{KEC_{(m)}} \vdash \varphi_1 \leftrightarrow \varphi_2$ implies both $\mathbf{KEC_{(m)}} \vdash E\varphi_1 \leftrightarrow E\varphi_2$ and $\mathbf{KEC_{(m)}} \vdash C\varphi_1 \leftrightarrow C\varphi_2$. (To see this, use the distribution rules (ED) and (CD), derived above.) Thus, we have rules E-SUB en C-SUB in $\mathbf{KEC_{(m)}}$, which can be used in the proof of SUB exactly in the same way as we used K-SUB in the proof of Exercise 1.5.1.2.

2.1.2.3 Let the sequence $K_{i_1}K_{i_2}\ldots K_{i_n}$ be given. Then the derivation looks as follows, where we write $E^k\varphi$ for φ, preceded by k occurrences of E.

1	$C\varphi \rightarrow EC\varphi$	(A8)
2	$EC\varphi \rightarrow EEC\varphi$	(KE; 1)
...	...	...
n	$E^{(n-1)}C\varphi \rightarrow E^nC\varphi$	(KE; n-1)
n+1	$E^nC\varphi \rightarrow E^n\varphi$	(n times KE; A7)
n+2	$EE^{(n-1)}\varphi \rightarrow K_{i_1}E^{(n-1)}\varphi$	(A1; A6)
n+3	$K_{i_1}E^{(n-1)}\varphi \rightarrow K_{i_1}K_{i_2}E^{(n-2)}\varphi$	(KD; A6)
...	...	...
2n+1	$K_{i_1}\ldots K_{i_{(n-1)}}E\varphi \rightarrow K_{i_1}\ldots K_{i_n}\varphi$	((n-1) times KD; A6)
2n+2	$C\varphi \rightarrow K_{i_1}\ldots K_{i_n}\varphi$	(HS; 1 ... (2n + 1))

2.1.3.1. We have to prove the soundness of (A6)—(A9) and (R3).

(A6) Suppose $(\mathbb{M}, s) \models E\varphi$. Then, for all t for which $s \rightarrow t$, $(\mathbb{M}, t) \models \varphi$. Now let u be such that for some $i \leq m$, $(s, u) \in R_i$. Obviously, we have $s \rightarrow u$, so $(\mathbb{M}, u) \models \varphi$. So, for each $i \leq m$, and each u such that $(s, u) \in R_i$, u verifies φ. This proves $(\mathbb{M}, s) \models (K_1\varphi \wedge K_2\varphi \wedge \ldots \wedge K_m\varphi)$. For the converse, suppose $(\mathbb{M}, s) \models (K_1\varphi \wedge K_2\varphi \wedge \ldots \wedge K_m\varphi)$, and let t be such that $s \rightarrow t$. This means that $(s, t) \in R_1 \cup \ldots \cup R_m$, so for some i, $(s, t) \in R_i$. Since $(\mathbb{M}, s) \models K_i\varphi$, we have $(\mathbb{M}, t) \models \varphi$, so $(\mathbb{M}, s) \models E\varphi$.

(A7) Suppose $(\mathbb{M}, s) \models C\varphi$, i.e. for all t such that $s \twoheadrightarrow t$, $(\mathbb{M}, t) \models \varphi$. However, since $s \rightarrow s$, we also have $s \twoheadrightarrow s$, so $(\mathbb{M}, s) \models \varphi$.

(A8) Suppose $(\mathbb{M}, s) \models C\varphi$, i.e. for all t such that $s \twoheadrightarrow t$, $(\mathbb{M}, t) \models \varphi$. Let u and v be such that $s \rightarrow u$ and $u \twoheadrightarrow v$. In order to show that $(\mathbb{M}, s) \models EC\varphi$, it is sufficient to show that $(\mathbb{M}, u) \models C\varphi$, for which it is sufficient to show that $s \twoheadrightarrow v$. But the latter is immediate from the definition of $\twoheadrightarrow$.

(R3) If $\models \varphi$, then φ is true in all world of all $\mathcal{K}_{(\mathbf{m})}$-models. In particular, φ will be true in any $\twoheadrightarrow$-

successor u of any world s, so that we have $\models C\varphi$.

2.1.4.1 We have to show: $\mathcal{K}_{(m)} \models \varphi \Leftrightarrow \mathcal{KEC}_{(m)} \models \varphi$. This follows from the following observation: any model $\mathbb{M} = \langle S, \pi, R_1, \ldots, R_m \rangle \in \mathcal{K}_{(m)}$ can be 'extended' to a model $\mathbb{M}' = \langle S, \pi, R_1, \ldots, R_m, R_E, R_C \rangle \in \mathcal{KEC}_{(m)}$ in such a way, that, for each $s \in S$, and all φ, $(\mathbb{M}, s) \models \varphi \Leftrightarrow (\mathbb{M}', s) \models \varphi$, such that the operator E is interpreted as the necessity operator for R_E, and C that for R_C. For atomic formulas, conjunctions, negations and K_i-formulas, the claim is obvious. To see it for $\varphi \in \{E\psi, C\psi\}$, it follows immediately from the truth definition for E- and C-formulas. From Definition 2.1.2 it follows that $E\varphi$ is true in s iff φ is true in all t such that $s \rightarrow t$. From Definition 2.1.1(ii), we see that this is equivalent to requiring φ to be true in all $(R_1 \cup \ldots \cup R_m)$-successors t of s. But this is exactly the same requirement as to make $E\varphi$ true in $(\mathbb{M}', s)$. Moreover, if $(\mathbb{M}, s) \models C\varphi$, then, by Definition 2.1.2, φ is true in all t for which $s \twoheadrightarrow t$. By Definition 2.1.1(iii), we see that this is equivalent to requiring φ to be true in all t that are reachable from s in the reflexive transitive closure of $(R_1 \cup \ldots \cup R_m)$. And this is exactly the same requirement as to make $C\varphi$ true in $(\mathbb{M}', s)$. Thus, we have $\mathcal{KEC}_{(m)} \models \varphi \Rightarrow \mathcal{K}_{(m)} \models \varphi$. For the converse, it is easily seen that any model $\mathbb{M}' = \langle S, \pi, R_1, \ldots, R_m, R_E, R_C \rangle \in \mathcal{KEC}_{(m)}$ can be considered to be a model $\mathbb{M} = \langle S, \pi, R_1, \ldots, R_m \rangle \in \mathcal{K}_{(m)}$ in such a way, that for each $s \in S$, $(\mathbb{M}', s)$ and $(\mathbb{M}, s)$ verify the same formulas.

2.1.5.3 Suppose Theorem 2.1.5.2 to be proven for ψ_1 and ψ_2 (IH). Then
$(\mathbb{M}, s) \models \neg\psi_1 \Leftrightarrow$ not $(\mathbb{M}, s) \models \psi_1 \Leftrightarrow_{IH}$ not $(\mathbb{N}, [s]) \models \psi_1 \Leftrightarrow (\mathbb{N}, [s]) \models \neg\psi_1$;
$(\mathbb{M}, s) \models \psi_1 \wedge \psi_2 \Leftrightarrow (\mathbb{M}, s) \models \psi_1$ and $(\mathbb{M}, s) \models \psi_2 \Leftrightarrow_{IH} (\mathbb{N}, [s]) \models \psi_1$ and $(\mathbb{N}, [s]) \models \psi_2 \Leftrightarrow (\mathbb{N}, [s]) \models \psi_1 \wedge \psi_2$.

2.1.6.1 (i)

φ_1: $(p_1 \vee p_2 \vee p_3 \vee p_4 \vee p_5)$

φ_2: $(p_1 \wedge p_2) \vee (p_1 \wedge p_3) \vee (p_1 \wedge p_4) \vee (p_1 \wedge p_5) \vee (p_2 \wedge p_3) \vee (p_2 \wedge p_4) \vee (p_2 \wedge p_5) \vee (p_3 \wedge p_4) \vee (p_3 \wedge p_5) \vee (p_4 \wedge p_5)$

ψ_1: $(p_1 \wedge \neg p_2 \wedge \neg p_3 \wedge \neg p_4 \wedge \neg p_5) \vee (\neg p_1 \wedge p_2 \wedge \neg p_3 \wedge \neg p_4 \wedge \neg p_5) \vee$
$(\neg p_1 \wedge \neg p_2 \wedge p_3 \wedge \neg p_4 \wedge \neg p_5) \vee (\neg p_1 \wedge \neg p_2 \wedge \neg p_3 \wedge p_4 \wedge \neg p_5) \vee$
$(p_1 \wedge \neg p_2 \wedge \neg p_3 \wedge \neg p_4 \wedge p_5)$

ψ_2: $\varphi_2 \wedge \neg\varphi_3$, or, made explicit:
$(p_1 \wedge p_2 \wedge \neg p_3 \wedge \neg p_4 \wedge \neg p_5) \vee (p_1 \wedge \neg p_2 \wedge p_3 \wedge \neg p_4 \wedge \neg p_5) \vee$
$(p_1 \wedge \neg p_2 \wedge \neg p_3 \wedge p_4 \wedge \neg p_5) \vee (p_1 \wedge \neg p_2 \wedge \neg p_3 \wedge \neg p_4 \wedge p_5) \vee$
$(\neg p_1 \wedge p_2 \wedge p_3 \wedge \neg p_4 \wedge \neg p_5) \vee (\neg p_1 \wedge p_2 \wedge \neg p_3 \wedge p_4 \wedge \neg p_5) \vee$
$(\neg p_1 \wedge p_2 \wedge \neg p_3 \wedge \neg p_4 \wedge p_5) \vee (\neg p_1 \wedge \neg p_2 \wedge p_3 \wedge p_4 \wedge \neg p_5) \vee$
$(\neg p_1 \wedge \neg p_2 \wedge p_3 \wedge \neg p_4 \wedge p_5) \vee (\neg p_1 \wedge \neg p_2 \wedge \neg p_3 \wedge p_4 \wedge p_5)$

(ii) Agent 4 does *not* know its own state, whereas it *does* know that state of the other agents, so the possible states for agent 4 are $<1, 0, 0, 1, 1>$ and $<1, 0, 0, 0, 1>$.

(iii) We consider the situation $s = <1, 0, 0, 1, 1>$. Then, obviously, R_iss holds, and, moreover, we have $R_1s<0, 0, 0, 1, 1>$, $R_2s<1, 1, 0, 1, 1>$, $R_3s<1, 0, 1, 1, 1>$, $R_4s<1, 0, 0, 0, 1>$ and $R_5s<1, 0, 0, 1, 0>$, and this are all the states that are reachable in one R_i-step $(1 \leq i \leq 5)$ from s. Obviously, in each world that is R_i-accessible from s, φ_1 holds. Hence we have $(\mathbb{M}, s) \models E\varphi_1$, and even $(\mathbb{M}, s) \models E\varphi_2$.
However, note thate we have $R_1s<0, 0, 0, 1, 1>$, $R_4 <0, 0, 0, 1, 1> <0, 0, 0, 0, 1>$ and $R_5 <0, 0, 0, 0, 1> <0, 0, 0, 0, 0>$.

In words: "child 1 holds a state possible in which two things hold:
- there are two muddy children;
- and child 4 considers a state possible in which two things hold:
    - there is one muddy child;
    - and child 5 considers a state possible in which:
        - there is no muddy child"

This shows that $(\mathbb{M}, s) \models \neg K_1K_4K_5\varphi_1$.

2.1.6.2 Recall that we assumed that the real world s equals $<1, 0, 0, 1, 1>$. After Father's first announcement, the world $t = <0, 0, 0, 0, 0>$ is known by every child to be an impossible one: no other state s' for which $s \twoheadrightarrow s'$ is related to t anymore (compare the analysis we made in the answer to Exercise 2.1.6.1) and thus we have $(\mathbb{M}, s) \models C\varphi_1$. Similar remarks hold for the worlds $<1, 0, 0, 0, 0>$, $<0, 0, 0, 1, 0>$ and $<0, 0, 0, 0, 1>$ after Father's second announcement, ensuring that after this second announcement, $(\mathbb{M}, s) \models C\varphi_2$ holds.

2.1.6.3 The difference between C and E is clear from the answers to Exercises 2.1.6.1 and 2.1.6.2; although, given s, nobody initially holds a state to be possible in which ψ_0 holds, child 1 considers a world in which child 2 considers a world in which child three considers a state in which ψ_0 *is* the case! If Father had initially whispered φ_1 in everybody's ear, we cannot conclude that $(\mathbb{M}, s) \models C\varphi_1$; since child 1 would not know the content of Father's whisper to child 2, we can repeat our analysis of the answer to Exercise 2.1.6.1 to show this.

2.2.7 $\mathbb{M} = \langle S, \pi, R_A, R_B, R_C \rangle$ is here

S: $\{(x, y, z) \mid x, y, z \in \{0, 1\}\}$.
For $s = (x_1, y_1, z_1)$ and $t = (x_2, y_2, z_2)$ we define:

R_A: $(s, t) \in R_A \Leftrightarrow x_1 = x_2$ (s and t in the same y-z plane).

R_B: $(s, t) \in R_B \Leftrightarrow y_1 = y_2$ (s and t in the same x-z plane).

R_C: $(s, t) \in R_C \Leftrightarrow z_1 = z_2$ (s and t in the same x-y plane).

π: $\forall s \in S: \pi(s)(p) = t$;
$\pi(s)(q) = f \Leftrightarrow s = (1, 1, 1)$.

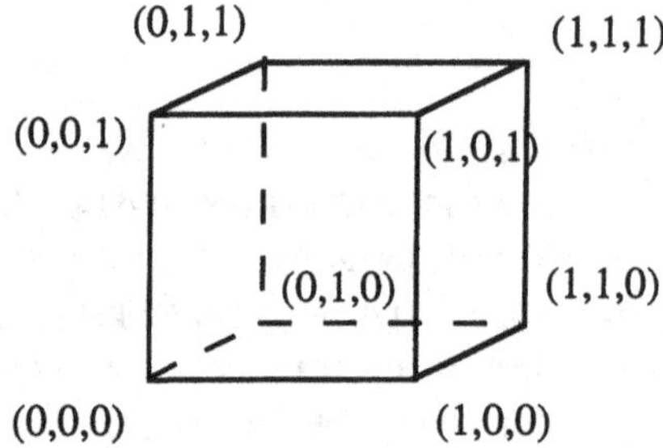

Obviously (since p is defined to be true everywhere) we have $\mathbb{M} \models Cp$. Moreover, if we choose $s = (0, 0, 0)$, we have $(\mathbb{M}, s) \models Eq$ (to see this, note that world $t = (x, y, z)$ is $(R_A \cup R_B \cup R_C)$-accessible from s iff $0 \in \{x, y, z\}$). Finally, since q is false in $(1, 1, 1)$, we have $\mathbb{M} \not\models Eq$.

2.2.8 (i) Suppose $\mathbb{M} \models \varphi$. Then, in all $s \in S$, $(\mathbb{M}, s) \models \varphi$. But then, in particular, φ is true in all R_C-successors of each world: let s and $t \in S$ such that $(s, t) \in R_C$. Since φ is true in all state of S, we have $(\mathbb{M}, t) \models \varphi$, and thus $(\mathbb{M}, s) \models C\varphi$.

(ii) Consider the model of Exercise 2.2.7; we have $(\mathbb{M}, (0, 0, 0)) \models q \wedge \neg Cq$, so that $\mathbb{M} \not\models q \rightarrow Cq$.

2.2.9 A simple model $\mathbb{M} = \langle S, \pi, R_1, R_2, R_E, R_C\rangle$ is obtained as follows: $S = \{a, b\}$; $\pi(x)(p) = t$ iff $x = a$ and $R_1 = R_2 = \{(a, a), (b, b)\}$. In the run $s \Rightarrow t$ it is the case that the common knowledge about $\neg p$ increases: we have $(\mathbb{M}, s) \models \neg C\neg p$ while $(\mathbb{M}, t) \models C\neg p$.

2.2.10 (i) First note that for each $\mathbb{M} = \langle S, \pi, R_1, \ldots, R_m, R_E, R_C\rangle \in \mathit{S5EC}_{(m)}$, R_E is reflexive. In particular, this means, that for each $x, y \in \mathbb{N}$, $\mathit{S5EC}_{(m)} \models E^{x+y}\varphi \rightarrow E^x\varphi$. Suppose that $(\mathbb{M}, s) \models E^n\varphi$. To show that $(\mathbb{M}, s) \models C\varphi$, let $t \in S$ be such that $s \twoheadrightarrow t$. This means that we have a sequence s_i such that $s = s_0 \rightarrow s_1 \rightarrow s_2 \ldots \rightarrow s_k = t$, where each '$s_j \rightarrow s_{j+1}$' ($j < k$) denotes some R_i-step ($i \leq m$). If $s = t$ then, by the reflexivity of R_E, we have $(\mathbb{M}, t) \models \varphi$. If $s \neq t$, we may assume that all s_j in this sequence are different: if t is $(R_1 \cup \ldots \cup R_m)$-accessible from s via some loop, it is also $(R_1 \cup \ldots \cup R_m)$-accessible from s without such a loop. So all states in $\{s_0, \ldots, s_k\}$ may be assumed to be different, so (since $|S| = n$) we have $k < n$. Thus, $(\mathbb{M}, s) \models E^k\varphi$, implying that for each $j \leq k$, $(\mathbb{M}, s_j) \models E^{n-j}\varphi$, and thus $(\mathbb{M}, s_k) \models E^{n-k}\varphi$, with $n - k > 0$. This implies that $(\mathbb{M}, s_k) \models E^0\varphi$, thus $(\mathbb{M}, s_k) \models \varphi$. Since $s_k = t$, this is what we had to prove. For the converse, suppose $(\mathbb{M}, s) \models C\varphi$. This means that all worlds t for which $s \twoheadrightarrow t$, $(\mathbb{M}, t) \models \varphi$. But if φ is true in worlds that are $(R_1 \cup \ldots \cup R_m)$-accessible from s in an arbitrary number of steps, then in particular, φ is true in all such worlds that are accessible in n such steps: so $(\mathbb{M}, s) \models E^n\varphi$.

(ii) For this item, we can in fact use the model of Figure 2.1. More precisely, we consider the following model $\mathbb{M} = \langle S, \pi, R_1, R_2, R_E, R_C\rangle \in \mathit{S5EC}_{(2)}$. $S = \mathbb{N}$, $(x, y) \in R_1 \Leftrightarrow x = y$ or (x is even and $y = x+1$) or (y is odd and $x = y - 1$); $(x, y) \in R_2 \Leftrightarrow x = y$ or (x is odd and $y = x + 1$) or (y is even or $x = y-1$). $\pi(x)(p) = t \Leftrightarrow x \neq 0$. Cf. the figure below, R_1 is the reflexive closure of the dotted arrows; R_2 is the reflexive closure of the black arrows.

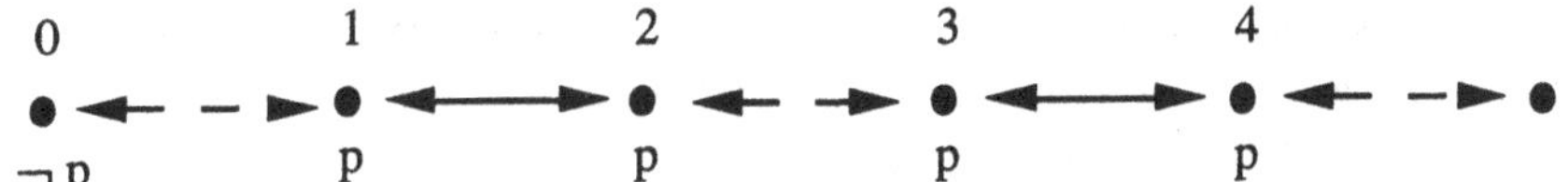

Note that, in each $n \in \mathbb{N}$, $(\mathbb{M}, n) \models \neg Cp$. However, in each world $(n + 1)$, the formula E^np is true (in world $(n + 1)$, doing at most n $(R_1 \cup R_2)$-steps, one only encounters p-worlds). Thus, we have $(\mathbb{M}, (n + 1)) \models E^np \wedge \neg Cp$. Hence, for every n, we can find a state in the model where E^np is not equivalent with Cp. Therefore, for every n, $\mathbb{M} \not\models E^np \leftrightarrow Cp$.

2.2.13 (i) From Theorem 2.2.12, we derive that such a run has to be 'simultaneous'. We can take a submodel $\mathbb{M}'$ of the model of Exercise 2.2.7, in which $S' = \{s, t\}$ with $s = (0, 0, 0)$ and $t = (1, 1, 1)$. Then we have $R_A' = R_B' = R_C' = \{(s, s), (t, t)\}$. If π' is the restriction of π to S' then q is true only in s. Then, in the run $s \Rightarrow t$ we not only have that common knowledge *increases* (from $\neg C\neg q$ to $C\neg q$), it also *changes;* in this run: there is a 'jump' from Cq to $C\neg q$.

(ii) We change the model of item (i) into a model $\mathbb{M}''$ as follows: for our valuation π'' we now require, for all atoms p, $\pi''(s)(p) = \pi''(t)(p)$; keeping the accessibility relations as they were. An easy induction on the complexity of φ shows that $(\mathbb{M}'', s) \models \varphi \Leftrightarrow (\mathbb{M}'', t) \models \varphi$. Since for any simultaneous run $x_1 \Rightarrow x_2 \Rightarrow \ldots \Rightarrow x_n$ in $\mathbb{M}''$ we have that all $x_i \in \{s, t\}$ ($i \leq n$), we even have that in *all* simultaneous runs C-knowledge is constant.

2.2.14

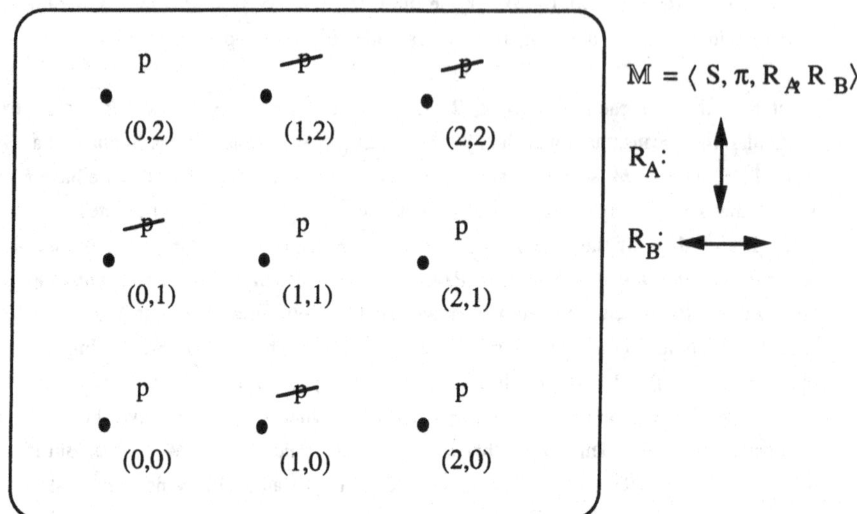

(i) Consider the run (0, 0) ➡ (0, 2) ➡ (2, 2). As is easily verified, this run is non-simultaneous, and thus, by Theorem 2.2.13, C-knowledge in this run is constant. In particular, this implies that common knowledge in (0, 0) and (2, 2) is the same.

(ii) Again, we find a non-simultaneous run: (0, 0) ➡ (0, 1) ➡ (2, 1) ➡ (2, 1). Thus, arguing as in item (i), we find that common konwledge in (0, 0) and (2, 2) is the same.

(iii) Obviously, all runs (0, 0) ➡ ... ➡ (2, 2) must be simultaneous. From Exercise 2.2.14(ii) we know that this does not imply that common knowledge in (0, 0) and (2, 2) must be different. However, in this case, C-knowledge *does* change in the run (0, 0) ➡ (2, 2). To see this, note that in (0, 0) formula Cp is true, in (2, 2) however, ¬Cp (even C¬p) is true.

2.2.15 (i)

M: ⟨S, π, R_1, R_2⟩ is here:

S: $\{(x, y) \mid x, y \in \{0, 1\}\}$;

R_1: the reflexive closure of the '→';

R_2: the reflexive closure of the '-->';

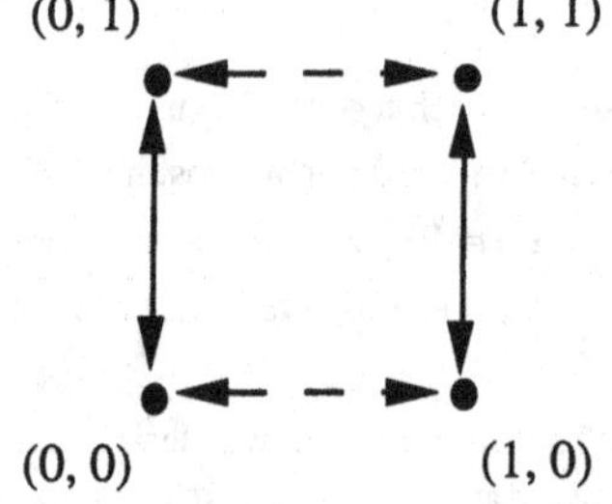

(ii) The largest j for which this holds is j = 0. Since φ_0 is true everywhere, we have $M_2 \models C\varphi_0$. To see that there is no bigger j, note that we have $(M_2, (0, 0)) \models \neg\varphi_1$, and thus $(M_2, (0, 0)) \models \neg C\varphi_1$.

(iii) Now, the state (0, 0) is not possible any more. Since now $\mathbb{M}' \models \varphi_1$, we have $\mathbb{M}' \models C\varphi_1$; however, since $\neg\varphi_2$ is true in (1, 0), we have $\mathbb{M}' \not\models C\varphi_2$.

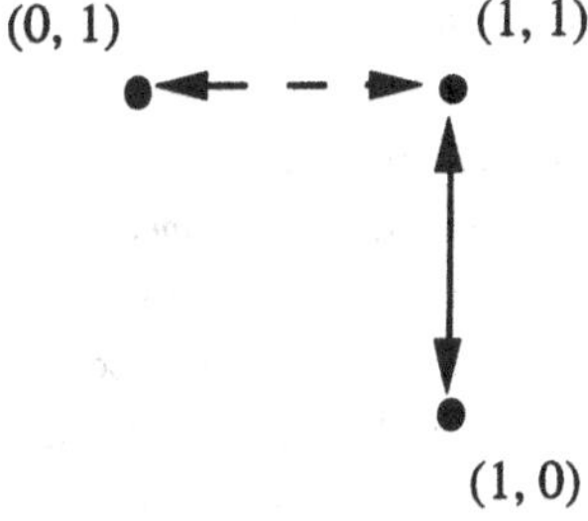

After Father's announcement that φ_2, the only possible world in the model $\mathbb{M}''$ is the state s = (1, 1), with $R_1 = R_2 = \{(s, s)\}$. Since $(\mathbb{M}'', s) \models \varphi_2$, we also have $\mathbb{M}'' \models C\varphi_2$.

2.3.1.1 In order to show $\models K_i\varphi \rightarrow I\varphi$, suppose $(\mathbb{M}, s) \models K_i\varphi$. Now, if t is such that $(s, t) \in (R_1 \cap \ldots \cap R_m)$, then surely R_ist, so that $(\mathbb{M}, t) \models \varphi$. Thus, $(\mathbb{M}, s) \models I\varphi$.

2.3.1.2 Suppose that $(s_\Theta, s_\Psi) \in R_I{}^c$, i.e.for all φ, $I\varphi \in \Theta \Rightarrow \varphi \in \Psi$. Suppose now that $K_i\varphi \in \Theta$. Since (A11) has been added to **K**, by Lemma 1.4.3(ii)(4) we have that $(K_i\varphi \rightarrow I\varphi) \in \Theta$. Hence, by Lemma 1.4.3(ii)(3), we have $I\varphi \in \Theta$, and hence $\varphi \in \Psi$. Since, for arbitrary $K_i\varphi \in \Theta$ we showed that $\varphi \in \Psi$, we may conclude that $(s_\Theta, s_\Psi) \in R_I{}^c$.

2.3.3 Let $\mathbf{XI}_{(\mathbf{m})}$ be the logic $\mathbf{KI}_{(\mathbf{m})} \setminus \{A11\}$. We will prove both (a) $\mathbf{XI}_{(\mathbf{m})} \cup \{A11\} \vdash (R4)$ and (b) $\mathbf{XI}_{(\mathbf{m})} \cup \{R4\} \vdash (A11)$. Note that, since $\mathbf{XI}_{(\mathbf{m})}$ contains also the K-axioms for I we have a distribution rule (ID) for I (analogous to rule (KD) for K), as well as the property (*):

$\mathbf{XI}_{(\mathbf{m})} \vdash I(\varphi \wedge \psi) \leftrightarrow (I\varphi \wedge I\psi)$ (*)

(Cf. Exercise 1.5.1.1, where this property was established for K).

(a)

1 $\mathbf{XI}_{(\mathbf{m})} \cup \{A11\} \vdash \psi_1 \wedge \ldots \wedge \psi_m \rightarrow \varphi$ (assumption)

2 $\mathbf{XI}_{(\mathbf{m})} \cup \{A11\} \vdash I(\psi_1 \wedge \ldots \wedge \psi_m) \rightarrow I\varphi$ (ID; 1)

3 $\mathbf{XI}_{(\mathbf{m})} \cup \{A11\} \vdash K_i\psi_i \rightarrow I\psi_i$ (A11)

4 $\mathbf{XI}_{(\mathbf{m})} \cup \{A11\} \vdash (K_1\psi_1 \wedge \ldots \wedge K_m\psi_m) \rightarrow (I\psi_1 \wedge \ldots \wedge I\psi_m)$ (CO; 3)

5 $\mathbf{XI}_{(\mathbf{m})} \cup \{A11\} \vdash (I\psi_1 \wedge \ldots \wedge I\psi_m) \rightarrow I(\psi_1 \wedge \ldots \wedge \psi_m)$ (EE; (*))

6 $\mathbf{XI}_{(\mathbf{m})} \cup \{A11\} \vdash (K_1\psi_1 \wedge \ldots \wedge K_m\psi_m) \rightarrow I\varphi$ (HS; 4,5,2)

(b) In the following we abbreviate **true** as T:

1 $\mathbf{XI}_{(\mathbf{m})} \cup \{R4\} \vdash (T \wedge \ldots \wedge T \wedge \varphi \wedge T \wedge \ldots \wedge T) \leftrightarrow \varphi$ (A1)

2 $\mathbf{XI}_{(\mathbf{m})} \cup \{R4\} \vdash (K_1T \wedge \ldots \wedge K_{i-1}T \wedge K_i\varphi \wedge K_{i+1}T \wedge \ldots \wedge K_mT) \rightarrow I\varphi$ (R4; 1)

3 $\mathbf{XI}_{(\mathbf{m})} \cup \{R4\} \vdash ((K_1T \wedge \ldots \wedge K_{i-1}T \wedge K_i\varphi \wedge K_{i+1}T \wedge \ldots \wedge K_mT) \rightarrow I\varphi) \rightarrow$
$((K_1T \wedge \ldots \wedge K_{i-1}T \wedge K_{i+1}T \wedge \ldots \wedge K_mT) \rightarrow (K_i\varphi \rightarrow I\varphi))$ (A1)

4 $\mathbf{XI}_{(\mathbf{m})} \cup \{R4\} \vdash K_1T \wedge \ldots \wedge K_{i-1}T \wedge K_{i+1}T \wedge \ldots \wedge K_mT \rightarrow (K_i\varphi \rightarrow I\varphi)$ (R1; 2,3)

5 $\mathbf{XI}_{(\mathbf{m})} \cup \{R4\} \vdash T$ (A1)

6 $\mathbf{XI}_{(\mathbf{m})} \cup \{R4\} \vdash K_rT \ (1 \leq r \leq m)$ (R2; 5)

7 $\mathbf{XI}_{(\mathbf{m})} \cup \{R4\} \vdash (K_1T \wedge \ldots \wedge K_{i-1}T \wedge K_{i+1}T \wedge \ldots \wedge K_mT)$ (A1,6)

8 $\mathbf{XI}_{(\mathbf{m})} \cup \{R4\} \vdash K_i\varphi \rightarrow I\varphi$ (R1; 4,7)

2.4.3.1.a

(i) Not satisfiable: if $(\mathbb{M}, s) \models B(p \wedge q)$, then is all t with Rst, $(\mathbb{M}, t) \models p \wedge q$, and in particular for such t, $(\mathbb{M}, t) \models p$, so that $(\mathbb{M}, s) \models Bp$.

(ii) From (i) we know that $(\mathbb{M}, s) \models B(p \wedge q)$ implies $(\mathbb{M}, s) \models Bp$; if moreover also $(\mathbb{M}, s) \models B\neg p$ would be true, this would mean that s has no R-successors, which is impossible in a $\mathbf{KD45}_{(m)}$-model. So the formula is not satisfiable.

(iii) Not satisfiable for the same reason as in (ii).

(iv) Satisfied in the following model $\mathbb{M}$ in state s: $S = \{s, t\}$, $\pi(s)(p) = \pi(t)(q) = t$; $\pi(s)(q) = \pi(t)(p) = f$, $R = S \times S$. Then, all successors of s verify $(p \vee q)$, not all verify p (t does not), neither do all satisfy q (s does not); $(\mathbb{M}, s) \models B(p \vee q) \wedge \neg Bp \wedge \neg Bq$.

(v) Not satisfiable: if all of s' R-successors have to satisfy $\neg p$ and $\neg q$, then in particular we know that there is such a t with Rst and $(\mathbb{M}, t) \models (\neg p \wedge \neg q)$, so that it is impossible for s to make $B(p \vee q)$ true.

(vi) Not satisfiable: suppose $(\mathbb{M}, s) \models B(p \vee q)$ and $(\mathbb{M}, s) \models B\neg p$. Let t be arbitrary such that R(s, t) holds (such a t exists by seriality). Then t satisfies both $p \vee q$ and $\neg p$, so $(\mathbb{M}, t) \models q$. Hence, $(\mathbb{M}, s) \models Bq$, and thus $(\mathbb{M}, s) \not\models \neg Bq$.

b Of course, since $\mathcal{KD}45_{(1)} \subseteq \mathcal{K}45_{(1)}$, $\mathcal{KD}45_{(1)}$-satisfiable formulas are also $\mathcal{K}45_{(1)}$-satisfiable. Thus we only have to consider items (i), (ii), (iii), (v) and (vi):

(i) We know from Proposition 1.3.5 that even on $\mathcal{K}_{(1)}$-models, we have that $\models (Bp \wedge B(p \rightarrow q)) \rightarrow Bq$, so that in particular we have on $\mathcal{K}45_{(1)}$-models that $\models B(p \wedge q) \rightarrow (Bp \wedge Bq)$: the formula of (i) is not $\mathcal{K}45_{(1)}$-satisfiable.

(ii) This formula is satisfied in the model $\mathbb{M}$ with one state s and R the empty relation: since s has no successors, is satisfies both $B(p \wedge q)$, $B\neg p$ and $B\neg q$.

(iii) Unsatisfiable: reason as in b(i).

(v) We notice that the model of b(ii) satisfies $(\mathbb{M}, s) \models B\varphi$ for all φ, so it satisfies also the formula $B(p \vee q) \wedge B\neg p \wedge B\neg q$.

(vi) Not satisfiable: suppose $(\mathbb{M}, s) \models \neg Bq$. Then there is a t with R(s, t) such that $(\mathbb{M}, t) \not\models q$. If one the other hand, also $(\mathbb{M}, s) \models B(p \vee q)$ and $(\mathbb{M}, s) \models B\neg p$, we have $(\mathbb{M}, t) \models p \vee q$ and $(\mathbb{M}, t) \models \neg p$ as well, and hence $(\mathbb{M}, t) \models q$, which yields a contradiction. (In fact, this proof also works for Exercise 2.4.3.1a (vi): an appeal to seriality there is not even needed.)

2.4.3.2

(i) Let $\mathcal{K}45_{(1)}$ be the class of models with m relations that are transitive and euclidean. Then, for all modal formulas φ, $\mathbf{K45}_{(m)} \vdash \varphi \Leftrightarrow \mathcal{K}45_{(1)} \models \varphi$.

(ii) We leave it to the reader to check soundness of $\mathbf{K45}_{(1)}$ with respect to simple $\mathcal{K}45_{(1)}$-models. For completeness, suppose that $\nvdash \varphi$, i.e., $\neg\varphi$ is consistent. It is now sufficient to prove that $\neg\varphi$ is satisfiable in a simple $\mathcal{K}45_{(1)}$-model. By our remarks in the answer to Exercise 2.4.3.1, we find that the canonical $\mathcal{K}45_{(1)}$-model $\mathbb{M}^c = \langle S^c, \pi^c, R_1{}^c \rangle$ has a state s such that $(\mathbb{M}^c, s) \models \neg\varphi$. We convert this into a simple $\mathcal{K}45_{(m)}$-model $\mathbb{M}' = \langle S', \pi', R_1' \rangle$ as follows. $S' = \{s' \mid \exists k \geq 0: s \rightarrow^k s'\}$ (see Definition 2.1.1), so, in particular, $s \in S'$; $\pi'(s')(p) = \pi(s')(p)$ for all atoms p, for all $s' \in S'$; further, we stipulate $R's's'' \Leftrightarrow Rs's''$, for all $s', s'' \in S'$. The model $\mathbb{M}'$ is also known as the *generated submodel* of $\mathbb{M}$. It is easy verified that $\mathbb{M}'$ is indeed simple if it does not hold that Rss. If the latter is the case, we add a 'copy' $s^{\not c}$ of s to S', with $\pi'(s^{\not c})(p) = \pi(s)(p)$, and moreover stipulate $R'ss^{\not c}$ and for all $s' \neq s$, $R's^{\not c}s'$. In this case, $\mathbb{M}'$ is again a simple $\mathcal{K}45_{(1)}$-model. Moreover, we claim that, for both cases, $(\mathbb{M}', s') \models \neg\varphi$. The proof of this claim follows the lines of that of Proposition 1.7.2. We conclude that $\neg\varphi$ is satisfiable in a simple $\mathcal{K}45_{(1)}$-model.

(iii) We take benefit of item (ii). Note that from (ii) it follows, that ψ is a $\mathbf{K45_{(1)}}$-theorem iff it is valid on a simple $\mathcal{K}45_{(1)}$-model, which is a simple $\mathcal{S}5_{(1)}$-model on a broom stick. We know that, for $\mathcal{S}5_{(1)}$-models, $(B\varphi \leftrightarrow BB\varphi)$ and $(\neg B\varphi \leftrightarrow B\neg B\varphi)$ are theorems (cf. 1.6.4, 1.6.7 and the axioms (A4) and (A5) for $\mathbf{S5_{(1)}}$– we only use the symbol 'B' instead of 'K' now). But if ψ is a $\mathcal{S}5_{(1)}$-valid, then, by the very nature of $\mathcal{K}45_{(1)}$-models, $B\psi$ is $\mathcal{K}45_{(1)}$-valid (the $\mathcal{S}5_{(1)}$ universe is put on a stick; transferred to the successors of the root). This proves the claim.

(iv) No, since the root of a simple $\mathcal{K}45$-model need not be reflexive; we can construct a model for which p is true in the balloon, but not in the root.

2.4.3.3 By combining the soundness and completeness results of Chapters 1 and 2, we see that $\mathbf{K(D)5_{(m)}}$ is a characterisation of the validities of euclidean (and serial, if **D** is present) models. We show that a serial euclidean model need not be transitive (which shows that there are models for all the axioms of $\mathbf{KD5_{(m)}}$ that do not verify axiom (A4). Such a model is conceived as follows. Let S = {s, t, u} and R = {(s, t), (t, u), (u, t), (t, t), (u, u)}. Note that R is serial and euclidean. Let us stipulate π such that p is true only in world t. Then we have $(\mathbb{M}, s) \models Bp$, but also $(\mathbb{M}, s) \not\models BBp$.

2.5.1

(LO1) This is axiom (A2), the validity of which in **K** is proven in Proposition 1.3.5(ii).

(LO2) This is rule (R2), the soundness of which in **K** is proven in Proposition 1.3.5(iv).

(LO3) Principle (KD) of Intermezzo E.1.

(LO4) Cf. Exercise 1.4.1.1(i).

(LO5) Cf. Exercise 1.4.1.2(i).

(LO6) Cf. Exercise 1.4.1.2(ii).

(LO7) Proof-theoretically: $B\varphi \wedge B\neg\varphi \Rightarrow B(\varphi \wedge \neg\varphi) \Rightarrow B\bot \Rightarrow_{(D)} \bot$. Semantically: $(\mathbb{M}, s) \models B\varphi$ implies that $(\mathbb{M}, t) \models \varphi$ for all t with R(s, t). Since we know that R is serial, we have that there exists a t with R(s, t). So there is a t with R(s, t) such that $(\mathbb{M}, t) \models \varphi$. Therefore, not for all t with R(s, t) it holds that $(\mathbb{M}, t) \not\models \varphi$, i.e., not for all t with R(s, t) it holds that $(\mathbb{M}, t) \models \neg\varphi$, i.e. $(\mathbb{M}, s) \not\models B\neg\varphi$, i.e. $(\mathbb{M}, s) \models \neg B\neg\varphi$.

(LO8) In a **KD45**-model we have that, for all s, t: $R(s, t) \Rightarrow R(t, t)$. (This follows from euclidicity.) So we have that, for all t with R(s, t): [for all u with R(t, u): $(\mathbb{M}, u) \models \varphi] \Rightarrow (\mathbb{M}, t) \models \varphi$, i.e. for all t with R(s, t), $(\mathbb{M}, t) \models B\varphi \Rightarrow (\mathbb{M}, t) \models \varphi$, i.e. for all t with R(s, t), $(\mathbb{M}, t) \models B\varphi \rightarrow \varphi$, i.e. $(\mathbb{M}, s) \models B(B\varphi \rightarrow \varphi)$.

(LO9) Directly from (LO2).

2.6.1.1

(i) Let $\mathbb{M}$ be a model with S = {s, t, u} and R = {(s, t), (s, u), (t, t), (u, u), (t, u), (u, t)}. It is easily seen that $\mathbb{M}$ is an $\mathbf{S5_{(1)}}$-model on a stick, and hence a $\mathbf{KD45_{(1)}}$-model (cf. Exercise 2.4.3.2). Let π be such that p is true in t, but not in u; moreover π makes q false everywhere, except for s. Then we have $(\mathbb{M}, t) \models p$ and $(\mathbb{M}, u) \models p \rightarrow q$, but for no successor x of s $(\mathbb{M}, x) \models q$; hence $(\mathbb{M}, s) \models Mp \wedge M(p \rightarrow q) \wedge \neg Mq$.

(ii) In the model of item (i) we have $(\mathbb{M}, s) \models Mp \wedge M\neg p \wedge \neg M(p \wedge \neg p)$.

(iii) In the same model: $(\mathbb{M}, s) \models Mp \wedge M\neg p$.

(iv) Suppose that we would have a $\mathbf{KD45_{(1)}}$-model with $(\mathbb{M}, s) \models \neg M(M\varphi \rightarrow \varphi)$ for some formula φ. Then we would have $(\mathbb{M}, s) \models B(M\varphi \wedge \neg\varphi)$ for that φ. This means that all successors t of s have some successor u for which φ is true, although $\neg\varphi$ is true in t itself. Since $\mathbf{KD45_{(1)}}$-models are serial, we also know that such a t exists. Now consider the state u for which φ is true; it satisfies

Rst and Rtu. Since R is transitive, we also have Rsu. Since u is a successor of s, it should satisfy $\neg\varphi$, which it does not: a contradiction.

(v) The formula $q \rightarrow Mq$ is not true in $(\mathbb{M}, s)$ as given in item (i).

(vi) Suppose $(\mathbb{M}, s) \models M\varphi$ for an arbitrary $\mathbf{KD45_{(1)}}$-model; then there is a t with Rst and $(\mathbb{M}, t) \models \varphi$. Since Rst and Rst hold, by euclidicity we have Rtt. So t has an R-successor (itself) in which φ is true, so that in s we have $(\mathbb{M}, s) \models M\varphi \rightarrow MM\varphi$. For the converse, suppose $(\mathbb{M}, s) \models MM\varphi$: there are t and u with Rst, Rtu and $(\mathbb{M}, u) \models \varphi$. By transitivity of R we find Rsu so that $(\mathbb{M}, s) \models M\varphi$.

(vii) Writing $\neg\psi$ for φ, we have to show that $\models B\psi \leftrightarrow MB\psi$. Suppose $(\mathbb{M}, s) \models B\psi$. So for all t with Rst we have $(\mathbb{M}, t) \models \psi$. Since R is serial, there exists a state u with Rsu. Now let v be an arbitrary state with Ruv. Since R is transitive, we have Rsv, so $(\mathbb{M}, v) \models \psi$. This shows $(\mathbb{M}, s) \models MB\psi$. Conversely, suppose $(\mathbb{M}, s) \models MB\psi$, i.e. there is a state t with Rst such that for all u with Rtu the formula ψ is true. Suppose x is arbitrary such that Rsx holds; by euclidicity of R Rtx now holds, and hence $(\mathbb{M}, x) \models \psi$ which implies $(\mathbb{M}, s) \models K\psi$.

(viii) Suppose $\models \varphi \leftrightarrow \psi$; then, in all states u of $\mathbf{KD45_{(1)}}$-models, we have that φ and ψ are equivalent. Now let s be a state in any $\mathbf{KD45_{(1)}}$-model. Suppose that $(\mathbb{M}, s) \models M\varphi$. Then there is some u with Rsu, satisfying φ. Clearly, now u also satisfies ψ. This proves $(\mathbb{M}, s) \models M\varphi \rightarrow M\psi$. The other implication is shown analogously, so that we obtain $(\mathbb{M}, s) \models M\varphi \leftrightarrow M\psi$.

2.6.2.1 (i) If $\models \varphi$, then in all states u of $\mathbf{KD45_{(1)}}$-models, we have $(\mathbb{M}, u) \models \varphi$. Let s be any state of a $\mathbf{KD45_{(1)}}$-model. Then, by seriality, there is a u with Rsu satisfying φ; so $(\mathbb{M}, s) \models M\varphi$.

(ii) Similar to the proof in answer 2.6.1.1 (viii).

(iii) Apply the previous item to $\models \varphi \rightarrow (\varphi \vee \psi)$ (which is of course valid in our class of models).

(iv) Apply item (i) to $\varphi = \mathbf{true}$.

(v) The '$\rightarrow$' direction follows from item (iii); for the converse, suppose that we have $(\mathbb{M}, s) \models M\varphi \vee M\psi$; s has either an R-successor t in which φ is true, or an R-successor u satisfying ψ. In both cases s has some successor in which $(\varphi \vee \psi)$ holds, so $(\mathbb{M}, s) \models M(\varphi \vee \psi)$.

2.7.1 Consider structures $\mathbb{M} = \langle S, \mathcal{B}, R, \pi_T, \pi_F \rangle$, where S, $\mathcal{B}$, π_T and π_F are as before, and where, moreover, R is such that:

(i) $R = S \times \mathcal{B}_0$, where $\mathcal{B}_0$ stands for the subset of *complete* situations in $\mathcal{B}$. Stipulate that $\mathcal{B}_0 \neq \emptyset$. This ensures that R is serial, euclidean and transitive.

(ii) Now the interpretation of $B\varphi$ is as follows (note that $(\mathbb{M}, t) \models_T \varphi$ for a complete situation t amounts to the classical notion of satisfaction, so that we may write just $(\mathbb{M}, t) \models \varphi$):

$(\mathbb{M}, s) \models_T B\varphi \Leftrightarrow \forall t(Rst \Rightarrow (\mathbb{M}, t) \models \varphi)$ $(\Leftrightarrow \forall t \in \mathcal{B}_0 \Rightarrow (\mathbb{M}, t) \models \varphi)$;

$(\mathbb{M}, s) \models_F B\varphi \Leftrightarrow (\mathbb{M}, s) \not\models_T B\varphi$.

From Section 2.4, it follows that B has the desired $\mathbf{KD45_{(1)}}$-properties. We now show that $\mathbb{M} \models_T B_e\varphi \rightarrow B\varphi$ for all such extended structures, which is the same as $(\mathbb{M}, s) \models_T \neg B_e\varphi \vee B\varphi$, for all s. To do so, we have to show that either $(\mathbb{M}, s) \models_T \neg B_e\varphi$ or $(\mathbb{M}, s) \models_T B\varphi$. Suppose $(\mathbb{M}, s) \not\models_T \neg B_e\varphi$ which is, $(\mathbb{M}, s) \not\models_F B_e\varphi$. This is equivalent to $(\mathbb{M}, s) \models_T B_e\varphi$. Let $u \in \mathcal{B}_0$. Then, since $(\mathbb{M}, s) \models_T B_e\varphi$, we have $(\mathbb{M}, u) \models \varphi$, which proves that $(\mathbb{M}, s) \models_T B\varphi$.

REMARK. Note that something strange is going on here. Although we did the obvious thing above to embed 'ordinary' KD45-belief into the model of Levesque, we obtain $B_e\varphi \rightarrow B\varphi$ as a validity in this approach. This is strange when φ is an incoherent assertion like $p \wedge \neg p$: since we have in KD45 that $\neg B(p \wedge \neg p)$ is valid, we obtain by contraposition that also $\neg B_e(p \wedge \neg p)$ would be valid, which is against the very idea of Levesque's approach, where it is possible to believe in incoherent information. The solution to this paradox is that in order to accommodate for the seriality condition of the relation R associated with the B-operator we have stipulated above that $\mathcal{B}_0 \neq \emptyset$. However, this condition excludes the possibility of *explicit* belief in incoherent information as well, since to evaluate a formula of the form $B_e\varphi$ we have to consider all situations in $\mathcal{B}$, including those in $\mathcal{B}_0$. Precisely in the case that $\mathcal{B}_0 \neq \emptyset$, we then have that no incoherencies can be believed explicitly, since in $\mathcal{B}_0$ these cannot be true. The conclusion is that when we really want to represent incoherent explicit belief, ordinary KD45-belief cannot be implemented by means of a 'submodel' as above (but a K45-notion of belief *can*, just by dropping the condition $\mathcal{B}_0 \neq \emptyset$).

2.7.2 a (i) $(\mathbb{M}, s) \models_T \varphi \rightarrow \psi$ iff $(\mathbb{M}, s) \models_F \varphi$ or $(\mathbb{M}, s) \models_T \psi$.

(ii) It is *not* the case that $(\mathbb{M}, s) \models_T \varphi \rightarrow \psi \Leftrightarrow ((\mathbb{M}, s) \models_T \varphi \Rightarrow (\mathbb{M}, s) \models_T \psi)$.
To see this, let $\pi_T(s)(x) = \pi_F(s)(x) = f$ for both $x = p$ and $x = q$; then obviously it is not the case that $(\mathbb{M}, s) \models_F p$ or $(\mathbb{M}, s) \models_T q$, although we *do* have $(\mathbb{M}, s) \models_T p \Rightarrow (\mathbb{M}, s) \models_T q$!

(iii) If we let s be a complete situation, we *do* have that

$$(\mathbb{M}, s) \models_T \varphi \rightarrow \psi \Leftrightarrow ((\mathbb{M}, s) \models_T \varphi \Rightarrow (\mathbb{M}, s) \models_T \psi).$$

This is seen by proving by induction on φ that one has, for all complete situations,

$$(\mathbb{M}, s) \models_T \varphi \Leftrightarrow \text{not } (\mathbb{M}, s) \models_F \varphi.$$

b (i) We claim that $\not\models (B_e\varphi \wedge B_e(\varphi \rightarrow \psi)) \rightarrow B_e\psi$. To see this, let $\mathcal{B} = \{t\}$, and s a complete situation. We stipulate $\pi_T(t)(p) = t$, $\pi_F(t)(p) = t$ and $\pi_T(t)(q) = f$. Then $(\mathbb{M}, s) \models_T B_ep$, $(\mathbb{M}, s) \models B_e(p \rightarrow q)$, but not $(\mathbb{M}, s) \models_T B_eq$.

(ii) We have to check whether $(\mathbb{M}, s) \models_T \neg B_e\bot$, for all complete situations s. This is equivalent to $(\mathbb{M}, s) \models_F B_e\bot$, and this is $(\mathbb{M}, s) \not\models_T B_e\bot$. If the latter did not hold, we would be able to find a situation s for which $(\mathbb{M}, s) \models_T B_e\bot$. In this case, we would have $(\mathbb{M}, t) \models_T \bot$, for all $t \in \mathcal{B}$. The latter is only possible if such a $\mathcal{B}$ is allowed to be empty, which is not excluded by the definition, so we conclude that $\not\models \neg B_e\bot$

(iii) Let s be a complete situation, and suppose that $(\mathbb{M}, s) \models_T B_e\varphi$. This means that, for all u in $\mathcal{B}$, one has $(\mathbb{M}, u) \models_T \varphi$. In order to show that $(\mathbb{M}, s) \models_T B_eB_e\varphi$, we have to show that $(\mathbb{M}, t) \models_T B_e\varphi$, for all $t \in \mathcal{B}$. But the latter amounts to showing that $(\mathbb{M}, u) \models_T \varphi$ for all $u \in \mathcal{B}$, which is already observed. This proves $\models B_e\varphi \rightarrow B_eB_e\varphi$.

(iv) We have to check whether $(\mathbb{M}, s) \models_T \neg B_e\varphi \rightarrow B_e\neg B_e\varphi$, for all complete situations s. By 2.7.2a, we may use a classical treatment of the implication here. So, suppose $(\mathbb{M}, s) \models_T \neg B_e\varphi$. This means that $(\mathbb{M}, s) \models_F B_e\varphi$, or, $(\mathbb{M}, s) \not\models_T B_e\varphi$. So, there is some $u \in \mathcal{B}$ for which $(\mathbb{M}, u) \not\models_T \varphi$. But then we can find such a u for every $t \in \mathcal{B}$, which says that $(\mathbb{M}, s) \models_T B_e\neg B_e\varphi$.

2.7.3 For all of the formulas that we claim to be satisfiable, we give one frame $\mathbb{F} = \langle S, \mathcal{B}\rangle$ and vary the valuations π_T and π_F, based on $\mathbb{F}$, for each item accordingly. We assume that $s \in S$ is a complete situation, and $\mathcal{B} = \{u, v\}$.

(i) $\pi_T(x)(p) = \pi_T(x)(q) = t$ for all $x \in \mathcal{B}$.

(ii) Note that $(\mathbb{M}, s) \models_T \neg B_e((p \wedge q) \rightarrow p)$ iff $(\mathbb{M}, s) \not\models_T B_e((p \wedge q) \rightarrow p)$, i.e. iff there is some $t \in \mathcal{B}$ fo which $(\mathbb{M}, t) \not\models_T (p \wedge q) \rightarrow p$, which is, by Exercise 2.7.2a (i), equivalent to the statement that there is some $t \in \mathcal{B}$ for which the negation of $(\mathbb{M}, t) \models_F p \wedge q$ or $(\mathbb{M}, t) \models_T p$ is true: so we have to specify a t in $\mathcal{B}$ for which $(\mathbb{M}, t) \not\models_F p \wedge q$ and $(\mathbb{M}, t) \not\models_T p$. For $u \in \mathcal{B}$, we stipulate $\pi_T(u)(p) = f$ (so that $(\mathbb{M}, u) \not\models_T p$) and $\pi_F(u)(q) = f$ and $\pi_F(u)(p) = f$ (so that $(\mathbb{M}, u) \not\models_F p \wedge q$).

(iii) This formula is not satisfiable. For suppose that s is such that $(\mathbb{M}, s) \models_T B_e(p \wedge q) \wedge \neg B_ep \wedge$

$\neg B_e q$; then, for all t in $\mathcal{B}$ we have $(\mathbb{M}, t) \models_T p \wedge q$, for which we must have $\pi_T(t)(p) = \pi_T(t)(q) =$ t. For s however, to also hold that $(\mathbb{M}, s) \models_T \neg B_e p$, there must be a u in $\mathcal{B}$ for which $(\mathbb{M}, u) \not\models_T p$, i.e., $\pi_T(u)(p) \neq t$, which is impossible.

(iv) This formula is satisfiable; to see this we stipulate $\pi_T(x)(p) = t$; $\pi_T(x)(q) = t$; $\pi_F(x)(p) = t$ and $\pi_F(x)(q) = t$, for all $x \in \{u, v\}$.

(v) We stipulate $\pi_T(u)(p) = f$; $\pi_F(u)(p) = t$; $\pi_T(v)(p) = t$ and $\pi_F(v)(p) = f$; then $(\mathbb{M}, u) \not\models_T p$ and $(\mathbb{M}, v) \not\models_T \neg p$ so that $(\mathbb{M}, s) \models_T \neg B_e p \wedge \neg B_e \neg p$.

(vi) This formula is satisfiable; it is true in s, if the π's are specified as in (v).

2.7.4.1 As in the answers to Exercise 2.7.3, we only need a model containing a complete situation s and $\mathcal{B} = \{u, v\}$.

(i) We gave a model for this set in the answer to Exercise 2.7.2(i).

(ii) We specify $\pi_T(u)(p) = f = \pi_F(u)(p)$, then $(\mathbb{M}, u) \not\models_T p \vee \neg p$.

(iii) Let $\pi_T(u)(q) = f = \pi_F(u)(q)$ and $\pi_T(u)(p) = t = \pi_T(v)(p)$.

(iv) Let $\pi_T(x)(p) = t$ $\pi_F(x)(p)$ for all x in $\mathcal{B}$; moreover stipulate $\pi_T(u)(q) = f$.

(v) Take the situation of (iv).

(vi) Take the situation of (iv).

2.7.4.2 Here, we will say that the logic does not suffer from LOi ($i \leq 10$) if the logical omniscience property denoted by LOi (cf. the introduction to Section 2.5) is not valid (in the approach of Levesque). We also say then that LOi does not hold.

(LO1) This does not hold: we showed this in the answer to Exercise 2.7.2(i).

(LO2) Not valid, as witnessed by Proposition 2.7.4.

(LO3) Note that validities are only checked at complete situations, so that one may easily verify that $\models (p \wedge q) \rightarrow p$; however, we know from the answer to Exercise 2.7.3(ii) that $\not\models B_e((p \wedge q) \rightarrow p)$.

(LO4) Not valid: note that $\models (p \vee \neg p) \leftrightarrow (q \vee \neg q)$, but $\not\models B_e(p \vee \neg p) \leftrightarrow B_e(q \vee \neg q)$. To see the latter, let s be a complete situation, let $\pi_T(u)(p) = t$; $\pi_T(u)(q) = f$ and $\pi_F(u)(q) = f$. Then we have $(\mathbb{M}, s) \models_T B_e(p \vee \neg p)$ but $(\mathbb{M}, s) \not\models_T B_e(q \vee \neg q)$.

(LO5) This is valid: suppose that $(\mathbb{M}, s) \models_T (B_e\varphi \wedge B_e\psi)$, that is, for all $u \in \mathcal{B}$ one has $(\mathbb{M}, u) \models_T \varphi$ and $(\mathbb{M}, u) \models_T \psi$, and hence $(\mathbb{M}, u) \models_T \varphi \wedge \psi$.

(LO6) Also valid: reason as with LO5.

(LO7) Not valid: cf. Proposition 2.7.4(v).

(LO8) Valid: if there was any s with $(\mathbb{M}, s) \not\models_T B_e(B_e\varphi \rightarrow \varphi)$, then there must be a $u \in \mathcal{B}$ with $(\mathbb{M}, u) \not\models_T B_e\varphi \rightarrow \varphi$, i.e. for this u we would have $(\mathbb{M}, u) \models_T B_e\varphi$ and $(\mathbb{M}, u) \not\models_T \varphi$, which is impossible.

(LO9) This depends on the definition of **true**: we have for instance $\not\models B_e(p \vee \neg p)$. However, if we define **true** $= \neg\bot$, then one has $\models B_e$**true** (cf. Exercise 2.7.2(ii)).

(LO10) Not valid, as verified in Proposition 2.7.4(iv).

2.8.1 In the following, when demonstrating that some formula is not valid, we only specify the relevant features of a counter-example: such a counter-example can always be embedded in a Kripke model $\mathbb{M} = \langle S, \pi, \mathcal{A}_1, \ldots, A_n, R_1, \ldots, R_n \rangle$ with all R_i serial, transitive and euclidean.

(a) (i) Not valid: we specify that for all t with $R_i st$ we have $\pi(t)(p) = \pi(t)(q) = t$, and also that $\mathcal{A}_i(s) = \{p, p \rightarrow q\}$; then $(\mathbb{M}, s) \not\models (B_{E,i}p \wedge B_{E,i}(p \rightarrow q)) \rightarrow B_{E,i}q$.

(ii) Since $B_{E,i}\varphi \leftrightarrow (A_i\varphi \wedge B_i\varphi)$ and we already observed in Section 2.4 that axiom (D) implies that $\neg B_i\bot$ is valid on $\mathcal{KD45}_{(m)}$-models, we now have $\models \neg B_{E,i}\bot$

(iii) Not valid: let $\mathcal{A}_i(s) = \{p\}$ and for all t with $R_i st$ we suppose that $\pi(t)(p) = t$. Then we have $(\mathbb{M}, s)$

$\models B_{E,i}p$, but not $(\mathbb{M}, s) \models B_{E,i}B_{E,i}p$ (since $B_{E,i}p \notin \mathcal{A}_i(s)$).

(iv) Not valid: let $\mathcal{A}_i(s) = \{p\}$. Then $(\mathbb{M}, s) \models \neg B_{E,i}q$ but also $(\mathbb{M}, s) \models \neg B_{E,i}\neg B_{E,i}q$.

(b) The following properties are sufficient, if required for all situations t.

(i) Demand that each $\mathcal{A}_i(t)$ is closed under subformulas. A weaker, but less natural property also makes the formula of this item valid: impose that for all φ, $\varphi \to \psi \in \mathcal{A}_i(t)$, one also has that $\psi \in \mathcal{A}_i(t)$.

(iii) $\mathcal{A}_i(t)$ should be closed under $B_{E,i}$: for all φ, $(\varphi \in \mathcal{A}_i(t) \Rightarrow B_{E,i}\varphi \in \mathcal{A}_i(t))$, and moreoever, $\mathcal{A}_i$ has to satisfy, for all φ and t: $(\varphi \in \mathcal{A}_i(t)$ and $R_itu) \Rightarrow \varphi \in \mathcal{A}_i(u)$.

(iv) Sufficient is: $\neg B_{E,i}\varphi \in \mathcal{A}_i(t)$, for all φ.

2.8.2 When demonstrating that some formula is satisfiable, we only specify the relevant features of the satisfying pair $(\mathbb{M}, s)$: we claim that it can always be embedded in a Kripke model $\mathbb{M} = \langle S, \pi, \mathcal{A}_1, \ldots, \mathcal{A}_n, R_1, \ldots, R_n\rangle$ with all R_i serial, transitive and euclidean.

(i) Satisfiable: require that all t with R_ist satisfy the properties that $\pi(t)(p) = \pi(t)(q) = t$ and $\{p \wedge q\} \subseteq \mathcal{A}_i(s)$.

(ii) Satisfied in the model of (i).

(iii) Satisfied in the model of (i).

(iv) Not satisfiable. The formula implies $B_i(p \wedge q) \wedge B_i\neg p \wedge B_i\neg q$: this is not satisfiable in a $\mathcal{KD}45_{(m)}$-model, as was observed in Exercise 2.4.3.1(a)(ii).

(v) Satisfiable: let R_ist and R_isu; stipulate $\pi(t)(p) = t$ and $\pi(u)(p) = f$.

(vi) Satisfied in the model of (v), if we moreover stipulate that $\{p \vee \neg p\} \subseteq \mathcal{A}_i(s)$.

2.8.3.1

(i) Satisfiability was demonstrated in the answer to Exercise 2.8.1(i).

(ii) Satisfied in any s with a t with R_ist and $(p \vee \neg p) \notin \mathcal{A}_i(s)$.

(iii) Satisfied in any s with $p \in \mathcal{A}_i(s)$, and such that for all t with R_ist it holds that $\pi(t)(p) = t$, and moreover $(p \wedge (q \vee \neg q)) \notin \mathcal{A}_i(s)$.

(iv) See (v).

(v) $B_{E,i}p \wedge B_{E,i}\neg p$ is not satisfiable: it implies $B_ip \wedge B_i\neg p$ which is obviously not $\mathcal{KD}45_{(m)}$-satisfiable (suppose the formula holds in state s; s then has an R_i-successor, which has to verify both p and $\neg p$: this is impossible).

(vi) $B_{E,i}(p \wedge \neg p)$ implies $B_i(p \wedge \neg p)$ which is not $\mathcal{KD}45_{(m)}$-satisfiable (Cf. (v)).

2.8.3.2

(LO1) Not valid in the awareness approach, as witnessed by Proposition 2.8.3(i).

(LO2) Not valid: see Proposition 2.8.3(ii).

(LO3) Not valid: an agent need not be aware of ψ. In the answer to Exercise 2.8.2(iii) we saw that $B_{E,i}(p \wedge q) \wedge \neg B_{E,i}p$ is satisfiable, although of course $\models (p \wedge q) \to p$.

(LO4) Not valid: although $\models (p \wedge q) \leftrightarrow (q \wedge p)$, it is possible that the agent is aware of one conjunction, without being aware of the other (stipulate $\mathcal{A}_i(s) = \{(p \wedge q), p, q\}$ and $\pi(t)(p) = \pi(t)(q) = t$ for all t with R_ist, then $(\mathbb{M}, s) \models B_{E,i}(p \wedge q) \wedge \neg B_{E,i}(q \wedge p)$).

(LO5) Not valid: in the situation above we have $(\mathbb{M}, s) \models B_{E,i}q \wedge B_{E,i}p \wedge \neg B_{E,i}(q \wedge p)$.

(LO6) Not valid: in the situation above we have $(\mathbb{M}, s) \models B_{E,i}q \wedge \neg B_{E,i}(q \vee p)$

(LO7) Valid: if $B_{E,i}\varphi$ holds, then we also have $B_i\varphi$, and hence (the models are serial) $\neg B_i\varphi$ and thus $\neg B_{E,i}\varphi$.

(LO8) Not valid: in the model that refuted (LO4), we have $(\mathbb{M}, s) \models \neg B_{E,i}(B_{E,i}p \rightarrow p)$.

(LO9) Not valid: as long as **true** $\notin \mathcal{A}_i(s)$, we have $(\mathbb{M}, s) \models \neg B_{E,i}$**true**.

(LO10) Valid: since we know from the answer to Exercise 2.8.3(v) that $B_{E,i}\varphi \wedge B_{E,i}\neg\varphi$ is never satisfied, and hence $\models (B_{E,i}\varphi \wedge B_{E,i}\neg\varphi) \rightarrow \bot$, and thus also (LO10) is valid.

2.9.1 In this exercise, we will not mention the assignment per world, but only specify the truth of formulas φ in clusters $T_1, T_2, \ldots$, all frames of mind of agent i in state s: all the T's are supposed to be members of $\mathcal{C}_i(s)$. Note that the dual $\neg B_i\neg\varphi$ is true in s iff for all clusters in $\mathcal{C}_i(s)$ there is some state in which φ is true.

(i) Not valid: let p be true in cluster T_1, and $\neg p$ be true in T_2, and suppose q to be valid in no cluster $T_j \in \mathcal{C}_i(s)$. Then $(\mathbb{M}, s) \models B_ip \wedge B_i(p \rightarrow q) \wedge \neg B_iq$.

(ii) Valid: a cluster $T_j \in \mathcal{C}_i(s)$ may not be empty, and cannot satisfy $\bot$.

(iii) Not valid. To see this, suppose $\mathcal{C}_i(s) = \{\{t\}\}$ and $\mathcal{C}_i(t) = \{\{u\}\}$; suppose p is true in t, but not in u. Then $(\mathbb{M}, s) \models B_ip \wedge \neg B_iB_ip$.

(iv) Not valid: in the situation of (iii) we have $(\mathbb{M}, s) \models \neg B_i\neg p \wedge \neg B_i\neg B_i\neg p$.

2.9.2 (i) Satisfiable: let s have a cluster T_j in which $(p \wedge q)$ is valid.

(ii) Not satisfiable: immediate from Exercise 2.9.1(ii).

(iii) Not satisfiable: if $B_i(p \wedge q)$ is true at s, i.e. there is a $T_j \in \mathcal{C}_i(s)$ in which $(p \wedge q)$ is valid: but in T_i then, both p and q are also valid.

(iv) This is satisfiable, let T_1, T_2 and T_3 be clusters in $\mathcal{C}_i(s)$, such that $(p \wedge q)$ is true in T_1, $\neg p$ in T_2 and $\neg q$ in T_3; then, the formula is true in $(\mathbb{M}, s)$.

(v) Satisfiable: we only need to require that for each cluster $T_j \in \mathcal{C}_i(s)$ there is a state in which p is true, and one in which $\neg p$ is true.

(vi) This is satisfied in the state s of item (v).

2.9.3.1

(i) Demonstrated in Exercise 2.9.1(i).

(ii) Note that $(p \vee \neg p)$ is true in each state, hence also in each state of some cluster $T_j \in \mathcal{C}_i(s)$, so that $B_i(p \vee \neg p)$ is true in each state s.

(iii) If B_ip is true in s, then there is a cluster $T_j \in \mathcal{C}_i(s)$ such that for all $t \in T_j$, p is true. Those states t are perfectly classical, so they also satisfy $(p \wedge (q \vee \neg q))$: hence $B_i(p \wedge (q \vee \neg q))$ must be true at s.

(iv) The satisfiability of this set is seen as follows. Suppose s has two clusters T_1 and T_2. In T_1, p is true in all states, but q is not, in T_2, $\neg p$ is true in all states, but q is not. Then $(\mathbb{M}, s) \models B_ip \wedge B_i\neg p \wedge \neg B_iq$.

(v) Satisfied in $(\mathbb{M}, s)$ of item (iv).

(vi) If this were true at s, there would be a cluster $T_j \in \mathcal{C}_i(s)$ such that all states in T_j verify $(p \wedge \neg p)$. Since T_j is non-empty, this is impossible.

2.9.3.2

(LO1) Not valid: see the answer to Exercise 2.9.1(i).

(LO2) Valid: there is always a cluster $T_j \in \mathcal{C}_i(s)$ that validates tautologies.

(LO3) Valid: if $\models \varphi \rightarrow \psi$, and $(\mathbb{M}, s) \models B_i\varphi$, then there is a cluster $T_j \in \mathcal{C}_i(s)$ that validates φ. By our assumption then, T_j must also validate ψ, so $(\mathbb{M}, s) \models B_i\psi$.

(LO4) Valid: reason as we did with LO3.

(LO5) Not valid, as follows from Proposition 2.9.3(v, vi).

(LO6) Valid, as follows immediately from the validity of (LO3).

(LO7) Not valid, as follows from Proposition 2.9.3(v).

(LO8) Not valid. Suppose $\mathcal{C}_i(s) = \{T_j\}_{j \in \mathcal{J}}$, and in each T_j there is some $t_j \in T_j$ such that $\neg p$ is true at t_j and $\mathcal{C}_i(t_j) = \{\{u\}\}$ for some state u with $\pi(u)(p) = t$. Then, the following holds at s: in each cluster $T_j \in \mathcal{C}_i(s)$ there is a state t_j such that $(\mathbb{M}, t_j) \models B_i p \wedge \neg p$, hence $(\mathbb{M}, s) \models \neg B_i(B_i p \rightarrow p)$.

(LO9) Valid, as follows from the validity of LO2.

(LO10) Not valid: this follows from Proposition 2.9.3(iv).

2.9.4 (i) Suppose that we have for all s' and s that $s' \in T \in \mathcal{C}_i(s)$ implies $T \in \mathcal{C}_i(s')$, and also that $(\mathbb{M}, s) \models B_i\varphi$, saying that there is some cluster T in $\mathcal{C}_i(s)$ such that for all $s' \in T$ it holds that $(\mathbb{M}, s') \models \varphi$. By our assumption, for all $s' \in T$ the cluster T is also a member of $\mathcal{C}_i(s')$, so that $(\mathbb{M}, s') \models B_i\varphi$ for all s' in the cluster $T \in \mathcal{C}_i(s)$. But this implies that $(\mathbb{M}, s) \models B_iB_i\varphi$.

(ii) Suppose that for all clusters $T \in \mathcal{C}_i(s)$, we have that $\mathcal{C}_i(t) \subseteq \mathcal{C}_i(s)$, for all $t \in T$, and also that $(\mathbb{M}, s) \models \neg B_i\varphi$. This means that each cluster $T \in \mathcal{C}_i(s)$ has a state t such that $(\mathbb{M}, t) \models \neg\varphi$. Let $T \in \mathcal{C}_i(s)$, and $t \in T$. If T' is some cluster in $\mathcal{C}_i(t)$, then $T' \in \mathcal{C}_i(s)$. So there is a state $t' \in T'$ with $(\mathbb{M}, t') \models \neg\varphi$. Thus, in no cluster T' of $\mathcal{C}_i(t)$, formula φ is valid. This means that $(\mathbb{M}, t) \models \neg B_i\varphi$, for all t in T, so that $(\mathbb{M}, s) \models B_i\neg B_i\varphi$.

2.10.1

(a) (i) Not valid: consider a state s such that there is a t with R_ist and $\pi(t)(q) = f$. Furthemore, let $\mathcal{P}_i(s) = \{p, p \rightarrow q\}$. Then $(\mathbb{M}, s) \models B_{I,i}p \wedge B_{I,i}(p \rightarrow q) \wedge \neg B_{I,i}q$.

(ii) Not valid: if $\bot \in \mathcal{P}_i(s)$ then immediately $(\mathbb{M}, s) \models B_{I,i}\bot$.

(iii) Not valid: let $p \in \mathcal{P}_i(s)$ and $B_{I,i}p \notin \mathcal{P}_i(s)$; furthermore let u be such that R_ist and R_itu for some state t, $B_{I,i}p \notin \mathcal{P}_i(t)$, and $\pi(u)(p) = f$. Then we have $(\mathbb{M}, s) \models B_{I,i}p \wedge \neg B_{I,i}B_{I,i}p$.

(iv) Not valid: let $p \notin \mathcal{P}_i(s)$, $\neg B_{I,i}p \notin \mathcal{P}_i(s)$, and choose t with R_ist, $\pi(t)(p) = f$ and $p \in \mathcal{P}_i(t)$. Then $(\mathbb{M}, s) \models \neg B_{I,i}p \wedge \neg B_{I,i}\neg B_{I,i}p$.

(b)(iii) For positive introspection, it is sufficient that $\mathcal{P}_i(s)$ is the whole language, for all s. A weaker, more natural condition is, for all formulas φ: $(\varphi \in \mathcal{P}_i(s) \Rightarrow B_{I,i}\varphi \in \mathcal{P}_i(s))$. To show this, assume the condition together with $(\mathbb{M}, s) \models B_{I,i}\varphi$. Then either $(\mathbb{M}, s) \models B_i\varphi$ or $(\mathbb{M}, s) \models P_i\varphi$; in the former case we have $(\mathbb{M}, s) \models B_iB_i\varphi$, and hence also $(\mathbb{M}, s) \models B_iB_{I,i}\varphi$, and thus $(\mathbb{M}, s) \models B_{I,i}B_{I,i}\varphi$. In the latter, since then $\varphi \in \mathcal{P}_i(s)$ holds, also $B_{I,i}\varphi \in \mathcal{P}_i(s)$, and so $(\mathbb{M}, s) \models P_iB_{I,i}\varphi$, and hence again $(\mathbb{M}, s) \models B_{I,i}B_{I,i}\varphi$.

(iv) Again, the constraint that $\mathcal{P}_i(s)$ is the whole language is sufficient. Also sufficient is, for all φ, $(\varphi \notin \mathcal{P}_i(s) \Rightarrow \neg B_{I,i}\varphi \in \mathcal{P}_i(s))$. To prove this, suppose this condition holds, and that $(\mathbb{M}, s) \models \neg B_{I,i}\varphi$. Then $(\mathbb{M}, s) \models \neg B_i\varphi \wedge \neg P_i\varphi$, implying $\varphi \notin \mathcal{P}_i(s)$. The condition gives $(\mathbb{M}, s) \models B_{I,i}\neg B_{I,i}\varphi$.

2.10.2 (i) Yes: satisfied at any state s with $(p \wedge q) \in \mathcal{P}_i(s)$.

(ii) Not satisfiable: note that $\neg B_{I,i}\varphi \equiv (\neg B_i\varphi \wedge \neg P_i\varphi)$. But we know from Proposition 1.3.5(ii) that, in any modal system, $\models B_i((p \wedge q) \rightarrow q)$ is valid.

(iii) Satisfiable: let s be a state with $\{p \wedge q\} = \mathcal{P}_i(s)$ and let t be such that R_ist and $\pi(t)(p) = \pi(t)(q) = f$. Then $(\mathbb{M}, s) \models B_{I,i}(p \wedge q) \wedge \neg B_{I,i}p \wedge \neg B_{I,i}q$.

(iv) Satisfied at any state s with $\{(p \wedge q), \neg p, \neg q\} \subseteq \mathcal{P}_i(s)$.

(v) Satisfied for s with $\{p, \neg p\} \cap \mathcal{P}_i(s) = \varnothing$, and with t, u with R_ist, R_isu such that $\pi(t)(p) = t$ and $\pi(u(p) = f$.

(vi) Satisfied in the state of (v).

2.10.3.1

(i) The set is satisfied in any state s with $q \notin \mathcal{P}_i(s) \supseteq \{p, p \to q\}$ and with a t with $R_i st$ and $\pi(t)(q) = f$.

(ii) We know from Proposition 1.3.5(iv) that $\models B_i(p \vee \neg p)$ and hence we have $\models B_{I,i}(p \vee \neg p)$.

(iii) Satisfied in any state s with $p \in \mathcal{P}_i(s) \not\ni (p \wedge (q \vee \neg q))$, with a state t with $R_i st$ and $\pi(t)(p) = f$.

(iv) Satisfied in any state s with $\{p, \neg p\} \subseteq \mathcal{P}_i(s) \not\ni q$, with a state t with $R_i st$ and $\pi(t)(q) = f$.

(v) Satisfied in s of (iv).

(vi) Satisfied in any state s with $\{(p \wedge \neg p)\} \subseteq \mathcal{P}_i(s)$.

2.10.3.2

(LO1) Not valid (cf. Proposition 2.10.3(i)).

(LO2) Valid: if $\models$ then (Proposition 1.3.5(iv)) we have $\models B_i\varphi$ and then, by definition of $B_{I,i}$, we also obtain $\models B_{I,i}\varphi$.

(LO3) Not valid, as follows immediately from Exercise 2.10.2(ii) and $\models (p \wedge q) \to p$.

(LO4) Not valid, as follows from Proposition 2.10.3(iii) and $\models p \leftrightarrow (p \wedge (q \vee \neg q))$.

(LO5) Not valid: let $\mathcal{P}_i(s) = \{p, \neg p\}$. Then $(\mathbb{M}, s) \models B_{I,i}p \wedge B_{I,i}\neg p \wedge \neg B_{I,i}(p \wedge \neg p)$.

(LO6) Not valid: let $\mathcal{P}_i(s) = \{p\}$ and $R_i ss$, $\pi(s)(p) = \pi(s)(q) = f$. Then $(\mathbb{M}, s) \models B_{I,i}p \wedge \neg B_{I,i}(p \vee q)$

(LO7) Not valid, as follows from Proposition 2.10.3(v).

(LO8) Not valid: let $(B_{I,i}p \to p) \notin \mathcal{P}_i(s)$, t a state with $R_i st$, $p \in \mathcal{P}_i(t)$ and $\pi(t)(p) = f$. Then $(\mathbb{M}, s) \models \neg P_i(B_{I,i}p \to p) \wedge \neg B_i(B_{I,i}p \to p)$, hence $(\mathbb{M}, s) \models \neg B_{I,i}(B_{I,i}p \to p)$.

(LO9) Valid: reason as for (LO2).

(LO10) Not valid: put $\mathcal{P}_i(s) = \{p, \neg p\}$. Then $(\mathbb{M}, s) \models B_{I,i}p \wedge B_{I,i}\neg p \wedge \neg B_{I,i}\bot$.

2.11.1 (i) Not valid: let s be such that $R_i sX$ only for $X = \{x_1, x_2\}$. For these worlds, we specify p to be true only at x_1 (so we have $(\mathbb{M}, s) \models B_i p$) and let q false in both x_1 and x_2. Now $(\mathbb{M}, s) \models B_i(p \to q)$, since in X there is a world (namely x_2) in which p is false. However, since there is no q-world in X, we have $(\mathbb{M}, s) \not\models B_i q$.

(ii) Not valid: suppose $R_i sX$ for no $X \subseteq S$. Then, for all T with $R_i sT$, any condition is true, in particular, any such T contains a state with $(\mathbb{M}, t) \models \bot$.

(iii) Not valid: let s be such that $R_i sX$ only for $X = \{t\}$ and $R_i tY$ only for $Y = \{u\}$. Furthermore, suppose $\pi(t)(p) = t$ and $\pi(u)(p) = f$. Then we have $(\mathbb{M}, s) \models B_i p \wedge \neg B_i B_i p$.

(iv) First note that $(\mathbb{M}, s) \models \neg B_i \neg\varphi \Leftrightarrow \exists T \subseteq S\ [R_i sT \text{ and } \forall t(t \in T \Rightarrow (\mathbb{M}, t) \models \varphi)]$. To show that negative introspection is not valid here, let s be such that $R_i sX$ only for $X = \{t\}$, $R_i tY$ only for $Y = \{u\}$. Let $\pi(t)(p) = f$; $\pi(u)(p) = t$. Then: $(\mathbb{M}, s) \models \neg B_i p \wedge \neg B_i \neg B_i p$.

2.11.2 In the following, we assume the R_i to be minimal: specifying $R_i sX$ implies that for no other Y, $R_i sY$.

(i) Yes: let $R_i s\{t\}$, $\pi(t)(p) = \pi(t)(q) = t$. Then $(\mathbb{M}, s) \models B_i(p \wedge q)$.

(ii) Not satisfiable: if t is an arbitrary state in an arbitrary cluster T, then $(\mathbb{M}, t) \models ((p \wedge q) \to q)$, so $(\mathbb{M}, s) \models B_i((p \wedge q) \to q)$ (recall that T is never empty).

(iii) Not satisfiable: if $(\mathbb{M}, s) \models B_i(p \wedge q)$, then in each cluster T there is a state t such that $(\mathbb{M}, t) \models (p \wedge q)$. Obviously, in each cluster T there must then also be a state t with both $(\mathbb{M}, t) \models p$ and $(\mathbb{M}, t) \models q$.

(iv) This is satisfiable: let $R_i s\{u,v\}$, p and q both true at u, both false at v. Then one has $(\mathbb{M}, s) \models B_i(p \wedge q) \wedge B_i\neg p \wedge B_i\neg q$.

(v) Satisfiable: let $R_i s\{t\}$ and $R_i s\{u\}$; let p be true at t but false at u. Then not in all clusters there is a p-world, nor is there in each cluster a $\neg p$-world: so $(\mathbb{M}, s) \models \neg B_i p \wedge \neg B_i \neg p$.

(vi) Satisfied in the situation of (v).

2.11.3.1

(i) The satisfiability is shown in the answer to Exercise 2.11.1(i).

(ii) The unsatisfiability is argued as we did in the answer to Exercise 2.11.2(ii): states in clusters are classical, so, since clusters are not empty, in every cluster we find a state t with $(\mathbb{M}, t) \models (p \vee \neg p)$, hence $(\mathbb{M}, s) \models B_i(p \vee \neg p)$.

(iii) We can argue as in (ii); if every cluster T with R_isT has a state t such that $(\mathbb{M}, t) \models p$ (which is necessary for $(\mathbb{M}, s) \models B_ip$), then every cluster T with R_isT also has a state t with $(\mathbb{M}, t) \models p \wedge (q \vee \neg q)$, so that $(\mathbb{M}, s) \models B_ip \rightarrow B_i(p \wedge (q \vee \neg q))$.

(iv) Satisfiable: let $R_is\{u,t\}$ such that q is false in both u and t, p is true at u but false at t. Then we have $(\mathbb{M}, s) \models B_ip \wedge B_i\neg p \wedge \neg B_iq$.

(v) Satisfied in the state s of (iv).

(vi) True in any state s for which no T exists with R_isT: cf. the answer to Exercise 2.11.1(ii).

2.11.3.2

(LO1) Not valid: cf. Exercise 2.11.1(i).

(LO2) Valid: if $\models \varphi$, then all states in each cluster T with R_isT verify φ; hence $(\mathbb{M}, s) \models B_i\varphi$ (Recall that a cluster T is never empty).

(LO3) Valid: if $\models \varphi \rightarrow \psi$, and $(\mathbb{M}, s) \models B_i\varphi$, then all clusters T with R_isT have a state t such that $(\mathbb{M}, t) \models \varphi$. Obviously, such t verify $(\mathbb{M}, t) \models \psi$, such that $(\mathbb{M}, s) \models B_i\psi$.

(LO4) Valid: reason as for (LO3).

(LO5) Not valid: cf. Exercise 2.11.2(iii).

(LO6) Valid: as follows immediately from the validity of (LO3).

(LO7) Not valid: cf. Proposition 2.11.3(v).

(LO8) Not valid. To see this, let s be such that $R_is\{t\}$ and $R_it\{u\}$. Suppose p is true at t, false at u. Then we have $(\mathbb{M}, t) \models B_ip \wedge \neg p$, i.e., $(\mathbb{M}, t) \models \neg(B_ip \rightarrow p)$. Since $\{t\}$ is the only cluster accessible from s, and it contains only t, we have $(\mathbb{M}, s) \not\models B_i(B_ip \rightarrow p)$.

(LO9) Valid: follows from the validity of (LO2).

(LO10) Not valid: in the situation s of the answer to Exercise 2.11.3.1(v), we have $(\mathbb{M}, s) \models B_ip \wedge B_i\neg p \wedge \neg B_i\bot$

2.12.1 In the following, (only) states with a superscript * are states in S^*.

(LO1) Let R_isx only for $x = s^*$, $\pi^*(s^*)(\varphi) = t$; $\pi^*(s^*)(\varphi \rightarrow \psi) = t$ and $\pi^*(s^*)(\psi) = f$.

(LO2) Not valid: note that, although $\models (p \vee \neg p)$ (we only evaluate formulas in classical worlds), $B_i(p \vee \neg p)$ is false at any s with a t^* and $\pi^*(t^*)((p \vee \neg p)) = f$.

(LO3) Not valid: although we have $\models ((p \wedge q) \rightarrow q)$, the formula $B_i((p \wedge q) \rightarrow q)$ is false at any s with a t^* such that R_ist^* and $\pi^*(t^*)((p \wedge q) \rightarrow q)) = f$.

(LO4) Not valid: reason as with (LO2); stipulate that only R_ist^* and stipulate $\pi^*(t^*)((p \vee \neg p)) = f$ whereas $\pi^*(t^*)((q \vee \neg q)) = t$.

(LO5) We only need one successor s^* of s to invalidate this formula: stipulate $\pi^*(s^*)(\varphi) = \pi^*(s^*)(\psi) = t$ and $\pi^*(s^*)(\varphi \wedge \psi) = f$.

(LO6) Suppose R_iss^*; stipulate $\pi^*(s^*)(\varphi) = t$ and $\pi^*(s^*)((\varphi \vee \psi)) = f$.

(LO7) Suppose R_iss^* and $\pi^*(s^*)(\varphi) = t = \pi^*(s^*)(\neg\varphi)$.

(LO8) Let s^* be a (non-normal) successor of s and stipulate $\pi^*(s^*)((B_i\varphi \rightarrow \varphi)) = f$.

(LO9) Let R_iss^* and stipulate $\pi^*(s^*)(\mathbf{true}) = f$.

(LO10) Recall that $\bot$ is defined as $(p_0 \wedge \neg p_0)$. Let $R_i sx$ only for one state $x = s^* \in S^*$ and let π^* and φ be such that $\pi^*(s^*)(\varphi) = \pi^*(s^*)(\neg\varphi) = t$, but $\pi^*(s^*)(p_0 \wedge \neg p_0) = f$. Since π^* has to be a function (assigning truth values to formulas), we see that we can invalidate $(B_i\varphi \wedge B_i\neg\varphi) \rightarrow B_i\bot$ for all $\varphi \neq (p_0 \wedge \neg p_0)$.

*2.13.5.1.1

Let us denote the class of models introduced in Section 2.13.3 by $\mathcal{M}$. Then the aim of this exercise is to prove that

$$\text{for all } \varphi \in \mathcal{L}^m_{\mathbf{KB}}(\mathbf{P})\text{: } \mathbf{KL} \vdash \varphi \text{ iff } \mathcal{M} \models \varphi$$

The proof of this statement roughly follows the lines we gave for the systems for knowledge in Section 2.1: in particular, soundness above (the '⇒' direction) will be proven in a way similar to the proof of Theorem 2.1.3, and completeness ('⇐') similar to the proof as given in Section *2.1.4.

To be more precise, the proof will proceed in the following steps.

1 We define a class of models $\mathcal{KL}$ that yield the same validities as $\mathcal{M}$, the models as defined in Section 2.13.3. This is done in definition Q1; in Lemma Q2 we observe the equivalence between the two classes. Thus, from that lemma on, we may reason about $\mathcal{KL}$ to prove completeness of **KL**.
2 In Lemma Q4 we show the soundness part of the statement above: $\mathbf{KL} \vdash \varphi \Rightarrow \mathcal{M} \models \varphi$.
3 In Definition Q5 we define the canonical model $\mathbb{M}$ for **KL**, and we observe in Q6 that it satisfies already some of the properties of $\mathcal{KL}$-models, though not all.
4 Given a consistent formula φ, we will define a suitable set Ψ for it (Definition Q7), and make a filtration of the canonical model $\mathbb{M}$ through this set Ψ. Thus, we obtain the model $\underline{\mathbb{M}}$, of which we will show that it is both a member of $\mathcal{KL}$ (Theorem Q10) and a model for Ψ (and hence for φ) (Theorem Q12).

The proof for the knowledge + belief case here is a bit more complicated than the case in which one has only to deal with knowledge (Section 2.1). In particular, the definition the relations T_i in the filtration deviate from the S_i-case, and the induction axiom for common belief differ from that of common knowledge. We will treat the proof in some detail.

DEFINITION Q1. Let us, for economic purposes, define the class of $\mathcal{KL}$-models of type $\mathbb{M} = \langle S, \pi, R_1, ..., R_m, T_1, ..., T_m, R_E, R_C, T_F, T_D\rangle$ in which:

(a) R_i $(i \leq m)$ is reflexive, transitive and euclidean, i.e. R_i is an equivalence relation.
(b) $R_E = R_1 \cup ... \cup R_m$.
(c) $(R_E)^+ = R_C$.
(d) T_i $(i \leq m)$ is serial, transitive and euclidean.

(e) $T_F = T_1 \cup \ldots \cup T_m$.
(f) $(T_F)^+ = T_D$.
(g) $T_i \subseteq R_i$ $(i \leq m)$.
(h) $\forall s, t, u \in S$: $((R_i st \wedge T_i tu) \rightarrow T_i su)$.
(i) $T_D \subseteq R_C$.

Obviously, if we use the modal operators K_i as the necessity operator for R_i, E for R_E, C for R_C, each B_i for T_i, F for R_F and D for T_D, we get the same truth conditions as were given for the same operators in structures for $\mathcal{L}^m_{\mathbf{KB}}(\mathbf{P})$ in 2.13.4 (there, for instance, the truth definition for $C\varphi$ was such that it allows us to regard C to be the transitive closure of R, which, in its turn was the union of the R_i's. Here, we have made such properties explicit in the models themselves.). Thus we have

LEMMA Q2. *$\mathcal{KL} \models \varphi$ iff $\mathcal{M} \models \varphi$.*

DIGRESSION. Let us spend one more remark on the class of models $\mathcal{KL}$. Note that property (i), $T_D \subseteq R_C$, is in some sense redundant: it follows from (b, c, e, f, g). This does not mean that the corresponding axiom (KL16) follows from the other axioms: there are some models for the system **KL** in which properties (c) or (f) do not hold; in those models, (i) need not be true as well. Let us give a model which we claim satisfies all axioms of **KL** except for (KL16); this means that indeed (KL16) is not entailed by the other axioms; we leave it to the reader to verify that the following model is a model for **KL** \ {(KL16)}. Let $\mathbb{N} = \langle S, \pi, R_1, \ldots, R_m, T_1, \ldots, T_m, R_E, R_C, T_F, T_D \rangle$.

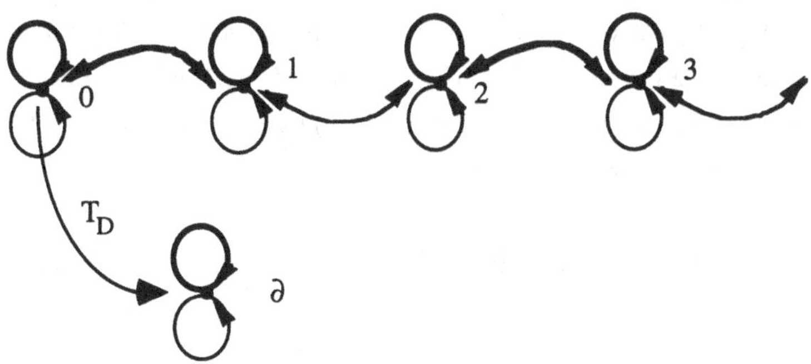

In this model $\mathbb{N}$, we define
$S = \mathbb{N} \cup \{\partial\}$,
$\pi(x)(p) = t \Leftrightarrow x \in \mathbb{N}$, and
$R_1 = T_1 = \{(x, y), (y, x) \mid x = y$ or x is even and $y = x + 1\}$;
$R_2 = T_2 = \{(x, y), (y, x) \mid x = y$ or x is odd and $y = x + 1\}$;

$R_E = R_1 \cup R_2$; $T_F = T_1 \cup T_2$;
$R_C = (R_E)^+$; $T_D = (T_F)^+ \cup \{(0, \partial)\}$.
Claim. $(\mathbb{N}, 0) \models$ **KL** $\setminus \{KL16\}$, $(\mathbb{N}, 0) \models \neg(Cp \to Dp)$. (Proof: left to the reader)

■digression

LEMMA Q3. *Let $\mathcal{KL} \models \varphi$ denote validity of φ in all $\mathcal{KL}$-models. Then*

(a) $\mathcal{KL} \models B_iB_i\varphi \leftrightarrow B_i\varphi$
(b) $\mathcal{KL} \models B_i\neg B_i\varphi \leftrightarrow \neg B_i\varphi$
(c) $\mathcal{KL} \models K_i\varphi \to B_i\varphi$
(d) $\mathcal{KL} \models B_i\varphi \to K_iB_i\varphi$

PROOF.
(a) The '←' direction follows in the same way as in Exercise 1.6.7.1(vi) (transitivity of T_i is needed). The '→' direction was also proven for K_i in 1.6.7.1, but here we may not assume that T_i is reflexive. So suppose that, for some $\mathcal{KL}$-model $\mathbb{M}$, we have $(\mathbb{M}, s) \models B_iB_i\varphi$. Let t be such that T_ist. By euclidicity, we have T_itt: t is an T_i-successor of some T_i-successor of s. But then $(\mathbb{M}, t) \models \varphi$ and thus $(\mathbb{M}, s) \models B_i\varphi$.
(b) This was proven for K_i in Exercise 1.7.6.1(ii), using only transitivity and euclidicity of R_i, hence it also holds for B_i, since T_i is transitive and euclidean in a $\mathcal{KL}$-model.
(c) Cf. Remark 2.13.3.1.
(d) Suppose $(\mathbb{M}, s) \models B_i\varphi$: for all t with T_ist, we have $(\mathbb{M}, t) \models \varphi$. Let u and v be such that R_isu and T_iuv. By property (h) of $\mathcal{KL}$-models, we notice T_isv, so that $(\mathbb{M}, v) \models \varphi$. Since u and v were arbitrary R_i and T_i-successors of s, respectively, we conclude $(\mathbb{M}, s) \models K_iB_i\varphi$. ■

LEMMA Q4 (Soundness). *We have* **KL** $\vdash \varphi \Rightarrow \mathcal{KL} \models \varphi$.

PROOF. The axioms (KL1), (KL4), (KL8) and (KL10) are valid $\mathcal{KL}$-valid by an argument as in Proposition 1.3.5(ii). $\mathcal{KL}$-validity of *modus ponens* is proven as in Proposition 1.3.5(iii) and validity of the rule (KLR1) follows like Proposition 1.3.5(iv). Validity of (KL2) is gurarantееd by reflexivity of R_i (cf. the proof of Theorem 1.6.4(i)), that of (KL3) by Euclidicity of R_i (cf. Theorem 1.6.4(iii)). Now we make the following observation:

OBSERVATION Q4.1. Suppose we have a Kripke model $\mathbb{M}$ in which we have two binary relations A and B with $A \subseteq B$, and that $\Box_A$ and $\Box_B$ are their respective necessity operators. Then $\mathbb{M} \models \Box_B\varphi \to \Box_A\varphi$.
PROOF. Let s be such that $(\mathbb{M}, s) \models \Box_B\varphi$. This means that all B-successors of s verify φ. Let t be an arbitrary A-successor of s: Ast. By assumption we the also have Bst, hence $(\mathbb{M}, t) \models \varphi$; since t was an arbitrary A-successor of s, we have $(\mathbb{M}, s) \models \Box_A\varphi$. ■

Continuing the proof of Q4, the observation above guarantees validity of KL5 (since $R_i \subseteq R_C$;

use (b) and (c) of Definition Q1); of (KL11) (since $T_F \subseteq T_D$; use item (f) of Definition Q1); of (KL14) (by item (g) of Q1) and of (KL16) (note that, since $T_i \subseteq R_i$, we also have $(T_1 \cup \ldots \cup T_m)^+ \subseteq (S_1 \cup \ldots \cup S_m)^+$).

In Theorem 2.1.3, we showed that in models in which R_C is the reflexive transitive closure of R_E, we have $C\varphi \rightarrow EC\varphi$ as a validity. Now observe that here we have that R_C is the transitive closure of R_E, but, since R_E is reflexive, this is the same as the reflexive transitive closure. Thus we have $\mathcal{KL} \models C\varphi \rightarrow EC\varphi$. By definition of E, we immediately obtain $\mathcal{KL} \models C\varphi \rightarrow K_iC\varphi$. Validity of (KL7) was demonstrated in the proof of Theorem 2.1.3; validity of (KL9) in $\mathcal{KL}$ follows as in the proof of Theorem 2.4.3. Validity of (KL12) and (KL13) follows in a similar way to that of (KL6) and (KL7), respectively. Finally we observe that $\mathcal{KL}$-validity of axiom (KL15) is proven in lemma Q3, item (d). ■

In order to achieve completeness with respect to the corresponding class of models, we again use the notion of a maximal consistent set and canonical model as in Section 1.4. Since we have that all modalities $K_1, \ldots, K_m, B_1, \ldots B_m$, C, D, E and F satisfy the basic properties of the basic system **K**, we have that all results of Section 1.4 are applicable in the present case. In particular, we can define a canonical model

$$\mathbb{M}^c = \langle S^c, \pi^c, R_1{}^c, \ldots, R_m{}^c, T_1{}^c, \ldots, T_m{}^c, R_E{}^c, R_C{}^c, T_F{}^c, T_D{}^c\rangle$$

defined as below. In the rest of this exercise, we will omit the superscript '^{c}'; moroever, we will interchangably write s, t, u and s_Θ, s_Ψ, t_Θ, t_Ψ for elements of S.

DEFINITION Q5. We define the following canonical model $\mathbb{M} = \langle S, \pi, R_1, \ldots, R_m, T_1, \ldots, T_m, R_E, R_C, T_F, T_D\rangle$ for **KL**.

$S = \{s_\Theta \mid \Theta$ is a **KL**-maximally consistent set of formulas$\}$

$$\pi(s_\Theta)(p) = \begin{cases} \mathfrak{t} \text{ if } p \in \Theta \\ \mathfrak{f} \text{ if } p \notin \Theta \end{cases}$$

$R_i = \{(s_\Theta, s_\Psi) \mid \Theta/K_i \subseteq \Psi\}$, $T_i = \{(s_\Theta, s_\Psi) \mid \Theta/B_i \subseteq \Psi\}$,
$R_E = \{(s_\Theta, s_\Psi) \mid \Theta/E \subseteq \Psi\}$, $T_F = \{(s_\Theta, s_\Psi) \mid \Theta/F \subseteq \Psi\}$,
$R_C = \{(s_\Theta, s_\Psi) \mid \Theta/C \subseteq \Psi\}$, $R_D = \{(s_\Theta, s_\Psi) \mid \Theta/D \subseteq \Psi\}$,

where, for each modal operator X, $\Theta/X = \{\varphi \mid X\varphi \in \Theta\}$. This canonical model satisfies the coincidence property: $\forall\varphi : (\mathbb{M}, s_\Phi) \models \varphi \Leftrightarrow \varphi \in \Phi$, and from this it follows as in Section 1.4 that we can satisfy any maximally consistent set of formulas in this canonical model.

To have completeness it would now be sufficient to show that the canonical model is of the right type.

LEMMA Q6. *As a first step, we observe that the canonical model* $\mathbb{M}$ *for* **KL** *has the following properties (cf. Section 2.1.4):*

(a) R_i $(i \leq m)$ *is reflexive, transitive and euclidean, i.e. is an equivalence relation.*
(b) $R_E = R_1 \cup \ldots \cup R_m$.
(c') $(R_E)^+ \subseteq R_C$.
(d) T_i $(i \leq m)$ *is serial, transitive and euclidean.*
(e) $T_F = T_1 \cup \ldots \cup T_m$.
(f') $(T_F)^+ \subseteq T_D$.
(g) $T_i \subseteq R_i$ $(i \leq m)$.
(h) $\forall s_\Psi, s_\Gamma, s_\Delta \in S$: $((R_i s_\Psi s_\Gamma \ \&\ T_i s_\Gamma s_\Delta) \Rightarrow T_i s_\Psi s_\Delta)$.
(i) $T_D \subseteq R_C$.

PROOF. First we observe that $R_i s_\Psi s_\Gamma \Leftrightarrow$ for all φ, $(K_i\varphi \in \Psi \Rightarrow \varphi \in \Gamma)$. Similar equivalences hold for the other canonical relations.
Then, properties (a)—(c') follow as in Theorem 2.1.4.2. Item (e) follows in a similar way as (b) follows in 2.1.4.2. Of item (d), transitivity and euclidicity of T_i follow similarly to that of R_i (in 2.1.4.2). Seriality of T_i is checked in Proposition 2.4.1. Property (e) is obtained similarly to (b) of 2.1.4.2, and (f') similarly to (c) of 2.1.4.2.
As for item (g), note that axioms of the form $K_i\varphi \rightarrow B_i\varphi$ (*) impose the canonical model to satisfy $T_i \subseteq R_i$. To see this, suppose $T_i s_\Gamma s_\Delta$. By definition of the canonical accessibility relation, this means that, for all φ, $(B_i\varphi \in \Gamma \Rightarrow \varphi \in \Delta)$. Now let $K_i\varphi \in \Gamma$. We now use the properties 3 and 4 of Lemma 1.4.3(ii), and the axiom (*) to conclude that $B_i\varphi \in \Gamma$. So, $\varphi \in \Delta$. But then we have proven that, for all φ, $(K_i\varphi \in \Gamma \Rightarrow \varphi \in \Delta)$, so that, by definition of R_i, we have $R_i s_\Gamma s_\Delta$. In the same way, property (i) follows from (KL16).
Finally, we prove item (h): Suppose we have $R_i s_\Psi s_\Gamma$ and $T_i s_\Gamma s_\Delta$. In order to show $T_i s_\Psi s_\Delta$, it is sufficient that, for all φ: $B_i\varphi \in \Psi \Rightarrow \varphi \in \Delta$. So suppose $B_i\varphi \in \Psi$. By axioms (KL15) and Lemma 1.4.3(ii)(4), we have $B_i\varphi \rightarrow K_iB_i\varphi \in \Psi$ and then, by Lemma 1.4.3(ii)3, $K_iB_i\varphi \in \Psi$. Since $R_i s_\Psi s_\Gamma$, we have $B_i\varphi \in \Gamma$ and, since $T_i s_\Gamma s_\Delta$, finally $\varphi \in \Delta$. This proves that we have $T_i s_\Psi s_\Delta$. ■

In what follows we shall refer to the class of models satisfying (a) ... (c') ... (f') ... (h) as $\mathcal{KL}^-$. Thus Lemma Q6 says that the canonical model $\mathbb{M}$ for **KL** is an element of $\mathcal{KL}^-$.

In the same way as we did in Theorem 2.1.4.4, one can show that the canonical model $\mathbb{M}$ for

KL does *not* satisfy $(R_E)^+ \supseteq R_C$, *neither* do we have $(T_F)^+ \supseteq T_D$.

DEFINITION Q7. Given a formula φ, we define a **KL**-suitable set (cf. Section 2.1.5):

$\Phi_1 = \{\psi, \neg\psi \mid \psi \text{ is a subformula of } \varphi, i \leq m\}$
$\Phi_2 = \{K_i\psi, \neg K_i\psi \mid E\psi \in \Phi_1, i \leq m\}$
$\Phi_3 = \{EC\psi, \neg EC\psi, K_iC\psi, \neg K_iC\psi \mid C\psi \in \Phi_1, \; i \leq m\}$
$\Phi_4 = \{B_i\psi, \neg B_i\psi \mid F\psi \in \Phi_1, i \leq m\}$
$\Phi_5 = \{FD\psi, \neg FD\psi, B_iD\psi, \neg B_iD\psi \mid D\psi \in \Phi_1, \; i \leq m\}$
$\Phi_6 = \{B_i\psi, \neg B_i\psi \mid K_i\psi \in \Phi_1 \cup \Phi_2 \cup \Phi_3, \; i \leq m\}$

Let $\Phi = \Phi_1 \cup \Phi_2 \cup \Phi_3 \cup \Phi_4 \cup \Phi_5 \cup \Phi_6$;

$\Psi_1 = \{B_iB_i\psi, \; \neg B_iB_i\psi, K_iB_i\,\psi, \neg K_iB_i\psi \mid B_i\psi \in \Phi, \; i \leq m\}$
$\Psi_2 = \{B_i\neg B_i\psi, \; \neg B_i\neg B_i\psi, \; B_iB_i\neg B_i\psi, \neg B_iB_i\neg B_i\psi,$
$\quad K_i\neg B_i\psi, \; \neg K_i\neg B_i\psi, \; K_iB_i\neg B_i\psi, \neg K_iB_i\neg B_i\psi \mid \neg B_i\psi \in \Phi, \; i \leq m\}$

$\Psi = \Phi \cup \Psi_1 \cup \Psi_2$;

LEMMA Q8. For every formula α, we have:

(i) if $B_i\alpha \in \Psi$ then there is some formula $B_iB_i\beta \in \Psi$ such that $\mathcal{KL}^- \models B_i\alpha \leftrightarrow B_iB_i\beta$;
(ii) if $\neg B_i\alpha \in \Psi$ then there is a formula $B_i\neg B_i\beta \in \Psi$ such that $\mathcal{KL}^- \models B_i\alpha \leftrightarrow B_i\beta$;
(iii) If $B_i\alpha \in \Psi$, and $\alpha \neq B_i\beta$, for any β, then also $K_iB_i\alpha \in \Psi$;
moreover, $(B_iB_i\beta \in \Psi \Rightarrow K_iB_i\beta \in \Psi)$;
(iv) for all $K_i\beta \in \Psi$ we have $B_i\beta \in \Psi$.

PROOF.
(i) If $B_i\alpha \in \Phi$, this follows from construction of Ψ. If $B_i\alpha \in \Psi_1$, then it must be itself of the form $B_iB_i\psi$, which also proves the lemma. If $B_i\alpha \in \Psi_2$ its equivalent counterpart $B_iB_i\alpha$ is also in Ψ_2.
(ii) If $\neg B_i\alpha \in \Phi$, then $B_i\neg B_i\alpha$ is an element of Ψ_2, and we are done. If $\neg B_i\alpha \in \Psi_1$, then $\neg B_i\alpha = \neg B_iB_i\psi$, for some $B_i\psi \in \Phi$. We claim that one may take $\beta = \psi$: first, note that, since $B_i\psi \in \Phi$, we also have $\neg B_i\psi \in \Phi$ (Φ_1 is closed under single negation and Φ_2—Φ_6 add a $B_i\gamma$ to Φ iff they also add $\neg B_i\gamma$). Moreover, if $\neg B_i\psi \in \Phi$, then also $B_i\neg B_i\psi \in \Psi_2 \subseteq \Psi$. In order to show that $\mathcal{KL}^- \models B_i\alpha \leftrightarrow B_i\psi$, we notice that $\mathcal{KL}^- \models B_iB_i\psi \leftrightarrow B_i\psi$. Finally, assume $\neg B_i\alpha \in \Psi_2$. Either it is of the form $\neg B_i \neg B_i\psi$, or of the form $\neg B_iB_i\neg B_i\psi$, for some $\neg B_i\psi \in \Phi$. In the first case, we choose $\beta = \neg B_i\psi$; in the second case $\beta = B_i\neg B_i\psi$.
iii First, notice that if $B_i\alpha \in \Psi$ and $\alpha \neq B_i\beta$, then $B_i\alpha$ already in Φ. But then, $K_iB_i\alpha$ is introduced in Ψ_1. If $B_iB_i\beta \in \Psi$, then $B_i\beta \in \Phi$, and we just observed that in that case also

$K_iB_i\beta \in \Psi$.

(iv) If $K_i\beta \in \Phi$, it follows from the clause of Φ_6. All the $K_i\beta$'s that are introduced at Ψ_k (k = 1, 2), have a corresponding $B_i\beta \in \Psi_k$. ■

DEFINITION Q9. Let $\mathbb{M} = \langle S, \pi, R_1, ..., R_m, T_1, ..., T_m, R_E, R_C, T_F, T_D\rangle$ be the canonical model as defined above, and let φ be a consistent formula. Furthermore, let Ψ be **KL**-suitable with respect to φ. Now define the model $\underline{\mathbb{M}} = \langle \underline{S}, \underline{\pi}, \underline{R}_1, ..., \underline{R}_m, \underline{T}_1, ..., \underline{T}_m, \underline{R}_E, \underline{R}_C, \underline{T}_F, \underline{T}_D\rangle$ by the following.

- $\underline{S} = \{[s]_\Psi \mid s \in S\}$. (Here $[s]_\Psi =_{def} \{t \mid (\mathbb{M}, t) \models \psi \Leftrightarrow (\mathbb{M}, s) \models \psi$ for all $\psi \in \Psi\}$. We will write [s] instead of $[s]_\Psi$. Note that $\underline{S}$ is finite since Ψ is finite.)
- For all $\underline{R}_i$ $(1 \leq i \leq m)$ it holds that:
  (i) for any [s] and [t] $\in$ W,
  $([s], [t]) \in \underline{R}_i \Leftrightarrow$ for all $K_i\psi \in \Psi$: $((\mathbb{M}, s) \models K_i\psi \Leftrightarrow (\mathbb{M}, t) \models K_i\psi)$
  (ii) $\underline{R}_E = (\underline{R}_1 \cup ... \cup \underline{R}_m)$
  (iii) $\underline{R}_C = (\underline{R}_E)^+$
  (iv) for any [s] and [t] $\in$ W,
  $([s], [t]) \in \underline{T}_i \Leftrightarrow$ for all $B_i\psi \in \Psi$: $((\mathbb{M}, s) \models B_i\psi \Rightarrow (\mathbb{M}, t) \models \psi)$
  (v) $\underline{T}_F = (\underline{T}_1 \cup ... \cup \underline{T}_m)$
  (vi) $\underline{T}_C = (\underline{T}_F)^+$
- $\underline{\pi}([s])(p) = \pi(s)(p)$.

Note the asimilarity between the definitions of $\underline{R}_i$ and $\underline{T}_i$. We will return to this at the end of the entire completeness proof.

THEOREM Q10. $\underline{\mathbb{M}}$ *is a* $\mathcal{KL}$*-model.*

PROOF. We have to check that all the properties of Definition Q1 above are satisfied:

(a) $\underline{R}_i$ $(i \leq m)$ is reflexive, transitive and euclidean, i.e. $\underline{R}_i$ is an equivalence relation.
(b) $\underline{R}_E = \underline{R}_1 \cup ... \cup \underline{R}_m$.
(c) $(\underline{R}_E)^+ = \underline{R}_C$.
(d) $\underline{T}_i$ $(i \leq m)$ is serial, transitive and euclidean.
(e) $\underline{T}_F = \underline{T}_1 \cup ... \cup \underline{T}_m$.
(f) $(\underline{T}_F)^+ = \underline{T}_D$.
(g) $\underline{T}_i \subseteq \underline{R}_i$ $(i \leq m)$.
(h) $\forall s, t, u \in S$: $((\underline{R}_ist \wedge \underline{T}_itu) \rightarrow \underline{T}_isu)$
(i) $\underline{T}_D \subseteq \underline{R}_C$

Properties (a), (b), (c) (e), and (f) are immediate from the definitions of the respective relations in $\underline{\mathbb{M}}$. (i) follows from (b, c, e, f and g). So let us concentrate on (d), (g), (h) and (i).

(d) $\underline{T}_i$ is serial: let $[s] \in \underline{S}$. In $\mathbb{M}$, s must have some T_i-successor, say t. For this successor, we obviously have, for *all* formulas φ, $(\mathbb{M}, s) \models B_i\varphi \Rightarrow (\mathbb{M}, t) \models \varphi$. In particular it is true of all formulas $B_i\varphi \in \Psi$, so $\underline{T}_i[s][t]$.
$\underline{T}_i$ is transitive: suppose we have $\underline{T}_i[s][t]$ and $\underline{T}_i[t][u]$. Let $B_i\varphi \in \Psi$, and suppose $(\mathbb{M}, s) \models B_i\varphi$. By Lemma Q8, $B_i\varphi$ is equivalent to some $B_iB_i\psi \in \Psi$, so $(\mathbb{M}, s) \models B_iB_i\psi$. Since $\underline{T}_i[s][t]$, we have $(\mathbb{M}, t) \models B_i\psi$, and thus by Lemma Q6(d) $(\mathbb{M}, t) \models B_iB_i\psi$ and, equivalently, $(\mathbb{M}, t) \models B_i\varphi$. Hence, since $(\mathbb{M}, u) \models \varphi$, we have $\underline{T}_i[s][u]$.
$\underline{T}_i$ is euclidean: suppose we have $\underline{T}_i[s][t]$ and $\underline{T}_i[s][u]$. Let $B_i\varphi \in \Psi$, and suppose $(\mathbb{M}, t) \models B_i\varphi$. We have to prove $(\mathbb{M}, u) \models \varphi$. Suppose not, then, since $\underline{T}_i[s][u]$, we have $(\mathbb{M}, s) \models \neg B_i\varphi$. Since $B_i\varphi \in \Psi$, by the definition of Ψ, $\neg B_i\varphi \in \Psi$ as well. By Lemma Q8(ii), we find a $B_i\neg B_i\beta \in \Psi$, such that $\mathcal{KL}^- \models B_i\varphi \leftrightarrow B_i\beta$. Since $\mathbb{M} \in \mathcal{KL}^-$, we obtain $(\mathbb{M}, s) \models \neg B_i\beta$. By Lemma Q3(b) we know that $(\mathbb{M}, s) \models B_i \neg B_i\beta$, and hence $(\mathbb{M}, t) \models \neg B_i\beta$, contradicting the fact $(\mathbb{M}, t) \models B_i\,\varphi$.
(g) $\underline{T}_i \subseteq \underline{R}_i$: Suppose $\underline{T}_i[s][t]$, that is, for all $B_i\varphi \in \Psi$, $(\mathbb{M}, s) \models B_i\varphi \Rightarrow (\mathbb{M}, t) \models \varphi$. Now suppose $K_i\varphi \in \Psi$ and $(\mathbb{M}, s) \models K_i\varphi$. By Lemma Q3(c) we know that $(\mathbb{M}, s) \models B_i\varphi$, and by Lemma Q8(iv) we have $B_i\varphi \in \Psi$. Since $\underline{T}_i[s][t]$, $(\mathbb{M}, t) \models \varphi$. Thus, $\underline{R}_i[s][t]$.
(h) for all s, t, u $\in$ S: $\underline{R}_i(s, t)$ and $\underline{T}_i(t, u)$ implies $\underline{T}_i(s, u)$: let $\underline{R}_i(s, t)$ and $\underline{T}_i(t, u)$. Suppose $B_i\varphi \in \Psi$ and $(\mathbb{M}, s) \models B_i\varphi$. In order to show that $(\mathbb{M}, u) \models \varphi$, we distinguish two cases:

i. $\varphi \neq B_i\beta$. By Lemma Q8(iii) we know that $K_iB_i\varphi \in \Psi$, and by Lemma Q3(d) we know that $(\mathbb{M}, s) \models K_iB_i\varphi$. Since $\underline{R}_i$st, we obtain $(\mathbb{M}, t) \models B_i\varphi$ and, since $\underline{T}_i$tu, we also have $(\mathbb{M}, u) \models \varphi$

ii. $\varphi = B_i\beta$, for some $B_i\beta \in \Psi$. Thus we have $(\mathbb{M}, s) \models B_iB_i\beta$ and, by Lemma Q2, also $(\mathbb{M}, s) \models B_i\beta$. From Lemma Q8(iii) we know that $K_iB_i\beta \in \Psi$; hence, since $\underline{R}_i[s][t]$ we have $(\mathbb{M}, t) \models B_i\beta$ and thus, by $\mathcal{KL}^- \models B_i\varphi \rightarrow B_iB_i\varphi$ and $\mathbb{M} \in \mathcal{KL}^-$, we obtain $(\mathbb{M}, t) \models B_iB_i\beta$, with $B_iB_i\beta \in \Psi$. Since $\underline{T}_i[t][u]$, we have $(\mathbb{M}, u) \models B_i\beta$, i.e. $(\mathbb{M}, u) \models \varphi$.

(i) To establish this property, we did not have to take care that $D\psi \in \Psi$ for any $C\psi \in \Psi$: (i) immediately follows from properties b, c, e f and g. ■

LEMMA Q11. *The model* $\underline{\mathbb{M}}$ *as defined in Definition Q9, given a model* $\mathbb{M}$ *and a suitable set of formulas* Ψ*, is a filtration of* $\mathbb{M}$ *through* Ψ*. In other words, all the relations of* $\underline{\mathbb{M}}$ *satisfy the* Min *and* Max *conditions of Definition 2.1.5.1. Those two conditions are equivalent to (cf. our remark proceeding Theorem 2.1.5.2):*
Min($\underline{R}$/R) *for all* s, t *in* S: Rst $\Rightarrow \underline{R}[s][t]$
Max($\underline{R}$) *for all* [s], [t] *in* $\underline{S}$: $\underline{R}[s][t] \Rightarrow$ *for all* $\Box_R\psi$ *in* Ψ: $((\mathbb{M}, s) \models \Box_R\psi \Rightarrow (\mathbb{M}, t) \models \psi)$.
where $\Box_R$ *is the necessity operator for R in the model* $\mathbb{M}$.

PROOF. The proof is basically the same as that of Theorem 2.1.5.9. There are some minor differences, though, and we give the details.

1. For the relations that deal with knowledge (i.e. $\underline{R}_1, \ldots, \underline{R}_m, \underline{R}_E, \underline{R}_C$) this is proven in Theorem 2.1.5.9.
2. To prove the minimality condition for $\underline{T}_i$, i.e. $\mathrm{Min}(\underline{T}_i/T_i)$, suppose that $T_i st$ holds. Let $B_i\varphi \in \Psi$. By the truth definition of B_i, $(\mathbb{M}, s) \models B_i\varphi \Rightarrow (\mathbb{M}, t) \models \varphi$, which immediately implies $\underline{T}_i[s][t]$. The condition $\mathrm{Max}(\underline{T}_i)$ immediately follows from the definition of $\underline{T}_i$ in the canonical model.
3. We consider $\underline{T}_F$. This relation satisfies $\mathrm{Min}(\underline{T}_F/T_F)$, as is seen as follows. Suppose $T_F st$. In the canonical model we have that $T_F = T_1 \cup \ldots \cup T_m$ (cf. Lemma Q6). So there must be some $i \le m$ with $T_i st$. Since $\underline{T}_i$ satisfies $\mathrm{Min}(\underline{T}_i/T_i)$, we have $\underline{T}_i[s][t]$. Finally, since $\underline{T}_F = \underline{T}_1 \cup \ldots \cup \underline{T}_m$, we have $\underline{T}_F[s][t]$. To show $\mathrm{Max}(\underline{T}_F)$, suppose $\underline{T}_F[s][t]$ and $(\mathbb{M}, s) \models F\varphi$, with $F\varphi \in \Psi$. Since Ψ is suitable (in particular, cf. the clause for Φ_4), we have $B_i\varphi \in \Psi$ $(i \le m)$, and, by definition of $F\varphi$, also $(\mathbb{M}, s) \models B_i\varphi$, for all $i \le m$. Since $\underline{T}_F[s][t]$, by definition of $\underline{T}_F$, there must be some $i \le m$ such that $\underline{T}_i[s][t]$. Since $\underline{T}_i$ satisfies $\mathrm{Max}(\underline{T}_i)$, we have $(\mathbb{M}, t) \models \varphi$.
4. Finally, we treat $\underline{T}_D$. To prove that $\underline{T}_D$ satisfies $\mathrm{Min}(\underline{T}_D/T_D)$, suppose $(s, t) \in T_D$. Let $A \subseteq \underline{S}$ be the set

$$A = \{[u] \in \underline{S} \mid ([s], [u]) \in \underline{T}_F^+\}.$$

We are done if we can prove that

$$(\mathbb{M}, s) \models D\sigma_A \tag{0}$$

(for the definition of the formula σ_A, see Lemma 2.1.5.8).

For this means that $(\mathbb{M}, t) \models \sigma_A$ and thus, by definition of σ_A, that $[t] \in A$, i.e. $[t]$ is a $\underline{T}_F^+$-successor of $[s]$, and hence $([s], [t]) \in \underline{T}_D$. To prove (0), we use the fact that $\mathbb{M}$ validates the induction axiom for common belief, in particular, that

$$(\mathbb{M}, s) \models D(\sigma_A \to F\sigma_A) \to (F\sigma_A \to D\sigma_A). \tag{1}$$

It appears that also the antecedent of this formula is true at $(\mathbb{M}, s)$, i.e. that

$$(\mathbb{M}, s) \models D(\sigma_A \to F\sigma_A). \tag{2}$$

To see this, suppose $(s, x) \in T_D$, and $(\mathbb{M}, x) \models \sigma_A$; we have to show $(\mathbb{M}, x) \models F\sigma_A$. So suppose $(x, y) \in T_F$. Since $(\mathbb{M}, x) \models \sigma_A$, by definition of A, $[x] \in A$, so $([s], [x]) \in \underline{T}_F^+$, i.e., $([s], [x]) \in \underline{T}_F^n$ for some $n \in \mathbb{N}$. Since $\underline{T}_F$ is a filtration of T_F, we have also $([x], [y]) \in \underline{T}_F$, and thus $([s], [y]) \in \underline{T}_F^{n+1}$, and so $([s], [y]) \in \underline{T}_F^+$. This implies that $[y] \in A$, and so $(\mathbb{M}, y) \models \sigma_A$, which completes the proof of (2).

Finally, we observe that

$$(\mathbb{M}, s) \models F\sigma_A \tag{3}$$

To see (3), let t be such that $(s, t) \in T_F$. Since $\underline{T}_F$ is a filtration through T_F, we have $([s], [t]) \in \underline{T}_F$, so $[t] \in A$ and $(\mathbb{M}, t) \models \sigma_A$.

It is easily seen that (1), (2) and (3) together imply (0), so we are done.

Next we have to show that $Max(\underline{T}_D)$ holds. Suppose $([s], [t]) \in \underline{T}_D$ and $(\mathbb{M}, s) \models D\psi$, with $D\psi \in \Psi$. We have to show that $(\mathbb{M}, t) \models \psi$. By definition of $\underline{T}_D$, we have that $([s]), [t]) \in \underline{T}_F^n$ for some $n \in \mathbb{N}$. This means that there are $[s_1] = [s], [s_2], \ldots, [s_n] = [t]$ with $([s_i], [s_{i+1}]) \in \underline{T}_F$, $i < n \geq 2$. Since $\mathbb{M}$ is a model for (KL12), we have that $(\mathbb{M}, s_i) \models D\psi \Rightarrow (\mathbb{M}, s_i) \models FD\psi$. Moreover, since $D\psi \in \Psi$ and Ψ is suitable (with respect to φ), we also have $FD\psi \in \Psi$. Together with the fact that $\underline{T}_D$ is a filtration through Ψ of T_D, the condition $Max(\underline{T}_D)$ guarantees that $(\mathbb{M}, s_i) \models FD\psi \Rightarrow (\mathbb{M}, s_{i+1}) \models D\psi$. Altogether we get that $(\mathbb{M}, s_i) \models D\psi \Rightarrow (\mathbb{M}, s_{i+1}) \models D\psi$ for all $i < n$. Since $(\mathbb{M}, s_1) = (\mathbb{M}, s) \models D\psi$, we eventually derive by means of induction $(\mathbb{M}, s_{n-1}) \models D\psi$. Since $(s_{n-1}, t) \in R_D$, we have $(\mathbb{M}, t) \models \psi$. ■

COROLLARY Q12. *Every* **KL**-*consistent formula is satisfied in some model and state* $(\underline{\mathbb{M}}, s)$ *where* $\underline{\mathbb{M}}$ *is a model in* $\mathcal{KL}$.

PROOF. Let φ be a **KL**-consistent formula. It is contained in a maximal consistent set Φ, hence it is satisfied at s_Φ in the canonical model for **KL**: $(\mathbb{M}^c, s_\Phi) \models \varphi$. Let Ψ be suitable for φ, and let $\underline{\mathbb{M}}$ be defined from $\mathbb{M}^c$ and Ψ, as in Definition Q9. From Theorem Q10 we know that $\underline{\mathbb{M}}$ is a $\mathcal{KL}$-model; and from Lemma Q11 we know that $\underline{\mathbb{M}}$ is a filtration of $\mathbb{M}^c$ through Ψ. Then if follows from Theorem 2.1.5.2 that $(\underline{\mathbb{M}}, [s]) \models \varphi$, so hence φ is satisfied in some $\mathcal{KL}$-model. ■

THEOREM Q13. (Completeness) *For all* φ, *we have* $\mathbf{KL} \vdash \varphi$ *iff* $\mathcal{KL} \models \varphi$.

PROOF. The 'only if' direction is proved in Lemma Q4, the 'if' direction follows immediately from Corollary Q12 above. ■

COROLLARY Q14. (Decidability). **KL** *is decidable.*

PROOF. Like that of Corollary 2.1.5.12. ■

REMARK Q15. As promised we return to the issue of the asimilarity between the definitions of $\underline{R}_i$ and $\underline{T}_i$ in Def. Q9. The definition of these accessibilty relations in $\underline{\mathbb{M}}$ has to establish two properties: the relations should satisfy the conditions of being relations in an $\mathcal{KL}$-model (which we verified in Theorem Q10), and at the same time, in order to ensure that this model still satisfies the given formula φ, we have to ensure that $\underline{\mathbb{M}}$ is a filtration through $\mathbb{M}$; for the relations, this means that they should satisfy the Max- and Min-conditions of Definition 2.1.5.1 (this was proved in Lemma Q11). If we would define $\underline{T}_i$ as we defined $\underline{R}_i$, the relation $\underline{T}_i$ would become reflexive, or, in other words, in general we would be unable to prove Max($\underline{T}_i$). We have to pay a price for this in the sense that we will have to do more work to show that $\underline{T}_i$ satisfies the required properties of seriality, transitivity and euclidicity (Theorem Q10); we essentially apply Lemma Q8 there, which, in its turn, was provable due to our careful definition of suitable sets (Definition Q7). Although proving the required properties of $\underline{T}_i$ takes some efforts, the properties Min($\underline{T}_i$/T_i) and Max($\underline{T}_i$) are almost encoded in the definition of $\underline{T}_i$ (see Lemma Q11). On the other hand, if we would have defined $\underline{R}_i$ in a similar way as we defined $\underline{T}_i$ (which, in principle, seems possible), we would have to be more careful about the definition of suitable sets regarding K_i-formulas. For the relations $\underline{R}_i$, we would have to do more work to prove the Max- and Min-conditions (we did this already in Theorem 2.1.5.9), whereas here the property of being 'of the right kind' (that is, an equivalence relation) is immediate from the definition of $\underline{R}_i$.

2.13.6.1 For both K_i and B_i we may use general modal properties that have already been established in Section 1.4; for K_i we use also the properties derived in Section 1.5 and for B_i those of Section 2.4. Moreover, we will also use a property like 'KD', *K-distribution*, for the operator B; let us refer to it by 'BD'. Of course, we will again use the derived rules for propositional logic extensively.

(T1)	1	$K_i\neg\varphi \rightarrow B_i\neg\varphi$	(KL14)
	2	$(K_i\neg\varphi \wedge B_i\varphi) \rightarrow (B_i\neg\varphi \wedge B_i\varphi)$	(KL0, 1)
	3	$(B_i\neg\varphi \wedge B_i\varphi) \rightarrow B_i(\varphi \wedge \neg\varphi)$	(Ex. 1.4.1.1(i))
	4	$B_i(\varphi \wedge \neg\varphi) \rightarrow B_i\bot$	(KL0, B_iD)
	5	$B_i\bot \rightarrow \bot$	(KL9, KL0)
	6	$(K_i\neg\varphi \wedge B_i\varphi) \rightarrow \bot$	(HS, 2, 3, 4, 5)
	7	$K_i\neg\varphi \rightarrow \neg B_i\varphi$	(NC, 6)
(T2)	1	$K_iB_i\varphi \rightarrow B_i\varphi$	(KL2)
	2	$B_i\varphi \rightarrow K_iB_i\varphi$	(KL15)
	3	$B_i\varphi \leftrightarrow K_iB_i\varphi$	(EI, 1, 2)

(T3)	1	$\neg B_i\varphi \to \neg K_iB_i\varphi$	(T2, KL0)
	2	$\neg K_iB_i\varphi \to K_i\neg K_iB_i\varphi$	(KL3)
	3	$\neg K_iB_i\varphi \to \neg B_i\varphi$	(T2, KL0)
	4	$K_i\neg K_iB_i\varphi \to K_i\neg B_i\varphi$	(3, B_iD)
	5	$\neg B_i\varphi \to K_i\neg B_i\varphi$	(HS, 1, 2, 4)
	6	$K_i\neg B_i\varphi \to \neg B_i\varphi$	(KL2)
	7	$\neg B_i\varphi \leftrightarrow K_i\neg B_i\varphi$	(EI, 5, 6)

(T4)	1	$K_i\varphi \to K_iK_i\varphi$	(Ex. 1.5.1.2(vi))
	2	$K_iK_i\varphi \to B_iK_i\varphi$	(KL14)
	3	$K_i\varphi \to B_iK_i\varphi$	(HS, 1, 2)
	4	$\neg K_i\varphi \to K_i\neg K_i\varphi$	(KL3)
	5	$K_i\neg K_i\varphi \to B_i\neg K_i\varphi$	(KL14)
	6	$\neg K_i\varphi \to B_i\neg K_i\varphi$	(HS, 4, 5)
	7	$(B_iK_i\varphi \wedge \neg K_i\varphi) \to (B_iK_i\varphi \wedge B_i\neg K_i\varphi)$	(KL0, 6)
	8	$(B_iK_i\varphi \wedge B_i\neg K_i\varphi) \to B_i\bot$	(Ex. 1.4.1.1(i))
	9	$B_i\bot \to \bot$	(KL14, KL0)
	10	$(B_iK_i\varphi \wedge \neg K_i\varphi) \to \bot$	(HS, 8, 9)
	11	$B_iK_i\varphi \to K_i\varphi$	(NC, 11)
	13	$K_i\varphi \leftrightarrow B_iK_i\varphi$	(EI, 3, 11)

(T5)	1	$\neg K_i\varphi \to K_i\neg K_i\varphi$	(KL3)
	2	$K_i\neg K_i\varphi \to B_i\neg K_i\varphi$	(KL14)
	3	$\neg K_i\varphi \to B_i\neg K_i\varphi$	(HS, 1, 2)
	4	$K_i\varphi \to B_iK_i\varphi$	(T4)
	5	$(B_i\neg K_i\varphi \wedge K_i\varphi) \to (B_i\neg K_i\varphi \wedge B_iK_i\varphi)$	(KL0, 4)
	6	$(B_i\neg K_i\varphi \wedge B_iK_i\varphi) \to B_i\bot$	(Ex. 1.4.1.1(i))
	7	$B_i\bot \to \bot$	(KL14, KL0)
	8	$(B_i\neg K_i\varphi \wedge K_i\varphi) \to \bot$	(HS, 5, 6, 7)
	9	$B_i\neg K_i\varphi \to \neg K_i\varphi$	(NC, 8)
	10	$\neg K_i\varphi \leftrightarrow B_i\neg K_i\varphi$	(EI, 3, 9)

(T6)	1	$B_i\varphi \to K_iB_i\varphi$	(KL15)
	2	$K_iB_i\varphi \to B_iB_i\varphi$	(KL14)
	3	$B_i\varphi \to B_iB_i\varphi$	(HHS, 1, 2)
	4	$B_i\varphi \to K_iB_i\varphi$	(T2, $\to$)
	5	$B_iB_i\varphi \to B_iK_iB_i\varphi$	(B_iD, 4)
	6	$B_iK_iB_i\varphi \to K_iB_i\varphi$	(T4, $\leftarrow$)
	7	$K_iB_i\varphi \to B_i\varphi$	(KL2)
	8	$B_iB_i\varphi \to B_i\varphi$	(HS, 5, 6, 7)
	9	$B_i\varphi \leftrightarrow B_iB_i\varphi$	(EI, 4, 8)

(T7)	1	$\neg B_i\varphi \to K_i\neg B_i\varphi$	(T3, $\to$)
	2	$K_i\neg B_i\varphi \to B_i\neg B_i\varphi$	(KL14)
	3	$\neg B_i\varphi \to B_i\neg B_i\varphi$	(HS, 1, 2)
	4	$(B_i\neg B_i\varphi \wedge B_i\varphi) \to (B_i\neg B_i\varphi \wedge B_iB_i\varphi)$	(KL0, T6, $\to$)

	5	$(B_i\neg B_i\varphi \wedge B_iB_i\varphi) \rightarrow B_i\bot$	(Ex. 1.4.1.1(i))
	6	$B_i\bot \rightarrow \bot$	(A9, KL0)
	7	$(B_i\neg B_i\varphi \wedge B_i\varphi) \rightarrow \bot$	(HS, 4, 5, 6)
	8	$B_i\neg B_i\varphi \rightarrow \neg B_i\varphi$	(NC, 7)
	9	$\neg B_i\varphi \leftrightarrow B_i\neg B_i\varphi$	(EI, 3, 8)

(T8)	1	$\neg(B_i\varphi \wedge \neg\varphi) \rightarrow (B_i\varphi \rightarrow \varphi)$	(KL0)
	2	$B_i\neg(B_i\varphi \wedge \neg\varphi) \rightarrow B_i(B_i\varphi \rightarrow \varphi)$	(K_iD, 1)
	3	$(\neg B_i\varphi \vee \varphi) \rightarrow \neg(B_i\varphi \wedge \neg\varphi)$	(KL0)
	4	$B_i(\neg B_i\varphi \vee \varphi) \rightarrow B_i\neg(B_i\varphi \wedge \neg\varphi)$	(K_iD, 3)
	5	$(B_i\neg B_i\varphi \vee B_i\varphi) \rightarrow B_i(\neg B_i\varphi \vee \varphi)$	(Ex. 1.4.1.1(ii))
	6	$(\neg B_i\varphi \vee B_i\varphi) \rightarrow (B_i\neg B_i\varphi \vee B_i\varphi)$	(T7, $\rightarrow$)
	7	$(\neg B_i\varphi \vee B_i\varphi) \rightarrow B_i(B_i\varphi \rightarrow \varphi)$	(HS, 6, 5, 4, 2)
	8	$\neg B_i\varphi \vee B_i\varphi$	(KL0)
	9	$B_i(B_i\varphi \rightarrow \varphi)$	(KLR0, 7, 8)

For proving the following theorems, it is important to recall the definitions

$$E\varphi \equiv (K_1\varphi \wedge \ldots \wedge K_m\varphi) \quad \text{and}$$
$$F\varphi \equiv (B_1\varphi \wedge \ldots \wedge B_m\varphi).$$

We also have the derived rules

$\vdash \varphi \Rightarrow \vdash X\varphi, X \in \{C, D, E, F, K_i, B_i, \mid i \leq m\}$	(R_X)
$\vdash \varphi \rightarrow \psi \Rightarrow \vdash X\varphi \rightarrow X\psi$	(XD)
$\vdash B_i\varphi$ for all $i \leq m \Rightarrow \vdash F\varphi$	($B_i$toF)
$\vdash K_i\varphi$ for all $i \leq m \Rightarrow \vdash E\varphi$	($K_i$toE)

PROOF.

R_X: For X = C this is is (KLR1), RK_i then follows with (KL5); RB_i from (KL14), and R_E follows from RK_i and the definition of E. R_D is from R_C and (KL16); R_F follows from RB_i and the definition of F.

XD: We proved this already for $X = K_i$; the case X = C is immediately obtained from (KL4); $X = B_i$ from (KL8), X = D from (KL10). The cases X = E and X = F follow from $X = K_i$ and $X = B_i$, respectively, by using the definitions of E and F.

Finally, the properties ($B_i$toF) and ($K_i$toE) are proved immediately from the definitions of F and E, respectively.

(T9)	1	$F\varphi \rightarrow (\varphi \rightarrow F\varphi)$	(KL0)
	2	$D(F\varphi \rightarrow (\varphi \rightarrow F\varphi))$	(1, R_D)
	3	$D(F\varphi \rightarrow (\varphi \rightarrow F\varphi)) \rightarrow (DF\varphi \rightarrow D(\varphi \rightarrow F\varphi))$	(KL10)
	4	$DF\varphi \rightarrow D(\varphi \rightarrow F\varphi)$	(2, 3, R0)
	5	$D(\varphi \rightarrow F\varphi) \rightarrow (F\varphi \rightarrow D\varphi)$	(KL13)
	6	$DF\varphi \rightarrow (F\varphi \rightarrow D\varphi)$	(4, 5, HS)
	7	$B_i(B_i\varphi \rightarrow \varphi)$	(T8)

	8	$F\varphi \to B_i\varphi$	(df F)
	9	$(B_i\varphi \to \varphi) \to (F\varphi \to \varphi)$	(KL0, 8)
	10	$B_i(B_i\varphi \to \varphi) \to B_i(F\varphi \to \varphi)$	(B_iD, 9)
	11	$B_i(F\varphi \to \varphi)$	(KLR0, 7, 10)
	12	$F(F\varphi \to \varphi)$	($B_i$toF, 11)
	13	$FF\varphi \to F\varphi$	(FD, 12)
	14	$DF\varphi \to FF\varphi$	(KL11)
	15	$DF\varphi \to F\varphi$	(HS, 14, 13)
	16	$(DF\varphi \to F\varphi) \to (DF\varphi \to D\varphi)$	(KL0, 6)
	17	$DF\varphi \to D\varphi$	(KLR0, 15, 16)
	18	$D(D\varphi \to FD\varphi)$	(R_D, 17)
	19	$D(D\varphi \to FD\varphi) \to (FD\varphi \to DD\varphi)$	(KL13)
	20	$FD\varphi \to DD\varphi$	(KLR0, 18, 19)
	21	$D\varphi \to FD\varphi$	(KL12)
	22	$D\varphi \to DD\varphi$	(HS, 21, 20)
	23	$D\varphi \to F\varphi$	(KL11)
	24	$DD\varphi \to DF\varphi$	(DD, 23)
	25	$D\varphi \to DF\varphi$	(HS, 22, 24)
	26	$D\varphi \leftrightarrow DF\varphi$	(KL0, 17, 25)

(T10)	1	$D\varphi \to FD\varphi$	(KL12)
	2	$FD\varphi \to DD\varphi$	(proof of T9, line 20)
	3	$D\varphi \to F\varphi$	(KL11)
	4	$DD\varphi \to DF\varphi$	(DD, 3)
	5	$DF\varphi \to D\varphi$	(T9, $\leftarrow$)
	6	$FD\varphi \to D\varphi$	(HS, 2, 4, 5)
	7	$D\varphi \leftrightarrow FD\varphi$	

(T11)	1	$DFD\varphi \to DD\varphi$	(T9, $\leftarrow$)
	2	$DD\varphi \to FD\varphi$	(KL11)
	3	$DFD\varphi \to FD\varphi$	(HS, 1, 2)
	4	$FD\varphi \to DD\varphi$	(proof of T9, line 20)
	5	$DD\varphi \to DFD\varphi$	(T9, $\to$)
	6	$FD\varphi \to DFD\varphi$	(HS, 4, 5)
	7	$FD\varphi \leftrightarrow DFD\varphi$	(KL0, 3, 6)

(T12)	1	$D\varphi \to DD\varphi$	(proof of T9 line 22)
	2	$DD\varphi \to DF\varphi$	(DD, KL11)
	3	$DF\varphi \to D\varphi$	(T9, $\leftarrow$)
	4	$DD\varphi \to D\varphi$	(KLR0, 2, 3)
	5	$D\varphi \leftrightarrow DD\varphi$	(KL0, 1, 4)

(T13), (T14) For the proof of those two theorems, see the answer to Exercise 1.4.1.1(i); by only using $\vdash \varphi \Rightarrow \vdash K_i\varphi$ and $\vdash K_i(\varphi \to \psi) \to (K_i\varphi \to K_i\psi)$ we were able to prove $\vdash K_i(\varphi \wedge \psi) \leftrightarrow (K_i\varphi \wedge K_i\psi)$. Since we now also have necessitation for C and D (R1 and R_D, respectively) and (KL4) (for C) and (KL10) (for D) we can give a similar proof to that of Exercise 1.4.1.1(i).

2.14.1

1 $B_iO\varphi \rightarrow OB_i\varphi$ (ass)
2 $B_i\varphi \rightarrow \neg K_i\neg\varphi$ (T1, KL0)
3 $O(B_i\varphi \rightarrow \neg K_i\neg\varphi)$ (ass (O-nec), 2)
4 $O(B_i\varphi \rightarrow \neg K_i\neg\varphi) \rightarrow (OB_i\varphi \rightarrow O\neg K_i\neg\varphi)$ (ass)
5 $OB_i\varphi \rightarrow O\neg K_i\neg\varphi$ (KLR0, 3, 4)
6 $B_iO\varphi \rightarrow O\neg K_i\neg\varphi$ (HS, 1, 5)
7 $K_iB_iO\varphi \rightarrow K_iO\neg K_i\neg\varphi$ (K_iD, 6)
8 $B_iO\varphi \rightarrow K_iB_iO\varphi$ (T2)
9 $B_iO\varphi \rightarrow K_iO\neg K_i\neg\varphi$ (HS, 8, 7)

2.15.1 Suppose that our model satisfies

$$\forall s_1, s_2\ [r_{do_i(act_1)}(s_1, s_2) \Rightarrow$$
$$\forall s_3(R_i(s_2, s_3) \Rightarrow \exists s_4(R_i\ (s_1, s_4)\ \wedge\ r_{do_i(act_1)}(s_4, s_3)\ ))]. \qquad (1)$$

Suppose furthermore that $(\mathbb{M}, s) \models K_i[do_i(act_1)]\varphi$. This means that

$$\forall v, u\ [R_i(s, v) \wedge r_{do_i(act_1)}(v, u) \Rightarrow (\mathbb{M}, u) \models \varphi]. \qquad (2)$$

In order to prove $(\mathbb{M}, s) \models [do_i(act_1)]\ K_i\varphi$, let t and u be such that $r_{do_i(act_1)}(s, t)$ and $R_i(t, u)$. By (1) above, we know that there is a v with $R_i(s, v)$ and $r_{do_i(act_1)}\ (v, u)$. By (2) we then have $(\mathbb{M}, u) \models \varphi$. Since u was an arbitrary world with $R_i(t, u)$ we have $(\mathbb{M}, t) \models K_i\varphi$; since t was an arbitrary world for which $r_{do_i(act_1)}(s, t)$, we have $(\mathbb{M}, s) \models [do_i(act_1)]\ K_i\varphi$.

2.16.3.1 Recall the definitions of $M_n\varphi = \neg L_n\neg\varphi$; $M_0\varphi = K_0\neg\varphi$; $\mathbf{M}_n\varphi = (M_{n-1}\varphi \wedge \neg M_n\varphi)$. Note that K_0 is the old K-operator, so we can use the derived rules for it (we call them now K_0-distribution, K_0D, etc.). Also, we have a dual of (Gr1) and (Gr2):

(Gr1') $K_0(\varphi \rightarrow \psi) \rightarrow (M_n\varphi \rightarrow M_n\psi)$

PROOF:

1 $(\varphi \rightarrow \psi) \rightarrow (\neg\psi \rightarrow \neg\varphi)$ (Gr0)
2 $K_0(\varphi \rightarrow \psi) \rightarrow K_0(\neg\psi \rightarrow \neg\varphi)$ (K_0D, 5)
3 $K_0(\neg\psi \rightarrow \neg\varphi) \rightarrow (K_n\neg\psi \rightarrow K_n\neg\varphi)$ (Gr1)
4 $(K_n\neg\psi \rightarrow K_n\neg\varphi) \rightarrow (\neg K_n\neg\varphi \rightarrow \neg K_n\neg\psi)$ (Gr0)
5 $(\neg K_n\neg\varphi \rightarrow \neg K_n\neg\psi) \rightarrow (M_n\varphi \rightarrow M_n\psi)$ (df M_n)
6 $K_0(\varphi \rightarrow \psi) \rightarrow (M_n\varphi \rightarrow M_n\psi)$ (HS, 2-5)

(Gr2') $M_{n+1}\varphi \rightarrow M_n\varphi$

PROOF:

1 $K_n\neg\varphi \rightarrow K_{n+1}\neg\varphi$ (Gr2)
2 $\neg K_{n+1}\neg\varphi \rightarrow \neg K_n\neg\varphi$ (CP, 1)
3 $M_{n+1}\varphi \rightarrow M_n\varphi$ (df M_n, 2)

(i) 1 $(\varphi \wedge \psi) \rightarrow \varphi$ (Gr0)
2 $(\varphi \wedge \psi) \rightarrow \psi$ (Gr0)
3 $K_0((\varphi \wedge \psi) \rightarrow \varphi)$ (R2, 1)
4 $K_0((\varphi \wedge \psi) \rightarrow \psi)$ (R2, 2)

5 $K_0((\varphi \wedge \psi) \to \varphi) \to (M_n(\varphi \wedge \psi) \to M_n\varphi)$ (Gr1')

6 $K_0((\varphi \wedge \psi) \to \psi) \to (M_n(\varphi \wedge \psi) \to M_n\psi)$ (Gr1')

7 $M_n(\varphi \wedge \psi) \to M_n\varphi$ (R1, 3, 5)

8 $M_n(\varphi \wedge \psi) \to M_n\psi$ (R1, 4, 6)

9 $(M_n(\varphi \wedge \psi) \to M_n\varphi) \to [(M_n(\varphi \wedge \psi) \to M_n\psi) \to (M_n(\varphi \wedge \psi) \to (M_n\varphi \wedge M_n\psi))]$ (Gr0)

10 $(M_n(\varphi \wedge \psi) \to M_n\psi) \to (M_n(\varphi \wedge \psi) \to (M_n\varphi \wedge M_n\psi))$ (R1, 7, 9)

11 $M_n(\varphi \wedge \psi) \to (M_n\varphi \wedge M_n\psi)$ (R1, 8, 10)

(ii) It is given that $n \neq m$; let us assume, without loss of generality, that $0 < n < m$.

1 $(M!_n\varphi \wedge M!_m\varphi) \to (M_{n-1}\varphi \wedge \neg M_n\varphi \wedge M_{m-1}\varphi \wedge \neg M_m\varphi)$ (Gr0, df M!)

2 $(M_{n-1}\varphi \wedge \neg M_n\varphi \wedge M_{m-1}\varphi \wedge \neg M_m\varphi) \to (\neg M_n\varphi \wedge M_{m-1}\varphi)$ (Gr0)

3 $(\neg M_n\varphi \wedge M_{m-1}\varphi) \to (\neg M_n\varphi \wedge M_n\varphi)$ ((m-1)-n applications of Gr2')

4 $(\neg M_n\varphi \wedge M_n\varphi) \to \bot$ (Gr0)

5 $(M!_n\varphi \wedge M!_m\varphi) \to \bot$ (HS, 1, 2, 3, 4)

(iii) 1 $(M!_n\varphi \wedge M!_m\varphi) \to \bot$, if $n \neq m$ (ii)

2 $\neg(M!_0\varphi \nabla M!_1\varphi \nabla \ldots \nabla M!_n\varphi) \to (\neg M!_0\varphi \wedge \neg M!_1\varphi \wedge \ldots \wedge \neg M!_n\varphi)$ (Gr0, 1, df M!)

3 $(\neg M!_0\varphi \wedge \neg M!_1\varphi \wedge \ldots \wedge \neg M!_n\varphi) \to (M_0\varphi \wedge (\neg M_0\varphi \vee M_1\varphi) \wedge \ldots \wedge (\neg M_{n-1}\varphi \vee M_n\varphi))$ (df M!)

4 $(M_0\varphi \wedge (\neg M_0\varphi \vee M_1\varphi) \wedge \ldots \wedge (\neg M_{n-1}\varphi \vee M_n\varphi)) \to (M_0\varphi \wedge M_1\varphi \wedge \ldots \wedge M_n\varphi)$ (Gr0)

5 $(M_0\varphi \wedge M_1\varphi \wedge \ldots \wedge M_n\varphi) \to M_n\varphi$ (Gr0, Gr2')

6 $M_n\varphi \to \neg K_n\neg\varphi$ (df M_n)

7 $\neg(M!_0\varphi \nabla M!_1\varphi \nabla \ldots \nabla M!_n\varphi) \to \neg K_n\neg\varphi$ (HS, 1, 2, 3, 4, 5, 6)

8 $K_n\neg\varphi \to (M!_0\varphi \nabla M!_1\varphi \nabla \ldots \nabla M!_n\varphi)$ (CP, 7)

(iv) 1 $\varphi \to (\varphi \vee \psi)$ (Gr0)

2 $K_0(\varphi \to (\varphi \vee \psi))$ (R2, 1)

3 $K_0(\varphi \to (\varphi \vee \psi)) \to (M_n\varphi \to M_n(\varphi \vee \psi))$ (Gr1')

4 $M_n\varphi \to M_n(\varphi \vee \psi)$ (R1, 2, 3)

(v) Now we have to reason about numbers explicitly, hence we will give up our strict regime of presenting proofs line by line.

1 $\neg(M_n\varphi \vee M_m\psi) \to (\neg M_n\varphi \wedge \neg M_n\psi)$ (Gr0)

2 $(\neg M_n\varphi \wedge \neg M_n\psi) \to (K_n\neg\varphi \wedge K_m\neg\psi)$ (df M_n)

3 $(K_n\neg\varphi \wedge K_m\neg\psi) \to (M!_{n_1}\varphi \wedge M!_{m_1}\psi)$ for some $n_1 \leq n$, $m_1 \leq m$ (Gr0, (iii))

4 $(M!_{n_1}\varphi \wedge M!_{m_1}\psi) \to (\neg M_{n_1}\varphi \wedge \neg M_{m_1}\psi)$ (Def. M!)

5 $(\neg M_{n_1}\varphi \wedge \neg M_{m_1}\psi) \to \neg M_{n_1}((\varphi \wedge \psi) \vee (\varphi \wedge \neg\psi)) \wedge \neg M_{m_1}((\varphi \wedge \psi) \vee (\neg\varphi \wedge \psi))$ (Sub, 4)

6 $\neg M_{n_1}((\varphi \wedge \psi) \vee (\varphi \wedge \neg\psi)) \wedge \neg M_{m_1}((\varphi \wedge \psi) \vee (\neg\varphi \wedge \psi)) \to$
$\neg M_{n_1}(\varphi \wedge \psi) \wedge \neg M_{n_1}(\varphi \wedge \neg\psi) \wedge \neg M_{m_1}(\varphi \wedge \psi) \wedge \neg M_{m_1}(\neg\varphi \wedge \psi)$ (Gr0, (iv))

7 $\neg M_{n_1}(\varphi \wedge \psi) \wedge \neg M_{n_1}(\varphi \wedge \neg\psi) \wedge \neg M_{m_1}(\varphi \wedge \psi) \wedge \neg M_{m_1}(\neg\varphi \wedge \psi) \to$
$M!_{n_{11}}(\varphi \wedge \psi) \wedge M!_{n_{12}}(\varphi \wedge \neg\psi) \wedge M!_{m_{11}}(\varphi \wedge \psi) \wedge M!_{m_{12}}(\neg\varphi \wedge \psi)$
for some $n_{11}, n_{12} \leq n_1$ and $m_{11}, m_{12} \leq m_1$ (Gr0, (iii))

Now we observe that, by (ii), $n_{11} = m_{11}$. Moreover, $n_{11} + n_{12} = n_1$, since we have

a $K_0\neg((\varphi \wedge \psi) \wedge (\varphi \wedge \neg\psi))$ (Gr0)

b $(M!_{n_{11}}(\varphi \wedge \psi) \wedge M!_{n_{12}}(\varphi \wedge \neg\psi)) \to M!_{(n_{11} + n_{12})}\varphi)$ (Gr0, Gr3, a)

c by, (iii), $M!_{(n_{11} + n_{12})}\varphi$ and $M!_{n_1}\varphi$ can only hold simultaneously if $n_{11} + n_{12} = n_1$, and, since by the arguments above, both $M!_{(n_{11}+n_{12})}\varphi$ and $M!_{n_1}\varphi$ follow from $\neg(M_n\varphi \vee M_m\psi)$, we must have $n_{11} + n_{12} = n_1$.

In a simular way, we have $m_{11} + m_{12} = m_1$. This gives:

8 $M!_{n_{11}}(\varphi \wedge \psi) \wedge M!_{n_{12}}(\varphi \wedge \neg\psi) \wedge M!_{m_{11}}(\varphi \wedge \psi) \wedge M!_{m_{12}}(\neg\varphi \wedge \psi) \rightarrow$
$M!_{n_{11}}(\varphi \wedge \psi) \wedge M!_{n_{12}}(\varphi \wedge \neg\psi) \wedge M!_{m_{12}}(\neg\varphi \wedge \psi)$ (7, $n_{11} = m_{11}$)

9 $M!_{n_{11}}(\varphi \wedge \psi) \wedge M!_{n_{12}}(\varphi \wedge \neg\psi) \wedge M!_{m_{12}}(\neg\varphi \wedge \psi) \rightarrow$
$M!_h((\varphi \wedge \psi) \vee (\varphi \wedge \neg\psi) \vee (\neg\varphi \wedge \psi))$, with $h = n_{11} + n_{12} + m_{21}$ (Gr0, K_0D, Gr3)

10 $M!_h((\varphi \wedge \psi) \vee (\varphi \wedge \neg\psi) \vee (\neg\varphi \wedge \psi)) \rightarrow M!_h(\varphi \vee \psi)$ (Gr0, Sub)

11 $M!_h(\varphi \vee \psi) \rightarrow \neg M_h(\varphi \vee \psi)$ (df M!)

Note that $h \le n_1 + m_1 \le n + m$;

12 $\neg M_h(\varphi \vee \psi) \rightarrow \neg M_{n+m}(\varphi \vee \psi)$ (applying Gr2' (n+m)-h times)

13 $\neg(M_n\varphi \vee M_m\psi) \rightarrow \neg M_{n+m}(\varphi \vee \psi)$ (HS, 1-12)

(vi) We do the proof in case $n \neq 0$; the other (but similar) case is left to the reader.

1 $M_m\varphi \rightarrow M_n\varphi$ (Gr2', $n < m$)

2 $M_n\varphi \rightarrow \neg(M_{n-1}\varphi \wedge \neg M_n\varphi)$ (Gr0)

3 $\neg(M_{n-1}\varphi \wedge \neg M_n\varphi) \rightarrow \neg M!_n\varphi$ (df M!)

4 $M_m\varphi \rightarrow \neg M!_n\varphi$ (HS, 1-3)

5 $(M!_n\varphi \wedge M_m\varphi) \rightarrow \bot$ (Gr0, 4)

(vii) 1 $\neg M_{n+m+1}\varphi \rightarrow \neg M_{n+m+1}((\varphi \wedge \psi) \vee (\varphi \wedge \neg\psi))$ (Sub, Gr0)

2 $\neg M_{n+m+1}((\varphi \wedge \psi) \vee (\varphi \wedge \neg\psi)) \rightarrow (\neg M_{n+m+1}(\varphi \wedge \psi) \wedge \neg M_{n+m+1}(\varphi \wedge \neg\psi))$ (iv)

3 $(\neg M_{n+m+1}(\varphi \wedge \psi) \wedge \neg M_{n+m+1}(\varphi \wedge \neg\psi)) \rightarrow M!_{n_1}(\varphi \wedge \psi) \wedge M!_{m_1}(\varphi \wedge \neg\psi)$,
for some $n_1, m_1 \le n + m + 1$ (iii)

4 $\neg M_{n+m+1}\varphi \rightarrow M!_{n_1}(\varphi \wedge \psi) \wedge M!_{m_1}(\varphi \wedge \neg\psi)$ (HS, 1-3)

5 $(M_n(\varphi \wedge \psi) \wedge M_m(\varphi \wedge \neg\psi) \wedge \neg M_{n+m+1}\varphi) \rightarrow M!_{n_1}(\varphi \wedge \psi) \wedge M!_{m_1}(\varphi \wedge \neg\psi)$ (Gr0, 4)

Now, we distinguish two subcases:

a $n_1 \le n$ or $m_1 \le m$

6a $(M_n(\varphi \wedge \psi) \wedge M_m(\varphi \wedge \neg\psi) \wedge \neg M_{n+m+1}\varphi) \rightarrow (\neg M!_{n_1}(\varphi \wedge \psi) \vee \neg M!_{m_1}(\varphi \wedge \neg\psi))$(Gr0, vi, a)

7a $(M_n(\varphi \wedge \psi) \wedge M_m(\varphi \wedge \neg\psi) \wedge \neg M_{n+m+1}\varphi) \rightarrow \bot$ (Gr0, 5, 6a)

8a $M_n(\varphi \wedge \psi) \wedge M_m(\varphi \wedge \neg\psi) \rightarrow M_{n+m+1}\varphi$ (Gr0, 7a)

b $n_1 > n$ and $m_1 > m$

Note that we now have $n_1 + m_1 \ge n + m + 2$ (B)

6b $M!_{n_1}(\varphi \wedge \psi) \wedge M!_{m_1}(\varphi \wedge \neg\psi) \rightarrow M!_{(n_1+m_1)}\varphi$ (Gr0, Gr3)

7b $M!_{(n_1+m_1)}\varphi \rightarrow M_{(n_1+m_1-1)}\varphi$ (df M!)

8b $M_{(n_1+m_1-1)}\varphi \rightarrow M_{n+m+1}\varphi$ (Gr2', Observation (B))

9b $(M_n(\varphi \wedge \psi) \wedge M_m(\varphi \wedge \neg\psi) \wedge \neg M_{n+m+1}\varphi) \rightarrow M_{n+m+1}\varphi$ (HS, 5-8b)

10b $(M_n(\varphi \wedge \psi) \wedge M_m(\varphi \wedge \neg\psi)) \rightarrow M_{n+m+1}\varphi$ (Gr0, 9b)

6 Now, observe that the cases a and b are mutual exclusive and exclude each other. In both cases, we derived the same conclusion. Thus, we have
$(M_n(\varphi \wedge \psi) \wedge M_m(\varphi \wedge \neg\psi)) \rightarrow M_{n+m+1}\varphi$ (8a, 10b, $a \equiv \neg b$)

REMARK. One may wonder whether the proof of item (vii) is really a proof within the logical calculus, and not also about numbers. Indeed, in the meta-proposition **Gr(S5)** $\vdash (M_n(\varphi \wedge \psi) \wedge M_m(\varphi \wedge \neg\psi)) \rightarrow M_{n+m+1}\varphi$ implicitly involves a quantification over the numbers n and m. We did make a distinction of cases by looking at the respective relations between n_1 and n, and also m_1

and m, respectively. One way to proceed form step 5, which is much more cumbersome in notation, but also does not need some explicit distinction of cases at a meta level, is as follows:

5' $(M_n(\varphi \wedge \psi) \wedge M_m(\varphi \wedge \neg\psi) \wedge \neg M_{n+m+1}\varphi) \rightarrow$
$(M_n(\varphi \wedge \psi) \wedge M_m(\varphi \wedge \neg\psi) \wedge \neg M_{n+m+1}\varphi) \wedge \nabla_{i\leq n+m+1} M!_i(\varphi \wedge \psi) \wedge \nabla_{j\leq n+m+1} M!_j(\varphi \wedge \neg\psi)$

and then proceed with a case-analysis within the system, considering all exclusive disjuncts

$$(M_n(\varphi \wedge \psi) \wedge M_m(\varphi \wedge \neg\psi) \wedge \neg M_{n+m+1}\varphi) \wedge M!_i(\varphi \wedge \psi) \wedge M!_j(\varphi \wedge \neg\psi)$$

and distinguish whether ($i \geq n$ or $j \geq m$) holds, or not, concluding for each disjunct that $\bot$ can be derived, so that the desired conclusion is eventually derived.

(viii)
1 $\neg(\varphi \wedge \psi) \rightarrow (\varphi \rightarrow ((\varphi \vee \psi) \wedge \varphi))$ (Gr0)
2 $\neg(\varphi \wedge \psi) \rightarrow (\psi \rightarrow ((\varphi \vee \psi) \wedge \neg\varphi))$ (Gr0)
3 $K_0(\neg(\varphi \wedge \psi) \rightarrow (\varphi \rightarrow ((\varphi \vee \psi) \wedge \varphi)))$ (K_0D, 1)
4 $K_0(\neg(\varphi \wedge \psi) \rightarrow (\psi \rightarrow ((\varphi \vee \psi) \wedge \neg\varphi)))$ (K_0D, 2)
5 $K_0\neg(\varphi \wedge \psi) \rightarrow (M_n\varphi \rightarrow M_n((\varphi \vee \psi) \wedge \varphi))$ (3, Gr1')
6 $K_0\neg(\varphi \wedge \psi) \rightarrow (M_m\psi \rightarrow M_m(\varphi \vee \psi) \wedge \neg\varphi))$ (4, Gr1')
7 $[K_0\neg(\varphi \wedge \psi) \wedge M_n\varphi \wedge M_m\psi] \rightarrow [M_n((\varphi \vee \psi) \wedge \varphi)) \wedge M_m(\varphi \vee \psi) \wedge \neg\varphi))]$ (Gr0, 5, 6)
8 $[M_n((\varphi \vee \psi) \wedge \varphi)) \wedge M_m(\varphi \vee \psi) \wedge \neg\varphi))] \rightarrow [M_{n+m+1}(\varphi \vee \psi)]$ (vii)
9 $[K_0\neg(\varphi \wedge \psi) \wedge M_n\varphi \wedge M_m\psi] \rightarrow [M_{n+m+1}(\varphi \vee \psi)]$ (HS, 7, 8)

2.16.7.1 The soundness of the rules (R1) and (R2) is proven in Proposition 1.3.5; the same holds for the axioms (Gr0) and (Gr1); the soundness of (Gr5) is proven in the answer to Exercise 1.6.4.1. So let us consider the typical numerical axioms (Gr2), (Gr3) and (Gr4);

(Gr2) Suppose $(\mathbb{M}, s) \models K_n\varphi$. We observed, immediately following 2.16.5, that this means that state s has at most n R-successors that verify φ. But then, of course, there also are at most (n+1) R-successors t with this property: hence $(\mathbb{M}, s) \models K_{n+1}\varphi$.

(Gr3) Suppose $(\mathbb{M}, s) \models K_0\neg(\varphi \wedge \psi)$ and $(\mathbb{M}, s) \models \mathbb{M}_m\varphi \wedge \mathbb{M}_m\psi$. By the truth definition for K_0 and that for M!, we obtain that no R-successor of s satisfies $(\varphi \wedge \psi)$ and also that s has exactly n φ-successors and m ψ-successors. But if the latter is the case, and we know that no world is counted in both ways (($\varphi \wedge \psi$) never occurs) we know that s has exactly (n + m) successors in which one of φ and ψ is true: $(\mathbb{M}, s) \models \mathbb{M}_{n+m}(\varphi \vee \psi)$.

(Gr4) Recalling the definition of M_n and the fact that (Gr4) is a *scheme* we observe that it is sufficient to prove that

(Gr4') $M_n\varphi \rightarrow K_0M_n\varphi$

is valid. So suppose $(\mathbb{M}, s) \models M_n\varphi$; s has more than n R-successors $x_1, \ldots, x_n, x_{n+1}$ that satisfy φ: $(\mathbb{M}, x_i) \models \varphi$ $(1 \leq i \leq n+1)$. Let t be an arbitrary R-successor of s. By euclidicity, we know that for all $1 \leq i \leq n$, we have Rtx_i. But then, t has also more than n R-successors in which φ is true; since t was an arbitrary R-successor, we have $(\mathbb{M}, s) \models K_0M_n\varphi$.

3.1.1.1

(i) The key-observation in the proof of '$\Rightarrow$' is that $(\varphi \rightarrow (\psi \rightarrow (\varphi \wedge \psi)))$ is a tautology in (classical) propositional logic, and thus, by (St 1), a member of Σ. The assumption is that $\varphi, \psi \in \Sigma$. Repeated application of (St 2) yields $(\psi \rightarrow (\varphi \wedge \psi)) \in \Sigma$ and $(\varphi \wedge \psi) \in \Sigma$, respectively. For the '$\Leftarrow$'-direction, it is sufficient to note that both $((\varphi \wedge \psi) \rightarrow \varphi)$ and $((\varphi \wedge \psi) \rightarrow \psi)$ are propositional tautologies and then to apply (St 2).

(ii) Let $(\varphi \leftrightarrow \psi)$ be a propositional tautology; by definition of '$\leftrightarrow$' this means that $((\varphi \rightarrow \psi) \wedge (\psi \rightarrow \varphi))$ is a tautology. By (St 1), we then have $((\varphi \rightarrow \psi) \wedge (\psi \rightarrow \varphi)) \in \Sigma$, for any stable Σ; by item (i) we then obtain $(\varphi \rightarrow \psi), (\psi \rightarrow \varphi) \in \Sigma$. Hence, if $\varphi \in \Sigma$, then, by (St 2), $\psi \in \Sigma$ and vice versa.

3.1.1.2

(i) If $\varphi \in \Sigma$, then, by (St 5), $\neg\varphi \notin \Sigma$ and hence, by (St 4), $\neg K \neg\varphi \notin \Sigma$.

(ii) We prove the claim with induction on $|w|$, the length of the word w. In order to apply the induction hypothesis properly on 'smaller' formulas, we will in fact prove a stronger statement. Let N(w) be the number of $\neg$'s occurring in w. Consider

$$\varphi \in \Sigma \Rightarrow [N(w) \text{ is even} \Leftrightarrow w\varphi \in \Sigma] \quad (*)$$

The proof of (*) is as follows:

- Suppose $N(w) = 0$, and $\varphi \in \Sigma$. Now N(w) is even, and, by $|w|$ applications of (St 3), we have $w\varphi \in \Sigma$. This proves [N(w) is even $\Leftrightarrow w\varphi \in \Sigma$].
- Suppose now that (*) has been proven for all v with $|v| < n$ $(n \geq 1)$, and suppose $|w| = n$.

 1 First, suppose $w = \neg v$.
 For '$\Leftarrow$', if $w\varphi \in \Sigma$, then, by (St 5), $v\varphi \notin \Sigma$, and, by the induction hypothesis, N(v) is odd, hence N(w) is even. For '$\Rightarrow$', we distinguish two cases:

 1a If N(w) is even, then N(v) is odd. Hence, by the induction hypothesis, $v\varphi \notin \Sigma$. We consider two sub-subcases; $v = \neg v_1$ and $v = Kv_1$. In the first case we have $w\varphi = \neg\neg v_1\varphi$, and since $N(v_1)$ is even, from $\varphi \in \Sigma$ we obtain $v_1\varphi \in \Sigma$ and thus (use $\vdash v_1\varphi \rightarrow \neg\neg v_1\varphi$) we have $w\varphi \in \Sigma$. If $v = Kv_1$, then $N(v_1)$ is odd. With $\varphi \in \Sigma$ it follows that $v_1\varphi \notin \Sigma$; with (St 4) we have $\neg K v_1 \varphi \in \Sigma$, so $w\varphi \in \Sigma$.

 1b If, on the other hand, N(w) is odd, then N(v) is even, and thus $\varphi \in \Sigma \Rightarrow v\varphi \in \Sigma$ and then, by (St 5), $w\varphi \notin \Sigma$.

 2 The other case is $w = Kv$. In that case we have $N(w) = N(v)$. For v, we have $\varphi \in \Sigma \Rightarrow$ [N(v) is even $\Leftrightarrow v\varphi \in \Sigma$]. However, by the observation above, N(v) is even $\Leftrightarrow$ N(w) is even, and by (St 3), $v\varphi \in \Sigma \Leftrightarrow w\varphi \in \Sigma$. This proves (*).

3.1.3.1 $(\neg K\varphi \vee (K\psi \vee \chi)) \in \Sigma \Leftrightarrow_{\text{Lemma 3.1.3(ii)}} \varphi \notin \Sigma$ or $(K\psi \vee \chi) \in \Sigma \Leftrightarrow_{\text{Lemma 3.1.3(i)}} \varphi \notin \Sigma$ or $\psi \in \Sigma$ or $\chi \in \Sigma$.

3.1.3.2 By (St 5), φ and $\neg\varphi$ cannot be simultaneously a member of Σ. To see that at least one of those formulas in sin Σ, first suppose $\varphi \equiv (K\psi \vee K\chi)$. Suppose $\varphi \notin \Sigma$. Then, by Lemma 3.1.3(i), $\psi \notin \Sigma$ and $\chi \notin \Sigma$. By (St 4), we then have $\neg K\psi, \neg K\chi \in \Sigma$, and, by Exercise 3.1.1.1(i), $(\neg K\psi \wedge \neg K\chi) \in \Sigma$. The latter formula is equivalent to $\neg\varphi$, and hence, by (St 1) and (St 2), $\neg\varphi \in \Sigma$. Secondly, suppose $\varphi \equiv (K\psi \wedge K\chi)$. If $\varphi \notin \Sigma$, then, by Exercise 3.1.1(i), $K\psi \notin \Sigma$ or $K\chi \notin \Sigma$. By (St 3), we see that $\psi \notin \Sigma$ or $\chi \notin \Sigma$ and, by (St 4), $\psi \notin \Sigma$ or $\neg K\chi \in \Sigma$. By Exercise 3.1.1.1(i) we get $(\neg K\psi \vee \neg K\chi) \in \Sigma$, and thus, by Exercise 3.1.1.1(ii) and propositional logic, $\neg\varphi \in \Sigma$.

*E.2. Intermezzo (for Exercise 3.1.4.3.1)

Proving whether an epistemic formula is by no means a trivial matter. In this intermezzo we develop some theory for this. Later we shall see how looking at things from a semantic perspective will make life easier (Exercise 3.1.10.3).

Let us denote our epistemic language by $\mathcal{L}$, and let $\mathcal{L}_n$ consist of all formulas $\varphi \in \mathcal{L}$ such that

$|\varphi| \leq n$, where $|\ |$ is the modal depth function as introduced in the proof of 3.1.2. Furthermore, in what follows we use the abbreviation $<\Phi>_0 = <\Phi> \cap \mathcal{L}_0$.

E.2.1. DEFINITION. Let A be a set of epistemic formulas. Define a sequence $\Sigma_0 \subseteq \Sigma_1 \subseteq \ldots$ as follows:

$$\Sigma_0 = <A>_0;$$
$$\Sigma_{n+1} = <\Sigma_n \cup \{K\sigma_n, \neg K\chi_n \mid \sigma_n \in \Sigma_n, \chi_n \notin \Sigma_n, |\sigma_n| = |\chi_n| = n\}> \cap \mathcal{L}_{n+1}.$$

Finally, let $\Sigma = \bigcup_i \Sigma_i$. We also write $\Sigma(A)$ for this set, and also $\Sigma_i(A)$ for the set Σ_i.

E.2.2. LEMMA. *If* A *is classically consistent, every* Σ_i *is classically consistent.*

PROOF. Use induction on i. We start with some preliminary work.

E.2.2.1. DEFINITION. Suppose we are given a classically consistent set $B \subseteq \mathcal{L}_0$. Let us define a *valuation* π *for B* such that $\pi(p) = t$ if $p \in <B> \cap \mathbf{P}$, and $\pi(p) = f$ if $\neg p \in <B> \cap \mathbf{P}$. (Note that π is not determined for atoms not mentioned in B but, since B is consistent, we know that such a valuation can be consistently extended for the whole set of atoms $\mathbf{P} \subseteq \mathcal{L}$.) Moreover, this π is straightforwardly extended to a 'valuation' π^* for the whole language $\mathcal{L}_0$ (satisfying $\pi^*(p) = \pi(p)$ for atoms p, $\pi^*(\varphi \wedge \psi) = t$ if and only both $\pi^*(\varphi)$ and $\pi^*(\psi)$ are true, $\pi^*(\neg\varphi) = t$ if and only if $\pi^*(\varphi) = f$) satisfying the property that $\pi^*(\varphi) = t$ if $\varphi \in <B> \cap \mathcal{L}_0$, and $\pi^*(\varphi) = f$ if $\neg\varphi \in <B> \cap \mathcal{L}_0$).

Now, let $\mathbf{P}^+$ be the set of quasi-atoms $\mathbf{P} \cup \{K\varphi \mid \varphi \in \mathcal{L}\}$. We argue that the quasi-atoms of the form $K\varphi$ can also be conceived as atoms: there is no way in which its truth value is depending on its parts. So, we will define 'supervaluations' $\Pi: \mathbf{P}^+ \to \{t, f\}$, that, in their turn, allow for a straightforward extension Π^* for the whole language $\mathcal{L}$, and also for the subsets $\mathcal{L}_n$ in it. For any classically consistent $C \subseteq \mathcal{L}_n$, we can define a supervaluation Π as we defined π above for B, now having the property that the extended valuation Π^* satisfies: $\Pi^*(\varphi) = t$ if $\varphi \in <C> \cap \mathcal{L}_n$, and $\Pi^*(\varphi) = f$ if $\neg\varphi \in <C> \cap \mathcal{L}_n$.

Let us make some remarks upon the construction above.

Firstly, this notion of supervaluation stresses the idea that we must refrain from imposing epistemically logical properties to sets of formulas. For instance, it is perfectly possible to find a supervaluation for the set $\{Kp, K\neg p, KKq, \neg Kq\}$.

Secondly, in each step we take restrictions to $\mathcal{L}_n$; otherwise, we obtain problems like the following: for $<C> \cap \mathcal{L}_0$, we do not want to bother about $\Pi(Kp \vee \neg Kp)$; its argument $Kp \vee \neg Kp$ would be in $<C>$, but it is not in $<C> \cap \mathcal{L}_0$.

Thirdly, note that the construction cannot always start with a general consistent subset A of $\mathcal{L}$: for instance, if one starts with A = {Kp → r, p, ¬r}, then, obviously A has a supervaluation, and we have $p \in \Sigma_1 = \langle A \rangle \cap \mathcal{L}_1$, and $\neg r \in \Sigma_1$. If we then move to the next layer, say Σ_2, then we are forced to add Kp to Σ_2, and it is not obvious how to maintain consistency, since then also r should be added. So note that in order to avoid these problems our construction starts with some consistent set in $\mathcal{L}_0$ rather than $\mathcal{L}$.

To apply induction properly in the proof of Lemma E.2.2, we strengthen it slightly.

E.2.2.2. LEMMA. *Let* $\Sigma_0, \Sigma_1, \ldots$ *be defined as above. Then, for all* n, *there is a supervaluation* Π_n *such that* $\Pi_n^*(\varphi) = t$ *if* $\varphi \in \Sigma_n$ *and* $\Pi_n^*(\varphi) = f$ *if* $\neg\varphi \in \Sigma_n$.

PROOF. For n = 0, we know that A is consistent, so it allows for a classical valuation, which is also a valuation for $\langle A \rangle \cap \mathcal{L}_0$. We now may take Π_0 to be π; we argued already above that $\pi^* = \Pi_0^*$ satisfies $\Pi_0^*(\varphi) = t$ if $\varphi \in \Sigma_0$, $\Pi_0^*(\varphi) = f$ if $\neg\varphi \in \Sigma_0$.
Now suppose Lemma E.2.2.2 has been proven for k: for Σ_k we have found a supervaluation Π_k such that $\Pi_k^*(\varphi) = t$ if $\varphi \in \Sigma_k$, $\Pi_k^*(\varphi) = f$ if $\neg\varphi \in \Sigma_k$. Now we observe the following: to obtain Σ_{k+1}, we add to Σ_k atoms of the form $K\sigma$ and $\neg K\chi$, that are not in Σ_k already, and for which we never have that there are σ and χ such that $(\sigma \leftrightarrow \chi) \in \Sigma_k$ (for then we would have both χ and $\neg\chi \in \Sigma_k$). But obiously, if we have a classical consistent set Σ_k with a valuation Π_k^* and we add to it a number of independent atoms, the valuation Π_{k+1} that extends Π_k such that $\Pi_{k+1}(K\sigma) = t$ for all the new $K\sigma$'s, and $\Pi_{k+1}(K\chi) = f$ for all the new $\neg K\chi$'s, is a valuation such that $\Pi_{k+1}^*(\varphi) = t$ if $\varphi \in \Sigma_{k+1}$, and $\Pi_{k+1}^*(\varphi) = f$ if $\neg\varphi \in \Sigma_{k+1}$. ■

This completes the proof of Lemma E.2.2.2 and, hence, of Lemma E.2.2.

E.2.3 THEOREM.
(i) $\Sigma(A)$ *is a stable set containing* A;
(ii) $\text{Prop}(\Sigma(A)) = \langle A \rangle \cap \mathcal{L}_0$.

PROOF.
(i) To prove that $\Sigma(A)$ is stable, let us check the items of Definition 3.1.1:

(St 1) Note that none of the Σ_i's is closed under $\langle\ \rangle$; Σ_i does not contain tautologies involving formulas with depth greater than i. However, let ψ be any tautology, with $|\psi| = n$. Clearly, $\psi \in \langle X \rangle \cap \Sigma_n$, for any X, hence $\psi \in \Sigma_n$.

(St 2) Let $n = \max\{i, j \mid \varphi \in \Sigma_i, \varphi \to \psi \in \Sigma_j\}$, then obviously $\psi \in \Sigma_n$.

(St 3) Obviously, if $\varphi \in \Sigma$, there must be some i such that $\varphi \in \Sigma_i$, and then $K\varphi \in \Sigma_{i+1} \subseteq \Sigma$. Conversely, if $K\varphi \in \Sigma$ but $\varphi \notin \Sigma$, we must have $K\varphi$, $\neg K\varphi$ in some Σ_i;

contradicting Lemma E.2.2 above.

(St 4) Let $|\varphi| = n$. If $\varphi \notin \Sigma$. then also $\varphi \notin \Sigma_n$, and then $\neg K\varphi \in \Sigma_{n+1} \subseteq \Sigma$. Conversely, if $\neg K\varphi \in \Sigma$ but $\varphi \in \Sigma$, we must have $\neg K\varphi$, $K\varphi$ in some Σ_i; contradicting Lemma E.2.2 above.

(St 5) Σ's classical consistency immediately follows from the consistency of each of the Σ_i's.

(ii) The $\supseteq$-direction follows from the definition of Σ and Σ_0.

We now first observe the following property of propositional logic:

E.2.3.1. CLAIM. Let $\alpha, \alpha_1, \ldots, \alpha_n, \beta_1, \ldots, \beta_k$ be propositional formulas, such that each α has no atoms in common with any of the formulas $\beta_1, \ldots, \beta_k$. Then

$$\alpha_1, \ldots, \alpha_n, \beta_1, \ldots, \beta_k \models_{prop} \alpha \Leftrightarrow \alpha_1, \ldots, \alpha_n \models_{prop} \alpha.$$

PROOF. From right to left is obvious; the other direction is argued as follows: suppose $\alpha_1, \ldots, \alpha_n \not\models_{prop} \alpha$, then there is a valuation π such that for its extension π^* to the whole propositional language holds that $\pi^*(\alpha_i) = t$ (all $i \leq n$), but $\pi^*(\alpha) = f$. If we change this π to a valuation π_1 that only differs from π in some atoms that are not involved in any of the α_i' or α, we still have that $\pi_1{}^*(\alpha_i) = t$ (all $i \leq n$) and $\pi_1{}^*(\alpha) = f$. Now, notice that any valuation $\underline{\pi}$ for which $\underline{\pi}(\alpha_i) = \underline{\pi}(\beta_j) = t$ ($i \leq n$, $j \leq k$) can be considered to be derived from π in such a way, hence we have $\alpha_1, \ldots, \alpha_n, \beta_1, \ldots, \beta_k \not\models_{prop} \alpha$. ■Claim

To complete the proof of item (ii), let $\alpha \in \text{Prop}(\Sigma(A))$. This implies that there is an n such that $\alpha \in \Sigma_n$. In Intermezzo E.3 introducing Exercise 3.4.14.1 we will show that for any two sets C and D, $<\,<C> \cup D\,> = <C \cup D>$. Iterating this property, we may conceive Σ_n as $\Sigma_n = <\sigma_{01}, \ldots, \sigma_{0k_0}, \sigma_{11}, \ldots, \sigma_{1k_1}, \sigma_{n-11}, \ldots, \sigma_{n-1k_{n-1}}>$, with $\sigma_{im} \in \Sigma_i$ ($i < n$, $m \leq k_i$), where each σ_{0j} ($j \leq k_0$) is purely propositional, and each σ_{it} ($0 < i < n$, $t \leq k_i$) is of the form $K\sigma$ or $\neg K\chi$, for some σ, χ. Now, keeping in mind the construction of supervaluations, we can apply Claim E.2.3.1 above to obtain the following:

$$\sigma_{01}, \ldots, \sigma_{0k_0}, \sigma_{11}, \ldots, \sigma_{1k_1}, \sigma_{n-11}, \ldots, \sigma_{n-1k_{n-1}} \models_{prop} \alpha \Leftrightarrow \sigma_{01}, \ldots, \sigma_{0k_0} \models_{prop} \alpha.$$

Notice that the left-hand side is equivalent to $\alpha \in \Sigma_n$, whereas the right-hand side is equivalent to $\alpha \in \Sigma_0$ ($= <A> \cap \mathcal{L}_0$). ■

E.2.4. COROLLARY. *A consistent propositional set of formulas* A *uniquely determines a stable set* Σ(A).

PROOF. Immediate from Proposition 3.1.2 and Theorem E.2.3 above. ∎

The following lemma may be useful in what follows:

E.2.5 LEMMA. *Let* φ *be an epistemic formula, and* A *be a set of propositional formulas. Suppose it holds that:*

(i) $\varphi \in \Sigma(A)$;

(ii) *for any stable set* Σ' *containing* φ *we have* $A \subseteq \Sigma'$.

Then φ *is honest, and* $\Sigma^{\varphi} = \Sigma(A)$.

PROOF. Property (i) guarantees that there is a stable set (i.e. $\Sigma(A)$) containing φ. We know of this stable set (Theorem E.2.3) that $Prop(\Sigma(A)) = \langle A \rangle \cap \mathcal{L}_0$. Let Σ' be any stable set containing φ; from property (ii) we know that $A \subseteq \Sigma'$, and, by St 1 and St 2 [and the compactness and deduction theorem: $\varphi \in \langle A \rangle \Rightarrow A \models_{prop} \varphi \Rightarrow A' \models_{prop} \varphi$ (for some finite $A' \subseteq A$) $\Rightarrow \models_{prop} A' \to \varphi$ (where A' now stands for the conjunction of the elements in A') $\Rightarrow$ (stability of Σ') $A' \to \varphi \in \Sigma' \Rightarrow$ (since $A' \subseteq A \subseteq \Sigma'$) $\varphi \in \Sigma'$], we also have $\langle A \rangle \subseteq \Sigma'$, and hence $Prop(\Sigma(A)) = \langle A \rangle \cap \mathcal{L}_0 \subseteq \Sigma' \cap \mathcal{L}_0 = Prop(\Sigma')$, and thus $Prop(\Sigma(A)) \subseteq Prop(\Sigma')$. Thus we have that $\Sigma(A)$ is a stable set containing φ and its propositional kernel is minimal among those sets; thus φ is honest and $\Sigma^{\varphi} = \Sigma(A)$. ∎

Now we are ready to answer Exercise 3.1.4.3.1:

*3.1.4.3.1 In the following, the phrase 'Σ^{φ} exists' means that there is a stable set Σ^{φ} containing φ with the property that for all stable sets Σ containing φ we have $Prop(\Sigma^{\varphi}) \subseteq Prop(\Sigma)$.

(i) $p \vee Kq$ is not honest.
From Lemma E.2.5 above, we know that $\Sigma^{p} = \Sigma(\{p\})$ and $\Sigma^{q} = \Sigma(\{q\})$ are unique stable sets, containing p and q, respectively, and both have a minimal propositional kernel, and hence $q \notin \Sigma^{p}$, $p \notin \Sigma^{q}$ (*). Moreover, in both of them, the formula $p \vee Kq$ occurs ($p \in \Sigma^{p}$; q and $Kq \in \Sigma^{q}$, and those sets are closed under their logical consequences, one of which is $p \vee Kq$).
Now suppose that $\Sigma^{(p \vee Kq)}$ exists. Since its propositional kernel is minimal amongst the stable sets containing $p \vee Kq$, from (*) we know that $\{p, q\} \cap \Sigma^{p \vee Kq} = \varnothing$. However, Lemma 3.1.3(i) implies that at least one of p and q should be a member of $\Sigma^{p \vee Kq}$; so that our assumption that $\Sigma^{p \vee Kq}$ exists — and hence that $p \vee Kq$ would be honest — cannot be true.

(ii) $p \wedge K\neg q$ is honest.
Let us consider $A = \{p, \neg q\}$; we will show that it satisfies the two conditions (i) and (ii) of Lemma E.2.5, with $\varphi = p \wedge K\neg q$: then we immediately have that $p \wedge K\neg q$ is honest. To prove property (i), note that, by construction, $p, \neg q \in \Sigma_0(A)$, $K\neg q \in \Sigma_1(A)$ and hence $(p \wedge K\neg q) \in \Sigma(A)$. Conversely, in any stable Σ' that contains $(p \wedge K\neg q)$, we must have $p, \neg q \in \Sigma'$ (apply Exercise

3.1.1.1(i) and St 3), which proves property (ii).

(iii) $\neg Kp \vee Kq \vee r$ is honest.
We again apply E.2.5; now with $A = \emptyset$ and $\varphi = (\neg Kp \vee Kq \vee r)$. To prove condition (i) of Lemma E.2.5, observe that $p \notin \langle A \rangle$ and hence $\neg Kp$ is added at $\in \Sigma_1(A)$, thus $\neg Kp \in \Sigma(A)$ and, by St 1 and St 2, also $(\neg Kp \vee \psi) \in \Sigma(A)$ for any ψ, hence $(\neg Kp \vee Kq \vee r) \in \Sigma(A)$. Property (ii) of E.2.5 is trivial, which proves that φ is honest.

(iv) $Kp \vee K\neg p$ is not honest.
Let $\varphi = Kp \vee K\neg p$. Suppose Σ^φ exists. By Lemma 3.1.3(i) and St 3 we know that either p or $\neg p$ must be a formula of Σ^φ. Consider $\Sigma(\{p\})$ and $\Sigma(\{\neg p\})$; they are both stable sets containing φ (use St 3, then St 1 and St 2). Thus Σ^φ satisfies $Prop(\Sigma^\varphi) \subseteq Prop(\Sigma(\{p\})) \cap Prop(\Sigma(\{\neg p\}))$; which is easily seen to be impossible ($p \notin Prop(\Sigma(\{\neg p\}))$, $\neg p \notin Prop(\Sigma(\{p\}))$).

(v) $p \vee q$ is honest.
Let $A = \{p \vee q\}$; the properties (i) and (ii) of E.2.5 are immediately obtained.

(vi) $Kp \vee \neg Kp$ is honest.
Again, apply E.2.5, with $A = \emptyset$. Obviously, by (St 2), we have $(Kp \vee \neg Kp) \in \Sigma(A)$, while $A \subseteq \Sigma'$ is true for any (stable) set Σ'.

(vii) $Kp \wedge Kq$ is honest.
We apply E.2.5, with $A = \{p, q\}$. Obviously, $(Kp \wedge Kq) \in \Sigma(A)$ (since $Kp, Kq \in \Sigma(A)$), and, any stable set containing $Kp \wedge Kq$ must also contain A.

(viii) $p \wedge \neg K\neg q$ is honest.
We now take $A = \{p\}$. Then, $p \in \Sigma_0(A) \subseteq \Sigma_1(A)$, and $\neg K\neg q \in \Sigma_1(A)$; so $(p \wedge \neg K\neg q) \in \Sigma_1(A)$, because of the logical closure property of each $\Sigma_i(A)$. Obviously, $A \subseteq \Sigma'$ for each stable set Σ' containing $(p \wedge \neg K\neg q)$.

(ix) $p \vee \neg K\neg q$ is honest.
Here, $A = \emptyset$; then, $\neg K\neg q \in \Sigma_1(A)$ and thus $p \vee \neg K\neg q \in \Sigma(A)$. $A \subseteq \Sigma'$ is obvious.

3.1.6.1 By Lemma 3.1.6, it is sufficient to design a Kripke model M such that $\neg K\neg\varphi \in K(M)$, but $\varphi \notin K(M)$. An example of such a model is $M = \langle S, R, \pi \rangle$ with $S = \{s, t\}$, $R = S \times S$ and $\pi(s)(p) = t$, $\pi(s)(q) = f$. Then we have $\neg K\neg p \in K(M)$, and $p \notin K(M)$.

3.1.6.2 Suppose $M' \models K(M)$. By definition of $\models$ and $K(M')$, this means that $K(M) \subseteq K(M')$. For the converse, suppose that $\varphi \notin K(M)$. Then, there is an s such that $(M, s) \models \neg\varphi$. Since M is a simple S5-model, we have $M \models \neg K\varphi$, or, $\neg K\varphi \in K(M)$. But then $M' \models \neg K\varphi$, which means that there must be an s' with $(M', s') \models \neg\varphi$, hence $M' \not\models \varphi$ and $\varphi \notin K(M')$.

3.1.7.1

(i) Suppose $M_1 \subseteq M_2$. Suppose $\alpha \in Prop(K(M_2))$ which means that $M_2 \models \alpha$, so $(M_2, s_2) \models \alpha$ for all $s_2 \in S_2$. Since α is propositional, the truth of α in s_2 only depends on $\pi(s_2)$; it is such that α is true. Now let $s_1 \in S_1$, by our assumption it follows that $s_1 \in S_2$ and hence α is true at s_1: $(M_1, s_1) \models \alpha$. Since this holds for arbitrary $s_1 \in S_1$, we have that $\alpha \in Prop(K(M_1))$.

(ii) Let $S_1 = \{s_1\}$, $S_2 = \{s_1, s_2\}$; moreover, suppose $s_1(q) = t$ and $s_2(q) = f$. Then, $\neg Kq \in K(M_2)$ but $\neg Kq \notin K(M_1)$.

3.1.7.2

(i) Since $M_i \subseteq M_1 \cup M_2$ (i = 1, 2) we have, by Exercise 3.1.7.1(i), $Prop(K(M_1 \cup M_2)) \subseteq Prop(K(M_i))$ (i = 1, 2) and hence $Prop(K(M_1 \cup M_2)) \subseteq Prop(K(M_1)) \cap Prop(K(M_2))$. For the converse, suppose $\alpha \in Prop(K(M_1)) \cap Prop(K(M_2))$, i.e. α is propositional, and $M_1 \models \alpha$, $M_2 \models \alpha$. Let s be a state in $(M_1 \cup M_2)$. Then s is a valuation making α true (since α is propositional, the truth of α at s only depends on the values s(p) for all atoms p occurring in α and we already know that $(M_i, s) \models \alpha$ for at least one $i \leq 2$) and hence $\alpha \in Prop(K(M_1 \cup M_2))$.

(ii) Let $\alpha \in (Prop(K(M_1)) \cup Prop(K(M_2)))$. Then for at least one $i \leq 2$, we have $\alpha \in Prop(K(M_i))$. Since $M_1 \cap M_2 \subseteq M_i$, an application of Exercise 3.1.7.1(i) yields $\alpha \in Prop(K(M_1 \cap M_2))$. To show that the converse does not hold, consider the following two models. Let $S_1 = \{s_1, s\}$, $S_2 = \{s_2, s\}$; let $s(p) = t$, $s_1(p) = s_2(p) = f$. Then $p \in Prop(K(M_1 \cap M_2))$, $p \notin Prop(K(M_1))$, $p \notin Prop(K(M_2))$.

3.1.8.1 Suppose $\alpha \in Prop(K(M_\Sigma))$, i.e. for all $s \in S$, $(M_\Sigma, s) \models \alpha$. Since α is propositional, we have $s \models \alpha$. This proves that, for all $s \in W$ with $s \models Prop(\Sigma)$, we have $s \models \alpha$, hence $Prop(\Sigma) \models \alpha$. Since Σ was a stable set, it is closed under propositional consequences. Hence we obtain $\alpha \in Prop(\Sigma)$. Conversely, suppose $\alpha \in Prop(\Sigma)$. Then, if $s \models Prop(\Sigma)$, then also $s \models \alpha$. This only depends on s(p) for those p that occur in α. So, viewing s as a state in S of M_Σ, we still have $(M_\Sigma, s) \models \alpha$, and hence $\alpha \in Prop(K(M_\Sigma))$.

*3.1.8.2(i) Let $i \in \mathbb{N}$ be given. We use induction on the structure of φ. If $\varphi = p_k$, we know that $k \leq i$, and, by definition of π_2, we have $\pi_2(x)(p_k) = \pi_2(y)(p_k) = t$. Conjunction follows easily, and so does negation. Let us consider $\varphi = K\psi$. Here, we do not need the induction hypothesis, since we are dealing with simple S5-structures. Let $x, y \geq i$. Then, $(M_2, x) \models \varphi \Leftrightarrow (M_2, x) \models K\psi \Leftrightarrow (M_2, z) \models \psi$ for all $z \in \mathbb{N} \cup \{\infty\} \Leftrightarrow (M_2, y) \models K\psi \Leftrightarrow (M_2, y) \models \varphi$

(ii) Immediate from (i) (any world $n \leq MI(\varphi)$ is a witness).

(iii) With induction on φ. For atoms p_i, this is immediate from the definition of π_1 and π_2. For conjunction and negation it follows immediately. Let $\varphi = K\psi$, and suppose the proposition holds for ψ, i.e. for all $n \in \mathbb{N}$: $((M_1, n) \models \psi \Leftrightarrow (M_2, n) \models \psi)$. Suppose $(M_1, n) \models K\psi$. Then for all $m \in \mathbb{N}$ we have $(M_1, m) \models \psi$, and, using induction, for all $m \in \mathbb{N}$ $(M_2, m) \models \psi$ (*). Furthermore, we now also have that $(M_2, \infty) \models \psi$, since if this would not be true, we would have $(M_2, \infty) \models \neg\psi$, and thus, using item (ii), that for some $k \in \mathbb{N}$, $(M_2, k) \models \neg\psi$, contradicting (*). Hence, we have for *all* worlds x in $\mathbb{N} \cup \{\infty\}$ that $(M_2, x) \models \psi$, and hence $(M_2, n) \models K\psi$. If, conversely, $(M_2, n) \models K\psi$, we have that for all $x \in \mathbb{N} \cup \{\infty\}$ $(M_2, x) \models \psi$, in particular for all $x \in \mathbb{N}$, and thus, by induction hypothesis, $(M_1, x) \models \psi$ for all $x \in \mathbb{N}$, hence $(M_1, n) \models K\psi$.

(iv) Now we prove $K(M_1) = K(M_2)$ as follows: suppose $\varphi \notin K(M_1)$, then there is some $n \in \mathbb{N}$ with $(M_1, n) \models \neg\varphi$. Item (iii) guarantees that $(M_2, n) \models \neg\varphi$ and thus $\varphi \notin K(M_2)$. Conversely, if $\varphi \notin K(M_2)$ there is some $y \in \mathbb{N} \cup \{\infty\}$ such that $(M_2, y) \models \neg\varphi$. By item (ii) we find some $n \in \mathbb{N}$ such that $(M_2, n) \models \neg\varphi$, and with item (iii) we know that $(M_1, n) \models \neg\varphi$, and hence $\varphi \notin K(M_1)$.

(v) Consider $\Sigma = K(M_1)$. From Lemma 3.1.6 we know that it is a stable set. We have found two different Kripke models M_1 and M_2 such that $\Sigma = K(M_1) = K(M_2)$.

3.1.8.3 The '$\Rightarrow$' direction is obvious. For the converse, suppose that $K(M) = K(M')$. By Lemma 3.1.6, K(M) is a stable set. By Proposition 3.1.8 that there must be a unique model N such that $K(N) = K(M)$. But if this N is unique, we must have $N = M = M'$.

3.1.8.4 If $M' \models K(M)$, we have, by Exercise 3.1.6.2, $K(M') = K(M)$. By Exercise 3.1.8.3 we then immediately obtain $M' = M$.

3.1.10.2 Let φ be purely propositional, and consistent. Then we know that there is a valuation s that verifies φ. Now consider $\mathbb{M}_\varphi$. This model is non-empty, since there exists a model $\mathbb{M} = \langle S, \pi \rangle$ with the aforementioned $s \in S$ and $\mathbb{M} \models \varphi$, and by definition we have $\mathbb{M} \subseteq \mathbb{M}_\varphi$. Next consider an arbitrary state t in $\mathbb{M}_\varphi$. Then, by definition of $\mathbb{M}_\varphi$ again, there must be at least one model $\mathbb{M} = \langle S, \pi \rangle$ with $t \in S$ and $\mathbb{M} \models \varphi$. This implies that $(\mathbb{M}, t) \models \varphi$. Since φ is propositional, it means that $t \models \varphi$, and this only depends on t(p) for those p occurring in φ. But obviously we then also have $(\mathbb{M}_\varphi, t) \models \varphi$. Since t was arbitrary in $\mathbb{M}_\varphi$, we have $\mathbb{M}_\varphi \models \varphi$.

3.1.10.3 In each item, φ will denote the epistemic formula of which we investigate honesty$_\mathbb{M}$. In all cases, the model $\mathbb{M}_\varphi = \langle S, \pi \rangle$ is defined as the union of all φ-models: other models for φ will be denoted by $\mathbb{M}_i = \langle S_i, \pi_i \rangle$, $i \in \mathbb{N}$. Recall that the truth definition for $K\varphi$ in $\mathbb{M}_\varphi$ reads as follows: $K\varphi$ is true in $s \in S$, iff φ is true in all $t \in S$.

(i) Not honest$_\mathbb{M}$: consider the following two 'singleton-models' $\mathbb{M}_1 = \langle \{s\}, \pi_1 \rangle$ and $\mathbb{M}_2 = \langle \{t\}, \pi_2 \rangle$. Let π_1 and π_2 be such that $\pi_1(s)(p) = \mathbf{t}$, $\pi_1(s)(q) = \mathbf{f}$, and $\pi_2(t)(p) = \mathbf{f}$, $\pi_1(s)(q) = \mathbf{t}$. Taking $\varphi = p \vee Kq$, it is easily verified that both $\mathbb{M}_1 \models \varphi$ and $\mathbb{M}_2 \models \varphi$, thus the models $\mathbb{M}_1$ and $\mathbb{M}_2$ are both contained in $\mathbb{M}_\varphi$. Now let us consider the truth of φ in $(\mathbb{M}_\varphi, s)$. The atom p is false in s, moreover; since t is a world in $\mathbb{M}_\varphi$ that falsifies q, we have $(\mathbb{M}_\varphi, s) \models \neg p \wedge \neg Kq$, i.e. $(\mathbb{M}_\varphi, s) \models \neg\varphi$, so $\mathbb{M}_\varphi \not\models \varphi$.

(ii) Honest$_\mathbb{M}$: let s be an arbitrary state in $\mathbb{M}_\varphi$. Then it occurs in a model $\mathbb{M}_1 = \langle S_1, \pi_1 \rangle$ for $p \wedge K\neg q$. We immediately see that we must have $\pi_1(s)(p) = \mathbf{t}$; $\pi_1(s)(q) = \mathbf{f}$. Thus, we also have $(\mathbb{M}_\varphi, s) \models p$. Let t be an arbitrary state in S; it was a state in a model $\mathbb{M}_2 = \langle S_2, \pi_2 \rangle$ for φ. As we did for s, we derive that $\pi_1(t)(q) = \mathbf{f}$. This proves that $(\mathbb{M}_\varphi, s) \models K\neg q$, so that we have $(\mathbb{M}_\varphi, s) \models p \wedge K\neg q$. Since s was an arbitrary state in S, we have $\mathbb{M}_\varphi \models \varphi$.

(iii) Honest$_\mathbb{M}$: consider the following singleton-model $\mathbb{M}_1 = \langle \{s\}, \pi_1 \rangle$, with $\pi_1(s)(p) = \mathbf{f}$. Since $\mathbb{M}_1 \models \neg Kp$, we have $\mathbb{M}_1 \models \varphi$, so $\mathbb{M}_1$ is a submodel of $\mathbb{M}_\varphi$. Now, let t be an arbitrary state in $\mathbb{M}_\varphi$. Not all states in S verify p (we saw that s does not), so we have $(\mathbb{M}_\varphi, t) \models \neg Kp$, so $(\mathbb{M}_\varphi, t) \models \varphi$ and thus $\mathbb{M}_\varphi \models \varphi$.

(iv) Not honest$_\mathbb{M}$: consider $\mathbb{M}_1 = \langle \{s\}, \pi_1 \rangle$ and $\mathbb{M}_2 = \langle \{t\}, \pi_2 \rangle$, π_1 and π_2 defined such that $\pi_1(s)(p) = \mathbf{t}$, and $\pi_2(t)(p) = \mathbf{f}$. Obviously, we have both $\mathbb{M}_1 \models \varphi$ and $\mathbb{M}_2 \models \varphi$. Let u be an arbitrary state in $\mathbb{M}_\varphi$. Then u cannot verify Kp (because the state $t \in S$ does not verify p) and u also does not verify $K\neg p$ (because the state $s \in S$ verifies p). Thus, $(\mathbb{M}_\varphi, u) \models \neg(Kp \wedge \neg Kp)$, and $\mathbb{M}_\varphi \not\models \varphi$.

(v) Honest$_\mathbb{M}$: as u is any state in S, it was contained in some $\mathbb{M}_1$ such that either $\pi(u)p = \mathbf{t}$ or $\pi(u)(q) = \mathbf{t}$. But then also $(\mathbb{M}_\varphi, u) \models p \vee q$, thus $\mathbb{M}_\varphi \models \varphi$.

vi) Honest$_\mathbb{M}$: no matter how $\mathbb{M}_\varphi$ was defined, as long as it is an *S5*-Kripke model, is validates propositional tautologies; hence $\mathbb{M}_\varphi \models \varphi$.

(vii) Honest$_\mathbb{M}$: let s be a state in S. This state is obtained in some S_1 from a model $\mathbb{M}_1$ for φ, in which we had $(\mathbb{M}_1, s) \models Kp \wedge Kq$. Thus, we have $(\mathbb{M}_1, s) \models p \wedge q$; so $\pi_1(s)(p) = \pi_1(s)(q) = \mathbf{t}$. Thus, any state in S verifies both p and q, thus we also have $(\mathbb{M}_\varphi, u) \models Kp \wedge Kq$ for any $u \in S$, thus $\mathbb{M}_\varphi \models \varphi$.

(viii) Honest$_\mathbb{M}$: consider the singleton-model $\mathbb{M}_1 = \langle \{s\}, \pi_1 \rangle$ with $\pi_1(s)(p) = \pi_1(s)(q) = \mathbf{t}$. Then $\mathbb{M}_1 \models p \wedge \neg K\neg q$, so $\mathbb{M}_1 \subseteq \mathbb{M}_\varphi$. Let u be an arbitrary state in $\mathbb{M}_\varphi$. It must be contained in some model $\mathbb{M}_2$, with $\mathbb{M}_2 \models p \wedge \neg K\neg q$, so $\pi_2(u)(p) = \mathbf{t}$ and thus $(\mathbb{M}_\varphi, u) \models p$. Moreover, since the state s is also contained in S, we have $(\mathbb{M}_\varphi, u) \models \neg K\neg q$. Since u was arbitrary, we have $\mathbb{M}_\varphi \models \varphi$.

(ix) Honest$_\mathbb{M}$: consider the singleton-model $\mathbb{M}_1 = \langle \{s\}, \pi_1 \rangle$ with $\pi_1(s)(q) = \mathbf{t}$. Then $\mathbb{M}_1 \models p \vee \neg K\neg q$, so $\mathbb{M}_1 \subseteq \mathbb{M}_\varphi$. Let u be an arbitrary state in $\mathbb{M}_\varphi$. Since the state s is also contained in S, we have

$(M_\varphi, u) \models \neg K \neg q$. Since u was arbitrary, we have $M_\varphi \models \varphi$.

REMARK. Note that honesty$_M$ is much easier to check than honesty$_S$, for which we had to develop a lot of technical tools to get a grip on it (cf. Exercise 3.1.4.3.1).

3.1.13.1 The '$\Leftarrow$' direction follows from the fact that for honest φ we have $\varphi \in \Sigma^\varphi$, and that stable sets are closed under **S5**-consequences (Corollary 3.1.9). For the '$\Rightarrow$' direction, we need to use the fact that ψ is honest. Suppose $\psi \in \Sigma^\varphi$, i.e. $\psi \in Prop(K(M_\varphi))$. We now show that $\varphi \models_{prop} \psi$. Suppose we have a classical valuation w with $w \models \varphi$. Let $\mathbb{M}$ be the simple S5-model with $S = \{w\}$. Then $\mathbb{M} \models \varphi$. And so for this $\mathbb{M}$ we have $\mathbb{M} \subseteq M_\varphi$ and hence, by Exercise 3.1.7.1(i), $Prop(K(M_\varphi)) \subseteq Prop(K(\mathbb{M}))$. Thus we obtain $\psi \in Prop(K(\mathbb{M}))$, and thus $\mathbb{M} \models \psi$, i.e. $w \models \psi$. Thus we have $\varphi \models_{prop} \psi$. Therefore, $\models \varphi \rightarrow \psi$.

3.1.14 Formula p is honest, because it is objective (cf. Corollary 3.1.12). $\neg Kp$ is also honest, as is seen as follows. Let $\mathbb{M} = \langle S, \pi \rangle$ be such that $S = \{s\}$ and $s(p) = f$. Then $\mathbb{M} \models \neg Kp$. So $\mathbb{M} \subseteq M_{\neg Kp}$. Let t be an arbitrary state in $M_{\neg Kp}$. Since s is a state in $M_{\neg Kp}$ as well, we have $(M_{\neg Kp}, t) \models \neg Kp$, so $M_{\neg Kp} \models \neg Kp$, which means that $K\neg p$ is honest$_M$ and hence, honest. Let us now consider the formula $\varphi = (p \wedge \neg Kp)$. We cannot have $M_\varphi \models \varphi$, since this would mean that, for all states s of M_φ, we would have both $(M_\varphi, s) \models p$ and $(M_\varphi, s) \models \neg Kp$, which is impossible.

3.1.19.1

(a) First we observe that, in all the items, the formulas at the left of $\mid\!\sim$ are indeed honest, so the relations are all defined. Recall that one way to check $\varphi \mid\!\sim \psi$ is by checking whether $M_\varphi \models \psi$; another is by checking whether $\psi \in \Sigma^\varphi$.

(i) Immediate from Exercise 3.1.13.1.

(ii) Immediate from Exercise 3.1.13.1 and $\models p \rightarrow (p \vee q)$.

(iii) From (i), we know that $p \in \Sigma^p$. Since this is a stable set, is satisfies (St 3), and thus $Kp \in \Sigma^p$.

(iv) Let s be a state such that $s(p) = t$; $s(q) = f$. The model $\mathbb{M}$ with only state s satisfies $\mathbb{M} \models Kp \wedge \neg q$. Now we observe that $\mathbb{M} \subseteq M_p$ and hence $(M_p, t) \models \neg Kq$, for any state t in M_p, so that $M_p \models \neg Kq$.

(v) We know that $p \in \Sigma^p$, a stable set. By (St 3), $Kp \in \Sigma^p$, and, since stable sets are closed under **S5**-consequences, we have $K(p \vee q) \in \Sigma^p$.

(vi) By Proposition 3.1.17, we see that $(p \wedge (p \rightarrow q)) \in \Sigma^{(p \wedge (p \rightarrow q))}$. Since stable sets are closed under **S5**-consequences, we get $q \in \Sigma^{(p \wedge (p \rightarrow q))}$ and, by (St 3), $Kq \in \Sigma^{(p \wedge (p \rightarrow q))}$.

(vii) We know that $(p \vee q) \in \Sigma^{(p \vee q)}$; by (St 3) then $K(p \vee q) \in \Sigma^{(p \vee q)}$.

(viii) Let us consider $M_{p \vee q}$. The following model $\mathbb{M}$ with two states s_1 and s_2 with $s_1(p) = s_2(q) = t$ and $s_1(q) = s_2(p) = f$ satisfies $\mathbb{M} \models p \vee q$ and hence is a submodel of $M_{p \vee q}$. Now, if t is an arbitrary state in $M_{p \vee q}$, we see that $(M_{p \vee q}, t) \models \neg Kq \wedge \neg Kp$.

(ix) We start with the observation that $p \wedge q \in \Sigma^{p \wedge q}$. By closure under **S5**-consequences we obtain p, q $\in \Sigma^{p \wedge q}$ and hence, by (St 3), Kp, $Kq \in \Sigma^{p \wedge q}$. By Exercise 3.1.1.1(i), we conclude that $(Kp \wedge Kq) \in \Sigma^{p \wedge q}$.

(x) The model $\mathbb{M}$ with only state s with $s(p) = s(q) = f$ satisfies $\mathbb{M} \models p \rightarrow q$ and hence is a submodel of $M_{p \rightarrow q}$. Hence $M_{p \rightarrow q} \models \neg Kp \wedge \neg Kq$, and, thus $\neg Kp \wedge \neg Kq \in \Sigma^{p \rightarrow q}$. We know that $p \rightarrow q \in \Sigma^{p \rightarrow q}$; by (St 3) we see $K(p \rightarrow q) \in \Sigma^{p \rightarrow q}$. We use Exercise 3.1.1.1(i) to see that $\neg Kp \wedge \neg Kq \wedge K(p \rightarrow q) \in \Sigma^{p \rightarrow q}$.

(xi) Since $K(p \rightarrow q) \in \Sigma^{K(p \rightarrow q)}$ and stable sets are closed under **S5**-consequences, we have $(Kp \rightarrow Kq)$

$\in \Sigma^{K(p \to q)}$.

(b) No. Observe that $M_{p \vee \neg p}$ is the union of *all* S5-models. This model obviously contains a state s with s(p) = f. If t is an arbitrary state in $M_{p \vee \neg p}$, we see that $(M_{p \vee \neg p}, t) \models \neg Kp$, hence $(M_{p \vee \neg p}, t) \not\models Kp \wedge \neg KKp$, hence $M_{p \vee \neg p} \not\models Kp \wedge \neg KKp$.

3.1.19.2

(i) No; we know (by Corollary 3.1.12) that the objective formula p is honest. From Examples 3.1.19(iii) we also know that it holds that $p \vdash Kp$, i.e. $Kp \in \Sigma^p$. Since stable sets are closed under S5-consequences, we obtain $(Kp \vee Kq) \in \Sigma^p$, or $p \vdash (Kp \vee Kq)$. However, from Example 3.1.4.1 we know that this $\vdash$-consequence $(Kp \vee Kq)$ of the honest formula p is itself not honest.

(ii) Let α be honest, and suppose $\alpha \vdash K\varphi \vee \psi$, i.e., $(K\varphi \vee \psi) \in \Sigma^\alpha$. By Lemma 3.1.3(i) we then have $\varphi \in \Sigma^\alpha$ or $\psi \in \Sigma^\alpha$, hence $\alpha \vdash \varphi$ or $\alpha \vdash \psi$.

3.1.22.1 This is immediate: suppose $\Gamma \vdash \varphi$. We have to show that, for all δ, $\delta \in \Sigma^{\Gamma^* \wedge \varphi} \Leftrightarrow \delta \in \Sigma^{\Gamma^*}$. But $\delta \in \Sigma^{\Gamma^* \wedge \varphi} \Leftrightarrow$ (use Corollary 3.1.18) $M_{\Gamma^* \wedge \varphi} \models \delta \Leftrightarrow$ (use Corollary 3.1.20.1) $M_{\Gamma^*} \models \delta \Leftrightarrow$ (by Corollary 3.1.18 again) $\delta \in \Sigma^{\Gamma^*}$.

3.1.23.1

(i) $p \vdash \neg Kq$; cf. the answer to Exercise 3.1.18.1(iv).

(ii) From Example 3.1.18(ix) we know that $(p \wedge q) \vdash Kp \wedge Kq$, i.e. $(Kp \wedge Kq) \in \Sigma^{(p \wedge q)}$. Now, stable sets are closed under S5-consequences, hence $Kq \in \Sigma^{(p \wedge q)}$, i.e. $(p \wedge q) \vdash Kq$.

(iii) From item (ii) we know that $Kq \in \Sigma^{(p \wedge q)}$. Since stable sets are propositionally consistent, we have $\neg Kq \notin \Sigma^{(p \wedge q)}$, i.e. it is *not* the case that $(p \wedge q) \vdash \neg Kq$.

3.1.23.2 By Exercise 3.1.23(i) we know $p \vdash \neg Kq$. We also claim that $\neg Kq \vdash \neg Kp$. To see this, first observe that $\neg Kq$ is honest: the union of all models in which $\neg Kq$ is valid (those models have at least one state in which q is false) is again a model for $\neg Kq$). Then, consider the state s with s(p) = s(q) = f. The model consisting of only this state is a submodel of $M_{\neg Kq}$; hence $M_{\neg Kq} \models \neg Kp$. Finally, observe that we do *not* have $p \vdash \neg Kp$ (this is because we *do* have $p \vdash Kp$, and stable sets are propositionally consistent).

3.2.5 Suppose $\models \varphi$; we have to show that both φ and $\neg\varphi$ are both preferentially valid. Rephrasing Proposition 3.2.4, we see that a formula ψ is preferentially valid if, for all models $\mathcal{M}$, we have $(\mathcal{M} \models \neg\psi \Rightarrow \exists \mathcal{M}', \mathcal{M} \lhd \mathcal{M}'$ and $\mathcal{M}' \models \neg\psi)$. Since we now have $\models \varphi$, the implication above is trivially true for $\psi = \varphi$. Now consider $\psi = \neg\varphi$ and take some model $\mathcal{M} \models \varphi$ (by $\models \varphi$, any model will do). By seriality of $\lhd$ we know that there is always a model $\mathcal{M}'$ with $\mathcal{M} \lhd \mathcal{M}'$. Since φ is valid, $\mathcal{M}'$ is also a model for φ: so we have found a model $\mathcal{M}'$ with both $\mathcal{M} \lhd \mathcal{M}'$ and $\mathcal{M}' \models \varphi$, so $\neg\varphi$ is preferentially valid.

3.2.7.1

$\models \varphi \Leftrightarrow$	definition of standard validity
$\neg\varphi$ is not satisfiable $\Leftrightarrow$	by Proposition 3.2.6
$\neg\varphi$ is not preferentially satisfiable $\Leftrightarrow$	Definition 3.2.3
$\models_\lhd \varphi$	

3.2.9.1.1

(i) Suppose that all preferred models of $\varphi \wedge \psi$ are also preferred models of φ. Now suppose also $\varphi \models_\lhd$

χ; for all $\mathcal{M}$: $\mathcal{M} \models_{\triangleleft} \varphi \Rightarrow \mathcal{M} \models \chi$. Now let $\mathcal{M}$ be an arbitrary preferred model of $\varphi \wedge \psi$: $\mathcal{M} \models_{\triangleleft} \varphi \wedge \psi$. By our first assumption, we have $\mathcal{M} \models_{\triangleleft} \varphi$, and the second assumption then yields $\mathcal{M} \models \chi$. This proves that $\varphi \models_{\triangleleft} \chi \Rightarrow \varphi \wedge \psi \models_{\triangleleft} \chi$, i.e. the logic is monotonic.

(ii) Let p and q be two distinct atoms. We now show that $p \models_{\triangleleft} \neg q$, while $p \wedge q \not\models_{\triangleleft} \neg q$. To show $p \models_{\triangleleft} \neg q$: assume that $w \models_{\triangleleft} p$. By the definition of $\triangleleft$ this means that w(p) = t, while w(r) = f, for all r $\neq$ p. In particular, w(q) = f, i.e. $w \models \neg q$. This proves $p \models_{\triangleleft} \neg q$. To show $p \wedge q \not\models_{\triangleleft} \neg q$: take (some) w such that $w \models_{\triangleleft} p \wedge q$. Then also $w \models p \wedge q$, and hence $w \models q$, and hence $w \not\models \neg q$. So we have found a counterexample against $p \wedge q \models_{\triangleleft} \neg q$.

(iii) We obtain an example of this phenomenon if φ is such that it does have a model, but $\triangleleft$ is such that φ has no preferred models. For example, take a preferential logic with classical propositional logic as a basis, and take the preferential structure on the classical propositional models such that $\triangleleft$ is serial (cf. Exercise 3.2.5). Let φ = p. Obviously φ has a (classical) model, so that φ is consistent. However, clearly in this case there is no preferred, i.e. maximal, model of p (by seriality we can always find a better one). So we have $\mathcal{M} \not\models_{\triangleleft} p$ for all $\mathcal{M}$. But then we also have for all $\mathcal{M}(\mathcal{M} \models_{\triangleleft} p \Rightarrow \mathcal{M} \models \chi)$, for all χ. In particular, the last assertion is true for both ψ and $\neg\psi$.

*3.2.12.1 Let $\mathcal{M}_0$ be a model that makes both p and r true, but q false. Moreover, stipulate $\mathcal{M}_0 \triangleleft \mathcal{M}'$ holds for no model $\mathcal{M}'$, whereas $\mathcal{M} \triangleleft \mathcal{M}_0$ for all models $\mathcal{M} \neq \mathcal{M}_0$. Then we have that $\mathcal{M}_0$ is the only preferred model of p: suppose that $\mathcal{M} \models_{\triangleleft} p$ for some model $\mathcal{M}$. If $\mathcal{M}$ would not be equal to $\mathcal{M}_0$, we would find a better model ($\mathcal{M}_0$) for p, contradicting the assumption $\mathcal{M} \models_{\triangleleft} p$. This implies that we also have $p \models_{\triangleleft} q \rightarrow r$. Let $\mathcal{M}_1$ be such that it is a model for p, q and $\neg r$; moreover, let $\mathcal{M}_1$ be a *best* model for $p \wedge q$: so we stipulate $\mathcal{M}_1 \models p \wedge q$ and for all $\mathcal{M}'$ with $\mathcal{M}' \models p \wedge q$, $\mathcal{M}' \triangleleft \mathcal{M}_1$. Now we have $\mathcal{M}_1 \models_{\triangleleft} p \wedge q$, but not $\mathcal{M}_1 \models r$, so $p \wedge q \not\models_{\triangleleft} r$.

3.2.16.1 $\mathcal{M}$ is a preferred model of $\varphi \Leftrightarrow$ — Definition 3.2.1
$\mathcal{M} \models \varphi$ and for no model $\mathcal{M}'$ $\mathcal{M} \triangleleft \mathcal{M}'$ and $\mathcal{M}' \models \varphi \Leftrightarrow$ — assumption about φ and ψ
$\mathcal{M} \models \psi$ and for no model $\mathcal{M}'$ $\mathcal{M} \triangleleft \mathcal{M}'$ and $\mathcal{M}' \models \varphi \Leftrightarrow$ — assumption about φ and ψ
$\mathcal{M} \models \psi$ and for no model $\mathcal{M}'$ $\mathcal{M} \triangleleft \mathcal{M}'$ and $\mathcal{M}' \models \psi \Leftrightarrow$ — Definition 3.2.1
$\mathcal{M}$ is a preferred model for ψ.

3.2.16.2 A counter-example is provided in the answer to Exercise *3.2.12.1: although we do have $\models (p \wedge q) \rightarrow p$, for the relation $\triangleleft$ in Exercise *3.2.12.1 we had $p \models_{\triangleleft} \neg q$; but also $p \wedge q \not\models_{\triangleleft} \neg q$.

3.4.3.1 We use Propositions 3.4.1 and 3.4.3 to note that

$$\Phi \models_X \varphi \Leftrightarrow \Phi \cup LX \cup \neg L\overline{X} \models_{prop} \varphi$$

We will usually drop the subscript 'prop' in $\Phi \models_{prop} \varphi$.

(i) We have to prove $\{Mp \rightarrow q\} \cup \{Lp\} \cup \neg L\overline{X} \models q$, with X = {p}. This is easy once one observes that $\neg p \notin X$ and thus $\neg L \neg p \in \neg L\overline{X}$ and uses the definition of M. We have $\{\neg L\neg p \rightarrow q\} \cup \{Lp\} \cup \{\neg L \neg p\} \models q$, and hence, by monotonicity, the desired result follows.

(ii) Notice that $\neg p \notin X$ again; so then $\{\neg L\neg p \rightarrow q\} \cup \{\neg L\neg p\} \models q$ implies, by monotonicity and the definition of M, that $\{Mp \rightarrow q\} \cup LX \cup \neg L\overline{X} \models q$.

(iii) Let M be the following $\{\neg p\}$-interpretation. Choose w such that q is false. Then $[w, \{\neg p\}] \models Mp \rightarrow q$ (since $[w, \{\neg p\}] \not\models Mp$, or, equivalently, $[w, \{\neg p\}] \models L\neg p$, which follows from $\neg p \in \{\neg p\}$), but $[w, \{\neg p\}] \models \neg q$, hence $Mp \rightarrow q \not\models_{\{\neg p\}} q$.

3.4.7.1 (i) Let X be stable and suppose $[w, X] \models_X LLp$. By the truth definition for AE-interpretations, this is equal to $Lp \in X$. Stability of X, (St 3), guarantees $p \in X$, hence $[w, X] \models_X Lp$.

(ii) Let X be stable with $Lp \in X$. By (St 3) then also $p \in X$. In order to show $Mp \rightarrow q \models_X q$, suppose $[w, X]$ is such that $[w, X] \models_X Mp \rightarrow q$, i.e., $[w, X] \models_X L\neg p \vee q$. Thus either $[w, X] \models_X L\neg p$ or $[w, X] \models_X q$. However, if $[w, X] \models_X L\neg p$ would be the case, we would have $\neg p \in X$, so that both $\neg p$ and p would be in X, which is impossible by (St 5). Hence we have $[w, X] \models_X q$.

E.3. Intermezzo

In order to tackle Exercise 3.4.14.1 it is convenient to consider the following properties of classical propositional closure, as stated in the following Lemma E.3.1 and Corollary E.3.2.

Recall that for any set of formulas X, $< X > = \{\varphi \mid X \vdash_{PC} \varphi\}$.

E.3.1. LEMMA. *Let* A *and* B *be two sets of formulas. Then* $A \subseteq B \subseteq < A > \Rightarrow < A > = < B >$.

PROOF. By monotonicity of $\vdash_{PC}$, we have $X \subseteq Y \Rightarrow < X > \subseteq < Y >$. Hence $< A > \subseteq < B >$, and also $< B > \subseteq << A >>$. Since $\vdash_{PC}$ is also idempotent ($<< X >> = < X >$), we have $< B > \subseteq < A >$. ∎

E.3.2. COROLLARY. *Let* C *and* D *be two sets of formulas. Then* $< < C > \cup D > = < C \cup D >$.

PROOF. Note that $C \cup D \subseteq < C > \cup D \subseteq < C \cup D >$ and apply Lemma E.3.1. ∎

3.4.14.1

(i) Let Φ be propositionally consistent, and assume $< \Psi_1 > = < \Psi_2 >$. Then:

Φ is an AE-extension of Ψ_1	$\Leftrightarrow$	Theorem 3.4.14(i)
$\Phi = < \Psi_1 \cup L\Phi \cup \neg L\overline{\Phi} >$	$\Leftrightarrow$	Corollary E.3.2
$\Phi = < < \Psi_1 > \cup L\Phi \cup \neg L\overline{\Phi} >$	$\Leftrightarrow$	assumption
$\Phi = < < \Psi_2 > \cup L\Phi \cup \neg L\overline{\Phi} >$	$\Leftrightarrow$	Corollary E.3.2
$\Phi = < \Psi_2 \cup L\Phi \cup \neg L\overline{\Phi} >$	$\Leftrightarrow$	Theorem 3.4.14(i)
Φ is an AE-extension of Ψ_2		

(ii) If Φ is an AE-extension of Ψ, then $\Phi = < \Psi \cup L\Phi \cup \neg L\overline{\Phi} >$. Now, let Ψ' be such that $\Psi \subseteq \Psi' \subseteq \Phi$. When we stipulate $A = \Psi \cup L\Phi \cup \neg L\overline{\Phi}$ and $B = \Psi' \cup L\Phi \cup \neg L\overline{\Phi}$, we notice that $A \subseteq B$, and also $B \subseteq <A>$. Hence, we can apply Lemma E.3.1 to conclude that $<A> = <B>$, i.e., $\Phi = < \Psi' \cup L\Phi \cup \neg L\overline{\Phi} >$, an AE-extension of Ψ'. When choosing $\Psi' = \Phi$, we see that Φ is its own AE-extension.

3.4.16.1

(i) $\Phi \supseteq < Prop(\Phi) \cup L\Phi \cup \neg L\overline{\Phi} >$ follows from stability and the fact that $Prop(\Phi) \subseteq \Phi$. The proof of $\Phi \subseteq < Prop(\Phi) \cup L\Phi \cup \neg L\overline{\Phi} >$ is obtained from the proof of Example 3.4.16, where in fact it is shown that $\Phi \subseteq < \Psi \cup L\Phi \cup \neg L\overline{\Phi} >$ for some Ψ with $<\Psi> = Prop(\Phi)$. Using Corollary E.3.2 we then also have that $\Phi \subseteq < <\Psi> \cup L\Phi \cup \neg L\overline{\Phi} > = < Prop(\Phi) \cup L\Phi \cup \neg L\overline{\Phi} >$.

(ii) Suppose $[w, \Phi] \models Prop(\Phi)$. By Lemma 3.4.2. we have that $[w, \Phi] \models L\Phi \cup \neg L\overline{\Phi}$. So together we have that $[w, \Phi] \models Prop(\Phi) \cup L\Phi \cup \neg L\overline{\Phi}$, and thus also $[w, \Phi] \models <Prop(\Phi) \cup L\Phi \cup \neg L\overline{\Phi}>$.

From 3.4.16.1(i) we know that for any stable set Φ it holds that $\Phi = \langle \text{Prop}(\Phi) \cup L\Phi \cup \neg I\overline{\Phi} \rangle$, so that we obtain $[w, \Phi] \vDash \Phi$.

3.4.17 We use again the abbreviation $\langle \Phi \rangle_0 = \langle \Phi \rangle \cap \mathcal{L}_0$.

(i) We can apply Example 3.4.16 to conclude that $\Phi = \langle \{p\} \cup L\Phi \cup \neg I\overline{\Phi} \rangle$ is an AE-extension of $\{p\}$. Since we already know that $\text{Prop}(\Phi) = \langle\{p\}\rangle_0$ and AE-extensions by their stability are uniquely determined by their objective formulas, there is only one solution Φ for $\Phi = \langle \{p\} \cup L\Phi \cup \neg I\overline{\Phi} \rangle$.

(ii) We apply Example 3.4.16 again to conclude that $\Phi = \langle \{p, q\} \cup L\Phi \cup \neg I\overline{\Phi} \rangle$ is the unique AE-extension of $\{p, q\}$.

(iii) We consider $\Psi = \{p \to Lp\}$ or, equivalently, $\Psi = \{\neg p \vee Lp\}$. Suppose that Φ is an AE-extension of Ψ. Then $\{\neg p \vee Lp\} \vDash_\Phi \Phi$. Since Φ is stable, and $(\neg p \vee Lp) \in \Phi$, we have (Lemma 3.1.3) that $p \in \Phi$ or $\neg p \in \Phi$. Suppose $p \in \Phi$. This is impossible, because the valuation w that makes p false, is a valuation such that $[w, \Phi] \vDash \neg p \vee Lp$ (since $[w, \Phi] \vDash Lp$, as $p \in \Phi$), but $[w, \Phi] \nvDash p$, so $[w, \Phi] \nvDash \Phi$. Thus $p \notin \Phi$. So we must have $\neg p \in \Phi$. We show that the stable set $\Phi_{\neg p}$ determined by $\text{Prop}(\Phi_{\neg p}) = \langle\{\neg p\}\rangle_0$ is an AE-extension of Ψ. We have to show that $\Psi \vDash_{\Phi_{\neg p}} \Phi_{\neg p}$. So suppose $[w, \Phi_{\neg p}] \vDash \Psi$. Then $[w, \Phi_{\neg p}] \vDash \neg p \vee Lp$, i.e., $[w, \Phi_{\neg p}] \vDash \neg p$ or $[w, \Phi_{\neg p}] \vDash Lp$. Since $p \notin \Phi_{\neg p}$, we know that $[w, \Phi_{\neg p}] \nvDash Lp$. Hence we have that $[w, \Phi_{\neg p}] \vDash \neg p$, i.e., $w \vDash \neg p$. So $[w, \Phi_{\neg p}] \vDash \text{Prop}(\Phi_{\neg p})$. By 3.4.16.1(ii) we immediately get $[w, \Phi_{\neg p}] \vDash \Phi_{\neg p}$. This proves that $\Phi_{\neg p}$ is an AE-extension of Ψ. Finally we note that any stable set Φ with $\text{Prop}(\Phi) \supset \text{Prop}(\Phi_{\neg p})$ (strictly bigger!) can be shown not to be an AE-extension of Ψ in a way similar to the proof above that a set containing p cannot be an AE-extension (by choosing a suitable valuation w). Since AE-extensions are stable sets, which — as we know — are determined uniquely by the objective formulas contained in them, this shows that there are no other AE-extensions of Ψ.

(iv) We consider $\Psi = \{Mp \to p\}$ or, equivalently, $\Psi = \{\neg p \to L\neg p\}$. Now we can exactly follow the lines of (iii) with $\neg p$ instead of p. This yields one unique AE-extension, namely Φ_p.

(v) We consider $\Psi = \{p \to L\neg p\}$ or, equivalently, $\Psi = \{\neg p \vee L\neg p\}$. Suppose that Φ is an AE-extension of Ψ (*). Since Φ is stable, and $(\neg p \vee L\neg p) \in \Phi$, we have (Lemma 3.1.3) that $\neg p \in \Phi$. Let w be such that it makes p true. Then $[w, \Phi] \vDash \neg p \vee L\neg p$ (since $\neg p \in \Phi$). On the other hand also $[w, \Phi] \vDash p$ (since $w \vDash p$), and so $[w, \Phi] \nvDash \neg p$ ($\in \Phi$), and hence $[w, \Phi] \nvDash \Phi$. This means $\{\neg p \vee L\neg p\} \nvDash_\Phi \Phi$, which yields a contradiction with (*), which implies that $\{\neg p \vee L\neg p\} \vDash_\Phi \Phi$. Thus there is no AE-extension of Ψ.

(vi) We consider $\Psi = \{Mp \to \neg q, Mq \to \neg p\}$ or, equivalently, $\Psi = \{q \to L\neg p, p \to L\neg q\}$ or, equivalently, $\Psi = \{\neg q \vee L\neg p, \neg p \vee L\neg q\}$. If Φ is an AE-extension of Ψ, then, from Lemma 3.1.3 we know that $\neg q$ or $\neg p$ must be in Φ. Moreover, for Φ it should hold that $\Psi \vDash_\Phi \Phi$. Suppose $\neg q$, $\neg p \in \Phi$. Let $w(q) = w(p) = t$, . Then $[w, \Phi] \vDash \Psi$ (since $[w, \Phi] \vDash L\neg p$ and $[w, \Phi] \vDash L\neg q$), but $[w, \Phi] \nvDash \Phi$ (since $w \nvDash \neg q$ and $w \nvDash \neg p$). This is a contradiction. So for Φ to be an AE-extension of Ψ, it cannot be the case that Φ contains both $\neg q$ and $\neg p$. We claim that the obvious remaining possibilities, namely the stable sets Φ_1, Φ_2 with $\text{Prop}(\Phi_1) = \langle\{\neg q\}\rangle$ and $\text{Prop}(\Phi_2) = \langle\{\neg p\}\rangle$ *are* AE-extensions of Ψ. We have to show that $\Psi \vDash_{\Phi_1} \Phi_1$. So suppose $[w, \Phi_1] \vDash \Psi$. Then $[w, \Phi_1] \vDash \neg q \vee L\neg p$, i.e., $[w, \Phi_1] \vDash \neg q$ or $[w, \Phi_1] \vDash L\neg p$. Since $\neg p \notin \Phi_1$, we know that $[w, \Phi_1] \nvDash L\neg p$. Hence we have that $[w, \Phi_1] \vDash \neg q$, i.e. $w \vDash \neg q$. So $[w, \Phi_1] \vDash \text{Prop}(\Phi_1)$. By 3.4.16.1(ii) we immediately get $[w, \Phi_1] \vDash \Phi_1$. This proves that Φ_1 is an AE-extension of Ψ. Likewise we can show that Φ_2 is an AE-extension of Ψ. Finally we note that any stable set Φ with $\text{Prop}(\Phi) \supset \text{Prop}(\Phi_1)$ or $\text{Prop}(\Phi) \supset \text{Prop}(\Phi_2)$ (strictly bigger!) can be shown not to be an AE-extension of Ψ in a way similar to the proof above that a set containing p cannot be an AE-extension (by choosing suitable valuations w). Since AE-extensions are stable sets, which are determined uniquely by the objective formulas contained in them, this shows that there are no other AE-extensions of Ψ.

E.4. Intermezzo (including answer to 4.2.0.1)

Let us first recall what the system **EDL** is; it is a one-agent **S5**-system together with the axioms AP2—AP9 that determine the behaviour of the P_i-modalities (note that the indexes here do not refer to agents, but to different frames of mind of the reasoner).

(A1) All (instances of) propositional tautologies
(A2) $(K\varphi \wedge K(\varphi \to \psi)) \to K\psi$
(A3) $K\varphi \to \varphi$
(A4) $K\varphi \to KK\varphi$
(A5) $\neg K\varphi \to K\neg K\varphi$

(R1) $$\frac{\varphi \quad \varphi \to \psi}{\psi}$$

(R2) $$\frac{\varphi}{K\varphi}$$

(AP2) $(P_i\varphi \wedge P_i(\varphi \to \psi)) \to P_i\psi$ $(i = 1, ..., n)$
(AP4) $P_i\varphi \to P_iP_i\varphi$ $(i = 1, ..., n)$
(AP5) $\neg P_i\varphi \to P_i\neg P_i\varphi$ $(i = 1, ..., n)$
(AP6) $K\varphi \to P_i\varphi$ $(i = 1, ..., n)$
(AP7) $KP_i\varphi \leftrightarrow P_i\varphi$ $(i = 1, ..., n)$
(AP8) $\neg P_i\bot \to (P_iP_j\varphi \leftrightarrow P_j\varphi)$ $(i, j = 1, ..., n)$
(AP9) $\neg P_i\bot \to (P_iK\varphi \leftrightarrow K\varphi)$ $(i = 1, ..., n)$

Before we start off, let us give an alternative presentation of **EDL**. Let the logic $\mathbf{EDL}^-$ be given by $(\mathbf{EDL} \setminus \{AP7, AP8, AP9\}) \cup \{P_i\varphi \to KP_i\varphi\}$. We claim that this is only a reduction in presentation, and not in strength:

CLAIM E.4.1. For all formulas φ, $\mathbf{EDL} \vdash \varphi$ iff $\mathbf{EDL}^- \vdash \varphi$.

PROOF. We are done if we show that $\mathbf{EDL}^- \vdash \{AP7, AP8, AP9\}$. We will give a compact derivation. Let $\vdash$ denote derivability in $\mathbf{EDL}^-$.

AP7 The '$\leftarrow$' direction is explicitly added to $\mathbf{EDL}^-$, the '$\to$'-direction follows immediately from the knowledge-axiom A3.

AP8 $\leftarrow$	1	$P_j\varphi \to KP_j\varphi$	(AP7, A1)
	2	$KP_j\varphi \to P_iP_j\varphi$	(AP6)
	3	$P_j\varphi \to P_iP_j\varphi$	(HS, 1, 2)

	4	$\neg P_i\bot \to (P_j\varphi \to P_iP_j\varphi)$	(3, A1)
AP9 ←	1	$K\varphi \to KK\varphi$	(A4)
	2	$KK\varphi \to P_iK\varphi$	(AP6)
	3	$K\varphi \to P_iK\varphi$	(HS, 1, 2)
	4	$\neg P_i\bot \to (K\varphi \to P_iK\varphi)$	(3, A1)
AP9 →	1	$(P_iK\varphi \wedge \neg K\varphi) \to (P_iK\varphi \wedge K\neg K\varphi)$	(A5, A1)
	2	$(P_iK\varphi \wedge K\neg K\varphi) \to (P_iK\varphi \wedge P_i\neg K\varphi)$	(AP6)
	3	$(P_iK\varphi \wedge P_i\neg K\varphi) \to P_i\bot$	(P_i is a modality, AP2, Exercise 1.4.1.2(i))
	4	$(P_iK\varphi \wedge \neg K\varphi) \to P_i\bot$	(HS, 1, 2, 3)
	5	$\neg P_i\bot \to (P_iK\varphi \to K\varphi)$	(A1, 4)
AP8 →	1	$P_iP_j\varphi \to P_iKP_j\varphi$	(A1, AP7, KD for P_i)
	2	$\neg P_i\bot \to (P_iKP_j\varphi \to KP_j\varphi)$	(AP9 →, which has now been proven)
	3	$\neg P_i\bot \to (P_iP_j\varphi \to KP_j\varphi)$	(A1, 1, 2)
	4	$\neg P_i\bot \to (P_iP_j\varphi \to P_j\varphi)$	(A1, 3, A3)

■Claim E.4.1

Now, in order to prove soundness and completeness of **EDL** with respect to $\mathcal{S5P}$, we can restrict ourselves to the axioms of **EDL**$^-$.

For both soundness and completeness of **EDL**$^-$ with respect to the class of $\mathcal{S5P}$ structures $\mathbb{M} = (S, \pi, S_1,..., S_n, \wp, \wp_1,..., \wp_n)$, we can benefit from a lot of work already done.

4.2.0.1(i) To start with soundness, we already know from Proposition 1.3.5 that the the axiom (A1) and the rule (R1) are sound with respect to the structures under consideration. Since both K and P_i are necessity-style operators, we also know from Proposition 1.3.5 that the axioms (A2) and (AP2) are sound, as is the rule (R2). Notice that K is the necessity operator for $\wp$, which is an equivalence relation. We already know from Theorem 1.6.4 that in such a case the axioms (A3), (A4) and (A5) are valid. As for the AP-axioms, note that each $\wp_i = S \times S_i$ is transitive and euclidean. From Exercise 1.6.7.1(vi) we know that transitivity makes (AP4) valid, and euclidicity (with transitivity) guarantees soundness of (AP5), as follows from Exercise 1.6.7.1(iv). In Exercise 2.13.5.1.1 we showed that the axiom $K_i\varphi \to B_i\varphi$ was sound on structures for which the relation for B_i is a subrelation of that for K_i, hence (AP6) is valid since we have $\wp_i \subseteq \wp$. One half of (AP7), to wit $P_i\varphi \to KP_i\varphi$ is proven to be sound in the same way as (A15) was proven sound for the system **KL** (note that we have that ($\wp st$ & $\wp_i tu$) implies $\wp_i su$, since by the fact that $\wp$ is the universal relation this is equivalent with "$\wp_i tu$ implies $\wp_i su$", and this is indeed what we have), and the other half is proven sound using reflexivity of $\wp$. Thus we have

LEMMA E.4.2 (Soundness). **EDL**$^- \vdash \varphi \Rightarrow \mathcal{S5P} \models \varphi$.

4.2.0.1(ii) For completeness, let us consider the canonical model $\mathbb{M}^c = \langle S^c, \pi^c, \wp^c, \wp_1{}^c,...,$

$\wp_n^c\rangle$ for **EDL**$^-$ in which, as a first instance, we omit the subclasses S_i ($i \leq n$). Again, we can use a lot of preliminary work (recall that we have $R^c_\Box\ s_\Sigma s_\Delta \Leftrightarrow (\Box\varphi \in \Sigma \Rightarrow \varphi \in \Delta)$): from Proposition 1.6.5 we know that $\wp^c$ is reflexive, transitive and Euclidean, and hence, by Proposition 1.6.2, an equivalence relation. We also know from Proposition 1.6.5 that each $\wp_i$ is transitive and Euclidean. The presence of AP6 and Exercise 2.13.5.1.1 guarantee that $\wp_i^c \subseteq \wp^c$. ■Lemma E.4.2

OBSERVATION E.4.3. $\forall i \leq n, \forall s_\Sigma, s_\Delta, s_\Omega \in S^c$: $((\wp^c s_\Sigma s_\Delta\ \&\ \wp_i^c s_\Delta s_\Omega) \Rightarrow \wp_i^c s_\Sigma s_\Omega)$.

PROOF. Suppose $\wp^c s_\Sigma s_\Delta\ \&\ \wp_i^c s_\Delta s_\Omega$. In order to show that $\wp_i^c s_\Sigma s_\Omega$, suppose that $P_i\varphi \in s_\Sigma$. Since maximal consistent sets are closed under consequences (cf. Lemma 1.4.3), we may use AP7 to conclude that also $KP_i\varphi \in \Sigma$. Since $\wp^c s_\Sigma s_\Delta$, we know that $P_i\varphi \in \Delta$ and, since $\wp_i^c s_\Delta s_\Omega$, we obtain $\varphi \in \Omega$. ■Observation E.4.3

Now, let φ be an **EDL**$^-$-consistent formula. It is contained in some maximal consistent set Φ, and we have $(\mathbb{M}^c, s_\Phi) \models \varphi$. Let us define the generated submodel $\mathbb{M} = \langle S, \pi, \wp, \wp_1, \ldots, \wp_n\rangle$ of $(\mathbb{M}^c, s_\Phi)$ as follows:

$$S = \{t \in S^c \mid (s_\Phi, t) \in \wp^c\}$$

and the other relations $\wp, \wp_1, \ldots, \wp_n$ and the truth assignment π are defined as the restrictions of $\wp^c, \wp_1^c, \ldots, \wp_n^c$ and π^c respectively, to this set S.

LEMMA E.4.4. *Now, we have that, for all formulas* ψ, *and all states* $t \in S$,

$$(\mathbb{M}^c, t) \models \psi \textit{ iff } (\mathbb{M}, t) \models \psi.$$

PROOF. With induction on ψ. If ψ is p, it follows immediately from the definition of π. Conjunction and negation are straightforward. Let us consider $\psi = K\alpha$, with the statement already proven for α. Notice that, since $\wp^c$ is an equivalence relation, we have for all u and v in S that $\wp uv$ in $\mathbb{M}$ and $\wp^c uv$ in $\mathbb{M}^c$.
$(\mathbb{M}^c, t) \models K\alpha \Leftrightarrow$ for all u in $\mathbb{M}^c$, if $(t,u) \in \wp^c$ then $(\mathbb{M}^c, u) \models \alpha \Leftrightarrow$ for all u in S, $(\mathbb{M}^c, u) \models \alpha \Leftrightarrow$ for all u in S, $(\mathbb{M}, u) \models \alpha$.
Finally, let us consider $\psi = P_i\alpha$. Note that for all u and v in S we have $\wp_i uv$ in $\mathbb{M}$ iff $\wp_i^c uv$ in $\mathbb{M}^c$. Now, $(\mathbb{M}^c, t) \models P_i\alpha \Leftrightarrow$ for all u in $\mathbb{M}^c$, if $(t, u) \in \wp_i^c$ then $(\mathbb{M}^c, u) \models \alpha \Leftrightarrow$ for all u in $\mathbb{M}$, if $(t, u) \in \wp_i$ then $(\mathbb{M}, u) \models \alpha \Leftrightarrow (\mathbb{M}, t) \models P_i\alpha$.
■Lemma E.4.4

As a corollary, we obtain that for the generated submodel $\mathbb{M}$ we have $(\mathbb{M}, s_\Phi) \models \varphi$. Note that in this model we have $\wp = S \times S$. We transform $\mathbb{M}$ into a model $\mathbb{M}' = \langle S, \pi, S_1, \ldots, S_n, \wp, \wp_1, \ldots, \wp_n\rangle$ by simply stipulating $S_i = \{t \mid \exists s \in S: (s, t) \in \wp_i\}$. Using Observation E.4.3, we see that for all x and y in S, $(x, y) \in \wp_i \Leftrightarrow y \in S_i$. Thus, the truth definition of P_i may be stated both as

$$(\mathbb{M}, s) \models P_i\varphi \Leftrightarrow \text{for all } y\ (\wp_i xy \Rightarrow (\mathbb{M}, y) \models \varphi), \text{ as well as}$$

$$(\mathbb{M}, s) \models P_i\varphi \Leftrightarrow \text{for all } y \in S_i, (\mathbb{M}, y) \models \varphi.$$

Thus, we see that $\mathbb{M}$, with its truth definition is an $\mathcal{S5P}$-model. By taking $s = s_\Phi$, with Φ a maximal consistent set containing the **EDL**$^-$-consistent formula φ, using the lemma we see that $(\mathbb{M}, s) \models \varphi$. Eventually, we derive

THEOREM E.4.5. *For all* φ: **EDL** $\vdash \varphi \Leftrightarrow \mathcal{S5P} \models \varphi$.

PROOF. The '$\Rightarrow$' direction follows from the equivalence between **EDL**$^-$ and **EDL** (Claim E.4.1) and soundness of **EDL**$^-$ (Lemma E.4.2). For '$\Leftarrow$' (completeness), let φ be consistent in **EDL**, or, equivalently, in **EDL**$^-$. We find a maximal consistent set Φ such that in the canonical model $\mathbb{M}^c = \langle S^c, \pi^c, \wp^c, \wp_1{}^c, \ldots, \wp_n{}^c\rangle$ we have $(\mathbb{M}^c, s_\Phi) \models \varphi$. The model $\mathbb{M}$ that we obtained from $\mathbb{M}^c$ by looking at the $\wp^c$-generated model from $(\mathbb{M}^c, s_\Phi)$ also satisfies $(\mathbb{M}, s_\Phi) \models \varphi$, and if we define $\mathbb{M}'$ derived from $\mathbb{M}$ by stipulating $S_i = \{t \mid \exists s \in S: (s, t) \in \wp_i\}$, we find an $\mathcal{S5P}$-model that satisfies φ in world s_Φ. Summarising, we see that any **EDL**-consistent formula φ is satisfied in some state in an $\mathcal{S5P}$-model, which is sufficient to prove completeness. ■

4.2.4.1 We are given the following premises:

(1)	$s \wedge h$	*(It is Sunday and a holiday.)*
(2)	$s \wedge M(f \wedge \neg l) \rightarrow P_1 f$	*(Normally on Sundays I go fishing unless I wake up late.)*
(3)	$h \wedge Ml \rightarrow P_2 l$	*(Normally on holidays I wake up late.)*
(4)	$M(f \wedge \neg l) \wedge Ml$	*(Possibly I go fishing and I am not late, and possibly I am late.)*

From (1)—(4) we want to derive the conclusion $P_1(s \wedge h \wedge f) \wedge P_2(s \wedge h \wedge l)$ in S5P. Recall that the necessitation rule (R2) may be applied to the premises in $\Phi = \{1, 2, 3, 4\}$. PL refers to (derivations in) propositional logic.

(5)	$K(s \wedge h)$	(R2, (1))
(6)	$P_1 f$	(PL, (1), (4), (2))
(7)	$P_1(s \wedge h)$	((5), PL, AP6)
(8)	$P_1(s \wedge h \wedge f)$	((6), (7), Cf. Exercise 1.4.1.1)
(9)	$P_2 l$	(PL, (1), (4), (3))
(10)	$P_2(s \wedge h)$	((5), PL, A6)
(11)	$P_2(s \wedge h \wedge l)$	((9), (10), Cf. Exercise 1.4.1.1)
(12)	$P_1(s \wedge h \wedge f) \wedge P_2(s \wedge h \wedge l)$	(PL, (8), (11))

4.2.7.1 Let r stand for being a republican, p for being a pacifist, q for being a quaker, f for being a football fan and a for anti-military. Then the scenario is formalised as follows:

(1) $r \wedge M(\neg p \wedge f) \rightarrow P_1(\neg p \wedge f)$

(2) $q \wedge Mp \rightarrow P_2 p$

(3) $p \wedge Ma \rightarrow P_3 a$

(4) $f \wedge M\neg a \rightarrow P_4 \neg a$

(5) $r \wedge q$

Now the question is whether Nixon is (presumably) anti-military. First note that the default (1) can be applied for Nixon, if we assume that it is consistent that Nixon is a non-pacifistic football fan, and that default (2) can be applied if it is assumed to be consistent that he is pacifist. To apply default (3), we also assume that it is consistent for Nixon to be anti-military; to apply default (4) we assume consistency of Nixon being non-anti-military as well. Since all these assumptions are about ignorance, (assuming that it is consistent that x here means Mx or, $\neg K \neg x$; not_x is not known) let us call these assumptions *ignorance assumptions*. Summarising, we have:

(ig_ass1) $M(\neg p \wedge f)$
(ig_ass2) Mp
(ig_ass3) Ma
(ig_ass4) $M\neg a$

Under these assumptions (in particular, ig_ass1), we conclude from (1) and (5) that, in frame 1, Nixon is a non-pacifistic football fan:

(6) $P_1(\neg p \wedge f)$.

In the same manner (now using ig_ass2), from (2) and (5) we obtain a frame 2 in which he is a pacifist:

(7) P_2p.

Reasoning within frame 2, we have that default (3) holds (expressed in (8)), that Nixon is a pacifist (see (7)) and that it is consistent for Nixon to be anti-military (we assume that our assumptions about consistency are inherited by the frames. Formally, this is justified by the theorem $M\varphi \rightarrow P_iM\varphi$, which, in its turn follows from the theorems $M\varphi \rightarrow KM\varphi$ (negative introspection) and $KM\varphi \rightarrow P_iM\varphi$ (axiom AP6)). The latter is expressed in (9).

(8) $P_2(p \wedge Ma \rightarrow P_3a)$
(9) P_2Ma

Obviously, within frame 2 reason with (7), (8) and (9) to obtain that P_3a is true in that frame (10) (Technically speaking, all the P_i's are ordinary modalities, for which we have P_i-distribution $(P_i(\varphi \rightarrow \psi) \rightarrow (P_i\varphi \rightarrow P_i\psi))$ and distribution over conjunction $(P_i(\varphi \wedge \psi) \leftrightarrow (P_i\varphi \wedge P_i\psi)$; Cf. Exercise 1.4.1.2.):

(10) P_2P_3a.

Similarly, reasoning with frame 1, we immediately obtain from (6):

(11) P_1f.

Moreover, in frame 1 the default (4) holds, together with ig_ass4:

(12) $P_1(f \wedge M\neg a \rightarrow P_4\neg a)$,

(13) $P_1M\neg a$.

Reasoning within frame 1, we get, combining (11), (12) and (13):

(14) $P_1P_4\neg a$.

Sentence (10) expresses that, in frame 2, it is true that in frame 3 Nixon is anti-military. Also, (14) says that, in frame 1, it is true that in frame 4 Nixon is non anti-military. Let us finally assume that the frames 1 and 2 are consistent; i.e. we have no contradictions in one of them. This is a kind of minimality assumption on the frames; since it does not follow that frame i is inconsistent, let us assume it is not. These assumptions are called *frame assumptions*: (Note: this terminology is *ad hoc*, and has nothing to do with either modal frames or the frame problem as discussed in Section 4.3.)

(f_ass1) $\neg P_1\bot$
(f_ass2) $\neg P_2\bot$

Now we reason as follows from (10) and f_ass2; if in frame 2 it is true that in frame 3 sentence a is true, and frame 2 makes sense, then a must be true in frame 3. (And similarly with (14) and f_ass1.) Formally, we use axiom (AP8) to derive (15) from (10) and f_ass2 and to derive (16) from (14) and f_ass1:

(15) P_3a,
(16) $P_4\neg a$.

Altogether, we have obtained two frames of reasoning: in one (frame 3) Nixon is anti-military, in the other (frame 4) he is not.

E.5. Intermezzo

In the answers to the exercises of section 4.2, we will use the following conventions (partly already motivated and used in the answer to Exercise 4.2.7.1);

P_i-nec — We already mentioned that K-necessitation may be applied to the premises of a default-theory (see our remark immediately following Exercise 4.2.0.1). Using axiom (AP6), we see that we may also apply P_i-necessitation to those premises. These premises may include default rules! So, from the default $\varphi \wedge M\psi \rightarrow P_k\chi$ we infer $P_i(\varphi \wedge M\psi \rightarrow P_k\chi)$.

P_i-mod — We observe that the P_i's are just K45-modalities, and we can apply properties that we have established for such modalities already. For instance, we will freely use P_i-distribution ($P_i(\varphi \rightarrow \psi) \rightarrow (P_i\varphi \rightarrow P_i\psi)$) and distribution over conjunction ($P_i(\varphi \wedge \psi) \leftrightarrow (P_i\varphi \wedge P_i\psi)$; cf. Exercise 1.4.1.2).

ig_ass(φ) — Assumptions of the form $M\varphi$. This is a special feature of **EDL**. An assumption of the form $M\varphi$ is justified, if $K\neg\varphi$

cannot be derived. In such a case, we will usually make this assumption. Note that such an assumption concerns the ignorance of the reasoner regarding a specific formula φ. If we add such an assumption, it means that the premises that are given are interpreted as 'all that is known'. (In fact, in Section 4.4 it is explained how these ignorance assumptions can be *inferred non-monotonically* from the premises; at this stage we just *assume* them to hold.)

f_ass(j) This is the assumption $\neg P_j\bot$. It says that the frame P_j is not empty, or, alternatively, one can consistently reason in the frame P_j. Such an assumption will often justify an application of the axiom (AP8) or (AP9), when applying a default within a frame. It allows us to conclude $P_j\varphi$ (instead of $\neg P_j\bot \rightarrow P_j\varphi$) when we have inferred $P_iP_j\varphi$.

4.2.8.1 Key: e = 'is_an_elephant'
g = 'is_grey'
r = 'is_royal_elephant'

We are given the following premises:

(1)	$r \rightarrow e$	*Royal elephants are elephants.*
(2)	$e \wedge Mg \rightarrow P_1g$	*Elephants tend to be grey.*
(3)	$r \wedge M\neg g \rightarrow P_2\neg g$	*Royal elephants tend to be non-grey.*
(4)	r	*Clyde is a royal elephant.*

Now, Clyde is non-grey in frame 2. That is, under the assumption that it is consistent for Clyde to assume that he is non-grey (an assumption of the format ig_ass($\neg$g)) we can apply default (3), and derive $P_2\neg g$. However, this is is not the whole story. We might, of course, equally well assume that Clyde is possibly grey, so that we can also use (1) and apply (2) to obtain that Clyde is grey in frame 1. However, this is not in accord with our intuitions about the situation: the default (3) regards more specific information about royal elephants and should be expected to overrule default (2) on elephants in general. So, if we want this, our representation above is not yet sufficient. To block a possible application of default (2), we might bluntly add a rule like:

(5) $r \rightarrow \neg g$ *Royal elephants are non-grey, for sure.*

Although this obviously does the job (since from r we obtain Kr by necessitation, and similarly $K(r \rightarrow \neg g)$ from (5), and hence $K\neg g$, i.e. $\neg Mg$, blocking application of (2)), this is not really a satisfactory solution. In fact, adding (5) makes the more subtly formulated default (3) superfluous. A more reasonable solution is weakening (2) to a modified default (with built-in priority):

(2') $e \wedge \neg P_2\neg g \rightarrow P_1g$

This default states somewhat more carefully that elephants that are not certainly non-grey *within frame 2* (rather than within the set of *all* possible worlds) are presumably grey (with respect to frame 1). Now in the situation above it works as desired: application of (3) yields $P_2\neg g$, which blocks application of (2'), so that we do *not* obtain P_1g as a conclusion.

4.2.8.2 Key: g = 'is_native_speaker_of_German'
a = 'is_born_in_America'
d = 'is_native_speaker_of_Pennsylvania_Dutch'
p = 'is_born_in_Pennsylvania'

We are given the following premises:

(1)	$g \wedge M\neg a \rightarrow P_1\neg a$	*Native speakers of German tend not to be born in America.*
(2)	$d \rightarrow g$	*All native speakers of Pennsylvania Dutch are native speakers of German.*
(3)	$d \wedge Mp \rightarrow P_2p$	*Native speakers of Pennsylvania Dutch tend to be born in Pennsylvania.*
(4)	d	*Hermann is a native speaker of Pennsylvania Dutch.*

Firstly, note the scope of the negation in the first default: we read it as 'Native speakers of German tend to be born not in America', rather than 'it is not the case that native speakers of German tend to be born in America'. Secondly, logically speaking, one cannot derive that Hermann is presumably born in America, since the theory on itself does not relate being born in Pennsylvania to being born in America. However, if one would add the intuitively correct premise (5),

(5)	$p \rightarrow a$	*Everyone who is born in Pennsylvania is born in America.*

we can indeed derive that, in some frame of reasoning, it is the case that Hermann is born in America. To see this, we only have to make the assumption ig_ass(p) (it is consistent to assume Hermann is born in Pennsylvania) and apply default (3) to conclude P_2p. From (5) we derive P_2a (cf. our remarks on P_i-Nec and P_i-mod in the intermezzo). Note that, if we also make the ignorance assumption ig_ass(¬a) we would also derive $P_1\neg a$, so that we have two contradictory frames of reasoning. Note that, using the criterion of specificity (d is more specific than g, so that (3) should get precendence over (1)), one might prefer the frame 2, and hence prefer the conclusion a over ¬a. We might then use a method like in Exercise 4.2.8.1 to deal with this form of specificity.

4.2.8.3 Key: b = 'wakes_up_before_noon'
a = 'wakes_up_after_noon'

We are given the following premises:

(1)	$Mb \rightarrow P_1b$	*People usually wake up before noon.*
(2)	$Ma \rightarrow P_2a$	*Tom usually wakes after noon.*

As represented, the theory immediately allows for the conclusion P_1a, provided that we make the ignorance assumption ig_ass(a). Note that the premises in no way relate a and b, for instance it is pertfectly consistent to assume that $(a \wedge b)$ holds. To do justice to the intuition, let us add the premise

(3) $a \leftrightarrow \neg b$ *Waking up after noon is not waking up before noon.*

Then we have, making the additional ignorance assumption ig_ass(b) two conclusions: $P_1 b$ and $P_2 a$, or, equivalently, $P_1 b$ and $P_2 \neg b$ (use P_i-nec and P_i-mod from the intermezzo). This does still no justice to the intuition that default (1) seems to be less relevant than default (2), and that the latter should take precedence. There is, however, also a way to represent the defaults in such a way, that specificity is recognised:

Key: b = 'wakes_up_before_noon'
a = 'wakes_up_after_noon'
h = 'is_a_human_being'
t = 'is_Tom'

We are given the following premises:

(1') $h \wedge Mb \rightarrow P_1 b$ *People usually wake up before noon.*
(2') $t \wedge Ma \rightarrow P_2 a$ *Tom usually wakes after noon.*

As before, we obtain, assuming ig_ass(b) and ig_ass(a) the conclusions $P_1 b$ and $P_2 a$, and, when adding premise (3), we find $P_1 b$ and $P_2 \neg b$. If we now add the hidden presumption that Tom is a human:

(4') $t \rightarrow h$ *Tom is a human.*

we may use specificity as an argument to prefer the conclusion a over b (or prefer the frame 2 over 1), as in Example 4.2.8 and the previous exercises.

4.2.8.4 Key: a = 'is_adult'
e = 'is_employed'
s = 'is_a_student'
y = 'is_younger_than_22'

(i) We are given the following premises:

(1) $a \wedge Me \rightarrow P_1 e$ *Adults tend to be employed.*
(2) $s \wedge M\neg e \rightarrow P_2 \neg e$ *University students tend to be unemployed.*
(3) $s \wedge Ma \rightarrow P_3 a$ *University students tend to be adults.*
(4) $s \wedge a$ *Fred is a university student and an adult.*

Indeed, we can derive that Fred is presumably unemployed, if we make the proper assumption ig_ass(¬e). From ig_ass(¬e) (saying M¬e), default (2) and premise (4) we then derive $P_2 \neg e$. Note that we also derive $P_1 e$ (assume ig_ass(e), use (1) and (4)). Specificity does not play a role here: both s and a are immediate consequences of (4). Note that also default (3) does not play a role in this case, since by (4) we know directly that Fred is an adult (a). In some sense, both pieces of information, Fred's being a student and his being an adult, are on an equal footing, so that both e and ¬e can be believed (in distinct frames). The situation would change if we replaced (4) by the weaker (4')

(4') s *Fred is a university student.*

In this case, assuming ig_ass($\neg$e), we can still derive $P_2\neg e$, using (2). Moreover, if we assume ig_ass(a), we would also be able to derive the defeasible conclusion that Fred is presumably an adult (P_3a). We can now use this information to derive that P_3P_1e, in a way similar to Exercise 4.2.7.1, and thus P_1e again, if we would assume f_ass(1) as well. However, in this case it is questionable whether this is the right outcome. We might tend to consider (2) a more specific default than (1), in view of the (albeit defeasible) relation (3) between s and a. Specificity then would make us prefer conclusion $\neg e$ over e (or, alternatively, frame 2 over frame 1). We might implement this in **EDL** by modifying (1) into

(1') $a \wedge \neg P_2\neg e \rightarrow P_1e$.

As desired in case (1'), (2), (3), (4'), we now can use (2) and (4') to get $P_2\neg e$, blocking inference of $(P_3)P_1e$ by means of (1'), using P_3a.

(ii) We are given the following premisses:

(1)	$a \wedge Me \rightarrow P_1e$	*Adults tend to be employed.*
(2)	$s \wedge M\neg e \rightarrow P_2\neg e$	*University students tend to be unemployed.*
(3)	$s \wedge Ma \rightarrow P_3a$	*University students tend to be adults.*
(4)	$a \wedge y \wedge Ms \rightarrow P_4s$	*Adults under 22 tend to be university students.*
(5)	$a \wedge y$	*Tom is an adult under 22.*

We can derive that Tom is presumably unemployed. First, we make the assumption ig_ass(s). Together with (4) and (5) this yields P_4s. Let us now also state ig_ass($\neg$e):

(6) $M\neg e$ *We may consistently assume that Tom is not employed.*

Applying P_4-nec to (6) and (2), we then derive $P_4M\neg e$, and $P_4(s \wedge M\neg e \rightarrow P_2\neg e)$, respectively. Since we already had derived P_4s, we use P_4-mod to conclude $P_4P_2\neg e$. If we assume that it is consistent to reason within frame 2, i.e. if we assume f_ass(4)

(7) $\neg P_4\bot$ *Reasoning within frame 4 is consistent.*

we then use axiom (AP8) to conclude $P_2\neg e$.

Note that, alternatively, one can derive P_1e (assuming ig_ass(e), but no frame assumption of type f_ass(j) is needed here). Note that we do not exactly have an example of specificity of (2) over (1) here: the conclusion s from $a \wedge y$ is not a strict one, but derived by default (4). This complicates the intuition about what should be the result here. In fact, in our opinion this kind of situations becomes so complicated that one loses the intuition of what the 'right' outcome should be. We refer to [Tou86] for an admirable attempt to systematise these cases. Here we leave the matter by noting that, by using the machinery of Example 4.2.8 in a nested way, one has great flexibility as to steering for the desired outcome whatever this may be.

4.2.8.5 Key: d = 'is_a_dancer'
b = 'is_a_ballerina'
g = 'is_graceful'

We are given the following premises:

(1)	$d \wedge M\neg b \rightarrow P_1\neg b$	*Dancers tend not to be ballerinas.*
(2)	$d \wedge Mg \rightarrow P_2g$	*Dancers tend to be graceful.*
(3)	$d \wedge g \wedge Mb \rightarrow P_3b$	*Graceful dancers tend to be ballerinas.*
(4)	d	*Noemi is a dancer.*

We can derive that Noemi is presumably a ballerina, if we add that it is consistent to assume that she is graceful and a ballerina: ig_ass(g) and ig_ass(b). To see this, note that from (4), default (2) and ig_ass(g), we derive P_2g. Applying P_2-nec and P_2-mod to this conclusion, (4) and ig_ass(b), gives $P_2(d \wedge g \wedge Mb)$. P_i-nec and (3) give $P_2(d \wedge g \wedge Mb \rightarrow P_3b)$, so that we get P_2P_3b. If we now make the frame assumption f_ass(2) we conclude P_3b. However, note that we also can conclude that $P_1\neg b$ holds (assume ig_ass($\neg$b), and use (1) and (4)). This shows that also this example is a difficult case: on the one hand, only knowing that Noemi is a dancer tends us to believe that she is not a ballerina (by default (1)). On the other hand, default (2) tends us to believe that Noemi is graceful, which then by (3) tends us to believe that she *is* a ballerina. This dilemma is nicely represented in our formal result, which is ambiguous. Again, if one would like to have that the line of reasoning which tends us to believe that Noemi is a ballerina is 'weaker' than that leading to the conclusion she is not (since the former uses an iterated chain of defaults, for instance), we might apply the techniques of Example 4.2.8 to implement this. For example, one might change (3) into

(3') $d \wedge g \wedge \neg P_1\neg b \rightarrow P_3b$,

the applicability of which is restricted to cases where default (1) has not been applied. But matters are even more complicated in this strange example. One might also view (3) as more specific than (1), since (3) concerns the more specific case of being a graceful dancer compared with a dancer in general in (1). This would be an argument for preferring the outcome that Noemi *is* a ballerina. Intuitions are not clear here, but if we would like to have this we should leave (3) unchanged and modify (1) into:

(1') $d \wedge \neg P_3b \rightarrow P_1\neg b$.

4.3.1.1.1 The soundness and completeness of the knowledge and preference-part of **DEDL** with respect to $\mathcal{S5P}^+$-structures has already been established in the answer to Exercise 4.2.0.1. Here, we will be concerned with the dynamic part.

As for soundness, we have to show that $\mathcal{S5P}^+$-structures satisfy the rule NEC(α) and the axioms (K) and (TD). For NEC(α) and (K), this is established in the same way as for the operator K: see Proposition 1.3.5, items (iv) and (ii), respectively. So, let us consider (TD). Let $\mathbb{M} \in \mathcal{S5P}^+$, we have to show that for each world s in $\mathbb{M}$, $(\mathbb{M}, s) \models [\alpha]\varphi \leftrightarrow \neg[\alpha]\neg\varphi$.

$(\mathbb{M}, s) \models [\alpha]\varphi$ means that for all t with $R_\alpha(s, t)$, we have $(\mathbb{M}, t) \models \varphi$. By our assumption on R_α being total, we know that there indeed is such a t (that satisfies φ). Hence not all R_α-successors of s satisfy $\neg\varphi$: $(\mathbb{M}, s) \models \neg[\alpha]\neg\varphi$. Conversely, suppose $(\mathbb{M}, s) \models \neg[\alpha]\neg\varphi$. It expresses that not all R_α-successors of s satisfy $\neg\varphi$, so there must be one, say t, for which $(\mathbb{M}, t) \models \varphi$. Now, we note that our assumption of R_α being deterministic implies that φ must be true in *all* of s' R_α-successors, i.e., $(\mathbb{M}, s) \models [\alpha]\varphi$.

For completeness, we have to look at the canonical model for **DEDL**. We will show that each $R_\alpha{}^c$ in this model satisfies $\forall s_\Theta \in S^c\ \exists_1 s_\Psi \in S^c\ [R_\alpha{}^c(s_\Theta, s_\Psi)]$. Let $s_\Theta \in S^c$, i.e. Θ is a **DEDL**-maximal consistent (m.c.) set. By Nec(α) we find that $[\alpha]\neg\bot \in \Theta$. Let $\Gamma = \{\gamma \mid [\alpha]\gamma \in \Theta\}$. Then Γ is **DEDL**-consistent. For, if it were not, we would find $\gamma_1, \ldots, \gamma_k \in \Gamma$ with $\vdash_{\mathbf{DEDL}} (\gamma_1 \wedge \ldots \wedge \gamma_k) \rightarrow \bot$. We can do some standard reasoning about the modality $[\alpha]$ to find that $\vdash_{\mathbf{DEDL}} ([\alpha]\gamma_1 \wedge \ldots \wedge [\alpha]\gamma_k) \rightarrow [\alpha]\bot$. Since $[\alpha]\gamma_1, \ldots, [\alpha]\gamma_k \in \Theta$, we also have (cf. Lemma 1.4.3) that $[\alpha]\bot \in \Theta$. By axiom (TD) we then find $\neg[\alpha]\neg\bot \in \Theta$, which is in contradiction to $[\alpha]\neg\bot \in \Theta$ and Θ is a (maximal) consistent set. This proves that Γ is consistent. Hence (Lemma 1.4.3(i)) there is a m.c. set $\Psi \supseteq \Gamma$. In $\mathbb{M}^c$, we have for s_Θ and s_Ψ that $R_\alpha{}^c(s_\Theta, s_\Psi)$ (cf. the definition of canonical models in Section 1.4). So we now have that for every $s_\Theta \in S^c$ there is an $s_\Psi \in S^c$ $[R_\alpha{}^c(s_\Theta, s_\Psi)]$.

To show that the canonical model is 'deterministic' for each $R_\alpha{}^c$, i.e. that for every $s_\Theta \in S^c$ there is *at most one* $s_\Psi \in S^c$ with $R_\alpha{}^c(s_\Theta, s_\Psi)$, we first state the following:

$$R_\alpha{}^c s_\Theta s_\Psi \Leftrightarrow (\text{for all } \psi, \psi \in \Psi \Rightarrow \langle\alpha\rangle\psi \in \Theta) \qquad (*)$$

To see (*), note that the definition of the canonical relation $R_\alpha{}^c$ is $\{(s_\Theta, s_\Psi) \mid \Theta/[\alpha] \subseteq \Psi\}$. Thus, we have

$$R_\alpha{}^c s_\Theta s_\Psi \Leftrightarrow (\text{for all } \omega, [\alpha]\omega \in \Theta \Rightarrow \omega \in \Psi). \qquad (**)$$

Using contraposition, (**) is equivalent to (for all ω, $\omega \notin \Psi \Rightarrow [\alpha]\omega \notin \Theta$), and this is, using Lemma 1.4.3, equivalent to (for all $\neg\omega$, $\neg\omega \in \Psi \Rightarrow \neg[\alpha]\omega \in \Theta$). Using the definition of $\langle\alpha\rangle$ and substituting ψ for $\neg\omega$, we see that the latter condition is equivalent to (*). Now, suppose we have m.c. sets s_Ψ and s_Σ for which both $R_\alpha{}^c s_\Theta s_\Psi$ and $R_\alpha{}^c s_\Theta s_\Sigma$. If $\Psi \neq \Sigma$, there must be a formula $\psi \in \Psi$, $\psi \notin \Sigma$. For this ψ, we have $\psi \in \Psi$ and $\neg\psi \in \Sigma$. Using (*), we see that $\langle\alpha\rangle\psi \in \Theta$, $\langle\alpha\rangle\neg\psi \in \Theta$. Using axiom (TD) and Lemma 1.4.3 we see that $[\alpha]\neg\psi$, $[\alpha]\psi \in \Theta$. Using (**), we obtain both $\neg\psi, \psi \in \Psi$, contradicting the fact that Ψ is a consistent set. This means that our assumption $\Psi \neq \Sigma$ cannot be true, i.e., s_Θ can have at most one $R_\alpha{}^c$-successor.

4.3.3.2 Key: a = 'the_turkey_is_alive'
h = 'the_turkey_is_hiding'
d = 'the_turkey_is_deaf'
l = 'the_gun_is_loaded'

We use the representation (H1) – (H6) again, and sketch the result (in particular we omit all the assumptions of the kind ig_ass(φ) and f_ass(j) that are needed):

$a \wedge \neg h \wedge \neg l \Rightarrow K(a \wedge \neg h \wedge \neg l) \Rightarrow Ka \wedge K\neg h \wedge K\neg l \Rightarrow a \wedge K\neg h \wedge \neg l \Rightarrow_{(H6)}$
$(a \wedge K\neg h \wedge \neg l \wedge Kd) \vee (a \wedge K\neg h \wedge \neg l \wedge K\neg d) \Rightarrow$

(P[load](a ∧ d∧ K¬h) ∧ K[load] Kl) ∨ (P[load](a ∧ ¬d) ∧ K[load](l ∧ h)) ⇒
(P[load](a ∧ d∧ K¬h) ∧ P[load] Kl) ∨ (P[load](a ∧ ¬d) ∧ P[load](l ∧ h)) ⇒
(P[load](a ∧ d∧ K¬h ∧ Kl) ∨ (P[load](a ∧ ¬d ∧ l ∧ h)) ⇒
(P[load](a ∧ d∧ K(¬h ∧ l)) ∨ (P[load](a ∧ ¬d ∧ l ∧ h)) ⇒
... ⇒
(P[load] P[wait] (a ∧ d∧ K(l ∧ ¬h))) ∨ (P[load] P[wait] (a ∧ ¬d ∧ l ∧ h)) ⇒
... ⇒
(P[load] P[wait] P[fire] (¬a ∧ d∧ ¬h ∧ ¬l)) ∨ (P[load] P[wait] P [fire] (a ∧ ¬d ∧ ¬l ∧ h)).

So we end up with two preferred clusters: one in which after loading it is preferred that after loading it is preferred that the turkey is not alive, deaf and not-hiding, and one in which it is preferred that after loading etc. it is preferred that the turkey is still alive, not deaf and hiding.
Note, furthermore, that again K¬d → ¬M[load]¬h is derivable (under the assumption that load does not fail), blocking the inference P[load]h in the second disjunct of the sixth formula above, as desired. Moreover, we can derive K(l ∧ ¬h) → ¬M¬[fire]¬a, and thus K(l∧¬h) → ¬M[fire]a (under the assumption that 'fire' does not fail), and hence also P[load]P[wait]K(l∧¬h) → P[load]P[wait]¬M[fire]a, blocking the inference P[load]P[wait](a ∧ d∧ K(l ∧ ¬h))) ⇒ P[load]P[wait]P[fire]a (under suitable consistency conditions), as desired, in a similar vein as in Example 4.3.2. (Note the crucial step above to use necessitation on ¬h to obtain *K*¬h!)

4.3.3.3 Key: r = 'the_engine_is_running'
s = 'starting_the_car'
d = 'there_is_tail-pipe_destroyer_around'
p = 'there_is_a_potato_in_the_tail-pipe'

(i) We represent this scenario as follows:

(1) ¬r
(2) M([s]r) → P([s]r)
(3) p → ¬[s]r

Since there is no evidence to the contrary, we may safely assume M[s]r (ig_ass(M[s]r)), so that we can conclude P[s]r. This is a classic illustration of what is known as the '*qualification problem*': it is not feasible in practice to qualify all effects of events given an open-ended list of ways the context affects these (cf. [McD87], [San91]). In the case above, we know that normally car engines run when one starts them. Since we do not have any clue about possible qualifications of this rule, such as that there is e.g. actually a potato put in the tail-pipe, which will prevent the engine from running, we will expect/believe that the engine will run after starting it. Note again the important difference between the outcome P[s]r and the assertion [s]r, which would say that actually the engine will run after starting it. The latter is certainly not true if, in fact, there will be a potato put in the tail-pipe, whereas in this case, as we are not aware of this, we may still ***believe*** that the engine will run after starting it!

Note, furthermore, that we did not represent the information that "nothing is known about a potato in the tail-pipe". Of course, we could have tried to represent this by the formula ¬Kp ∧ ¬K¬p, or equivalently M¬p ∧ Mp, which would just state another two ignorance assertions, viz. ig–

ass(M¬p) and ig_ass(Mp), which, by the way, would have no effect on the outcome. (In fact, in Intermezzo E.6 below, we will show a method to derive (1') — defeasibly — from the rest.) However, we have not done this, since here the information "nothing is known about a potato in the tail-pipe" is meant to say something else entirely, more on a meta-level: one is *not even aware* of the the possibility of there being a potato in the tail-pipe. It actually says that (2) is the right default to use. This will change drastically if there is an awareness of this possibility, as we'll see below.

(ii) Now we know additionally:

(4) d

(5) $d \rightarrow Mp$

Although logically speaking there is not much difference with just assuming the ignorance assertion ig_ass(Mp), the way the scenario is stated now changes the situation profoundly. The intent of it is that we are now *aware* of a possible problem with the car, and might consider it possible that the tail-pipe is blocked. This means that we cannot use the default (2) any more: it is not the case that by default the car engine will run after starting it, since there may well be a problem. This forces us to change our beliefs, *including our defaults*. The most obvious way to represent this situation is to modify (2) into

(2') $K\neg p \wedge M([s]r) \rightarrow P([s]r)$.

This illustrates the qualification problem again. Here we know about the concrete possible problem p, so that we can incorporate this in our defaults, but there can be yet another host of problems that we are not aware of. In fact, what happens here is that we have a piece of information (Mp) that undercuts the application of a default (2) and arriving at the conclusion P[s]r. And there is no guarantee that if we obtain additional information we do not have to change our defaults again! In some sense this can be viewed as a kind of non-monotonic reasoning on a meta-level: the defaults *themselves* have to be changed when additional information becomes available. In other words, what *normally* is the case changes: going *knowingly* to an abnormal situation (such as having a tail-pipe destroyer around) changes your expectations.

Note that this is a really subtle situation (cf. [San91]). We would not need the modification (2') if one changed (5) to

(5') $d \rightarrow p$

which states that having the destroyer around will for certain entail that there is a potato in the tail-pipe (since then we could derive: $d \Rightarrow_{(nec)} Kd \Rightarrow_{(5')} Kp \Rightarrow_{(3)} K\neg[s]r \Rightarrow \neg M[s]r$, which would block the default (2), as desired). However, (5') is not what we intend to represent: we do not want to say that, once there is a tail-pipe destroyer around, it is certain that the tail-pipe will be blocked by a potato! Moreover, we do not even want to say that this is normally the case, which would result in the default

(5'') $d \wedge Mp \rightarrow P_1 p$,

which would give us $P_1\neg[s]r$, which we could then use conveniently to block the application of a modified version of (2):

(2") $\neg P_1\neg([s]r) \rightarrow P_2([s]r)$,

as we did in Example 4.2.8. This is simply not what we want here either! What we want to express by (5) is not a default.

4.4.4.1 Given $\Theta = (W, \Delta)$, $W = \{q \rightarrow (\neg p \wedge \neg r)\}$ and $\Delta = \{Mp \rightarrow P_1p, Mq \rightarrow P_1q, Mr \rightarrow P_2r\}$. We search for $Cons(\Theta) = \{\psi \mid\ \vdash_\Theta \psi\}$. We have:

$q \rightarrow (\neg p \wedge \neg r) \mathrel{|\!\sim} K(q \rightarrow (\neg p \wedge \neg r)) \wedge Mp \wedge Mq \wedge Mr$
$\vdash_{\mathbf{EDL},\Delta} K(q \rightarrow (\neg p \wedge \neg r)) \wedge P_1p \wedge P_1q \wedge P_2r$
$\vdash_{\mathbf{EDL}} P_1(q \rightarrow (\neg p \wedge \neg r)) \wedge P_1p \wedge P_1q \wedge P_2(q \rightarrow (\neg p \wedge \neg r)) \wedge P_2r$
$\vdash_{\mathbf{EDL}} (P_1q \rightarrow P_1(\neg p \wedge \neg r)) \wedge P_1p \wedge P_1q \wedge P_2(q \rightarrow (\neg p \wedge \neg r)) \wedge P_2r$
$\vdash_{\mathbf{EDL}} P_1(\neg p \wedge \neg r) \wedge P_1p \wedge P_2(q \rightarrow (\neg p \wedge \neg r)) \wedge P_2r$
$\vdash_{\mathbf{EDL}} P_1\neg p \wedge P_1\neg r \wedge P_1p \wedge P_2(q \rightarrow (\neg p \wedge \neg r)) \wedge P_2r$
$\vdash_{\mathbf{EDL}} P_1\bot \wedge P_2(q \rightarrow (\neg p \wedge \neg r)) \wedge P_2r$
$\vdash_{\mathbf{EDL}} P_1\bot \wedge P_2((p \vee r) \rightarrow \neg q) \wedge P_2r$
$\vdash_{\mathbf{EDL}} P_1\bot \wedge (P_2(p \vee r) \rightarrow P_2\neg q) \wedge P_2(p \vee r) \wedge P_2r$
$\vdash_{\mathbf{EDL}} P_1\bot \wedge P_2\neg q \wedge P_2r$

We obtain two frames or extensions: S_1 is empty (and hence $P_1\varphi$ is true for every φ) and S_2 is such that $S_2 \models r \wedge \neg q$.

E.6. Intermezzo

What we really have to do in the answers to Exercise 4.4.4.2 is to derive formally all the ignorance assertions of type ig_ass, as used in Exercise 4.2.7.1 and following exercises, and explained in the Intermezzo to those exercises. For, if we can do this, we can add these now to the old derivations (which were derivations within **EDL**), and thus obtain the desired conclusions. Such an ig_ass is typically of the form $M\alpha$, where α is a propositional formula. So, what we have to do is to show that $\varphi \mathrel{|\!\sim}_\Theta M\alpha$, where φ and $\Theta = (W, \Delta)$ have to be specified in each example. Thus, the general picture looks like this:

In Section 4.2, we were able to derive conclusions of the form

$$\psi \in Th_{\mathbf{EDL}}(W \cup \Delta \cup Ig\_ass)$$

where W was some set of given facts, and Δ some set of defaults. In such a derivation, we sometimes needed to make additional assumptions in a postulated set Ig_ass of type $M\alpha$. In this section, we want to derive the formulas $M\alpha$ as appearing in these sets Ig_ass, using the minimization of knowledge techniques of Chapter 3, according to Definition 4.4.2 of default entailment:

$$\psi \in Th_{\mathbf{EDL}}(\Sigma_{\varphi \wedge W^*} \cup \Delta).$$

So, in fact, we use the set $\Sigma^{\varphi \wedge W^*}$ for both the factual information W and the ignorance information that we had to postulate earlier in a set Ig_ass, completely in line with Halpern & Moses' original intent of this set. The following lemma will prove useful: it says that, when 'circumscribing' some propositional formula φ, for any ψ that does not propositionally follow from φ, we can non-monotonically derive that $\neg K\psi$: ψ is not known.

E.6.1. LEMMA. *Let φ and ψ be propositional formulas such that $\varphi \nvdash \psi$. Then $\varphi \mid\!\sim \neg K\psi$.*

PROOF. We know that φ is honest. Now recall from Intermezzo E.5 and Exercise 3.1.4.2.1 that $\Sigma(\{\varphi\})$ is a stable set. From Lemma I.5 of that Intermezzo, we conclude that $\Sigma(\{\varphi\}) = \Sigma^{\varphi}$. From the construction of $\Sigma(\{\varphi\})$, we see that, since $\varphi \nvdash \psi$, $\psi \notin \Sigma_0$ and hence $\neg K\psi \in \Sigma_1$, so $\neg K\psi \in \Sigma^{\varphi}$, so $\varphi \mid\!\sim \neg K\psi$. ■

REMARK. We will use this lemma in the format $W \nvdash \neg\beta$, where $M\beta$ is the ig_ass we are aiming for. Note that the lemma guarantees $W^* \mid\!\sim \neg K \neg\beta$, hence $W^* \mid\!\sim M\beta$.

REMARK. In the following, the general reasoning pattern will be as follows. We will specify the relevant

$$W = \{\varphi_1, \ldots, \varphi_n\},$$
$$\Delta = \{\alpha_1 \wedge M\beta_1 \to P_1\gamma_1, \ldots, \alpha_k \wedge M\beta_k \to P_k\gamma_k\},$$
$$\text{ig\_ass} = \{M\beta_1, \ldots, M\beta_k\}.$$

In each specific case, $\Theta = (W, \Delta)$ will refer to the specific W and Δ. Sometimes, Δ will also include formulas of the form $\alpha_r \wedge \neg P_h \neg\beta_1 \to P_r\gamma_r$. In the general case, we will show that $W \nvdash \neg\beta_i$ (and hence $W^* \mid\!\sim M\beta_i$); and also that $W \vdash \alpha_i$. If we can do both we may apply the i-th default in Δ and conclude $P_i\gamma$. Sometimes we will claim that a default $\alpha_i \wedge M\beta_i \to P_i\gamma_i$ is *blocked* (Example 4.2.8): in such a case we mean that $W \vdash \neg\beta_i$, which implies $W^* \mid\!\sim K\neg\beta_i$, and hence $\mid\!\sim_\Theta \neg M\beta_i$. By the consistency of the stable set $\Sigma^{\varphi \wedge W^*}$, we then know that $\not\mid\!\sim_\Theta M\beta_i$. In such a case, the idea is that the default $\alpha_i \wedge M\beta_i \to P_i\gamma_i$ cannot be applied and we will act as if $P_i\gamma_i$ cannot be derived; formally, we must exclude *each* possible way to derive $P_i\gamma_i$. In the examples and exercises below we will not go into such detail: the reader may use semantic means to verify that, if we claim that the default $\alpha_i \wedge M\beta_i \to P_i\gamma_i$ is blocked, the conclusion $P_i\gamma_i$ is indeed refutable. This also applies to those cases where an applicable default of type $\alpha_i \wedge M\beta_i \to P_i\gamma_i$ is claimed to block a default of type $\alpha_r \wedge \neg P_i\gamma_i \to P_r\gamma_r$ (Exercises 4.2.8.1, 4.2.8.4(a)).

4.4.4.2 Example 4.2.3

$W = \{(\neg p \vee \neg t)\}$,

$\Delta = \{Mp \to P_1p, Mt \to P_2t\}$

ig_ass = $\{Mp, Mt\}$.

To see that they follow from W, observe that $\neg p \vee \neg t \nvdash \neg p$, $\neg p \vee \neg t \nvdash \neg t$ and apply Lemma E.6.1.

Example 4.2.4 / Exercise 4.2.4.1

$W = \{s \wedge h\}$,

$\Delta = \{s \wedge M(f \wedge \neg l) \rightarrow P_1 f, h \wedge Ml \rightarrow P_2 l\}$,
ig_ass = $\{M(f \wedge \neg l), Ml\}$.
To see that they follow from W, observe that $s \wedge h \nvdash \neg (f \wedge \neg l)$ and that $s \wedge h \nvdash \neg l$, and apply Lemma E.6.1.

Example 4.2.5
$W = \{w_1 \vee w_2 \vee \ldots \vee w_{1000}\}$,
$\Delta = \{M\neg w_i \rightarrow P_i \neg w_i \mid 1 \leq i \leq 1000\}$
ig_ass = $\{M\neg w_i \mid 1 \leq i \leq 1000\}$.
To apply Lemma E.6.1, observe that
$w_1 \vee w_2 \vee \ldots \vee w_{1000} \nvdash w_i$.

Example 4.2.6
$W = \{s \vee h\}$,
$\Delta = \{s \wedge Mf \rightarrow P_1 f, h \wedge Mf \rightarrow P_2 f\}$
ig_ass = $\{Mf\}$.
To apply Lemma E.6.1, observe that
$s \vee h \nvdash \neg f$.

Example 4.2.7
$W = \{r \wedge q\}$,
$\Delta = \{r \wedge M\neg p \rightarrow P_1 \neg p, q \wedge Mp \rightarrow P_2 p\}$
ig_ass = $\{M\neg p, Mp\}$.
To apply Lemma E.6.1, observe that
$r \wedge q \nvdash \neg p$ and $r \wedge q \nvdash p$.

Exercise 4.2.7.1
$W = \{r \wedge q\}$,
$\Delta = \{r \wedge M(\neg p \wedge f) \rightarrow P_1(\neg p \wedge f), q \wedge Mp \rightarrow P_2 p, p \wedge Ma \rightarrow P_3 a, f \wedge M\neg a \rightarrow P_4 \neg a\}$
ig_ass = $\{M(\neg p \wedge f), Mp, Ma, M\neg a\}$
To apply Lemma E.6.1, observe that
$r \wedge q \nvdash \neg(\neg p \wedge f)$; $r \wedge q \nvdash \neg p$; $r \wedge q \nvdash \neg a$, and $r \wedge q \nvdash a$.

Example 4.2.8
$W = \{r \wedge a\}$,
$\Delta = \{r \wedge Mb \rightarrow P_1 b, r \wedge a \wedge M\neg b \rightarrow P_2 \neg b\}$
ig_ass = $\{Mb, M\neg b\}$.
To apply Lemma E.6.1, observe that
$r \wedge a \nvdash \neg b$ and $r \wedge a \nvdash b$.

In the (2^*)-case, we have
$W' = \{r \wedge a, r \wedge a \rightarrow \neg b\}$,
$\Delta' = \{r \wedge Mb \rightarrow P_1 b, r \wedge a \wedge M\neg b \rightarrow P_2 \neg b\}$
ig_ass' = $\{Mb, M\neg b\}$.
Now we see that indeed the first default ($r \wedge Mb \rightarrow P_1 b$) is blocked, since we have $r \wedge a, r \wedge a \rightarrow \neg b \vdash \neg b$ (and still $r \wedge a, r \wedge a \rightarrow \neg b \nvdash b$). In other words, the ig_ass Mb cannot be

derived here, while the ig_ass $M\neg b$ is still derivable.

In the (1^*)-case, we have
$W'' = \{r \wedge a\}$,
$\Delta'' = \{r \wedge \neg P_2\neg b \rightarrow P_1 b, r \wedge a \wedge M\neg b \rightarrow P_2\neg b\}$
ig_ass'' = $\{M\neg b\}$
Although the only ig_ass here is $M\neg b$, we want to make another derivation from the minimal stable set: we want to derive $P_2\neg b$ to block the first default, and one way to achieve this is by deriving $M\neg b$.
Now, since $r \wedge a \nvdash b$, we have $r \wedge a \vdash M\neg b \vdash_{\mathbf{EDL}} P_2\neg b$.

Exercise 4.2.8.1

$W = \{r \rightarrow e, r\}$,
$\Delta = \{e \wedge Mg \rightarrow P_1 g, r \wedge M\neg g \rightarrow P_2\neg g\}$
ig_ass = $\{Mg, M\neg g\}$.
To apply Lemma E.6.1, observe that
$r \rightarrow e, r \nvdash \neg g$ and $r \rightarrow e, r \nvdash g$.

When adding rule (5), we get
$W' = \{r \rightarrow e, r, r \rightarrow \neg g\}$,
$\Delta' = \{e \wedge Mg \rightarrow P_1 g, r \wedge M\neg g \rightarrow P_2\neg g\}$
ig_ass' = $\{Mg, M\neg g\}$.
Indeed, the first default cannot be applied, since we have
$r \rightarrow e, r, r \rightarrow \neg g \vdash \neg g$ and hence $r \rightarrow e, r, r \rightarrow \neg g \vdash K\neg g$, i.e. $r \rightarrow e, r, r \rightarrow \neg g \vdash \neg Mg$, and consequently *not* $r \rightarrow e, r, r \rightarrow \neg g \vdash Mg$.

When replacing (2) by (2'), we obtain:
$W'' = \{r \rightarrow e, r\}$,
$\Delta'' = \{e \wedge \neg P_2\neg g \rightarrow P_1 g, r \wedge M\neg g \rightarrow P_2\neg g\}$
ig_ass'' = $\{M\neg g\}$.
We obtain $W'' \nvdash g$, so we obtain $M\neg g$, and, since the default $r \wedge M\neg g \rightarrow P_2\neg g$ can be applied we obtain $P_2\neg g$, so that the first default is blocked and for the default theory $\Theta'' = (W'', \Delta'')$ we do *not* have $\vdash_\Theta P_1 g$.

Exercise 4.2.8.2

We will immediately consider the case where premise (5), $p \rightarrow a$, is included in the theory. This is the most general case: if $W_1 \subseteq W_2$ then $W_2{}^* \vdash M\alpha \Rightarrow W_1{}^* \vdash M\alpha$ (the non-monotonic inference $\vdash$ here even behaves *anti*-monotonically!).
$W = \{d \rightarrow g, d, p \rightarrow a\}$,
$\Delta = \{g \wedge M\neg a \rightarrow P_1\neg a, d \wedge Mp \rightarrow P_2 p\}$
ig_ass = $\{M\neg a, Mp\}$.
To apply Lemma E.6.1, observe that
$d \rightarrow g, d, p \rightarrow a \nvdash a$ and $d \rightarrow g, d, p \rightarrow a \nvdash \neg p$. Note that indeed we obtain that $\vdash_\Theta P_2 a$ and $\vdash_\Theta P_1\neg a$.

Exercise 4.2.8.3

We start with the theory containing $a \leftrightarrow \neg b$:
$W = \{a \leftrightarrow \neg b\}$,
$\Delta = \{Mb \rightarrow P_1b, Ma \rightarrow P_2a\}$
ig_ass = {Mb, Ma}.
To apply Lemma E.6.1, observe that
$a \leftrightarrow \neg b \nvdash \neg b$ and $a \leftrightarrow \neg b \nvdash \neg a$.

For the extended theory, we obtain
$W' = \{a \leftrightarrow \neg b, t \rightarrow h\}$,
$\Delta' = \{h \wedge Mb \rightarrow P_1b, t \wedge Ma \rightarrow P_2a\}$
ig_ass = {Mb, Ma}.
To apply Lemma E.6.1, observe that
$a \leftrightarrow \neg b, t \rightarrow h \nvdash \neg b$ and $a \leftrightarrow \neg b, t \rightarrow h \nvdash \neg a$.

Exercise 4.2.8.4(a)
$W = \{s \wedge a\}$,
$\Delta = \{a \wedge Me \rightarrow P_1e, s \wedge M\neg e \rightarrow P_2\neg e, s \wedge Ma \rightarrow P_3a\}$
ig_ass = {Me, M¬e, Ma}.
To apply Lemma E.6.1, observe that
$W \nvdash \neg e$, $W \nvdash e$ and $W \nvdash \neg a$.

Of course, we derive the same conclusions if W is weakened to $W' = \{s\}$:
$W' \nvdash \neg e$, $W' \nvdash e$ and $W' \nvdash \neg a$.

Bringing in specificity, we obtain
$W'' = \{s\}$
$\Delta'' = \{a \wedge \neg P_2\neg e \rightarrow P_1e, s \wedge M\neg e \rightarrow P_2\neg e, s \wedge Ma \rightarrow P_3a\}$
ig_ass'' = {M¬e, Ma}.
Now, we have $s \nvdash \neg e$, $s \nvdash e$ and $s \nvdash \neg a$, hence $\vdash_{\Theta''} s \wedge Me \wedge M\neg e \wedge Ma$ and $\vdash_{\Theta''} P_2\neg e \wedge P_3a$ and we see that the first default rule is blocked by the fact that we have $P_2\neg e$: we cannot use it to derive P_3P_1e (and thus P_1e) from P_3a.

Exercise 4.2.8.4(b)
$W = \{a \wedge y\}$,
$\Delta = \{a \wedge Me \rightarrow P_1e, s \wedge M\neg e \rightarrow P_2\neg e, s \wedge Ma \rightarrow P_3a, a \wedge y \wedge Ms \rightarrow P_4s\}$
ig_ass = {Me, M¬e, Ma, Ms}.
To apply Lemma E.6.1, observe that
$a \wedge y \nvdash \neg e$, $a \wedge y \nvdash e$ and $a \wedge y \nvdash \neg a$ and $a \wedge y \nvdash \neg s$.
Hence we have $\vdash_\Theta P_2\neg e$; note that for this conclusion we still need the f_assumption $\neg P_4\bot$.

4.4.4.3 (i) Key: ha = 'block_A_is_heavy'
hb = 'block_B_is_heavy'
ta = 'block_A_is_on_the_table'
tb = 'block_B_is_on_the_table'

We are given the following premises:

(1)	$ha \wedge hb$	*Blocks A and B are heavy.*
(2a)	$(ha \wedge Mta \rightarrow P_1ta)$	
(2b)	$(hb \wedge Mtb \rightarrow P_1tb)$	*Heavy blocks are normally located on the table.*
(3)	$\neg ta$	*Block A is not on the table.*

Note the effect of our mimicking first-order logic: a perhaps better translation of default (2) would be (with B(x): x_is_a_block, H(x): x_is_heavy and T(x): x_is_located_on_the_table):

(2') $\forall x((B(x) \wedge H(x) \wedge M\, T(x)) \rightarrow P_1\, T(x))$

Since we do not use this full language, we have in fact some more freedom to represent the default (2); we are free to choose different frames here and use $(a \wedge Mt \rightarrow P_1t) \wedge (b \wedge Mu \rightarrow P_2u)$; in an n-blocks-world we then would obtain n different clusters: in each of them, one of the heavy blocks is believed to be located on the table. In this case, it does not matter whether we take different frames or not.

In order to verify whether u holds, we must check ig_ass(u). Thus, we now have:
$W = \{(ha \wedge hb), \neg ta\}$;
$\Delta = \{(ha \wedge Mta \rightarrow P_1ta), (hb \wedge Mtb \rightarrow P_1tb)\}$;
ig_ass = {Mta, Mtb}.
Since $(ha \wedge hb), \neg ta \nvdash \neg tb$, we get $\vdash_\Theta hb \wedge Mtb \vdash_{\mathbf{EDL}} P_1tb$, hence $\vdash_\Theta P_1tb$. Furthermore, $W \vdash \neg ta$, so we do *not* have $\vdash_\Theta$ Mta, so that application of (2a) is blocked.

(ii) Key: ha = 'block_A_is_heavy'
hb = 'block_B_is_heavy'
ta = 'block_A_is_on_the_table'
tb = 'block_B_is_on_the_table'
ra = 'block_A_is_red'
rb = 'block_B_is_red'

We immediately classify the premises in their parts W and Δ. Since we want to verify whether 'tb' and 'ra' are preferred beliefs, we can also identify ig_ass. Since, beforehand, we do not want to commit ourselves to collapse of clusters, we give them variable names:
$W = \{(ha \wedge hb), \neg ta, \neg rb\}$;
$\Delta = \{(ha \wedge Mta \rightarrow P_wta), (hb \wedge Mtb \rightarrow P_xtb), (ha \wedge Mra \rightarrow P_yra), (hb \wedge Mrb \rightarrow P_zrb)\}$;
ig_ass = {Mta, Mtb, Mra, Mrb}.

Obiously, for a generic reading of the default (there is one kind of belief in which heavy blocks are assumed to be on the table, and (possibly another one) in which they are assumed to be red), we must assume w = x and y = z.

Now, we have $W \nvdash \neg tb$, $W \nvdash \neg ra$; but on the other hand we have $W \vdash \neg ta$, $W \vdash \neg rb$. Hence $\vdash_\Theta$ $(hb \wedge Mtb) \wedge (ha \wedge Mra)$, but *not* $\vdash_\Theta$ Mta and *not* $\vdash_\Theta$ Mrb, so that the rules $(ha \wedge Mta \rightarrow P_wta)$ and $(hb \wedge Mrb \rightarrow P_zrb)$ are blocked. Obiously, we derive that $\vdash_\Theta P_xtb \wedge P_yra$.

Our conclusion is that we can derive that both 'B is on the table' and 'A is red' are preferred beliefs: however, if we do not make additional constraints, we cannot derive that 'B is on the table and A is red' as a preferred belief. If we want this conclusion as well, we should explicitly demand that x = z. Finally, note that if we replace Δ by Δ'

$$\Delta' = \{(\mathrm{ha} \wedge \mathrm{M}(\mathrm{ta} \wedge \mathrm{ra}) \rightarrow \mathrm{P_w}(\mathrm{ta} \wedge \mathrm{ra})), (\mathrm{hb} \wedge \mathrm{M}(\mathrm{tb} \wedge \mathrm{rb}) \rightarrow \mathrm{P_x}(\mathrm{tb} \wedge \mathrm{rb}))\}$$

expressing that heavy blocks are normally both on the table and red, neither of the defaults would be applicable, since we now have $W \vdash \neg(\mathrm{ta} \wedge \mathrm{ra})$ and $W \vdash \neg(\mathrm{tb} \wedge \mathrm{rb})$.

4.6.1.1. **ECL** is the union of **K**, **S5**, **EDL** and the axioms AP10-AP16:

K:
- (A1) All (instances of) propositional tautologies
- (A2) $(K\varphi \wedge K(\varphi \rightarrow \psi)) \rightarrow K\psi$
- (R1) $\dfrac{\varphi \quad \varphi \rightarrow \psi}{\psi}$
- (R2) $\dfrac{\varphi}{K\varphi}$

S5:
- (A3) $K\varphi \rightarrow \varphi$
- (A4) $K\varphi \rightarrow KK\varphi$
- (A5) $\neg K\varphi \rightarrow K\neg K\varphi$

EDL
- (AP2) $(P_\sigma\varphi \wedge P_\sigma(\varphi \rightarrow \psi)) \rightarrow P_\sigma\psi \quad (\sigma \in I^*)$
- (AP4) $P_\sigma\varphi \rightarrow P_\sigma P_\sigma\varphi \quad (\sigma \in I^*)$
- (AP5) $\neg P_\sigma\varphi \rightarrow P_\sigma\neg P_\sigma\varphi \quad (\sigma \in I^*)$
- (AP6) $K\varphi \rightarrow P_\sigma\varphi \quad (\sigma \in I^*)$
- (AP7) $KP_\sigma\varphi \leftrightarrow P_\sigma\varphi \quad (\sigma \in I^*)$
- (AP8) $\neg P_\sigma\bot \rightarrow (P_\sigma P_\tau\varphi \leftrightarrow P_\tau\varphi) \quad (\sigma, \tau \in I^*)$
- (AP9) $\neg P_\sigma\bot \rightarrow (P_\sigma K\varphi \leftrightarrow K\varphi) \quad (\sigma \in I^*)$

ECL
- (AP10) $A(\varphi \wedge \psi) \leftrightarrow A\varphi \wedge A\psi$
- (AP11) $A\neg\varphi \leftrightarrow \neg A\varphi$
- (AP12) $K\varphi \rightarrow A\varphi$
- (AP13) $A\varphi \rightarrow KA\varphi$
- (AP14) $AP_\sigma\varphi \leftrightarrow P_\sigma\varphi \quad (\sigma \in I^*)$
- (AP15) $\neg P_\sigma\bot \rightarrow (P_\sigma A\varphi \leftrightarrow A\varphi) \quad (\sigma \in I^*)$
- (AP16) $P_\sigma\varphi \rightarrow P_{\sigma,i}\varphi \quad (\sigma \in I^*, i \in I)$

Models here are of the kind $\mathbb{M} = (\{S_\sigma \mid \sigma \in I^*\}, \pi, \rho, \{\wp_\sigma \mid \sigma \in I^*\})$, where $S_{<>} = S$, the set of all worlds, $\rho \in S$ denotes 'the real world'; $\wp_{<>} = \wp = S \times S$, the universal relation on S; $S_{\sigma,i} \subseteq S_\sigma$; $\wp_\sigma = S \times S_\sigma \subseteq \wp$. We refer to the soundness and completeness proof for the system **EDL** (Exercise 4.2.0.1) to check soundness and completeness of the axioms up to AP9. In fact, as we did in Exercise 4.2.0.1, we can again give a more economical presentation of **ECL**. Let $\mathbf{ECL}^- = (\mathbf{ECL} \setminus \{\text{AP7, AP8, AP9, AP14, AP15}\}) \cup \{P_\sigma\varphi \to KP_\sigma\varphi\}$.

CLAIM 1. For all formulas φ, $\mathbf{ECL} \vdash \varphi$ iff $\mathbf{ECL}^- \vdash \varphi$.

PROOF. The axioms AP7, AP8 and AP9 are derived as in Exercise 4.2.0.1. So let us give derivations of AP14 and AP15.

AP14 ←	1	$P_\sigma\varphi \to KP_\sigma\varphi$	AP7, A1
	2	$KP_\sigma\varphi \to AP_\sigma\varphi$	AP12
	3	$P_\sigma\varphi \to AP_\sigma\varphi$	HS, 1, 2
AP14 →	1	$\neg P_\sigma\varphi \to \neg KP_\sigma\varphi$	AP7, A1
	2	$\neg KP_\sigma\varphi \to K\neg KP_\sigma\varphi$	A5
	3	$K\neg KP_\sigma\varphi \to K\neg P_\sigma\varphi$	KD, A1, AP7
	4	$K\neg P_\sigma\varphi \to A\neg P_\sigma\varphi$	AP12
	5	$A\neg P_\sigma\varphi \to \neg AP_\sigma\varphi$	AP11, A1
	6	$\neg P_\sigma\varphi \to \neg AP_\sigma\varphi$	HS, 1, 2, 3, 4, 5
	7	$AP_\sigma\varphi \to P_\sigma\varphi$	CP, 6
AP15	1	$A\varphi \to KA\varphi$	AP13
	2	$KA\varphi \to P_\sigma A\varphi$	AP6
	3	$A\varphi \to P_\sigma A\varphi$	HS, 1, 2
	4	$\neg P_\sigma\bot \to (A\varphi \to P_\sigma A\varphi)$	A1, 3, R1
	5	$P_\sigma A\varphi \to P_\sigma KA\varphi$	P_σ-distribution (cf. Ex. 4.2.7.1), 1
	6	$\neg P_\sigma\bot \to (P_\sigma A\varphi \to P_\sigma KA\varphi)$	A1, 5, R1
	7	$\neg P_\sigma\bot \to (P_\sigma KA\varphi \to KA\varphi)$	AP9, A1
	8	$\neg P_\sigma\bot \to (KA\varphi \to A\varphi)$	A3, A1, R1
	9	$\neg P_\sigma\bot \to (P_\sigma A\varphi \to A\varphi)$	A1, R1, 6, 7, 8
	10	$\neg P_\sigma\bot \to (P_\sigma A\varphi \leftrightarrow A\varphi)$	A1, R1, 6, 9

■Claim 1

LEMMA 2 (Soundness). *For all* φ, $\mathbf{ECL}^- \vdash \varphi \Rightarrow \mathcal{S5AP} \models \varphi$.

PROOF. Using the results of Exercise 4.2.0.1, and Claim 1, we only have to consider the axioms (AP10)—(AP13) plus (AP16). Note that we may conceive the models here of the kind $\mathbb{M} = \langle\{S_\sigma \mid \sigma \in I^*\}, \pi, \wp_\rho, \{\wp_\sigma \mid \sigma \in I^*\}\rangle$, with the property that

$$\exists\rho \in S(\forall s,t \in S(\wp_\rho st \leftrightarrow t = \rho)) \tag{*}$$

and which allows us to interpret A as the necessity operator of $\wp_\rho$. Then, soundness of the axiom (AP10) is checked as in Exercise 1.3.5.3 for the operator K. Concerning (AP11), we observe that

$(\mathbb{M}, s) \models A\neg\varphi \Leftrightarrow$
for all t with $\wp_\rho st$, $(\mathbb{M}, t) \models \neg\varphi \Leftrightarrow$
$(\mathbb{M}, \rho) \models \neg\varphi \Leftrightarrow$ not $(\mathbb{M}, \rho) \models \varphi \Leftrightarrow$

not for all t with $\wp_\rho st$, $(\mathbb{M}, t) \models \varphi \Leftrightarrow$
$(\mathbb{M}, s) \models \neg A\varphi$.

Soundness of (AP12) follows from the obervation that $\wp_\rho \subseteq \wp$ (which holds because of the following: suppose that s and t are such that $\wp_\rho st$. By (*), we know that $t = \rho$, thus (since $\wp$ is the universal relation) $\wp st$) and Exercise 2.13.5.1.1. Validity of (AP13) follows immediately from observation (*): suppose that $(\mathbb{M}, s) \models A\varphi$. By (*), we have $(\mathbb{M}, \rho) \models \varphi$. Now, let t be such that $\wp st$. This means simply that $t \in S$, so still we have $(\mathbb{M}, t) \models A\varphi$. Since t was an arbitrary $\wp$-successor of s, we have $(\mathbb{M}, s) \models KA\varphi$. Thus, $(\mathbb{M}, s) \models A\varphi \rightarrow KA\varphi$. Finally, soundness of (AP16) follows directly from $S_{\sigma,i} \subseteq S_\sigma$. ■Lemma 2

For completeness, we almost copy the procedure of Exercise 4.2.0.1; we first build the canonical model $\mathbb{M}^c = \langle S^c, \pi^c, \wp^c, \wp_\rho{}^c, \{\wp_\sigma{}^c \mid \diamond \neq \sigma \in I^*\}\rangle$ for any **ECL**-consistent formula $\varphi \in \Phi$, such that $(\mathbb{M}^c, s_\Phi) \models \varphi$. Because of the axioms (A1)—(AP9), we know that $\wp^c$ is an equivalence relation, that each $\wp_\sigma{}^c$ is transitive and euclidean, and that we have, for all $\sigma \in I^*$, $\forall s_\Sigma, s_\Delta, s_\Omega \in S^c$: $((\wp^c s_\Sigma s_\Delta \;\&\; \wp_\sigma{}^c s_\Delta s_\Omega) \Rightarrow \wp_\sigma{}^c s_\Sigma s_\Omega)$ (cf. Observation 3 in Exercise 4.2.0.1). Moreover, by axiom (AP16) and Exercise 2.13.5.1.1 we have that $\wp_{\sigma,i}{}^c \subseteq \wp_\sigma{}^c$.

Let us now consider $\wp_\rho$. Axiom (AP12) and Exercise 2.13.5.1.1 guarantee that $\wp_\rho{}^c \subseteq \wp^c$. Now we want to establish property (*) in this canonical model. First, we will show that there is a *unique* s_Δ representing ρ for each $\wp^c$-equivalence class, that is, we show that

(i) for each s_Σ, we have $\wp_\rho{}^c s_\Sigma s_\Delta$ for exactly one s_Δ;
(ii) for all $s_\Sigma, s_\Gamma, s_{\Delta_1}, s_{\Delta_2}$: $\wp^c s_\Sigma s_\Gamma \Rightarrow (\wp_\rho{}^c s_\Sigma s_{\Delta_1} \;\&\; \wp_\rho{}^c s_\Gamma s_{\Delta_2} \Rightarrow \Delta_1 = \Delta_2)$. (**)

For (i) we argue as follows: note that we have $\mathbf{ECL} \vdash \neg A\bot$ ($A\bot \Rightarrow_{AP11} \neg A\, \mathbf{true} \Rightarrow_{A1,\, R2,\, AP12} \bot$) and hence, by Proposition 2.4.1, we know that $\wp_\rho{}^c$ is serial. Hence, for each s_Σ, we have $\wp_\rho{}^c s_\Sigma s_\Delta$ for at least one s_Δ. Now suppose that $\wp_\rho{}^c s_\Sigma s_{\Delta_1}$ and $\wp_\rho{}^c s_\Sigma s_{\Delta_2}$, with $\Delta_1 \neq \Delta_2$. So, there is some ψ with $\psi \in \Delta_1$, $\psi \notin \Delta_2$. Since $\wp_\rho{}^c s_\Sigma s_{\Delta_1}$, we have $\neg A \neg\psi \in \Sigma$, and since $\wp_\rho{}^c s_\Sigma s_{\Delta_2}$, we have $\neg A\psi \in \Sigma$. Using (AP11), we derive that both $A\psi \in \Sigma$ and $\neg A\psi \in \Sigma$, which is impossible for a maximal consistent set Σ. So every m.c. set is $\wp_\rho{}^c$-accessible to exactly one world Δ.

In order to prove (ii), suppose that s_Σ and s_Γ are such that $\wp^c s_\Sigma s_\Gamma$, and suppose $\wp_\rho{}^c s_\Sigma s_{\Delta_1}$ and $\wp_\rho{}^c s_\Gamma s_{\Delta_2}$. We want to show that $\Delta_1 = \Delta_2$. Let $A\varphi$ be any formula in Σ. By (AP13), we have $KA\varphi \in \Sigma$, and, since $\wp^c s_\Sigma s_\Gamma$, $A\varphi \in \Gamma$. Since $\wp_\rho{}^c s_\Gamma s_{\Delta_2}$, we have $\varphi \in \Delta_2$. Thus, we have obtained that $\wp_\rho{}^c s_\Sigma s_{\Delta_2}$ holds. But we also have $\wp_\rho{}^c s_\Sigma s_{\Delta_1}$, and we observed above that s_Σ can only have one $\wp_\rho{}^c$-successor; hence $\Delta_1 = \Delta_2$.

Now, let φ be an $\mathbf{ECL}^-$-consistent formula. It is contained in some maximal consistent set Φ, and we have $(\mathbb{M}^c, s_\Phi) \models \varphi$. Let us define the generated submodel $\mathbb{M} = \langle S, \pi, \wp, \wp_\rho, \{\wp_\sigma \mid \diamond \neq \sigma \in I^*\}\rangle$ of $(\mathbb{M}^c, s_\Phi)$ as follows:

$S = \{t \in S^c \mid (s_\Phi, t) \in \wp^c\}$

and the other relations $\wp$, $\wp_\rho$, $\wp_\sigma$ ($\sigma \in I^*$, $\sigma \neq \langle\rangle$) and the truth assignment π are defined as the restrictions of $\wp^c$, $\wp_\rho{}^c$, $\wp_\sigma{}^c$ ($\sigma \in I^*$, $\sigma \neq \langle\rangle$) and π^c respectively, to this set S. Note that this entails that $\wp_{\sigma,i} \subseteq \wp_\sigma$.

As in Lemma E.4.4 of Exercise 4.2.0.1, one easily sees that

$$(\mathbb{M}^c, t) \models \psi \text{ iff } (\mathbb{M}, t) \models \psi.$$

As a corollary, we obtain that for the generated submodel $\mathbb{M}$ we have $(\mathbb{M}, s_\Phi) \models \varphi$.
Note that in this model we have $\wp = S \times S$. Since from (**) we know that each equivalence class in $\mathbb{M}^c$ has a unique s_P, in $\mathbb{M}$ we have *exactly one* actual world, say ρ. We transform $\mathbb{M}$ into a model $\mathbb{M}' = \langle S, \pi, \rho, \{S_\sigma \mid \langle\rangle \neq \sigma \in I^*\}, \wp, \{\wp_\sigma \mid \langle\rangle \neq \sigma \in I^*\}\rangle$, where ρ is *the* state such that $\wp_\rho(s, \rho)$ for every $s \in S$, and $S_\sigma = \{t \mid \exists s \in S: (s, t) \in \wp_\sigma\}$. Note that $\wp_{\sigma,i} \subseteq \wp_\sigma$ yields immediately that $S_{\sigma,i} \subseteq S_\sigma$. Now, the clause for $A\varphi$ reads

$(\mathbb{M}, s) \models A\varphi \Leftrightarrow (\mathbb{M}, \rho) \models \varphi$, where in $\mathbb{M}^c$ it was
$(\mathbb{M}^c, x) \models A\varphi \Leftrightarrow$ for all y ($\wp_\rho xy \Rightarrow (\mathbb{M}, y) \models \varphi$).

Thus, the truth definition of A has become real '*S5AP*-like'.

Using Observation E.4.3 of Exercise 4.2.0.1, we see that for all x and y in S, $(x, y) \in \wp_\sigma \Leftrightarrow y \in S_\sigma$. Thus, the truth definition of P_σ may be stated both as

$(\mathbb{M}, s) \models P_\sigma\varphi \Leftrightarrow$ for all y ($\wp_\sigma xy \Rightarrow (\mathbb{M}, y) \models \varphi$), as well as
$(\mathbb{M}, s) \models P_\sigma\varphi \Leftrightarrow$ for all $y \in S_\sigma$, $(\mathbb{M}, y) \models \varphi$.

By taking $s = s_\Phi$, with Φ a maximal consistent set containing the $\mathbf{ECL}^-$-consistent formula φ, we see that $(\mathbb{M}, s) \models \varphi$, where $\mathbb{M}$ is an *S5AP*-model. Eventually, we derive

THEOREM 3. *For all* φ, $\mathbf{ECL} \vdash \varphi \Leftrightarrow$ *S5AP* $\models \varphi$.

PROOF The $\Rightarrow$-direction follows from the equivalence between $\mathbf{ECL}^-$ and $\mathbf{ECL}$ (Claim 1) and soundness of $\mathbf{ECL}^-$ (Lemma 2). For '$\Leftarrow$' (completeness), let ψ be consistent in $\mathbf{ECL}$, or, equivalently, in $\mathbf{ECL}^-$. As we have seen above, we can now find an *S5AP*-model $\mathbb{M}$ and world s such that $(\mathbb{M}, s) \models \psi$. This is sufficient for completeness. ■

4.6.3.2 (i) Take, for simplicity, $T = \langle\emptyset\rangle$ and suppose $p >_{0,1} q$ and $p >_{0,2} \neg q$ for atoms p, q. Then we also have that $(p >_0 q)$ and $(p >_0 \neg q)$. We now show that we do not have $p >_0 (q \wedge \neg q)$. By $p >_{0,1} q$ we have that $[T \cup \{P_0p\} \vdash \neg P_0\neg q \;\&\; T \cup \{P_0p\} \vdash P_{0,1}q]$. Likewise, by $p >_{0,2} \neg q$ we have that $[T \cup \{P_0p\} \vdash \neg P_0 q \;\&\; T \cup \{P_0p\} \vdash P_{0,2}\neg q]$. (An *S5AP*-model for this situation might be such that $S_0 = \{s_1, s_2\}$, and $S_1 = \{s_1\}$, $S_2 = \{s_2\}$. In both s_1 and s_2 p is true, and only in s_1 q is true.) However, we do not have that $p >_0 (q \wedge \neg q)$, or equivalently $p >_0 \bot$, since this would imply $[T \cup \{P_0p\} \vdash \neg P_0\neg\bot$, or equivalently $T \cup \{P_0p\} \vdash \bot$, which contradicts our assumption that $\vdash$ maintains consistency.

(ii) This is false: a counterfactual implication in our sense only involves a hypothetical frame S_0, which in our setting is very loosely coupled to the real world ρ. (This means that our approach to counterfactual reasoning cannot be used for 'factual' reasoning as well. This must be done within **ECL** by means of reasoning about the A-operator directly. We note that this differs from 'traditional' approaches to counterfactuals (conditional logic) such as in [Lew73] or [Sta68], where such a form of 'conditional modus ponens' *does* hold. In [Bou94], p. 68, 69, where counterfactual reasoning is also compared with default reasoning, a similar discrepancy with 'traditional' counterfactual reasoning is noted. Interestingly, Boutilier ascribes the reason for this difference to the *epistemic* nature of a default reasoning-based approach to counterfactuals.) We now give a formal countermodel: Consider a frame S_0, in which p and q hold everywhere, and a non-empty subframe $S_{0,1}$ (in which there is thus a state where q holds). Furthermore we stipulate that in ρ it holds that p and ¬q (thus $\rho \notin S_0$). Now, obviously we have both Ap and $p >_0 q$ (since we have $p >_{0,1} q$), while Aq is *not* true. Finally we have to check whether schema (Δ) is satisfied for the relevant cases, namely ψ = p and ψ = ¬q. Clearly $Ap \wedge \neg P_0\neg p \rightarrow P_{0,1}p$ holds, since P_0p is true and this implies $P_{0,1}p$. Since we also have that P_0q, we trivially obtain $A\neg q \wedge \neg P_0 q \rightarrow P_{0,1}q$ as well.

(iii) Even this is not true. From the fact that in ρ it holds that φ, and the fact that $[T \cup \{P_0\varphi\} \vdash \neg P_0\neg\psi \ \&\ T \cup \{P_0\varphi\} \vdash P_{0,i}\psi]$, for some i, we cannot derive that $P_{0,i}\psi$. Take for φ an atom p. Application of (Δ) yields $Ap \wedge \neg P_0\neg p \rightarrow P_{0,j}p$. Even if we assume that $\neg P_0\neg p$ holds (which is not guaranteed, but might hold if e.g. $\rho \in S_0$), we obtain $P_{0,j}p$, which is not enough to use the assumption $T \cup \{P_0p\} \vdash P_{0,i}\psi$ to derive $P_{0,i}\psi$.

4.6.4.1

(G1) A formal counterexample can be found in the answer to Exercise 4.6.3.2(i).

(G2) We have to show $[T \cup \{P_0\varphi\} \vdash \neg P_0\neg \mathbf{true} \ \&\ T \cup \{P_0\varphi\} \vdash P_{0,i}\mathbf{true}]$, for some i and arbitrary (consistent) theory T, under the additional assumption that $(T \cup \{P_0\varphi\} \vdash)\ \neg P_0\bot$. The first conjunct follows directly from the assumption (is in fact the assumption).

(G4) We have to show $[T \cup \{P_0\varphi\} \vdash \neg P_0\neg\varphi \ \&\ T \cup \{P_0\varphi\} \vdash P_{0,i}\varphi]$, for some i and arbitrary (consistent) theory T, under the additional assumption that $T \cup \{P_0\varphi\} \vdash \neg P_0\neg\varphi$. So we only have to check the second conjunct. This is obvious, since $S_{0,i} \subseteq S_0$, so that $P_0\varphi \rightarrow P_{0,i}\varphi$ is valid. Moreover, from $\neg P_0\neg\varphi$ it follows that $\neg P_0\bot$, so that $P_i\varphi \leftrightarrow P_{0,i}\varphi$. So we can infer: $P_0\varphi \Rightarrow_{\mathbf{ECL}} P_i\varphi \Rightarrow_{\mathbf{ECL}} P_{0,i}\varphi$, and since we had that ⊢ extends $\vdash_{\mathbf{ECL}}$, we are done.

(G5) Suppose $\varphi >_0 \chi$, i.e. $[T \cup \{P_0\varphi\} \vdash \neg P_0\neg\chi \ \&\ T \cup \{P_0\varphi\} \vdash P_{0,i}\chi]$, for some i and arbitrary (consistent) theory T. Since we are also given $K(\varphi \leftrightarrow \psi)$, we know that by (an **ECL**-analogue of) Exercise 1.4.1.1(ii), we may substitute φ by ψ in the above formula, and obtain: $[T \cup \{P_0\psi\} \vdash \neg P_0\neg\chi \ \&\ T \cup \{P_0\psi\} \vdash P_{0,i}\chi]$, i.e. $\psi >_0 \chi$.

(G6) Suppose $K(\varphi \wedge \psi)$. We have to show $[T \cup \{P_0\varphi\} \vdash \neg P_0\neg\psi \ \&\ T \cup \{P_0\varphi\} \vdash P_{0,i}\psi]$, for some i and arbitrary (consistent) theory T, under the additional assumption that $T \cup \{P_0\varphi\} \vdash \neg P_0\bot$. Now we reason: $K(\varphi \wedge \psi) \Rightarrow K\psi \Rightarrow P_0\psi \Rightarrow \neg P_0\neg\psi$ (the last step uses the assumption that $\neg P_0\bot$), and, furthermore, $P_0\psi \Rightarrow$ (since $S_{0,i} \subseteq S_0$) $P_{0,i}\psi$.

(G7) That this does not hold is obvious: a counterfactual implication only states something about a subframe S_0, and induces no constraints on the whole set S (where the K-operator is pertaining to).

(G7*) That this holds can be seen as follows: assume $\varphi >_{0,i} \psi$, i.e., $[T \cup \{P_0\varphi\} \vdash \neg P_0\neg\psi \ \&\ T \cup \{P_0\varphi\} \vdash P_{0,i}\psi]$, and now suppose Kφ. By Kφ we also have $P_0\varphi$. So, in the context of T, we can derive $P_{0,i}\psi$.

(G8) Given $\varphi >_0 \chi$, i.e., $[T \cup \{P_0\varphi\} \vdash \neg P_0\neg\chi \ \&\ T \cup \{P_0\varphi\} \vdash P_{0,i}\chi]$, for some i, and $\psi >_0 \chi$, i.e. [T

$\cup \{P_0\psi\} \vdash \neg P_0\neg\chi$ & $T \cup \{P_0\psi\} \vdash P_{0,j}\chi]$, for some j, we would have to show $\varphi \vee \psi >_0 \chi$, i.e. $[T \cup \{P_0(\varphi \vee \psi)\} \vdash \neg P_0\neg\chi$ & $T \cup \{P_0(\varphi \vee \psi)\} \vdash P_{0,k}\chi]$, for some k. However, from the premises $T \cup \{P_0(\varphi \vee \psi)\}$ we can neither derive $T \cup \{P_0\varphi\}$ nor $T \cup \{P_0\psi\}$, so that the given statements are useless in trying to derive $T \cup \{P_0(\varphi \vee \psi)\} \vdash P_{0,k}\chi$.

(G9*) Assume $\varphi >_0 \psi$, i.e. $[T \cup \{P_0\varphi\} \vdash \neg P_0\neg\psi$ & $T \cup \{P_0\varphi\} \vdash P_{0,i}\psi]$, for some i, and furthermore that $T \cup \{P_0\varphi, P_0\chi\} \vdash \neg P_0\neg\psi$. We have to show that $\varphi \wedge \chi >_0 \psi$, i.e. $[T \cup \{P_0(\varphi \wedge \chi)\} \vdash \neg P_0\neg\psi$ & $T \cup \{P_0(\varphi \wedge \chi)\} \vdash P_{0,i}\psi]$ (for some i), or equivalently, $[T \cup \{P_0\varphi \wedge P_0\chi)\} \vdash \neg P_0\neg\psi$ & $T \cup \{P_0\varphi \wedge P_0\chi)\} \vdash P_{0,i}\psi]$ (for some i). The first conjunct follows from the assumption; the second from the fact that the inference $T \cup \{P_0\varphi\} \vdash P_{0,i}\psi$ can still 'fire' in the presence of the additional information $P_0\chi$, since the latter does not block this inference by the assumption $T \cup \{P_0\varphi, P_0\chi\} \vdash \neg P_0\neg\psi$, which implies $\{P_0\varphi, P_0\chi\} \nvdash P_0\neg\psi$.

R REFERENCES

[AKPT91] J.E. Allen, H.A. Kautz, R.N. Pelavin & J.D. Tenenberg, *Reasoning about Plans*, Morgan Kaufmann, San Mateo CA, 1991.

[AP88] P. Atzeni & D.S. Parker, Set Containment Inference and Syllogisms, *Theoretical Computer Science* 62, 1988, pp. 39—65.

[Bak80] J.W. de Bakker, *Mathematical Theory of Program Correctness*, Prentice-Hall International, Englewood Cliffs NJ, 1980.

[Bes89] Ph. Besnard, *An Introduction to Default Logic*, Springer, Berlin, 1989.

[Bou94] C. Boutilier, Unifying Default Reasoning and Belief Revision in a Modal Framework, *Artificial Intelligence* 68, 1994, pp. 33—85.

[Bre91] G. Brewka, *Nonmonotonic Reasoning: Logical Foundations of Commonsense*, Cambridge University Press, Cambridge, 1991.

[Bro87] F.M. Brown (ed.), *The Frame Problem in Artificial Intelligence (Proceedings of the 1987 Workshop)*, Morgan Kaufmann, Los Altos CA, 1987.

[Che80] B.F. Chellas, *Modal Logic: An Introduction*, Cambridge University Press, Cambridge/London 1980.

[ChM85] M. Chandy & J. Misra, How Processes Learn, in: *Proceedings of the 4th ACM Symp. on Principles of Distributed Computing*, 1985, pp. 204—214.

[ChM86] M. Chandy & J. Misra, How Processes Learn, Distributed Computing 1(1), 1986, pp. 40—52.

[Coo71] S.A. Cook, The Complexity of Theorem-Proving Procedures, in: *Proceedings of the 3rd Annual ACM Symposium on the Theory of Computing*, 1971, pp. 151—158.

[dCar88] F. de Caro, Graded Modalities II, *Studia Logica* 47, 1988, pp. 1—10.

[Del88] J.P. Delgrande, An Approach to Default Reasoning Based on a First-Order Conditional Logic, *Artificial Intelligence* 36, 1988, pp. 63—90.

[Doh91] P. Doherty, NM3 — A Three-Valued Cumulative Non-Monotonic Formalism, in: J. van Eijck (ed.), *Logics in AI*, LNCS 478, Springer, Berlin, 1991, pp. 196—211.

[Doy79] J. Doyle, A Truth Maintenance System, *Artificial Intelligence* 12, 1979, pp. 231—272.

[DR92] F. Dignum & R.P. van de Riet, Addition and Removal of Information for a Knowledge Base with Incomplete Information, *Data and Knowledge Engineering* 8, 1992, pp. 293—307.

[Dun86] J.M. Dunn, Relevance Logic and Entailment, in: D. Gabbay & F. Guenthner (eds.), *Handbook of Philosophical Logic, Vol. III*, Reidel, Dordrecht, 1986, pp. 117—224.

[Eth88] D.W. Etherington, *Reasoning with Incomplete Information,* Pitman/Morgan Kaufmann, London /Los Altos, 1988.

[FC85] M. Fattorosi-Barnaba & F. de Caro, Graded Modalities I, *Studia Logica* 2, 1985, pp. 197—221.

[FC88] M. Fattorosi-Barnaba & C. Cerrato, Graded Modalities III, *Studia Logica* 47, 1988, pp. 99—110.

[FG92] M. Finger & D.M. Gabbay, Adding a Temporal Dimension to a Logic System, *Journal of Logic, Language and Information* 1(3), 1992, pp. 203—233.

[FH88] R. Fagin & J.Y. Halpern, Belief, Awareness and Limited Reasoning, *Artificial Intelligence* 34, 1988, pp. 39—76.

[FHV84] R. Fagin, J.Y. Halpern & M.Y. Vardi, A Model-Theoretic Analysis of Knowledge, in: *Proceedings of the 25th IEEE Symp. on Foundations of Computer Science*, 1984, p.268—278.

[FHV91] R. Fagin, J.Y. Halpern & M.Y. Vardi, A Model-Theoretic Analysis of Knowledge, *J. ACM* 38(2), 1991, pp. 382—428.

[FI86] M.J. Fischer & N. Immerman, Foundations of Knowledge for Distributed Systems, in: J.Y. Halpern (ed.), *Proceedings of the 1st Conference on Theoretical Aspects of Knowledge*, Morgan Kaufmann, Los Altos, 1986, pp. 171—185.

[Fin72] K. Fine, In So Many Possible Worlds, *Notre Dame Journal of Formal Logic* 13 (4), 1972, pp. 516—520.

[FS9?] K. Fine & G. Schurz, Transfer Theorems for Stratified Mulitimodal Logics, in: *Proceedings of the Arthur Prior Memorial Conference*, Christchurch, New Zealand, to appear.

[FV85] R. Fagin & M.Y. Vardi, An Internal Semantics for Modal Logic, in: *Proceedings of the 17th ACM Symposium on Theory of Computing*, 1985, p.305—315.

[FV86] R. Fagin & M.Y. Vardi, Knowledge and Implicit Knowledge in a Distributed Environment, in: J.Y. Halpern (ed.), *Proceedings of the 1st Conference on Theoretical Aspects of Knowledge*, Morgan Kaufmann, Los Altos, 1986, pp. 187—206.

[Gab85] D.M. Gabbay, Theoretical Foundations for Non-Monotonic Reasoning in Expert Systems, in: K.R. Apt (ed.), *Proceedings of the NATO Advanced Study Institute on Logics and Models of Concurrent Systems*, Springer, Berlin, 1985, pp. 439—457.

[Gal90] A. Galton, *Logic for Information Technology*, Wiley, Chichester, 1990.

[Gam91] L.T.F. Gamut, *Logic, Language and Meaning Vol. II, Intensional Logic and Logical Grammar*, University of Chicago Press, Chicago, 1991.

[GG90] E. Gillet & P. Gochet, La logique de la connaissance; le problème de l' omniscience logique, Université de Liège, Séminaire de Logique et d'Epistémologie, 1990.

[GG91] P. Gochet & E. Gillet, On Professor Weingartner's Contribution to Epistemic Logic, in: G. Schurz & G.J.W. Dorn (eds.), *Advances in Scientific Philosophy*, Rodopi, 1991, pp. 97—115.

[Gin86] M.L. Ginsberg, Counterfactuals, *Artificial Intelligence* 30, 1986, pp. 35—79.

[Gin87] M.L. Ginsberg (ed.), *Readings in nonmonotonic reasoning,* Morgan Kaufmann, Los Altos, 1987.

[GN87] M.R. Genesereth & N.J. Nilsson, *Logical Foundations of Artificial Intelligence,* Morgan Kaufmann, Los Altos, 1987.

[Gol87] R. Goldblatt, *Logics of Time and Computation*, CSLI Lecture Notes 7, Stanford, 1987.

[Gär78] P. Gärdenfors, Conditionals and Changes of Belief, *Acta Philos. Fennica* 30, 1978, pp. 381—404.

[Gär88] P. Gärdenfors, *Knowledge in Flux (Modeling the Dynamics of Epistemic States)*, Bradford / MIT Press, Cambridge, Massachusetts, 1988.

[Hal86] J.Y. Halpern (ed.), *Theoretical Aspects of Reasoning about Knowledge, Proceedings of the 1986 Conference, Monterey*, Morgan Kaufmann, Los Altos, 1986.

[Hal87] J.Y. Halpern, Using Reasoning about Knowledge to Analyze Distributed Systems, *Ann. Rev. Comput. Sci.* 2, 1987, pp. 37—68.

[Har84] D. Harel, Dynamic Logic, in: D.M. Gabbay & F. Guenther (eds.), *Handbook of Philosophical Logic, Vol.II*, Reidel, Dordrecht / Boston, 1984.

[HC68] G.E. Hughes & M.J. Cresswell, *An Introduction to Modal logic,* Methuen & Co. Ltd, London, 1968.

[HC84] G.E. Hughes & M.J. Cresswell, *A Companion to Modal Logic*, Methuen, London, 1984.

[Hei80] J.F. Heiser et al., Can Psychiatrics Distinguish a Computer Simulation of Paranoia from the Real Thing?, *Journal of Psychiatric Research* 15, 1980, pp. 149—162.

[HF89] J.Y. Halpern & R. Fagin, Modelling Knowledge and Action in Distributed Systems, *Distributed Computing* 3, 1989, pp. 159—177.

[HHM93] W. van der Hoek, M. van Hulst & J.-J. Ch. Meyer, Towards an Epistemic Approach to Reasoning about Concurrent Programs, in: J.W. de Bakker, W.P. de Roever & G. Rozenberg (eds.),*Semantics — Foundations and Applications, Proceedings of the REX Workshop Beekbergen 1992* , LNCS 666, Springer, Berlijn, 1993, pp. 261—287.

[Hin62] J. Hintikka, *Knowledge and Belief*, Cornell University Press, Ithaca (N.Y.), 1962.

[Hin86] J. Hintikka, Reasoning about Knowledge in Philosophy: The Paradigm of Epistemic Logic, in: J.Y. Halpern (ed.), *Proceedings of the 1st Conference on Theoretical Aspects of Knowledge*, Morgan Kaufmann, Los Altos, 1986, pp. 63—80.

[HK91] Z. Huang & K. Kwast, Awareness, Negation and Logical Omniscience, in: J. van Eijck (ed.), *Logics in AI (Proc. JELIA '90)*, LNCS 478, Springer, 1991, pp. 282—300.

[HLM94a] W. van der Hoek, B. van Linder & J.-J. Ch. Meyer, A Logic of Capabilities, in: A. Nerode & Yu.V. Matiyasevich (eds.), *Proceedings of the 3rd Int. Symp. on the Logical Foundations of Computer Science (LFCS'94)*, LNCS 813, Springer-Verlag, Berlin, 1994, pp. 366—378.

[HLM94b] W. van der Hoek, B. van Linder & J.-J. Ch. Meyer, Unravelling Nondeterminism: On Having the Ability to Choose, in: P. Jorrand & V. Sgurev (eds.), *Proceedings of the 6th Int. Conf. on Artificial Intelligence: Methodology, Systems, Applications (AIMSA'94)*, World Scientific, 1994, pp. 163—172.

[HM84a] J.Y. Halpern & Y.O. Moses, Knowledge and Common Knowledge in a Distributed Environment, in: *Proceedings of the 3rd ACM Symp. on Principles of Distributed Computing*, 1984a, pp. 50—61.

[HM84b] J.Y. Halpern & Y.O. Moses, Towards a Theory of Knowledge and Ignorance, in: *Proceedimgs of the Workshop on Non-Monotonic Reasoning*, AAAI, 1984b, pp. 125—143.

[HM85] J.Y. Halpern & Y.O. Moses, A Guide to the Modal Logics of Knowledge and Belief, in: *Proceedings of the 9th International Joint Conference on Artificial Intelligence*, 1985, pp. 480—490.

[HM90] J.Y. Halpern & Y.O. Moses, Knowledge and Common Knowledge in a Distributed Environment, *J. ACM* 37(3), 1990, pp. 549—587 (revised and expanded version of [HM84a]).

[HM92] J.Y. Halpern & Y.O. Moses, A Guide to Completeness and Complexity for Modal Logics of Knowledge and Belief, *Artificial Intelligence* 54, 1992, pp. 319—379.

[HMcD87] S. Hanks & D. McDermott, Nonmonotonic Logic and Temporal Projection, *Artificial Intelligence* 33 (1987), pp. 379—412.

[Hoa69] C.A.R. Hoare, An Axiomatic Basis for Computer Programming, *Comm. ACM* 12, 1969, p.576—580.

[HR93] W. van der Hoek & M. de Rijke, Generalized Quantifiers and Modal Logic, *Journal of Logic, Language and Information.* 2, 1993, pp. 19—58.

[HU79] J.E. Hopcraft & J.D. Ullman, *Introduction to Automata Theory, Languages and Computation*, Addison-Wesley, 1979.

[Hua90] Z. Huang, Dependency of Belief in Distributed Systems, in: M. Stokhof & L. Torenvliet (eds.), *Proceedings of the 7th Amsterdam Colloquium*, ITLI, University of Amsterdam, 1990, pp. 637—662.

[HvEB91] Z. Huang & P. van Emde Boas, The Schoenmakers Paradox: Its Solution in a Belief Dependence Framework, ITLI Prepublication Series LP-91-05, University of Amsterdam, 1991.

[HZ87] J.Y. Halpern & L.D. Zuck, A Little Knowledge Goes a Long Way: Simple Knowledge-Based Derivations and Correctness Proofs for a Family of Protocols, in: *Proceedings of the 6th ACM Symp. on Pronciples of distributed Computing*, 1987, pp. 269—280.

[Jas91] J.O.M. Jaspars, Fused Modal Logic and Inconsistent Belief, in: M. De Glas & D. Gabbay (eds.), *Proceedings of the 1st World Conference on the Fundamentals of Artificial Intelligence (WOCFAI'91)*, Paris, 1991, pp. 267—275.

[Jas93] J.O.M. Jaspars, Logical Omniscience and Inconsistent Belief, in: M. de Rijke (ed.), *Diamonds and Defaults*, Kluwer Academic Publishers, Dordrecht, 1993, pp. 129—146.

[KL86] S. Kraus & D. Lehmann, Knowledge, Belief and Time, in: L. Kott (ed.), *Proceedings of the 13th Int. Colloquium on Automata, Languages and Programming, Rennes,* LNCS 226, Springer, Berlin, 1986.

[KLM90] S. Kraus, D. Lehmann & M. Magidor, Nonmonotonic Reasoning, Preferential Models and Cumulative Logics, *Artificial Intelligence* 44, 1990, pp. 167—207.

[Kon86] K. Konolige, *A Deduction Model of Belief,* Pitman / Morgan Kaufmann, London / Los Altos, 1986.

[Kon88] K. Konolige, On the Relation between Default and Autoepistemic Logic, *Artificial Intelligence* 35, 1988, pp. 343—382.

[Kri63] S. Kripke, Semantic Analysis of Modal Logic, *Zeitschrift für Mathematische Logik und Grundlagen der Mathematik* 9, 1963, pp. 67—96.

[Kri65] S. Kripke, Semantic Analysis of Modal Logic II: Non-Normal Modal Propositional Calculi, in: *Symposium on the Theory of Models,* North-Holland, Amsterdam, 1965.

[KT86] S. Katz & G. Taubenfeld, What Processes Know: Definitions and Proof Methods, in: *Proceedings of the 5th ACM Symp. on Principles of Distributed Computing,* 1986, pp. 249—262.

[KW91] M. Kracht & F. Wolter, Properties of Independently Axiomatizable Bimodal Logics, *J. of Symbolic Logic* 56(4), 1991, pp. 1469—1485.

[Lad77] R.E. Ladner, The Computational Complexity of Provability in Systems of Modal Propositional Logic, *SIAM Journal on Computing* 6(3), 1977, pp. 467—480.

[Leh84] D.J. Lehmann, Knowledge, Common Knowledge, and Related Puzzles, in: *Proceedings of the 3rd ACM Symp. on Principles of Distributed Computing,* 1984, pp. 62—67.

[Len80] W. Lenzen, *Glauben, Wissen und Wahrscheinlichkeit,* Springer, Wien / New York, 1980.

[Lev84] H.J. Levesque, A Logic of Implicit and Explicit Belief, in: *Proceedings of the National Conference on Artificial Intelligence,* 1984, pp.198—202.

[Lev90] H.J. Levesque, All I Know: A Study in Autoepistemic Logic, *Artificial Intelligence* 42, 1990, pp. 263—309.

[Lew73] D.K. Lewis, *Counterfactuals*, Basil Blackwell, Oxford, 1973.

[LHM94a] B. van Linder, W. van der Hoek & J.-J. Ch. Meyer, Tests as Epistemic Updates, in: A.G. Cohn (ed.), *Proceedings of 11th European Conference on Artificial Intelligence (ECAI'94),* Amsterdam, Wiley, Chichester, 1994, pp. 331—335.

[LHM94b] B. van Linder, W. van der Hoek & J.-J. Ch. Meyer, Communicating Rational Agents, in: B. Nebel & L. Dreschler-Fischer (eds.), *Proceedings of KI-94: Advances in Artificial Intelligence,* LNCS 861, Springer, Berlin, 1994, pp. 202—213.

[LHM94c] B. van Linder , W. van der Hoek & J.-J. Ch. Meyer, The Dynamics of Default Reasoning, Technical Report UU-CS-1994-48, Utrecht University, 1994; to appear in *Proceedings of ECSQARU'95.*

[Lif89] V. Lifschitz, Benchmark Problems for Formal Non-Monotonic Reasoning, Version 2.00, in: M. Reinfrank, J. de Kleer, M. Ginsberg & E. Sandewall (eds.), *Proceedings Non-Monotonic Reasoning, 2nd Int. Workshop*, LNCS 346, Springer, Berlin, 1989, pp. 202—219.

[LM91] Ph. Lejoly & M. Minsoul, A Subjective Logic of Knowledge, Technical Report, Université de Liège, 1991.

[LMRT90] K. Lodaya, M. Mukund, R. Ramanujam & P.S. Thiagarajan, Models and Logics for True Concurrency, SPIC Science Foundation, School of Mathematics, Technical Report TCS-90-3, Madras, 1990.

[Lok94] G.-J. C. Lokhorst, Counting the Minds of Split-Brain Patients, Technical Report Erasmus University, Dept of Philosophy, Rotterdam, 1994.

[LS90] F. Lin & Y. Shoham, Epistemic Semantics for Fixed-Points Non-Monotonic Logics, in: R. Parikh (ed.), *Proceedings of the 3rd Conference on Theoretical Aspects of Reasoning about Knowledge,* Morgan Kaufmann, San Mateo CA, 1990, pp. 111—120.

[LS92] F. Lin & Y. Shoham, A Logic of Knowledge and Justified Assumptions, *Artificial Intelligence* 57, 1992, pp. 271—289.

[Luk84] V. Lukaszewicz, Considerations of Default Logic, in: *Proceedings of the AAAI Workshop on Nonmonotonic Reasoning*, 1984, p.165—193.

[Luk90] W. Lukaszewicz, *Non-Monotonic Reasoning (Formalisation of Commonsense Reasoning)*, Ellis Horwood, New York, 1990.

[LvdG91]P. Lucas & L. van der Gaag, *Principles of Expert Systems*, Addison Wesley, Wokingham, 1991.

[Mak89] D. Makinson, General Theory of Cumulative Inference, in: M. Reinfrank, J. de Kleer, M. Ginsberg & E. Sandewall (eds.), *Proceedings Non-Monotonic Reasoning, 2nd Int. Workshop*, LNCS 346, Springer, Berlin, 1989, pp. 1—18.

[McC80] J. McCarthy, Circumscription: A Form of Non-Monotonic Reasoning, *Artificial Intelligence* 13, 1980, pp. 27—39.

[McD82] D. McDermott, Nonmonotonic Logic II: Nonmonotonic Modal Theories, *J. ACM* 29, 1982, pp. 33—57.

[McD87] D. McDermott, AI, Logic and the Frame Problem, in: F. Brown (ed.), *Proceedings of the 1987 Workshop on the Frame Problem in Artificial Intelligence* Lawrence, Kansas, Morgan Kaufmann, Los Altos, 1987.

[McDD80] D. McDermott & J. Doyle, Non-Monotonic Logic I, *Artificial Intelligence* 13, 1980, pp. 41—72.

[Men64] E. Mendelson, *Introduction to Mathematical Logic*, Van Nostrand, New York, 1964.

[Mey90] J.-J. Ch. Meyer, An Analysis of the Yale Shooting Problem by Means of Dynamic Epistemic Logic, in: M. Stokhof & L. Torenvliet (eds.), *Proceedings of the 7th Amsterdam Colloquium*, ITLI, University of Amsterdam, 1990, pp. 317—326.

[MH91a] J.-J.Ch. Meyer & W. van der Hoek, Non-Monotonic Reasoning by Monotonic Means, in: J. van Eijck (ed.), *Logics in AI (Proc. JELIA '90)*, LNCS 478, Springer, 1991, pp. 399—411.

[MH91b] J.-J. Ch. Meyer & W. van der Hoek, A Modal Contrastive Logic, Technical Report IR-245, Free University, Amsterdam, 1991; revised version to appear in the *Annals of Mathematics and Artificial Intelligence.*

[MH92] J.-J.Ch. Meyer & W. van der Hoek, A Modal Logic for Nonmonotonic Reasoning, in: W. van der Hoek, J.-J. Ch. Meyer, Y.H. Tan & C. Witteveen (eds.), *Non-Monotonic Reasoning and Partial Semantics*, Ellis Horwood, Chichester, 1992, pp. 37—77.

[MH93a] J.-J. Ch. Meyer & W. van der Hoek, A Default Logic Based on Epistemic States (extended abstract), in: M. Clarke, R. Kruse & S. Moral (eds.), *Symbolic and Quantitative Approaches to Reasoning and Uncertainty (Proceedings of ECSQARU '93, Granada)*, Springer-Verlag, Berlin, 1993, pp. 265—273;

[MH93b] J.-J. Ch. Meyer & W. van der Hoek, Counterfactual Reasoning by (Means of) Defaults, *Annals of Mathematics and Artificial Intelligence* 9 (III-IV), 1993, pp. 345—360.

[MH93c] J.-J. Ch. Meyer & W. van der Hoek, An Epistemic Logic for Defeasible Reasoning Using a Meta-Level Architecture Metaphor, VU-Report IR-329, Amsterdam, 1993.

[MH95] J.-J. Ch. Meyer & W. van der Hoek, A Default Logic Based on Epistemic States, *Fundamenta Informaticae* 23(1), 1995, pp. 33—65.

[MHV91] J.-J. Ch. Meyer, W. van der Hoek & G.A.W. Vreeswijk, Epistemic Logic for Computer Science: A Tutorial, Part 1 in *Bulletin of the EATCS* 44, 1991, pp. 242—270; Part 2 in *Bulletin of the EATCS* 45, 1991, pp. 256—287.

[Min88] J. Minker (ed.), *Foundations of Deductive Databases and Logic Programming*, Morgan Kaufmann, Los Altos CA, 1988.

[Moo84] R.C. Moore, Possible-World Semantics for Autoepistemic Logic, in: *Proceedings of the Non-Monotonic Reasoning Workshop*, New Paltz NY, 1984, pp. 344—354.

[Moo85a] R.C. Moore, Semantical Considerations on Nonmonotonic Logic, *Artificial Intelligence* 25, 1985, pp. 75—94.

[Moo85b] R.C. Moore, A Formal Theory of Knowledge and Action, in: J.R. Hobbs & R.C. Moore (eds.), *Formal Theories of the Commonsense World*, 1985, Ablex, Norwood, New Jersey, pp. 319—358.

[Mor86] L. Morgenstern, A First Order Theory of Planning, Knowledge, and Action, in: J.Y. Halpern (ed.), *Proceedings of the 1st Conference on Theoretical Aspects of Knowledge*, Morgan Kaufmann, Los Altos, 1986, pp. 99—114.

[Morr92] M. Morreau, Conditionals in Philosophy and Artificial Intelligence, PhD Thesis, University of Amsterdam, 1992.

[Mos88] Y. Moses, Resource-Bounded Knowledge, in: M. Vardi (ed.), *Proceedings of the 2nd Conference on Theoretical Aspects of Knowledge*, Morgan Kaufmann, Los Altos, 1988, pp. 261—275.

[Mos92] Y. Moses, Knowledge and Communication, in: Y. Moses (ed.), *Proceedings of the 4th Conference on Theoretical Aspects of Knowledge*, Morgan Kaufmann, San Mateo, 1992, pp. 1—14.

[MT89] V.W. Marek & M. Truszczynski, Relating Autoepistemic and Default Logics, in: R.J. Brachman, H.J. Levesque & R. Reiter (eds.), *Proceedings of the 1st Int. Conference on Principles of Knowledge Representation and Reasoning (KR'89)*, Toronto, Morgan Kaufmann, San Mateo CA, 1989, pp. 276—288.

[MT91] V.W. Marek & M. Truszczynski, Autoepistemic Logic, *J. ACM* 38(3), 1991, pp. 588—619.

[MT93] V. W. Marek & M. Truszczynski, *Nonmonotonic Logic, Context-Dependent Reasoning*, Springer-Verlag, Berlin, 1993.

[Nau63] P. Naur (ed.), Revised Report on the Algorithmic Language ALGOL 60, *Comm. ACM* 6, 1963, pp. 1—17.

[Nut84] D. Nute, Conditional Logic, in: D. Gabbay & F. Guenther (eds.), *Handbook of Philosophical Logic, Vol. II*, Reidel, Dordrecht / Boston, 1984, pp. 387—439.

[Pol86] J.L. Pollock, *Contempory Theories of Knowledge*, Hutchinson, London, 1986.

[Ram88] A. Ramsay, *Formal Methods in Artificial Intelligence*, Cambridge University Press, Cambridge, 1988.

[Ran82] V. Rantala, Impossible World Semantics and Logical Omniscience, *Acta Philosophica Fennica* 35, 1982, pp. 106—115.

[RB80] N. Rescher & R. Brandom, *The Logic of Inconsistency*, Basil Blackwell, London, 1980.

[RC81] R. Reiter & G. Criscuolo, On Interacting Defaults, in: *Proceedings of the 7th Int. Joint Conference on Artificial Intelligence,* 1981, pp. 270—276.

[RD88] G.A. Ringland & D.A. Duce (eds.), *Approaches to Knowledge Representation: An Introduction*, RSP/Wiley, New York, 1988.

[Rei80] R. Reiter, A Logic for Default Reasoning, *Artificial Intelligence* 13, 1980, p.81—132.

[Rei87] R Reiter, Nonmonotonic Reasoning, *Annual Reviews of Computer Science* 2, 1987, pp. 147—187.

[Res75] N. Rescher, Belief-Contravening Suppositions and the Problem of Contrary-to-Fact Conditionals, in: E. Sosa (ed.), *Causation and Conditionals*, Oxford University Press, Oxford, 1975, pp. 156—164.

[Res76] N Rescher, *Plausible Reasoning, An Introduction to the Theory and Practice of Plausibilistic Inference*, Van Gorcum, 1976.

[San91] E. Sandewall, Features and Fluents, Review version of 1991, Technical Report LiTH-IDA-R-91-29, IDA, Linköping University, 1991.

[San95] E. Sandewall, *Features and Fluents: A Systematic Approach to the Representation of Knowledge about Dynamical Systems*, Oxford University Press, 1995.

[Sch86] W.J. Schoenmakers, A Problem in Knowledge Acquisition, *SIGART Newsletter* 95. 1986, pp. 56—57.

[Seg70] K. Segerberg, Modal Logics with Linear Alternative Relations, *Theoria* 36, 1970, pp. 301—322.

[Sho87] Y. Shoham, A Semantical Approach to Nonmonotonic Logics, in: M.L. Ginsberg (ed.), *Readings in Nonmonotonic Reasoning,* Morgan Kaufmann, Los Altos, 1987, pp. 227—250.

[Sho88] Y. Shoham, *Reasoning about Change*, MIT Press, Cambridge, Massachusetts, 1988.

[SK88] B. Smith & G. Kelleher (eds.), *Reason Maintenance Systems and Their Applications*, Ellis Horwood, Chichester, 1988.

[SM89] Y. Shoham & Y. Moses, Belief as Defeasible Knowledge, in: *Proceedings of the 11th Int. Joint Conference on Artificial Intelligence*, 1989, pp. 1168—1173.

[SMDP88] Ph. Smets, E.H. Mamdani, D. Dubois & H. Prade, *Non-standard Logics for Automated Reasoning*, Academic Press, 1988.

[Sos75] E. Sosa (ed.), *Causation and Conditionals*, Oxford University Press, Oxford, 1975.

[Sta68] R. Stalnaker, A Theory of Conditionals, in: N. Rescher (ed.), *Studies in Logical Theory*, American Philosophical Quarterly Monograph Series, No. 2, Basil Blackwell, Oxford, 1968.

[SWM95] P.A. Spruit, R.J. Wieringa & J.-J. Ch. Meyer, Axiomatization, Declarative Semantics and Operational Semantics of Passive and Active Updates in Logic Databases, *Journal of Logic and Computation*. 5(1), 1995, pp. 27-70.

[Tan92] Y.-H. Tan, Aspects of Non-Monotonic Reasoning, PhD Thesis, Free University, Amsterdam, 1992.

[Tha88] A. Thayse (ed.), *From Standard Logic to Logic Programming*, Wiley, Chichester, 1988.

[Tha89] A. Thayse (ed.), *From Modal Logic to Deductive Databases*, Wiley, Chichester, 1989.

[Tho84] R.H. Thomason, Combinations of Tense and Modality, in: D. Gabbay & F. Guenthner (eds.), *Handbook of Philosophical Logic, Vol. II*, Reidel, Dordrecht, 1984, pp. 135—165.

[Thy92] E. Thijsse, Partial Logic and Knowledge Representation, PhD Thesis, Tilburg University, 1992.

[Tou86] D.S. Touretzky, *The Mathematics of Inheritance Systems*, Pitman, London, 1986.

[TT91] Y.-H. Tan & J. Treur, A Bi-Modular Approach to Non-Monotonic Reasoning, in: M. De Glas & D. Gabbay (eds.), *Proceedings of the 1st World Conference on the Fundamentals of Artificial Intelligence (WOCFAI'91)*, Paris, 1991, pp. 461—475.

[Tur84] R. Turner, *Logics for Artificial Intelligence*, Ellis Horwood / Wiley, Chichester / New York, 1984.

[Var88] M.Y. Vardi (ed.), *Proceedings of the 2nd Conf. on Theoretical Aspects of Reasoning about Knowledge*, Pacific Grove, Morgan-Kaufmann Los Altos, 1988.

[vB83] J.F.A.K. van Benthem, *Modal Logic and Classical Logic*, Bibliopolis, Naples, 1983.

[vdH91a] W. van der Hoek, Systems for Knowledge and Belief, in: J. van Eijck (ed.), *Logics in AI (Proc. JELIA '90)*, LNCS 478, Springer, 1991, pp. 267—281; extended version in: *Journal of Logic and Computation* 3(2), 1993, pp. 173—195.

[vdH91b] W. van der Hoek, Qualitative Modalities, in: B. Mayoh (ed.), *Proceedings of the Scandinavian Conference on Artificial Intelligence '91*, IOS Press, Amsterdam, 1991, pp. 322—327.

[vdH92a] W. van der Hoek, Modalities for Reasoning about Knowledge and Quantities, PhD Thesis, Free University, Amsterdam, 1992.

[vdH92b] W. van der Hoek, On the Semantics of Graded Modalities, *Journal of Applied Non-Classical Logics*, 2(1), 1992, pp. 81—123.

[vdHM89] W. van der Hoek & J.-J. Ch. Meyer, Possible Logics for Belief, in *Logique et Analyse* 127-128, 1989, pp.177—194.

[vdHM92a] W. van der Hoek & J.-J. Ch. Meyer, Knowledge and Uncertainty, Lecture Notes Nordic Graduate Studies Course on "Partial Semantics and Non-Monotonic Reasoning for Knowledge Representation", Linköping University, Linköping, Sweden, 1992.

[vdHM92b] W. van der Hoek & J.-J. Ch. Meyer, Making Some Issues of Implicit Knowledge Explicit, in *Int. J. of Foundations of Computer Science* 3(2), 1992, pp. 193—223.

[vdHM92c] W. van der Hoek & J.-J. Ch. Meyer, Graded Modalities in Epistemic Logic, in: A. Nerode & M. Taitslin (eds.), *Proceedings Logical Foundations of Computer Science —*

Tver'92, 2nd Int. Symp., Tver, Russia, LNCS 620, Springer, Berlijn, 1992, pp. 503—514; extended version in *Logique et Analyse*.133-134 (Special issue on Int. Symposium on Epistemic Logic), 1991 [published in 1994], pp. 251—270.

[Vel91] F. Veltman, Defaults in Update Semantics, ITLI Prepublications Series No 91-82, University of Amsterdam, Amsterdam, 1991.

[vHM92] M. van Hulst & J.-J. Ch. Meyer, A Taxonomy of Knowledge in Distributed Systems, in: J.L.G. Dietz (ed.), *Proceedings of Computer Science in the Netherlands '92*, SION, Utrecht, 1992, pp. 42—53.

[vHM93] M. van Hulst & J.-J. Ch. Meyer, An Epistemic Proof System for Parallel Processes, Techn. Report No. 93—17, KUN, Nijmegen, 1993; extended abstract in: R. Fagin (ed.), *Proceedings of the 5th Conference on Theoretical Aspects of Reasoning about Knowledge (TARK V), Pacific Grove,* Morgan Kaufmann, San Francisco, 1994, pp. 243—254.

[Voo91a] F. Voorbraak, The Logic of Objective Knowledge and Rational Belief, in: J. van Eijck (ed.), *Logics in AI (Proceedings of JELIA '90)*, LNCS 478, Springer, 1991, pp. 499—516.

[Voo91b] F. Voorbraak, A Preferential Model Semantics for Default Logic, in R. Kruse & P. Siegel (eds.), *Symbolic and Quantitative Approaches to Uncertainty*, LNCS 548, Springer, 1991, pp. 344—351.

[Voo92] F. Voorbraak, Generalized Kripke Models for Epistemic Logic, in: Y. Moses (ed.), *Proceedings of the 4th Conference on Theoretical Aspects of Knowledge*, Morgan Kaufmann, San Mateo, 1992, pp. 214—228.

[Voo93] F. Voorbraak, As Far as I Know: Epistemic Logic and Uncertainty, PhD Thesis, Utrecht University, Utrecht, 1993.

[Vre91] G.A.W. Vreeswijk, A Complete Logic for Autoepistemic Membership, in J. van Eijck (ed.), *Logics in AI (Proceedings of JELIA '90)*, LNCS 478, Springer, 1991, pp. 516—525.

[Wan90] H. Wansing, A General Possible Worlds Framework for Reasoning about Knowledge and Belief, *Studia Logica* 49, 1990, pp. 523—539.

[Wei82] P. Weingartner, Conditions for the Rationality of Belief, Knowledge and Assumption, *Dialectica* 36, 1982, pp. 243—263.

[Win90] M. Winslett, *Updating Logical Databases*, Cambridge University Press, Cambridge, 1990.

I INDEX